# INTERNATIONAL TRADE THEORY AND POLICY

# ECONOMICS HANDBOOK SERIES

# INTERNATIONAL TRADE THEORY AND POLICY

**Miltiades Chacholiades, Ph.D.**

*Research Professor of Economics*
*Georgia State University*

Foreword by Harry G. Johnson

**McGraw-Hill Book Company**

New York   St. Louis   San Francisco   Auckland   Bogotá
Düsseldorf   Johannesburg   London   Madrid   Mexico
Montreal   New Delhi   Panama   Paris   São Paulo
Singapore   Sydney   Tokyo   Toronto

ABOUT THE AUTHOR

Miltiades Chacholiades did his undergraduate work at the
Athens School of Economics and Business Science in Athens, Greece,
and received his Ph.D. from the Massachusetts Institute of Technology.
He has taught at New York University and the University of California
in Los Angeles, and is presently Research Professor of Economics at
Georgia State University. His articles have been published in
a number of international professional economics journals.

INTERNATIONAL TRADE THEORY AND POLICY

1 2 3 4 5 6 7 8 9 0 D O D O 7 8 3 2 1 0 9 8 7

This book was set in Times. The editor was J. S. Dietrich and
the production supervisor was David Damstra.
R. R. Donnelley & Sons Company was printer and binder.

**Library of Congress Cataloging in Publication Data**

Chacholiades, Miltiades.
    International trade theory and policy.

    (Economics handbook series)
    First ed. published in 1973 under title: The pure
theory of international trade.
    Includes index.
    1. Commerce.   2. International economic relations.
3. Commercial policy.   I. Title.
HF1007.C385   1978          382          77-5119
ISBN 0-07-010344-5

*To Mary, Lea, Marina, and Linda*

# CONTENTS

## I. INTRODUCTION

### 1. Introduction     3

# II. THE CLASSICAL THEORY

# III. THE NEOCLASSICAL THEORY

## IV. THE MODERN THEORY

## 9. Factor Proportions, Factor Prices, and Commodity Prices   235

## 10. The Cause and Effect of International Trade   255

## V. ECONOMIC GROWTH AND TRADE

## 12. The Effects of Economic Growth on Trade    313

## VI. TRADE AND WELFARE

## VII. INTERNATIONAL TRADE POLICY

## 21. The Infant-Industry Argument and Noneconomic Objectives    525

### PART A. THE INFANT-INDUSTRY ARGUMENT    525

### PART B. THE THEORY OF NONECONOMIC OBJECTIVES    530

## 22. The Theory of Customs Unions: I. The Partial Equilibrium Approach    542

## 23.  The Theory of Customs Unions: II. The General Equilibrium Approach  563

### PART A. FREE-TRADE EQUILIBRIUM AND THE EFFECTS OF TARIFFS    564

# FOREWORD

There has long been a need for a systematic introduction to the modern pure theory of international trade that would take the student through a careful introduction to the tools of analysis and the main logical propositions into the application of the theory to practical problems of international economic policy. Too often, the student who has learned sophisticated analytical techniques in his price theory course is thrown back in his trade theory course into a morass of strange concepts and problems—such as absolute versus comparative advantage, or why free trade that theoretically benefits everyone should be one of the most unpopular of policy proposals—which could be understood and solved easily if only the appropriate price theory tools were applied and their use understood. Trade theory should be part and parcel of price theory, distinguished only by the fact that other countries form part of the natural opportunities—and natural constraints—that a country confronts in its efforts to bend nature to its desire to produce utility-yielding goods and services; but its exposition is often confused by the attachment of its expositors to obsolete problems and obsolete analytical techniques.

The great virtue of the present volume by Miltiades Chacholiades is that it concentrates on the analytical issues and techniques, and expounds them in a careful and straightforward fashion that should enable students to grasp them and hold them once-and-for-all in their intellectual bag of tools. The book is a workmanly exposition of what the student needs to know, pitched at a level that requires sustained application but no feats of imagination to follow. It does not attempt to deal with major issues of current economic policy, though students and their instructors using it should have little difficulty in applying its analysis to current policy problems. Nevertheless, it does deal with several issues of keen contemporary interest, such as the relation between economic growth and international trade, the effects of trade on social and individual welfare, and the effects of various taxes on international trade, all of which figure prominently in recent discussions of American international economic policy.

The book may seem a trifle abstract and austere to those who would like easy answers to complex problems phrased in facile literary form and buttressed by the insertion of bite-sized chunks of theoretical analysis. But the purpose of any good book in economics, as Lord Keynes once remarked, is not to provide answers but to provide a way of thinking about the problem; and this objective is better served by a rigorous exposition of existing theory—at the appropriate level of difficulty and comprehension—than by a literary exposition that plays down the analytical apparatus and plays up the policy conclusions (which may well be wrong, or wrong in certain possible circumstances). Professor Chacholiades has followed the former course; he may not—in fact, does not—provide obvious answers to all the problems that society throws upon the area of international trade theory and policy; but neither does he provide soft answers that will not stand up to criticism. What he provides is the tools needed to arrive at answers that the economist can live by; and if the reader takes the trouble to master the tools, he should be able to arrive at answers that he can conscientiously defend.

This revised edition should meet the requirements of students even better than the previous edition, since the author has incorporated material on empirical evidence (including a new chapter on the Leontief paradox and its explanation), intermediate goods, domestic distortions and the theory of noneconomic objectives, and customs unions.

Harry G. Johnson
*University of Chicago*

# PREFACE

The aim of *International Trade Theory and Policy* is to present in a logical and sufficiently systematic manner those principles and tools of trade theory and policy which every serious student of international economics ought to know. Students and instructors can easily supplement it with other readings on current policy problems.

The present book provides a smooth transition from price theory to trade theory so that the reader who has mastered the principles and techniques of elementary price theory will not get the feeling that trade theory is a totally different and strange field. Quick reviews of relevant price-theory tools are provided where necessary. In addition, the development of the subject matter is honest, rigorous, up to date, and, at the same time, pitched at the appropriate level to serve the needs of advanced undergraduates and first-year graduates as well as the needs of the general economist.

In an effort to communicate with the masses of students, the exposition does not make use of advanced mathematical techniques. It relies rather heavily on geometry which, in addition to being simpler, is often more flexible than mathematical analysis. Nevertheless, several appendices (and sections) have been added to deal with more advanced material. These appendices (and sections) may be omitted without interrupting the continuity of the book. Hopefully, this will insure maximum flexibility in the book's use. All theorems are proved with great care, and all assumptions are stated and explained clearly. Although it is presumed that the student has some acquaintance with the tools and principles of elementary price theory, acquaintance with elementary calculus, though desirable, is not absolutely necessary.

The book is divided into seven parts. Part one is a simple overview of the book. Part two (chapters 2 and 3), dealing with the classical theory, is the simplest. It is nevertheless an important part of the book and should not be ignored, for in addition to providing an explanation of what the classical theory really is, it serves as a general introduction to the pure theory of trade and thus facilitates the understanding of the rest of the book. Parts three and four cover essential material which should be read before parts five to seven are read. Nevertheless, chapter 4, "Opportunity Cost," which offers a quick review of some of the tools and principles of price theory, may be omitted by those whose background in price theory is rather strong. In addition, chapter 7, "Increasing Returns," may be omitted on a first reading without interrupting the continuity of the book. After parts two to four are read, part five, "Economic Growth and Trade," can be taken up either before or after parts six and seven. Chapter 14, "Growth in a Simple Open Economy," which is more advanced than the rest of the book, can be omitted without interrupting the continuity of the book. Finally, although parts six and seven can be taken up in any order after parts two to four are read, it is recommended that part six be read before part seven.

Selected bibliographies are provided at the end of each chapter. No attempt was made to provide exhaustive bibliographies.

It should be noted that the last section of chapter 5, "Neoclassical Demonstration of Comparative Advantage," is a revised version of the author's *Metroeconomica* paper "Multiple Pre-Trade Equilibria and the Theory of Comparative Advantage." Similarly, chapter 7, "Increasing Returns," is an expanded version of the author's *Southern Economic Journal* paper "Increasing Returns and Comparative Advantage." I wish to thank the editors of both *Metroeconomica* and *Southern Economic Journal* for their permission to reproduce the above papers.

This book does not aim to push forward the frontiers of international economic analysis. Any new results which may be noticed are mere by-products of the more important aim of careful and systematic exposition.

My indebtedness to other economists is very great. To my former teachers, Robert L. Bishop, Charles P. Kindleberger, Paul A. Samuelson, and Robert M. Solow, I owe a special debt of gratitude for the knowledge and inspiration they gave me during my graduate years (1962–65) at M.I.T. Special thanks are due to Alan V. Deardorff and Heidermarie Sherman whose comments and suggestions were invaluable in improving the final product. Also, I am happy to acknowledge the influence of numerous authors of books and journal articles. Unfortunately, I cannot make specific acknowledgments (beyond those in the text itself), partly because the list would be too long and partly because I find it difficult to identify each idea I have with the source from which it came. Above all I am infinitely indebted and grateful to Professor Harry G. Johnson who made numerous invaluable suggestions and criticisms of my *Pure Theory of International Trade* (Aldine Publishing Co., 1973) which formed the basis for the present book.

Any remaining deficiencies are mine. Further, I wish to thank Stephen Dietrich, the Economics Editor of the McGraw-Hill Book Company, for his assistance in preparing the manuscript and for expediting the publication process. I would like to thank Marilyn King for making my job a lot easier with her efficient preparation of a lengthy and technical manuscript, and June Shipley and Fred Horne who helped her. Thanks are also due to Carlos Nunes for his assistance in compiling the indexes.

Miltiades Chacholiades

# INTERNATIONAL TRADE THEORY AND POLICY

# PART
# ONE

## INTRODUCTION

# INTRODUCTION

This chapter deals briefly with the relationship between international economics and general economic theory, the role of international trade in raising the standards of living of all countries of the world, and the overall organizational structure of the book.

## 1.1 THE MAIN BRANCHES OF ECONOMIC THEORY

Economics is a social science. Broadly speaking, it is concerned with the use of scarce resources (e.g., labor and skills of all kinds, land of various qualities, and the innumerable capital goods that modern technology requires) for the satisfaction of human wants.

Like most other disciplines, economics is divided into several branches and subbranches; the two major branches are *microeconomics* and *macroeconomics*. Microeconomics is the study of the behavior of individuals and well-defined groups of individuals in the society, such as households, firms, and industries. On the other hand, macroeconomics is the study of broad aggregates, such as national income, employment, consumption, and investment. In a sense, the micro-macro distinction is artificial because the actual decisions about production, consumption, employment, investment, and so on, are made by the microunits of the economy. Therefore, the basic principles of economic theory are those which explain the behavior of these microunits. However, the distinction is justified by the basic differences in the objectives and methods of the two branches.

Microeconomics deals primarily with the analysis of price determination and the allocation of specific resources to particular uses. On the other hand, macroeconomics deals with the determination of the levels of national income and aggregate resource employment. While microeconomics deals with individual prices and their relations to one another, macroeconomics deals only with aggregate price indices. As a result, the relationship between individual units and aggregates is not clear in macroeconomics. Nevertheless, the simplifications introduced by aggregation are quite useful. Despite the great usefulness of microeconomics (and, in particular, the general-equilibrium theory) to an understanding of the way in which the individual decision-making units of the economy fit together to form a coherent whole, its practical use in explaining aggregate behavior is severely limited by its enormous complexity. A more practical approach is offered by macroeconomics, which attempts to describe the behavior of the economic system in terms of a few simple aggregates and aims explicitly at influencing public policy.

When properly understood, microeconomics and macroeconomics become complementary rather than competitive branches of economic theory. Thus, macroeconomics can enable the policy makers to pursue appropriate economic policies to ensure an economic environment which will validate the verities of microeconomics. Microeconomics, on the other hand, can often be a fruitful source of hypotheses which can be used, with suitable modifications, to explain aggregate behavior.

Microeconomics is further subdivided into *positive economics* and *welfare economics*. The former is the study of what actually *is*. That is, positive economics deals with the problem of how the economic system actually functions, why it produces the results it does, and how changes in the fundamental data of the economy (such as factor endowments, factor ownership, tastes, and technology) affect the solution of the economic problem. It is important to observe that positive economics is, in principle, independent of ethical judgements, and its propositions can be tested against the facts of the real world which they purport to explain.

Welfare economics, on the other hand, is the study of what *ought* to be. It deals with propositions which are themselves logical deductions from a set of assumptions which may or may not be ethical in nature. In contrast with positive economics, the propositions of welfare economics cannot be tested against the facts of the real world for the simple reason that welfare is not an observable quantity. Usually, welfare propositions are tested indirectly by testing the assumptions from which they have been derived—and this is an extremely delicate task. The conclusions of welfare economics depend crucially on ethical judgements.

Perhaps an example might make clearer the distinction between positive and welfare economics. Consider an economy which is contemplating the removal of a tariff on an imported commodity, $M$. What effects would the removal of the tariff have on the domestic production, consumption, imports, and price of commodity $M$ and of each and every other commodity? Would the removal of the tariff tend to raise or lower real wages and other factor rewards? These questions belong to the realm of positive economics. Notice that the accuracy of the answers given to the above questions (i.e., the conclusions of positive economics) can be tested directly against the actual events which will take place after the removal of the tariff.

Consider the following questions. (*a*) Will the removal of the tariff make the workers (of the economy contemplating the removal of the tariff) better off or worse off? (*b*) What about the effects of the removal of the tariff on the welfare of the owners of land and capital? (*c*) Should the tariff be removed or not? These questions belong to the realm of welfare economics. They all involve a comparison between two situations: the situation which actually exists before and that which will exist after the removal of the tariff. Therefore, any answers that welfare economics has to offer necessarily rest on a prediction about the consequences of doing one thing rather than another, a prediction that must be based on positive economics.

What ethical judgements are involved in answering questions (*a*) through (*c*)? Questions (*a*) and (*b*) can be handled simultaneously. Consider the case of a single individual, whether worker, landlord, or capitalist. Positive analysis can show whether, after the removal of the tariff, he moves to a higher or lower indifference curve. To be specific, assume that he moves to a higher indifference curve. Does this mean that this particular individual is better off after the removal of the tariff? Not unless we make the ethical judgement that no one else but the individual himself is the best judge of his well-being. Without this ethical judgement, we may say that he moves to a higher indifference curve, but we are then only describing how he acts—we are not judging his welfare.

Consider now question (*c*): should the tariff be removed or not? If social welfare increases with the removal of the tariff, the tariff should be removed; if social welfare decreases, it should not be removed; and if social welfare remains constant, it makes no difference. But what is social welfare? And how can we find out whether it increases or decreases with the removal of the tariff? To answer these questions, additional ethical judgements are required. For instance, we can postulate that social welfare depends on the welfare of the individuals comprising the society, and on nothing else. The mathematical expression of this statement is the Bergson–Samuelson social-welfare function in its general form, discussed in chaps. 5 and 16. This function is usually made a little more specific by attributing to it an ethical property, namely, that social welfare increases when one individual becomes better off, with no one else being worse off. Now, if the removal of the tariff were to make everybody better off, we could immediately conclude, on the basis of the ethical judgements made so far, that the tariff should be removed. But this is a big *if*. What if the removal of the tariff made some people better off and others worse off? In this more likely case, several alternatives are open to us, and they will be considered in detail in chap. 16. What is important right now, however, is that the propositions of welfare economics depend on ethical judgements whereas the propositions of positive economics do not.

## 1.2 THE SCOPE OF INTERNATIONAL ECONOMICS

While general economic theory deals with the problems of a single, closed economy, international economics deals with the problems of two or more open economies. In particular, international economics deals with the same economic problems as those studied by general economic theory, but it deals with these problems in their international setting. Thus, international economics studies how a number of distinct economies interact upon each other in the process of allocating scarce resources to satisfy human wants. Clearly, international economics is more general than the economics of a closed economy, the latter being a special case of international economics where the number of trading countries has been reduced to one. Further, the study of general economic theory dealing with the problems of a closed economy is only a first (but necessary) step toward the study of the behavior of a real economy, because there is actually no closed economy except the world economy.

Parallel to the division of economic theory into microeconomics and macroeconomics is the breakdown of international economics into two major branches: international trade theory (or the pure theory of trade) and international monetary economics. The latter is centered upon the monetary aspects of international monetary relations. Its approach is mainly macroeconomic in nature, and it particularly deals with the short-run problems of balance-of-payments disequilibrium and adjustment.

The subject matter of this book is the pure theory of trade, which, in contrast to international monetary economics, is a long-run, static-equilibrium theory of barter. Here the short-run monetary adjustment process is assumed completed, with money having no influence whatsoever on the nature or position of long-run equilibrium. Its approach is basically microeconomic in nature. Like microeconomics, the pure theory of trade can be divided into two main branches: one branch dealing with problems of positive economics and the other dealing with problems of welfare economics. Thus, the analysis of the effects of free trade on domestic consumption, production, commodity prices, factor rewards, and so on, belongs to what might be called international positive economics. On the other hand, the question of whether free trade is better than restricted or no trade is clearly an issue which belongs to the realm of (international) welfare economics.

## 1.3 THE ROLE OF TRADE

The importance of trade springs from the extensive degree of specialization observed in our society. Even in the most primitive societies people cooperate in the use of their scarce resources, because through such cooperation more goods and services are produced than if everyone tried to do many different jobs at once.

The high degree of specialization in our society increases the standard of living of all by making more goods and services available. *But specialization necessarily implies trade and cannot occur without it.* This follows from the fact that people usually want to have a " balanced diet." The specialized producer uses only a small part—maybe none—of his own product for his personal consumption, and he exchanges his surplus for the goods and services of other specialized producers. For instance, a shoemaker does not and cannot consume only shoes. He needs, in addition, food, clothing, shelter, transportation, and so on. Therefore, he exchanges his surplus production of shoes (which, for practical purposes, may be identified with his total output of shoes) for the specialized outputs of farmers, supermarkets, auto producers, physicians, tailors, and the like. Such exchange of goods and services among specialized producers is exactly what is meant by trade.

The exchange of goods and services among residents of the same country is usually called *domestic trade*. The present book is, however, concerned with *international trade*, i.e., the exchange of goods and services among residents of different countries. Countries cannot live alone any more effectively than individuals can. Thus, each country tends to specialize in the production of those commodities which it can produce relatively more cheaply than other countries, exchanging its surplus for the surplus of other countries of goods and services which they produce relatively more cheaply, or which the first country cannot produce at all. This process brings about an international division of labor which makes it possible to make more goods and services available to all countries. Therefore, the international division of labor and specialization increases the standard of living in all countries in the same way that the division of labor and specialization within a single, closed economy increases the standard of living of all of its residents. In the same way that the division of labor and specialization within a single, closed economy necessarily implies domestic trade and cannot occur without it, the international division of labor and specialization necessarily implies international trade and cannot occur without it.

## 1.4 PLAN OF THE BOOK

This book is mainly concerned with the basic theoretical principles that govern international trade, and also with empirical evidence and trade policy. In particular, chaps. 2 and 3 deal with the classical theory of comparative advantage associated with Robert Torrens, David Ricardo, and John Stuart Mill. But chaps. 2 and 3 actually do more than this. Because of the inherent complexity of the pure theory of trade due mainly to its general-equilibrium character, it was considered useful to introduce, within the context of the simple labor theory of value, most of the tools which are used later in the book. Hence, chaps. 2 and 3 can also be considered as a general introduction to the pure theory of trade. Familiarity with the contents of these chapters will definitely improve the student's chances of understanding the rest of the book. The appendix to chap. 3 extends the analysis to many countries and many commodities. This appendix can be omitted without interrupting the continuity of the book.

Chapters 4 through 7 cover the neoclassical theory of international trade associated with Alfred Marshall, Jacob Viner, Gottfried Haberler, F. Y. Edgeworth, Abba P. Lerner, Wassily W. Leontief, and James E. Meade. In particular, chap. 4 deals with the theory of production and cost minimization, the concept of the production-possibilities frontier and opportunity cost. Chapter 5 deals with the concept of social indifference, and the problem of general equilibrium and comparative advantage. Chapter 6 deals with Meade's ingenious geometric technique and the stability of international equilibrium. Finally, chap. 7 deals with the problem of increasing returns to scale. Because of its more technical character, chap. 7 may be omitted without interrupting the continuity of the book. In addition, all appendices to chaps. 4 through 7 may be omitted.

Chapters 8 through 11 deal with the modern theory of trade associated with Eli F. Heckscher, Bertil Ohlin, Paul A. Samuelson, and Abba P. Lerner. In particular, chap. 8 deals with the concepts of factor intensity and factor abundance. Chapter 9 deals with the relationship among factor proportions, factor prices, and commodity prices. Chapter 10 deals with (a) the factor price-equalization theorem (namely, that the effect of trade is to tend to equalize factor prices between countries, thus serving to some extent as a substitute for factor mobility) and (b) the Heckscher–Ohlin theorem (namely, that the cause of trade is to be found largely in differences between the factor endowments of different countries). Finally, chap. 11 deals with the Leontief paradox. Again the appendices to chaps. 8 and 10 may be omitted.

Chapters 12 through 14 deal with the effects of economic growth due either to growth of factor endowments or to technical progress. Chapters 12 and 13 are largely based on Harry G. Johnson's comparative-statics model of growth. Chapter 14, on the other hand, is a dynamic model which could be considered an integration of the growth models of Robert M. Solow and Hirofumi Uzawa. Chapter 14 can easily be omitted.

Chapters 15 and 16 deal with the effects of international trade on economic welfare. In particular, chap. 15 discusses the effects of international trade on the welfare of the citizens of the trading countries; and chap. 16 covers the evaluation of the effects of international trade on social welfare.

Chapters 17 through 23 deal with international trade policy. Chapters 17 through 19 deal primarily with what H. G. Johnson calls the standard theory of tariffs. In particular, chap. 17 deals with the forms of trade control and the effects of import and export taxes and subsidies when the tax-imposing country is small (i.e., a price taker in the international market); chap. 18 deals with the effects of import and export taxes, subsidies, and quantitative restrictions when the tax-imposing country is large; and chap. 19 deals with the welfare effects of trade taxes and subsidies, the Stolper–Samuelson theorem, and optimum tariffs and retaliation. Chapter 20 deals with the theory of domestic distortions which is applied in chap. 21 to the infant-industry argument for protection as well as the theory of noneconomic objectives. Finally, chaps. 22 and 23 deal with the theory of customs unions.

## SELECTED BIBLIOGRAPHY

Listed below are several selected readings in the areas of mathematical economics, microeconomics, and international economics. This list is neither exhaustive nor required for the understanding of the different aspects of the pure theory of international trade presented in this study. However, it was considered useful to provide a convenient guide to the literature relevant to the present study. More specific references will be found at the end of each chapter.

## Mathematics and Mathematical Economics

Allen, R. G. D. (1959). *Mathematical Economics*. Macmillan and Company, London.
—— (1960). *Mathematical Analysis for Economists*. Macmillan and Company, London.
Apostol, T. M. (1960). *Mathematical Analysis*. Addison-Wesley Publishing Company, Reading, Mass.
—— (1964). *Calculus*, 2 vols. Blaisdell Publishing Company, New York.
Chiang, A. C. (1967). *Fundamental Methods of Mathematical Economics*. McGraw-Hill Book Company, New York.
Courant, R. (1936). *Differential and Integral Calculus*, 2 vols. Blackie and Son, Ltd., London.
—— and H. Robbins (1963). *What Is Mathematics?* Oxford University Press, Oxford.
Samuelson, P. A. (1947). *Foundations of Economic Analysis*. Harvard University Press, Cambridge, Mass.
Yamane, T. (1968). *Mathematics for Economists*, 2d ed. Prentice-Hall, Inc., Englewood Cliffs, N.J.

## Microeconomics

Becker, G. S. (1971). *Economic Theory*. Alfred A. Knopf, Inc., New York.
Ferguson, C. E. (1972). *Microeconomic Theory*, 3d ed. Richard D. Irwin, Inc., Homewood, Ill.
Friedman, M. (1962). *Price Theory: A Provisional Text*. Aldine Publishing Company, Chicago, Ill.
Graaff, J. de V. (1967). *Theoretical Welfare Economics*. Cambridge University Press, London.
Henderson, J. M., and R. E. Quandt (1971). *Microeconomic Theory*, 2d ed. McGraw-Hill Book Company, New York.
Hicks, J. R. (1946). *Value and Capital*, 2d ed. Clarendon Press, Oxford.
Hirshleifer, J. (1976). *Price Theory and Applications*. Prentice-Hall, Inc., Englewood Cliffs, N.J.
Johnson, H. G. (1973). *The Theory of Income Distribution*. Gray-Mills Publishing, Ltd., London.
Lancaster, K. (1969). *Introduction to Modern Microeconomics*. Rand McNally and Company, Chicago, Ill.
Quirk, J., and R. Saposnik (1968). *Introduction to General Equilibrium Theory and Welfare Economics*. McGraw-Hill Book Company, New York.

## International Economics

American Economic Association (1950). *Readings in the Theory of International Trade*. R. D. Irwin, Inc., Homewood, Ill.
—— (1968). *Readings in International Economics*. R. D. Irwin, Inc., Homewood, Ill.
Balassa, B. (1961). *The Theory of Economic Integration*. R. D. Irwin, Inc., Homewood, Ill.
Baldwin, R. E., and J. D. Richardson (1974). *International Trade and Finance: Readings*. Little, Brown and Company, Boston, Mass.
Bhagwati, J. (1964). "The Pure Theory of International Trade." *Economic Journal*, vol. 74, pp. 1–78.
Caves, R. E. (1960). *Trade and Economic Structure*. Harvard University Press, Cambridge, Mass.
—— and R. W. Jones (1973). *World Trade and Payments*. Little, Brown and Company, Boston, Mass.
Chacholiades, M. (1973). *The Pure Theory of International Trade*. Aldine Publishing Company, Chicago, Ill.
Chipman, J. S. (1965). "A Survey of the Theory of International Trade: Part 1, The Classical Theory." *Econometrica*, vol. 33, pp. 477–519.
—— (1965). "A Survey of the Theory of International Trade: Part 2, The Neoclassical Theory." *Econometrica*, vol. 33, pp. 685–760.
—— (1966). "A Survey of the Theory of International Trade: Part 3, The Modern Theory." *Econometrica*, vol. 34, pp. 18–76.
Clement, M. O., R. L. Pfister, and K. J. Rothwell (1967). *Theoretical Issues in International Economics*. Houghton-Mifflin Company, Boston, Mass.
Corden, W. M. (1965). *Recent Developments in the Theory of International Trade*. Princeton University Special Papers in International Economics, no. 7, Princeton, N.J.

Ellsworth, P. T., and J. C. Leith (1975). *The International Economy*, 5th ed. The Macmillan Company, New York.

Enke, S., and V. Salera (1957). *International Economics*. Prentice-Hall, Inc., Englewood Cliffs, N.J.

Freeman III, A. M. (1971). *International Trade*. Harper and Row, Publishers, New York.

Friedrich, K. (1974). *International Economics*. McGraw-Hill Book Company, New York.

Haberler, G. (1936). *The Theory of International Trade*. William Hodge and Company, London.

——— (1961). *A Survey of International Trade Theory*. Princeton University Special Papers in International Economics, no. 1, 2d ed., Princeton, N.J.

Harrod, R. (1973). *International Economics*. Cambridge University Press, Cambridge.

Heller, H. R. (1973). *International Trade*, 2d ed. Prentice-Hall, Inc., Englewood Cliffs, N.J.

Horwich, G., and P. A. Samuelson (Eds.) (1974). *Trade, Stability, and Macroeconomics*. Academic Press, New York.

Johnson, H. G. (1958). *International Trade and Economic Growth*. George Allen and Unwin, Ltd., London.

——— (1962). *Money, Trade and Economic Growth*. Harvard University Press, Cambridge, Mass.

——— (1972). *Aspects of the Theory of Tariffs*. Harvard University Press, Cambridge, Mass.

Kemp, M. C. (1964). *The Pure Theory of International Trade*. Prentice-Hall, Inc., Englewood Cliffs, N.J.

——— (1969). *The Pure Theory of International Trade and Investment*. Prentice-Hall, Inc., Englewood Cliffs, N.J.

——— (1969). *A Contribution to the General Equilibrium Theory of Preferential Trading*. Amsterdam: North-Holland Publishing Co.

Kindleberger, C. P. (1973). *International Economics*, 5th ed. R. D. Irwin, Inc., Homewood, Ill.

Krauss, M. B., and H. G. Johnson (1975). *General Equilibrium Analysis*. Aldine Publishing Company, Chicago, Ill.

Lerner, A. P. (1953). *Essays in Economic Analysis*. Macmillan and Company, London.

Magee, S. P. (1976). *International Trade and Distortions in Factor Markets*. Marcel Dekker, Inc., New York.

Meade, J. E. (1952). *A Geometry of International Trade*. George Allen and Unwin, Ltd., London.

——— (1955). *The Theory of International Economic Policy*, vol. 2: *Trade and Welfare*. Oxford University Press, Oxford.

Meier, G. M. (1963). *International Trade and Development*. Harper and Row, New York.

Metzler, L. A. (1948). "The Theory of International Trade." In H. S. Ellis (Ed.), *A Survey of Contemporary Economics*. Blackiston Company, Philadelphia, Pa.

Mookerjee, S. (1958). *Factor Endowment and International Trade: A Study and Appraisal of the Heckscher-Ohlin Theory*. Asia Publishing House, Bombay.

Mosak, J. L. (1944). *General Equilibrium Theory in International Trade*. Principia Press, Bloomington, Ind.

Mundell, R. A. (1960). "The Pure Theory of International Trade." *American Economic Review*, vol. 40, pp. 301–22.

——— (1968). *International Economics*. The Macmillan Company, New York.

Ohlin, B. (1933). *Interregional and International Trade*. Harvard University Press, Cambridge, Mass.

Scammell, W. M. (1974). *International Trade and Payments*. St. Martin's Press, New York.

Snider, D. A. (1975). *Introduction to International Economics*, 6th ed. R. D. Irwin, Inc., Homewood, Ill.

Vanek, J. (1962). *International Trade: Theory and Economic Policy*. R. D. Irwin, Inc., Homewood, Ill.

Viner, J. (1965). *Studies in the Theory of International Trade*. Augustus M. Kelly, Publishers, New York.

Walter, I. (1968). *International Economics: Theory and Policy*. Ronald Press, New York.

Yntema, T. O. (1932). *A Mathematical Reformulation of the General Theory of International Trade*. University of Chicago Press, Chicago, Ill.

Young, D. (1970). *International Economics*. Intext Educational Publishers, Scranton, Pa.

# PART TWO

# THE CLASSICAL THEORY

# TWO

# SUPPLY

## 2.1 THE PROBLEM

The pure theory of trade, as expounded by the classical economists Torrens, Ricardo, and Mill, is mainly concerned with the following three questions:

1. Which goods are exported and imported; i.e., what is the direction or pattern of trade in commodities and services among the nations of the world?
2. What are the terms of trade; i.e., at what prices are the exported and imported goods exchanged internationally?
3. What are the gains from trade; i.e., is trade profitable from the point of view of the world as a whole, on the one hand, as well as from the point of view of each country separately, on the other? If so, how are these gains or profits divided among the participating countries?

The first two questions belong to the realm of positive economics, while the third belongs to the realm of welfare economics. However, in a presentation of the pure theory, the three questions cannot be considered apart from each other. This follows from the fact that the pattern of trade of a country, i.e., which commodities it exports and which it imports, depends on the terms of trade; further, the division of the gains from trade among the trading partners also depends on the terms of trade; and, finally, the gains from trade form the motivating force of all trade.

Despite the strong interdependence that exists among the three questions raised by the classical economists, for pedagogical reasons each question is dealt with separately. Before getting down to specifics, however, let us see how the classical theory answers the three questions in a rather general fashion.

To the first question (which goods are exported and which are imported by a country?), the classical theory gives the following simple answer. Each country will concentrate on the production of those goods that it can produce relatively more cheaply than other countries and exchange the surplus (i.e., whatever it produces above the requirements for its own needs) *against the surplus goods other countries produce relatively more cheaply*, or goods which the first country cannot produce at all. From this point, it is easy to derive the answer to the third question (what are the gains from trade?), because the preceding process brings about an international division of labor that makes it possible to produce more of every commodity on a worldwide basis, with the surplus production representing the gains from trade to be distributed among the trading partners. Finally, as far as the second question is concerned, the classical theory shows that the equilibrium terms of trade will be determined by international supply and demand relations and that they (i.e., the terms of trade) will provide the basis for the division of the gains from trade among the participating nations. This is the classical theory in a nutshell.

## 2.2 THE LABOR THEORY OF VALUE

The classical economists adopted the simplifying assumption of the labor theory of value. This theory asserts that labor is the only factor of production and that in a closed economy the prices of all commodities are determined by their labor content. In particular, since our interest lies mainly in relative as opposed to absolute prices with regard to the pure theory of trade, according to the labor theory of value, goods are exchanged against one another according to the relative amounts of labor they represent. For example, assume that there are two commodities, $X$ and $Y$. Let the symbol $a_x$ denote the amount of labor that is required for the production of 1 unit of commodity $X$; and the symbol $a_y$, the amount of labor that is required for the production of 1 unit of commodity $Y$. If $w$ is used to denote the money wage rate, then the long-run average cost of production of the two commodities is given by the following equations:†

$$\text{Average cost of } X = wa_x$$

$$\text{Average cost of } Y = wa_y$$

Note that a common wage rate is used for both commodities because of the implicitly assumed mobility of labor between the two industries.

The coefficients of production $a_x$ and $a_y$ were assumed by the classical economists to be constant in the sense that they were independent of the level of output of each industry. In other words, the coefficients $a_x$ and $a_y$ are assumed to remain the same whether 10 or 1000 or any other number of units of $X$ and $Y$ are produced. Under these circumstances, it follows that the supply curves of $X$ and $Y$ are horizontal at the levels $wa_x$ and $wa_y$, respectively. Consequently, the long-run equilibrium prices of $X$ and $Y$ ($p_x$ and $p_y$, respectively) must necessarily be given by the equations

$$p_x = wa_x \qquad p_y = wa_y \tag{2.1}$$

provided that both commodities are produced.

---

† Here and elsewhere the symbols $X$ and $Y$ stand both for names and for quantities.

*Not produced because price is less than cost so $P_y = w a_y$ would not hold $P_y < w a_y$ unless $P_y = w a_y$ at point where demand = supply = 0*

The requirement that both commodities be produced for the validity of eqs. (2.1) is seen from the fact that the price of a commodity that is not produced—in the sense of the maximum price that the consumers might be willing to pay if they were to consume a positive amount of the said commodity—is usually less than the average cost of production, except in the limiting case where the market supply and demand curves happen to have a common price-axis intercept. From eqs. (2.1) it follows that relative prices ($p$) are entirely determined by relative labor requirements; that is,

$$w = \frac{p_x}{a_x} = \frac{p_y}{a_y} \implies p \equiv \frac{p_x}{p_y} = \frac{a_x}{a_y} \tag{2.2}$$

The constancy of the coefficients $a_x$ and $a_y$ does not necessarily imply that the average cost of production of each firm, as opposed to each industry, is constant, with the optimum size of each firm being indeterminate. It may very well be that the production function of each firm is characterized successively by increasing, constant, and decreasing returns. In other words, as $X$ and $Y$ increase from zero, their respective coefficients $a_x$ and $a_y$ decrease continuously (increasing returns) until they reach their respective minima (momentary constant returns), and then they increase (decreasing returns). Under these circumstances, the average cost curve of each firm will be U-shaped, as usually assumed. However, if the production functions of all producers in each industry separately are the same, then each long-run industry supply curve will still be horizontal at the level of minimum average cost of each producer in each individual industry, as the reader should be able to verify. What this means is that, despite the fact that the coefficients $a_x$ and $a_y$ are actually variable, we can rest assured that Adam Smith's invisible hand will guide industries to choose their minimum values which are uniquely determined. Thus, the analysis presented earlier is more general than what it appears to be. In fact, the perfect identity of production functions of firms producing the same commodity is not actually needed. The only requirement for our conclusion is that the production functions of all firms in the same industry give rise to the same minimum value of the labor coefficient—and this may very well occur at varying levels of production among the various firms.

That the labor theory of value is an oversimplification of reality is well known. Broadly speaking, it is valid under the assumptions that labor is the only factor of production, that it is homogeneous (i.e., all labor is of the same quality), that every occupation is open to all, and that perfect competition rules everywhere. These assumptions are too restrictive; in reality, some of them are never true and some are not always true. In particular, the element of time is a difficulty the theory cannot surmount. Thus, with a positive rate of interest, the average cost of a commodity, and hence its price, is influenced not merely by the amount of labor required to produce it but also by the length of time for which it is embodied in production. For instance, if one worker can produce 1 unit of $X$ in one year while it requires one worker two years to produce 1 unit of $Y$, the relative price of $X$ in terms of $Y$ will be smaller than one-half—i.e., the price predicted by the simple labor theory of value—because the producers of $Y$ will necessarily incur a certain amount of interest expense over and above their wage bill. In particular, assume that each worker is paid $\$w$ at the end of each year. Then

$$p_x = \$w$$

$$p_y = \$[w(1 + i) + w]$$

*when you sell good you must charge for the wages you had tied up for a year.*

$$\frac{p_x}{p_y} = \frac{w}{w(1 + i) + w} = \frac{1}{2 + i} < \frac{1}{2}$$

where $i \equiv$ the rate of interest. Thus, relative prices do not depend only on the relative amounts of labor required for the production of the two commodities; they also depend on the rate of interest.

Despite the obvious shortcomings of the labor theory of value, we shall adopt it as our point of departure for three reasons. First, it will enable us, with relatively little effort, to bring out quite sharply the nature of the problem of international specialization and the gains from trade. Second, if the interest rate remains constant, the relative price structure will be fixed. Third, it will enable us to construct a fairly simple model of international equilibrium that will serve as an introduction to the more complicated models of the neoclassical and modern writers. As noted in the introductory chapter, the pure theory of trade is a general-equilibrium theory which is inherently more difficult than the Marshallian approach of partial equilibrium. Thus, students lacking a fairly good background in general-equilibrium theory would probably give the subject up if we were to start directly with the neoclassical and modern theories. However, a student who understands well the analysis of chaps. 2 and 3—which is fairly elementary—will be at an advantage in understanding the more complex theories in later chapters.

## 2.3 ABSOLUTE ADVANTAGE

Adam Smith (1937) emphasized the importance of free trade in increasing the wealth of all trading nations. He stated that "it is a maxim of every prudent master of a family never to attempt to make at home what it will cost him more to make than to buy." He later continued that

> What is prudence in the conduct of every private family, can scarce be folly in that of a great kingdom. If a foreign country can supply us with a commodity cheaper than we ourselves make it, better buy it of them with some part of the produce of our own industry employed in a way in which we have some advantage. . . . By means of glasses, hotbeds, and hotwalls, very good grapes can be raised in Scotland, and very good wine too can be made of them at about thirty times the expense for which at least equally good can be bought from foreign countries. Would it be a reasonable law to prohibit the importation of all foreign wines, merely to encourage the making of claret and burgundy in Scotland? . . . As long as the one country has those advantages, and the other wants them, it will always be more advantageous for the latter, rather to buy of the former than to make (pp. 424–426).

### An Illustration

This can best be understood with a simple illustration. Let there be two countries, $A$ and $B$, endowed with labor alone and producing two commodities, $X$ and $Y$. In particular, assume that country $A$ can produce a unit of commodity $X$ with 4 units of labor and a unit of commodity $Y$ with 2 units of labor, and that in country $B$ the corresponding costs (in labor units) of $X$ and $Y$ are 2 and 4, respectively. This state of affairs is usually expressed by saying that $A$ has an *absolute advantage* in the production of $Y$, because 1 unit of $Y$ requires more units of labor in $B$ than in $A$. Similarly, $B$ has an absolute advantage in the production of $X$ because 1 unit of $X$ requires more units of labor in $A$ than in $B$. Notice that we speak of an *absolute advantage* because each country can produce one commodity at an absolutely lower cost—measured in labor units—than the other country.

Assuming that labor is immobile between the two countries, is profitable trade in commodities possible between them? Adam Smith would say yes. He would also go on to say that it would be to the advantage of both countries if $A$ specialized in (or confined itself to) the production of $Y$, and $B$ in the production of $X$.

Before going any further, it can be shown quite explicitly that the international division of labor postulated by Smith will indeed increase the total world output of every commodity.

Assume that, up to this moment in time, the two countries have been isolated by prohibitive trade barriers. In their isolated general-equilibrium states, they have been producing and consuming the following quantities of $X$ and $Y$ per unit of time: $X_A$, $Y_A$ (country $A$), and $X_B$, $Y_B$ (country $B$), where the subscripts $A$ and $B$ indicate the country. Thus, up to now, the total world production of $X$ (denoted by $X_W$) and $Y$ (denoted by $Y_W$) per unit of time has been

$$X_W = X_A + X_B \qquad Y_W = Y_A + Y_B \qquad (2.3)$$

As long as $A$ produces a positive amount of $X$ and $B$ a positive amount of $Y$ (i.e., as long as $X_A > 0$, $Y_B > 0$) in their isolated general-equilibrium states, it can be shown that it is possible to increase the total world production of every commodity if $A$ specializes in the production of $Y$ and $B$ in $X$. Thus, suppose that, starting from the isolated general-equilibrium states, country $A$ transfers 4 units of labor from the production of $X$ to the production of $Y$, and $B$ transfers 4 units of labor from $Y$ to $X$. On the basis of the assumed labor coefficients of production, the outputs of $X$ and $Y$ in the two countries, and the world as a whole, will change as follows:

$$\Delta X_A = -1 \qquad \Delta X_B = +2$$
$$\Delta Y_A = +2 \qquad \Delta Y_B = -1$$
$$\Delta X_W \equiv \Delta X_A + \Delta X_B = +1 \qquad (2.4)$$
$$\Delta Y_W \equiv \Delta Y_A + \Delta Y_B = +1$$

This process can continue for as long as $X_A > 0$ and $Y_B > 0$.

The conclusion that the world output of both commodities can increase if $A$ specializes in $Y$ and $B$ in $X$ does not necessarily imply that the world output of every commodity actually increases with free trade. The outcome, as is shown later, depends on tastes.

## The Optimum Distribution of Labor Between Countries

Observe that, in the above illustration of absolute advantage, labor will not necessarily migrate from one country to another, even if it were perfectly mobile between countries, for after the removal of trade barriers each country will continue to produce one product because it is more efficient than the other (in that product) in an absolute sense. Thus, the optimum distribution of labor in the sense of maximizing world output would depend ultimately on the strength of the demand for each commodity. For instance, suppose that all consumers in both countries consume the two commodities in the fixed proportion $1X : 1Y$. Then, in equilibrium, the total number of units of $X$ produced (and consumed) must be equal to the total number of units of $Y$ produced (and consumed). Now, since with perfect labor mobility $A$ will be producing all units of $Y$ and $B$ all units of $X$; it follows that half of the total world labor force must be working in $A$ and the other half in $B$. (Remember that the labor coefficient of $X$ in $B$ is by assumption equal to the labor coefficient of $Y$ in $A$.) This is the optimum distribution of labor between the two countries. If it existed to begin with, labor would not move internationally even if it were perfectly mobile. On the other hand, if the actual distribution of labor were different from the optimal, a limited migration would be required from the more heavily populated country to the less heavily populated country until the optimum distribution was established. Further, on the assumption that labor is perfectly mobile internationally, relative prices under conditions of free trade will be determined by the relative amounts of labor embodied in the two commodities, as in the case of a closed economy. The best way to see this is to observe that the present case does not differ at all from the case where $A$ and $B$ are simply two different regions of the same country, instead of being two independent countries. In this case, of course, it is obvious that relative prices are indeed determined according to the labor theory of value. However, if labor is completely immobile between countries, relative prices cannot be determined so easily. This topic will be taken up in a later section of this chapter.

## Absolute Advantage Is Not Needed for Profitable Trade

What is the fundamental reason why the international division of labor postulated by Adam Smith does indeed result in an increased output of both commodities? Some, including Smith himself, would hasten to point out that this is so because $A$ has an absolute advantage in $Y$ and $B$ in $X$. But this is a superficial answer and does not really get to the crux of the matter. Suppose that $A$ had an absolute advantage in both $X$ and $Y$. What should we conclude then? That $A$ should produce both $X$ and $Y$ and $B$ nothing? This would make sense only if $A$ and $B$ were two regions of the same country, or if labor was free to migrate from country $B$ to country $A$. But what if $A$ and $B$ are indeed separate countries and labor cannot move from $B$ to $A$? Is it not then reasonable to conclude that even the more inefficient country $B$ must produce something? It appears, then, that the fundamental reason for profitable trade is not to be found in the absolute differences in labor cost between the two countries. In other words, it appears that *profitable international trade does not necessarily require an exporter to have an absolute advantage over his foreign rivals.* But if this is so, then what is the *raison d'être* for profitable international trade? This particular question is taken up below in secs. 2.4 and 2.5, where it is shown that absolute labor-cost differences are not necessary for profitable trade.

## 2.4 COMPARATIVE ADVANTAGE

### The Setting

To gain further insight into the problem of international specialization, consider the following illustration. Assume again two countries, $A$ and $B$, two commodities, $X$ and $Y$, and a single homogeneous factor of production, labor. As before, assume that $A$'s labor requirements in the production of $X$ and $Y$ are 4 and 2 units of labor, respectively. However, in complete contrast to the preceding illustration of absolute advantage, assume that $B$'s labor requirements in the production of $X$ and $Y$ are 6 and 12 units of labor, respectively—i.e., three times as much as those assumed in the preceding illustration of absolute advantage. Table 2.1 summarizes the data.

   In the present illustration, which Ricardo considered as the typical state of affairs, one of the two countries (that is, $A$) can produce both goods with a smaller expenditure (cost) of labor than the other (that is, $B$). It should be obvious that if $A$ and $B$ were two regions of the same country, or if labor were perfectly mobile among countries, all goods would eventually end up being produced in that region (or country) where costs are lower in an absolute sense. But what happens in the presence of labor immobility among countries?

### Arguments Against Free Trade

It is interesting to note some of the arguments against free trade that could be advanced in each of the two countries. Thus, in $B$, some politicians might argue that $A$'s efficiency is so great that it would undersell $B$'s producers in every line of production. Therefore, import tariffs are needed to protect $B$'s (honest) workers from ruinous foreign competition. On the other hand, in country $A$, some politicians might argue that $B$'s wage rate will definitely be lower than that of $A$, since the latter is more productive than the former. Therefore, it might be argued, if $A$'s workers are subjected to the competition of $B$'s cheap labor, the real wage of $A$'s

**Table 2.1**

|  | Country $A$ | Country $B$ |
| --- | --- | --- |
| Labor requirements per unit of output of: |  |  |
|    Commodity $X$ | 4 | 6 |
|    Commodity $Y$ | 2 | 12 |
| Relative price (or cost) of $X$ in terms of $Y$ | 2 | $\frac{1}{2}$ |
| Relative price (or cost) of $Y$ in terms of $X$ | $\frac{1}{2}$ | 2 |

workers will drastically fall; hence, protective tariffs are needed. Thus, both countries could provide pseudoarguments against free trade. The greatest contribution of Ricardo and Torrens† was to show that both of these arguments are wrong. The workers of both countries can indeed benefit from international trade.

### Definition of Comparative Advantage

Consider again table 2.1. Country $A$ has an absolute advantage in the production of both $X$ and $Y$ because $4 < 6$ and $2 < 12$, respectively. However, its absolute advantage is greater in the production of $Y$ than in $X$ because $\frac{2}{12} < \frac{4}{6}$. In other words, $A$ requires 2 and $B$ requires 12 units of labor for the production of 1 unit of $Y$. Or $A$ requires $\frac{2}{12}$ (approximately 17 percent) of the amount of labor that $B$ requires for the production of the same amount of output of $Y$. On the other hand, $A$ requires $\frac{4}{6}$, or approximately 67 percent, of the amount of labor that $B$ requires for the production of the same amount of output of $X$. Hence, $A$'s advantage is greater in the production of $Y$ than in $X$. It can be said that $A$ has a *comparative advantage* in the production of $Y$ and a *comparative disadvantage* in the production of $X$.

Similarly, country $B$ has an *absolute disadvantage* in the production of both $X$ and $Y$ for the same reasons that $A$ has an absolute advantage in both commodities. However, its disadvantage is smaller in the production of $X$ than in $Y$, since $\frac{6}{4} < \frac{12}{2}$. This is expressed by saying that $B$ has a comparative *advantage* in the production of $X$ and necessarily a comparative *disadvantage* in the production of $Y$.

Note that comparative advantage, as opposed to absolute advantage, is a relative term. Essentially, the same inequality was used to determine the commodity in whose production each of the two countries has a comparative advantage. In other words, the inequalities $\frac{2}{12} < \frac{4}{6}$ and $\frac{6}{4} < \frac{12}{2}$ are equivalent. Therefore, in a two-country, two-commodity model, once it is determined that, for instance, $A$ has a comparative advantage in $Y$, the rest (i.e., that $A$ has a comparative disadvantage in $X$ and that $B$ has a comparative advantage in $X$ and a comparative disadvantage in $Y$) follows automatically.

### Comparative Advantage and the Gains from Trade

*multiply both sides by 9*

Can international trade be profitable even when one country has an absolute advantage in the production of every commodity? The great classical achievement was to demonstrate that, even under the present circumstances where one country is more efficient than the other in every line of production, an international division of labor would also take place that could (potentially) increase the world output of every commodity. What is even more surprising is that the truth of this theorem can be demonstrated in exactly the same way as in the simple case where each country has an absolute advantage in the production of only one

---

† The theory of *comparative advantage* is usually associated with Ricardo (1821). However, an increasing number of economists tend to believe that we owe the theory to Torrens (1808, 1815). Therefore, it seems reasonable to call it the *Ricardo–Torrens theory*. See also Chipman (1965, pp. 480–483).

commodity—Adam Smith's case. In fact, for the proof of the theorem, the same equations can be used (i.e., eqs. (2.4)) that were used in Adam Smith's case. The equations are reproduced below for convenience:

$$\Delta X_A = -1 \qquad \Delta X_B = +2$$
$$\Delta Y_A = +2 \qquad \Delta Y_B = -1$$
$$\Delta X_W \equiv \Delta X_A + \Delta X_B = +1 \tag{2.4}$$
$$\Delta Y_W \equiv \Delta Y_A + \Delta Y_B = +1$$

Starting again from the isolated general-equilibrium states of the two countries, let country $A$ transfer 4 units of labor from the production of $X$ to the production of $Y$—as before—and let country $B$ transfer 12 units of labor from $Y$ to $X$—i.e., three times as many as before, since $B$ is assumed to be three times less efficient now than before. With the qualifications made earlier, it is clear that the resulting changes in the world outputs of both commodities will again be given by eqs. (2.4). The proof is complete.

The general conclusion that can be derived from the preceding analysis is that, if each country specializes in the production of that commodity in which it has a comparative advantage, the total world output of every commodity necessarily increases potentially (*the law of comparative advantage*). However, it should be noted that specialization according to comparative advantage does not enable the world to produce the maximum output that could be produced if all labor were free to migrate to the most efficient country. Free commodity trade will, nevertheless, enable the world to produce more of everything, as compared with the case where each country is a closed economy with no international trade relations. Finally, free international trade is profitable (i.e., it increases potentially the world output of every commodity) if, and only if, there exists a difference in the relative labor requirements between countries. That is, if country $A$ is more efficient than $B$ in the production of every commodity, but the degree of its superiority is the same everywhere, then there is no basis for trade.

## The General Validity of the Law of Comparative Advantage

The principle of comparative advantage has general validity: it applies to the division of labor between individual persons. Examples are not difficult to find. A business manager, though a great typist himself, employs somebody else to do his typing because it pays him to concentrate upon those tasks in which his superiority, and thus his comparative advantage, is greatest. The same is true of the doctor who employs a gardener or the teacher who employs an assistant to grade his papers.

## 2.5 OPPORTUNITY COST

### The Theory of Opportunity Costs

So far, it has been demonstrated that international trade does not require offsetting absolute advantages but is possible—and profitable to both trading countries in general—where a comparative advantage exists. However, the analysis and conclusions seem to depend on the restrictive assumption of the labor theory of value. As noted earlier, the labor theory of value is not generally accepted as valid, because labor is neither homogeneous nor the sole factor of production. Labor consists of numerous qualitatively different subgroups known as "noncompeting" groups. For instance, if the demand for medical services increases while the demand for servicing automobiles decreases, it would hardly be conceivable to expect auto mechanics to assume the role of physicians; the wage rate of the two groups would, in at least the short run, tend to move in opposite directions. But even if labor were indeed homogeneous and commanded a single wage rate in a perfectly competitive market, there remains the more fundamental objection that labor is not the only factor of production; goods are usually produced by various combinations of land, labor, and capital.† This makes it impossible to use the labor theory of value, however qualified. But if we shall have to discard eventually the labor theory of value as invalid, do we also have to discard the important classical conclusion that specialization according to comparative advantage increases potentially the total world output of every commodity? Fortunately, this is not the case. Gottfried Haberler (1936) succeeded in developing his *theory of opportunity costs*, which actually frees the classical theory from the restrictive assumption of the labor theory of value.

## Definitions

Consider again the example summarized in table 2.1. Country $A$'s labor coefficients for $X$ and $Y$ are 4 and 2, respectively, and $B$'s corresponding labor coefficients are 6 and 12. In the preceding section, the inequality $\frac{2}{12} < \frac{4}{6}$ was used to determine that $A$ has a comparative advantage in $Y$ and $B$ in $X$. But this inequality can also be written as $\frac{2}{4} < \frac{12}{6}$. Clearly, the two inequalities are equivalent, but the interpretation of the latter is much more interesting and useful.

Consider the ratio $\frac{2}{4}$, keeping in mind that 4 and 2 are $A$'s labor coefficients of $X$ and $Y$, respectively. What is the meaning of the ratio $\frac{2}{4}$? Suppose that country $A$ is currently employing all of its labor in the production of some positive amounts of $X$ and $Y$. How much $X$ would country $A$ have to give up if it wished to increase the output of $Y$ by 1 unit by transferring sufficient amounts of labor from $X$ to $Y$? Since, for the production of an additional unit of $Y$, 2 units of labor are required, and since, as the output of $X$ falls, labor is being released at the rate of 4 units per unit of $X$ given up, it follows that only $\frac{2}{4}$, or half a unit, of $X$ must be given up for the production of an additional unit of $Y$. *This minimum amount of X (that is, $\frac{2}{4}$) which A has to give up in order to produce an additional unit of Y is called the opportunity cost of Y in terms of X in country A.*

Similarly, the ratio $\frac{12}{6}$ shows $B$'s opportunity cost of $Y$ in terms of $X$, since 6 and 12 are $B$'s labor coefficients of $X$ and $Y$. Therefore, the inequality $\frac{2}{4} < \frac{12}{6}$ simply tells us that $A$'s opportunity cost of $Y$ in terms of $X$ is lower than $B$'s.

---

† Frank Taussig (1927, chap. 7) attempted to circumvent this objection by his belief that the proportion in which labor was used with other factors was usually the same in all industries. This seems to amount to what Marx called "equal organic composition of capital."

It should be noted that the opportunity cost of $X$ in terms of $Y$ is nothing but the reciprocal of the opportunity cost of $Y$ in terms of $X$. Thus, in the example of table 2.1, $A$'s opportunity cost of $X$ in terms of $Y$ is 2 and its opportunity cost of $Y$ in terms of $X$ is $\frac{1}{2}$. The same relationship can be verified in the case of country $B$. Thus, referring back to the example of table 2.1, it is obvious that the information given in only one of the last two rows is sufficient for our purposes.

## Comparative Advantage Defined in Terms of Opportunity Costs

It follows that, if a country, $A$, has a comparative advantage (in the sense of sec. 2.4) in the production of a commodity, $Y$, the opportunity cost of $Y$ in terms of $X$ must be lower in $A$ than in $B$. Conversely, if the opportunity cost of a commodity, $Y$, is lower in $A$ than in $B$, then $A$ necessarily has a comparative advantage (in the sense of sec. 2.4) in the production of $Y$. Accordingly, it must be obvious that comparative advantage can be defined in terms of opportunity costs directly. Therefore, given two countries ($A$ and $B$) and two commodities ($X$ and $Y$), we say that a country, $A$, has a comparative advantage in the production of a certain commodity, $Y$, if, and only if, the opportunity cost of $Y$ in terms of $X$ is lower in $A$ than in $B$. This is verified by the example of table 2.1. Thus, the third row of table 2.1 shows that the opportunity cost of $X$ in terms of $Y$ is 2 in $A$ and $\frac{1}{2}$ in $B$; this confirms our earlier conclusion that $B$ has a comparative advantage in $X$. Further, in the last row of table 2.1, the opportunity cost of $Y$ in terms of $X$ is seen to be $\frac{1}{2}$ in $A$ and 2 in $B$; this again confirms our conclusion that $A$ has a comparative advantage in $Y$.

Our main conclusion is: where two countries are producing two different commodities, one country should specialize in the production of that commodity in which the country's opportunity cost is lower than the second country's opportunity cost of the same commodity. Thus, if $A$'s opportunity cost of $Y$ in terms of $X$ is $\frac{1}{2}$ while $B$'s is 2, $A$ should specialize in $Y$ and $B$ in $X$. That this pattern of specialization necessarily increases the total world output of every commodity must be obvious by now. Thus, for every additional unit of $Y$ produced in $A$, half a unit of $X$ must be given up (because $A$'s opportunity cost of $Y$ in terms of $X$ is $\frac{1}{2}$). However, the production of half a unit of $X$ in $B$ (to restore the total world output of $X$ to its original level) requires the sacrifice of only $\frac{1}{2} \times \frac{1}{2} = \frac{1}{4}$ of $Y$ (because $B$'s opportunity cost of $X$ in terms of $Y$ is $\frac{1}{2}$). Hence, while the total world output of $X$ remains constant, the output of $Y$ increases by $1 - \frac{1}{4} = \frac{3}{4}$. Note that instead of increasing $B$'s output of $X$ by $\frac{1}{2}$, we could have increased it by $\Delta X_B$, where $\frac{1}{2} < \Delta X_B < 2$. The outputs of both commodities would then increase.

## Significance of the Theory of Opportunity Costs

What is the significance of this analysis? Is it more than a mere restatement of the conclusions of the preceding section on comparative advantage? To begin with, in the preceding discussion it is immaterial whether $A$ produces $Y$ with less labor than $B$, or $B$ produces $X$ with less labor than $A$. What this means is that offsetting absolute advantages are not required for the existence of profitable trade. This is no doubt an important conclusion, but we can go beyond it. Once comparative advantage is defined in terms of opportunity cost reflecting foregone production of other commodities, *it makes no difference whether commodities are actually produced by labor alone.* This accounts for the superiority of the theory of opportunity costs which, like the *deus ex machina*, saves the classical conclusions. What is important, in other words, is only the opportunity cost of one commodity in terms of the other in each of the two countries, and nothing else. Once these opportunity costs are given, we can determine the desirable pattern of international specialization, irrespective of what theory of production is being adopted. It is, therefore, important to realize labor cost is only a transitional consideration in the previous analysis. As Haberler repeatedly emphasized, the sole purpose of the labor theory of value is to determine the opportunity cost of one commodity in terms of the other in each of two countries.

## Opportunity Costs Versus Relative Commodity Prices

Note that within the context of the labor theory of value, the opportunity cost of $X$ in terms of $Y$ in a country coincides with that country's pretrade relative price of $X$ in terms of $Y$. For instance, given that $A$'s labor coefficients of $X$ and $Y$ are 4 and 2, respectively, $A$'s pretrade price ratio, $p_x/p_y$, and $A$'s opportunity cost of $X$ in terms of $Y$ are both given by the ratio $\frac{4}{2}$. Therefore, within the context of the labor theory of value, comparative advantage can be defined alternatively in terms of pretrade relative prices instead of opportunity costs. Thus, we can say that a country, $A$, has a comparative advantage in $X$ (and should specialize in the production of $X$) if, and only if, $A$'s relative price of $X$, before trade, is smaller than $B$'s. Does it follow, then, that comparative advantage can in general be defined in terms of pretrade prices? This can be done only under the proviso that relative prices do reflect opportunity costs.

## 2.6 LIMITS OF THE TERMS OF TRADE AND WAGE RATES

The analysis so far has shown that, if each country specializes in that commodity in whose production it is relatively more efficient, the world output of every commodity increases (potentially). It is shown in this section that the introduction of free international trade will necessarily generate forces which cause this to happen.

The rest of the analysis of this chapter applies both to Adam Smith's case of absolute advantage and to the Ricardo–Torrens case of comparative advantage. Therefore, no sharp distinction needs to be drawn between the two cases for the rest of this chapter.

### Labor Mobility

The main distinguishing feature of international trade singled out by Ricardo was the international immobility of labor coupled with its perfect mobility within countries. On the other hand, goods were regarded as perfectly mobile within and among countries (at zero transport cost). Now the perfect mobility of labor within a country causes, in the absence of international trade (in commodities), an allocation of labor among the various branches of production that ensures everywhere the equality between its marginal productivity and the wage rate—which is another way of saying that eqs. (2.1) above are satisfied, since the marginal physical product of labor in the $i$th industry is equal to $1/a_i$ and thus

$$p_x \frac{1}{a_x} = p_y \frac{1}{a_y} = w \qquad MPP = \frac{1}{a} \qquad (2.5)$$

Therefore, the perfect mobility of labor is a necessary condition for the validity of the labor theory of value.

## The Terms of Trade

In our two-country, two-commodity model, before trade starts, one distinct domestic price ratio exists for each of the two countries. These pretrade price ratios are, of course, determined by the labor requirements in the production of each of the two commodities. With the opening up of trade relations, these two (in general) different price ratios will necessarily be replaced by a single ratio—the "law of one price." This international price ratio is generally referred to as the *terms of trade*. What the following analysis shows is that the actual pattern of specialization in each of the two countries (considered separately) depends on the value of the international terms of trade; further, the equilibrium value of the terms of trade will be such as to cause each country to specialize in that commodity in whose production it is relatively more efficient, i.e., the commodity in whose production it has a comparative advantage.

## The Similarity Between the Opportunity to Trade and Technical Progress

Given the data summarized in table 2.1, the pretrade price ratios in each of the two countries can be determined as follows:

$$\left(\frac{p_x}{p_y}\right)_A \equiv A\text{'s price ratio} = \frac{4}{2} = 2$$

$$\left(\frac{p_x}{p_y}\right)_B \equiv B\text{'s price ratio} = \frac{6}{12} = 0.5$$

In other words, in $A$, 1 unit of $X$ exchanges for 2 units of $Y$ (or the price of $X$ is twice as high as the price of $Y$), whereas in $B$, 1 unit of $X$ exchanges for only 0.5 units of $Y$ (or the price of $X$ is one-half the price of $Y$).

Consider now country $A$ by itself and assume that it has access to a huge international market where it can buy and sell unlimited quantities of $X$ and $Y$ at prices that are fixed internationally and cannot be substantially influenced by the purchases and sales of country $A$. This case can be compared with the case of a purely competitive firm that faces an infinitely elastic demand curve for its products, or with the case of a consumer who faces fixed prices. Suppose for the

**Table 2.2**

| | A's labor coefficients | |
|---|---|---|
| | Direct production | Acquisition through trade |
| Commodity $X$ | 4 | $10 \times 2 = 20$ |
| Commodity $Y$ | 2 | $\frac{1}{10} \times 4 = \frac{2}{5}$ |

moment that the international price ratio $(p_x/p_y)$ is higher than 2 (that is, $A$'s domestic price ratio). Assume that the international price ratio is 10. What does the possibility of international trade imply for country $A$, and how will country $A$ react to this new opportunity?

This new opportunity to trade is similar to the discovery of two new production techniques, one for producing $X$ and another one for producing $Y$. Thus, country $A$ can obtain each commodity through the application of labor in either of the following two ways: (*a*) it can directly produce the commodity, as it did before the opportunity to trade was available, or (*b*) it can produce the other commodity directly and then exchange it in the international market for the desired commodity. It will be to the advantage of country $A$ to choose that production technique which requires less expenditure of labor; in fact, this will necessarily be dictated by the forces of competition.

Table 2.2 shows the labor requirements of each commodity both for the case of direct domestic production and for the case where each commodity is indirectly obtained through trade. The first column of table 2.2 simply repeats the first column of table 2.1. The entries in the second column ("acquisition through trade") have been determined as follows. First consider commodity $X$. To obtain 1 unit of $X$ from the international market, country $A$ has to surrender 10 units of $Y$, the direct domestic production of which requires $10 \times 2 = 20$ units of labor. On the other hand, in order to obtain 1 unit of $Y$ from the international market, country $A$ has to surrender only $\frac{1}{10}$ of a unit of $X$, the direct domestic production of which requires $\frac{1}{10} \times 4 = \frac{2}{5}$ of a unit of labor. From these results, it follows that country $A$ will find it cheaper to import commodity $Y$ and produce domestically commodity $X$ only. This conclusion will continue to hold for as long as the international price ratio is higher than $A$'s pretrade domestic price ratio.

However, when the international price ratio falls below $A$'s pretrade price ratio, the conclusion is reversed; that is, $A$ will find it cheaper to import commodity $X$ and produce domestically commodity $Y$ only. This is illustrated in table 2.3

**Table 2.3**

| | A's labor coefficients | |
|---|---|---|
| | Direct production | Acquisition through trade |
| Commodity $X$ | 4 | $\frac{1}{4} \times 2 = \frac{1}{2}$ |
| Commodity $Y$ | 2 | $4 \times 4 = 16$ |

Export when relative price is higher (Numerator), otherwise import (opposite case for denominator.

(which is similar to table 2.2) where it is assumed that the international price ratio is $\frac{1}{4}$.

Finally, note that if the international price ratio happens to coincide with $A$'s pretrade price ratio, the labor coefficients of both commodities for their direct production will necessarily be equal to the corresponding expenditure of labor for obtaining each commodity through trade. In other words, country $A$ will be indifferent between producing a commodity directly and obtaining it indirectly through trade. For this reason, its structure of production is indeterminate in this case. *not of, all but for all.*

Observe that $A$ will always find it cheaper to import one commodity and export another. In other words, it is impossible for acquisition through trade to be cheaper than direct production for all goods. This can be seen as follows. Let $a_x$ and $a_y$ stand for the labor requirements of $X$ and $Y$, respectively, and let $p$ stand for the international price ratio. Then, from the preceding analysis it follows that the labor requirements for $X$ and $Y$, if they were to be obtained indirectly through trade, are $pa_y$ and $(1/p)a_x$, respectively. Suppose $X$ is cheaper to produce domestically, i.e., $a_x < pa_y$. This inequality can also be written as follows: $(1/p)a_x < a_y$, which implies that $Y$ is cheaper to obtain indirectly through trade. Thus, given the first inequality, we can derive the second, and vice versa.

When the international price ratio is different from $A$'s pretrade price ratio, free trade will enable country $A$ to increase (potentially) its consumption of every commodity. Thus country $A$ can obtain one commodity indirectly through trade with less labor than it otherwise would have to use, while it can continue to produce the other commodity with the same labor as in the pretrade state.

## The Pattern of Specialization: Summary

Figure 2.1 summarizes the pattern of specialization of country $A$. The international terms of trade are measured along the horizontal line of fig. 2.1. The vertical rule at the point $\alpha$ indicates where the international terms of trade are equal to $A$'s pretrade price ratio. To the right of point $\alpha$, the international price ratio is higher than $A$'s pretrade price ratio and $A$ specializes in the production of $X$: it exports $X$ and imports $Y$. To the left of $\alpha$, the international price ratio is smaller than $A$'s

### $A$'s PATTERN OF SPECIALIZATION

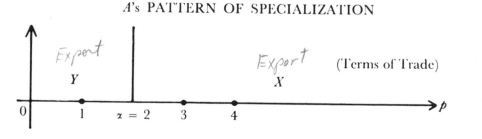

**Figure 2.1**

*Export (also implies production + domestic consumption?)*

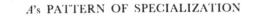

A's PATTERN OF SPECIALIZATION

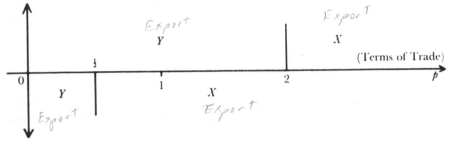

B's PATTERN OF SPECIALIZATION

**Figure 2.2**

pretrade price ratio and $A$ specializes in the production of $Y$: it exports $Y$ and imports $X$.

A similar analysis holds for country $B$, so there is no need for repetition. Figure 2.2 summarizes the conclusions for both countries. It is similar to fig. 2.1 except that above the terms-of-trade line, $A$'s pattern of specialization is indicated, whereas below it, $B$'s pattern of specialization is shown.

## Limits of the Terms of Trade and Comparative Advantage

Figure 2.2 is important because it will enable us to answer the question with which we began the discussion of this section: will free international trade generate forces that will make it profitable for each country to specialize in that commodity in whose production it has a comparative advantage? For this purpose, it is necessary to introduce one additional assumption about demand, namely, that both commodities are consumed somewhere in the world for all values of the terms of trade. The two commodities do not have to be consumed simultaneously by one or the other or both countries. It will be sufficient for our purposes if one country consumes only $X$ and the other consumes only $Y$. The only requirement is that the total world consumption of every commodity is always positive. This does not appear to be an unreasonable assumption.

Figure 2.2 shows that, unless the international price ratio lies in the closed region $\{\frac{1}{2}, 2\}$,† both countries will end up specializing in the production of the same commodity. Thus, for values of $p$ higher than 2, both countries will tend to specialize in the production of $X$, whereas for values of $p$ lower than $\frac{1}{2}$, both countries will tend to specialize in the production of $Y$. Neither of these situations is viable in the long run if both commodities are to be consumed. Therefore, long-run international equilibrium cannot exist for values of the terms of trade that lie outside the closed region $\{\frac{1}{2}, 2\}$. The only possible values of the terms of trade that are consistent—from the point of view of long-run equilibrium—with

† The *closed region* $\{\frac{1}{2}, 2\}$ includes all those numbers which lie between $\frac{1}{2}$ and 2, including the numbers $\frac{1}{2}$ and 2 themselves. The *open region* $(\frac{1}{2}, 2)$ differs from the closed region $\{\frac{1}{2}, 2\}$ in that the former does not include the numbers $\frac{1}{2}$ and 2 whereas the latter does.

the assumption that both commodities are always consumed are those that lie in the closed region $\{\frac{1}{2}, 2\}$, which is, of course, determined by the pretrade price ratios in the two countries.

For any value of the terms of trade in the open region $(\frac{1}{2}, 2)$ country $A$ specializes in $Y$ and $B$ in $X$; that is, *each country specializes in that commodity in whose production it has a comparative advantage.* In this more general case, both countries benefit from trade.

In the specific case where the equilibrium terms of trade coincide with either country's pretrade price ratio, one of the two countries—the one whose pretrade price ratio is equal to the terms of trade—gains nothing while the other becomes the sole beneficiary of the gains from trade. This could very well happen if the two countries are not of equal size, because then it is possible that the total world consumption of the commodity in which the smaller country has a comparative advantage may be larger than the latter's maximum output of the said commodity, thus causing the larger country to produce both commodities. Under these circumstances, the terms of trade will necessarily coincide with the larger country's pretrade price ratio, with all gains from trade accruing to the smaller country. The larger country will merely be forced to change its internal allocation of labor between the two commodities to satisfy the needs of the smaller country.

## The Terms of Trade and the Division of the Gains from Trade

The division of the gains of trade between the two countries depends on the equilibrium terms of trade. Thus, if the terms of trade coincide with $A$'s ($B$'s) pretrade price ratio, $A$ ($B$) gains nothing. Further, the closer to $A$'s ($B$'s) pretrade price ratio the terms of trade lie, the larger is $B$'s ($A$'s) share of the gains. Thus, if the terms of trade are initially equal to $\frac{1}{2}$ (that is, $B$'s pretrade price ratio) and, as a result of a continuous change in tastes in favor of commodity $X$, they increase continuously until they reach the value 2 (that is, $A$'s pretrade terms of trade), the division of the gains from trade is affected as follows. Initially all the gains accrue to $A$. As the terms of trade increase, the division of gains shifts continuously in favor of country $B$ until the terms of trade become equal to 2. Then all gains accrue to country $B$. This conclusion, of course, makes sense because tastes are assumed to shift continuously in favor of $X$, which is the commodity in which $B$ has a comparative advantage.

The truth of the above conclusion can be demonstrated as follows. Let $p$ stand for the terms of trade. As we have seen, $p$ must satisfy the condition

$$\tfrac{1}{2} \le p \le 2 \tag{2.6}$$

Further, on the basis of the analysis of the present section, it should be clear that the labor coefficients for the production or acquisition through trade of commodities $X$ and $Y$ in countries $A$ and $B$ are those given in table 2.4. Two of the four coefficients are constant; the other two, however, are variable depending on the value of $p$. Observe that as $p$ increases, the amount of labor required in $A$ for the acquisition of 1 unit of $X$ (that is, $2p$) tends to *increase*, whereas the amount of labor required in $B$ for the acquisition of 1 unit of $Y$ (that is, $6/p$) tends to *decrease*.

*[handwritten: See pg 18 +19 of notes]*
*[handwritten: Bertrand's class]*
*[handwritten: P is used for acquisition units — ie for (A) Y is produced for (B) X is produced]*

**Table 2.4**

|  | Country A | Country B |
|---|---|---|
| Commodity X | 2p | 6 |
| Commodity Y | 2 | $\dfrac{6}{p}$ |

*[handwritten: Producing]* *[handwritten: Importing]*

Therefore, as $p$ increases, country $A$ will find out that it can consume less $X$ for any given consumption of $Y$ because the acquisition of $X$ becomes more costly. Country $B$, however, will be delighted to find out that the acquisition of $Y$ becomes cheaper, and thus for any level of consumption of $X$ it can consume a higher amount of $Y$. Consequently, as $p$ increases, the division of the gains from trade shifts in favor of country $B$ and against country $A$.

## Real Wage Rates

The data given in table 2.4 can also help answer the question of the real wage in the two countries. The real wage rate—as opposed to the money wage rate—can be expressed in terms of either commodity. Actually, it is equal to the amount of the commodity in terms of which it is being measured that can be directly produced, or acquired through trade, with the expenditure of 1 unit of labor.

Strictly speaking, the real wage rate expressed in terms of the $i$th commodity is given by the marginal physical productivity of labor in the production of the $i$th commodity. Since the preceding definition refers to the average, as opposed to the marginal, physical productivity of labor, it is quite possible that some confusion might arise. However, in the context of our model, the marginal and the average physical productivity of labor are identical.

The real wage rate expressed in either commodity in each of the two countries is given in table 2.5. Note that the entries in table 2.5 correspond to the entries in table 2.4. This should be obvious from the fact that when $z$ units of labor are required for the production of 1 unit of the $i$th commodity ($z$ being the entry in table 2.4), $1/z$ units of the $i$th commodity can be produced with 1 unit of labor ($1/z$ being the entry in table 2.5).

The most important observation that can be made about the information given in table 2.5 is this: whether the real wage rate is expressed in terms of $X$ or $Y$

**Table 2.5**

|  | Country A | Country B |
|---|---|---|
| Real wage rate expressed in terms of: | | |
| Commodity X | $\dfrac{1}{2p}$ | $\dfrac{1}{6}$ |
| Commodity Y | $\dfrac{1}{2}$ | $\dfrac{p}{6}$ |

(in both countries), the two rates will be proportional to each other, with $A$'s real wage rate always $3/p \times B$'s wage rate. (That is, $(1/2p)/(\frac{1}{6}) = (\frac{1}{2})/(p/6) = 3/p$.)

Inequality (2.6) can be used to show that the factor of proportionality, $3/p$, must, in the long run, satisfy the following inequality:

$$1 < \frac{3}{2} \le \frac{3}{p} \le 6 \tag{2.7}$$

*ie.* if $\frac{1}{2} \le p \le 2$

$\Rightarrow$ $\frac{3}{p}$

Thus, the factor of proportionality will always be greater than unity. This implies, of course, that *A's wage rate will definitely be higher than B's.* This is what we should have been expecting, because, after all, *country A was assumed to be more productive than country B in every line of production.*

## Money Wage Rates

The above conclusion can also be established in terms of money wage rates—even though, within the context of our model, money wage rates cannot be uniquely determined. Consider the following problem. Suppose that $B$'s money wage rate is arbitrarily fixed at \$1. Then, from inequality (2.7), it follows that $A$'s money wage rate ($w_A$), also expressed in dollars for convenience, must necessarily satisfy the inequality \$1.5 $\le w_A \le$ \$6. It can be shown that if $w_A >$ \$6, the average cost of production of every commodity in country $A$ will be higher than the corresponding cost in $B$. Thus, $B$ will undersell $A$ in every line of production. But this is not a viable situation in the long run, because $A$ will not be able to finance its purchases from $B$ indefinitely. On the other hand, if $w_A <$ \$1.5, $A$ will undersell $B$ in every line of production. But again, this is not a viable situation in the long run.

In the context of the present model, the argument that country $A$ cannot compete with country $B$ because the latter's wage rate is lower is absolutely fallacious. When inequality (2.7) is satisfied, inequality (2.6) is also satisfied, and each country specializes in the production of that commodity in which it has a comparative advantage. In general, both countries benefit from trade. The other argument for protection in $B$ (i.e., because of $A$'s superiority in every line of production) is equally fallacious: every country necessarily has a comparative advantage by definition.

## 2.7 PRODUCTION-POSSIBILITIES FRONTIERS

We now proceed to introduce the concept of the *production-possibilities frontier*. This will make it possible to restate the preceding analysis graphically, which will be helpful in two different ways: (*a*) in assimilating the conclusions established so far, particularly that the major classical conclusions remain valid even if the labor theory of value is discarded, and (*b*) in understanding the neoclassical theory of international trade, which is the subject matter of part three of the book.

### Definition

In general, the production-possibilities frontier of a country producing two commodities, $X$ and $Y$, shows, on the basis of given factor endowments and technology, the maximum amount of $Y$ that the economy can produce for any given

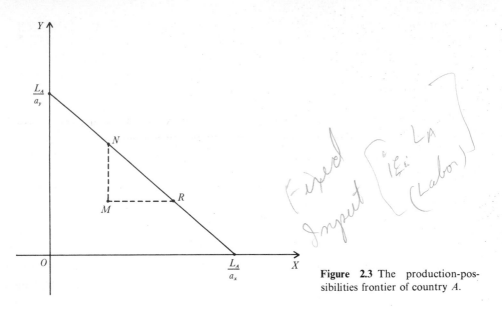

Figure 2.3 The production-possibilities frontier of country $A$.

amount of $X$. Thus, assuming that country $A$ is endowed with $L_A$ units of (homogeneous) labor and that the production of $X$ and $Y$ requires, respectively, $a_x$ and $a_y$ units of labor per unit of output, its production-possibilities frontier will be given by the following equation:

$$L_A = a_x X + a_y Y \tag{2.8}$$

Equation (2.8) is linear and is represented graphically by a straight line, as shown in fig. 2.3.

Since the production-possibilities frontier is in this case linear, it can be easily determined by first finding its intercepts with the two axes and then connecting them with a straight line. The x-axis intercept shows the maximum quantity of commodity $X$ that the economy can produce—under the constraints of given factor endowments and technology—when the output of $Y$ is zero; it is given by the ratio $L_A/a_x$, as shown in fig. 2.3. A similar interpretation holds for the y-axis intercept, which is given by $L_A/a_y$. Any point inside the production-possibilities frontier, such as point $M$, implies that the economy is not making full use of its resources. Since the pure theory of trade is a full-employment, general-equilibrium theory, in what follows it will be assumed that each economy is always producing somewhere on its production-possibilities frontier.

### The Marginal Rate of Transformation

The absolute slope of $A$'s production-possibilities frontier is given by the ratio

$$\frac{L_A/a_y}{L_A/a_x} = \frac{a_x}{a_y} \tag{2.9}$$

What is the meaning of the ratio $a_x/a_y$?

Suppose that country $A$ is producing at point $N$ (fig. 2.3) and that, as a result of a change in tastes in favor of $X$, it moves to point $R$. In other words, it transfers sufficient amounts of resources from the production of $Y$ to the production of $X$ so that the production of $X$ increases by $MR$ units while the production of $Y$ falls by $NM$ units. How many units of $Y$ did $A$ have to give up per extra unit of $X$? The answer is $MN/MR$, which actually is the absolute slope of $A$'s production-possibilities frontier. Therefore, the absolute slope of $A$'s production-possibilities frontier, or, as is usually called, the *marginal rate of transformation*, has an important meaning: it shows the opportunity cost of $X$ in terms of $Y$. Further, combining eqs. (2.2) and (2.9), it follows that the absolute slope of $A$'s production-possibilities frontier is identical to the ratio of commodity prices, that is, $p_x/p_y$. This important conclusion can be expressed as follows:

*ay given => w determines*
*Px which gives MCx*

$$-\frac{\Delta Y}{\Delta X} = \frac{a_x}{a_y} = \frac{p_x}{p_y} = P \tag{2.10}$$

Actually, it is more accurate to say that the slope of $A$'s production-possibilities frontier (PPF) shows the ratio of marginal costs of $X$ and $Y$, that is,

$$\text{Absolute slope of } A\text{'s PPF} = \frac{\text{marginal cost of } X}{\text{marginal cost of } Y}$$

This observation becomes important shortly when international trade is introduced, since the terms of trade (equivalent to the relative prices prevailing in each country) are different from the absolute slope of each country's PPF.

Country $B$'s production-possibilities frontier can be derived in a similar way, so there is no need to repeat the preceding discussion. However, it is useful to introduce some additional symbols. Assume that $B$ is endowed with $L_B$ units of labor; its labor requirements per unit of output are $b_x$ and $b_y$ for commodities $X$ and $Y$, respectively. Therefore, $B$'s production-possibilities frontier is given by the equation

$$L_B = b_x X + b_y Y \tag{2.11}$$

Its absolute slope (or the opportunity cost of $X$ in terms of $Y$) is, of course, given by the ratio $b_x/b_y$.

## The Law of Comparative Advantage Again

Notice that $A$ will have a comparative advantage in $X$ and $B$ in $Y$ if the following inequality holds:

$$\frac{a_x}{a_y} < \frac{b_x}{b_y} \tag{2.12a}$$

*A Exports X*

On the other hand, $A$ will have a comparative advantage in $Y$ and $B$ in $X$ if the opposite inequality holds, that is,

$$\frac{a_x}{a_y} > \frac{b_x}{b_y} \tag{2.13a}$$

*A exports Y*

*opportunity costs shown with these ratios*

This should become obvious if inequalities (2.12*a*) and (2.13*a*) are rewritten as follows:

*A exports X* (handwritten)

$$\frac{a_x}{b_x} < \frac{a_y}{b_y} \tag{2.12b}$$

*A exports Y* (handwritten)

$$\frac{a_x}{b_x} > \frac{a_y}{b_y} \tag{2.13b}$$

These are actually the inequalities used in sec. 2.4 for the definition of comparative advantage. The importance of inequalities (2.12*a*) and (2.13*a*)—which from a strictly mathematical point of view are equivalent to the inequalities (2.12*b*) and (2.13*b*), respectively—follows from the fact that they define comparative advantage directly in terms of opportunity costs.

## 2.8 THE WORLD PRODUCTION-POSSIBILITIES FRONTIER

The quite useful concept of the world production-possibilities frontier is illustrated in fig. 2.4, which shows the maximum amount of $Y$ that both countries together can produce for any given amount of $X$, under the assumption that labor is completely immobile between countries. Its construction is rather simple. The triangle $TUR$ represents the production-possibilities frontier of country $A$, with $T$ as its point of origin. The triangle $VRZ$ represents $B$'s production-possibilities frontier, with $V$ as its point of origin. The intercept $Z$ of the world production-possibilities frontier is determined by the sum of the maximum quantities of $Y$ that both countries could produce if they were to channel all of their resources in the

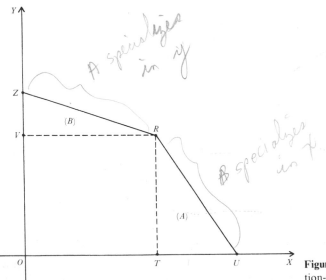

**Figure 2.4** The world production-possibilities frontier.

production of $Y$, that is, $OZ = TR + VZ$. Similarly, the intercept $U$ is determined by the sum of the maximum quantities of $X$ that both countries could produce if they were to channel all of their resources in the production of $X$, that is, $OU = VR + TU$.

The world frontier can now be derived. Note that $B$'s production-possibilities frontier has been assumed flatter than $A$'s; i.e., the opportunity cost of $X$ in terms of $Y$ was assumed to be lower in $B$. Suppose that we are at point $Z$—with both countries producing $Y$ only—and assume that we would like to produce an extra unit of $X$. Which country should undertake the production of the extra unit of $X$? Obviously, country $B$, because its opportunity cost of $X$ in terms of $Y$ is lower. This will continue for the second, third, etc., units of $X$ until $B$ specializes completely in $X$, that is, until we reach point $R$. From then on, i.e., from $R$ to $U$, any additional amounts of $X$ can only be extracted from $A$. Thus, in the region $ZR$, country $A$ specializes in $Y$ while $B$ produces both commodities. On the other hand, in the region $RU$, country $A$ produces both commodities while $B$ completely specializes in $X$. In particular, at the specific point $R$, country $A$ specializes in the production of $Y$ and $B$ in $X$. Thus, point $R$ can be recognized as the *Ricardian point* of complete specialization in each country according to the comparative advantage of each.

The world production-possibilities frontier, as illustrated in fig. 2.4, is not a straight line—except in the special case of equal-opportunity costs (i.e., when the production-possibilities frontiers of $A$ and $B$ have the same slope). In general, it consists of two straight-line segments, such as $ZR$ and $RU$. Along each of these straight-line segments, opportunity costs are constant. However, the absolute slope of $ZR$ is different from, and significantly smaller than, that of $RU$. At the Ricardian point $R$, the slope of the world production-possibilities frontier ($\equiv$ opportunity cost of $X$ in terms of $Y$) is indeterminate. This indeterminacy of the slope of point $R$ accounts for the failure of the Ricardo–Torrens theory of comparative advantage to explain the equilibrium value of the terms of trade. From fig. 2.4, it should be obvious that the slope at point $R$ can range from the slope of $B$'s production-possibilities frontier to the slope of $A$'s. This coincides with our previous conclusion that the equilibrium terms of trade must necessarily lie between the pretrade price ratios of the two countries or coincide with one or other of them.

## The Gains from Trade Again

The world production-possibilities frontier can be used in several ways. In the following chapter, it will be used to demonstrate the international equilibrium of the two-country model. In this section, it can be used to illustrate the important idea of the gains from trade.

Consider now fig. 2.5. It is similar to fig. 2.4 but includes some additional information. Country $A$'s production-possibilities frontier has been drawn with respect to the origin of the diagram, as shown by the line $VS$. Thus, the triangles $OSV$ and $TUR$ are similar in all respects. Assume that country $A$ is producing at point $E$; place $B$'s production-possibilities frontier in such a way as to have its

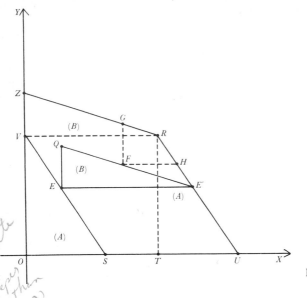

**Figure 2.5** The gains from trade.

origin at point *E*, as shown by the triangle *EE'Q*. Note that *B*'s production-possibilities frontier, *EE'Q*, must necessarily lie inside the world production-possibilities frontier—except at the singular point *E'*—because *A*'s production-possibilities frontier is steeper than *B*'s. Finally, assume that *B* produces at any point on its frontier—other than *E'*—such as point *F*. It can be shown that the coordinates of point *F* with respect to the origin *O* give the total world output of the two commodities. But point *F* lies inside the world production-possibilities frontier, which means that, with a different pattern of specialization, the world as a whole could move to the boundaries of the world production-possibilities frontier. The workers do not have to move internationally; nor do they have to work harder. If *A* specializes in *X* and *B* in *Y*, the world can reach point *R*, which implies higher output of all commodities.

It should be obvious, however, that whether or not the world moves from point *F* to point *R* depends on demand. Thus, it is conceivable that, with free commodity trade, the world might move from point *F* to some point on the world production-possibilities frontier in the region *ZG*, where the world output of *X* is smaller after trade, or in the region *HU*, where the posttrade world output of *Y* is smaller than before trade started. In both of these cases, it should not be concluded that the world does not necessarily gain from trade. The fact that the consumption of one commodity is reduced while the consumption of the other is increased is not sufficient to support the conclusion that trade may not be profitable. The world can always move to point *R*—where the output of every commodity increases with trade—so at least potentially everybody could be made better off with trade. If the world chooses a different point than *R*, it must be assumed that it does so because that other point is preferred to point *R*. However, the concept of the gains from trade is much more subtle than what this paragraph suggests. This problem is discussed in chap. 16.

### International Mobility of Labor

Finally, it should be noted that what is called in this section the "world production-possibilities frontier" is not what the world can actually achieve, because this frontier has been derived under the assumption that labor is internationally immobile. Therefore, in cases where one country is superior to another country in every line of production, the world could reach a frontier that includes inside it the frontier of fig. 2.4 merely by allowing labor to move to the most productive nation. The same is also true in the case of absolute advantage.

## 2.9 TRADE IN INTERMEDIATE PRODUCTS: A DIGRESSION†

The classical theory of comparative advantage has been developed so far on the assumption that the commodities ($X$ and $Y$) which are traded internationally are final consumption goods. Yet intermediate products play an important and obvious role in international trade—the bulk of world trade is in intermediate products (see Maizels, 1963; and Yates, 1959). What difference does it make to our preceding conclusions if $X$ and $Y$ are also used in the production process (in a Leontief-type world) as intermediate goods? This question was first raised by McKenzie (1954, 1955) who observed that the introduction of trade in intermediate products modifies the classical theory considerably. Additional contributions in this area have been made by Amano (1966), Jones (1961), McKinnon (1966), Melvin (1969a, 1969b, 1970), and Warne (1971).

### The Production-Possibilities Frontier in the Presence of Intermediate Products

Suppose that the production of $X$ and $Y$ requires not only labor but also $X$ and $Y$ as well, just as the production of steel and coal may require, in addition to labor, steel and coal. Assume constant returns to scale and smooth substitutability in production. What is the production-possibilities frontier of a country which is endowed with a fixed amount of labor?

For a *closed* economy, Samuelson's (1951) substitution theorem (or, rather, *non*-substitution theorem) guarantees that even though an infinite number of production processes are possible, only one production process is always optimal for the production of each commodity. In other words, even though the coefficients of production are not technically fixed, the *optimal* coefficients of production always assume the same constant values. Hence, the closed economy's production-possibilities frontier is necessarily linear, and no significant difference arises between the present case (in which $X$ and $Y$ serve both as inputs and final products) and our earlier case (in which $X$ and $Y$ were strictly final products).

McKenzie (1954) showed that Samuelson's theorem is no longer true when the economy is open and trade in intermediate products allowed. The reason is simple: when intermediate products can be imported, the optimum production

† This section is slightly more technical than the rest of chap. 2 and may be skipped on a first reading.

processes need no longer coincide with those processes which minimize *domestic* labor inputs.

The production functions of industries $X$ and $Y$ may be written as follows:

$$X = F(Y_x, L_x) - X_y \tag{2.14}$$

$$Y = G(X_y, L_y) - Y_x \tag{2.15}$$

where

$X \equiv net$ output of industry $X$

$Y \equiv net$ output of industry $Y$

$X_y \equiv$ amount of $X$ used in the production of $Y$

$Y_x \equiv$ amount of $Y$ used in the production of $X$

$L_i \equiv$ amount of labor allocated to the $i$th industry

For simplicity, we ignore the complication that a commodity may be used directly in its own production. The function $F(Y_x, L_x)$ gives the amount of $X$ which results from the application of $Y_x$ units of $Y$ and $L_x$ units of labor, and after the amount of $X$ needed for its own production has been subtracted. Thus, the function $F(Y_x, L_x)$ gives the amount of $X$ which becomes available to the economy and can be used either for the production of $Y$, or for domestic consumption, or even for export to the rest of the world. A similar interpretation holds for the function $G(X_y, L_y)$.

The derivation of the economy's production-possibilities frontier is given in fig. 2.6. Outputs are shown along the positive direction while inputs are shown along the negative direction of both axes. The curve $OUS$ (second quadrant) is the total product curve of industry $Y$ assuming that all available labor $(\bar{L})$ is employed by industry $Y$. Similarly, the curve $OVT$ (fourth quadrant) is the total product curve of industry $X$ when all available labor $(\bar{L})$ is employed by industry $X$. At point $S$, the marginal physical product of $X$ in the production of $Y$ (i.e., the slope of the total product curve at $S$) is zero. Similarly, at $T$ the marginal physical product of $Y$ in the production of $X$ is zero—the tangent at $T$ is vertical.

Because of constant returns to scale, convex combinations of the two production processes are possible (see chap. 4 below). Accordingly, maximal output combinations are those which lie on the common tangent $(UV)$ to both total product curves. When the economy is *closed*, only the combinations shown by the linear segment $MN$ are possible—negative production must be excluded. This is, of course, consistent with Samuelson's substitution theorem. On the other hand, when the economy is *open* and trade in intermediate commodities is allowed, the economy can produce anywhere along the curve $SUMNVT$. Hence, the open economy's production-possibilities frontier is given by $SUMNVT$. (See also McKinnon, 1966, pp. 601–604, and Melvin, 1969b, pp. 141–143.)†

---

† For a viable system, the functions $F(Y_x, L_x)$ and $G(X_y, L_y)$ must be such that their common tangent passes through the first quadrant. Otherwise positive outputs are not possible. On the other hand, as Melvin (1969a) has shown, this model is capable of exploding. In other words, the production-possibilities frontier may not have finite existence.

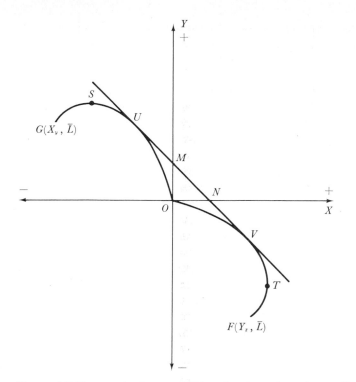

**Figure 2.6** The production-possibilities frontier when intermediate products are traded internationally.

Observe that along the *curved* segment $SU$ there is no domestic production of commodity $X$, that is, $F(Y_x, L_x) = 0$ since $L_x = 0$. Similarly, along the curved segment $VT$ there is no domestic production of commodity $Y$, that is, $G(X_y, L_y) = 0$ since $L_y = 0$. On the other hand, along the straight-line segment $UV$ (excluding the endpoints $U$ and $V$) both $X$ and $Y$ are produced domestically, that is, $G(X_y, L_y) > 0$, $F(Y_x, L_x) > 0$. Nevertheless, only along the straight-line segment $MN$ are the *net* outputs of both commodities positive, that is, $F(Y_x, L_x) - X_y > 0$, $G(X_y, L_y) - Y_x > 0$.

## Production Behavior

As before, the economy's autarkic price ratio coincides with the absolute slope of the closed economy's production-possibilities frontier ($MN$). This is in agreement with Samuelson's substitution theorem. Consider now the production behavior of an open economy which faces given commodity prices in the international market. If the international price ratio coincides with the economy's autarkic price ratio, production is indeterminate. However, because of the existence of intermediate commodities and the opportunity to trade them internationally, production is not restricted to the linear segment $MN$ in the first quadrant but extends from $U$ to $V$.

When the international price ratio differs from the autarkic price ratio, the economy necessarily specializes completely in the production of one commodity only. For instance, when $X$ is cheaper in the international market, the economy produces somewhere between $S$ and $U$, and in particular at the point where the absolute slope of $SU$ is equal to the given international price ratio. On the other hand, when $Y$ is cheaper in the international market, the economy produces at a point between $V$ and $T$ where the absolute slope of the curved segment $VT$ is again equal to the given international price ratio.

Suppose that the international price ratio is such that the economy specializes completely in the production of either commodity. Two conclusions follow immediately from the preceding analysis: (a) as McKenzie (1954) pointed out, the economy no longer uses the production techniques implied by points $U$ and $V$, and this shows that Samuelson's substitution theorem is no longer true for an open economy; and (b) as McKinnon (1966) emphasized, the economy's gains from trade are necessarily larger when trade in intermediate commodities is allowed. Thus the economy's consumption-possibilities frontier lies further away from the origin when trade in intermediate commodities is allowed as compared with the case where intermediate commodities are excluded from trade and the economy is restricted to produce somewhere along the linear segment $MN$ (i.e., in the positive quadrant).

## The World Production-Possibilities Frontier

Consider now two countries, $A$ and $B$, producing two commodities, $X$ and $Y$. Their respective production-possibilities frontiers are qualitatively similar to that shown in fig. 2.6. To make room for profitable international trade, assume that $A$'s production functions of $X$ and $Y$ are different from the corresponding production functions of country $B$. To fix ideas, assume that before trade commodity $X$ is relatively cheaper in $A$ than in $B$.

To derive the world production-possibilities frontier merely rotate $B$'s frontier by 180° and place it tangent to $A$'s production frontier as shown in fig. 2.7 by the broken curve $T'N'M'P'S'$. Let $B$'s production block slide along $A$'s frontier in such a way that the two frontiers remain tangential. The corner of $B$'s production block now traces the line $O'CDE$ which is the world production-possibilities frontier. (Ignore points in the second and fourth quadrants because they imply negative world production of one of the commodities.) For any given point on the world frontier $O'CDE$, such as $D$, the corresponding tangency between the individual frontiers, such as $D'$, gives the precise production points on the individual frontiers of $A$ and $B$.

The world production-possibilities frontier $O'CDE$ gives the maximum *net* output of one commodity that the world as a whole can produce for any nonnegative net output of the other. This world frontier consists of three parts: (a) the linear segment $O'C$ whose absolute slope is equal to $A$'s autarkic price ratio ($O'C$ is parallel to $MN$); (b) the linear segment $DE$ which is parallel to $N'M'$; and (c) the curved segment $CD$ in the middle. Depending on the characteristics of the production functions in $A$ and $B$, either linear segment ($O'C$ or $DE$) can be made to disappear together with the curved segment $CD$, as the reader should be able to show (see Melvin, 1969b).

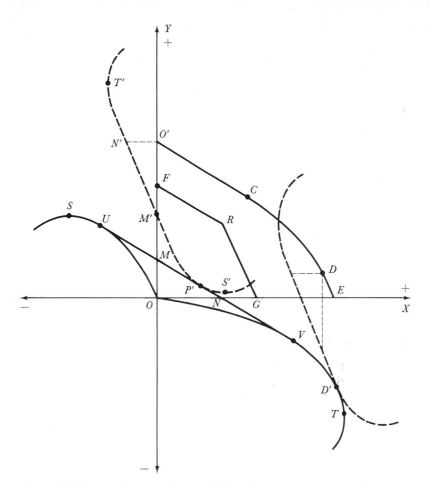

**Figure 2.7** The world production-possibilities frontier when intermediate products are traded internationally.

It becomes immediately obvious from fig. 2.7 that when trade in intermediate products is allowed, the world production-possibilities frontier becomes larger than the corresponding frontier $(FRG)$ which is derived under the assumption that no trade in intermediate products takes place, i.e., that no country is allowed to produce negative net outputs. This means, of course, that the world gains from trade are larger when intermediate products are traded.

Melvin (1969b) showed that the introduction of the opportunity to trade intermediate products, though beneficial to the world as a whole, *may* hurt a country; i.e., trade in intermediate products may reduce the gains which a country could have reaped if only final consumption goods were traded. Such a reduction in the gains from trade of a country occurs through a deterioration in its terms of trade which in turn reflects the resultant changes in the basic supply and demand relations. This phenomenon is indeed very similar to the phenomenon of immiserizing growth (see chap. 12).

# SELECTED BIBLIOGRAPHY

Amano, A. (1966). "Intermediate Goods and the Theory of Comparative Advantage: A Two-Country, Three-Commodity Case." *Weltwirtschaftliches Archiv*, vol. XCVI, no. 2, pp. 340–345.

Balassa, B. (1963). "An Empirical Demonstration of Comparative Cost." *Review of Economics and Statistics*, vol. 45, pp. 231–238.

Chipman, John S. (1965). "A Survey of the Theory of International Trade, Part 1: The Classical Theory." *Econometrica*, vol. 33, pp. 477–519.

Haberler, G. (1936). *The Theory of International Trade*. W. Hodge and Company, London, chaps. 9 to 11.

Jones, R. W. (1961). "Comparative Advantage and the Theory of Tariffs: A Multi-Country, Multi-Commodity Model." *Review of Economic Studies*, vol. 28 (3), no. 77 (June), pp. 161–175.

MacDougall, G. D. A. (1951). "British and American Exports: A Study Suggested by the Theory of Comparative Costs, Part I." *Economic Journal*, vol. 61, pp. 697–724. Reprinted in AEA *Readings in International Economics*. R. D. Irwin, Inc., Homewood, Ill., 1968.

——— (1952). "British and American Exports: A Study Suggested by the Theory of Comparative Costs, Part II. *Economic Journal*, vol. 62, pp. 487–521.

McKenzie, L. W. (1954). "Specialization and Efficiency in World Production." *Review of Economic Studies*, vol. 21 (3), no. 56 (June), pp. 165–180.

——— (1955). "Specialization in Production and the Production Possibility Locus." *Review of Economic Studies*, vol. 23 (1), no. 60 (October), pp. 56–64.

McKinnon, R. I. (1966). "Intermediate Products and Differential Tariffs: A Generalization of Lerner's Symmetry Theorem." *Quarterly Journal of Economics*, vol. 80, no. 4 (November), pp. 584–615.

Maizels, A. (1963). *Industrial Growth and World Trade*. Cambridge University Press, London.

Meade, J. E. (1955). *The Theory of International Economic Policy*, vol. 2: *Trade and Welfare*. Oxford University Press, Oxford, chap. 9.

Melvin, J. R. (1969a). "Intermediate Goods in Production Theory: The Differentiable Case." *Review of Economic Studies*, vol. 36 (January), pp. 124–131.

——— (1969b). "Intermediate Goods, the Production Possibility Curve, and Gains from Trade." *Quarterly Journal of Economics*, vol. 83, no. 1 (February), pp. 141–151.

——— (1970). "The Production Set When Labor Is Indispensable." *International Economic Review*, vol. 11, no. 2 (June), pp. 305–314.

Mill, J. S. (1902). *Principles of Political Economy*. Appleton, New York, chaps. 17, 18, and 25.

Ricardo, David (1821). *The Principles of Political Economy and Taxation*. J. Murray, London, chap. 7.

Samuelson, P. A. (1951). "Abstract of a Theorem Concerning Substitutability in Open Leontief Models." In T. C. Koopmans (Ed.), *Activity Analysis of Production and Allocation*. John Wiley and Sons, New York. Reprinted in J. Stiglitz (Ed.), *The Collected Scientific Papers of Paul A. Samuelson*, vol. 1. The MIT Press, Cambridge, Mass., 1966.

Smith, Adam (1937). *The Wealth of Nations*. Modern Library, New York.

Stern, R. (1962). "British and American Productivity and Comparative Costs in International Trade." *Oxford Economic Papers*, vol. 14, pp. 275–296.

Taussig, F. W. (1927). *International Trade*. The Macmillan Company, New York.

Torrens, R. (1808). *The Economists Refuted*. S. A. and H. Oddy, London. Reprinted in R. Torrens, *The Principles and Practical Operation of Sir Robert Peel's Act of 1844 Explained and Defended*, 3d ed. Longmans, London, 1858.

——— (1815). *An Essay on the External Corn Trade*. J. Hatchard, London.

Warne, R. D. (1971). "Intermediate Goods in International Trade with Variable Proportions and Two Primary Inputs." *Quarterly Journal of Economics*, vol. 85, no. 2 (May), pp. 225–236.

Williams, J. H. (1929). "The Theory of International Trade Reconsidered." *Economic Journal*, vol. 39, pp. 195–209. Reprinted in AEA *Readings in the Theory of International Trade*. R. D. Irwin, Inc., Homewood, Ill., 1949.

Yates, P. L. (1959). *Forty Years of Foreign Trade*. The Macmillan Company, New York.

# CHAPTER THREE

# DEMAND AND
# INTERNATIONAL EQUILIBRIUM

Even if comparative advantage explains why trade takes place, it certainly cannot explain on what terms. (Ricardo (1821) is widely regarded as having maintained that the terms of trade would settle "halfway between" the comparative cost ratios.) For this purpose, as John Stuart Mill (1902) emphasized, it is required that demand be introduced into the picture. This is done in the present chapter.

## 3.1 INDIFFERENCE CURVES†

Economists following Pareto, Slutsky, and Hicks usually depict the tastes of the consumer via the concept of indifference curves. As is well known, an indifference curve is the geometric locus of all alternative combinations of, say, commodities $X$ and $Y$ which enable the consumer to attain a given level of satisfaction, or utility. Thus, each indifference curve corresponds to a certain level of satisfaction. The collection of all indifference curves forms the indifference map. This is shown in fig. 3.1, where only three indifference curves have been drawn. Some general properties of indifference curves are noted briefly: ($a$) they slope downward; ($b$) they are convex to the origin, as illustrated in fig. 3.1; ($c$) they never intersect each other; and ($d$) a movement from a lower to a higher indifference curve (such as from $I_1$ to $I_2$ in fig. 3.1) implies an increase in the satisfaction or utility enjoyed by the consumer. Finally, note that the object of the consumer is to reach the highest possible indifference curve, i.e., attain the highest level of satisfaction, under the

† In the following analysis, mastery of the concept of indifference curves is assumed. Those who wish to refresh their memory should consult any price-theory textbook.

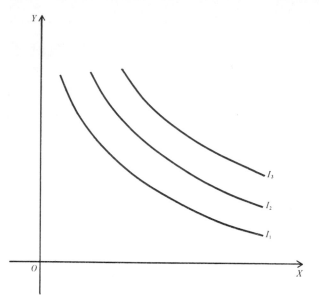

**Figure 3.1** The indifference map.

assumptions of a fixed money income and fixed commodity prices. The first-order condition for this maximization is that the *marginal rate of substitution* of X for Y (i.e., the maximum number of units of Y that the consumer could give up for an extra unit of X and still continue to enjoy the same level of satisfaction or utility), which is simply the absolute slope of the indifference curve passing through the equilibrium point, be equal to the price ratio $p_x/p_y$.

### Social Indifference Curves

The neoclassical theory makes the simplifying assumptions that the tastes of a society—as opposed to the tastes of the individual consumer—can be conveniently summarized by a *social indifference map* qualitatively similar to the indifference map of an individual consumer, and that the society behaves as if it were trying to attain the highest possible social indifference curve. The validity of this assumption will be examined in chap. 5. For the moment, assume that a meaningful social indifference map exists. Once this is done, the general equilibrium of each country separately, but also the general equilibrium of the world as a whole, can be shown graphically.

### General Equilibrium in a Closed Economy

Figure 3.2 shows the general equilibrium of a closed economy. The straight line RS is the production-possibilities frontier and the curves $I_1$, $I_2$, and $I_3$ are three social indifference curves. Equilibrium is seen to occur at point E, where the production-possibilities frontier is tangent to the social indifference curve $I_2$.

The analogy between the general equilibrium of the whole economy, on the one hand, and the equilibrium of the individual consumer, on the other, should be noted. In the case of the consumer, the straight line RS represents his budget constraint; in the case of general equilibrium, the line RS represents the

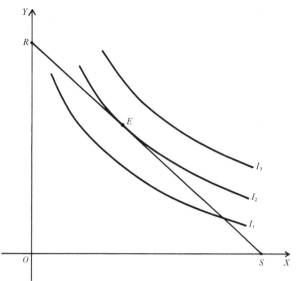

**Figure 3.2** Equilibrium in a closed economy.

production-possibilities frontier. In both cases, the line $RS$ serves as a constraint. In the former case it is the familiar budget constraint, while in the latter case it is the society's technological constraint: the society cannot produce beyond the boundaries of its production-possibilities frontier. Further, in both cases, the indifference map represents tastes, and the assumption is that both the consumer and the society will move to the highest possible indifference curve. At the equilibrium point (i.e., point $E$) the slope of the straight line $RS$ is equal to the slope of the indifference curve $I_2$. In the case of the consumer, the slope of $RS$ is equal to the price ratio $p_x/p_y$. In the case of the society, the slope of $RS$ gives the opportunity cost of $X$ in terms of $Y$, which under competitive conditions is equal to the price ratio $p_x/p_y$. Finally, the slope of the indifference curve $I_2$ at point $E$ is, in the case of the consumer, the individual consumer's marginal rate of substitution of $X$ for $Y$; in the case of the society, it is the *social* marginal rate of substitution of $X$ for $Y$.

## International Equilibrium

Figure 3.3 extends the preceding analysis to international equilibrium. To simplify the analysis, it is assumed that the tastes of the world as a whole can be represented by a single social indifference map. In other words, the world is assumed to behave like a single rational individual whose budget constraint is the line $ZRU$, which is similar in all respects to the world production-possibilities frontier depicted in fig. 2.4. Observe that this assumption is even more restrictive than the assumption that a separate social indifference map exists for each country. It is used here merely because the analysis of international equilibrium is greatly simplified. Incidentally, it should be noted that John Stuart Mill in his theory of international values made such assumptions about demand conditions as to guarantee the existence of a world indifference map. On this point, see Chipman (1965, sec. 1.2).

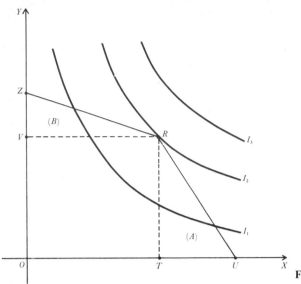

**Figure 3.3** International equilibrium.

International equilibrium occurs at the Ricardian point $R$. It should be obvious that international equilibrium need not take place at point $R$. Depending upon tastes, it can occur anywhere on the world production-possibilities frontier. Point $R$ is selected because the classical economists considered this to be the usual case; in addition, we want to show how the equilibrium terms of trade can be rigorously determined at this point.

The slope of the production-possibilities frontier $ZRU$ at point $R$ is indeterminate. Thus the equilibrium value of relative prices cannot be determined from the characteristics of the world production-possibilities frontier alone—only the limits of the relative prices can be so determined. However, with the introduction of demand, this indeterminacy disappears. In equilibrium, relative prices must necessarily be equal to the marginal rate of substitution which is perfectly determinate at point $R$. Therefore, the equilibrium terms of trade (that is, $p_x/p_y$) are given by the slope of the indifference curve $I_2$ at point $R$.

Figure 3.3 can also be used to verify our earlier conclusion that the terms of trade must lie between the pretrade price ratios of the two countries. This should be obvious, because, if point $R$ is to be the equilibrium point, the marginal rate of substitution of $X$ for $Y$ (i.e., the absolute slope of the indifference curve $I_2$ at $R$) must necessarily lie between the absolute slopes of the straight-line segments $ZR$ and $RU$, which show, respectively, $B$'s and $A$'s pretrade price ratios. If the indifference curve $I_2$ were steeper (flatter) at point $R$ than the slope of the straight-line segment $RU$ ($ZR$), the indifference curve would simply intersect the world production-possibilities frontier at point $R$ and equilibrium would occur somewhere on the $RU$ ($ZR$) straight-line segment, with the equilibrium terms of trade given by $A$'s ($B$'s) pretrade price ratio (i.e., the pretrade price ratio of the country which is producing both commodities at the final international equilibrium position).

The preceding general-equilibrium solution shows: (*a*) the equilibrium terms of trade; (*b*) the pattern of specialization; (*c*) the total world output and consumption of each commodity; and (*d*) the potential role of free commodity trade in improving the welfare of the world as a whole. However, it conceals much important information, such as the consumption levels of $X$ and $Y$ in the two countries, the quantities of $X$ and $Y$ exported or imported by the two countries, and the manner in which the gains from trade are divided between the two countries. In the following section, it will be shown how this information can be recovered.

## 3.2 INTERNATIONAL EQUILIBRIUM IN TERMS OF PRICE-CONSUMPTION CURVES

To demonstrate international equilibrium in a more disaggregated form than is given in the preceding section, it is necessary to make use of another known tool, namely, the price-consumption curve.

Suppose that, instead of having a single social indifference map for the world as a whole, there are two—one for each country. How, then, can international equilibrium be demonstrated? This can be done geometrically in two ways. First, international equilibrium will be established in terms of price-consumption curves. This is done in the present section, and it is a useful way of demonstrating international equilibrium when the production-possibilities frontiers are linear. However, this method cannot be used in general. For this reason, the following section extends the analysis to show international equilibrium in terms of *offer curves*. The latter method is much more general than the former, and it can be easily grasped, at least in the context of the classical theory, once international equilibrium in terms of price-consumption curves has been understood.

It is necessary to explain how a single economy which can buy and sell unlimited quantities of commodities $X$ and $Y$ at given prices attains general equilibrium. This problem can be divided into two subproblems:

1. What should the economy produce to maximize its income (i.e., the value of its output)?
2. Subject to the answer given to question 1, what should the economy consume to maximize social welfare (i.e., reach the highest possible social indifference curve)?

Let us consider both of these questions in the order in which they have been presented.

### Optimization of Production

Since our interest lies mainly in relative prices, as opposed to absolute prices, the value of output produced, $Q$, is expressed in terms of commodity $Y$. As before, let $p$ stand for the international terms of trade (that is, $p \equiv p_x/p_y$). Accordingly, the value of total output is given by

$$Q = pX_p + Y_p \tag{3.1}$$

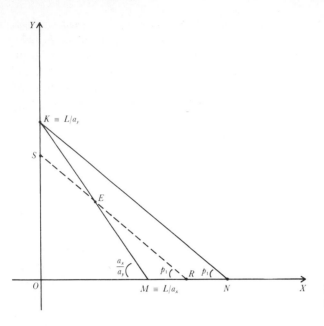

**Figure 3.4** Optimization of production.

where $X_p$ and $Y_p$ are the production levels of commodities $X$ and $Y$, respectively. The object is to maximize $Q$, as given by eq. (3.1), subject to the production-possibilities frontier of the economy, such as eq. (2.8) above.

The solution is given graphically in fig. 3.4. The straight line $KM$ is the economy's production-possibilities frontier. Its slope (i.e., the opportunity cost of $X$ in terms of $Y$) is given by the ratio of labor requirements, that is, $a_x/a_y$. In fig. 3.4, it is assumed that the given terms of trade, $p_1$, are lower than $a_x/a_y$, that is, $p_1 < a_x/a_y$; which is to say, the opportunity cost of $X$ in the economy was assumed to be higher than the relative price of $X$ in the world economy. It should be obvious that the economy has to produce somewhere on the production-possibilities frontier. On the one hand, it cannot produce outside of the frontier and, on the other, from any point within the frontier it can always move to some region of the frontier where the outputs of both commodities are higher than the corresponding outputs implied by the original point, and thus increase the total value of the economy's output.

Now consider any point on the production-possibilities frontier, such as point $E$, and assume that the economy is for the moment producing there. Then draw the *income line* of the economy, as defined by eq. (3.1). This income line (whose absolute slope is given by $p_1$) is a kind of consumption line for the economy; i.e., on the assumption that the economy produces at $E$ and the relative price of $X$ in terms of $Y$ (as given by the international market) is $p_1$, the income line shows the maximum combinations of $X$ and $Y$ that the economy can consume. Observe that this particular income line, as illustrated in fig. 3.4 by the broken line through $E$, must necessarily pass through point $E$: if the economy produces at $E$ it can also consume at $E$, irrespective of prices. In addition, it must be flatter than the production-possibilities frontier because of our original assumption that

$p_1 < a_x/a_y$. Thus, through any arbitrarily chosen production point, such as $E$, an income line can be drawn with slope equal to the given terms of trade $p_1$. The problem is to determine the optimum production point, i.e., the point which will maximize the economy's value of output produced. What this means in terms of fig. 3.4 is that a point on the production-possibilities frontier should be determined on the basis of which the income line will lie as far from the origin as possible.

The optimum production point is $K$. As the production point slides downward on the production-possibilities frontier (i.e., from $E$ to $M$), the income line shifts inward. On the other hand, as the production point slides upward on the frontier (i.e., from $E$ to $K$), the income line shifts outward, reaching its optimum position when the production point coincides with $K$. This should come as no surprise, because at point $K$ the economy specializes completely in the production of commodity $Y$, whose opportunity cost is smaller at home than abroad. The income line $KN$, which corresponds to the highest possible value of output, is given a special name: *consumption-possibilities frontier*. The determination of the consumption-possibilities frontier answers the first of the two questions raised earlier.

Note that the consumption-possibilities frontier lies totally outside the production-possibilities frontier, except at the singular point $K$. This is important, because it follows that while an economy is necessarily constrained by its production-possibilities frontier as far as production is concerned, it is by no means so constrained with respect to consumption. That is, *free trade makes it possible to consume beyond the boundaries of the production-possibilities frontier*. Free trade expands the consumption-possibilities set beyond the boundaries of the production-possibilities frontier; herein lies the whole essence of the gains from trade.

Note also the relationship between the (domestic) opportunity cost of $X$ in terms of $Y$ and the international price ratio. In fig. 3.4, it is assumed that $p_1 < a_x/a_y$. To complete the analysis, however, it must be shown what happens when $p \geq a_x/a_y$. The answer is simple. If $p > a_x/a_y$, the family of income lines† will be steeper than the production-possibilities frontier, so for income maximization the economy will have to specialize completely in the production of $X$ ($X$ being relatively cheaper domestically); i.e., the consumption-possibilities frontier will pass through $M$ and be steeper than the production-possibilities frontier. What is important is that the consumption-possibilities frontier will lie beyond the economy's production-possibilities frontier, except at the singular (production) point $M$.

If $p = a_x/a_y$, the consumption-possibilities frontier coincides with the production-possibilities frontier. In this particular case, the economy obviously gains nothing from international trade. In addition, its structure of production is indeterminate: it can produce anywhere on the production-possibilities frontier and end up with the same consumption-possibilities frontier.

---

† We speak of a "family of income lines" because an income line passes through every point on the production-possibilities frontier.

## Optimization of Consumption

Let us turn now to the second question: what should the economy consume? The answer is given graphically in fig. 3.5, which contains the pertinent information given in fig. 3.4 together with the economy's social indifference map. Actually, to avoid confusion, only two social indifference curves have been drawn in fig. 3.5. Equilibrium before trade obviously occurs at point $E_1$, where the production-possibilities frontier is tangent to the highest possible social indifference curve (that is, $I_1$). In other words, before trade, the economy produces *and* consumes at point $E_1$. However, a distinction between consumption and production equilibria must necessarily be made when the country has access to international trade. As was already shown, production in this particular case (i.e., when $p < a_x/a_y$) takes place at point $K$, with $KN$ being the consumption-possibilities frontier. Consumption, however, will have to take place at point $E_2$, where the consumption-possibilities frontier is tangent to the highest possible social indifference curve (that is, $I_2$).

## Exports and Imports

Once the posttrade production and consumption equilibria are determined, the exports and imports of the economy can be easily determined by completing the right-angled triangle $RKE_2$. Thus, since the economy produces $OK$ units of $Y$ and consumes only $OR$ units, it must necessarily be exporting $RK$ units of $Y$ to the rest of the world. Further, since the economy consumes $RE_2$ units of $X$ and produces none, it must necessarily be importing $RE_2$ units of $X$ from the rest of the world.

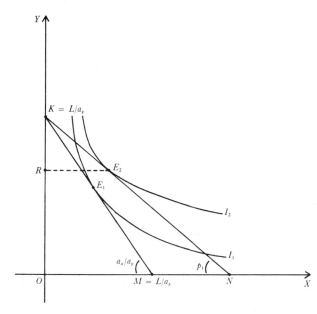

**Figure 3.5** Optimization of consumption.

Further, note that

$$p_1 \equiv \frac{OK}{ON} = \frac{RK}{RE_2}$$

or

$$p_1 RE_2 = RK$$

i.e., the value of exports is equal to the value of imports, both being expressed in terms of commodity $Y$. This is no accident; it follows, rather, from the assumption that our economy spends on $X$ and $Y$ exactly as much as it receives in the form of income from the production of $Y$. In other words, our economy does indeed consume on the consumption-possibilities frontier, which means that the value of production equals the value of consumption.

## The Price-Consumption Curve

What has been done for a single value of $p$ can be repeated for every other value. The general conclusion can be summarized as follows. For all values of $p$ satisfying the inequality $p < a_x/a_y$, the consumption-possibilities frontier will always start from point $K$ (fig. 3.5) and be flatter than the production-possibilities frontier. Further, as $p$ falls from $a_x/a_y$ toward zero, the consumption-possibilities frontier rotates through the production equilibrium point $K$, becoming continuously flatter. But while the production equilibrium point remains unique, the consumption equilibrium point varies with $p$. The locus of all consumption equilibrium points is the price-consumption curve. This is illustrated in fig. 3.6(a), where the social indifference map has been omitted to keep the diagram simple. The straight line $KM$ is the economy's production-possibilities frontier, and the curve labeled PCC is the price-consumption curve.

For all values of $p$ satisfying the inequality $p > a_x/a_y$, the economy produces at $M$ and consumes along the price-consumption curve (PCC) as shown in

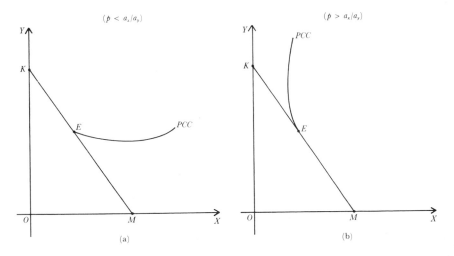

**Figure 3.6** The price-consumption curve.

fig. 3.6($b$). In this case, the consumption-possibilities frontier is always steeper than the production-possibilities frontier. Further, as $p$ increases, the consumption-possibilities frontier rotates through point $M$, becoming continuously steeper.

### International Equilibrium

Let us now return to the problem of international equilibrium. Assume that $A$ has a comparative advantage in the production of $Y$ and $B$ in $X$; that is, $A$'s production-possibilities frontier is steeper than $B$'s. International equilibrium is shown in fig. 3.7. The triangle $O_B KN$ represents $B$'s production-possibilities frontier, with $O_B$ being its origin. The curve $\mathrm{PCC}_B$ is $B$'s price-consumption curve derived under the assumption that $b_x/b_y < p$, that is, that $B$'s opportunity cost of $X$ in terms of $Y$ is always smaller than the international terms of trade $p$. On the other hand, the triangle $O_A MK$ is $A$'s production-possibilities frontier, having been rotated through its origin $O_A$ by 180°. The curve $\mathrm{PCC}_A$ is $A$'s price-consumption curve derived under the assumption that $a_x/a_y > p$, that is, that $A$'s opportunity cost of $X$ in terms of $Y$ is higher than the international terms of trade $p$. Therefore, country $B$ is seen to specialize completely in the production of $X$, whereas country $A$ specializes in the production of $Y$. Accordingly, the total world output of $X$ is given by the horizontal distance $O_B K$ (that is, $B$'s maximum output of commodity $X$), and that of $Y$ is given by the vertical distance $O_A K$ (that is, $A$'s maximum output of $Y$).

Since we have assumed thus far that each country behaves as a single rational individual, it is obvious that the problem is essentially reduced to that of two individuals, $A$ and $B$, with one (that is, $A$) endowed with a fixed quantity of $Y$ and the other (that is, $B$) with a fixed quantity of $X$. From price theory, we know that general equilibrium occurs at the point of intersection between the price-

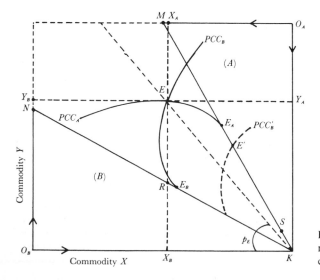

**Figure 3.7** International equilibrium in terms of price-consumption curves.

consumption curves of the two consumers.† This is shown by point $E$ of fig. 3.7. Thus, at point $E$, $A$ consumes $X_A$ and $Y_A$ (measured from $O_A$) while $B$ consumes $X_B$ and $Y_B$ (measured from $O_B$) units of commodities $X$ and $Y$, respectively. Supply is equal to demand in both markets, and therefore general equilibrium prevails. Country $B$ $(A)$ is exporting (importing) $X_B K$ units of $X$ while it is importing (exporting) $X_B E$ units of $Y$. The equilibrium terms of trade $(p_E)$ are given by the absolute slope of the vector $KE$. Observe that $b_x/b_y < p_E < a_x/a_y$, and that $KE$ is steeper than $NK$ but flatter than $MK$.

## The Gains from Trade

Figure 3.7 shows the gains from trade and their division between the two countries. Without trade, each country will necessarily have to consume on its production-possibilities frontier. With trade, as fig. 3.7 shows, both countries consume beyond their respective production-possibilities frontiers, because they both specialize completely. In fact, the gains from trade correspond to the area $NKM$ of fig. 3.7. The larger this area, the larger the gains from trade. In addition, observe that the area $NKM$ is divided into two parts by the terms-of-trade line $KE$—the area $EKM$ going to $A$ and the area $EKN$ going to $B$, so to speak. Therefore, the closer the terms-of-trade line $KE$ lies to $B$'s production-possibilities frontier (i.e., the smaller the difference between $b_x/b_y$ and $p_E$), the smaller will be $B$'s share of the gains. Similarly, the closer $KE$ lies to $A$'s production-possibilities frontier (i.e., the smaller the difference between $a_x/a_y$ and $p_E$), the smaller will be $A$'s share of the gains.

  As pointed out earlier, the concept of the gains from trade is much subtler than it appears. In general, the introduction of free international trade will make (within each country) some people better off and others worse off compared with the pretrade equilibrium position. But it is not clear whether the society actually becomes better off or worse off when some of its members gain and some lose. Within the context of the classical theory, however, this difficulty does not arise. Labor is the only factor of production, and if any worker becomes better off, all of them do. In fact, the production-possibilities frontier of each country can be scaled down to the relative size of the representative citizen and the analysis carried out on the basis of the data on the production-possibilities frontiers and indifference maps of all individuals. Such analysis would, of course, be more complicated without any distinct advantage, except that it would probably enable us to see better the relationship between the equilibrium value of $p$ and the division of the gains from trade. However, the latter should be obvious when it is realized that, in this particular case, the production-possibilities frontier of the country as a whole is merely the sum of all individual frontiers with no interaction whatsoever between them.

---

  † The analysis of the text assumes that both $A$ and $B$ behave as price takers. It is well known that this assumption may be violated in the case of two consumers and that our problem may end up being a problem of bilateral monopoly. However, this assumption is quite legitimate for our purposes because we are not actually dealing with two individuals; rather, we are dealing with two countries, each composed of many individuals.

There is no general rule according to which one can decide which distribution of the gains from trade between countries is the best. International competition will, of course, give rise to a certain distribution, but we cannot be sure that this distribution is the best. Further, it is not unusual for any or all countries of the world to interfere with the free workings of the competitive system through tariffs and other barriers to trade, in an effort to turn the terms of trade in their favor and thus end up with a bigger share of the gains from trade.

## Graham

Frank B. Graham (1923, 1932, 1948) believed that the equilibrium terms of trade were, as a rule, equal to the pretrade equilibrium price ratio of one of the trading countries; intermediate or "limbo" price ratios were, he thought, the exception. An important feature of a "limbo" price ratio is that changes in tastes cause changes in prices only with production and supply remaining constant in each country. If "limbo" price ratios were the rule, Graham argued, one would observe violent fluctuations in prices because of the (assumed) highly volatile nature of demand. Since the terms of trade were empirically stable, "limbo" price ratios must be ruled out.

Graham believed that relative prices are determined by opportunity costs rather than reciprocal demand, as illustrated in the following section by the Marshallian offer curves. The theory of reciprocal demand (he said) relies on changes in the terms of trade as the fundamental means of international adjustment, which is useless and misleading given the observed stability of relative prices. ("Stability" in this context should be interpreted as "constancy" or "rigidity.") Graham believed that international adjustment was more likely to take place through the possibility of transferring resources from one commodity to another under conditions of constant opportunity costs.

Later econometric studies did not support Graham's belief about the volatile nature of demand. In fact, demand stability rather than instability was borne out by such studies. Actually, if demand was volatile and the equilibrium terms of trade coincided with the pretrade equilibrium price ratio of one of the trading countries, one would observe violent fluctuations in production which seems quite contrary to the facts.

Of greater interest was Graham's effort to liberate the pure theory of trade from the assumption of two commodities and two countries—an effort that had already been begun by Mill and continued by Mangoldt, Edgeworth, and Viner. This topic is treated briefly in the appendix to this chapter.

In the context of the classical model discussed so far, Graham's conclusion is possible when the two trading countries are of unequal size. This is illustrated in fig. 3.7. If $B$ were a small country with a production-possibilities frontier given by the triangle $X_B KR$ (instead of $O_B KN$) and if its price-consumption curve were the broken curve labeled $PCC'_B$, equilibrium would occur on $A$'s production-possibilities frontier, with the terms of trade being equal to $A$'s pretrade price ratio. Country $B$ would specialize completely in the production of $X$, but $A$ would produce both $X$ and $Y$. Note that at $A$'s pretrade price ratio, $B$ will consume at point $E'$, and $A$ at $E_A$ (as before trade). However, since the consumption points $E'$

and $E_A$ do not coincide, supply cannot equal demand in any market if $A$ specializes in $Y$ and $B$ in $X$ (that is, if the supplies of $X$ and $Y$, respectively, are given by the sides of the original parallelogram of fig. 3.7), for then there would be an excess demand for $X$ and an excess supply of $Y$. The problem is solved if country $A$ produces at point $S$ on its production-possibilities frontier, which is determined in such a way as to satisfy the equation $E'E_A = KS$.

Note that essentially the same result could have been reached if $B$ were not a small country but its tastes were heavily biased in favor of commodity $X$ and, as a result, the $PCC'_B$ were its original price-consumption curve. Therefore, the "size" of a country is not an absolute magnitude which can be measured objectively. Demand considerations are indeed important in this respect. Nevertheless, there is one objectively measurable magnitude which can serve as a sufficient condition for the emergence of the preceding phenomenon. Suppose that $B$ is so small that the maximum amount of $X$ it can produce falls short of the amount of $X$ that $A$ consumes before trade. Then, provided that $X$ is not a Giffen commodity† in country $A$, international equilibrium will always imply that $A$ produces both commodities, with the terms of trade being equal to $A$'s pretrade price ratio and all the gains from trade accruing to the small country $B$. This is the importance of being unimportant!

In one of his numerical examples, Graham (1923) assumed that commodities were consumed in fixed proportions. As Chipman (1965, pp. 493–494) points out, the assumption of fixed coefficients in consumption "practically guarantees the extreme solution."

The implications of the assumption that commodities are consumed in fixed proportions are illustrated in fig. 3.8, which is similar to fig. 3.7 except that now it is assumed that $A$ consumes the commodities $X$ and $Y$ in the proportion shown by the slope of the vector $O_A E_A$ and $B$ in the proportion shown by the slope of the vector $O_B E_B$. Equilibrium does indeed occur at point $E$, but it is unstable. That is, if the terms of trade happen to be equal to the slope of the vector $KE$, say $p_E$, all markets will be cleared and general equilibrium would prevail. However, any displacement of the terms of trade from their equilibrium value $p_E$ will generate forces which will push them further from equilibrium. For instance, if $p$ were to rise above $p_E$, an excess demand for $X$ and an excess supply of $Y$ would emerge— as can be verified from fig. 3.8. The price ratio $p_x/p_y$ will thus tend to rise on both counts, instead of falling back to $p_E$. On the other hand, should $p$ ever fall below $p_E$, it will go on falling because when the terms of trade are lower than $p_E$, an excess supply of $X$ and an excess demand for $Y$ emerge. Therefore, point $E$ is unstable. But there are another two possible equilibrium points which are indeed stable. These are $E_S$ and $E'_S$. At each of these points, one country produces both commodities, with the equilibrium terms of trade given by its pretrade price ratio and all gains from trade going to the other country. Thus, at $E'_S$, country $A$ produces both commodities, while at $E_S$ country $B$ does.

The assumption that commodities are consumed in fixed proportions is not sufficient to guarantee that the intersection between the two consumption paths

† For the concept of "Giffen commodity," see any textbook on price theory.

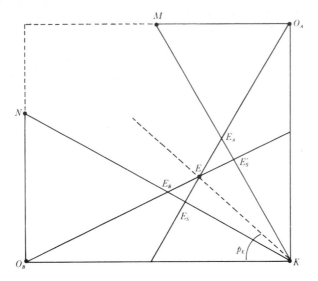

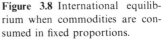

Figure 3.8 International equilibrium when commodities are consumed in fixed proportions.

(i.e., point $E$ of fig. 3.8) is an unstable equilibrium. To see this, draw a straight line connecting the origins $(O_A, O_B)$ of the two production-possibilities frontiers. If the intersection of the two consumption paths takes place in the cone $NKM$ but to the northwest of the line connecting $O_A$ and $O_B$, that intersection will give rise to a stable equilibrium.

## The Need for a Better Geometrical Solution

The analysis of the present section has relaxed the assumption made in the preceding section, namely, that there exists a world social indifference map. But although the analysis has given further insights into the problems of international equilibrium and the gains from trade, it suffers from two disadvantages. In the first place, figs. 3.7 and 3.8 were drawn on the assumption that the terms of trade must lie between the pretrade price ratios of the two countries, which actually was the conclusion derived earlier. However, it appears desirable to have a geometrical solution which does not depend on conclusions derived otherwise. In the second place, figs. 3.7 and 3.8 can hardly be used to find the general-equilibrium solutions to the neoclassical and modern theories of trade, notwithstanding the fact that they contain all the necessary ingredients. The purpose of the following section is mainly to remedy these two deficiencies.

## 3.3 OFFER CURVES

### Equilibrium Conditions in Terms of Excess Demands

International equilibrium requires that for every commodity the world supply must be equal to the world demand. In particular, within the context of our two-country, two-commodity model, the following equations must be satisfied:

$$X_A^P + X_B^P = X_A^C + X_B^C \tag{3.2a}$$

$$Y_A^P + Y_B^P = Y_A^C + Y_B^C \tag{3.3a}$$

where the superscripts $P$ and $C$ indicate production and consumption, respectively, and the subscripts $A$ and $B$ indicate the countries. Figures 3.7 and 3.8 have been interpreted as showing general equilibrium in precisely this manner, i.e., by showing that world supply is equal to world demand in every market. However, general equilibrium can be shown in another way, namely, in terms of the excess demand for each commodity by each country. Figures 3.7 and 3.8 could also be interpreted in this fashion.

The equilibrium conditions (3.2a) and (3.3a) can be rewritten as follows:

$$(X_A^C - X_A^P) + (X_B^C - X_B^P) = 0 \tag{3.2b}$$

$$(Y_A^C - Y_A^P) + (Y_B^C - Y_B^P) = 0 \tag{3.3b}$$

The four pairs of parentheses in these equations enclose the excess demands of the two countries for each of the two commodities. For instance, the expression $(X_A^C - X_A^P)$ is $A$'s excess demand for $X$, which may be either positive or negative. A similar interpretation holds for every other difference in these equations.

Actually, the above equations can be simplified by introducing the symbol $E_i^j$ to indicate the excess demand of the $j$th country for the $i$th commodity. Thus, eqs. (3.2b) and (3.3b) can be simplified as follows:

$$E_X^A + E_X^B = 0 \tag{3.2c}$$

$$E_Y^A + E_Y^B = 0 \tag{3.3c}$$

In other words, for general equilibrium it is required that $A$'s excess demand for $X$ plus $B$'s excess demand for $X$ be zero, and that $A$'s excess demand for $Y$ plus $B$'s excess demand for $Y$ be zero.

From eqs. (3.2c) and (3.3c) it is quite obvious that $E_X^A$ and $E_X^B$ cannot be of the same sign—unless they are both zero. The same is true of $E_Y^A$ and $E_Y^B$. That is, in equilibrium, when one country's excess demand for $X$ (or $Y$) is positive, the other country's excess demand for $X$ (or $Y$) must be negative. In other words, when a country imports a commodity, the other country exports it. What is more, the former country's imports must necessarily match the latter country's exports. To verify this, note that in fig. 3.7 the coordinates of the equilibrium point $E$ with respect to $K$ as origin give the exports and imports of $X$ and $Y$ for both countries and that eqs. (3.2c) and (3.3c) are indeed satisfied.

## The Demand for Imports and Supply of Exports as Functions of the Terms of Trade

The excess demands $E_X^A$, $E_Y^A$, $E_X^B$, and $E_Y^B$ depend on the terms of trade. These excess demands can be rigorously derived. It suffices to show how this can be done for only one of the two countries, country $A$.

Figure 3.6 has shown how $A$'s price-consumption curve can be derived. Figure 3.9 shows how to derive $A$'s excess demand for $X$ and $Y$ on the basis of the information given in fig. 3.6. Panel ($a$) reproduces in the lower part the information contained in panel ($a$) of fig. 3.6. The only additional information in fig. 3.9($a$) is the introduction of the consumption-possibilities frontier for the specific value of the terms of trade $p_0$. As has been pointed out, the price-consumption curve

(PCC) is the locus of consumption equilibrium points. For instance, for $p = p_0$, the economy will produce at $K$ and consume at $R$. But this implies that $A$ will be willing to offer to the rest of the world the quantity $SR$ of $Y$ in exchange for the quantity $KS$ of $X$. Now draw a horizontal line at the level of $K$ (as in fig. 3.9) and measure from $K$, in the positive direction, $A$'s imports of $X$ (i.e., $A$'s positive excess demand for $X$). Then extend the vertical axis beyond $K$ and measure vertically $A$'s supply of exports of $Y$ (i.e., $A$'s negative excess demand for $Y$). Finally, determine point $R'$ as the mirror image of point $R$ on the PCC curve. The coordinates of point $R'$ with respect to $K$ as origin show $A$'s exports of $Y$ and imports of $X$. In addition, the vector $KR'$ is the mirror image of the consumption-possibilities frontier $KR$. The vector $KR'$ is called the terms-of-trade line; its slope is equal to the given terms of trade $p_0$.

## A's Offer Curve

Point $R'$ is a point on $A$'s *offer curve*, which shows the quantities of $X$ and $Y$ that $A$ is willing to export to, or import from, the rest of the world, as the case may be, at alternative values of the terms of trade. Repeating the same experiment for all values of $p$ which satisfy the inequality $p \leq a_x/a_y$, we determine one part of $A$'s offer curve as the mirror image of the price-consumption curve. This is shown by the curve $E'R'$ in fig. 3.9(*a*).

For the specific value $p = a_x/a_y$, the country will consume at $E$, but as noted earlier, its production point is indeterminate. For the moment, assume that pro-

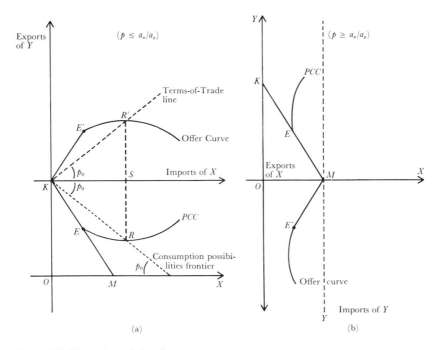

**Figure 3.9** Derivation of $A$'s offer curve.

duction takes place somewhere in the region $KE$. (Figure 3.9($b$) explains what happens when production takes place in the region $EM$.) If production takes place at $E$, both the demand for imports and the supply of exports of country $A$ will be zero. This will give rise to point $K$ of the offer curve. On the other hand, if production takes place at $K$, the relevant point on the offer curve is $E'$. Finally, as the production point slides from $K$ to $E$, the point on the offer curve slides from $E'$ to $K$. Note again that the linear part $KE'$ of the offer curve is the mirror image of $KE$ of $A$'s production-possibilities frontier.

Figure 3.9($b$) shows how the second and final part of $A$'s offer curve can be derived. Country $A$'s offers for all values of $p$ greater than $a_x/a_y$ are now considered. The upper half of the diagram reproduces the information given in fig. 3.6($b$). The reader who has mastered the analysis of fig. 3.9($a$) will have no trouble proving that the second part of $A$'s offer curve is again the mirror image of the price-consumption curve (PCC), with $M$ as its point of origin and the horizontal axis the axis of symmetry. The linear part $ME''$ corresponds to the case where $p = a_x/a_y$, and production takes place in the region $EM$ of $A$'s production-possibilities frontier.

The two branches of $A$'s offer curve are brought together in fig. 3.10. In the first quadrant is the part of the offer curve derived in fig. 3.9($a$), and in the third quadrant is the part derived in fig. 3.9($b$). Thus, fig. 3.10 gives $A$'s full offer curve.

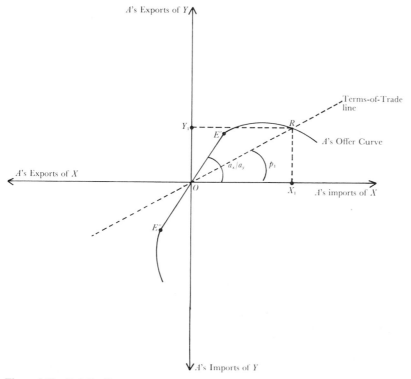

**Figure 3.10** $A$'s full offer curve.

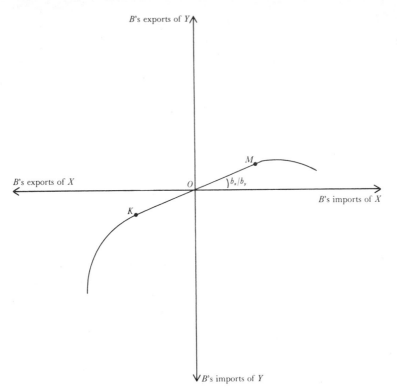

**Figure 3.11** *B*'s offer curve.

Notice that it necessarily lies in the first and third quadrants only. This follows from the fact that any point on the offer curve necessarily satisfies the equation "value of exports = value of imports." Therefore, a country cannot export or import both commodities simultaneously by assumption. Any point of the offer curve in the first quadrant shows how much $Y$ country $A$ is willing to export for a given quantity of imports of $X$. On the other hand, any point in the third quadrant shows how much $X$ the country is willing to export for a given quantity of imports of $Y$. To determine the precise offer of the economy at any particular value of the terms of trade, simply draw through the origin a straight line with slope equal to the given value of the terms of trade—called the terms-of-trade line—and determine the point of intersection between it and the offer curve. The coordinates of the point of intersection show $A$'s exports and imports. Thus, for $p = p_1 < a_x/a_y$, $A$'s offer is given by the coordinates of point $R$; that is, $A$ is willing to export $OY_1$ units of $Y$ for $OX_1$ units of imports of $X$. Note that $p_1 = OY_1/OX_1$. Finally, notice that the straight-line portion $E''OE'$ of the offer curve corresponds precisely to the mirror image of $A$'s production-possibilities frontier, with the origin of the offer curve corresponding to the pretrade equilibrium point on the production-possibilities frontier.

Remember that the offer curve does not depend on demand alone. It also depends on supply. Both the production-possibilities frontier (supply) and the social indifference map (demand) were used for its derivation. This point is made here because Graham believed that the offer curve depended only on demand.

## B's Offer Curve

The offer curve of any other country can be similarly derived. Figure 3.11 shows B's offer curve. It is similar to fig. 3.10 except that now it is B's exports and imports that are being measured along the corresponding axes. Again, the straight-line segment KOM is the mirror image of B's production-possibilities frontier, and its slope is equal to $b_x/b_y$, that is, the absolute slope of B's production-possibilities frontier.

## International Equilibrium

As noted earlier (see eqs. (3.2c) and (3.3c)), general equilibrium occurs when A's excess demand plus B's excess demand for each and every commodity is zero. The offer curves given in figs. 3.10 and 3.11 give each country's excess demand ($\pm$) for each commodity for all values of the terms of trade. This information can be used to demonstrate international equilibrium in terms of these offer curves.

It is important to note that the corresponding axes of figs. 3.10 and 3.11 do not measure the same variables that are relevant for the analysis of general equilibrium. For instance, along the positive direction of the horizontal axis are measured, in fig. 3.10, the quantity of A's imports of X and, in fig. 3.11, the quantity of B's imports of X. Along the negative direction of the horizontal axis are measured, in fig. 3.10, the quantity of A's exports of X and, in fig. 3.11, the quantity of B's exports of X. But what we are actually interested in comparing is not A's demand for imports of X and B's demand for imports of X but, rather, A's demand for imports of X and B's supply of exports of X, or A's supply of exports of X and B's demand for imports of X. Similar observations hold for commodity Y. To remedy the situation simply rotate either one of the two diagrams by 180°, so that all axes will correspond to what we would like to compare. In the following analysis, B's diagram has been rotated.

Figure 3.12 brings together the two offer curves, with B's offer curve rotated by 180°. International equilibrium occurs at the intersection of the two offer curves in the first quadrant (i.e., point E). Country A exports Y and imports X, and B exports X and imports Y. The precise quantities of X and Y imported and exported by the two countries are given by the coordinates of the equilibrium point E. Further, the equilibrium terms of trade are given by the slope of the vector OE (not drawn). Obviously, the equilibrium terms of trade lie between the pretrade price ratios of the two countries; i.e., the vector OE lies between the vectors OE' and OK. In addition, the two offer curves intersect each other in the first quadrant only.

## The Limits of the Equilibrium Terms of Trade

It might seem at this point that the conclusion that the vector OE (showing the equilibrium terms of trade) lies between the vectors OE' and OK is an artificial one because the offer curves might be drawn in a different way and give rise to international equilibrium that might violate our conclusion. However, in the first quadrant, A's offer curve does not exist for $p > a_x/a_y$ and B's offer curve does not exist for $p < b_x/b_y$, because these are the assumptions under which they have been

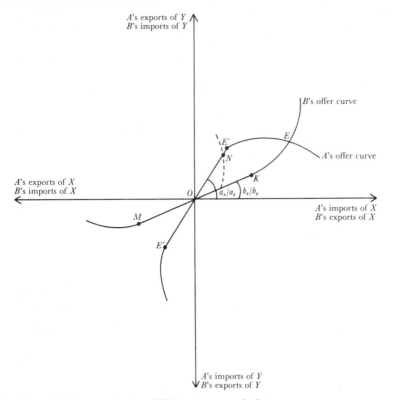

**Figure 3.12** International equilibrium in terms of offer curves.

drawn. The parts of these offer curves which correspond to $p > a_x/a_y$ and $p < b_x/b_y$ lie in the third quadrant. Thus, as long as $a_x/a_y > b_x/b_y$, international equilibrium will occur in the first quadrant, with the equilibrium terms of trade $p_E$ satisfying the condition $b_x/b_y \leq p_E \leq a_x/a_y$. The analysis can be extended to the case where equilibrium occurs in the third quadrant, i.e., when $a_x/a_y < b_x/b_y$.

The equilibrium terms of trade coincide with one country's pretrade price ratio if, and only if, the intersection of the two offer curves takes place on the linear part of either offer curve. The broken offer curve in fig. 3.12 illustrates the case where equilibrium occurs at point $N$ on the straight-line segment of $A$'s offer curve, with the equilibrium terms of trade coinciding with $A$'s pretrade price ratio and all gains from trade going to $B$.

## Verification of the Law of Comparative Advantage

On the basis of the above observations, it should be clear that it is impossible to have intersections of the two offer curves in the first and third quadrants simultaneously. However, this does not necessarily imply that international equilibrium is unique, because it is quite possible to have several intersections of the two offer curves in the same quadrant. What is implied is that when $a_x/a_y > b_x/b_y$, and thus $E''E'$ is steeper than $MK$, international equilibrium will necessarily occur in the first quadrant; i.e., country $A$ will definitely export $Y$ and import $X$ while $B$ will export $X$ and import $Y$, which is in perfect agreement with the law of comparative advantage. If $a_x/a_y < b_x/b_y$, international equilibrium will necessarily occur in the third quadrant: $A$ $(B)$ will export $X$ $(Y)$ and import $Y$ $(X)$, which again is in agreement with the law of comparative advantage.

## Stability of International Equilibrium

Is international equilibrium stable? To aid in answering this question, the first quadrant of fig. 3.12 is reproduced in fig. 3.13. Again, international equilibrium occurs at point $E$, with the equilibrium terms of trade given by the slope of the vector $OE$ (not drawn). What happens when the system is out of equilibrium? Will the system return to point $E$ (i.e., is the system stable?) or not (i.e., is the system unstable?). To answer this question, let us use the Walrasian stability condition that the price of a commodity tends to rise (fall) when its excess demand is positive (negative). On the basis of this condition, it can easily be shown that the international equilibrium in fig. 3.13 is indeed stable.

Consider any value of the terms of trade which is lower than the equilibrium terms of trade. This can be presented graphically by a terms-of-trade (TOT) line flatter than the vector $OE$, such as the broken line $\text{TOT}_1$. For the specific value of the terms of trade implied by $\text{TOT}_1$, $A$'s offer is given by the coordinates of point $S$ (i.e., the intersection between $\text{TOT}_1$ and $A$'s offer curve) and $B$'s offer by the coordinates of point $R$ (i.e., the intersection between $\text{TOT}_1$ and $B$'s offer curve). That is, $A$ is offering $OY_2$ units of $Y$ in exchange for $OX_2$ units of $X$, and $B$ is offering $OX_1$ units of $X$ in exchange for $OY_1$ units of $Y$. Since $OX_2 > OX_1$ and $OY_2 > OY_1$ (that is, since the world excess demand for $X$ is positive while that for $Y$ is negative), the price of $X$ will tend to rise and the price of $Y$ will tend to fall. On both counts, the price ratio $p_x/p_y$ will tend to rise and the terms-of-trade line

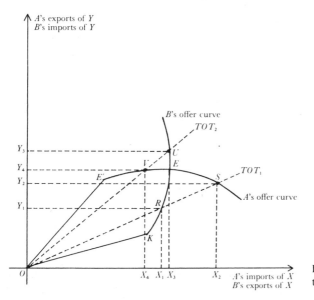

**Figure 3.13** Stability of international equilibrium.

$TOT_1$ will rotate through the origin and move closer to the vector $OE$; that is, the system will tend to move back to the equilibrium point $E$.

On the other hand, for any value of the terms of trade higher than the equilibrium value (such as that implied by $TOT_2$), the world excess demand for $X$ will be negative and that for $Y$ positive. This is also illustrated in fig. 3.13. Thus, for the terms of trade implied by $TOT_2$, country $A$ will be offering $OY_4$ units of $Y$ in exchange for $OX_4$ units of $X$ and $B$ will be offering $OX_3$ units of $X$ in exchange for $OY_3$ units of $Y$. Since $OY_3 > OY_4$ and $OX_3 > OX_4$, the price of $X$ will tend to fall and the price of $Y$ will tend to rise; the price ratio $p_x/p_y$ will tend to fall and the terms-of-trade line $TOT_2$ will rotate through the origin and move closer to the vector $OE$. Therefore, when the system is not in equilibrium, forces are generated which will push it back to equilibrium. Accordingly, $E$ is a stable equilibrium point.

Not all equilibrium points are stable. Some are indeed unstable. (A case of an unstable equilibrium has already been given in fig. 3.8.) One of the problems that will have to be investigated later relates to the necessary and sufficient conditions for stability.

## 3.4 WALRAS'S LAW AND INTERNATIONAL EQUILIBRIUM

The preceding section shows how the problem of international equilibrium can be handled in terms of offer curves. But however useful the geometrical apparatus of offer curves may be, it is important to notice that they give (directly) more information than is actually necessary for the determination of international equilibrium. The purpose of the present section is to show the redundancy of the information given by the offer curves and to provide a simpler way of dealing with the problem of international equilibrium.

### Walras's Law

International equilibrium requires that eqs. (3.2c) and (3.3c) be satisfied. In other words, supply must equal demand in every market. However, eqs. (3.2c) and (3.3c) are not independent. When one of them is satisfied, the other is necessarily satisfied as well. This is actually what has come to be known as *Walras's law*: in a system of $n$ markets, when $(n - 1)$ markets are in equilibrium, then by necessity the last market is also in equilibrium. This conclusion should give some assurance to those who have already noticed that each of eqs. (3.2c) and (3.3c) contains only one unknown, $p$, and that each could be solved for $p$; hence, there arises the possibility of inconsistent solutions. Walras's law is seen to eliminate the problem of inconsistency by declaring that eqs. (3.2c) and (3.3c) are not independent.

As has been repeatedly pointed out, the value of output produced is equal to the value of output consumed in each of the two countries. Accordingly, the following equations must be satisfied:

$$pX_A^P + Y_A^P = pX_A^C + Y_A^C \tag{3.4a}$$

$$pX_B^P + Y_B^P = pX_B^C + Y_B^C \tag{3.5a}$$

These equations can be rewritten thus:

$$pE_X^A + E_Y^A = 0 \qquad (3.4b)$$

$$pE_X^B + E_Y^B = 0 \qquad (3.5b)$$

Combining eqs. (3.4b) and (3.5b) gives

$$p(E_X^A + E_X^B) + (E_Y^A + E_Y^B) = 0 \qquad (3.6)$$

Equation (3.6) shows that eqs. (3.2c) and (3.3c) are indeed dependent; any solution of (3.2c) is also a solution of (3.3c), and vice versa. This should be obvious from eq. (3.6), because whenever the expression $(E_X^A + E_X^B)$ is zero, the expression $(E_Y^A + E_Y^B)$ is also zero, and vice versa.

We therefore conclude that it is not necessary to solve both eqs. (3.2c) and (3.3c) in order to determine the equilibrium value of $p$. It is sufficient to solve only one of them, for its solution will necessarily satisfy the other equation. The following discussion concentrates on eq. (3.2c).

## The Excess Demand for Commodity $X$

Figure 3.14 illustrates country $A$'s excess demand for commodity $X$ (that is, $E_X^A$). The horizontal segment $ME_1K$ corresponds to the horizontal base of $A$'s production-possibilities frontier. At the pretrade equilibrium price ratio, $OE_1$, $A$'s excess demand for $X$ is indeterminate because its structure of production is indeterminate. If $A$ specializes in the production of $Y$, it will have to import whatever amount of $X$ will be domestically consumed, given by the distance $E_1K$. As $A$ continuously reshuffles its resources in favor of $X$, the output of $X$ increases and the output of $Y$ decreases continuously (i.e., the production point slides along $A$'s production-possibilities frontier, as given by fig. 3.6, from $K$ to $M$). Since $A$'s

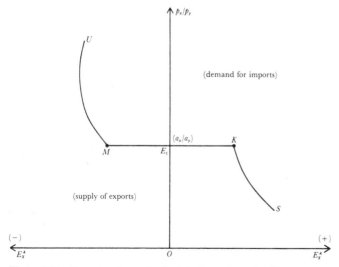

**Figure 3.14** $A$'s excess-demand schedule for commodity $X$.

consumption of $X$ remains the same, its excess demand for $X$ falls continuously, as indicated by the movement from $K$ to $M$. When $A$ specializes in the production of $X$, its excess demand for $X$ is negative (that is, $A$ is willing to export $X$), its precise value being determined by the difference between domestic production and consumption.

So much for the particular value $OE_1 = a_x/a_y$ of $p_x/p_y$. As $p_x/p_y$ falls below $a_x/a_y$, country $A$ will specialize in the production of $Y$ and consume along the PCC curve as shown in fig. 3.6(a). The domestic consumption of $X$ is, in this case, $A$'s excess demand for $X$, as shown by the portion $KS$ of the curve in fig. 3.14. On the other hand, as $p_x/p_y$ increases above $a_x/a_y$, country $A$ specializes in the production of $X$ and consumes along the price-consumption curve as shown in fig. 3.6(b). The difference between domestic production and consumption constitutes $A$'s supply of exports of $X$, as shown in fig. 3.14 by the curve $MU$.

## International Equilibrium

Country $B$'s excess-demand curve for commodity $X$ (that is, $E_X^B$) can be determined in a similar fashion. Qualitatively, it is similar to $A$'s excess demand for $X$ as shown in fig. 3.14. However, for equilibrium in the market for commodity $X$, it is required that $A$'s demand for imports be equal to $B$'s supply of exports, or that $A$'s supply of exports be equal to $B$'s demand for imports. For this reason, $B$'s excess-demand curve for $X$ ideally should be drawn on a diagram where $B$'s supply of exports of $X$ is measured in the positive direction, and $B$'s demand for imports of $X$ is measured in the negative direction of the horizontal axis. In other words, the mirror image of $B$'s excess-demand curve must be used.

$B$'s excess-demand curve (properly drawn) is superimposed on $A$'s excess-demand curve for $X$, as shown in fig. 3.15. Equilibrium occurs at the intersection

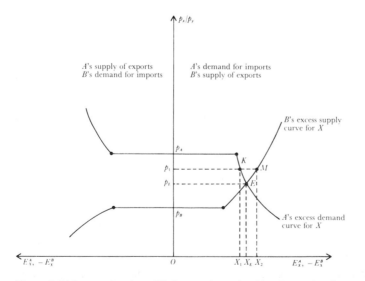

**Figure 3.15** International equilibrium as determined by the market for commodity $X$.

of the two curves, point $E$. The equilibrium terms of trade are given by $Op_E$, and the quantity of $X$ traded internationally (i.e., exported from $B$ to $A$) is given by the distance $OX_E$.

Again, notice that $Op_E$ lies between the pretrade price ratios of $A$ and $B$, that is, $Op_A$ and $Op_B$, respectively. Observe that for values of the terms of trade outside the region $p_B p_A$ (that is, the region defined by the pretrade price ratios of the two countries), the supply curve for exports of one country and the demand curve for imports of the other lie in opposite quadrants. Thus, equilibrium is impossible outside the region $p_B p_A$, assuming, of course, that both commodities are always consumed. The importance of the last qualification is discussed in chap. 5.

## The Missing Information on the Market for Commodity $Y$

Figure 3.15 appears to be a much simpler geometrical device than that of the offer curves. It may seem that the price of this simplicity is a lack of information for the market of $Y$, but this is actually not so. Whatever information is needed for the market of commodity $Y$ can be easily recovered from fig. 3.15. This can be illustrated by rewriting eqs. (3.4$b$) and (3.5$b$) as follows:

$$E_Y^A = -pE_X^A \tag{3.4c}$$

$$E_Y^B = -pE_X^B \tag{3.5c}$$

Thus, the excess demand for $Y$ by either country is equal to the negative of the value of the same country's excess demand for $X$ expressed in terms of commodity $Y$. For example, in fig. 3.15, country $B$ is exporting $OX_E$ units of $X$ to country $A$ at the equilibrium terms of trade $Op_E$. But from eqs. (3.4$c$) and (3.5$c$), it can also be deduced that country $A$ is exporting to $B$ an amount of commodity $Y$ equal to the area of the rectangle $OX_E Ep_E$.

## Stability of International Equilibrium

Figure 3.15 is also useful to the discussion of stability. For any value of $p$ (such as $p_1$) higher than the equilibrium value $p_E$, $B$'s supply of exports of $X$ is larger than $A$'s demand for imports of $X$. In addition, $B$'s demand for imports of $Y$ (as given by the area of the rectangle $OX_2 Mp_1$) is greater than $A$'s supply for exports of $Y$ (as given by the area of the rectangle $OX_1 Kp_1$). Thus, the terms of trade will tend to fall. The opposite will, of course, happen when $p$ takes a value lower than $p_E$.

## 3.5 LIMITATIONS OF THE CLASSICAL THEORY

The classical theory explains that profitable international trade takes place because of the existence of comparative cost differences. But, then, why do comparative cost differences exist? Within the context of the labor theory of value, it appears that a necessary condition for the existence of comparative cost differences is the existence of different production functions between countries. If production functions were the same between countries, the labor requirements for the production of any commodity would, by necessity, be the same in all countries; i.e., every country would be equally productive in every line of production. This state of affairs, however, leaves no room for international trade. Therefore, it appears that the *sine qua non* for the existence of international trade is the non-identity of production functions between countries. But if this is so, why do production functions differ between countries? Unfortunately, the classical theory does not offer any answers—although implicitly, in Ricardo's classic example, the reason was climatic differences. Without a satisfactory answer to this important question, the classical theory loses most of its explanatory usefulness. As we shall see later, the modern theory of trade starts with the assumption that production functions are indeed identical among countries and explains the existence of comparative advantage with differences in factor proportions.

The classical theory offers a clear explanation of the gains from trade and as such has made an important contribution to welfare as opposed to positive economics. In addition, it demonstrates convincingly that trade barriers are harmful to the world economy and that free trade is potentially the best policy.

## 3.6 EMPIRICAL EVIDENCE

The first serious attempt to test empirically the predictive capacity of the classical theory was made by MacDougall (1951, 1952). Additional similar studies supporting MacDougall's initial empirical findings were more recently made by Balassa (1963) and Stern (1962). All three studies were carried out on the basis of data for the United States and the United Kingdom for the years 1937 (MacDougall), 1950 (Balassa), and 1950 and 1959 (Stern).

The hypothesis which MacDougall (1951, p. 697) tested is this: given two countries, say $A$ and $B$, "each will export those goods for which the ratio of its output per worker to that of the other exceeds the ratio of its money wage-rate to that of the other." For instance, country $A$ will export to country $B$ commodity $X$ when $(1/a_x)/(1/b_x) > w_a/w_b$, or $b_x/a_x > w_a/w_b$, or $b_x w_b > a_x w_a$.

To test his hypothesis, MacDougall calculated for some 25 industry groups both the ratio of American to British exports and the ratio of American to British output per worker. In calculating the export ratio, MacDougall excluded the mutual trade between the United States and the United Kingdom because (*a*) as a result of the high American and British tariffs the bulk (more than 95 percent) of American and British exports in 1937 went to Third Countries, and (*b*) the height of both the American and the British tariff varied from sector to sector and tended to offset differences in labor productivity. In general, in the rest of the world both the American and the British exporters faced the same tariff walls.

MacDougall's results are summarized in fig. 3.16, which is drawn on a double logarithmic scale. The observed points lie fairly close to a positively sloped straight line $(KMUL)$. This proves that *there is a tendency for each country to capture a larger share of the export markets as its comparative advantage becomes higher.*

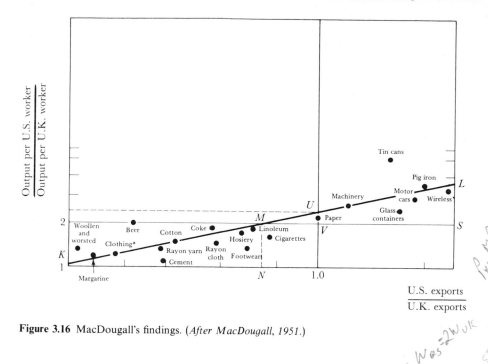

**Figure 3.16** MacDougall's findings. (*After MacDougall, 1951.*)

MacDougall found that in 1937 American wages were about double those in Britain. He concluded that, approximately, American money costs of production are equal to, lower, or higher than British money costs according as the productivity ratio (output per U.S. worker/output per U.K. worker) is equal to, lower, or higher than 2. Thus, for productivity ratios lower than 2, Britain had the cost advantage; for productivity ratios higher than 2, America had the cost advantage; and for productivity ratios equal to 2, neither country enjoyed a significant cost advantage.

Two questions arise in relation to MacDougall's results summarized in fig. 3.16. First, one may expect the export ratio to be about 1 when the productivity ratio is about 2 (that is, that the line $KMUL$ should intersect the horizontal line $MVS$ at $V$—not $M$), and clearly this is not the case. The productivity ratio needs to be significantly higher than 2 (about 2.5) for the export ratio to be equal to 1. MacDougall gives two reasons for this discrepancy.

1. The productivity data reflect the direct labor requirements only, and he observed that the American indirect labor requirements (for transporting, distributing, and servicing) were more than half the corresponding British indirect labor requirement. MacDougall concluded that on balance the figures probably exaggerated the overall American superiority.
2. British exports to Commonwealth countries faced lower tariffs than American exports because of the discriminatory arrangement called imperial preference (see chap. 22).

Another theoretical reason for the discrepancy stressed by Caves and Jones (1973, pp. 190–191) is the fact that the classical theory predicts nothing about the "sharing of an export market between two countries when neither has a cost advantage."

The second question which arises in relation to fig. 3.16 is: why does the country which has the cost advantage not capture the whole export market as the classical theory would lead us to believe? MacDougall attributes this phenomenon to the existence of imperfect markets (monopolistic and oligopolistic), nonhomogeneous products, transport costs, and the like.

Bhagwati (1964, pp. 10–17) argued that MacDougall's data do not reveal any systematic relationship between export price ratios and labor productivity ratios. Since, Bhagwati argued, market shares should be compared with export price ratios and not with labor productivity ratios, MacDougall's results cannot be trusted. Nevertheless, as Caves and Jones (1973, p. 191) point out, Bhagwati is in error. Posttrade prices are necessarily equalized by competition. Thus, while a productivity advantage leads to a larger market share, it does not lead to a lower price in the posttrade equilibrium configuration. Bhagwati's formulation would be correct if pretrade prices were observed.

Until future research refutes the important results of MacDougall (which were confirmed by Balassa and Stern) we must conclude that they provide strong evidence that the classical theory really works. The greatest defect of the classical theory remains, though, the fact that it does not shed any light on what determines comparative advantage, and how comparative advantage may be expected to change in the future.

# APPENDIX TO CHAPTER THREE.
# MANY COMMODITIES AND MANY COUNTRIES

## A3.1 TRADE IN MANY COMMODITIES AND TWO COUNTRIES

The analysis of chaps. 2 and 3 can be easily extended to the case where not two but any number of commodities are produced in two countries.

Let there be $n$ commodities, $X_1, X_2, \ldots, X_n$, and let the labor requirements for the production of 1 unit of the $i$th commodity in country $A$ be denoted by $a_i$ and in country $B$ by $b_i$ ($i = 1, 2, \ldots, n$). In addition, let us adopt the following notation:

$C_i^A = A$'s consumption of commodity $X_i$

$Q_i^A = A$'s production of commodity $X_i$

$D_A^A = A$'s indirect demand (i.e., through the consumption of commodities produced in $A$) for its own labor

$D_B^A = A$'s indirect demand for $B$'s labor

Similar notation with superscript $B$ will be used with the first four terms of country $B$.

$D_A$ = total demand (by both $A$ and $B$) for $A$'s labor

$D_B$ = total demand for $B$'s labor

$L_A$ = total supply of labor in $A$

$L_B$ = total supply of labor in $B$

## A3.2 ARRANGEMENT OF COMMODITIES IN ORDER OF COMPARATIVE ADVANTAGE

Following the analysis of chap. 2, we can say that $A$ has a comparative advantage in the production of $X_i$ and $B$ in $X_j$ when

$$\frac{a_i}{b_i} < \frac{a_j}{b_j} \qquad (i, j = 1, 2, \ldots, n) \tag{A3.1}$$

On the basis of this definition, the $n$ commodities can be arranged in the order of comparative advantage of country $A$ over country $B$. Thus, assume that the following inequalities hold:

$$\frac{a_1}{b_1} < \frac{a_2}{b_2} < \frac{a_3}{b_3} < \cdots < \frac{a_{n-1}}{b_{n-1}} < \frac{a_n}{b_n} \tag{A3.2}$$

It should be obvious that country $A$ is relatively more efficient in the production of $X_1$ as compared with $X_2$; $X_2$ as compared with $X_3$; $\ldots$; $X_{n-1}$ as compared with $X_n$. From inequalities (A3.2) it is also evident that these relationships are transitive. That is, since $A$ is relatively more efficient in the production of $X_1$ compared with $X_2$, and in the production of $X_2$ compared with $X_3$, country $A$ must also be relatively more efficient in the production of $X_1$ compared with $X_3$.

## A3.3 WAGES AND PRICES

Denote the money wage rate in $A$ by $w_A$ and in $B$ by $w_B$. Before trade starts, the absolute money prices in countries $A$ and $B$ are given, respectively, by

$$P_i^A = w_A a_i \qquad (i = 1, 2, \ldots, n) \tag{A3.3}$$
$$P_i^B = w_B b_i \tag{A3.4}$$

While absolute prices depend upon the absolute money wage rates in the two countries, relative prices are given by relative labor requirements as explained in chap. 2. Since this discussion concerns mainly relative prices and wages, let us assume, without any loss of generality, that $w_A$ is arbitrarily set equal to unity with only $w_B$ allowed to vary. Actually, $w_B$, which for convenience will be denoted from this point on simply by $w$, can vary only within certain limits, which will presently be determined.† As the analysis of chap. 2 showed, international equilibrium requires that each country export at least one commodity to secure enough revenue to pay for its imports. Thus, if $w$ increases beyond a certain limit, $B$'s unit costs of production will be higher than the corresponding costs in $A$, and $B$ will be unable to export anything. On the other hand, if $w$ falls below a certain limit, everything will cost less in $B$, and $A$ will be unable to export anything.

**Theorem A3.1** The upper limit for $w$ is given by the ratio $a_n/b_n$ and the lower limit by $a_1/b_1$; that is,

$$\frac{a_1}{b_1} \leq w \leq \frac{a_n}{b_n} \tag{A3.5}$$

PROOF The upper limit for $w$ is determined in such a way as to make $B$'s unit cost of production of $X_n$ (that is, the commodity in whose production $B$ has a comparative advantage compared with any other commodity) equal to $A$'s. That is, the upper limit for $w$ is given by the solution to the equation $a_n = wb_n$. To see why this is so, observe that for any commodity $X_i$ $(i \neq n)$ the following inequality holds:

$$\frac{a_i}{b_i} < \frac{a_n}{b_n} \tag{A3.6}$$

Thus, if $w = a_n/b_n$, it follows from inequality (A3.6) that

$$a_i < wb_i \qquad (i \neq n) \tag{A3.7}$$

In other words, $A$'s unit costs of production of every commodity except $X_n$ are lower than $B$'s. Since $B$ can conceivably export $X_n$, the value $w = a_n/b_n$ cannot be ruled out as a possible equilibrium value. However, should $w$ rise slightly above $a_n/b_n$, country $A$'s costs will be everywhere lower than $B$'s, and long-run equilibrium is ruled out. Therefore, the value $a_n/b_n$ is indeed the upper limit for $w$.

The lower limit for $w$, on the other hand, is determined in such a way as to make $B$'s unit cost of production of $X_1$ (that is, the commodity in whose production $A$ has a comparative advantage compared with any other commodity) equal to $A$'s. That is, the lower limit for $w$ is given by the solution to the equation $a_1 = wb_1$. This follows from the fact that for any commodity $X_i$ $(i \neq 1)$ the following inequality holds:

$$\frac{a_1}{b_1} < \frac{a_i}{b_i} \tag{A3.8}$$

Therefore, if $w = a_1/b_1$, we must have

$$wb_i < a_i \qquad (i \neq 1) \tag{A3.9}$$

† The ratio of wage rates, $w_B/w_A$, is usually called the "factoral terms of trade." It shows the number of units of $A$'s labor that can be exchanged for 1 unit of $B$'s labor.

That is, $B$ will undersell $A$ in every commodity except $X_1$. Since $A$ can conceivably export $X_1$, the value $w = a_1/b_1$ cannot be ruled out as a possible equilibrium value. However, should $w$ fall slightly below $a_1/b_1$, $B$'s costs will be everywhere lower than $A$'s, and long-run equilibrium cannot exist. Therefore, the value $a_1/b_1$ is indeed the lower limit for $w$.

## A3.4 DIRECTION OF TRADE

**Theorem A3.2** In any general-equilibrium configuration, each country enjoys a comparative advantage (over the other country) in all its export commodities relative to all its import commodities.

PROOF Consider the problem from the point of view of country $A$. Assume that $A$ exports commodity $X_t$ and imports commodity $X_s$. Then the following inequalities must hold:

$$a_t < wb_t \tag{A3.10}$$

$$a_s > wb_s \tag{A3.11}$$

These inequalities can be rearranged as follows:

$$\frac{a_t}{b_t} < w < \frac{a_s}{b_s} \tag{A3.12}$$

This proves the theorem.

It is conceivable that one of the inequalities (A3.10) and (A3.11) may be an equality. However, as long as inequalities (A3.2) hold, at least one of the two will be a strict inequality, and this is sufficient for our proof. If inequalities (A3.2) are not strict inequalities, however, and if in particular we have $a_t/b_t = a_s/b_s$, commodities $X_t$ and $X_s$ are identical from the point of view of comparative advantage. In fact, if the equilibrium value of $w$ is such that $a_t = wb_t$ and $a_s = wb_s$, it will be impossible to determine whether $X_s$ or $X_t$ or both will be exported from $A$ to $B$, or vice versa. This can be seen as follows. As in the two-commodity case, the consumption levels of all commodities are perfectly determined in both countries once the value of $w$ is given. Further, given $w$, each country will certainly be producing all those commodities (and at levels equal to the world consumption of each) which it can produce more cheaply than the other. But the production and direction of trade as far as commodities $X_t$ and $X_s$ are concerned are not so certain. Thus, since the production levels in each of all other commodities (except $X_t$ and $X_s$) are known, it is easy to determine the quantity of labor required for their production. Hence, it is easy to determine the residual amount of labor left in each country for the production of $X_s$ and $X_t$. Denote these residual amounts of labor in $A$ and $B$ by $L_A^0$ and $L_B^0$, respectively, and form the following two equations:

$$L_A^0 = a_s Q_s^A + a_t Q_t^A \tag{A3.13}$$

$$L_B^0 = b_s Q_s^B + b_t Q_t^B \tag{A3.14}$$

These equations can be considered as the production-possibilities frontiers of two countries, $A$ and $B$, producing two commodities, $X_s$ and $X_t$. If $a_s/b_s = a_t/b_t$, the opportunity costs will be the same in the two countries, i.e., the production-possibilities frontiers will have the same slope. As the analysis of chap. 3 shows, despite the fact that the consumption equilibria of the two countries are unique, the production equilibria are indeterminate and so is the pattern of trade as far as these two commodities are concerned.

Inequality (A3.12) is useful in another way. Given any value of $w$, say $w^*$, the export and import commodities of country $A$ (and country $B$, for that matter) can easily be determined as follows. All those commodities for which the inequality $w^* > a_i/b_i$ holds are exported from $A$ to $B$, and all those commodities for which the inequality $w^* < a_i/b_i$ holds are exported from $B$ to $A$. (If for a particular commodity, say $X_t$, we have $w^* = a_t/b_t$, this commodity will in general be produced in both countries. Without further information about demand, it is impossible to say which country will be exporting it.) Thus, given $w^*$, we can draw a line and break the chain of commodities $X_1, X_2, \ldots, X_n$ into two groups: those at the beginning of the chain which satisfy the inequality $w^* > a_i/b_i$ and thus are exported from $A$ to $B$, and those at the end of the chain which satisfy the inequality $w^* < a_i/b_i$ and are exported from $B$ to $A$.

A corollary of the above result is that, if we know that at the existing international equilibrium commodity $X_m$ is exported from $A$ to $B$, we can then conclude without any further information that all commodities in the chain before $X_m$, that is, $X_1, X_2, \ldots, X_{m-1}$, are also exported from $A$ to $B$. Or, if commodity $X_t$ is known to be exported from $B$ to $A$, then without any further information we can conclude that commodities $X_{t+1}, X_{t+2}, \ldots, X_n$ must also be exported from $B$ to $A$.

Finally, it should be noted that when $a_1/b_1 < w < a_n/b_n$, both countries gain from trade; when $w = a_1/b_1$, all gains accrue to $A$; and when $w = a_n/b_n$, all gains accrue to $B$.

## A3.5 COMMODITY PRICES

The relative prices in the international market depend on $w$ and nothing else. Thus, for any specific value of $w$, say $w^*$, $A$'s export and import commodities can be determined as in the preceding section. Assume provisionally that, when $w = w^*$, the first $m$ commodities (that is, $X_1, X_2, \ldots, X_m$) are exported from $A$ to $B$ while the rest (that is, $X_{m+1}, X_{m+2}, \ldots, X_n$) are exported from $B$ to $A$. Then the $n$ equilibrium prices will be given by the following equations:

$$P_i = a_i \qquad (i = 1, 2, \ldots, m) \tag{A3.15}$$

$$P_j = w^* b_j \qquad (j = m+1, \ldots, n) \tag{A3.16}$$

Any commodity could be used as numeraire, and these prices could be converted into price ratios, but that is not necessary for our purposes. As they now stand, eqs. (A3.15) and (A3.16) give the $n$ commodity prices in terms of $A$'s labor units, and this is sufficient for the ensuing analysis.

From eqs. (A3.15) and (A3.16), it becomes apparent that, as $w$ increases, only the prices of the commodities exported by $B$ are increased. However, this process does not continue forever. In particular, the price $P_{m+1}$ will continue to increase until $wb_{m+1} = a_{m+1}$. When that happens, $X_{m+1}$ will be produced in $A$ and any further increases in $w$ will not affect $P_{m+1}$. As noted earlier, for the particular value of $w$ which satisfies the equation $wb_{m+1} = a_{m+1}$, commodity $X_{m+1}$ can be imported or exported by $A$. However, as $w$ rises above this value, $X_{m+1}$ definitely shifts into the category of $A$'s export commodities. As $w$ continues to increase, the same will successively happen to commodities $X_{m+2}$, $X_{m+3}$, and so on. Therefore, we conclude that as $w$ increases, $A$'s export commodities tend to become cheaper relative to $A$'s import commodities.

## A3.6 INTERNATIONAL EQUILIBRIUM

As in the case of two commodities, the determination of the equilibrium prices requires the introduction of demand data. It might appear that, since there are $n$ commodity markets, we might have to solve simultaneously $n$ equations, which, of course, cannot be done graphically. However, things are not as bad as they look. As the discussion in the preceding section showed, all prices depend on $w$ only. Therefore, if we could somehow determine the equilibrium value of $w$, we would be able to determine indirectly all equilibrium prices and also break the chain of commodities $X_1, X_2, \ldots, X_n$ into export and import commodities from the point of view of either country. The following remarkable theorem shows that this can be done.

**Theorem A3.3** International equilibrium occurs when the following condition is satisfied:

$$D_B^A = L_B - D_B^B \qquad (A3.17)$$

PROOF Consider any value of $w$ satisfying condition (A3.5) and assume that the first $m$ commodities (that is, $X_1, X_2, \ldots, X_m$) are exported from $A$ to $B$ and the last $(n - m)$ commodities (that is, $X_{m+1}, \ldots, X_n$) are exported from $B$ to $A$. Then form the following equations, which follow directly from the definitions given at the beginning of this appendix:

$$D_A^A = \sum_{i=1}^{m} a_i C_i^A \qquad (A3.18)$$

$$D_A^B = \sum_{i=1}^{m} a_i C_i^B \qquad (A3.19)$$

$$D_B^A = \sum_{j=m+1}^{n} b_j C_j^A \qquad (A3.20)$$

$$D_B^B = \sum_{j=m+1}^{n} b_j C_j^B \qquad (A3.21)$$

$$D_A = D_A^A + D_A^B \qquad (A3.22)$$

$$D_B = D_B^A + D_B^B \qquad (A3.23)$$

General equilibrium occurs when each country can actually produce all commodities that it finds profitable to produce at the given value of $w$ and at the precise amounts that are being demanded by both countries together. Now, given that country $A$ produces $X_1, \ldots, X_m$ and $B$ produces $X_{m+1}, \ldots, X_n$, we can determine all alternative combinations of commodities that can be produced in each country as follows:

$$L_A = \sum_{i=1}^{m} a_i Q_i^A \qquad \qquad \text{(A3.24)}$$

$$L_B = \sum_{j=m+1}^{n} b_j Q_j^B \qquad \qquad \text{(A3.25)}$$

For general equilibrium, it is required that the following conditions be satisfied:

$$Q_i^A = C_i^A + C_i^B \qquad (i = 1, \ldots, m) \qquad \text{(A3.26)}$$

$$Q_j^B = C_j^A + C_j^B \qquad (j = m+1, \ldots, n) \qquad \text{(A3.27)}$$

Substituting eqs. (A3.26) and (A3.27) into eqs. (A3.24) and (A3.25), respectively, we get

$$L_A = \sum_{i=1}^{m} a_i(C_i^A + C_i^B) = D_A \qquad (i = 1, \ldots, m) \qquad \text{(A3.28)}$$

$$L_B = \sum_{j=m+1}^{n} b_j(C_j^A + C_j^B) = D_B \qquad (j = m+1, \ldots, n) \qquad \text{(A3.29)}$$

Therefore, general equilibrium occurs when eqs. (A3.28) and (A3.29) are satisfied. But these equations are not independent; one of them is redundant. To see why, let us start with the following community budget equations:

$$L_A = \sum_{i=1}^{m} a_i C_i^A + w \sum_{j=m+1}^{n} b_j C_j^A = D_A^A + w D_B^A \qquad \text{(A3.30)}$$

$$w L_B = \sum_{i=1}^{m} a_i C_i^B + w \sum_{j=m+1}^{n} b_j C_j^B = D_A^B + w D_B^B \qquad \text{(A3.31)}$$

Adding eqs. (A3.30) and (A3.31) and manipulating them slightly, we get

$$(L_A - D_A) + w(L_B - D_B) = 0 \qquad \text{(A3.32)}$$

Now equation (A3.32) must always be satisfied, whether or not international equilibrium exists. But if this is so, then it should be obvious that, if $(L_A - D_A) = 0$ (that is, if eq. (A3.28) is satisfied), then $(L_B - D_B) = 0$ (that is, eq. (A3.29) is also satisfied), and vice versa. In the following analysis, let us eliminate eq. (A3.28) and work with eq. (A3.29). The latter is simply a variant of eq. (A3.17). This completes the proof of the theorem.

Figure A3.1 shows how, on the basis of the preceding theorem, international equilibrium can be determined in terms of two curves: $A$'s demand for $B$'s labor ($D_B^A$) and $B$'s supply of labor to $A$ ($L_B - D_B^B$). Start with $A$'s demand curve for $B$'s

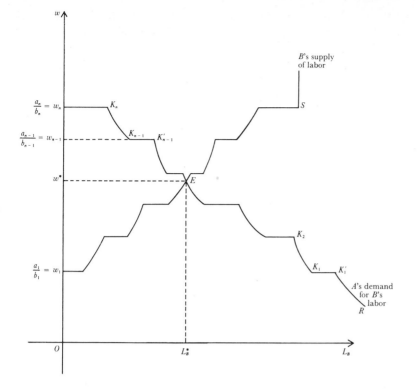

**Figure A3.1** International equilibrium as determined by the market for $B$'s labor.

labor. For $w > a_n/b_n$, $D_B^A$ must be zero, because, as shown above, $A$'s costs of production will be lower than $B$'s in every line of production and $A$ will demand no commodities and hence no labor from $B$. Thus, for $w > a_n/b_n$, $A$'s demand curve for $B$'s labor coincides with the vertical axis. For the specific value $w = a_n/b_n$, however, $B$ produces $X_n$ at the same cost as $A$, while everything else is still produced cheaper in $A$. The relative commodity prices are still the same in $A$ (compared with the case where $w > a_n/b_n$), and therefore $A$ will continue to consume the same quantities of $X_1, \ldots, X_n$ as before. Nevertheless—and this is the difference now—$A$ does not have to produce commodity $X_n$ at the level of domestic consumption of $X_n$, although it has to continue producing the rest of the commodities, that is, $X_1, \ldots, X_{n-1}$. Now, if $\bar{C}_n^A$ is the equilibrium consumption of $X_n$ in $A$ when $w = a_n/b_n$, country $A$ may be importing all, or nothing, or any fraction of this amount of $X_n$ from $B$. This gives rise to the horizontal segment $w_n K_n$ on $A$'s demand curve for $B$'s labor. In particular, the distance $w_n K_n$ is given by the product $b_n \bar{C}_n^A$. As $w$ falls below $a_n/b_n$ but remains above $a_{n-1}/b_{n-1}$, that is, when $a_{n-1}/b_{n-1} < w < a_n/b_n$, commodity $X_n$ will be cheaper in $B$ and it will have to be imported from $B$. On the other hand, all other commodities will continue to be cheaper in $A$, and therefore none will have to be imported from $B$. But as $w$ falls below $a_n/b_n$, commodity $X_n$ becomes cheaper relative to all other commodities, and $A$'s consumers will tend to substitute $X_n$ for other, more expensive commodities.† This will tend to increase the amount of $B$'s labor demanded by $A$, as shown by the negatively sloped segment $K_n K_{n-1}$. When $w = a_{n-1}/b_{n-1}$, then $B$'s costs of production of $X_{n-1}$ are equal to $A$'s. Therefore, $A$ can import, in addition to $X_n$, all or any part of $X_{n-1}$ that it consumes domestically. This gives rise to the straight-line segment $K_{n-1} K'_{n-1}$.

The above process continues until $w = a_1/b_1$, when $B$'s costs of production of $X_1$ are equal to $A$'s while $A$'s costs are higher than $B$'s in every other line of production. The straight-line segment $K_1 K'_1$ corresponds to the amount of labor that $B$ will have to use for the production of that amount of $X_1$ consumed by $A$ at $w = a_1/b_1$. For values of $w$ below $a_1/b_1$, $A$'s demand for $B$'s labor is part of the rectangular hyperbola given by the equation $L_A = wD_B^A$. This follows from the fact that $A$'s income is $L_A$ (measured in terms of $A$'s labor units); $A$ would like to spend this income totally on commodities produced by $B$, because $B$'s costs are everywhere lower than $A$'s. Hence, $A$'s budget equation becomes

$$L_A = w(b_1 C_1^A + b_2 C_2^A + \cdots + b_n C_n^A) = wD_B^A$$

Country $B$'s supply curve of labor to $A$ is derived in a similar fashion. It coincides with the vertical axis for $w < a_1/b_1$, because in this region $B$'s costs are lower than $A$'s and $B$ consumes everything it produces. In the region $a_1/b_1 \le w \le a_n/b_n$, we have again a step function, as shown in fig. A3.1. The various steps in its derivation have been omitted because the analysis is similar to that provided for the derivation of $A$'s demand curve for $B$'s labor. For $w > a_n/b_n$, $A$'s costs are lower in every line of production and therefore $B$ would be willing to consume nothing that is produced domestically, which means that $B$ would be willing to supply all of its labor to $A$. Thus, $B$'s supply curve becomes vertical in the region $w > a_n/b_n$. It should be noted that the number of horizontal segments of both curves depicted in fig. A3.1 is equal to the number of commodities, or, more precisely, it is equal to the number of distinct ratios $a_i/b_i$.

Equilibrium is seen to occur at point $E$, where country $B$ exports indirectly $L_B^*$ units of labor to $A$ in exchange for $L_A^*$ units of $A$'s labor, where $L_A^* =$ area of rectangle $OL_B^* Ew^*$.

Once $w^*$ is determined, all other prices in the system can be determined as explained earlier. In addition, the chain of commodities $X_1, X_2, \ldots, X_n$ can be split into $A$'s export and import commodities. However, what cannot be determined without additional information are the precise amounts of these commodities traded internationally, despite the fact that the aggregate value of $A$'s exports and imports expressed in terms of either $A$'s or $B$'s labor units is in general perfectly determined.‡

---

† For simplicity, it is assumed that as the relative price of a commodity falls, more of it is being demanded.

‡ This is true except in the limiting case where $w^*$ is equal to one of the ratios $a_i/b_i$, say $a_s/b_s$, and commodity $X_s$ is being produced in both countries. Then, as a result of the indeterminacy of the amounts of $X_s$ produced by the two countries (though the total production of $X_s$ is given by the sum of the equilibrium consumption levels of $X_s$ in the two countries), the aggregate value of exports and imports cannot be uniquely determined, although an upper and a lower limit can be established.

From the above observation follows the important conclusion that shifts in demand within each group of commodities (that is, $A$'s export commodities and $A$'s import commodities) do not affect the equilibrium value of $w$ and, therefore, relative commodity prices—as long as the aggregate expenditure on each group of commodities remains constant. The important condition, in other words, for international equilibrium is the equality between $A$'s demand for $B$'s labor and $B$'s supply of labor to $A$, irrespective of the allocation of $D_A^A$ among the commodities produced by $A$; the allocation of $D_B^A$ among the commodities produced by $B$; the allocation of $D_A^B$ among the commodities produced by $A$; and the allocation of $D_B^B$ among the commodities produced by $B$.

However, shifts in demand which involve a redistribution of expenditure from $A$'s export to $A$'s import commodities, or vice versa, will in general affect the equilibrium value of $w$. In this latter case, the shift in demand will not have a substantial effect on $w$, or will have none at all, if $w^*$ is equal to one of the ratios $a_i/b_i$. The importance of this qualification, though, shrinks as the number of commodities increases. This can be seen as follows. The average length of the horizontal segments of the curves depicted in fig. A3.1 decreases as the number of commodities increases, for the average length of the horizontal segments of $B$'s supply curve is given by the ratio $L_B/n$ and the average length of the horizontal segments of $A$'s demand curve is given by $[L_A(a_1/b_1)]/n$. Thus, as $n$ increases, they both decrease. In fact, as $n \to \infty$, both curves become smoothly continuous in the region $a_1/b_1 < w < a_n/b_n$, and a shift of either curve will definitely affect the equilibrium value of $w$.

If the number of commodities is small and if the two curves of fig. A3.1 coincide along a horizontal segment—whose length will be relatively large because of the small number of commodities—a shift in demand which causes either curve to shift totally to the left or right will, within limits, fail to produce any change in $w^*$. If a change in $w^*$ does take place, it will most certainly be smaller than what it would have been had the number of commodities been larger.

## A3.7 TWO COMMODITIES AND MANY COUNTRIES

The model of chap. 2 can be generalized easily from another point of view. The number of commodities can be kept to two while the number of countries can be allowed to increase to $m$ ($m > 2$). This case can be handled quite easily in terms of the concept of the world production-possibilities frontier.

Figure A3.2 shows how the world production-possibilities frontier can be derived when there are five countries, $A$, $B$, $C$, $D$, and $E$, producing two commodities, $X$ and $Y$. The x-axis intercept $X_0$ shows the maximum amount of $X$ that all countries together can produce when the output of $Y$ is zero. Thus, $OX_0 = K'K + L'L + M'M + N'N + SX_0$, where $K'K$, $L'L$, $M'M$, $N'N$, and $SX_0$ are the maximum quantities of $X$ that countries $A$, $B$, $C$, $D$, and $E$, respectively, can produce. Similarly, the y-axis intercept $Y_0$ shows the maximum amount of $Y$ that all countries together can produce when the output of $X$ is zero. Thus, $OY_0 = K'Y_0 + L'K + M'L + N'M + SN$, where $K'Y_0$, $L'K$, $M'L$, $N'M$, and $SN$ are

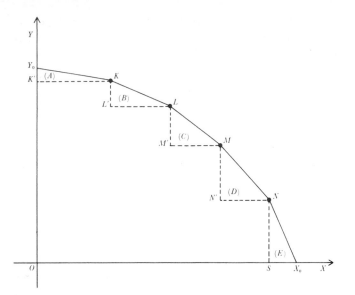

**Figure A3.2** The world production-possibilities frontier of many countries and two commodities.

the maximum quantities of $Y$ that countries $A$, $B$, $C$, $D$, and $E$, respectively, can produce. The reader should be able to verify that the triangles $K'KY_0$, $L'LK$, $M'ML$, $N'NM$, and $SX_0N$ are the production-possibilities frontiers of countries $A$, $B$, $C$, $D$, and $E$, respectively. Further, on the basis of the analysis of chap. 2, the reader should be able to show why the five production-possibilities frontiers have been arranged in the order in which they appear in fig. A3.2.

Given the world production-possibilities frontier, international equilibrium can be determined by the introduction of demand. If demand could be introduced in the form of a world indifference map, the analysis would closely approximate that of sec. 3.1. The only difference is that now the world production-possibilities frontier does not consist of only two straight-line segments but many. In fact, the number of straight-line segments of the world production-possibilities frontier is given by the number of countries whose opportunity costs are different from those of all other countries.

Demand could very well be introduced in terms of separate social indifference maps, one for each country. Then general equilibrium could be shown by adding horizontally the excess-demand curves for $X$ of all countries, as shown in chap. 3. Thus, the analysis is essentially the same as that of the simple two-country, two-commodity model.

Finally, it should be pointed out that the introduction of many countries with different opportunity costs increases the probability that the equilibrium terms of trade will coincide with some country's, say country $C$'s, pretrade price ratio. In that case, country $C$ will gain nothing from international trade; and what is more, any changes in demand (within limits) will merely affect $C$'s internal allocation of resources without having any effect on the terms of trade. It is, of course, conceivable that wider shifts in world demand might shift the equilibrium point from the linear segment $LM$ to another linear segment, say $MN$. Then country $D$ will assume the role of country $C$, with the terms of trade shifting from $C$'s to $D$'s pretrade price ratio.

## A3.8 MANY COUNTRIES AND MANY COMMODITIES

The analysis can be extended to the general case of $m$ countries and $n$ commodities. However, the rigorous treatment of this case seems to require the application of mathematical tools that go beyond the scope of this book. Therefore, no attempt will be made now to provide a general-equilibrium solution. The discussion will be limited to some general conclusions which follow easily from the preceding analysis.

In this general case, as well as in simpler ones, international equilibrium requires that each country export at least one commodity. In addition, the problem of international equilibrium can be formulated in either one of the following two ways: ($a$) in terms of a system of $n$ equilibrium conditions, one for each of the $n$ commodity markets, which by Walras's law can be reduced to a system of $(n - 1)$ equations in $(n - 1)$ price ratios, or ($b$) in terms of a system of $m$ equilibrium conditions, one for each country's labor market, which can be reduced (by Walras's law) to a system of $(m - 1)$ equations in $(m - 1)$ wage ratios. Both approaches will necessarily give rise to identical results.

If $n = m$, either approach will give rise to the same number of equations. Each country will specialize in the production of at least one commodity, and once the equilibrium wage ratios are determined, the price ratios can be determined, and vice versa.

If $n \neq m$, it might appear that the two approaches would give rise to inconsistent results. However, this is not so. For instance, if $n > m$, the first approach would give rise to $(n - 1)$ equations in $(n - 1)$ unknowns while the second approach would give rise to $(m - 1)$ equations in $(m - 1)$ unknowns. But, as has been shown earlier in this appendix in the case of two countries and many commodities, the $(n - 1)$ price ratios are necessarily functions of the $(m - 1)$ wage ratios. Thus, in the final analysis, the $(n - 1)$ equations are actually functions of only $(m - 1)$ unknowns, and the question naturally arises as to whether the set of $(n - 1)$ equations is consistent. That this is so follows from the fact that $(n - m)$ commodities will have to be produced in one country or another along with other commodities, and therefore their relative prices will be determined by relative labor requirements. Actually, the system can be thought of as consisting of $m$ composite commodities, each of which is being produced by a single country—although these composite commodities cannot be decided a priori. The actual proportions of the various commodities making up each composite good are immaterial from the point of view of international equilibrium. Thus, any shifts in the composition of each and every composite good as a result of a shift in demand will necessarily leave relative prices undisturbed.

If $n < m$, at least $(m - n)$ commodities will have to be produced in more than one country. The $(m - 1)$ wage ratios can be seen to be uniquely determined by the $(n - 1)$ price ratios. The reader is referred to the discussion of the simple case of two commodities and $m$ countries.


## SELECTED BIBLIOGRAPHY

Balassa, B. (1963). "An Empirical Demonstration of Comparative Cost." *Review of Economics and Statistics*, vol. 45, pp. 231–238.

Bhagwati, J. (1964). "The Pure Theory of International Trade: A Survey." *Economic Journal*, vol. 74, pp. 1–78.

Caves, R. E., and R. W. Jones (1973). *World Trade and Payments.* Little, Brown and Company, Boston, Mass., chap. 10.

Chipman, John S. (1965). "A Survey of the Theory of International Trade, Part 1: The Classical Theory. *Econometrica*, vol. 33, pp. 477–519.

Graham, F. D. (1923). "The Theory of International Values Re-examined." *Quarterly Journal of Economics*, vol. 28, pp. 54–86. Reprinted in AEA *Readings in the Theory of International Trade.* R. D. Irwin, Inc., Homewood, Ill., 1949.

———— (1932). "The Theory of International Values." *Quarterly Journal of Economics* (August), pp. 581–616.

———— (1948). *The Theory of International Values.* Princeton University Press, Princeton, N.J.

Haberler, G. (1936). *The Theory of International Trade.* W. Hodge and Company, London, chaps. 9 to 11.

Heller, H. R. (1968). *International Trade.* Prentice-Hall, Inc., Englewood Cliffs, N.J., chap. 2.

MacDougall, G. D. A. (1951). "British and American Exports: A Study Suggested by the Theory of Comparative Costs, Part I. *Economic Journal*, vol. 61, pp. 697–724. Reprinted in AEA *Readings in International Economics.* R. D. Irwin, Inc., Homewood, Ill., 1968.

———— (1952). "British and American Exports: A Study Suggested by the Theory of Comparative Costs, Part II." *Economic Journal*, vol. 62, pp. 487–521.

Meade, J. E. (1955). *The Theory of International Economic Policy*, vol. 2: *Trade and Welfare.* Oxford University Press, Oxford, chap. 9.

Melvin, J. R. (1969). "On a Demand Assumption Made by Graham." *Southern Economic Journal*, vol. 36, pp. 36–43.

Metzler, L. A. (1950). "Graham's Theory of International Values." *American Economic Review*, vol. 50, pp. 67–110.

Mill, J. S. (1902). *Principles of Political Economy.* Appleton, Century and Crofts, Inc., New York, chaps. 17, 18, and 25.

Ricardo, David (1821). *The Principles of Political Economy and Taxation.* J. Murray, London, chap. 7.

Smith, Adam (1937). *The Wealth of Nations.* Modern Library, New York.

Stern, R. (1962). "British and American Productivity and Comparative Costs in International Trade." *Oxford Economic Papers*, vol. 14, pp. 275–296.

———— (1975). "Testing Trade Theories." In P. B. Kenen (Ed.), *International Trade and Finance.* Cambridge University Press, New York.

Williams, J. H. (1929). "The Theory of International Trade Reconsidered." *Economic Journal*, vol. 39, pp. 195–209. Reprinted in AEA *Readings in the Theory of International Trade.* R. D. Irwin, Inc., Homewood, Ill., 1949.

# PART
# THREE

## THE NEOCLASSICAL THEORY

# FOUR

## OPPORTUNITY COST

The neoclassical theory of international values is based on the fundamental concepts of opportunity cost and social indifference. It is an improvement over the classical theory because it frees the classical conclusions from the restrictive assumption of the labor theory of value. The main architects of the neoclassical theory are Edgeworth, Haberler, Leontief, Lerner, Marshall, and Meade.

The neoclassical theory is discussed in this and the following three chapters. In particular, the present chapter discusses at some length the concept of opportunity cost; chap. 5, the concept of social indifference and comparative advantage; chap. 6, the problem of general equilibrium; and chap. 7, the problem of increasing returns.

As discussed in chap. 2, Haberler insisted that the sole purpose of the labor theory of value was to determine the pretrade price ratios in the two countries. By means of the concept of the production-possibilities frontier (or substitution curve, as he called it), Haberler (1936, p. 126) demonstrated that the restrictive assumption of the labor theory of value can be dispensed with "without having to discard the results obtained from it: these will remain, just as a building remains after the scaffolding, having served its purpose, is removed."

Chapter 2 introduced the concept of the production-possibilities frontier but within the context of the labor theory of value. The latter is now being dropped to make room for a more general theory of production. This discussion therefore begins with a brief survey of the theory of production.

## 4.1 PRODUCTION FUNCTIONS

Consider a firm using two factors of production, labor, $L$, and land, $T$, and producing a single output, $q$. Its *production function* is merely a statement of the maximum quantity of output that it can produce with any specified quantities of labor and land. This can be expressed algebraically as

$$q = f(L, T) \tag{4.1}$$

The production function is a purely physical concept; i.e., it is a relationship between the physical quantities of output and input—not their values. The symbol $f$ in eq. (4.1) could be thought of as an engineer who could tell us the maximum amount of $q$ that he can possibly produce with given amounts of $L$ and $T$, irrespective of price.

### The Isoquant Map

The production function is usually illustrated graphically by means of the *isoquant map*, as shown in fig. 4.1. Each curve, or *isoquant*, is the locus of alternative combinations of labor and land, all of which are capable of producing the same amount of output. Once the production function (4.1) is given, an isoquant can be derived by assigning a particular value to $q$. Equation (4.1) then becomes an

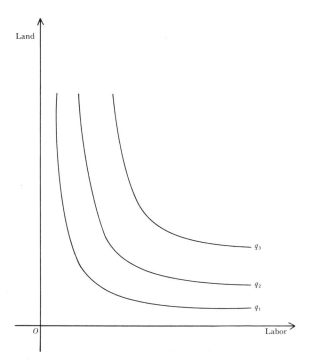

**Figure 4.1** The isoquant map.

equation in two variables ($L$ and $T$) and is graphically depicted by means of an isoquant. Thus, isoquant $q_2$ is simply the graphical representation of the function $f(L, T) = q_2$. The totality of all isoquants, which can be derived by assigning different values to $q$ in eq. (4.1), is the isoquant map. Therefore, an isoquant map gives, in principle, all the information included in eq. (4.1)—no more and no less.

Qualitatively, an isoquant map looks like an indifference map. However, in the case of an isoquant map, the quantity produced is objectively measurable, whereas in the case of an indifference map the utility attached to each indifference curve is not objectively measurable. As $q$ increases, we move to isoquants which lie farther from the origin.

## The Marginal Rate of Substitution

Isoquants have normally a negative slope—at least within a certain range. Within this range, factors of production are substitutable for one another. The absolute value of the slope of an isoquant is known as the *marginal rate of substitution* of labor for land ($\mathrm{MRS}_{LT}$). It shows the maximum number of units of land that can be given up for an extra unit of labor if the firm is to continue producing the same amount of output. This is illustrated in fig. 4.2.

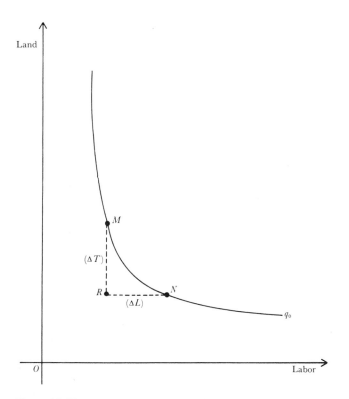

**Figure 4.2** The marginal rate of substitution.

Assume that the firm is at point $M$ and that $RM$ (or $\Delta T$) units of land are given up for the additional amount of $RN$ (or $\Delta L$) units of labor. The firm moves from point $M$ to point $N$; since it remains on the same isoquant, its output does not change. For each additional unit of labor acquired, it gave up, on the average, $RM/RN$ units of land. The ratio $RM/RN = -(\Delta T/\Delta L)$ gives the absolute slope of the straight line passing through points $M$ and $N$. Now imagine that point $N$ travels along the isoquant toward $M$; the slope of the line $MN$ will move closer and closer to the slope of the tangent at $M$. Actually, the limit of the sequence of numbers given by the various values of the slope of $MN$ as $N$ tends to $M$ is simply the slope of the tangent at $M$. Thus,

$$\text{MRS}_{LT} = -\frac{dT}{dL} \qquad (4.2)$$

where $dT/dL$ stands for the slope of the isoquant.†

## Marginal Physical Products and the Marginal Rate of Substitution

There is a close relationship between the *marginal physical products* of the two factors of production and the marginal rate of substitution of labor for land. (The marginal physical product of a factor, say labor, is the extra amount of output that can be secured by increasing labor by 1 unit while leaving all other factors unchanged.) To see this, let us go back to fig. 4.2 and assume again that we are moving from $M$ to $N$. It is useful, however, to divide this movement into two parts: (a) a movement from $M$ to $R$ and (b) a movement from $R$ to $N$. In the first step, $\Delta T$ units of land are given up, and output necessarily falls. In particular, output will fall by $\Delta T(\text{MPP}_T)$ (where $\text{MPP}_T \equiv$ marginal physical product of land). On the other hand, moving from $R$ to $N$ implies that the employment of labor is increased by $\Delta L$ units. Output necessarily increases this time by the amount $\Delta L(\text{MPP}_L)$ (where $\text{MPP}_L \equiv$ marginal physical product of labor). Now, since we end up on the same isoquant (i.e., points $M$ and $N$ lie on the same curve), it follows that the reduction of output, $\Delta T(\text{MPP}_T)$, is equal to the increase in output, $\Delta L(\text{MPP}_L)$. In other words, the following equation necessarily holds:

$$\Delta T(\text{MPP}_T) + \Delta L(\text{MPP}_L) = 0 \qquad (4.3)$$

Making use of eq. (4.2), we can rearrange eq. (4.3) as follows:

$$\text{MRS}_{LT} = -\frac{\Delta T}{\Delta L} = \frac{\text{MPP}_L}{\text{MPP}_T} \qquad (4.4)$$

Consequently, the marginal rate of substitution of labor for land is equal to the ratio of the marginal physical product of labor over the marginal physical product of land.

---

† The term $dT/dL$ is the first derivative of $T$ with respect to $L$. Since the isoquant is negatively sloped, $dT/dL$ is negative. However, we are interested in the absolute value of $dT/dL$ and, hence, eq. (4.2).

## The Isocost Map

Each point on an isoquant corresponds to a different technological method of producing the specified output. Given these technological methods, a real choice remains to be made among the alternative methods. This choice is an economic one, because it is not determined by wholly technical or engineering considerations. It depends, in addition, on factor prices and the behavioral assumption that firms try to minimize cost, which is part and parcel of the profit-maximization assumption. Accordingly, given any factor prices, the firm will choose that production technique which minimizes cost. This problem is illustrated in fig. 4.3. No further explanation is needed for the two isoquants appearing in this figure.

The straight lines $T_1 L_1$, $T_2 L_2$, and $T_3 L_3$ are three illustrative *isocost lines*. Each isocost line shows the alternative combinations of labor and land which can be purchased with a fixed sum of money. Algebraically, these isocost lines are given by the simple equation

$$C = wL + rT \tag{4.5}$$

where $C$ = total amount of expenditure, $w$ = wage rate, and $r$ = rent for land services. (The factor prices, $w$ and $r$, are assumed constant because each firm is assumed to be a price taker in the factor markets.) For any given value of $C$, eq. (4.5) can be represented graphically in the $(L, T)$ plane by a straight line whose absolute slope is equal to the ratio of factor prices. Thus, as shown in fig. 4.3, when $C = C_1$, we get the isocost line $T_1 L_1$; when $C$ increases to $C_2$, we get the line $T_2 L_2$; and when $C$ increases further to $C_3$, we get the line $T_3 L_3$. Observe that in

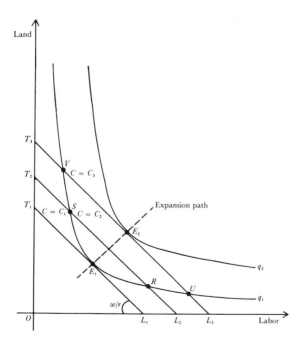

**Figure 4.3** The expansion path.

each case, the $L$-axis intercept is given by the ratio $C/w$, while the $T$-axis intercept is given by the ratio $C/r$. Thus, as $C$ increases, the isocost line shifts outward (i.e., away from the origin).

## Cost Minimization

It should be obvious from fig. 4.3 that if the firm wants to produce $q_1$ units of output (and, therefore, a combination of labor and land must be selected in such a way as to coincide with the coordinates of some point on the $q_1$ isoquant), to minimize costs it will have to produce at point $E_1$; anywhere else, its costs are higher. (Compare points $U$, $R$, $S$, and $V$ with point $E_1$.) Also, if the firm wants to produce $q_2$, it will produce at point $E_2$. Observe that at points $E_1$ and $E_2$ the isocost lines are tangent to the respective isoquants. The locus of all such tangencies, as illustrated by points $E_1$ and $E_2$, is called the *expansion path*. This is illustrated in fig. 4.3 by the broken curve through points $E_1$ and $E_2$.

It should be noted that the expansion path gives all the information necessary for the derivation of the firm's *long-run total-cost curve*. An isoquant and an isocost line pass through any point along the expansion path. The former gives the amount of output produced, and the latter gives the (minimum) total cost of production. Further, when the total-cost curve is determined, the average cost is determined as the ratio $C/q$ while the marginal cost is given by the slope of the total-cost curve, or the derivative $dC/dq$.

From the preceding analysis, it follows that a necessary condition for cost minimization is that the slope of the isocost line be equal to the slope of the isoquant, that is,

$$\frac{w}{r} = \frac{\text{MPP}_L}{\text{MPP}_T} \tag{4.6}$$

This condition can also be written in the form

$$\frac{w}{\text{MPP}_L} = \frac{r}{\text{MPP}_T} = \text{MC} \tag{4.7a}$$

The ratio $w/\text{MPP}_L$ is the marginal cost of production if labor were to increase sufficiently and raise output by 1 unit. The ratio $r/\text{MPP}_T$ is the marginal cost of production if land were to increase and raise output by 1 unit. That is, increasing total cost by $w$, we increase the employment of labor by 1 unit, which in turn increases output by $\text{MPP}_L$ units. Thus, the per-unit cost on the margin (i.e., for the last unit of labor employed) is given by the ratio $w/\text{MPP}_L$. A similar reasoning holds for land as well. In the long run, as eq. (4.7a) shows, the two ratios must be equal to the unique long-run marginal cost. If that is not the case, total costs can be reduced (while keeping output constant) by transferring expenditure from the factor whose "marginal cost" is higher to the other. It can be shown that at $S$ (fig. 4.3) we have $w/\text{MPP}_L < r/\text{MPP}_T$ and at $R$ we have $w/\text{MPP}_L > r/\text{MPP}_T$.

Thus, in both cases, a movement toward point $E_1$ reduces costs.

Equation (4.7a) can also be arranged as follows:

$$\frac{\text{MPP}_L}{w} = \frac{\text{MPP}_T}{r} = \frac{1}{\text{MC}} \qquad (4.7b)$$

where the ratio $\text{MPP}_L/w$ ($\text{MPP}_T/r$) shows the extra output which can be produced by spending an extra dollar on $L$ ($T$).

## 4.2 LINEAR HOMOGENEOUS PRODUCTION FUNCTIONS

An important production function playing a prominent role in economics in general and international economics in particular is the so-called *linear homogeneous production function*, or the class of production functions characterized by *constant returns to scale*.

The term *returns* refers in general to what happens to output (measured either in physical units or in value) when an input or some combination of inputs are increased. In particular, the term *returns to scale* refers to the relationship between changes in the physical quantity of output and a proportionate change in the physical quantity of all inputs. If the physical quantity of output changes in the same proportion as all physical inputs, we say that the production function is characterized by *constant returns to scale* for the range of input combinations under consideration. That is, if output doubles when all inputs are doubled, returns to scale are constant. On the other hand, if the physical quantity of output changes faster (slower) than all physical inputs, we say that the production function is characterized by *increasing (decreasing) returns to scale*. That is, if output more than doubles when all inputs are doubled, returns to scale are increasing, and if output increases but falls short of being doubled when all inputs are doubled, returns to scale are decreasing.

A linear homogeneous (production) function is the name that mathematicians use to describe (production) functions subject to constant returns to scale. A production function is linear homogeneous if, and only if, it satisfies the equation

$$mq = f(mL, mT) \qquad (4.8)$$

where $m$ is any positive real number.

A linear homogeneous production function has the following properties.

1. The *average physical product* (APP) of either factor depends only on the proportion in which the factors $L$ and $T$ are used; it does not depend on their absolute amounts. Thus, putting $m = 1/L$, eq. (4.8) becomes

$$\text{APP}_L \equiv \frac{q}{L} = f\left(1, \frac{T}{L}\right) = g\left(\frac{T}{L}\right) \qquad (4.9)$$

Or, putting $m = 1/T$, we get

$$\text{APP}_T \equiv \frac{q}{T} = f\left(\frac{L}{T}, 1\right) = h\left(\frac{T}{L}\right) \tag{4.10}$$

The symbol APP means "average physical product"; the subscripts $L$ and $T$ indicate the factors of production.

2. The marginal physical products, $\text{MPP}_L$ and $\text{MPP}_T$, can likewise be expressed as functions of the ratio $T/L$ alone. This proposition can be proved as follows:

$$\text{MPP}_L = \frac{\partial q}{\partial L} = \frac{\partial[Lg(T/L)]}{\partial L} = g\left(\frac{T}{L}\right) - \left(\frac{T}{L}\right)g'\left(\frac{T}{L}\right) = \phi\left(\frac{T}{L}\right)$$

$$\text{MPP}_T = \frac{\partial q}{\partial T} = \frac{\partial[Lg(T/L)]}{\partial T} = g'\left(\frac{T}{L}\right)$$

where primes indicate partial differentiation. Note that in these calculations use was made of eq. (4.9); that is, $q = L(\text{APP}_L)$.

3. Total output equals the $\text{MPP}_L$ multiplied by the quantity of $L$ used plus the $\text{MPP}_T$ multiplied by $T$. That is,

$$q = L(\text{MPP}_L) + T(\text{MPP}_T) \tag{4.11}$$

This is *Euler's theorem*. From the economic point of view, this property means that under conditions of constant returns to scale, if each factor is paid the amount of its marginal physical product, the total product will be exhausted exactly by the distributive shares of all factors. For this reason, this property is sometimes referred to as the *adding-up theorem*.

The proof of Euler's theorem is not difficult to establish. Thus, substituting the above results into the right-hand side of eq. (4.11), we get

$$L(\text{MPP}_L) + T(\text{MPP}_T) = L\left[g - \left(\frac{T}{L}\right)g'\right] + Tg'$$

$$= Lg - Tg' + Tg' = Lg = q$$

The independent variable $T/L$ has been omitted for simplicity.

4. As a result of property 2 (i.e., that the MPP of every factor depends only on the ratio $T/L$) and eq. (4.4) (i.e., that the $\text{MRS}_{LT}$ is given by the ratio $\text{MPP}_L/\text{MPP}_T$), it follows that any straight line through the origin (implying a fixed ratio $T/L$) will cut all isoquants at points which have the same slope (i.e., the same $\text{MRS}_{LT}$).

5. If any one isoquant is given, the whole isoquant map can be constructed without any further information. This is illustrated in fig. 4.4, where for simplicity it is assumed that the unit isoquant is given. To determine a point (such as $N$) on the (unknown) isoquant which is the locus of alternative combinations of $L$ and $T$ which are capable of producing $x$ units of output, simply draw a straight line through the origin (such as $OMN$). It will cut the unit isoquant at a certain point (such as point $M$). Then measure the distance $OM$ and determine

point $N$ on the ray through the origin in such a way that the distance $ON$ is equal to $x$ times the distance $OM$ (that is, $ON = xOM$). Point $N$ will lie on the isoquant $q = x$. That this should be so follows from the definition of constant returns to scale, because the movement from point $M$ to point $N$ implies that all factors are multiplied by the factor $x$, and therefore output at point $N$ must be $x$ times the output at point $M$. (Note that the tangents at points $M$ and $N$ in fig. 4.4 are parallel.) In the same way, we can determine all other points on the isoquant $q = x$. Since $x$ stands for any particular value of $q$, it should be obvious that the whole isoquant map can be so constructed.

6. *When production techniques can be combined without any interaction between them*, then the isoquants are convex to the origin.† Consider any two points on an isoquant, such as $S$ and $V$ (fig. 4.4). These points correspond to two production techniques which for convenience we may call technique $S$ and technique $V$. Let $q_S$ and $q_V$ stand for the rates of output at points $S$ and $V$, respectively. By assumption, $q_S = q_V = x$, where $x$ is the rate of output produced along the chosen isoquant.

Consider a weighted average of points $S$ and $V$, that is, $W = \lambda S + (1 - \lambda)V$, where $0 \leq \lambda \leq 1$. Point $W$ necessarily lies somewhere on the straight-

---

† Strictly speaking, this is not a general property of linear homogeneous production functions. For instance, the "Pythagorean" production function $Q = \sqrt{L^2 + T^2}$ gives rise to isoquants which are *concave* to the origin.

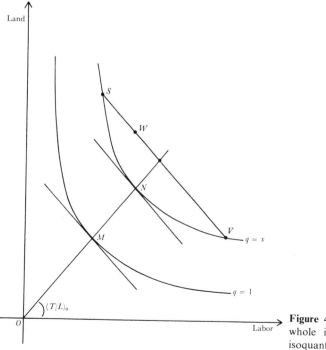

**Figure 4.4** How to construct the whole isoquant map when one isoquant is given.

line segment $SV$ (see appendix (b) to this chapter). What is the rate of output at $W$? If techniques $S$ and $V$ only are used, the rate of output at $W(q_w)$ is

$$q_w = \lambda q_S + (1 - \lambda)q_V = \lambda x + (1 - \lambda)x = x$$

Thus, by using techniques $S$ and $V$ only, the rate of output at $W$ is the same as that at points $S$ and $V$.

As $\lambda$ varies from 0 to 1, point $W$ travels from $V$ to $S$ along the straight-line segment $SV$. Thus, by arbitrarily combining the production techniques $S$ and $V$, we can achieve the same output $q = x$ along the straight-line segment $SV$. But in general we can do better than that as more efficient techniques are available. Therefore, the true isoquant between points $S$ and $V$ must lie below the straight-line segment $SV$, as illustrated in fig. 4.4. This proves convexity.

7. *When the isoquants are convex to the origin, the marginal physical products of labor and land are diminishing.*† We wish to show that

$$\frac{\partial MPP_L}{\partial L} = +\frac{T^2}{L^3}g'' < 0$$

$$\frac{\partial MPP_T}{\partial T} = \frac{1}{L}g'' < 0$$

Since $T$ and $L$ are positive numbers, we only have to show that $g'' < 0$.

Consider the marginal rate of substitution of labor for land:

$$MRS_{LT} = \frac{MPP_L}{MPP_T} = \frac{g - (T/L)g'}{g'} = \frac{g}{g'} - \frac{T}{L}$$

(The argument $T/L$ of the functions $g$ and $g'$ has been omitted for convenience.) Since the isoquants are convex to the origin (property 6), the marginal rate of substitution must be diminishing. In other words, the convexity of the isoquants implies:

$$\frac{\partial MRS_{LT}}{\partial(T/L)} > 0$$

But

$$\frac{\partial MRS_{LT}}{\partial(T/L)} = \left(\frac{1}{g'}\right)^2(g'g' - gg'') - 1 = -\frac{g}{(g')^2}g'' > 0$$

Given that $g > 0$, and for efficient production $g' > 0$ also, it follows that $-g'' > 0$, or $g'' < 0$. This proves the proposition.

8. For any given factor prices ($w$ and $r$), the expansion path is always a straight line through the origin. This follows from the fact that for cost minimization, it

---

† Again this is not a general property of linear homogeneous production functions. The "Pythagorean" production function $Q = \sqrt{L^2 + T^2}$ is an example of a linear homogeneous production function with *increasing* marginal physical products.

is required that the $\text{MRS}_{LT}$ be equal to the factor-price ratio $w/r$. According to property 4, the $\text{MRS}_{LT}$ will remain constant (and equal to the ratio $w/r$) along a certain ray through the origin.

9. As a result of property 8, the average cost of production (AC) remains constant at all levels of output. This can be seen as follows. By definition,

$$AC = \frac{wL + rT}{q} \tag{4.12}$$

Given $w$ and $r$, factors $L$ and $T$ are always used in the same proportion. When $L$ and $T$ increase by a certain percentage, $q$ also increases by the same percentage (because of the assumption of constant returns to scale). Therefore, both the numerator and the denominator on the right-hand side of eq. (4.12) change by the same percentage, and thus, their ratio (that is, AC) remains constant.

If both $w$ and $r$ increase by a certain percentage, their ratio, $w/r$, will of course remain the same and so will the expansion path. The average cost curve, however, will shift upward by the percentage by which $w$ and $r$ have gone up. This can be seen more rigorously as follows. Starting with eq. (4.12) and making use of eqs. (4.11), (4.6), and (4.7), we obtain

$$
\begin{aligned}
AC &= \frac{wL + rT}{q} \\[2mm]
&= \frac{wL + rT}{L(\text{MPP}_L) + T(\text{MPP}_T)} \\[2mm]
&= \frac{r}{\text{MPP}_T} \frac{(w/r)L + T}{(\text{MPP}_L/\text{MPP}_T)L + T} \\[2mm]
&= \frac{r}{\text{MPP}_T} = \frac{w}{\text{MPP}_L} = MC
\end{aligned}
$$

Thus, for given $w$ and $r$, AC is equal to MC. In addition, if the ratio $w/r$ is kept constant, the ratio $L/T$ and the marginal physical productivities of $L$ and $T$ also remain constant. Accordingly, AC is proportional to $w$ and $r$.

On the other hand, if $w$ falls while $r$ remains constant, more labor will be used per unit of land (i.e., the ratio $L/T$ will rise); the marginal physical product of labor will fall and the marginal physical product of land will rise; and, finally, the marginal and average cost of production will fall. This can be proved as follows. At the original factor prices, say $(w^0, r^0)$, the following equality is, for cost-minimization purposes, satisfied:

$$\frac{w^0}{r^0} = \frac{\text{MPP}_L^0}{\text{MPP}_T^0}$$

or

$$\frac{w^0}{\text{MPP}_L^0} = \frac{r^0}{\text{MPP}_T^0} = MC^0 = AC^0 \tag{4.13}$$

where $\text{MPP}_L^0$ and $\text{MPP}_T^0$ stand, respectively, for the marginal physical product of labor and land at the initial equilibrium state. When $w$ falls to, say, $w^1$, equality (4.13) is immediately converted into the inequality

$$\frac{w^1}{\text{MPP}_L^0} < \frac{r^0}{\text{MPP}_T^0} \tag{4.14}$$

As explained in the section on production functions, costs can be reduced if labor is substituted for land, i.e., if the ratio $L/T$ rises. As this happens, and because of diminishing returns to a variable factor, the $\text{MPP}_L$ will tend to fall and the $\text{MPP}_T$ will tend to rise. Thus, the left-hand side of inequality (4.14) will tend to increase while the right-hand side will tend to fall. Accordingly, if this substitution proceeds sufficiently, inequality (4.14) will again be converted into an equality as follows:

$$\frac{w^1}{\text{MPP}_L^1} = \frac{r^0}{\text{MPP}_T^1} = \text{MC}^1 = \text{AC}^1 \tag{4.15}$$

where the superscript 1 indicates the values at the new equilibrium state. Now recall that $\text{MPP}_T^1 > \text{MPP}_T^0$. Hence,

$$\text{AC}^0 = \text{MC}^0 = \frac{r^0}{\text{MPP}_T^0} > \frac{r^0}{\text{MPP}_T^1} = \text{MC}^1 = \text{AC}^1 \tag{4.16}$$

This completes the proof.

## 4.3 THE PRODUCTION FUNCTION OF THE INDUSTRY

### Does an Industry Production Function Exist?

The discussion of sec. 4.1 refers to the production function of the firm as opposed to the production function of a whole industry. However, sec. 4.2 is silent on this point, for the very good reason that, typically, the production function of a firm is not characterized by constant returns to scale throughout. Instead, increasing returns at the beginning (i.e., the familiar fact of "economies of large-scale production") are followed by constant and decreasing returns successively, presumably because of increasing difficulties of supervision. Accordingly, we observe the usual U-shaped average-cost curve for the firm instead of the horizontal average-cost curve implied by the linear homogeneous production function. But if the typical production function of a firm is not characterized by constant returns to scale, why study the linear homogeneous production function? The answer follows from the fact that neoclassical and modern writers usually postulate the existence of an industry production function, and for the whole industry, constant returns to scale is not an unrealistic assumption.

Before proceeding any further, we have to question whether it is meaningful or legitimate to bypass the firm and postulate a production function for the industry. In other words, the question is whether it is possible to predict the amount of output produced by an industry when only the *total* amounts of labor and land employed by all firms in the industry are known. Obviously, the actual output produced depends not only on the total $L$ and $T$ used but also on their allocation among the various firms. Whether this can be done in general seems to be an open question. The rest of this section shows that this can be done if the assumptions enumerated below are satisfied.

## The Assumptions

For the rest of our discussion we make the following simplifying assumptions:

1. Each firm produces a single commodity.
2. Whatever the number of *active* firms in an industry at a given time, there is an indefinitely large number of *potential* producers.
3. Entrepreneurship is not a distinct factor of production. That is, the organizing and operating of a firm call for only routine ability and effort, exactly comparable to what is demanded of a hired worker—and hence require the same remuneration.†
4. All firms in an industry are alike in the sense that they have access to the same production function. Assume that the common production function will give rise to the usual U-shaped average-cost curve for each individual firm at every possible combination of factor prices. Therefore, the present formulation is consistent with the phenomenon of "economies of large-scale production." However, it will be assumed that the output where each firm is able to attain minimum average cost is sufficiently low relative to the total industry output that many firms will be able to operate for the industry to remain purely competitive.
5. The common production function of firms is of the type illustrated by eq. (4.1). In other words, output $q$ depends only on the amounts of $L$ and $T$ used by the firm and nothing else. Therefore, the phenomenon of technological external effects‡ is assumed away.

---

† In equilibrium, the entrepreneur will receive wages for his labor and rent for his land that are neither more nor less than other suppliers of labor and land receive. However, it is clear that the function of the entrepreneur is quite distinct in that, in disequilibrium, he may enjoy a temporary profit or suffer a temporary loss. Nevertheless, assume that the entrepreneurs receive no compensation for their risk-bearing function. This can be justified on the grounds that profits and losses do cancel out over time and that all entrepreneurs have a neutral attitude toward these balanced chances of profit and risks of loss.

‡ When technological external effects are present, the output of a typical firm depends not only on the amounts of $L$ and $T$ used by the firm itself but also on the amounts of $L$ and $T$ used by all other firms in the industry as well as the aggregate industry output. This phenomenon is discussed briefly in chap. 7.

## The Long-Run Industry Supply Curve

Under these assumptions, the equilibrium price of the commodity produced by the industry must necessarily be equal to the minimum average cost of production. In other words, given any combination of $w$ and $r$, the expansion path for a typical firm can be determined and the average-cost curve derived therefrom. Since, by assumption, there is an infinite number of potential producers with the same average-cost curve, the equilibrium price must necessarily be equal to the common minimum average cost. Thus, if the price were lower than the minimum average cost, no firm would be willing to produce, and if the price were higher than the minimum average cost of production, all active producers would be enjoying positive profits which would attract additional firms into the industry and cause the price to fall. In summary, the long-run industry supply curve is horizontal at the level of the minimum average cost of production, and the long-run equilibrium price is necessarily equal to this minimum average cost.

## The Optimal Scale of Operations of Each Active Firm

The preceding analysis shows that all active firms in the industry will use, in the long run, the same production technique and that their scale of operations will always be determined at the point where the average cost of production is at a minimum. In other words, given any combination of factor prices $(w, r)$, the optimum combination of labor and land that each and every firm will be using can be determined under conditions of long-run equilibrium. The scale of operations of each firm is perfectly determined, and the only unknown that remains to be determined is the number of active firms. The latter obviously depends upon demand. If, at the minimum average cost, the consumers would like to consume an output $Q_0$ and if each firm is producing $q_0$, then the number of active firms must be equal to $Q_0/q_0$.

## From Output to Inputs

If the quantity demanded increases, the number of firms will increase—with each individual firm doing exactly what each and every other firm was doing before the change in demand. In particular, if the quantity demanded doubles, the number of firms (and, therefore, the employment of $L$ and $T$) doubles as well. In general, if the quantity demanded is multiplied by the positive number $m$, the number of firms (and, therefore, the employment of $L$ and $T$) will be multiplied by the number $m$. This sounds like constant returns to scale, for both output and inputs always seem to change by the same percentage. Does this mean that we have proved that, under assumptions 1 to 5 above, there exists an industry production function that is linear homogeneous? Not quite. We are very close to providing such a proof, but we are not there yet.

What has just been shown (i.e., that as output doubles, inputs double as well) seems to be the reverse of the order followed in the definition of the (linear homogeneous) production function. In the latter case, output was the dependent variable while inputs were the independent variables. In the present case, though, output appears to be the independent variable while inputs are the dependent variables. In addition, the conclusion that inputs double as output demanded doubles was derived under the assumption that factor prices $(w, r)$ were given. This is closely related to the first observation.

## From Inputs to Output

The real question is whether, under assumptions 1 to 5, industry output $Q$ can be expressed as a function of the total quantities of $L$ and $T$ employed by all firms in the industry. This depends upon whether the allocation of the totals $L$ and $T$ among the firms in the industry will be such as to give rise to a unique industry output.

From the preceding analysis, it follows that, in the long run, all active firms always use the factors $L$ and $T$ in exactly the same proportion, because of the assumed identity of production functions. This being the case, when the total quantities of labor and land, say $L_0$ and $T_0$ respectively, are given, only one thing is certain: every active firm will be using the two factors in the proportion $T_0/L_0$. However, this alone is not sufficient for the determination of the industry output. To do so, we would have to know, in addition to the proportion in which the two factors are being used, the optimum scale of operations of each firm. But, as we saw earlier, the optimum scale of operations depends on factor prices. If we were to conclude that the industry output depends not only on the total quantities of $L$ and $T$ employed by the industry but also on factor prices, we would also have to conclude that an industry production function does not exist.

Prior knowledge of factor prices for the determination of industry output is unnecessary when a one-to-one correspondence exists between the factor-price ratio $w/r$ and the optimum ratio $T/L$ in which each firm uses $L$ and $T$ in the long run. Under these circumstances, the totals $L_0$ and $T_0$ fix the proportion $T_0/L_0$, which in turn can be optimum if, and only if, a single factor-price ratio exists. Therefore, the ratio $T_0/L_0$ does, in this case, imply a unique scale of operations for each firm, and when that scale is known, the industry output can easily be determined as the product $nq^*$, where $q^*$ is the optimum output for each firm and $n$ is the number of firms which can be accommodated by the totals $L_0$ and $T_0$.

Figure 4.5 illustrates the point. The solid curves $OM$, $ON$, and $OR$ are three illustrative expansion paths corresponding to the factor-price ratios $(w/r)_1$, $(w/r)_2$, and $(w/r)_3$, respectively, with $(w/r)_3 < (w/r)_2 < (w/r)_1$. The points $M$, $N$, and $R$ are assumed to be the optimum production points in the three cases. The broken curve through points $M$, $N$, and $R$ is assumed to be the locus of all optimum production points as $w/r$ varies from zero to infinity. The one-to-one correspondence between $w/r$ and the optimum ratio $T/L$ implies that any ray through the origin will intersect the $MNR$ curve only once. Thus, assuming that (given $T_0$ and $L_0$) the ratio $T_0/L_0$ is given by the slope of the vector $ON$ (not drawn), $N$ would be

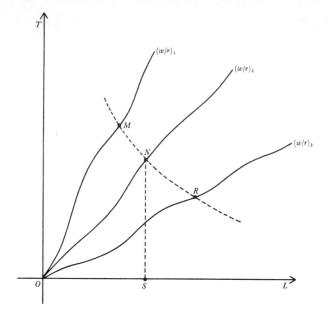

**Figure 4.5** Optimal scale of operations of a firm for alternative factor-price ratios.

the optimum production point for each and every firm and the implied factor-price ratio would be $(w/r)_2$. Further, the ratio $L_0/OS$ would give the number of active firms in the industry.

The real question now is this: does a one-to-one correspondence exist between factor prices and factor proportions at the level of the firm? Yes. The rigorous proof of this proposition is relegated to appendix (a) to this chapter.

In summary, on the basis of assumptions 1 to 5, an industry production function exists which expresses the industry output as a function of the specific aggregate quantities of $L$ and $T$. Under these assumptions, this industry production function is linear homogeneous, i.e., it is characterized by constant returns to scale.

## An Important Property of the Industry Production Function

An important property of the industry production function is that any given totals of labor and land, such as $L_0$ and $T_0$, are allocated among the active firms of the industry in such a way as to maximize the industry output. This follows from the following two equilibrium conditions:

1. The marginal physical product of every factor is the same in all active firms. This follows directly from the assumed identity of production functions among firms and the fact that each firm is using the same combination of labor and land.

2. Consider the composite factor of production $Z$ that consists of 1 unit of land and $L_0/T_0$ units of labor. (Remember that $L_0$ and $T_0$ are the given totals of labor and land available to the industry.) Then the average physical product of $Z$ ($APP_Z$) in every firm is necessarily at a maximum. The easiest way to see this is to note that the average cost of production (AC) is given by

$$AC = \frac{\text{total cost in terms of } T}{\text{total output}} = \frac{p_z Z}{Z(APP_Z)} = \frac{p_z}{APP_Z} = \frac{1 + (w/r)(L_0/T_0)}{APP_Z}$$

Thus, for the given ratio $L_0/T_0$, the (implied) equilibrium factor-price ratio $w/r$ is perfectly determined and so is the rental of the composite factor $Z$ (that is, $p_z = 1 + (w/r)(L_0/T_0)$). Therefore, minimization of AC necessarily implies maximization of $APP_Z$.

How do conditions 1 and 2 guarantee that the allocation of $L_0$ and $T_0$ among firms is such as to maximize the industry output? Condition 1 implies that, given the number of firms in the industry, the industry output cannot be increased by transferring either labor or land from one firm to another—the marginal physical products of both factors being equal and diminishing everywhere. On the other hand, condition 2 implies that the industry output cannot be increased by increasing or decreasing the number of active firms—through a decrease or increase of the scale of operations of each firm, with condition 1 always being satisfied.

## 4.4 THE BOX DIAGRAM

### Assumptions

Let us consider an economy endowed with fixed quantities of labor and land, $L_0$ and $T_0$, respectively, and producing two commodities, $X$ and $Y$. It is assumed that each industry's technology is summarized by a linear homogeneous production function as described in the preceding section. All this information can be conveniently summarized by means of the so-called Edgeworth–Bowley box diagram.† This has been done in fig. 4.6.

### Interpreting the Axes

The sides of the parallelogram $O_X M O_Y N$ are determined by the given amounts of labor and land. Thus, the distance $O_X M$ equals $L_0$ while the distance $O_X N$ equals $T_0$. Along the lower horizontal axis $O_X M$, we measure, moving from $O_X$ toward $M$, the amount of labor used in the production of $X$. Along the left-hand vertical axis, we measure, moving from $O_X$ toward $N$, the amount of land used in the

---

† Edgeworth (1881, especially pp. 21, 28–29, and 34–38) was the originator of the box-diagram idea. Nevertheless, the diagram itself was first used by Bowley (1924, p. 5), even though Edgeworth's (1881, p. 28) Fig. 1 has all the necessary ingredients.

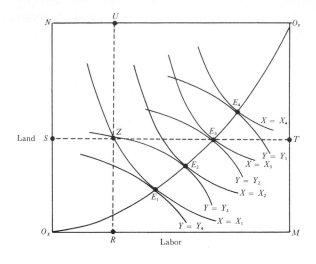

**Figure 4.6** Derivation of the contract curve.

production of $X$. Because the amount of each factor not used in the production of $X$ must be employed in the production of $Y$ by assumption, the upper horizontal axis indicates, moving from $O_Y$ toward $N$, the amount of labor used in the production of $Y$. Similarly, along the right-hand vertical axis, we measure, moving from $O_Y$ toward $M$, the amount of land used in the production of $Y$. Any point in the box represents four quantities: the amounts of labor and land used in the production of $X$ and $Y$. For instance, the coordinates of point $Z$ with respect to $O_X$, that is, $(O_X R, O_X S)$, give us the amounts of labor and land, respectively, that are used in the production of $X$, while the coordinates of the same point, $Z$, with respect to $O_Y$, that is, $(O_Y U, O_Y T)$, give us the amounts of labor and land, respectively, that are used in the production of $Y$. Finally, note that

$$O_X R + O_Y U = L_0 \quad \text{and} \quad O_X S + O_Y T = T_0$$

## The Isoquant Maps

Let us now introduce the isoquant maps of $X$ and $Y$ into the box. Thus, the isoquant map of industry $X$ has been drawn with respect to the origin $O_X$, and the isoquant map of industry $Y$ has been drawn with respect to the origin $O_Y$. In order to keep the diagram as clear as possible, there are only four isoquants for each commodity. Now, any point in the box taken at random corresponds to a definite allocation of $L$ and $T$ between the two industries, giving rise to definite production levels of both commodities. Thus, at point $Z$, in addition to knowing how much $L$ and $T$ are used in the production of both $X$ and $Y$, we can also read, from the isoquants passing through $Z$, the amounts of $X$ and $Y$ produced, that is, $X_1$ and $Y_3$, respectively. Therefore, this diagram is indeed remarkable because it enables us to represent the relations among six variables in only two dimensions.

## The Contract Curve

As was seen earlier, the $MRS_{LT}$ in each industry must necessarily be equal to the factor-price ratio $w/r$ in long-run equilibrium. Since factor prices are assumed uniform throughout the economy, it follows that in the long run the economy must be allocating $L$ and $T$ in a way that equalizes the $MRS_{LT}$ in the two industries. Therefore, long-run equilibrium will necessarily occur at a point within the box diagram where the isoquants of $X$ and $Y$ happen to be tangential to one another. The locus of all such tangencies between the two sets of isoquants corresponds to Edgeworth's *contract curve*. In fig. 4.6, the contract curve is illustrated by the curve $O_X E_1 E_2 E_3 E_4 O_Y$.

Edgeworth (1881, especially pp. 21, 28–29, and 34–38) actually uses the term *contract curve* to describe the case of a pure exchange economy. In this case, the dimensions of the box (fig. 4.6) will represent the total available quantities of the two consumer goods, and the two sets of contour lines will represent the indifference maps of the two consumers. The contract curve will be given by the locus of tangencies between the two sets of indifference curves. Observe that any point on the contract curve is Pareto-optimal in the sense that each consumer's utility is at a maximum given the utility level of the other consumer.

The term *optimum efficiency locus* might describe the present case of production better than the term contract curve. However, the less accurate term contract curve is used here because it is used by the majority of economists writing in the area of international economics.

## Perfect Competition and Efficient Allocation of Resources

An important property of all points on the contract curve is this: if the economy is on the contract curve, it is impossible to increase the outputs of both $X$ and $Y$ by a mere reallocation of resources. Thus, an increase in the production of $X$ necessarily implies a decrease in the production of $Y$, and vice versa. Conversely, if the economy is not on the contract curve, the outputs of both $X$ and $Y$ can be increased by a mere reallocation of resources which moves the economy to the contract curve. For instance, if the economy were at point $Z$ of fig. 4.6, the output of both commodities could be increased by reallocating resources in such a way as to move from $Z$ to some point on the contract curve in the region $E_1 E_2$. However, this is not possible if the economy is already on the contract curve. Accordingly, the existence of perfect competition, which implies that the economy (in the long run) is producing somewhere along the contract curve, achieves economic efficiency in the sense that resources are optimally used.

## The Contract Curve Never Crosses the Diagonal

Under the assumption of linear homogeneous production functions, the contract curve must lie on one side of the diagonal of the box diagram; i.e., it can never cross it, although it may happen to coincide with it. To see why, consider the following two cases.

1. When a point of the contract curve lies on the diagonal, the diagonal itself becomes the contract curve. This follows from the fact that along the diagonal the marginal rates of substitution of labor for land in both industries remain the same, and if they are equal at one point they must be equal everywhere.

2. Consider a typical pair of isoquants intersecting each other on the diagonal, as shown in fig. 4.7. In panel ($a$), the two isoquants intersect each other at point $K$. (A single pair of isoquants is sufficient for our purposes because the same relationship between the $MRS_{LT}$ in $X$ and the $MRS_{LT}$ in $Y$ will necessarily hold at any other point along the diagonal, as a result of the assumed homogeneity.) The straight lines $KZ$ and $RKS$ are the tangents to the isoquants of $X$ and $Y$, respectively. Thus, at point $K$, the $MRS_{LT}$ in the production of $X$ ($MRS_{LT}^X$) is given by the slope $c$, while the $MRS_{LT}$ in the production of $Y$ ($MRS_{LT}^Y$) is given by slope $a$, which is equal to slope $b$. It is obvious that $MRS_{LT}^X < MRS_{LT}^Y$. Since in every industry the $MRS_{LT}$ diminishes as the ratio $L/T$ increases, it should be clear that all tangencies between the two sets of isoquants must occur in the northwest triangle, above and to the left of the diagonal.

Above and to the left of the diagonal, the proportion $L/T$ is lower in the $X$ industry but higher in the $Y$ industry than the overall proportion, $L_0/T_0$, along the diagonal. Thus, the $MRS_{LT}^X$ is higher and the $MRS_{LT}^Y$ is lower at points above and to the left of the diagonal, compared with their respective values (i.e., slopes $c$ and $b$) along the diagonal. On the other hand, below and to the right of the diagonal, the $MRS_{LT}^X$ is lower and the $MRS_{LT}^Y$ is higher than their respective values along the diagonal. Since along the diagonal $MRS_{LT}^X < MRS_{LT}^Y$, below and to the left of the diagonal the inequality between marginal rates of substitution is accentuated. Thus, no tangency can ever occur in this region. At points above and to the left of the diagonal, however, the divergence between marginal rates of substitution tends to disappear on two counts: ($a$) the $MRS_{LT}^X$ increases and ($b$) the $MRS_{LT}^Y$ decreases. All tangencies (and, therefore, the contract curve)

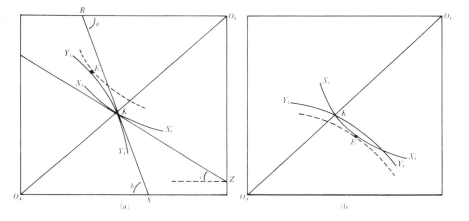

**Figure 4.7** When two typical isoquants intersect each other on the diagonal, the contract curve lies either above or below (and never intersects) the diagonal.

necessarily lie above and to the left of the diagonal, as illustrated by point $E$ in fig. 4.7($a$), where a broken isoquant of industry $X$ touches the isoquant of industry $Y$.

In fig. 4.7($b$) the inequality $\text{MRS}_{LT}^X > \text{MRS}_{LT}^Y$ prevails along the diagonal. All tangencies (and, therefore, the contract curve) lie below and to the right of the diagonal, as illustrated by point $E$.

## 4.5 THE PRODUCTION-POSSIBILITIES FRONTIER

The main objective of the preceding analysis is to prepare the ground for the derivation of the production-possibilities frontier (also known as the transformation curve). This is precisely the purpose of this section.

The production-possibilities frontier shows the maximum obtainable amount of one commodity for each amount of the other. Also, as noted earlier, it depends on two fundamental data: factor endowments and production functions.

The discussion of the box-diagram technique of the preceding section enables us to derive an important conclusion: when the economy allocates its resources along the contract curve, it is impossible to increase the output of one commodity without decreasing the output of the other commodity. Hence each point on the contract curve corresponds to a point on the production-possibilities frontier (and vice versa). Further, perfect competition leads the economy to allocate its resources along the contract curve. Accordingly, perfect competition implies that the economy actually produces on the production-possibilities frontier, the precise equilibrium point being determined by demand.

### A Modified Box Diagram

The one-to-one correspondence between points on the contract curve and the production-possibilities frontier can be illustrated graphically by a slightly modified box diagram. Measure again labor and land horizontally and vertically, respectively, but place the origins $O_X$ and $O_Y$ in the northwest and southeast corners, respectively, as shown in fig. 4.8. Further, measure the outputs of $X$ and $Y$ with respect to the southwest corner ($O$), with $X$ being measured horizontally and $Y$ vertically. Now consider a point along the diagonal $O_X O_Y$, such as point $M$. Observe that the coordinates of point $M$ with respect to the southwest corner ($O$) show (horizontally) the quantity of labor allocated to $X$ ($L_X$) and (vertically) the quantity of land allocated to $Y$ ($T_Y$).

Since the units of measurement of both $X$ and $Y$ (and $L$ and $T$, for that matter) are arbitrary, adopt the following convention: if the economy were to allocate its resources according to some point on the diagonal $O_X O_Y$, the amount of $X$ produced will be equal to the number of units of $L$ used for its production, and, similarly, the amount of $Y$ produced will be equal to the number of units of $T$ used for its production. This is possible because of the assumption of constant returns to scale. Thus, at point $M$ on fig. 4.8 the economy must be producing $KM$

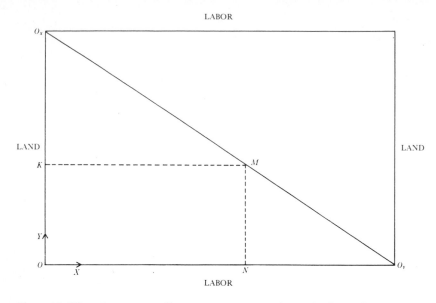

**Figure 4.8** When the economy allocates resources at a point on the diagonal, say $M$, the amounts of $X$ and $Y$ produced are by convention measured by the coordinates of $M$ with respect to $O$, that is, $L_x$, $T_y$.

(or $ON$) units of commodity $X$ and $NM$ (or $OK$) units of $Y$. We now have a way to measure the amounts of $X$ and $Y$ implied by the isoquants for $X$ and $Y$, respectively, passing through point $M$. Since all isoquants necessarily cross the diagonal of the box only once, this appears to be a unique way of assigning values to $X$ and $Y$ at any given point in the box. All we have to do is draw the isoquants through the specified point and determine their intersections with the diagonal. We then follow the same procedure as with point $M$ to determine the amounts of $X$ and $Y$ produced.

## Derivation of the Production-Possibilities Frontier

Figure 4.9 shows how to determine a point on the production-possibilities frontier when a point on the contract curve is given. Consider point $E$, where the two isoquants, $X_1 X_1$ and $Y_1 Y_1$, are tangent to each other. Point $E$ is a point on the contract curve. The isoquant $X_1 X_1$ intersects the diagonal at point $M$, and therefore the quantity of $X$ produced is given by the distance $OR$. On the other hand, the $Y_1 Y_1$ isoquant intersects the diagonal at point $N$, and therefore the quantity of $Y$ produced is given by the distance $OS$. It should now be clear that the coordinates of point $E'$ show the quantities of $X$ and $Y$ produced (when the economy is allocating its resources according to point $E$ on the contract curve), with $X$ measured horizontally along the lower horizontal side of the box and $Y$ measured vertically along the left-hand side of the box, and with $O$ being, of course, the point of origin. Notice that point $E'$ always lies above and to the right of the diagonal. In

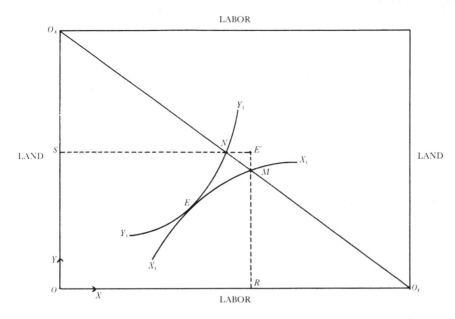

LABOR

LAND

LAND

$O$

$X$

LABOR

**Figure 4.9** Derivation of the production-possibilities frontier.

fact point $E'$ lies above and to the right of the diagonal even if point $E$ lies above and to the right of the diagonal.

Once we know how to determine a point on the production-possibilities frontier given a point on the contract curve, we can derive the whole production-possibilities frontier by repeating the same process for each and every point on the contract curve.

## The Shape of the Production-Possibilities Frontier

If the contract curve coincides with the diagonal of the box, it should be obvious that the production-possibilities frontier is necessarily a straight line. In particular, with the procedure of fig. 4.9, the production-possibilities frontier would coincide with the diagonal, with $O$ being its point of origin. It should be pointed out that the numerical value of the slope of the linear frontier is arbitrary, depending upon the units of measurement of $L$ and $T$. Further, this is the case which Taussig (1927, chap. 7) had in mind in his effort to show that the classical theory is logically correct even though other factors besides labor are used in the production of commodities.

If the contract curve does not coincide with the diagonal, then the production-possibilities frontier will be concave to the origin, as shown in fig. 4.10($a$). To see why, first note that the economy can always reach the broken straight line $MK$ by allocating its resources arbitrarily along the diagonal. However, by assumption, the contract curve does not coincide with the diagonal, and therefore the

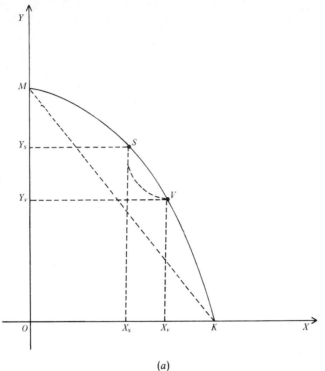

(a)

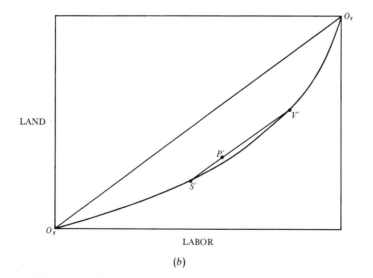

(b)

**Figure 4.10** (a) The production-possibilities frontier is concave to the origin when the contract curve does not coincide with the diagonal. (b) Points S' and V' correspond to points S and V in (a).

production-possibilities frontier will definitely lie beyond the straight line $MK$—except for the intercepts $M$ and $K$. But does this necessarily mean that the production-possibilities frontier is concave to the origin? This will be the case if it can be shown that no part of the frontier $MSVK$ can be convex to the origin. For this purpose, consider any two points on the frontier, such as points $S$ and $V$. At $S$ the economy produces $X_S$ units of $X$ and $Y_S$ of $Y$. Similarly, at $V$ the economy produces $X_V$ of $X$ and $Y_V$ of $Y$. What can easily be shown is that the economy can always reach all points that lie on the straight-line segment $SV$ (not drawn). Therefore, the convex broken curve $SV$ can be ruled out.

Consider fig. 4.10($b$). It represents the box diagram from which the production-possibilities frontier of fig. 4.10($a$) has been derived. The curve $O_X S'V'O_Y$ is the contract curve. Points $S'$ and $V'$ on the contract curve correspond to points $S$ and $V$, respectively, on the production-possibilities frontier. Point $S'$ corresponds to a certain production technique for producing $X$ and another technique for producing $Y$. Similarly, point $V'$ corresponds to two more production techniques—one for each commodity. In what follows, assume that no other techniques are used.

Consider the straight-line segment $S'V'$ (fig. 4.10($b$)). As shown in appendix ($b$) to this chapter, the line $S'V'$ is nothing but the set of all points ($P'$) of the form

$$P' = (1 - \lambda)S' + \lambda V'$$

where $0 \leq \lambda \leq 1$. This is true whether we measure the coordinates of $S'$, $V'$, and $P'$ with respect to $O_X$ or $O_Y$. What are the output levels of $X$ and $Y$ at $P'$? Because of constant returns to scale, we have

$$X = (1 - \lambda)X_S + \lambda X_V$$

$$Y = (1 - \lambda)Y_S + \lambda Y_V$$

Consider now the point $P = (X, Y)$ in fig. 4.10($a$). We obviously have

$$P = (X, Y)$$

$$= [(1 - \lambda)X_S + \lambda X_V , (1 - \lambda)Y_S + \lambda Y_V]$$

$$= (1 - \lambda)(X_S , Y_S) + \lambda(X_V , Y_V) = (1 - \lambda)S + \lambda V$$

Thus, point $P$ (fig. 4.10($a$)) must lie somewhere along the straight-line segment $SV$. As $\lambda$ increases from 0 to 1, and thus point $P'$ (fig. 4.10($b$)) moves from $S'$ to $V'$ along the straight line $S'V'$, point $P$ (fig. 4.10($a$)) moves along the straight line $SV$ from $S$ to $V$. Accordingly, the broken curve $SV$ (fig. 4.10($a$)) is ruled out. (An alternative proof of the concavity of the production-possibilities frontier will be given in chaps. 9 through 10.)

In general, the economy will be able to do better than the straight line $SV$, as illustrated in fig. 4.10($a$). This follows from the fact that the straight-line segment $S'V'$ (fig. 4.10($b$)) does not coincide with the contract curve—more efficient techniques are available than those which are associated with points $S'$ and $V'$.

## Increasing Opportunity Costs

The absolute slope of the production-possibilities frontier (known as the marginal rate of transformation), as shown in fig. 4.10(a), shows the opportunity cost of $X$ in terms of $Y$, that is, the minimum amount of $Y$ that the economy can possibly give up to obtain an extra unit of $X$, or, the maximum amount of $Y$ that the economy can obtain by giving up 1 unit of $X$. Because of the concavity of the production-possibilities frontier, the opportunity cost of $X$ in terms of $Y$ increases as more $X$ is produced. Thus, as we move from point $S$ to point $V$ (see fig. 4.10(a)), the tangent to the production-possibilities frontier becomes steeper, indicating increasing opportunity cost. It can be verified that in fig. 4.10(a) increasing opportunity costs exist for every commodity. (*Hint:* the opportunity cost of $X$ in terms of $Y$ is the reciprocal of the opportunity cost of $Y$ in terms of $X$.)

It should also be emphasized that a movement along the production-possibilities frontier is much more complicated than what it appears to be from fig. 4.10(a). Thus, a movement from $S$ to $V$ implies that labor and land are transferred from industry $Y$ to industry $X$. Since the two industries do not use the two factors in the same proportion (the latter occurring, by the way, only when the production-possibilities frontier is linear), new production techniques will necessarily become optimum in both industries. Therefore a whole reorganization of production takes place. This is an important phenomenon.

## The Marginal Rate of Transformation and Marginal Costs

The marginal rate of transformation (or the opportunity cost of $X$ in terms of $Y$) can be shown to be equal to the ratio of the marginal cost of $X$ ($MC_X$) to the marginal cost of $Y$ ($MC_Y$). Before rigorous proof of this proposition is provided, it is useful to consider the following heuristic argument. Consider point $S$ on the production-possibilities frontier of fig. 4.10(a) as corresponding to point $S'$ (fig. 4.10(b)) on the contract curve. Now consider a slight movement along the contract curve in the neighborhood of $S'$, implying an infinitesimal transfer of resources from industry $Y$ to industry $X$. The production of $X$ increases infinitesimally by $dX$ and the production of $Y$ decreases infinitesimally by $dY$. For this infinitesimal transfer of resources, the increase in the total cost of production of $X$ (that is, $dC_X$) must be equal to the reduction of the total cost of production of $Y$ (that is, $dC_Y$). That is,

$$dC_X + dC_Y = 0 \tag{4.17}$$

But, by definition, we have

$$MC_X \equiv \frac{dC_X}{dX} \quad \text{and} \quad MC_Y \equiv \frac{dC_Y}{dY} \tag{4.18}$$

Introducing eqs. (4.18) into (4.17) and reorganizing, we obtain

$$-\frac{dY}{dX} = \frac{MC_X}{MC_Y} \tag{4.19}$$

That is to say, the absolute slope of the production-possibilities frontier is equal to the ratio of the marginal cost of $X$ to $Y$.

Since, under perfectly competitive conditions, marginal costs are also equal to prices, eq. (4.19) can be extended as follows:

$$-\frac{dY}{dX} = \frac{MC_X}{MC_Y} = \frac{\text{price of } X}{\text{price of } Y} \qquad (4.20)$$

Thus, under competitive conditions, the marginal rate of transformation (or absolute slope of the production-possibilities frontier) shows relative commodity prices. When perfect competition in the product markets (only) breaks down, the absolute slope of the frontier will continue to show the ratio of marginal costs, but it will, in general, fail to show relative prices.

### Geometric Proof of the Equality Between Opportunity Costs and Marginal Costs

The rigorous proof of eq. (4.20) follows. Consider fig. 4.11. As before, measure labor horizontally and land vertically, and place the origins $O_X$ and $O_Y$ in the northwest and southeast corners, respectively, of the box diagram. Consider now point $E_0$, which, by assumption, lies on the contract curve. The corresponding point on the production-possibilities frontier (following our earlier convention) is, of course, $P_0$. What is the slope of the production-possibilities frontier at $P_0$? Consider another point on the contract curve, such as $E_1$. Obviously, point $P_1$ on

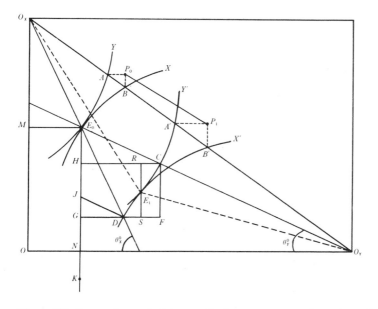

**Figure 4.11** Geometric proof of the equality between opportunity and marginal costs.

the production-possibilities frontier corresponds to $E_1$. Consider the slope of the straight line $P_0 P_1$ and imagine that point $E_1$ moves closer to $E_0$, causing point $P_1$ to move closer to point $P_0$. The limit of the slope of the straight line $P_0 P_1$, as $P_1$ moves closer to $P_0$, is simply the slope of the production-possibilities frontier at $P_0$. How is this limit determined?

Consider the percentage changes in the outputs of $X$ and $Y$ as we move from $E_0$ to $E_1$. Because of the assumed linear homogeneity, we have

$$\frac{\Delta X}{X_0} = \frac{E_0 D}{O_X E_0} \quad \text{and} \quad -\frac{\Delta Y}{Y_0} = \frac{E_0 C}{O_Y E_0}$$

where $X_0$ and $Y_0$ are the outputs of commodities $X$ and $Y$, respectively, at point $P_0$ (or $E_0$). Now observe that the triangles $O_X M E_0$ and $E_0 G D$ are similar. Hence,

$$\frac{\Delta X}{X_0} = \frac{E_0 D}{O_X E_0} = \frac{GD}{ME_0} \tag{4.21}$$

In addition, the triangles $O_Y E_0 N$ and $C E_0 H$ are similar. Hence,

$$-\frac{\Delta Y}{Y_0} = \frac{E_0 C}{O_Y E_0} = \frac{HC}{O_Y N} \tag{4.22}$$

Taking now the ratio of the percentage change in $Y$ to $X$, we obtain

$$-\frac{\Delta Y}{\Delta X} \frac{X_0}{Y_0} = \frac{HC}{O_Y N} \frac{ME_0}{GD} \tag{4.23}$$

Observe that the distance $ME_0$ shows the amount of labor allocated to the production of $X$ at $P_0$ (that is, $L_X^0$) and that the distance $O_Y N$ shows the amount of labor allocated to the production of $Y$ at $P_0$ (that is, $L_Y^0$). Introducing these new symbols ($L_X^0$ and $L_Y^0$) into eq. (4.23) and multiplying both sides by $Y_0/X_0$, we obtain

$$-\frac{\Delta Y}{\Delta X} = \frac{HC}{GD} \frac{L_X^0}{L_Y^0} \frac{Y_0}{X_0} \tag{4.24}$$

Now determine the limit of the expression on the right-hand side of eq. (4.24) as $\Delta X \to 0$. Since the quantities $L_X^0$, $L_Y^0$, $Y_0$, and $X_0$ remain constant, let us concentrate on the limit of the ratio $HC/GD$.

Draw a straight line through $D$ and parallel to $O_Y C E_0$. Let it intersect the perpendicular line $E_0 N$ at $J$. In addition, imagine a straight line through points $C$ and $D$ and let it intersect $E_0 N$ at $K$. Given all this, the ratio $HC/GD$ can be rewritten as follows:

$$\frac{HC}{GD} = \frac{HC}{GD} \frac{KE_0}{KE_0} = \frac{HC}{GD} \frac{GE_0 + KG}{HE_0 + KH}$$

$$= \frac{(GE_0/GD) + (KG/GD)}{(HE_0/HC) + (KH/HC)}$$

$$= \frac{\theta_X^0 + (KG/GD)}{\theta_Y^0 + (KH/HC)} = \frac{\theta_X^0 + (KG/GD)}{\theta_Y^0 + (KG/GD)} \tag{4.25}$$

where $\theta_X^0$ and $\theta_Y^0$ are the optimum land/labor ratios in industries $X$ and $Y$, respectively, at point $E_0$. Again, $\theta_X^0$ and $\theta_Y^0$ remain constant. The only thing that will change continuously as we move from $E_1$ to $E_0$ is the ratio $KG/GD$. What is the limit of this ratio? Observe that

$$\frac{KG}{GD} = \frac{CF}{DF} = \frac{RE_1 + E_1 S}{DS + RC} = \frac{RE_1[1 + (E_1 S/RE_1)]}{RC[1 + (DS/RC)]} \tag{4.26}$$

In the limit, the slope of $E_1 C$ and the slope of $DE_1$ will tend to the common slope of the isoquants of $X$ and $Y$ at $E_0$, that is, $(w/r)_0$. In other words, in the limit the following will be true:

$$\frac{RE_1}{RC} = \frac{E_1 S}{DS} = \left(\frac{w}{r}\right)_0 \tag{4.27}$$

Hence,

$$\frac{E_1 S}{RE_1} = \frac{DS}{RC} \tag{4.28}$$

Substituting eqs. (4.27) and (4.28) into (4.26), we get (in the limit)

$$\frac{KG}{GD} = \frac{RE_1}{RC} = \left(\frac{w}{r}\right)_0 \tag{4.29}$$

Therefore, the value of the ratio $HC/GD$ as given by eq. (4.25) can now be rewritten (in the limit) as follows:

$$\frac{HC}{GD} = \frac{\theta_X^0 + (w/r)_0}{\theta_Y^0 + (w/r)_0} \tag{4.30}$$

Finally, introducing the preceding result into eq. (4.24), we obtain

$$-\frac{dY}{dX} = \frac{\theta_X^0 + (w/r)_0}{\theta_Y^0 + (w/r)_0} \frac{L_X^0}{L_Y^0} \frac{Y_0}{X_0} \tag{4.31}$$

Observe that the symbol $\Delta Y/\Delta X$ has now been replaced by $dY/dX$.

What is the meaning of the right-hand side of eq. (4.31)? For completeness, the equation can be rewritten as follows:

$$\frac{\theta_X^0 + (w/r)_0}{\theta_Y^0 + (w/r)_0} \frac{L_X^0}{L_Y^0} \frac{Y_0}{X_0} = \frac{(T_X^0/L_X^0) + (w_0/r_0)}{(T_Y^0/L_Y^0) + (w_0/r_0)} \frac{L_X^0}{L_Y^0} \frac{Y_0}{X_0}$$

$$= \frac{(r_0 T_X^0 + w_0 L_X^0)/X_0}{(r_0 T_Y^0 + w_0 L_Y^0)/Y_0}$$

$$= \frac{AC_X^0}{AC_Y^0} = \frac{MC_X^0}{MC_Y^0} = \frac{p_x^0}{p_y^0}$$

Accordingly, our general conclusion can be stated thus:

$$-\frac{dY}{dX} = \frac{AC_X}{AC_Y} = \frac{MC_X}{MC_Y} = \frac{p_x}{p_y} \tag{4.32}$$

This completes our geometric proof.

## Mathematical Proof of the Equality Between Opportunity Costs and Marginal Costs

For the mathematically inclined reader an additional mathematical proof of eq. (4.20) is provided.

Consider the following production functions:

$$X = X(L_x, T_x) \tag{4.33}$$

$$Y = Y(L_y, T_y) \tag{4.34}$$

where $L_i$ and $T_i$ $(i = x, y)$ indicate the amounts of labor and land, respectively, employed by the $i$th industry.

Full employment requires that the following equations be satisfied:

$$L_0 = L_x + L_y \tag{4.35}$$

$$T_0 = T_x + T_y \tag{4.36}$$

Take the total differentials of eqs. (4.33) through (4.36) as follows:

$$dX = \text{MPP}_{LX}\, dL_x + \text{MPP}_{TX}\, dT_x \tag{4.37}$$

$$dY = \text{MPP}_{LY}\, dL_y + \text{MPP}_{TY}\, dT_y \tag{4.38}$$

$$0 = dL_x + dL_y \tag{4.39}$$

$$0 = dT_x + dT_y \tag{4.40}$$

Solve eqs. (4.39) and (4.40) for $dL_y$ and $dT_y$ and substitute into eq. (4.38) to obtain

$$-dY = \text{MPP}_{LY}\, dL_x + \text{MPP}_{TY}\, dT_x \tag{4.41}$$

Now take the ratio of eq. (4.41) to eq. (4.37):

$$-\frac{dY}{dX} = \frac{\text{MPP}_{LY}\, dL_x + \text{MPP}_{TY}\, dT_x}{\text{MPP}_{LX}\, dL_x + \text{MPP}_{TX}\, dT_x}$$

$$= \frac{\text{MPP}_{TY}\, (\text{MPP}_{LY}/\text{MPP}_{TY})\, dL_x + dT_x}{\text{MPP}_{TX}\, (\text{MPP}_{LX}/\text{MPP}_{TX})\, dL_x + dT_x}$$

$$= \frac{\text{MPP}_{TY}}{\text{MPP}_{TX}} \tag{4.42}$$

The last equation follows from the efficiency condition: $(\text{MPP}_{LY}/\text{MPP}_{TY}) = (\text{MPP}_{LX}/\text{MPP}_{TX})$, which is satisfied when resources are allocated along the contract curve.

Finally, substitute the profit-maximization conditions

$$p_x\, \text{MPP}_{TX} = p_y\, \text{MPP}_{TY} = r \tag{4.43}$$

into eq. (4.42) to obtain eq. (4.20). This completes the mathematical proof.

## The Significance of Increasing Opportunity Costs

When, as in the classical theory, the production-possibilities frontier is a straight line, relative pretrade prices are uniquely given by the slope of the production-possibilities frontier. However, in the presence of increasing opportunity costs, this is not so. The pretrade prices will be determined by the slope of the production-possibilities frontier at the pretrade equilibrium point, which can only be determined if demand is introduced into the picture. This particular problem will be taken up in the next chapter.

## 4.6 INTERINDUSTRY FLOWS AND THE PRODUCTION-POSSIBILITIES FRONTIER†

Jaroslav Vanek (1963) showed how to derive the production-possibilities frontier when each commodity is used as an intermediate product and in *fixed* proportions in the production of the other commodity. Vanek's model of interindustry flows is interesting because it captures an additional dimension of reality. It nevertheless suffers from two drawbacks: (*a*) Vanek excludes the possibility of substitution in production between primary factors and intermediate products; and (*b*) he also ignores the possibility of negative net production (when trade in intermediate goods is allowed). For this reason, we presently follow Warne (1971) who showed how these two drawbacks can be handled. See also Guisinger (1969) and Chang and Mayer (1973).

## The Model of Interindustry Flows

The general system of interindustry flows may be written as follows:

$$X = F(L_x, T_x, Y_x) - X_y \tag{4.44}$$

$$Y = G(L_y, T_y, X_y) - Y_x \tag{4.45}$$

$$L_0 = L_x + L_y \tag{4.46}$$

$$T_0 = T_x + T_y \tag{4.47}$$

where $X$ and $Y$ are the *net* outputs, $F(L_x, T_x, Y_x)$ and $G(L_y, T_y, X_y)$ are the *gross* outputs, and $L_0$ and $T_0$ are the fixed amounts of the primary factors, labor and land, available to the economy. Both production functions are assumed to be linear homogeneous.

† This section is slightly more technical and may be skipped without interrupting the continuity of the book.

## The Production-Possibilities Frontier

The derivation of the production-possibilities frontier is sketched in fig. 4.12. Consider the positive quadrant first. The concave curve $MN$ shows the maximum obtainable *net* (nonnegative) amount of one commodity for each net and nonnegative amount of the other. That this curve is necessarily concave can be easily shown by an argument similar to that provided earlier when interindustry flows did not exist: *because of constant returns to scale, convex combinations of any two points on the curve are always feasible.* For a rigorous proof, see Chang and Mayer (1973).

In a closed economy, only the curve $MN$ is relevant. However, for an open economy which can also import intermediate products, the production-possibilities frontier must be extended into the second and fourth quadrants also, as we have done in sec. 2.9.

The curve $OUS$ (second quadrant) is the total-product curve of industry $Y$ on the assumption that all available labor $L_0$ and land $T_0$ are employed by industry $Y$. The negative amounts of $X$ read off this curve show merely imports of $X$.

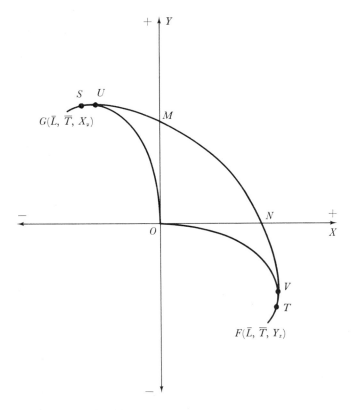

**Figure 4.12** The production-possibilities frontier of the interindustry flows model.

Similarly, the curve $OVT$ (fourth quadrant) is the total-product curve of industry $X$ when all available labor $L_0$ and land $T_0$ are employed by industry $X$, and any $Y$ requirements in the production of $X$ are imported from abroad. The open-economy's production-possibilities frontier is now given by $SUMNVT$, as in sec. 2.9.

Note that the segments $UM$ and $NV$ are now *curvilinear*. Along these segments both commodities are produced by the economy. Between $M$ and $U$, however, the domestic production of $X$ is not sufficient to satisfy the production requirements of $Y$, and thus $X$ (as an intermediate product) is imported from the rest of the world. Similarly, along $NV$, commodity $Y$ is imported from the rest of the world to serve as an intermediate input in the production of $X$.

At $U(V)$ the economy specializes completely in the production of $Y(X)$ and such specialization continues until $S(T)$, where the tangent to the curve $OUS(OVT)$ becomes horizontal (vertical). Thus, along $SU$, all $X$ requirements in the production of $Y$ are imported. Similarly, along $VT$, all $Y$ requirements in the production of $X$ are imported.

## The Slope of the Production-Possibilities Frontier

The absolute slope of the production-possibilities frontier continues to be equal to the commodity price ratio $p_x/p_y$, even when interindustry flows are introduced. The proof is straightforward.

The negative of the ratio of the total differentials of eqs. (4.44) through (4.45) reduces to

$$-\frac{dY}{dX} = \frac{\text{MPP}_{LY}\, dL_x + \text{MPP}_{TY}\, dT_x - \text{MPP}_{XY}\, dX_y + dY_x}{\text{MPP}_{LX}\, dL_x + \text{MPP}_{TX}\, dT_x + \text{MPP}_{YX}\, dY_x - dX_y} \tag{4.48}$$

where $\text{MPP}_{XY} \equiv$ marginal physical product of $X$ in the production of $Y$, $\text{MPP}_{YX} \equiv$ marginal physical product of $Y$ in the production of $X$, $dL_y = -dL_x$, and $dT_y = -dT_x$.

Profit maximization requires that $\text{MPP}_{LY} = w/p_y$, $\text{MPP}_{TY} = r/p_y$, $\text{MPP}_{XY} = p_x/p_y$, $\text{MPP}_{LX} = w/p_x$, $\text{MPP}_{TX} = r/p_x$, and $\text{MPP}_{YX} = p_y/p_x$. Substituting these conditions into eq. (4.48) and simplifying, we obtain

$$-\frac{dY}{dX} = \frac{(1/p_y)(w\, dL_x + r\, dT_x - p_x\, dX_y + p_y\, dY_x)}{(1/p_x)(w\, dL_x + r\, dT_x + p_y\, dY_x - p_x\, dX_y)} = \frac{p_x}{p_y} \tag{4.49}$$

Thus, under perfectly competitive conditions, the absolute slope of the (*net*) production-possibilities frontier gives the market price ratio.

## The World Production-Possibilities Frontier

Warne (1971) shows (and the reader can easily verify) that in the present case of *increasing* opportunity costs, the world production-possibilities frontier *with* trade in intermediate products does not uniformly lie beyond the world production-possibilities frontier *without* trade in intermediate products. The two frontiers necessarily coincide over a certain (middle) range. This result is, of course, different from the conclusion we reached earlier in sec. 2.9 in terms of the single primary-factor model.

## 4.7 SOME DIFFICULTIES WITH THE PRODUCTION-POSSIBILITIES FRONTIER

The preceding analysis assumes implicitly that factors of production are perfectly mobile and indifferent as between different employments. Problems, however, arise when the assumption of perfect mobility is dropped.

If all factors are perfectly immobile between industries (assuming that factor-price flexibility prevails), the production-possibilities frontier becomes a rectangle and the economy (whether *closed* or *open*) will always be producing a fixed combination of $X$ and $Y$. However, in the intermediate case of imperfect mobility, whether or not a production-possibilities frontier can be derived, with its slope at any point showing relative prices, is still an open question.

Finally, it should be noted that several attempts have been made to derive the production-possibilities frontier when the factor supplies are variable. Unfortunately, the production-possibilities frontiers so derived lack the important property referred to earlier, namely, that the slope of the frontier at any point shows relative prices. In general, the production-possibilities frontier derived under the assumption that factor supplies are variable can be regarded as a locus of points which lie on a family of production-possibilities frontiers derived from a family of successively different fixed-factor supplies.

## APPENDIX TO CHAPTER FOUR. (a) FACTOR PRICES AND FACTOR PROPORTIONS FOR THE FIRM

This part of the appendix attempts to prove rigorously that there exists a one-to-one correspondence between factor prices and factor proportions at the level of the firm.

Given the factor-price ratio $w/r$, we can determine uniquely the optimum scale of operations of the firm; i.e., we can determine the optimum amounts of labor and land, $L^*$ and $T^*$ respectively, that a typical firm will employ in order to minimize its average cost of production. This can be expressed formally as follows:

$$L^* = L\left(\frac{w}{r}\right) \tag{A4.1}$$

$$T^* = T\left(\frac{w}{r}\right) \tag{A4.2}$$

Equations (A4.1) and (A4.2) express the absolute quantities $L^*$ and $T^*$ as functions of the factor-price ratio $w/r$. However, what we are interested in at the moment is not the relationship between the absolute quantities $L^*$ and $T^*$ and $w/r$ but, rather, the relationship between the optimum factor ratio $\mu = T^*/L^*$ and the factor-price ratio $w/r$. Let us therefore concentrate on

$$\mu = \frac{T^*}{L^*} = \frac{T(w/r)}{L(w/r)} \tag{A4.3}$$

Is there a one-to-one correspondence between $\mu$ and $w/r$? This will be the case if, and only if, the function (A4.3) is monotonic, i.e., if $\mu$ is either a strictly increasing, or a strictly decreasing, function of $w/r$. In turn, this condition will be satisfied if the derivative of $\mu$ with respect to $w/r$ is either strictly positive, or strictly negative, for all values of $w/r$. In other words, a one-to-one correspondence exists between the factor ratio $\mu$ and the factor-price ratio $w/r$ if, and only if, the derivative $d\mu/d(w/r)$ is nonzero and retains the same sign for all values of $w/r$. Is this condition met?

Differentiating $\mu$ as given by eq. (A4.3) with respect to $w/r$, we get

$$\frac{d\mu}{d(w/r)} = \frac{T'L - L'T}{L^2} \tag{A4.4}$$

where $L$ and $T$ are the functions (A4.1) and (A4.2), respectively, and primes indicate differentiation. From eq. (A4.4) it is obvious that

$$\text{Sign of } \frac{d\mu}{d(w/r)} = \text{sign of } (T'L - L'T)$$

Is the sign of $(T'L - L'T)$ unique? If it is, then a one-to-one correspondence exists between $\mu$ and $w/r$. To answer this question, a way to determine the derivatives $L'$ and $T'$ must be found. First formalize the cost-minimization problem.

Express the average cost of production (AC) as follows, using $T$ as the numeraire:

$$AC = \frac{(w/r)L + T}{f(L, T)} \tag{A4.5}$$

where $f(L, T)$ is the production function of a typical firm. For minimization of AC, it is required that the partial derivatives of AC with respect to $L$ and $T$ be equal to zero. Thus,

$$\frac{\partial(AC)}{\partial L} = \frac{(w/r)f(L, T) - [(w/r)L + T]f_L(L, T)}{[f(L, T)]^2} = 0 \tag{A4.6a}$$

$$\frac{\partial(AC)}{\partial T} = \frac{f(L, T) - [(w/r)L + T]f_T(L, T)}{[f(L, T)]^2} = 0 \tag{A4.7a}$$

where the subscripts $L$ and $T$ indicate partial differentiation with respect to labor and land, respectively.

Equations (A4.6a) and (A4.7a) can be reduced to

$$\left(\frac{w}{r}\right)f = \left(\frac{w}{r}L + T\right)f_L \tag{A4.6b}$$

$$f = \left(\frac{w}{r}L + T\right)f_T \tag{A4.7b}$$

where the arguments of the functions $f, f_L$, and $f_T$ have been omitted for simplicity. Note that the ratio of eqs. (A4.6b) and (A4.7b) gives the familiar condition

$$\frac{w}{r} = \frac{f_L}{f_T} \tag{A4.8}$$

That is, for cost minimization it is required that the marginal rate of substitution of labor for land be equal to the factor-price ratio $w/r$. This condition will necessarily be satisfied at the point where AC is at a minimum. In addition, substituting (A4.8) into (A4.7b), we get

$$f = \left(\frac{f_L}{f_T}L + T\right)f_T = Lf_L + Tf_T \tag{A4.9}$$

In other words, at the point where AC is at a minimum, Euler's equation must be satisfied. Put differently, AC is minimized at a point where returns to scale are momentarily constant.

Equations (A4.6a) and (A4.7a) are known as the first-order conditions for minimization of AC. Unfortunately, however, for the problem at hand we shall have to go beyond the first-order conditions and determine the second-order conditions as well.

Consider the following Hessian matrix:

$$H \equiv \begin{bmatrix} \dfrac{\partial^2(AC)}{\partial L^2} & \dfrac{\partial^2(AC)}{\partial L \, \partial T} \\[2ex] \dfrac{\partial^2(AC)}{\partial T \, \partial L} & \dfrac{\partial^2(AC)}{\partial T^2} \end{bmatrix} \tag{A4.10}$$

It is well known that the second-order condition for AC minimization is that the Hessian matrix $H$ be positive definite (on this point, see Samuelson (1947), Mathematical Appendix A). The Hessian matrix $H$ will be positive definite if, and only if,

$$\frac{\partial^2(AC)}{\partial L^2} > 0 \qquad \frac{\partial^2(AC)}{\partial T^2} > 0 \qquad \text{and} \qquad |H| > 0$$

where $|H|$ is the determinant of $H$, that is, the Hessian determinant. These second-order partial derivatives must be evaluated to see whether the above conditions are satisfied, or rather to determine the restrictions (that must be placed on these second-order partial derivatives) for minimization of AC. We have:

$$\frac{\partial^2(AC)}{\partial L^2} = \left\{ \left[ \frac{w}{r} f_L - f_{LL}\left(\frac{w}{r}L + T\right) - \frac{w}{r}f_L \right] f^2 \right.$$
$$\left. - 2ff_L \left[ \frac{w}{r}f - f_L\left(\frac{w}{r}L + T\right) \right] \right\} \bigg/ f^4$$

$$\frac{\partial^2(AC)}{\partial L\,\partial T} = \left\{ \left[ \frac{w}{r} f_T - f_{LT}\left(\frac{w}{r}L + T\right) - f_L \right] f^2 \right.$$
$$\left. - 2ff_T \left[ \frac{w}{r}f - f_L\left(\frac{w}{r}L + T\right) \right] \right\} \bigg/ f^4$$

$$\frac{\partial^2(AC)}{\partial T^2} = \left\{ \left[ f_T - f_{TT}\left(\frac{w}{r}L + T\right) - f_T \right] f^2 \right.$$
$$\left. - 2ff_T \left[ f - f_T\left(\frac{w}{r}L + T\right) \right] \right\} \bigg/ f^4$$

$$\frac{\partial^2(AC)}{\partial T\,\partial L} = \left\{ \left[ f_L - f_{TL}\left(\frac{w}{r}L + T\right) - f_T\frac{w}{r} \right] f^2 \right.$$
$$\left. - 2ff_L \left[ f - f_T\left(\frac{w}{r}L + T\right) \right] \right\} \bigg/ f^4$$

These second-order partial derivatives have to be evaluated at the point where AC is at a minimum. This means that eqs. (A4.6$b$) and (A4.7$b$) as well as eqs. (A4.8) and (A4.9) must necessarily hold. Making use of these equations, we can easily simplify the above second-order partial derivatives to

$$\frac{\partial^2(AC)}{\partial L^2} = -\frac{f_{LL}[(w/r)L + T]}{f^2} \tag{A4.11a}$$

$$\frac{\partial^2(AC)}{\partial L\,\partial T} = -\frac{f_{LT}[(w/r)L + T]}{f^2} \tag{A4.12a}$$

$$\frac{\partial^2(AC)}{\partial T^2} = -\frac{f_{TT}[(w/r)L + T]}{f^2} \tag{A4.13a}$$

$$\frac{\partial^2(AC)}{\partial T\,\partial L} = -\frac{f_{TL}[(w/r)L + T]}{f^2} \tag{A4.14a}$$

Note that the ratio $[(w/r)L + T]/f^2$ is a factor common to all expressions on the right-hand side of eqs. (A4.11$a$) to (A4.14$a$). Therefore, eqs. (A4.11$a$) to (A4.14$a$) can be simplified as follows:

$$\frac{\partial^2(AC)}{\partial L^2} = -cf_{LL} \tag{A4.11$b$}$$

$$\frac{\partial^2(AC)}{\partial L\, \partial T} = -cf_{LT} \tag{A4.12$b$}$$

$$\frac{\partial^2(AC)}{\partial T^2} = -cf_{TT} \tag{A4.13$b$}$$

$$\frac{\partial^2(AC)}{\partial T\, \partial L} = -cf_{TL} \tag{A4.14$b$}$$

where $c \equiv [(w/r)L + T]/f^2 > 0$.

The Hessian matrix $H$ (see eq. (A4.10)) will thus be positive definite if, and only if, the following conditions are satisfied:

$$-cf_{LL} > 0$$

$$-cf_{TT} > 0$$

$$|H| = \begin{vmatrix} -cf_{LL} & -cf_{LT} \\ -cf_{TL} & -cf_{TT} \end{vmatrix} = c^2 \begin{vmatrix} f_{LL} & f_{LT} \\ f_{TL} & f_{TT} \end{vmatrix} > 0$$

Since $c > 0$, these conditions can be simplified to

$$f_{LL} < 0 \qquad f_{TT} < 0 \qquad \begin{vmatrix} f_{LL} & f_{LT} \\ f_{TL} & f_{TT} \end{vmatrix} > 0 \tag{A4.15}$$

These conditions imply that the Hessian matrix of the production function is negative definite. (This implies that the production function must be strictly concave in the neighborhood of the point where AC is at a minimum.) In what follows assume that these conditions are indeed satisfied. Note that the conditions $f_{LL} < 0$ and $f_{TT} < 0$ are simply the mathematical expression of the familiar law of diminishing returns to a variable factor.

Having derived the first-order and second-order conditions for minimization of the average cost of production, we return to the problem of whether or not there exists a one-to-one correspondence between the factor-price ratio $w/r$ and the optimum factor ratio $\mu$. As we saw earlier (see eq. (A4.4)), the problem reduces to whether or not the sign of $(T'L - LT')$ is unique. For this purpose, let us evaluate the derivatives $T'$ and $L'$.

Given the factor-price ratio $w/r$, eqs. (A4.6$b$) and (A4.7$b$) can be solved simultaneously for the optimum values of labor and land employed by the firm, that is, $L^*$ and $T^*$. But we are not interested in these absolute quantities at the moment. Our first step is the determination of the partial derivatives $L'$ and $T'$; that is, we want to find out how the optimum quantities $L^*$ and $T^*$ vary as the factor-price ratio varies. For this purpose, differentiate eqs. (A4.6b) and (A4.7b) totally with respect to $w/r$, to get

$$\left[\frac{w}{r}f_L + \left(\frac{w}{r}L + T\right)f_{LL} - \frac{w}{r}f_L\right]\frac{dL}{d(w/r)}$$

$$+ \left[f_L + \left(\frac{w}{r}L + T\right)f_{TL} - \frac{w}{r}f_T\right]\frac{dT}{d(w/r)} = f - Lf_L$$

$$\left[\frac{w}{r}f_T + \left(\frac{w}{r}L + T\right)f_{LT} - f_L\right]\frac{dL}{d(w/r)}$$

$$+ \left[f_T + \left(\frac{w}{r}L + T\right)f_{TT} - f_T\right]\frac{dT}{d(w/r)} = - Lf_T$$

Making use of equations (A4.8) and (A4.9), we can simplify the above equations to

$$f_{LL}\frac{dL}{d(w/r)} + f_{TL}\frac{dT}{d(w/r)} = \frac{f - Lf_L}{(w/r)L + T} \tag{A4.16}$$

$$f_{LT}\frac{dL}{d(w/r)} + f_{TT}\frac{dT}{d(w/r)} = -\frac{Lf_T}{(w/r)L + T} \tag{A4.17}$$

or, in matrix notation,

$$\begin{bmatrix} f_{LL} & f_{TL} \\ f_{LT} & f_{TT} \end{bmatrix}\begin{bmatrix} L' \\ T' \end{bmatrix} = \begin{bmatrix} \dfrac{Tf_T}{(w/r)L + T} \\ -\dfrac{Lf_T}{(w/r)L + T} \end{bmatrix} \tag{A4.18}$$

Note that the matrix of this system is simply the Hessian matrix of the production function. Hence, it must be negative definite. The determinant

$$\Delta \equiv \begin{vmatrix} f_{LL} & f_{TL} \\ f_{LT} & f_{TT} \end{vmatrix}$$

must be positive (see (A4.15)).

Solving system (A4.18) by means of Cramer's rule, we get

$$L' = \frac{1}{\Delta}\begin{vmatrix} \dfrac{Tf_T}{(w/r)L + T} & f_{TL} \\ -\dfrac{Lf_T}{(w/r)L + T} & f_{TT} \end{vmatrix}$$

$$= \frac{f_T}{\Delta[(w/r)L + T]}(Tf_{TT} + Lf_{TL}) \tag{A4.19}$$

$$T' = \frac{1}{\Delta} \begin{vmatrix} f_{LL} & \dfrac{Tf_T}{(w/r)L + T} \\ f_{LT} & -\dfrac{Lf_T}{(w/r)L + T} \end{vmatrix}$$

$$= \frac{-f_T}{\Delta[(w/r)L + T]}(Lf_{LL} + Tf_{LT}) \tag{A4.20}$$

Now substitute these results into the expression $T'L - L'T$ to get

$$T'L - L'T = -\left\{\frac{f_T}{\Delta[(w/r)L + T]}\right\}[L(Lf_{LL} + Tf_{LT}) + T(Tf_{TT} + Lf_{TL})] \tag{A4.21}$$

Since

$$\frac{-f_T}{\Delta[(w/r)L + T]} < 0$$

the sign of $(T'L - L'T)$ is necessarily the opposite of the sign of $[L(Lf_{LL} + Tf_{LT}) + T(Tf_{TT} + Lf_{TL})]$. What is the sign of this latter expression? Observe that

$$L(Lf_{LL} + Tf_{LT}) + T(Tf_{TT} + Lf_{TL}) = (L, T)\begin{bmatrix} f_{LL} & f_{TL} \\ f_{LT} & f_{TT} \end{bmatrix}\begin{pmatrix} L \\ T \end{pmatrix}$$

Therefore, what we are actually looking for is the sign of a quadratic form, the matrix of which is the Hessian matrix of the production function of the firm. This Hessian matrix is negative definite at the point where the average cost of production is at a minimum. Hence, the expression in brackets at the far right-hand side of eq. (A4.21) must be negative. Accordingly,

$$T'L - L'T > 0 \tag{A4.22}$$

$$\frac{d\mu}{d(w/r)} > 0 \tag{A4.23}$$

This means that $\mu \equiv T/L$ is a strictly increasing function of $w/r$. That is, as labor becomes relatively cheaper (i.e., as $w/r$ falls), each firm will be using relatively more labor per unit of land (i.e., each firm will be using a smaller $\mu \equiv T/L$) at the new minimum average-cost point as compared with the old. This being the case, it must be obvious that, given $\mu$, there is only one factor-price ratio $w/r$ consistent with perfectly competitive conditions. That is, given $\mu$, only one expansion path will give rise to a minimum average-cost point at that value of $\mu$. Hence, any ray through the origin will intersect the "optimality locus" of fig. 4.5 only once. This completes the proof of the proposition that there exists a one-to-one correspondence between $\mu$ and $w/r$.

## (b) POINTS AND VECTORS

This part of the appendix discusses briefly the concepts of points and vectors and some of their properties. Comments are restricted to points and vectors in the plane (i.e., the two-dimensional space).

A point in the plane, such as point $P_0$ in fig. A4.1, can be denoted either by the letter $P_0$ or in the coordinate form $P_0 = (x_0, y_0)$. Since a point in the plane is associated with an ordered pair $(x, y)$ of real numbers, the geometric term *plane* can be interpreted as the set of all ordered pairs $(x, y)$ of real numbers.

The operation of addition of real numbers can be generalized to provide a way to add points. If

$$P_0 = (x_0, y_0)$$
$$P_1 = (x_1, y_1)$$

we define their sum to be the point

$$P_2 = P_0 + P_1 = (x_0 + x_1, y_0 + y_1) = (x_2, y_2)$$

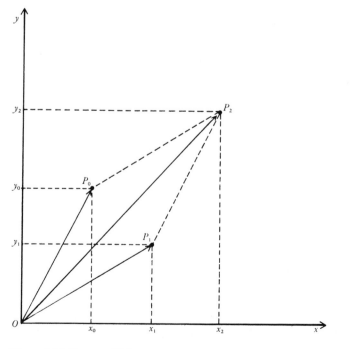

**Figure A4.1** Vector addition.

R( Pete) Parcells

where, of course, $x_2 = x_0 + x_1$ and $y_2 = y_0 + y_1$, as shown in fig. A4.1. Further, the product of a point $P = (x, y)$ by a real number $\lambda$ is given by the new point $\lambda P = (\lambda x, \lambda y)$.

At the most elementary level in physics, a vector is defined as a quantity which has both magnitude and direction. Vectors are often represented geometrically by a line with an arrowhead on the end of it. The length of the line indicates the magnitude of the vector, and the arrow denotes its direction. Some vectors lying in a plane are shown in fig. A4.1. In general, a vector may originate at any point in space and terminate at any point. However, it is convenient to have a vector start at the origin of the coordinate system rather than at some other point in space. Once this convention is adopted, a vector becomes perfectly determined when the terminal point of the vector is specified. Thus, there is a one-to-one correspondence between all points in the plane and all vectors which emanate from the origin. This is illustrated in fig. A4.1; points $P_0$, $P_1$, and $P_2$ correspond to the synonymous vectors, and vice versa.

The algebraic operations of addition of points and multiplication of points by real numbers have simple geometric interpretations in the plane (and in space). Here, we speak of addition of vectors and multiplication of vectors by *scalars*. The addition of points defined earlier corresponds exactly to the parallelogram rule for adding geometric vectors as illustrated in fig. A4.1. Similarly, multiplication of points by real numbers corresponds to expansion or contraction of the associated vector by the appropriate factor, with negative numbers effecting reversal.

An important geometric concept is the straight line determined by two distinct points, such as points $P_1$ and $P_2$ in fig. A4.1. As we saw earlier, $P_0 + P_1 = P_2$, or $P_0 = P_2 - P_1$. Looking at fig. A4.1, we see that every point $(P)$ on the straight-line segment $P_1 P_2$ can be obtained by adding to the point $P_1$ some positive fraction of the vector (point) $P_0 = P_2 - P_1$. Thus,

$$P = P_1 + \lambda P_0 = P_1 + \lambda(P_2 - P_1) = (1 - \lambda)P_1 + \lambda P_2 \qquad (A4.24)$$

where $0 \leq \lambda \leq 1$. When $\lambda = 0$, $P$ coincides with $P_1$; and when $\lambda = 1$, $P$ coincides with $P_2$. Further, as $\lambda$ increases continuously from 0 to 1, $P$ slides along the straight-line segment $P_1 P_2$, moving from $P_1$ to $P_2$. In particular, when $\lambda = \frac{1}{2}$, $P$ lies halfway between $P_1$ and $P_2$. More generally, the distance from $P_1$ to $P$ is given by $\lambda$ times the distance from $P_1$ to $P_2$. This follows directly from eq. (A4.24), which can be rewritten as $P - P_1 = \lambda(P_2 - P_1)$.

Consider fig. A4.2. It is a box diagram similar to that of fig. 4.6. (No isoquants have been drawn, because they are not needed for our purposes.) The sides of the box are given by the total amounts of labor and land $(L_0, T_0)$ available to an economy. The coordinates of any point $P$ in the box with respect to $O_x$ show the quantities of labor and land allocated to the production of $X$ (that is, $L_x, T_x$). The coordinates of the same point $P$ with respect to $O_y$ show the quantities of labor and land allocated to the production of $Y$ (that is, $L_y, T_y$). Since there are two origins, $O_x$ and $O_y$, and there might be confusion as to which origin is the relevant one, write $P$ with a superscript $x$ or $y$ to distinguish between the two. Thus, $P^x$ refers to point $P$ with its coordinates measured with respect to $O_x$, while $P^y$ refers

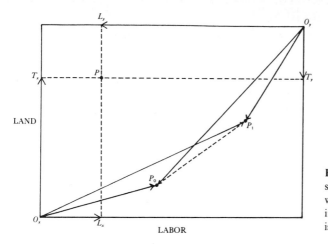

**Figure A4.2** Each point along the straight-line segment $P_0P_1$ is a weighted average of $P_0$ and $P_1$, irrespective of whether $O_x$ or $O_y$ is used as origin.

to point $P$ with its coordinates measured with respect to $O_y$. Accordingly, $P^x = (L_x, T_x)$, and $P^y = (L_y, T_y)$. Note that the sum of the points $P^x$ and $P^y$ is given by

$$P^x + P^y = (L_x + L_y, T_x + T_y) = (L_0, T_0) \tag{A4.25}$$

Consider now points $P_0$ and $P_1$. Looking at them from the point of view of $O_x$, we can express every point $(P^x)$ along the broken straight-line segment $P_0P_1$ as

$$P^x = (1 - \lambda)P_0^x + \lambda P_1^x \tag{A4.26}$$

where $0 \leq \lambda \leq 1$.

On the other hand, looking at $P_0$, $P_1$ from the point of view of $O_y$, we can express every point $(P^y)$ along the broken straight-line segment $P_0P_1$ as

$$P^y = (1 - \lambda)P_0^y + \lambda P_1^y \tag{A4.27}$$

where $0 \leq \lambda \leq 1$.

**Theorem A4.1** For any given value of $\lambda$ in the interval $[0, 1]$, the points $P^x$ and $P^y$ in eqs. (A4.26) and (A4.27) are identical.

PROOF Because of eq. (A4.25), it is only necessary to show that the sum $P^x + P^y$ equals $(L_0, T_0)$. Thus, substituting directly from eqs. (A4.26) and (A4.27) and making use of eq. (A4.25) we get

$$P^x + P^y = (1 - \lambda)P_0^x + \lambda P_1^x + (1 - \lambda)P_0^y + \lambda P_1^y$$

$$= (1 - \lambda)(P_0^x + P_0^y) + \lambda(P_1^x + P_1^y)$$

$$= (L_0, T_0)$$

This completes the proof.

## SELECTED BIBLIOGRAPHY

Bowley, A. L. (1924). *Mathematical Groundwork of Economics*. Clarendon Press, Oxford, chap. 1.

Chang, W. W., and W. Mayer (1973). "Intermediate Goods in a General Equilibrium Trade Model." *International Economic Review*, vol. 14, no. 2 (June), pp. 447–459, June, 1973.

Edgeworth, F. Y. (1881). *Mathematical Psychics*. C. Kegan Paul and Company, London.

Guisinger, S. E. (1969). "Negative Value Added and the Theory of Effective Protection." *Quarterly Journal of Economics*, vol. 83(3), pp. 415–433.

Haberler, G. (1936). *The Theory of International Trade*. W. Hodge and Company, London, chap. 12.

Lerner, A. P. (1932). "The Diagrammatical Representation of Cost Conditions in International Trade." *Economica*, vol. 12, pp. 346–356. Reprinted in A. P. Lerner, *Essays in Economic Analysis*. Macmillan and Company, London, 1953.

Samuelson, P. A. (1947). *Foundations of Economic Analysis*. Harvard University Press, Cambridge, Mass.

Savosnik, K. M. (1958). "The Box Diagram and the Production Possibility Curve." *Ekonomisk Tidskrift*, vol. 60, pp. 183–197.

Taussig, F. W. (1927). *International Trade*. The Macmillan Company, New York.

Vanek, J. (1963). "Variable Factor Proportions and Interindustry Flows in the Theory of International Trade." *Quarterly Journal of Economics*, vol. 80 (November), pp. 129–142.

Viner, J. (1937). *Studies in the Theory of International Trade*. Harper and Brothers, New York, chaps. 7 and 9.

Warne, R. D. (1971). "Intermediate Goods in International Trade with Variable Proportions and Two Primary Inputs." *Quarterly Journal of Economics*, vol. 85 (May), pp. 225–236.

(Additional references may be found at the end of chap. 5.)

# CHAPTER FIVE

# COMMUNITY INDIFFERENCE AND COMPARATIVE ADVANTAGE

This chapter is divided into two parts. The first part discusses the fundamental concept of social indifference. The second part discusses the problems of how to portray general equilibrium (*a*) in a closed economy, and (*b*) in a simple open economy which is a price taker in the international market; in addition, it provides a neoclassical demonstration of comparative advantage.

## PART A. COMMUNITY INDIFFERENCE

In addition to the concept of opportunity cost studied in chap. 4, the neoclassical theory of international trade is also based on the fundamental concept of social indifference. In other words, the neoclassical theory of international trade assumes the existence of a logically acceptable social indifference map, i.e., an indifference map qualitatively similar to the well-known indifference map of an individual consumer that portrays the tastes of the society at large. Several questions arise. First, what meaning should be attached to a social indifference curve? Further, do social indifference maps having the same properties as the indifference map of an individual consumer exist? If they do, how can they be derived? This section is concerned mainly with these questions. It should be noted that the main justification for the continued use of social indifference curves is, besides their simplicity, the fact that they give rise to results which are qualitatively similar to those derived more laboriously by the use of a totally disaggregated model.

## 5.1 DEFINITION AND DIFFICULTIES

An individual consumer's indifference curve shows all the alternative combinations of two commodities ($X$ and $Y$) which are capable of providing the consumer with the same amount of utility. The consumer is thus indifferent to the alternatives. One might be inclined to apply this definition to a social indifference curve. But in what sense does social welfare remain constant along a social indifference curve? Since interpersonal comparisons of consumer welfare levels are impossible, this seems to be a rather difficult question.

### The Scitovsky Social Indifference Curves

Tibor Scitovsky (1942) defines an indifference curve as the locus of all those minimal combinations of $X$ and $Y$ that are capable of putting each and every consumer in the society on arbitrarily prescribed levels of well-being. That is, given the indifference maps of all consumers, an indifference curve is arbitrarily selected from every map. What minimal combinations of $X$ and $Y$ are needed to put every consumer on his arbitrarily selected indifference curve? Note that, since every consumer remains by assumption on the same indifference curve, the society may be said to be indifferent between one or another combination on the social indifference curve (SIC).

Scitovsky's definition is illustrated in fig. 5.1. Assume two consumers, $A$ and $B$. Given their indifference maps, select arbitrarily an indifference curve from each map, as shown in fig. 5.1 by the indifference curves $I'_A I''_A$ and $I'_B I''_B$, where the subscripts indicate the individuals. Note that $A$'s indifference map is drawn with respect to the $O_A$ origin and $B$'s with respect to $O_B$. That is, $B$'s indifference map has actually been rotated by $180°$ and placed in such a way that the two arbitrarily selected indifference curves, $I'_A I''_A$ and $I'_B I''_B$, are tangent to each other at point $K$.

What are the minimal combinations of $X$ and $Y$ (measuring them with respect to the origin $O_A$) which are capable of putting consumer $A$ on indifference curve $I'_A I''_A$ and $B$ on $I'_B I''_B$? One such combination is already known: the origin $O_B$ itself. To determine all such combinations, and thus the social indifference curve, simply slide $B$'s indifference curve, $I'_B I''_B$, along $A$'s indifference curve so that they are always tangent to each other, and let the origin $O_B$ trace out the curve $SIC_K$. The latter is the social indifference curve we have been looking for. The slope of the $SIC_K$ curve at a particular point is necessarily equal to the slope of the corresponding point of the indifference curves $I'_A I''_A$ and $I'_B I''_B$ at which they are tangent to each other. (For a proof of this statement, i.e., that the slope of a Scitovsky social indifference curve at a certain point is equal to the corresponding slope of the corresponding indifferences curves of $A$ and $B$, see the appendix to this chapter.) For instance, the slope of $SIC_K$ at $O_B$ is equal to the common slope of $I'_A I''_A$ and $I'_B I''_B$ at $K$. The slope at $N'$, determined by the origin of $B$'s indifference map when the $I'_B I''_B$ curve is tangent to $I'_A I''_A$ at point $N$, is equal to the slope of $I'_A I''_A$ at $N$ (or the slope of $I'_B I''_B$ at $N''$).

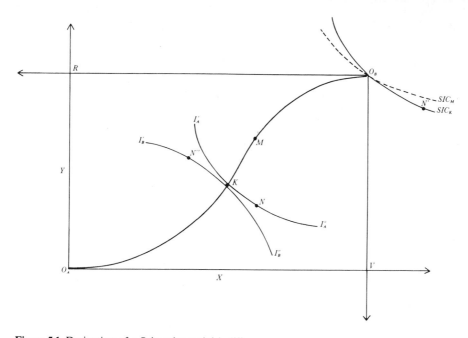

**Figure 5.1** Derivation of a Scitovsky social indifference curve.

The social indifference curve $SIC_K$ has been derived on the basis of the arbitrarily selected indifference curves $I'_A I''_A$ and $I'_B I''_B$. In order to bring out clearly the consequences of this construction, suppose for the moment that the rectangle $O_A V O_B R$ is a box diagram. Our two-man economy is endowed with the fixed quantities $O_A V$ and $O_A R$ of $X$ and $Y$, respectively. The indifference maps of $A$ and $B$ have been drawn as before, with the solid curve $O_A K O_B$ being the contract curve, i.e., the locus of tangencies between the two sets of indifference curves. It should be noted again that all points on the contract curve are Pareto-optimum points. In other words, starting from a point on the contract curve, it is impossible to improve the well-being of one consumer without making the other consumer worse off. No other points in the box have this important property. Now arbitrarily select some other point (besides $K$) on the contract curve, such as $M$. Obviously, the two indifference curves passing through point $M$ are by construction tangential to each other at $M$. Suppose now that another social indifference curve is defined in relation to the indifference curves passing through $M$. How would this new social indifference curve compare with $SIC_K$? Obviously, it will necessarily pass through point $O_B$, but, in general, it will intersect $SIC_K$ at $O_B$ instead of coinciding with it throughout. This is illustrated by the broken curve $SIC_M$, which intersects the curve $SIC_K$ at $O_B$. That the two curves will, in general, intersect each other at point $O_B$ follows from the fact that the common slope of the indifference curves at $K$ is different from the slope at $M$.

In general, there will be an infinite number of social indifference curves passing through point $O_B$, each curve being associated with a certain distribution of welfare between the two individuals (in other words, a point on the contract curve). Thus, in general, nonintersecting social indifference curves cannot be drawn. Accordingly, an infinite number of social indifference curves (usually intersecting one another) pass through any point of the positive quadrant. This makes it impossible to assign a single social utility index to any given combination of $X$ and $Y$ available to the society. In addition, we cannot predict the social marginal rate of substitution of $X$ for $Y$ by knowing the aggregate of the two commodities available to the society. We have no way of knowing which social indifference curve (out of the infinite number of social indifference curves passing through the chosen point in the commodity space) will eventually be the relevant one.

## The Utility Frontier

Social welfare does not depend only on the total quantities of $X$ and $Y$ available to the society. It also depends on their distribution among the various members of the society. To put it differently, it depends on the distribution of income. Figure 5.2 shows the so-called (unique) utility frontier of the society, which is derived on the basis of the information given in fig. 5.1. Consumer $A$'s total utility $(U_A)$ is measured along the horizontal axis and $B$'s $(U_B)$ is measured along the vertical axis. Each point on the utility frontier (fig. 5.2) corresponds to a point on the contract curve (fig. 5.1). The utility frontier necessarily slopes downward because, as we move along the contract curve, one consumer becomes better off and the other worse off. In other words, when the economy is on the contract curve (and

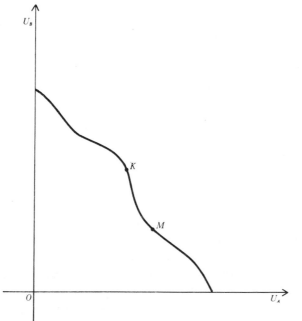

**Figure 5.2** The utility frontier.

thus on the utility frontier), it is impossible to make one consumer better off without making the other consumer worse off. Thus, every point on the contract curve or the utility frontier is Pareto-optimal. Points $K$ and $M$ on the utility frontier (fig. 5.2) correspond to the synonymous points on the contract curve (fig. 5.1).

Every point on the utility frontier necessarily corresponds to a certain level of social welfare, although we have no way of knowing what that level is at the moment. But a point on the utility frontier corresponds not to a single combination of $X$ and $Y$ available to the society but to an infinite number of combinations of $X$ and $Y$ that lie on a Scitovsky social indifference curve as previously derived. Each combination of $X$ and $Y$ (that is, each point in the commodity space, such as point $O_B$ in fig. 5.1) corresponds to an infinite number of points in the utility space, i.e., the whole utility frontier. Thus, the points $K$ and $M$ (and all other points on the utility frontier) of fig. 5.2 correspond to the single point $O_B$ in fig. 5.1. A different combination of $X$ and $Y$ in the commodity space gives rise to a new utility frontier which might or might not intersect the original utility frontier.

## 5.2 JUSTIFICATION OF SOCIAL INDIFFERENCE CURVES IN SOME SPECIAL CASES

The analysis of the preceding section shows convincingly that, in general, social indifference curves with the desired properties do not exist. However, there are several cases in the literature where the use of social indifference curves can be justified. The purpose of this section is to review these cases.

### Two Types of Social Indifference Curve

Before proceeding with the discussion of these cases, let us distinguish between two concepts of social indifference curves. Social indifference curves can be drawn (*a*) to describe *positive behavior* irrespective of the level of social welfare attached to each social indifference curve, or (*b*) to represent *social welfare*. In addition, welfare statements can be made if either (1) we have an optimizing income-redistribution policy or (2) we talk about potential welfare as opposed to actual welfare.

Note that, when an optimizing income-redistribution policy is pursued, the social indifference map can be used to describe both the consumption behavior of the economy and changes in social welfare. But in the absence of an optimizing income-redistribution policy, the social indifference map need not indicate changes in social welfare. Thus, a movement from a lower to a higher social indifference curve need not imply an increase in social welfare; it may very well imply a decrease if the income distribution becomes worse. Under these circumstances, we can only talk about potential welfare. For instance, as is shown in chap. 16, although we cannot be sure that free trade improves actual welfare, we can prove that free trade could potentially make everybody better off; i.e., free trade improves potential welfare.

## A Robinson Crusoe Economy

The simplest and at the same time most trivial case is where the economy is composed of a single individual (i.e., a Robinson Crusoe economy). Here the problem of aggregation of indifference maps does not arise because there exists only one indifference map, which is also the social indifference map. Nevertheless, this case cannot be taken seriously.

## A Totalitarian State

In a totalitarian state (or even when a planning bureau exists), the indifference map of a dictator (or of the planning bureau) becomes the social indifference map. Here, as in the preceding case, the problem of aggregation does not arise.

## Identical Tastes and Factor Endowments

An apparently more realistic case is a country inhabited with individuals having identical tastes and factor endowments. Thus, these individuals must be equally endowed capitalists (or land owners) and also equally productive workers. The identity of tastes is not unrealistic, particularly within one nation and culture. However, the identity of factor endowments is most certainly violated in the real world. This case corresponds to Pigou's (1932) concept of the *representative citizen*.

The box-diagram technique used in the preceding section can be used in the present case to yield a single nonintersecting social indifference map. Thus, considering again two individuals, $A$ and $B$, endowed with $X_0$ and $Y_0$ units of commodities $X$ and $Y$, respectively, study the box diagram in fig. 5.3. The contract curve must necessarily pass through point $K$ (on the diagonal) which lies halfway between points $O_A$ and $O_B$. This must be so because of the assumed identity of tastes. Thus, at $K$ both consumers consume the same bundle of commodities, and therefore their marginal rates of substitution must be identical. Now, since both consumers have the same income, the consumption of quantities $X_0$ and $Y_0$ necessarily implies that $K$ is the equilibrium point on the contract curve. The Scitovsky social indifference curve $\text{SIC}_K$ has been derived as before on the basis of the indifference curves passing through $K$. On the assumption of the identity of incomes, this is a unique curve. Observe that any point on $\text{SIC}_K$, such as $S$, implies that both consumers are consuming exactly the same bundles of commodities, as shown by points $S_A$ and $S_B$. Point $S_A$ is the midpoint of the straight-line segment joining points $O_A$ and $S$; point $S_B$ is the point whose distance from $O_B$ is equal to $O_A S_A$. That this is so follows from the fact that the slopes at $S_A$ and $S_B$ must be equal; because tastes are assumed identical, this occurs only when both consumers consume exactly the same bundles of commodities.

What this analysis shows is that, in the present case of identical tastes and endowments (or incomes), a social indifference curve can be constructed as follows. Draw a ray through the origin intersecting a common (to all consumers)

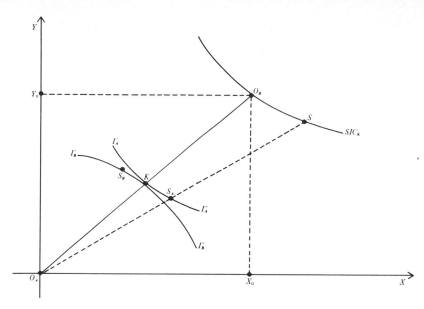

**Figure 5.3** Construction of social indifference curves when tastes and factor endowments are identical between individuals.

indifference curve at a point, such as $K$. Then, in the case of two consumers, determine the point on the ray whose distance from the origin is twice as long as that of $K$. For instance, $O_A O_B = 2(O_A K)$ and $O_A S = 2(O_A S_A)$. When the number of consumers is not two but $n$, the point on the social indifference curve is that point on the ray which lies $n$ times the distance $O_A K$ from the origin. Repeating the same experiment for all points on the chosen indifference curve, we can construct the whole social indifference curve that corresponds to it.

Note that in this case we have been able to select only one Scitovsky social indifference curve passing through a point in the commodity space, because of the assumed identity of incomes and tastes. If these assumptions are dropped, then according to the analysis of the preceding section, there does not exist a noninter-secting social indifference map.†

It should be obvious that a social indifference curve corresponds to a single curve of the common indifference map of all consumers. Repeating, therefore, the same experiment for all such common indifference curves, we can construct the whole social indifference map.

A fundamental property of this social indifference map is that a movement from a lower to a higher indifference curve implies that the economy as a whole becomes better off because the welfare of each and every consumer goes up; i.e.,

---

† Eisenberg (1961) has shown that a nonintersecting social indifference map also exists in the case where all individuals have the same proportionate share in total resources and homogeneous (*but not necessarily identical*) tastes.

every consumer necessarily moves from a lower to a higher indifference curve. Thus, the present social indifference map can be used for predicting both the consumption behavior of the economy and changes in social welfare.

## Identical and Homothetic Tastes

Another case in which the use of a social indifference map is justified is when all individuals have identical tastes which are, in addition, *homothetic* in the sense that all income-consumption curves are straight lines through the origin. In this case, the contract curve in the box diagram coincides with the diagonal which intersects all indifference curves at points with the same slope. This case also yields a single nonintersecting social indifference map which is actually identical with any of the individual indifference maps. The technique of the preceding section can be used to show that, whatever point on the contract curve is chosen, the same social indifference curve will be derived.

Although this social indifference map is capable of describing the *consumption behavior* of the economy, it cannot be used to discuss changes in social welfare. This follows from the fact that *the present social indifference map is independent of the distribution of income*, on which it gives absolutely no information. Put differently, through any point in commodity space there pass an infinite number of social indifference curves which happen to be identical. Each social indifference curve, however, corresponds to a different distribution of income and thus social welfare. Even though this social indifference map can be used to predict the marginal rate of substitution in consumption when only the aggregates of $X$ and $Y$ are given, there is no way of knowing what the distribution of income is and how it changes as we move from a lower to a higher social indifference curve. As a result, there is no way of knowing (by looking at the aggregates of $X$ and $Y$) whether social welfare improves as the society moves from a lower to a higher indifference curve.

## Samuelson's Social Indifference Curves

Samuelson (1956) has shown that, if a social welfare functions exists and if income is always reallocated among individuals in such a way as to maximize social welfare, it is possible to derive a social indifference map with all the usual properties of an individual consumer's indifference map.

A social welfare function is a function of the form $W = f(U_1, U_2, \ldots, U_n)$, where $W \equiv$ social welfare and $U_i \equiv$ utility enjoyed by the $i$th individual. For the case of a society consisting of two individuals, the social welfare function can be represented graphically by a family of contour lines in the utility space $(U_A, U_B)$. Welfare maximization can be determined by superimposing these contour lines on the utility frontier (fig. 5.2) and finding the point where the utility frontier touches the highest welfare contour line.

A Samuelson social indifference curve gives all alternative combinations of commodities $X$ and $Y$ which, if distributed optimally among the members of the society, produce the same amount of welfare. We wish to show that Samuelson's social indifference curves have the following properties:

1. They do not intersect each other (i.e., only one Samuelson social indifference curve passes through each point in the commodity space).
2. They slope downward.
3. They are convex to the origin.
4. A movement from a lower to a higher indifference curve implies an increase in social welfare.

Consider fig. 5.4. Panel ($a$) gives a welfare contour line $WW'$ associated with a given level of welfare $W_0$. (Because the utility indicators $U_A$ and $U_B$ are arbitrary, the welfare contour line $WW'$ can be made to assume any curvature.) To derive Samuelson's social indifference curve for $W = W_0$, determine all alternative combinations of $X$ and $Y$ in panel ($b$) which generate utility frontiers just touching the given welfare contour line $WW'$. Suppose that $S$ is such a combination. The utility curve $S'S''$ in panel ($a$), which is tangent to the welfare contour line $WW'$ at $V$, corresponds to point $S$ in panel ($b$). From this we can immediately conclude that point $S$ is always associated with the *unique* level of welfare $W_0$, and therefore only one Samuelson social indifference curve can pass through $S$. This proves the first property ("Samuelson's social indifference curves do not intersect").

Turn now to the second property ("Samuelson's social indifference curves slope downward"). Clearly any point in region I (i.e., the rectangle $ONSM$ including the boundaries) cannot generate the same social welfare as point $S$ (panel ($b$)). The utility frontiers associated with these points necessarily lie inside the utility frontier $S'S''$ (panel ($a$)). On the other hand, it must also be clear that any point in region II generates higher welfare than $S$. Accordingly, only points in regions III and IV can produce the same welfare as $S$. This is sufficient to conclude that the slope of the Samuelson social indifference curve at $S$ is negative since it must pass from region III to region IV. This also proves the fourth property ("a movement from a lower to a higher Samuelson social indifference curve implies an increase in social welfare").

As it turns out, we can restrict the Samuelson social indifference curve through $S$ even more. Consider the downward-sloping Scitovsky social indifference curve through $S$ (panel ($b$)). By definition, any point on this curve generates a utility frontier (panel ($a$)) which passes through $V$. In general, all other points, besides $S$, on Scitovsky's social indifference curve generate utility frontiers which actually intersect the welfare contour line $WW'$ at $V$. In any case, the Scitovsky social indifference curve is an upper limit for the Samuelson social indifference curve through $S$. We therefore conclude that the Samuelson social indifference curve through $S$ must lie in the two shaded areas below the Scitovsky curve.

Consider finally the third property ("Samuelson's social indifference curves are convex to the origin"). To prove convexity, Samuelson assumes that the social-welfare function satisfies the following convexity property: as equal amounts of a good are taken away from one individual, increasing amounts must

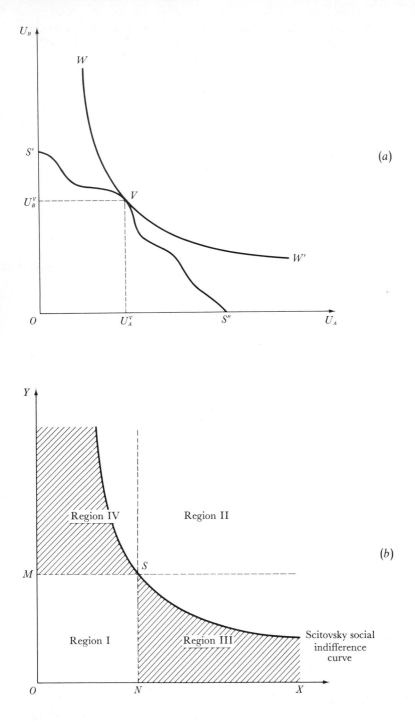

**Figure 5.4** (*a*) Maximization of social welfare. (*b*) The Samuelson social indifference curve through *S* must lie in the shaded areas.

be given to another if social welfare is to remain constant. This, of course, implies a diminishing social marginal rate of substitution of consumption by one individual for consumption by another. As Samuelson (1956, p. 17) points out, this assumption "is stronger than realism can justify." Once made, though, the convexity of Samuelson's social indifference curves is immediate.

Consider two specific commodity distributions between individuals A and B as follows: $D_1 = D_1(X_A^1, Y_A^1; X_B^1, Y_B^1)$ and $D_2 = D_2(X_A^2, Y_A^2; X_B^2, Y_B^2)$. Assume that these commodity distributions are associated with two points on a Samuelson social indifference curve: $P_1 = P_1(X_A^1 + X_B^1, Y_A^1 + Y_B^1)$ and $P_2 = P_2(X_A^2 + X_B^2, Y_A^2 + Y_B^2)$, respectively. Because of the assumed convexity of the social-welfare function, any weighted average of $D_1$ and $D_2$, say $D_w$, must generate a maximum social welfare which is at least as high as that attained by either $D_1$ or $D_2$. Further, the commodity distributions $D_w = \lambda D_1 + (1 - \lambda)D_2$, for any $0 \le \lambda \le 1$, necessarily give rise to points $P_w = \lambda P_1 + (1 - \lambda)P_2$ which lie on the straight line joining points $P_1$ and $P_2$. Accordingly, the Samuelson social indifference curve must lie below the straight-line $P_1 P_2$, that is, it must be convex to the origin.

## Each Individual as a Separate Country?

Samuelson (1956) suggests that the problem of aggregation can be bypassed by treating each individual within a country as a separate country. If factor endowments are the same among individuals, or proportional to aggregate endowments, the production-possibilities frontier of each country can be scaled down in proportion to the relative factor endowments of each individual. In this case, we can follow Samuelson's suggestion and treat each individual as a separate country. In the case of the classical theory where there is a single factor of production, this suggestion can indeed be carried through because the condition of proportionality in factor endowments is indeed satisfied. However, with dissimilar factor endowments, the income distribution changes continuously as the economy moves along the production-possibilities frontier, and the simple idea of scaling down the production-possibilities frontier becomes exceedingly complex—though not impossible.

## Johnson's Approach

The cases considered so far refer to total aggregation of individual indifference maps. Harry G. Johnson (1959) offers what appears to be a more fruitful approach to this problem, which is actually a compromise between total disaggregation, on the one hand, and total aggregation, on the other. In particular, Johnson considers the two factors of production (which he calls *labor* and *capital*) as separate consuming groups, with each group behaving as a single rational individual. Since the income distribution is perfectly fixed at any point on the production-possibilities frontier (although it usually varies when we move from one point to another), the aggregate quantities consumed are thus perfectly determined for any given commodity price ratio.

## PART B. GENERAL EQUILIBRIUM AND COMPARATIVE ADVANTAGE

Assuming that the concept of a social indifference map can be made logically acceptable, the problems arise of how to portray general equilibrium (*a*) in a closed economy, (*b*) in a simple open economy which is a price taker in the international market, and (*c*) in a two-country, two-commodity model. The first two problems will be considered rigorously and the third problem only tentatively. Chapter 6 considers the question of international equilibrium in detail.

## 5.3 GENERAL EQUILIBRIUM IN A CLOSED ECONOMY

Despite all the limitations and shortcomings of the social indifference map, let us employ it as a tool of analysis. The only justification for its use, as mentioned earlier, is the great simplification that it makes possible with regard to the problem of general equilibrium; in addition, the conclusions so derived are similar to those derived by more rigorous and laborious ways.

Figure 5.5 portrays the general equilibrium of a closed economy. Curve *RS* is the production-possibilities frontier of the economy. It is a curve concave† to the origin and exhibits increasing opportunity costs. As explained in the previous chapter, such a production-possibilities frontier is derived under the assumptions of fixed endowments of labor and land and constant returns to scale. In addition, superimposed on the same diagram are three illustrative social indifference curves. General equilibrium occurs at point *E*, where the production-possibilities frontier is tangent to the highest possible social indifference curve (that is, $\text{SIC}_2$). Therefore, the economy will produce and consume $X_E$ units of commodity $X$ and $Y_E$ units of $Y$. The common absolute slope of the production-possibilities frontier and the $\text{SIC}_2$ at point *E* gives the equilibrium price ratio $p_X/p_Y$, or $p$ for short. *Therefore, in general equilibrium, p is equal both to the marginal rate of transformation, or the opportunity cost of X in terms of Y* (that is, the absolute slope of the production-possibilities frontier at the equilibrium point), *and to the marginal rate of substitution in consumption of X for Y.*

It is usually said that the economy maximizes social welfare at point *E*. As the analysis of part *A* of the present chapter reveals, this may be legitimate under certain conditions. However, this statement is not generally true. For this reason, let us refrain from passing a judgement on social welfare by means of the tenuous

---

† The description of the curve *RS* of fig. 5.5 as a concave curve may give rise to some confusion. Some would like to say that the set of points lying within the production-possibilities block *OSER* is convex in the sense that any straight line joining two points of the set lies totally within the set. There is nothing wrong with either characterization, but confusion can occur.

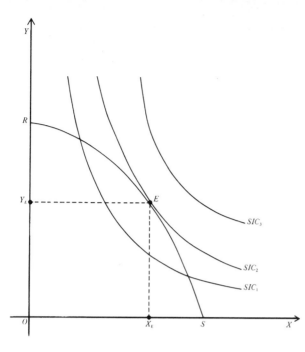

**Figure 5.5** General equilibrium in a closed economy.

concept of the social indifference map. For the moment, let us use the social indifference map for predicting the demand behavior of the economy alone. The question of the effects of trade on welfare is taken up later in chaps. 15 and 16.

In the classical theory, the production-possibilities frontier is a straight line and the (pretrade) equilibrium price ratio can be predicted from the production data (i.e., the labor coefficients) alone without any knowledge about demand—assuming, of course, that both commodities are produced and consumed in equilibrium. Under the more general assumptions of the neoclassical theory, however, increasing opportunity costs are the rule (and constant costs the exception). Therefore, we can no longer predict the (pretrade) equilibrium price ratio without full information about demand, which now becomes as important as supply. In the presence of increasing opportunity costs, the most that can be accomplished without full information about demand (assuming only that both commodities are consumed in equilibrium) is finding the limits within which the pretrade equilibrium price ratio must lie. These limits are, of course, given by the slope of the production-possibilities frontier at the intercepts (i.e., points $R$ and $S$ in fig. 5.5).

## 5.4 EQUILIBRIUM IN A SIMPLE OPEN ECONOMY

The preceding analysis can easily be extended to a simple open economy which is too small relative to the rest of the world to have any appreciable influence on the formation of international prices. Therefore, assume now that our economy can buy and sell unlimited quantities of $X$ and $Y$ at given international prices, $p_X^*$ and $p_Y^*$. Actually, we are only interested in relative prices, that is $p_X^*/p_Y^*$, or simply $p^*$. The problem is to show how equilibrium is reached when trade with the rest of the world is possible.

As in the case of the classical theory, our economy will reach general equilibrium in the following two steps:

1. Given $p^*$, the economy will choose to produce at that particular point on the production-possibilities frontier where national income (expressed in either $X$ or $Y$) is at a maximum. Mathematically, this problem can be stated as follows: maximize $Q = p^*X + Y$ subject to the constraint $F(X, Y) = 0$, where $Q$ is national income expressed in $Y$ and the function $F(X, Y) = 0$ is the algebraic expression for the production-possibilities frontier.
2. Having chosen the production point, the economy will then have to decide what to consume.

## Optimization of Production

The determination of the optimum production point is illustrated in fig. 5.6. The curve $RS$ is the familiar production-possibilities frontier of the economy. The family of parallel straight lines with slope equal to $p^*$ is the geometric representation of the function

$$Q = p^*X + Y \qquad (5.1)$$

It is a family of contour lines, with each line being the locus of all those combinations of $X$ and $Y$ which have the same value in the international market. The object of the economy is to maximize national income $Q$. In this effort, it is constrained by the production-possibilities frontier. (Remember that the economy can produce at any point that lies inside or on the production-possibilities frontier, but not beyond it.)

From fig. 5.6, it should be obvious that national income is maximized when the economy produces at point $E$, that is, at the point where the production-possibilities frontier becomes tangent to the highest income contour line, $Q_3$. Production at a point other than $E$ either is impossible (such as $Z$) or gives rise to a national income smaller than $Q_3$ (such as $K$). Accordingly, the economy cannot reach a higher income contour line than $Q_3$ because of the constraint imposed by the production-possibilities frontier. With technological progress, labor growth, and capital accumulation, the production-possibilities frontier will, of course, shift outward and enable the economy to reach a higher income contour line. However, with given technology and factor endowments, giving rise to the production-possibilities frontier $RS$ (fig. 5.6), the maximum income that the economy can possibly reach is $Q_3$.

Following the terminology introduced in chap. 3, let us call the highest income contour line, $Q_3$, the *consumption-possibilities frontier*. In other words, the economy, by producing at point $E$, can consume at any point on the consumption-

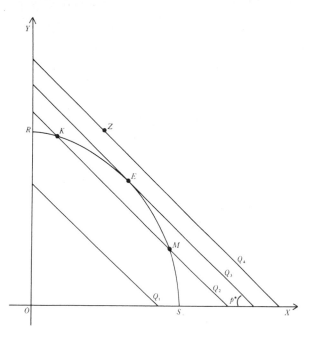

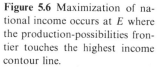

Figure 5.6 Maximization of national income occurs at $E$ where the production-possibilities frontier touches the highest income contour line.

possibilities frontier, i.e., the income contour line $Q_3$, because of the possibility of international trade. Therefore, as the classical theory demonstrates, international trade makes it possible for an economy to consume beyond its production-possibilities frontier despite the fact that it can never produce beyond the boundaries of the production-possibilities frontier. To use Haberler's metaphor, the building (i.e., the possibility of consuming beyond the production-possibilities frontier) remains after the scaffolding (i.e., the labor theory of value) is removed.

Observe that the income contour line $Q_3$ lies totally outside the production-possibilities frontier $RS$, except at the singular point $E$. Therefore, neglecting the singular point $E$, we can say immediately that free trade increases potential welfare, for it is possible, with an appropriate distribution of income after trade, to make everybody better off relative to the pretrade position. This question is discussed in detail in chap. 16.

The preceding discussion shows that national income is maximized if the economy produces at point $E$. But how do we know that the economy will actually produce at $E$? This is a legitimate question, because in a perfectly competitive economy there is no "planning board" to make this important decision. Nevertheless, this important function is performed by the forces of competition. Since our economy is a price taker in the world market and transportation costs are assumed zero, domestic prices will necessarily coincide with international prices. Point $E$ is the only point on the production-possibilities frontier where domestic and international prices are equal. In addition, observe that at any other point on the production-possibilities frontier, the value of output produced at world prices could increase by merely changing the production pattern. Therefore, Adam Smith's invisible hand will sooner or later guide the economy to produce at point $E$.

In summary, the economy will produce at that point on the production-possibilities frontier whose absolute slope is equal to the international price ratio $p^*$. The tangent to the production-possibilities frontier at the production point so selected becomes the consumption-possibilities frontier of the economy.

## Optimization of Consumption

Once the consumption-possibilities frontier is determined, the next step is to find out where the economy should consume. Figure 5.7 shows how this part of the problem can be handled. The curves $RPS$ and $KPV$ are the production-possibilities and consumption-possibilities frontiers, respectively. In addition, on the same diagram are three illustrative social indifference curves. Consumption equilibrium occurs at point $C$, where the consumption-possibilities frontier touches the highest possible social indifference curve. Therefore, the economy produces at $P$ and consumes at $C$; that is, it produces $X_P$ and $Y_P$ units of $X$ and $Y$, respectively, and consumes $X_C$ and $Y_C$ units of $X$ and $Y$, respectively. Accordingly, the economy must be exporting $DP$ units of $Y$ while importing $DC$ units of $X$.

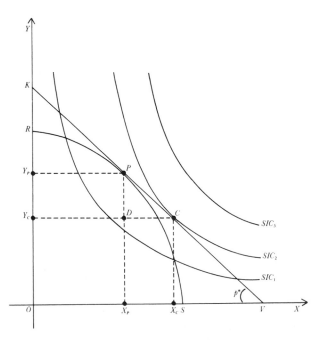

**Figure 5.7** Optimization of consumption occurs at $C$ where the consumption-possibilities frontier $KV$ touches the highest possible social indifference curve.

Finally, note that the value of $DC$ units of $X$ is equal to the value of $DP$ units of $Y$. Geometrically, this follows from the fact that the ratio $DP/DC$ gives the absolute slope of the consumption-possibilities frontier that is equal to the international price ratio $p^*$. Thus, $DP/DC = p^*$, or $DP = p^*(DC)$. That is, the value of exports is equal to the value of imports. From an economic point of view, this equality follows from the fact that the value of output produced is equal to the value of output consumed; i.e., both the production and consumption points lie on the same income contour line. Thus,

$$p^*X_P + Y_P = p^*X_C + Y_C$$

or
$$Y_P - Y_C = p^*(X_C - X_P) \tag{5.2}$$

But $Y_P - Y_C = DP$ and $X_C - X_P = DC$. Therefore, eq. (5.2) reduces to the equation $DP = p^*(DC)$.

## The Offer Curve

The preceding analysis shows how to determine the quantities of $X$ and $Y$ that the economy would be willing to export or import, as the case may be, for a given value of the international price ratio $p$. But this is precisely the information that is required for the determination of a point on the offer curve of the economy involved. Therefore, repeating the same process for all possible values of $p$, we can determine all points on the country's offer curve; i.e., we can determine the country's offer curve.

Compared with the classical theory, the determination of the offer curve in the present case becomes much more complicated because of the existence of increasing opportunity costs. Recall that, in the classical theory where the production-possibilities frontier is linear, the production point coincides with the vertical-axis intercept of the production-possibilities frontier for all values of $p$ lower than the pretrade price ratio. Similarly, for all values of $p$ higher than the pretrade price ratio, the production point coincides with the horizontal-axis intercept of the production-possibilities frontier. As a result of this simplification, the derivation of the offer curve did not seem to be an impossible task. In the presence of increasing opportunity costs, the production point necessarily changes as $p$ changes. This makes the derivation of the offer curve much more difficult. However, thanks to Meade's ingenious technique (explained in the following chapter), the offer curve can still be derived with little effort.

## Consumption and Production Gains

Note that the preceding analysis can be used to improve our understanding of the gains from trade. For this purpose, assume that the social indifference map describes not only consumption behavior but also changes in social welfare. As noted in part A of the present chapter, this assumption is legitimate only under certain conditions. In particular, it is legitimate in all the special cases discussed in part A with only one exception—the case of identical and homothetic tastes.

Given a social indifference map describing social welfare in addition to consumption behavior, it is obvious (see fig. 5.7) that free international trade enables the economy to move from a lower to a higher social indifference curve, i.e., to increase social welfare.

The total gain from trade is usually divided into the following two components:

1. The *gain from international exchange*, or the *consumption gain*, which accrues to the economy when the same bundle of commodities that was produced under autarky is also produced under free trade.
2. The *gain from specialization*, or the *production gain*, which accrues to the economy over and above the consumption gain as a result of the shift of the production point due to the difference between the pretrade and posttrade commodity prices.

Figure 5.8 illustrates the reduction of the total gain into a consumption and a production gain. The curve $MP_1 P_0 N$ is the economy's production-possibilities frontier. Before trade, equilibrium occurs at point $P_0$, where the production-possibilities frontier touches the highest possible social indifference curve ($SIC_1$). When trade opens up, the economy produces at $P_1$ and consumes at $E_2$. The straight line that passes through $P_1$ and $E_2$ is the economy's consumption-possibilities frontier. Social welfare improves because the economy moves from a lower social indifference curve ($SIC_1$) to a higher one ($SIC_3$). To isolate the consumption

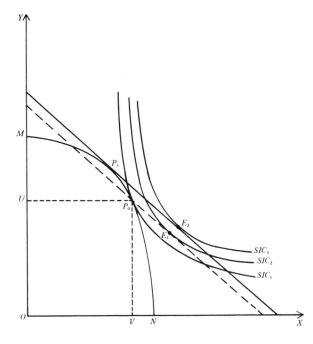

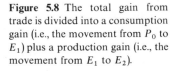

**Figure 5.8** The total gain from trade is divided into a consumption gain (i.e., the movement from $P_0$ to $E_1$) plus a production gain (i.e., the movement from $E_1$ to $E_2$).

gain, assume for the moment that with the opening up of trade, the production point is frozen at $P_0$. This could be identified as the case of perfect factor immobility between industries and factor-price flexibility, where the economy's production-possibilities frontier becomes the rectangle $OVP_0U$. Even though production is frozen at $P_0$, the economy will still benefit from trade. Its consumption point would move from $P_0$ to $E_1$. That is, the economy would move from a lower social indifference curve ($SIC_1$) to a higher one ($SIC_2$). The movement from $SIC_1$ to $SIC_2$ is the consumption gain. The production gain is represented by the movement from $E_1$ to $E_2$ as a result of the change in the production pattern (from $P_0$ to $P_1$).

## 5.5 NEOCLASSICAL DEMONSTRATION OF COMPARATIVE ADVANTAGE

### The Setting

Assume two countries, $A$ and $B$, endowed with fixed quantities of two factors of production, labor ($L$) and land ($T$), and producing two commodities, $X$ and $Y$, under constant returns to scale. Denote the pretrade equilibrium price ratios $p_X/p_Y$ in countries $A$ and $B$ by $p_A^0$ and $p_B^0$, respectively. Figure 5.9 summarizes the pretrade equilibrium positions of the two countries. Panel ($a$) illustrates $A$'s pretrade general equilibrium and panel ($b$) illustrates $B$'s. The curve $ME_AN$ ($KE_BR$) is $A$'s ($B$'s) production-possibilities frontier, while the curve $SIC_A$ ($SIC_B$) is the highest social indifference curve that $A$'s ($B$'s) production-possibilities frontier can reach. Thus, before trade, $A$ ($B$) produces and consumes at $E_A$ ($E_B$). Country $A$'s

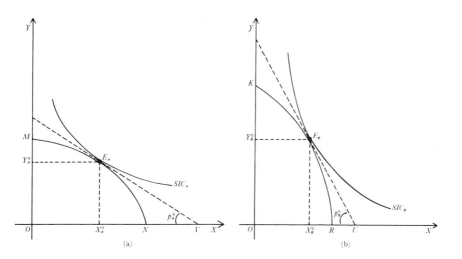

**Figure 5.9** Autarkic equilibria.

($B$'s) pretrade price ratio is given by the slope of the tangent $E_A V$ ($E_B U$). It has been assumed that $p_A^0 < p_B^0$, that is, that $X$ is relatively cheaper in $A$ and $Y$ in $B$ before trade.

## Limits of the Terms of Trade and Structure of Trade

Under the preceding assumptions, it can be said that country $A$ has a comparative advantage in the production of $X$ and $B$ in $Y$. Thus, when trade is opened up, $A$ will export commodity $X$ and import $Y$ (or $B$ will export $Y$ and import $X$). Finally, it can be shown that the equilibrium terms of trade $p_E$ will definitely lie between the pretrade price ratios of the two countries; that is,

$$p_A^0 < p_E < p_B^0 \tag{5.3}$$

The preceding statements can be proved as follows. First, show that international equilibrium is impossible when the international terms of trade take a value lower than $p_A^0$, that is, a value lower than both pretrade price ratios. Figure 5.10 shows why. It illustrates the behavior of a typical country whose pretrade price ratio is higher than the international price ratio. Thus, before trade, the country produces and consumes at $E$. However, for any international price ratio lower than the pretrade price ratio, the production point moves into the region $KE$ of the production-possibilities frontier, as illustrated by point $P$. Under these circumstances, the consumption-possibilities frontier (as illustrated by the straight line $PFCD$) necessarily intersects the social indifference curve SIC at two points, such as $F$ and $D$. Consumption equilibrium should occur somewhere in the region $FD$

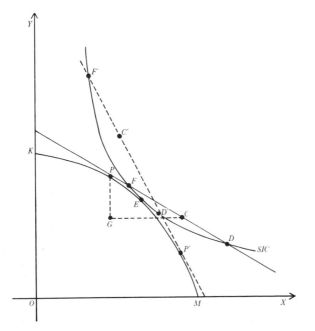

**Figure 5.10** Equilibrium in a typical country when trade is possible.

of the consumption-possibilities frontier, as shown by point $C$. Therefore, the typical country of fig. 5.10 wants to export commodity $Y$ and import $X$. When the international price ratio is smaller than both $p_A^0$ and $p_B^0$, both countries ($A$ and $B$) want to export $Y$ and import $X$. As the analysis of chap. 3 shows, international equilibrium is impossible under these circumstances.

International equilibrium is also impossible when the international price ratio is higher than $p_B^0$, that is, when it is higher than both pretrade price ratios. Under these circumstances, both countries will want to export $X$ and import $Y$, as illustrated by the broken consumption-possibilities frontier $F'C'D'P'$ of fig. 5.10, with production occurring at $P'$ and consumption at $C'$.

Having eliminated all values of the international price ratio that lie outside the open region $(p_A^0, p_B^0)$, we can now show that international equilibrium will necessarily take place for some value of the terms of trade between $p_A^0$ and $p_B^0$. In order to prove this assertion as briefly as possible, let us concentrate on the market for commodity $X$ only. The reader is reminded that, in a two-commodity model, when the market for one commodity is in equilibrium the market for the other is necessarily in equilibrium (Walras's law). Therefore, general equilibrium can be discussed in terms of either market alone. This has already been explained in detail in chap. 3.

Adopt the symbol $p$ as a shorthand expression for the international terms of trade and consider the following extreme values: $p = p_A^0$ and $p = p_B^0$. When $p = p_A^0$, $A$'s excess demand for commodity $X$ from the rest of the world is necessarily zero. However, as the preceding analysis shows, at $p = p_A^0$ country $B$ has a positive excess demand for commodity $X$. Therefore, when $p = p_A^0$, the combined excess demand for $X$ by both countries is necessarily positive. On the other hand, when $p = p_B^0$, $B$'s excess demand for $X$ is necessarily zero while $A$'s becomes negative. Therefore, when $p = p_B^0$, the combined excess demand for $X$ by both countries is necessarily negative. It should be obvious that, because of the (assumed) continuity of the combined excess-demand curve for $X$, there must exist a value of $p$ satisfying the inequality $p_A^0 < p < p_B^0$ at which the combined excess demand for $X$ becomes zero, i.e., the market for $X$ is in equilibrium. Finally, it should be noted that when inequality (5.3) is satisfied, country $A$ will export commodity $X$ and import $Y$.


## Multiple Pretrade Equilibria

The preceding conclusions are in full agreement with the conclusions of the classical theory. However, these conclusions depend crucially on the assumption that the tastes of each country can be logically portrayed by a nonintersecting social indifference map. What is the implication of the assumption that a nonintersecting social indifference map exists? It eliminates the possibility of multiple pretrade equilibria which might violate some (but not necessarily all) classical conclusions. Thus, in the presence of multiple pretrade equilibria, we cannot be sure that a country will export the commodity which, in the pretrade equilibrium position, it produces relatively more cheaply than the other country. In addition, the equilibrium terms of trade need not satisfy inequality (5.3).

Figure 5.11 illustrates the preceding statements. Panels $(a)$, $(b)$, and $(c)$ show $A$'s, $B$'s, and the combined excess demand for $X$, respectively. The solid curves illustrate the case where the pretrade equilibrium prices, $p_A^0$ and $p_B^0$, are unique. The relationship among these curves is illustrated for the two values of $p$, $p_A^0$ and $p_B^0$. Note that $UV = U'V'$ and $MN = M'N'$. Thus, the equilibrium terms of trade are $p_E$, where $p_A^0 < p_E < p_B^0$. Now distort $A$'s excess-demand curve as shown by the broken curve in panel $(a)$ and assume that the equilibrium price ratio in $A$ before trade is still $p_A^0$. This distortion of $A$'s excess-demand curve distorts the combined excess-demand curve as shown in panel $(c)$ by the broken curve. Note that $NS = N'S'$. The equilibrium terms of trade are now $p_E'$, where the broken combined curve intersects the vertical axis. But $p_E' > p_B^0 > p_A^0$. Therefore, when trade is introduced, both countries tend to specialize in the production of $X$; that is, they both increase the production of $X$ and decrease the production of $Y$. Further, when $p = p_E'$, *country A exports commodity Y and B commodity X—quite contrary to the classical expectations.* It should be pointed out that, had $A$'s pretrade price ratio been $p_A^2$ instead of $p_A^0$, the classical conclusions would have been entirely correct.

The existence of multiple pretrade equilibria does not affect the classical conclusions in the following special case. In the presence of increasing opportunity costs, the pretrade equilibrium price ratio of a country cannot be determined without full information about demand. However, the limits within which the pretrade equilibrium price ratio will necessarily lie can be determined under the reasonable assumption that both commodities are consumed by the economy. Denote the lower limit of the pretrade price ratio of the $i$th country by the symbol $p_i^L$ and the upper limit by $p_i^M$. Thus, any pretrade equilibrium price ratio in country $A$ $(p_A)$ must satisfy the condition

$$p_A^L < p_A < p_A^M \tag{5.4}$$

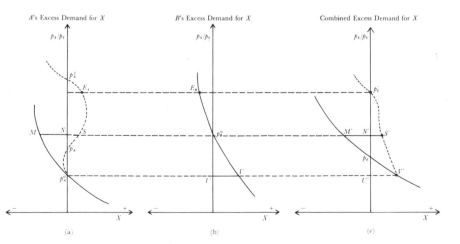

**Figure 5.11** Pretrade multiple equilibria.

Similarly, the following condition must be satisfied by country $B$'s pretrade price ratio $(p_B)$:

$$p_B^L < p_B < p_B^M \tag{5.5}$$

It can be shown that if the two regions $(p_A^L, p_A^M)$ and $(p_B^L, p_B^M)$ do not overlap, all classical conclusions remain valid. For instance, if $p_A^M < p_B^L$, country $A$ will be producing $X$ relatively more cheaply than $B$ before trade, and it will definitely (i.e., whether or not multiple pretrade equilibria exist) specialize in the production of $X$ and export it to $B$, while $B$ will specialize in the production of $Y$ and export it to $A$. A similar statement can be made when $p_B^M < p_A^L$, with $B$ specializing in the production of $X$ and exporting it to $A$, and $A$ in $Y$.

Finally, whether or not multiple pretrade equilibria invalidate the classical conclusions regarding the direction of trade and the limits of the equilibrium terms of trade, the marginal rates of transformation of the participating countries will always be equalized with trade (except in the case of complete specialization). This automatically ensures that the world as a whole will be operating on the world production-possibilities frontier (and not inside it), with the result that all countries can be made potentially better off with trade. Thus, this important classical contribution indeed remains unassailable.

# APPENDIX TO CHAPTER FIVE. SCITOVSKY'S SOCIAL INDIFFERENCE CURVES

This appendix considers (a) how the Scitovsky social indifference curves can be derived and (b) what their slope is equal to.

Let $X_i$ and $Y_i$ ($i \equiv A, B$) stand for the quantities of $X$ and $Y$, respectively, allocated to the $i$th individual, and let $\bar{U}_A = U_A(X_A, Y_A)$ and $\bar{U}_B = U_B(X_B, Y_B)$ be the equations for two arbitrarily selected indifference curves of $A$ and $B$, respectively, such as $I_A' I_A''$ and $I_B' I_B''$ of fig. 5.1. The problem can be formalized as follows. Given a fixed amount of $X$, say $X_0$, to be allocated (in a way which will be determined below) between $A$ and $B$, what is the minimum amount of $Y$ needed so that its allocation between $A$ and $B$, along with the allocation of $X_0$, will put $A$ on indifference curve $I_A' I_A''$ and $B$ on $I_B' I_B''$? In other words, we would like to minimize

$$Y = Y_A + Y_B$$

subject to

$$X_A + X_B - X_0 = 0$$

$$U_A(X_A, Y_A) - \bar{U}_A = 0$$

$$U_B(X_B, Y_B) - \bar{U}_B = 0$$

Form the lagrangian function

$$Z = Y_A + Y_B + \lambda_1[U_A(X_A, Y_A) - \bar{U}_A]$$
$$+ \lambda_2[U_B(X_B, Y_B) - \bar{U}_B] + \lambda_3(X_A + X_B - X_0) \quad (A5.1)$$

where $\lambda_i$ ($i = 1, 2, 3$) are the lagrangian multipliers. For minimization of $Y$, it is required that the following partial derivatives be zero:

$$\frac{\partial Z}{\partial X_A} = \lambda_1 \frac{\partial U_A}{\partial X_A} + \lambda_3 = 0 \quad (A5.2)$$

$$\frac{\partial Z}{\partial X_B} = \lambda_2 \frac{\partial U_B}{\partial X_B} + \lambda_3 = 0 \quad (A5.3)$$

$$\frac{\partial Z}{\partial Y_A} = 1 + \lambda_1 \frac{\partial U_A}{\partial Y_A} = 0 \quad (A5.4)$$

$$\frac{\partial Z}{\partial Y_B} = 1 + \lambda_2 \frac{\partial U_B}{\partial Y_B} = 0 \quad (A5.5)$$

$$\frac{\partial Z}{\partial \lambda_1} = U_A(X_A, Y_A) - \bar{U}_A = 0 \quad (A5.6)$$

$$\frac{\partial Z}{\partial \lambda_2} = U_B(X_B, Y_B) - \bar{U}_B = 0 \quad (A5.7)$$

$$\frac{\partial Z}{\partial \lambda_3} = X_A + X_B - X_0 = 0 \quad (A5.8)$$

Equations (A5.6) through (A5.8) imply that the three constraints of the problem are indeed satisfied. Combining eqs. (A5.2) and (A5.3), we get

$$\frac{\partial U_A/\partial X_A}{\partial U_B/\partial X_B} = \frac{\lambda_2}{\lambda_1} \quad (A5.9)$$

Further, combining eqs. (A5.4) and (A5.5), we get

$$\frac{\partial U_A/\partial Y_A}{\partial U_B/\partial Y_B} = \frac{\lambda_2}{\lambda_1} \quad (A5.10)$$

Finally, substituting eq. (A5.10) into eq. (A5.9), we get

$$\frac{\partial U_A/\partial X_A}{\partial U_B/\partial X_B} = \frac{\partial U_A/\partial Y_A}{\partial U_B/\partial Y_B}$$

or

$$\frac{\partial U_A/\partial X_A}{\partial U_A/\partial Y_A} = \frac{\partial U_B/\partial X_B}{\partial U_B/\partial Y_B} \quad (A5.11)$$

That is, a necessary condition for minimization of $Y$ is that the two commodities are allocated between $A$ and $B$ in such a way that the marginal rates of substitution of the two consumers are equal. This is illustrated in fig. 5.1, where the two indifference curves, $I'_A I''_A$ and $I'_B I''_B$, are tangent to each other.

What is the slope of a Scitovsky social indifference curve at a certain point, say $(X_0, Y_0)$? To answer this question, rewrite eq. (A5.11) in the following form:

$$\frac{dY_A}{dX_A} = \frac{dY_B}{dX_B} \tag{A5.12a}$$

or
$$dY_A = \frac{dY_B}{dX_B} dX_A \tag{A5.12b}$$

Consider now the differentials

$$dX_0 = dX_A + dX_B \tag{A5.13}$$

$$dY_0 = dY_A + dY_B \tag{A5.14}$$

Substitute eq. (A5.12b) into eq. (A5.14) and get

$$dY_0 = \frac{dY_B}{dX_B} dX_A + dY_B \tag{A5.15}$$

Now consider the ratio

$$\frac{dY_0}{dX_0} = \frac{(dY_B/dX_B)\,dX_A + dY_B}{dX_A + dX_B} = \frac{(dY_B/dX_B)\,dX_A + (dY_B/dX_B)\,dX_B}{dX_A + dX_B} = \frac{dY_B}{dX_B} \tag{A5.16}$$

Combining eqs. (A5.12a) and (A5.16), we finally get

$$\frac{dY_0}{dX_0} = \frac{dY_B}{dX_B} = \frac{dY_A}{dX_A} \tag{A5.17}$$

Therefore, the slope of a Scitovsky social indifference curve at a certain point is equal to the corresponding slope of the corresponding indifference curves of $A$ and $B$ (at which the latter are tangent to each other).

## SELECTED BIBLIOGRAPHY

Chacholiades, M. (1972). " Pre-trade Multiple Equilibria and the Theory of Comparative Advantage." *Metroeconomica*, vol. XXIV, fasc. II, pp. 128–139.

Eisenberg, E. (1961). "Aggregation of Utility Functions." *Management Science*, vol. 7, pp. 337–350.

Haberler, G. (1936). *The Theory of International Trade*. W. Hodge and Company, London, chap. 12.

Johnson, H. G. (1959). "International Trade, Income Distribution, and the Offer Curve." *Manchester School of Economic and Social Studies*, vol. 27, pp. 241–260; Reprinted in *AEA Readings in International Economics*. R. D. Irwin, Inc., Homewood, Ill., 1968.

———— (1960). " Income Distribution, the Offer Curve, and the Effects of Tariffs." *Manchester School of Economic and Social Studies*, vol. 28, pp. 215–242.

Leontief, W. W. (1933). "The Use of Indifference Curves in the Analysis of Foreign Trade." *Quarterly Journal of Economics*, vol. 47, pp. 493–503.

Lerner, A. P. (1932). "The Diagrammatical Representation of Cost Conditions in International Trade." *Economica*, vol. 12, pp. 346–356. Reprinted in A. P. Lerner, *Essays in Economic Analysis.* Macmillan and Company, London, 1953.

—— (1934). "The Diagrammatical Representation of Demand Conditions in International Trade." *Economica*, N.S. 1, pp. 319–334. Reprinted in A. P. Lerner, *Essays in Economic Analysis.* Macmillan and Company, London, 1953.

Marshall, A. (1924). *Money, Credit and Commerce.* Macmillan and Company, New York, app. J.

Pigou, A. C. (1932). "The Effect of Reparations on the Ratio of International Exchange." *Economic Journal*, vol. 42 (December), pp. 532–543.

Samuelson, P. A. (1956). "Social Indifference Curves." *Quarterly Journal of Economics*, vol. 70, pp. 1–22.

Savosnik, K. M. (1958). "The Box Diagram and the Production Possibility Curve." *Ekonomisk Tidskrift*, vol. 60, pp. 183–197.

Scitovsky, T. (1942). "A Reconsideration of the Theory of Tariffs." *Review of Economic Studies*, vol. 9, pp. 89–110. Reprinted in AEA *Readings in the Theory of International Trade.* R. D. Irwin, Inc., Homewood, Ill., 1949.

Vanek, J. (1959). "An Afterthought on the Real Cost-Opportunity Cost Dispute and Some Aspects of General Equilibrium under Conditions of Variable Factor Supplies." *Review of Economic Studies*, vol. 26, pp. 198–208.

Viner, J. (1937). *Studies in the Theory of International Trade.* Harper and Brothers, New York, chaps. 7 and 9.

# CHAPTER SIX

# INTERNATIONAL EQUILIBRIUM

As we saw in chap. 3, international equilibrium is usually portrayed in terms of offer curves. Our first problem is to derive the offer curve of a single country. This can be repeated for a second country, and then the analysis of international equilibrium can proceed along the familiar lines of chap. 3.

The derivation of the offer curve in the absence of constant opportunity costs is not an easy task. Edgeworth (1905, p. 70) summarized the difficulties in the following well-known statement: "There is more than meets the eye in Professor Marshall's foreign trade curves. As it has been said by one who used this sort of curve, a movement along a supply-and-demand curve of international trade should be considered as attended with rearrangements of internal trade; as the movement of the hand of a clock corresponds to considerable unseen movements of the machinery." Edgeworth was actually quoting himself (Edgeworth, 1894, pp. 424–425).

In the early 1930s, Leontief (1933) and Lerner (1934) provided a geometric technique for obtaining a country's offer curve from its social indifference curves and production-possibilities frontier. Twenty years later, the technique introduced by these two writers was finally perfected by James E. Meade in his *Geometry of International Trade* (1952)†. Meade's ingenious geometric technique is the subject of part A of this chapter. Part B deals with the problem of stability of international equilibrium.

---

† In retrospect, it becomes evident that Edgeworth (1894) did indeed use offer curves which were all derivable by the techniques of Leontief, Lerner, and Meade. See, for instance, his fig. 8 on p. 433 along with his commentary on pp. 433–434. Chipman (1965, p. 689) expresses the same opinion.

# PART A. MEADE'S GEOMETRIC TECHNIQUE

## 6.1 INTRODUCTION

The previous chapter shows how, for a given value of the terms of trade, a point on a country's offer curve can be derived from its social indifference curves and production-possibilities frontier. In particular, given the terms of trade, production occurs at the point on the production-possibilities frontier where national income is being maximized, i.e., at the point on the production-possibilities frontier at which the latter is tangent to the highest income contour line, known as the consumption-possibilities frontier. Further, consumption occurs at the point on the consumption-possibilities frontier at which the latter is tangent to the highest social indifference curve. Finally, the quantities traded (i.e., the coordinates of a point on the offer curve) are shown by the differences between the quantities consumed and the quantities produced. This procedure can be repeated for all possible values of the terms of trade, until the whole offer curve is derived. Obviously, the same procedure can be repeated for a second country; and then the analysis of international equilibrium can proceed along the familiar lines of chap. 3.

This procedure, though formally correct, is abandoned for three reasons. First, it is cumbersome: too much time and effort are required for the job. Second, it is inadequate for the analysis of the effects of, say, tariffs on the welfare of the tariff-imposing country, assuming that the social indifference map does indeed portray welfare. The imposition of a tariff causes the offer curve of the tariff-imposing country to shift, and it is extremely difficult to determine whether the country moves to a higher social indifference curve after the imposition of the tariff. Third, there exists an alternative approach distinctly superior to the cumbersome procedure above. This alternative approach is Meade's technique, to which we now turn.

## 6.2 THE NEED FOR A TRADE INDIFFERENCE MAP

As we saw in chap. 3, international equilibrium requires that the value of exports be equal to the value of imports. Consider now a simple open economy which can buy or sell unlimited amounts of $X$ and $Y$ in the international market at the fixed prices $p_x^0$ and $p_y^0$, respectively. Denote the given international terms of trade (i.e., the price ratio $p_x^0/p_y^0$) by the symbol $p_0$. This information can be summarized by the equation

$$p_0 E_X + E_Y = 0 \qquad (6.1)$$

where $E_X$ and $E_Y$ denote our country's excess demand for $X$ and $Y$, respectively. (Since $p_0$ is positive, it should be obvious that $E_X$ and $E_Y$ must necessarily have opposite signs, unless they are both zero.)

Figure 6.1 illustrates graphically the information summarized by eq. (6.1). The straight line $ROK$, which is usually called the *terms-of-trade line*, is the locus of points which satisfy eq. (6.1).

Observe that when $E_X > 0$, commodity $X$ is imported, and when $E_X < 0$, commodity $X$ is exported. A similar interpretation holds for $E_Y$. The first quadrant of fig. 6.1 shows exports of $X$ (that is, negative $E_X$) and inports of $Y$ (that is, positive $E_Y$), and the third quadrant shows imports of $X$ (that is, positive $E_X$) and exports of $Y$ (that is, negative $E_Y$).

The terms-of-trade line $ROK$ is another form of the budget constraint for our economy. It shows all combinations of exports and imports of $X$ and $Y$ which satisfy the requirement that the value of exports be equal to the value of imports. Thus, for a given amount of exports, such as $OV$ units of $X$, our economy will be able to get only $VU$ units of $Y$. Although it could get less than $VU$ units of $Y$ (by destroying, for instance, part of $VU$), it can never get more. This suggests that our economy can never reach any point which lies above and to the left of the terms-of-trade line. It can, however, reach points in the shaded area, i.e., below and to the right of the terms-of-trade line. Nevertheless, our economy will not be able to reach the highest social indifference curve unless it actually operates on the terms-of-trade line. Accordingly, in what follows, let us concentrate on the points which lie on the terms-of-trade line and ignore the rest.

Once it is understood that the terms-of-trade line is a budget constraint, it must be clear that, given $p_0$, the corresponding point on our country's offer curve, i.e., the optimum *trade point*, could easily be determined if, somehow, indifference

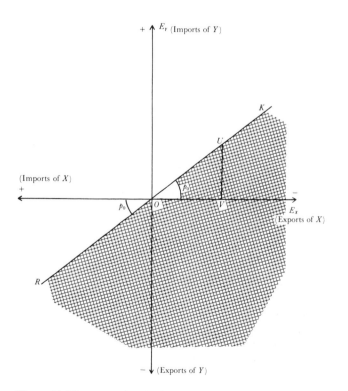

**Figure 6.1** The terms-of-trade line $ROK$ is another form of the budget constraint for the economy.

curves for trade,† not indifference curves for consumption, could be plotted in fig. 6.1. Then the optimum trade point would be determined by the tangency of the terms-of-trade line to the highest indifference curve for trade. Hence, the real question is: do indifference curves for trade, or, as Meade called them, *trade indifference curves*, exist? If they do exist, how can they be derived?

## 6.3 DERIVATION OF TRADE INDIFFERENCE CURVES

### A Simple Edgeworth Exchange Economy

The main tool of Meade's analysis is the concept of the trade indifference map. Figure 6.2 illustrates this concept in the simplest possible case. We measure vertically, moving upward from the origin $O$, the total amount of $Y$ consumed by the economy, and we measure horizontally, moving leftward from $O$, the total amount of $X$ consumed by the economy. Accordingly, the social indifference curves have been drawn in the second quadrant with 180° rotation. Each social indifference curve shows (with respect to the origin $O$) the alternative combinations of consumption levels of $X$ and $Y$ which yield the same level of social welfare.

Assume now that the economy under consideration is an Edgeworth exchange economy endowed with $OO'$ units of commodity $X$ only. Consider point $O'$ as a new origin. Measure vertically, moving upward from $O'$, the imports of $Y$; horizontally, moving leftward from $O'$, the imports of $X$; and rightward from $O'$, the exports of $X$. The indifference curves $I_1, I_2, I_3, \ldots$, viewed with respect to $O'$ as origin, automatically become *trade indifference curves*. That is, each indifference curve shows, with respect to the origin $O'$, all export-import combinations which, given the initial endowment of $OO'$ of $X$, allow the economy to reach the consumption levels indicated by the same curve with respect to the origin $O$ (that is, to reach a certain level of welfare).

For instance, the coordinates of point $A$ with respect to the origin $O$ (that is, $OU$ and $OV$) show one combination of consumption levels of $X$ and $Y$ which enables the economy to reach the level of social welfare indicated by the social indifference curve $I_2$. At the same time, the coordinates of point $A$ with respect to the origin $O'$ (that is, $O'U$ and $UA$) show one combination of exports of $X$ and imports of $Y$ which enables the economy to reach the same social indifference curve $I_2$. Notice that, at point $A$, we have

Imports of $Y = UA = OV$ = consumption of $Y$

Exports of $X = O'U = OO' - OU = OO'$ − consumption of $X$

Similarly, we can say that the coordinates of points $A$, $B$, $C$, and $D$ (which lie on the social indifference curve $I_2$) give us, with respect to the origin $O$, four

---

† Edgeworth (1894) did actually draw such indifference curves for trade. For instance, see his fig. 8, p. 433 and his comments on pp. 433–434.

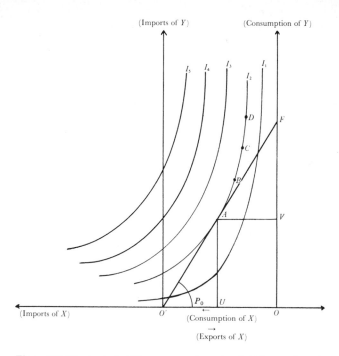

**Figure 6.2** The trade indifference map in a simple Edgeworth exchange economy.

alternative combinations of consumption levels of $X$ and $Y$ which enable the economy to reach the level of social welfare indicated by the social indifference curve $I_2$. The coordinates of the same points $A$, $B$, $C$, and $D$ give us, with respect to the origin $O'$, four alternative export-import combinations which (given the initial endowment of $X$) enable the economy to reach the same level of social welfare.

In general, then, the indifference curves in fig. 6.2, when viewed with respect to the origin $O$, are the familiar social indifference curves (which, following Meade, we might call *consumption indifference curves*). (To avoid confusion, the term "consumption indifference curve" will be used instead of the term "social indifference curve" which we have been using so far.) The same indifference curves become trade indifference curves, however, when viewed with respect to the origin $O'$.

Assume now that the international terms of trade are given by $p_x/p_y = p_0$. Draw a straight line through $O'$ (fig. 6.2) with slope equal to $p_0$, as shown by $O'AF$. The straight line $O'AF$ is simply our economy's consumption-possibilities frontier viewed with respect to the origin $O$. Consumption equilibrium necessarily occurs at point $A$, where the consumption-possibilities frontier is tangent to the highest consumption indifference curve. What is the interpretation of the straight line $O'AF$ when viewed with respect to the origin $O'$? It is simply our economy's terms-of-trade line. Hence, the tangency at point $A$ can also be viewed as the point where the terms-of-trade line becomes tangent to the highest trade indifference curve. If we assume that the concept of the trade indifference map can be made acceptable in the general case where the economy's production-possibilities frontier is a concave curve (and not merely a point, as in the present case), this latter interpretation becomes quite useful: the optimum trade point, as illustrated in fig. 6.2 by point $A$, when viewed with respect to $O'$, can be identified as the tangency between the terms-of-trade line and the highest trade indifference curve. In addition, the economy becomes better off when it moves from a lower to a higher trade indifference curve. The concept of the trade indifference map becomes a powerful tool.

## Trade Indifference Curves in the General Case

So far, the concept of the trade indifference map has been illustrated by means of a simple exchange economy endowed with a fixed amount of commodity $X$ only. But how is the trade indifference map derived in the general case where the economy's domestic availability of commodities is given by a production-possibilities frontier exhibiting increasing opportunity costs? The information needed for the construction of such a trade indifference map is contained in the consumption indifference map *and* the production-possibilities frontier. How can we condense all this information into a trade indifference map?

Consider fig. 6.3. Measure vertically along the axis $OY$ (that is, moving north from the origin $O$) positive quantities of $Y$, and along the axis $OY'$ (that is, moving south) negative quantities of $Y$. Similarly, measure horizontally along the axis $OX'$ (that is, moving west) positive quantities of $X$, and along the axis $OX$ (that is, moving east) negative quantities of $X$. A set of consumption indifference curves, $I_i^c$ ($i = 1, 2, 3, 4$), has been drawn in the second quadrant as in fig. 6.2. The block $OMPN$ is the economy's production-possibilities frontier. It is tangent to the highest consumption indifference curve at point $P$. Hence, before trade, the economy produces and consumes at point $P$, enjoying the level of social welfare implied by the consumption indifference curve $I_1^c$.

What are the alternative export-import combinations which enable the economy to reach the consumption indifference curve $I_1^c$? These export-import combinations are given by a trade indifference curve which can be derived as follows. Imagine that the block $OMPN$ (that is, the production-possibilities frontier) is moved up the consumption indifference curve $I_1^c$ in such a way that the curve $MPN$ remains tangent to $I_1^c$, and the line $MO$ remains in a horizontal position. The corner of the block $OMPN$ traces out the required trade indifference curve $I_1^t$.

In interpreting fig. 6.3, recall that imports are shown as positive quantities and exports as negative quantities.

How do we know that the trade indifference curve $I_1^t$ gives us the information we are looking for? Concentrate on a single point on $I_1^t$, because what is true for one point is true for all. Consider, therefore, point $V$. At $V$ the country exports $OC$ ($= DV$) units of $X$ in exchange for $OD$ ($= CV$) units (of imports) of $Y$. Does this export-import combination enable our economy to consume somewhere on the social indifference curve $I_1^c$? Further, is it not possible that with this particular combination our economy might be able to reach a higher social indifference

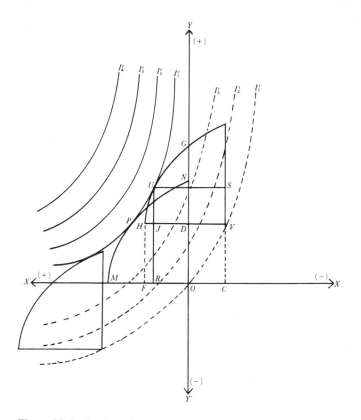

**Figure 6.3** Derivation of the trade indifference curves in the general case.

curve than $I_1^c$? The answers become obvious when it is seen that, after our economy makes the exchange of $OC$ units of $X$ for $OD$ units of $Y$, the best it can do is to consume along the curve $FHUG$, where the straight line $FH$ is perpendicular. Thus, it actually consumes at point $U$ (where the production block is tangent to $I_1^c$). It produces $VJ$ units of $X$, out of which it exports $DV$ units and consumes only $JD$. Similarly, it produces $VS$ ($= JU$) units of $Y$ which along with the imports of $Y$ given by $CV$ (or $RJ$) make up the total domestic consumption of $Y$ (that is, $RU$). Similar reasoning applies to all other points lying on $I_1^t$. Therefore, the trade indifference curve $I_1^t$ shows the alternative export-import combinations which enable the economy to reach the consumption indifference curve $I_1^c$.

In general, a trade indifference curve can be derived for each consumption indifference curve. Imagine the block $OMPN$ (that is, the production-possibilities frontier) placed tangentially against a consumption indifference curve, such as $I_2^c$, and then moved along this $I_2^c$ curve. A new trade indifference curve is traced by the corner of the block $OMPN$, as illustrated by the $I_2^t$ curve. Observe that $I_2^t$ lies consistently above and to the left of $I_1^t$, since $I_2^c$ lies consistently above and to the left of $I_1^c$. In general, one trade indifference curve corresponds to one consumption indifference curve; the higher the consumption indifference curve, the higher the corresponding trade indifference curve. Thus, suppose that the trade indifference curve $I_i^t$ corresponds to the consumption indifference curve $I_i^c$ (for $i = 1, 2, \ldots$). Then, if $I_5^c$ is higher than $I_3^c$, $I_5^t$ must lie totally to the left and above $I_3^t$, and so on.

## 6.4 PROPERTIES OF THE TRADE INDIFFERENCE MAP

Some of the most important properties of the trade indifference map are described as follows.

1. There exists a one-to-one correspondence between trade indifference curves and consumption indifference curves. The higher the consumption indifference curve, the higher is the corresponding trade indifference curve.
2. The slope of a trade indifference curve at any point is equal to the slope of the corresponding consumption indifference curve and the slope of the production-possibilities frontier at the corresponding point.

In terms of fig. 6.4, the slope of the trade indifference curve $I_1^t$ at point $T_1$ is necessarily equal to the slope of the consumption indifference curve $I_1^c$ and the slope of the production-possibilities frontier at point $C_1$. This can be proved as follows. Let the production block slide along $I_1^c$ from $C_1$ to $C_2$, with its corner moving from $T_1$ to $T_2$. The movement from $T_1$ to $T_2$ implies that the exports of $X$ increase by $T_1 N$ and the imports of $Y$ by $N T_2$. Further, the increase in exports of $X$ (that is, $T_1 N$) can be decomposed into (a) a decrease in the consumption of $X$ by $MC_2$ (since on $I_1^c$ we move from $C_1$ to $C_2$) plus (b) an increase in the production of $X$ by $C_2 K$ (since on the production block $T_2 C_2$ we move from $C_1'$ to $C_2$). Therefore, $T_1 N = MC_2 + C_2 K$. Similarly, the increase in imports of $Y$ (that is, $N T_2$) can be decomposed into (a) an increase in the consumption of $Y$ by $C_1 M$ plus (b) a decrease in the production of $Y$ by $KC_1'$. Thus, $N T_2 = C_1 M + KC_1'$. (Note that point $C_1'$ on the production block $T_2 C_2$ corresponds to point $C_1$ on the production block $T_1 C_1$.)

The slope of the straight-line segment joining points $T_1$ and $T_2$ on $I_2^t$ equals $N T_2/T_1 N = (C_1 M + KC_1')/(MC_2 + C_2 K)$. Let the production block $T_2 C_2$ slide along the consumption indifference curve $I_1^c$ until it coincides with the production block $T_1 C_1$. The ratio $C_1 M/MC_2$ approaches the slope of the $I_1^c$ curve at point $C_1$, and the ratio $KC_1'/C_2 K$ approaches the slope of the production block at point $C_1$ (or $C_1'$). Since at point $C_1$ the production block is tangent to the $I_1^c$ curve, we must have (in the limit)

$$\frac{C_1 M}{MC_2} = \frac{KC_1'}{C_2 K} \quad \text{or} \quad \frac{C_2 K}{MC_2} = \frac{KC_1'}{C_1 M}$$

Therefore,

$$\frac{N T_2}{T_1 N} = \frac{C_1 M + KC_1'}{MC_2 + C_2 K} = \frac{C_1 M[1 + (KC_1'/C_1 M)]}{MC_2[1 + (C_2 K/MC_2)]} = \frac{C_1 M}{MC_2} = \frac{KC_1'}{C_2 K}$$

In words, the slope of the $I_1^t$ curve at $T_1$ is equal to the slope of the $I_1^c$ curve and the slope of the production block at the point $C_1$.

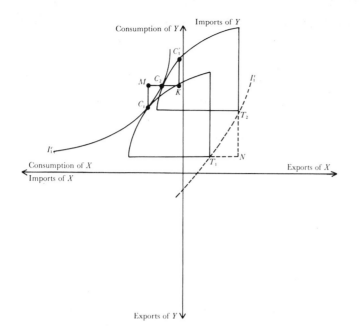

**Figure 6.4** The slope of $I_1^t$ at $T_1$ equals the slope of $I_1^c$ and the slope of the production block $T_1C_1$ at $C_1$.

3. As a result of property 2, it follows that if the $I_i^c$ curve is negatively sloped, the $I_i^t$ curve will also be negatively sloped.
4. Likewise, if the $I_i^c$ curve is always convex, the $I_i^t$ curve will also be convex under conditions of increasing opportunity costs.†

These properties are also discussed (more rigorously) in the appendix to this chapter.

## 6.5 THE OFFER CURVE

### Derivation of the Offer Curve

The trade indifference map can be used for the purpose of deriving the offer curve. As the preceding section demonstrates, there is a trade indifference curve corresponding to every consumption indifference curve; the higher the consumption indifference curve, the higher the corresponding trade indifference curve. Further, for any given international price ratio, the economy consumes on the consumption-possibilities frontier at the point where the latter is tangent to the highest consumption indifference curve. But as should be clear by now, the optimum trade point can be determined by the tangency of the terms-of-trade line,

---

† For the derivation of trade indifference curves under conditions of decreasing opportunity costs as well as for some other important properties of the trade indifference map, see Meade (1952).

which is parallel to the consumption-possibilities frontier, to the highest possible trade indifference curve. As the international price ratio changes, the terms-of-trade line rotates through the origin so that its slope is again equal to the (new) international price ratio. A new tangency is determined between the (new) terms-of-trade line and the highest possible trade indifference curve, giving us another point on the offer curve. By allowing the international terms of trade to vary from zero to infinity, we can thus trace out all tangencies between the successive terms-of-trade lines and the trade indifference curves, i.e., all optimum trade points. The locus of all these tangencies, or optimum trade points, is the economy's offer curve.

Figure 6.5 illustrates the derivation of the offer curve. Consider the terms-of-trade line $TOT_1$, which is tangent to the trade indifference curve $I_1^t$ at the origin. For the terms of trade implied by $TOT_1$, say $p_1$, our economy does not wish to participate in international trade. (Put differently, $p_1$ corresponds to our economy's pretrade equilibrium price ratio.) Imagine that commodity $X$ becomes progressively more expensive in the international market. The terms-of-trade line rotates through the origin, becoming steeper and steeper, as illustrated by the terms-of-trade lines $TOT_2$ and $TOT_3$. As this happens, the optimum trade point (i.e., the tangency between the rotating terms-of-trade line and the trade indifference curves) moves from the origin into the first quadrant, as illustrated by points $E_2$ and $E_3$. The locus of all optimum trade points in the first quadrant is given by the continuous curve $OE_2E_3$. In particular, this is the part of the offer curve which corresponds to terms of trade higher than $p_1$. The remaining part of the offer curve is derived by allowing the international terms of trade to fall continuously from $p_1$ to zero. As this happens, the terms-of-trade line rotates through the origin, becoming flatter and flatter than $TOT_1$, as illustrated by the terms-of-trade lines $TOT_4$ and $TOT_5$. The optimum trade point moves from the origin into the third quadrant, as illustrated by points $E_4$ and $E_5$. The locus of all optimum trade points in the third quadrant (that is, $OE_4E_5$) is the other part of the offer curve. Accordingly, the offer curve is given by the solid curve $E_5E_4OE_2E_3$.

It should be clearly understood why fig. 6.5 has *three* trade indifference curves but *five* terms-of-trade lines. First, note that the $I_1^t$ curve passes through the origin. It follows that the $I_1^t$ curve corresponds to the consumption indifference curve (say $I_1^c$) which the country's production-possibilities frontier touches tangentially in the absence of international trade. Further, the slope of $I_1^t$ at the origin, as shown by the slope of the terms-of-trade line $TOT_1$, necessarily corresponds to the pretrade price ratio, i.e., the slope of the $I_1^c$ curve at the pretrade equilibrium point. From the analysis so far, it must be clear that our economy consumes on the $I_1^c$ curve—and therefore the optimum trade point will be on the $I_1^t$ curve—if, and only if, the international price ratio is equal to the pretrade price ratio, as shown by the slope of $TOT_1$. Accordingly, the only point of the $I_1^t$ curve that belongs to the offer curve is the origin $O$.

For any international price ratio other than the one that coincides with the pretrade price ratio (i.e., the slope of $TOT_1$), our economy consumes on a higher consumption indifference curve than the $I_1^c$ curve and, therefore, trades on a higher trade indifference curve than the $I_1^t$ curve. For this reason, all trade indiffer-

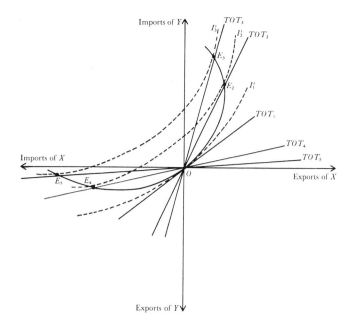

**Figure 6.5** Derivation of the offer curve.

ence curves lower than the $I'_1$ curve have been omitted from fig. 6.5 as irrelevant to our problem. However, given any other trade indifference curve higher than the $I'_1$ curve,† the terms-of-trade line necessarily becomes tangent to it at two different points for two different values of the international price ratio. For instance, points $E_2$ and $E_4$ lie on the same trade indifference curve $I'_2$ and points $E_3$ and $E_5$ lie on $I'_3$. Why is this so?

Consider fig. 6.6 which provides the explanation in terms of more familiar tools. The curve $RP_3E_1P_2S$ is the economy's production-possibilities frontier, while $I^c_1$ and $I^c_2$ are two consumption indifference curves. In the absence of international trade, the economy produces and consumes at point $E_1$ (which corresponds to the origin of fig. 6.5). For the international price ratio given by the slope of the consumption-possibilities frontier $P_2E_2$ and which is higher than the pre-trade price ratio (i.e., the slope of $I^c_1$ at $E_1$), the economy produces at $P_2$ and consumes at $E_2$ on the consumption indifference curve $I^c_2$. This situation corresponds to point $E_2$ of fig. 6.5. In addition, our economy can consume on the consumption indifference curve $I^c_2$ if the international price ratio becomes equal to the slope of the consumption-possibilities frontier $P_3E_3$. This situation corresponds to point $E_4$ of fig. 6.5. Thus, the economy can reach the same consumption indifference curve $I_2$ for two distinct values of the international price ratio—one

---

† We are now interested in trade indifference curves which lie partially in the first and third quadrants. Any trade indifference curves higher than the $I'_1$ curve but lying totally in the second quadrant are out of reach for our economy. The possibility of a trade indifference curve lying in the first and second, or the second and third, quadrants has been ignored for convenience.

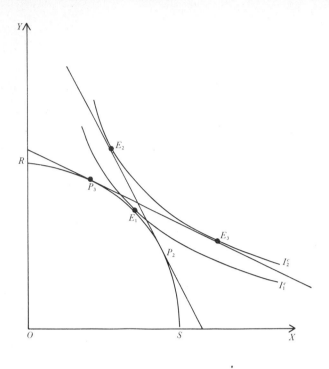

Figure 6.6 The economy can reach a consumption indifference curve at two distinct values of the international terms of trade.

higher and one lower than the pretrade price ratio. At the higher terms of trade, the economy exports $X$ and imports $Y$ (that is, the optimum trade point lies in the first quadrant of fig. 6.5), and at the lower terms of trade, the economy imports $X$ and exports $Y$ (that is, the optimum trade point lies in the third quadrant of fig. 6.5).

## Two Important Properties of the Offer Curve

The offer curve illustrated in fig. 6.5 has two important properties: (*a*) it passes through the origin and lies totally above and to the left of the terms-of-trade line $TOT_1$, whose slope is equal to the pretrade price ratio, and (*b*) the terms-of-trade line $TOT_1$ is tangent to the offer curve at the origin, i.e., the slope of the offer curve at the origin shows the pretrade price ratio. The first property follows directly from the fact that all trade indifference curves higher than $I_1^t$ (that is, the trade indifference curve passing through the origin) lie above and to the left of $I_1^t$. The second property follows from the assumed continuity of the offer curve and the fact that the terms-of-trade line $TOT_1$ is tangent to $I_1^t$ at the origin.

A more rigorous proof of the second property—the first should be obvious from fig. 6.5—is as follows. We know that for any point on the offer curve, eq. (6.1), reproduced below for convenience, must be satisfied:

$$pE_X + E_Y = 0 \tag{6.1}$$

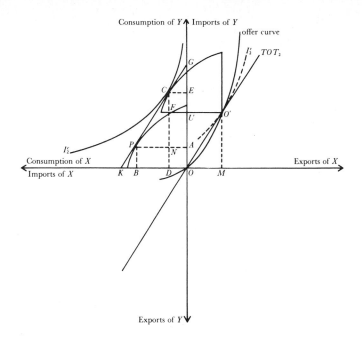

**Figure 6.7** The offer curve can be used along with the production-possibilities frontier and the consumption indifference map to show the optimum points for trade, production, and consumption.

Taking the total differential, we have $E_X\, dp + p\, dE_X + dE_Y = 0$, or

$$\frac{dE_Y}{dE_X} = -p - E_X\left(\frac{dp}{dE_X}\right)$$

When $E_X = 0$, this last equation reduces to

$$\frac{dE_Y}{dE_X} = -p$$

This proves our proposition.

## How to Use the Offer Curve to Determine Trade, Consumption, and Production

Having derived the offer curve, we can determine the optimum trade, consumption, and production points for any given value of the terms of trade. Assume that in fig. 6.7 the terms of trade are given by the slope of $\text{TOT}_2$, which intersects the offer curve at point $O'$. Place the production block in position with its corner at $O'$. By the nature of the construction of the trade indifference curve ($I_2^t$) passing through $O'$, the production block must be tangent to the corresponding consumption indifference curve ($I_2^c$) at the corresponding point ($C$). The common slope of the production block and the consumption indifference curve at point $C$ is equal to the slope of the trade indifference curve at $O'$. That is, the slope of the terms-of-trade line $\text{TOT}_2$ is equal to the slope of the consumption-possibilities frontier $KPCG$.

The coordinates of point $O'$ (in the first quadrant) with respect to the origin $O$ show the quantities of $X$ and $Y$ that our economy is willing to export and import, respectively, at the given terms of trade. The quantities of $X$ and $Y$ consumed are shown by the coordinates of point $C$ (in the second quadrant) with respect to the origin $O$. Finally, the quantities produced are shown by the coordinates of point $C$ with respect to the corner of the production block $O'$.

The value of output consumed in terms of commodity $X$ is given by the horizontal distance $OK$. If commodity $Y$ is used as the numeraire, however, the value of output consumed is given by the vertical distance $OG$. In addition, the same measurements show the value of output produced. This is easily verified if we imagine the production block sliding downward along the consumption-possibilities frontier and the terms-of-trade line until its corner $O'$ coincides with the origin of the diagram $(O)$. Since the production block continues to be tangential to the consumption-possibilities frontier (say at point $P$), the value of output produced must be equal to the value of output consumed.

It might be useful to consider the following relationships in fig. 6.7:

$$AP = OB = O'F = MD$$

$$OA = BP = FC = UE$$

$$EC = UF = OD$$

$$DC = OE$$

$$OB - OD = DB = NP = UO' = OM = \text{exports of } X$$

$$OE - OA = AE = NC = DC - FC = DF = OU = MO' = \text{imports of } Y$$

## 6.6 INTERNATIONAL EQUILIBRIUM

The same procedure can be repeated to derive the offer curve of a second country. International equilibrium can then be shown in terms of the two offer curves by superimposing one diagram on the other, after one country's diagram has been rotated 180° to match the axes of the other.

Figure 6.8 illustrates how international equilibrium can be determined. Assume that $B$'s diagram has been rotated 180°. In the first quadrant of fig. 6.8, measure along the horizontal axis $A$'s exports of $X$ and $B$'s imports of $X$, and along the vertical axis measure $A$'s imports of $Y$ and $B$'s exports of $Y$. Similarly, in the third quadrant, measure along the horizontal axis $A$'s imports of $X$ and $B$'s exports of $X$, and along the vertical axis $A$'s exports of $Y$ and $B$'s imports of $Y$. In the second quadrant, measure along the horizontal axis $A$'s consumption of $X$, and along the vertical axis $A$'s consumption of $Y$. In the fourth quadrant, measure along the horizontal axis $B$'s consumption of $X$, and along the vertical axis $B$'s consumption of $Y$.

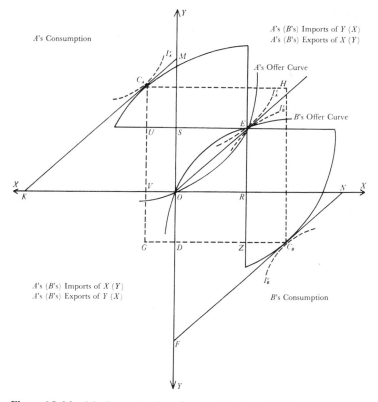

**Figure 6.8** Meade's demonstration of international equilibrium.

International equilibrium occurs at point $E$ in the first quadrant where the two offer curves intersect each other. Country $A$ exports $OR$ units of $X$ to $B$, and $B$ exports $OS$ units of $Y$ to $A$. The equilibrium terms of trade are given by the slope of the vector $OE$, which is equal to the ratio $OS/OR$. Country $A$ is consuming at point $C_A$ in the second quadrant (that is, $OV$ units of $X$ and $VC_A$ units of $Y$), and country $B$ at point $C_B$ in the fourth quadrant (that is, $OD$ units of $Y$ and $DC_B$ units of $X$). Country $A$ is producing $EU$ units of $X$ and $UC_A$ units of $Y$, while $B$ is producing $EZ$ units of $Y$ and $ZC_B$ units of $X$. Thus, the total production of $X$ by both countries is given by $EU + ZC_B = GZ + ZC_B = GC_B$, and the total production of $Y$ is given by $EZ + UC_A = GU + UC_A = GC_A$.

The sides of the rectangle $GC_B HC_A$ show the total production of $X$ and $Y$. But the sides of the same rectangle also show the total consumption of $X$ and $Y$, because $SU + DC_B = GD + DC_B = GC_B$ and $VC_A + RZ = GV + VC_A = GC_A$. In other words, the rectangle $GC_B HC_A$ can be considered a *production box*. The coordinates of point $E$ with respect to the corner $C_A$ show $A$'s production (or endowments) of $X$ and $Y$, while the coordinates of $E$ with respect to $C_B$ show $B$'s production of $X$ and $Y$. Similarly, the coordinates of point $O$ with respect to $C_A(C_B)$ show $A$'s ($B$'s) consumption of $X$ and $Y$, and the coordinates of $O$ with respect to $E$ (or vice versa) show $A$'s exports of $X$ and imports of $Y$.

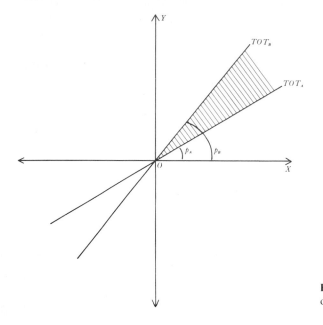

**Figure 6.9** The limits of the terms of trade.

Note that the terms-of-trade line $OE$ is tangent to $A$'s trade indifference curve $I_A^t$ and $B$'s curve $I_B^t$ at point $E$. Note, too, that $A$'s consumption-possibilities frontier $KC_A M$ is tangent to $A$'s consumption indifference curve $I_A^c$ and that $B$'s consumption-possibilities frontier is tangent to $B$'s consumption indifference curve $I_B^c$. Therefore, all equilibrium conditions are indeed satisfied.

Figure 6.8 brings together production, consumption, and trade in an ingenious way. A multitude of relationships are brought to light in fig. 6.8. This diagram, which we owe to Meade, is the culmination of the neoclassical model.

## The Limits of the Terms of Trade Again

Figure 6.8 can also be used to show that the equilibrium terms of trade have to lie between the pretrade price ratios of the two countries. This is shown in fig. 6.9, where only the tangents to the two offer curves of fig. 6.8 at the origin have been drawn. Thus, the line $TOT_A$ has a slope equal to $A$'s pretrade price ratio $(p_A)$ and $TOT_B$ has a slope equal to $B$'s pretrade price ratio $(p_B)$. Country $A$'s offer curve must lie above and to the left of $TOT_A$, and $B$'s below and to the right of $TOT_B$. Therefore, the only area where the two offer curves can intersect is the shaded cone in the first quadrant. This means that the equilibrium terms of trade will definitely lie between $p_A$ and $p_B$.

What the preceding analysis and fig. 6.9 show is that, if international equilibrium exists, it will necessarily occur in the region $(p_A, p_B)$. But how do we know that international equilibrium necessarily exists?

Country $A$'s offer curve necessarily lies above $TOT_A$ (fig. 6.9). Assume, therefore, that the international price ratio is initially equal to $p_A$ and let it rise continuously. Country $A$'s offer curve will start from the origin and lie above $TOT_A$.

How would $A$'s offer curve behave as the international price ratio tends to infinity, i.e., as commodity $X$ tends to become infinitely more expensive relative to $Y$? Obviously, as $p \to \infty$, country $A$ can acquire unlimited amounts of $Y$ by offering only an infinitesimal amount of $X$. But this means that, as $p \to \infty$, $A$'s offer curve will tend to approach asymptotically the vertical axis. Thus, $A$'s offer curve will not remain in the shaded area of fig. 6.9 but will eventually go beyond it.

Applying the same argument to country $B$, we observe that, as $p \to 0$, $B$'s offer curve will start from the origin with slope equal to $p_B$, lie below $\text{TOT}_B$, and approach the horizontal axis asymptotically. Therefore, on the assumption that the two offer curves are indeed continuous, they will necessarily intersect each other at least once in the shaded area of fig. 6.9.

It should be noted that if $p_A > p_B$, then $\text{TOT}_A$ will become steeper than $\text{TOT}_B$ and the shaded cone will move into the third quadrant.

The above conclusion depends upon the assumption that the pretrade equilibrium price ratios are unique. As was shown earlier, the existence of multiple pretrade equilibria might violate this conclusion.

## PART B. ELASTICITIES, STABILITY, AND MULTIPLE EQUILIBRIA

This section is devoted to the properties of international equilibrium, in particular, whether or not it is stable and unique. The necessary and sufficient conditions for stability are discussed also.

## 6.7 THREE IMPORTANT ELASTICITIES

Consider the offer curve in fig. 6.10. Define three elasticities in relation to this offer curve at any selected point, such as $K$, as follows.

(a) The *elasticity of the offer curve*, denoted by $\varepsilon$, is defined as

$$\varepsilon \equiv \frac{\% \text{ change in imports}}{\% \text{ change in exports}} = \frac{dY/Y}{dX/X} = \frac{dY}{dX}\frac{X}{Y} \qquad (6.2a)$$

The ratio $Y/X$ along the offer curve is the country's *average* terms of trade which show the number of units of $Y$ imported for each unit of $X$ exported *on the average*. On the other hand, the ratio (derivative) $dY/dX$ gives the rate at which the country exchanges $X$ for $Y$ *on the margin*. For this reason, the ratio $dY/dX$ is usually called the *marginal terms of trade*. The elasticity of the offer curve is obviously given by the ratio of the marginal to the average terms of trade, that is,

$$\varepsilon = \frac{\text{marginal terms of trade}}{\text{average terms of trade}} \qquad (6.2b)$$

Given eq. (6.2a), the elasticity of the offer curve at point $K$ can be determined as follows. First draw the tangent to the offer curve at $K$ and let it intersect the horizontal axis at point $D$. Then draw a vertical line through $K$ and let it intersect the horizontal axis at point $C$. Now the slope of the tangent to the offer curve at $K$ coincides with the derivative $dY/dX$ at $K$. Therefore,

$$\varepsilon = \frac{CK}{DC}\frac{OC}{CK} = \frac{OC}{DC} \tag{6.3}$$

As long as point $D$ lies between the origin and point $C$ (as in fig. 6.10), the elasticity of the offer curve is positive and greater than unity. When the offer curve is a straight line through the origin, point $D$ coincides with the origin and $\varepsilon$ becomes equal to unity at all points of the offer curve. When the offer curve is backward bending, as shown by the broken curve in fig. 6.10, and $\varepsilon$ is estimated at a point (such as $M$) on the backward-bending portion of the curve, then point $D$ lies to the right of point $C$; the distance $DC$ is negative and so is $\varepsilon$. (This is also seen from the fact that the derivative $dY/dX$, that is, the marginal terms of trade, at the backward-bending portion of the offer curve is negative.) At the point where the offer curve stops sloping upward and begins bending backward, i.e., the point (such as $N$) where the tangent becomes perpendicular, $\varepsilon$ becomes infinite, because $OC$ is strictly positive, while $DC$ becomes zero.

(b) The *elasticity of demand for imports*, denoted by $e$, is defined as

$$e \equiv \frac{\%\text{ change in imports}}{\%\text{ change in the relative price of imports}}$$

Since, along the offer curve, the value of exports equals the value of imports, that is, $p_x X = p_y Y$, the relative price of imports (that is, $p_y/p_x$) is given by the ratio $X/Y$. Thus, the above formula becomes

$$e = \frac{(dY/Y)}{[d(X/Y)]/(X/Y)} = \frac{dY}{d(X/Y)}\frac{X}{Y^2} = \frac{dY}{(Y\,dX - X\,dY)/Y^2}\frac{X}{Y^2}$$

$$= \frac{(dY/dX)(X/Y)}{1 - [(dY/dX)(X/Y)]} = \frac{\varepsilon}{1 - \varepsilon} \tag{6.4a}$$

Using eq. (6.3), the elasticity of demand for imports, $e$, can be measured as follows:

$$e = \frac{\varepsilon}{1 - \varepsilon} = \frac{OC/DC}{1 - (OC/DC)} = \frac{OC}{DC - OC} \tag{6.5}$$

From eqs. (6.4a) and (6.5), it follows that when the elasticity of the offer curve $\varepsilon$ is positive and greater than unity, the elasticity of demand for imports $e$ is negative and greater than unity (in absolute terms), i.e., the demand for imports is elastic. When $\varepsilon$ is infinite, $e = -1$. As was noted earlier, $\varepsilon$ becomes infinite when the tangent to the offer curve becomes vertical and $DC = 0$. Thus, from eq. (6.5),

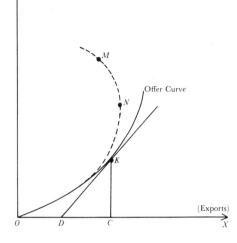

$Y$ (Imports)

$M$

Offer Curve

$N$

$K$

(Exports)

$0$   $D$   $C$   $X$

**Figure 6.10** The elasticity of the offer curve, of the demand for imports, and of the supply of exports.

when $DC = 0$, $e = -1$. The same conclusion can be derived from eq. $(6.4a)$ after it is rearranged as follows:

$$e = \frac{1}{(1/\varepsilon) - 1} \qquad (6.4b)$$

Thus, as $\varepsilon \to \infty$, $(1/\varepsilon) \to 0$ and $e \to (-1)$.

Furthermore, when $\varepsilon$ tends to unity from above (i.e., when $\varepsilon$ assumes a sequence of values such as 2, 1.9, 1.8, 1.7, ..., 1), then $e$ tends to $-\infty$, that is, the demand for imports becomes infinitely elastic. Also note that when $0 < \varepsilon < 1$, the elasticity of demand for imports necessarily becomes positive, which means that imports are necessarily a Giffen good.† Finally, notice that when $\varepsilon$ is negative (i.e., when the offer curve is backward bending), the elasticity of demand for imports is necessarily negative but less than unity in absolute terms.

It seems more interesting to consider $\varepsilon$ as a function of $e$ instead of considering $e$ as a function of $\varepsilon$, as we have been doing so far. Thus, solving eq. $(6.4a)$ for $\varepsilon$, we get

$$\varepsilon = \frac{e}{1 + e} \qquad (6.6)$$

In general, the elasticity of demand for imports is expected to be negative.‡ If it is also greater than unity in absolute terms (that is, $e < -1$), then $\varepsilon > +1$ and the

---

† A Giffen good is a commodity whose consumption falls as its price falls. Notice that while it is necessary that the imported commodity be a Giffen good for the imports demand elasticity to be positive, this is not a sufficient condition (see the note below).

‡ Even if the imported commodity were a Giffen good, the elasticity of demand for imports might still be negative because imports ≡ domestic consumption − domestic production. Thus, even if domestic consumption falls as imports become cheaper, it does not necessarily follow that imports also fall because domestic production falls too. Imports fall if, and only if, domestic consumption falls faster than domestic production. This is ruled out as unrealistic.

offer curve is upward sloping, i.e., it looks like the solid curve of fig. 6.10. On the other hand, if the demand for imports is inelastic (that is, $-1 < e < 0$), then $\varepsilon < 0$, which implies that the offer curve is backward bending (in the region where $\varepsilon < 0$). Conversely, if the offer curve is backward bending, the demand for imports is necessarily inelastic in that region.

(c) The *elasticity of supply of exports*, denoted by $\eta$, is defined as

$$\eta \equiv \frac{\%\ \text{change in exports}}{\%\ \text{change in relative price of exports}}$$

The relative price of exports is simply the ratio $p_x/p_y$, which along the offer curve is given by the ratio $Y/X$. Substituting the ratio $Y/X$ for the relative price of exports in the above formula, we get

$$\eta \equiv \frac{dX/X}{[d(Y/X)]/(Y/X)} = \frac{dX}{d(Y/X)}\frac{Y}{X^2}$$

$$= \frac{dX}{(X\ dY - Y\ dX)/X^2}\frac{Y}{X^2} = \frac{1}{[(dY/dX)(X/Y)] - 1} = \frac{1}{\varepsilon - 1} \qquad (6.7)$$

In addition, using eq. (6.3), we can measure the elasticity of supply of exports $\eta$ as

$$\eta = \frac{1}{\varepsilon - 1} = \frac{1}{(OC/DC) - 1} = \frac{DC}{OC - DC} \qquad (6.8)$$

Finally, adding the elasticity of demand for imports as given by eq. (6.4) to the elasticity of supply of exports as given by eq. (6.7), we get

$$e + \eta = -1 \qquad (6.9a)$$

or
$$\eta = -(1 + e) \qquad (6.9b)$$

That is to say, the sum of the elasticities of the demand for imports $e$ and supply of exports $\eta$ is always equal to $-1$. Therefore, when the demand for imports is elastic (that is, $e < -1$), the elasticity of supply of exports must be positive, i.e., the supply of exports must be upward sloping. However, when the demand for imports becomes inelastic (that is, $-1 < e < 0$), the elasticity of supply of exports is necessarily negative and the supply curve for exports becomes backward bending.

As noted earlier, when $e < -1$, the offer curve is positively sloped, and when $-1 < e < 0$, it is backward bending. Therefore, when the supply of exports becomes backward bending, so does the offer curve, and when the supply for exports is upward sloping, the offer curve is also upward sloping. These relationships can be easily verified. Let $Z$ and $M$ stand for exports and imports, respectively, and denote their prices by $p_z$ and $p_m$. Along the offer curve, we necessarily have

$(p_m/p_z)M = Z$; that is, the value of imports equals the value of exports. In other words, *the offer curve may be looked at as a total-revenue curve which is derived from the demand schedule for imports*, as explained in elementary books on price theory. If the demand for imports $M$ is elastic, then as $p_m/p_z$ falls, the product $(p_m/p_z)M$ rises. But $(p_m/p_z)M = Z$; hence $Z$ rises too. Thus, when the demand for imports $M$ is elastic, $Z$ ($\equiv$ supply of exports) rises as $p_m/p_z$ falls, or as $p_z/p_m$ rises. Now the supply of exports is the relationship between $Z$ and $p_z/p_m$. Thus, when the demand for imports is elastic, $Z$ is an increasing function of $p_z/p_m$ and the supply curve for exports is upward sloping. In addition, $M$ is a decreasing function of $p_m/p_z$, or an increasing function of $p_z/p_m$. It follows that, when the demand for imports is elastic, both $Z$ and $M$ change in the same direction as $p_m/p_z$ changes, and thus the offer curve is upward sloping.

Assume the demand for imports is inelastic. As $p_m/p_z$ falls (or as $p_z/p_m$ rises), the product $(p_m/p_z)M$, and therefore $Z$, falls. Hence, as $p_z/p_m$ rises, $Z$ falls, which shows that the supply of exports is backward bending. In addition, $M$ is an increasing function of $p_z/p_m$. Hence, as $p_m/p_z$ changes, $Z$ and $M$ necessarily move in opposite directions, and the offer curve becomes backward bending.

The relationships among the three elasticities ($e$, $\eta$, and $\varepsilon$) and the shape of the offer curve are summarized in table 6.1, where it is assumed that the elasticity of demand for imports is strictly negative.

## Table 6.1

| $e$ (elasticity of demand for imports) | $\eta = -(1 + e)$ (elasticity of supply of exports) | $\varepsilon = e/(1 + e)$ (elasticity of the offer curve) | Shape of the offer curve |
|---|---|---|---|
| Case 1 $\quad e = -\infty$ | $\eta = \infty$ | $\varepsilon = 1$ | Elasticity of offer curve is, in general, unity at origin. When offer curve is a straight line through origin, $\varepsilon = 1$ throughout its length. |
| Case 2 $\quad e < -1$ | $\eta > 0$ | $\varepsilon > 1$ | Offer curve is upward sloping. Its tangent (at any point in this region) intersects the horizontal axis at latter's positive part, as shown in fig. 6.10. |
| Case 3 $\quad e = -1$ | $\eta = 0$ | $\varepsilon = \infty$ | Offer curve is perpendicular. This is illustrated in fig. 6.10 by point $N$. |
| Case 4 $\quad -1 < e < 0$ | $\eta < 0$ | $\varepsilon < 0$ | Offer curve is backward bending. |

## 6.8 STABILITY

### Extension of Walras's Law to Stability

As indicated in chap. 3, the general equilibrium of a two-commodity model can be demonstrated in terms of a single market because of Walras's law. Thus, if the market for $X$ is in equilibrium, the market for $Y$ must also be in equilibrium, and vice versa. This is seen from the fact that eq. (6.1) holds for both countries. Using the superscripts $A$ and $B$ to indicate the countries and adding these two equations together, we get

$$p(E_X^A + E_X^B) + (E_Y^A + E_Y^B) = 0 \tag{6.10}$$

Thus, when $E_X^A + E_X^B = 0$, it follows that $E_Y^A + E_Y^B = 0$, and vice versa. Therefore, general equilibrium in a two-commodity model can be determined by concentrating on a single market. Is it also possible to study the stability of a two-commodity model by concentrating on a single market? In other words, is it true that, when an equilibrium point in the market for commodity $X$ is stable, the corresponding equilibrium in the market for commodity $Y$ is also stable? This is indeed the case. *When the market for $X$ is stable, the market for $Y$ is also stable, and vice versa.*

Suppose that $p = p_0$ is an equilibrium price; i.e., at $p = p_0$ both the market for $X$ and the market for $Y$ are cleared. Suppose, further, that the equilibrium reached in the market for $X$ is stable. That is, for relative prices higher than $p_0$, the supply of $X$ is greater than the demand for $X$, and for relative prices lower than $p_0$, the demand for $X$ is larger than the supply of $X$. Does it necessarily follow that the corresponding equilibrium in the market for $Y$ is also stable? That is, does it follow that for relative prices higher than $1/p_0$ the supply of $Y$ is larger than the demand for $Y$, and for relative prices lower than $1/p_0$ the demand for $Y$ is larger than the supply of $Y$? The answer is "Yes."

As we have seen, whether or not the system is in equilibrium, the following equation holds:

$$p(E_X^A + E_X^B) + (E_Y^A + E_Y^B) = 0 \tag{6.10}$$

Given that $p > 0$, it follows that, when the sum $(E_X^A + E_X^B)$ is positive, the sum $(E_Y^A + E_Y^B)$ is necessarily negative, and when $(E_X^A + E_X^B)$ is negative, the sum $(E_Y^A + E_Y^B)$ is positive. Thus, the statement "for $p > p_0$, we have $(E_X^A + E_X^B) < 0$" is equivalent to "for $1/p < 1/p_0$, we have $(E_Y^A + E_Y^B) > 0$," and the statement "for $p < p_0$, we have $(E_X^A + E_X^B) > 0$" is equivalent to "for $1/p > 1/p_0$, we have $(E_Y^A + E_Y^B) < 0$," and vice versa. Therefore, when the equilibrium in the market for $X$ is stable, the corresponding equilibrium in the market for $Y$ is also stable; and when the equilibrium in the market for $Y$ is stable, the corresponding equilibrium in the market for $X$ is also stable. Similarly, when the equilibrium in one market is unstable, the corresponding equilibrium in the other market is also unstable. Let us discuss the stability of the system by concentrating on a single market. (Refer back to the analysis of sec. 3.4.)

## The Marshall–Lerner Condition

Whether a particular position of equilibrium is stable or not depends on the process of adjustment that is specified. Unfortunately, there is not a unique process of adjustment that one can specify. The main drawback of the process we are using is the implicit assumption that the value of exports equals the value of imports at all times, i.e., that both countries are always on their respective offer curves. This is in the spirit of the Walrasian *tâtonnement* process, in which no trade takes place except at the final equilibrium. Alfred Marshall, on the other hand, analyzed stability in terms of points which were off the offer curves. (The mathematical formulation of Marshall's analysis is given in Samuelson, 1947.) The stability condition derived below depends crucially on the assumed specific dynamical generalization of the static model. For other dynamic assumptions, it should not be surprising if a different stability condition or conditions are found.

Let us discard the market for $Y$ and concentrate on the market for $X$. Suppose that at the equilibrium point, commodity $X$ is being exported from $B$ to $A$. (It should be noted that this is not a restrictive assumption.) What are the necessary and sufficient conditions for the equilibrium to be stable?

On the basis of the notation adopted earlier in this chapter, the equilibrium condition for the market of commodity $X$ is given by

$$E_X^A + E_X^B = 0 \tag{6.11}$$

In other words, the sum of $A$'s and $B$'s excess demand for commodity $X$ must be zero. Observe that both $E_X^A$ and $E_X^B$ are functions of the price ratio $p_x/p_y$, which we simply denote by the letter $p$. For stability, it is required that the excess demand curve for $X$ at the equilibrium point be downward sloping, as shown in fig. 6.11 by the solid curve $DD$. Thus, for any $p$ higher than $p_0$, the aggregate excess demand for $X$ is negative, causing $p$ to fall. For instance, at $p = p_2$, there is negative excess demand (or positive excess supply) for $X$ equal to the horizontal distance $Kp_2$, and the price ratio tends to fall toward $p_0$, as shown by the arrow on the diagram. Similarly, for any $p$ lower than $p_0$, the excess demand for $X$ is positive, causing $p$ to rise. Thus, for $p = p_1$, there is a positive excess demand (or negative excess supply) for $X$ equal to the horizontal distance $p_1 M$, and $p$ tends to rise toward $p_0$.

The slope of the demand curve $DD$ of fig. 6.11 is given by the first derivative of the function $(E_X^A + E_X^B)$ with respect to $p$. For stability, it is required that the slope of $DD$ at the equilibrium point be negative, that is,

$$\frac{dE_X^A}{dp} + \frac{dE_X^B}{dp} < 0 \tag{6.12}$$

for the value of $p$ satisfying eq. (6.11).

Inequality (6.12) can be rewritten as

$$\left(\frac{dE_X^A}{dp} \frac{p}{E_X^A}\right) \frac{E_X^A}{p} + \left(\frac{dE_X^B}{dp} \frac{p}{E_X^B}\right) \frac{E_X^B}{p} < 0 \tag{6.13a}$$

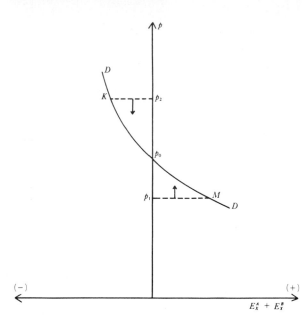

Figure 6.11 An equilibrium point, say $p_0$, is stable when the aggregate excess-demand schedule is downward sloping at that point.

The term in the first pair of parentheses is the elasticity of $A$'s demand for imports (which we denote by the symbol $e_A$). The term in the second pair of parentheses is the elasticity of $B$'s supply of exports (which we denote by $\eta_B$).† Inequality (6.13a) can now be simplified to

$$\frac{1}{p}\left(e_A E_X^A + \eta_B E_X^B\right) < 0 \tag{6.13b}$$

Since $p$ is necessarily positive and, further, at the equilibrium point we necessarily have (see eq. (6.11))

$$E_X^A = -E_X^B > 0$$

inequality (6.13b) reduces to

$$e_A - \eta_B < 0 \tag{6.14}$$

(Remember that we have been assuming that $X$ is exported from $B$ to $A$. Thus, $E_X^A > 0$ and $E_X^B < 0$.)

Inequality (6.14) is a necessary and sufficient condition for the stability of international equilibrium. It is expressed in terms of $A$'s demand elasticity for imports and $B$'s supply elasticity of exports. By making use of eq. (6.9b), condition (6.14) can be expressed in terms of the demand elasticities for imports of the two countries. Thus, substituting (6.9b) into (6.14), we arrive at

$$e_A + e_B < -1 \tag{6.15}$$

---

† Let us use the symbols adopted in the preceding section for the three elasticities. The subscripts $A$ and $B$ indicate the country whose elasticity is being considered.

Inequality (6.15) is known as the *Marshall–Lerner condition*. However, it seems more accurate to say that this is the Marshallian condition, because only Marshall was interested in the stability of a pure trade model such as the one discussed in this chapter.† Lerner's interest was with the foreign exchange market.

Since both demand elasticities for imports are generally negative, the Marshallian condition (which is both necessary and sufficient for the stability of the present model) requires that the sum of the elasticities of demand for imports in absolute terms be greater than unity. It follows that a sufficient (but not necessary) condition for stability is that the demand for imports of one of the two countries be elastic at the equilibrium point. In terms of offer curves, therefore, a sufficient (but not necessary) condition for stability is that the offer curve of one of the two countries be upward sloping (i.e., not backward bending) around the equilibrium point.

A necessary (but not sufficient) condition for *instability* is that both demand curves for imports (that is, $A$'s demand for imports of $X$ and $B$'s demand for imports of $Y$) be inelastic at the equilibrium point. In terms of the offer curves, this means that both offer curves must necessarily be backward bending around an unstable equilibrium point. It should be emphasized that this is only a necessary condition. That is, it is quite possible for both offer curves to be backward bending at the equilibrium point and yet equilibrium be stable—because condition (6.15) is satisfied. An example of this case is given in the following section.


## 6.9 MULTIPLE EQUILIBRIA

The preceding analysis deals with the problem of *local stability*. An equilibrium point is said to be *locally stable* if, for any small displacements around it, the system returns to the original equilibrium. On the other hand, if the system returns to the equilibrium point irrespective of how large the displacement is, the system is called *globally stable*. A globally stable equilibrium is necessarily unique. For instance, if a second equilibrium exists, a displacement from the first equilibrium point which shifts the economy to the second cannot possibly generate forces to bring the system back to the original equilibrium. If it did, the second point would not be an equilibrium point.

The history of the pure theory of trade is replete with cases of (posttrade) multiple equilibria. Marshall (1879, pp. 24–25; 1923, pp. 352–354) provided a geometric argument to the effect that offer curves have an odd number of intersections, with each unstable point bounded by two stable ones. Several modern economists, most notably Bhagwati and Johnson,‡ Scarf, and Gale, have provided

---

† In fact, as noted earlier, Marshall had postulated a different dynamic system than the one discussed in the text (see Samuelson, 1947).

‡ Johnson (private correspondence) has changed his mind on this particular point.

examples where Marshall's proposition is not generally true. From the point of view of pure theory, many strange possibilities cannot be ruled out by a priori reasoning.

The case of multiple (posttrade) equilibria is illustrated in fig. 6.12 which shows three equilibria, $E_1$, $E_2$, and $E_3$. Point $E_2$ is unstable while points $E_1$ and $E_3$ are stable. This is in agreement with the Marshallian proposition that the number of equilibria is odd, with each unstable equilibrium bounded by two stable ones. For any terms of trade $(p_x/p_y)$ smaller than the slope of the vector $OE_2$ (not drawn), the system tends to move to point $E_1$. On the other hand, for any terms of trade higher than the slope of the vector $OE_2$, the system converges to $E_3$.

The multiplicity of equilibria illustrated in fig. 6.12 is necessarily due to the inelasticity of demand for imports of both countries which gives rise to backward-bending offer curves. If at least one of the offer curves were upward sloping (and not backward bending) throughout, there would be only one stable intersection. This can be seen geometrically from fig. 6.12, and also from the fact that the elasticity of demand for imports of the country whose offer curve is upward sloping is necessarily greater than unity. Thus, condition (6.15) is satisfied, and equilibrium must be stable. Further, when one offer curve is upward sloping, there cannot be more than one equilibria, for if there were, all of them would be stable, which is impossible.

The existence of multiple equilibria raises the question of whether equilibrium is determinate. Given sufficiently large disturbances, the system would move from one (stable) equilibrium to another, thus leading to very volatile price fluctuations. In fact, as the number of equilibrium points tends to infinity, we approach the state of "neutral equilibrium." An extreme case would be when the two offer curves coincide over a certain region.

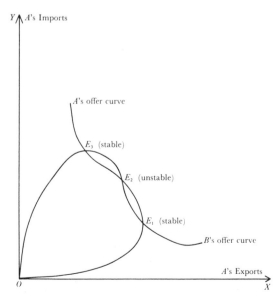

**Figure 6.12** Multiple equilibria.

The existence of multiple equilibria has important policy implications. An equilibrium point which is considered "optimum" from the point of view of one country is not, in general, "optimum" from the point of view of the other country. For instance, in the presence of two stable equilibria, with the first being more favorable to $A$ and the second more favorable to $B$, countries $A$ and $B$ may pursue inconsistent policies. Thus, the real question is whether there exists a stable equilibrium point corresponding to a division of the gains from trade which can be considered as "fair" by all participating countries.

# APPENDIX TO CHAPTER SIX. TRADE INDIFFERENCE CURVES

This appendix gives an alternative proof (in terms of differential calculus) of the fundamental property of trade indifference curves, namely, that the slope of a trade indifference curve at any point is equal to the slope of the corresponding consumption indifference curve and the slope of the production-possibilities frontier at the corresponding point. The curvature of trade indifference curves is briefly discussed.

Let

$$Y_c = U(X_c) \tag{A6.1}$$

be the equation of the $I_1^c$ curve, and let

$$Y_p = F(X_p) \tag{A6.2}$$

denote the production-possibilities frontier. When the production block is tangent to the consumption indifference curve, the following condition is necessarily satisfied:

$$\frac{dY_c}{dX_c} = \frac{dY_p}{dX_p} \tag{A6.3a}$$

or
$$U' = F' \tag{A6.3b}$$

where primes indicate differentiation.

Now define $E_X$ and $E_Y$ as

$$E_X \equiv X_c - X_p \tag{A6.4}$$

$$E_Y \equiv Y_c - Y_p = U(X_c) - F(X_p) \tag{A6.5a}$$

Thus, $E_X$ and $E_Y$ show the excess demand for $X$ and $Y$, respectively.

Solving (A6.4) for $X_c$ and substituting into (A6.5a), we get

$$E_Y = U(E_X + X_p) - F(X_p) \tag{A6.5b}$$

Differentiating $E_Y$ totally with respect to $E_X$, we get

$$\frac{dE_Y}{dE_X} = [U'(E_X + X_p)]\left(1 + \frac{dX_p}{dE_X}\right) - F'(X_p)\frac{dX_p}{dE_X}$$

$$= U'(E_X + X_p) + [U'(E_X + X_p) - F'(X_p)]\frac{dX_p}{dE_X} \qquad (A6.6a)$$

Equation (A6.6a) reduces to

$$\frac{dE_Y}{dE_X} = U' = F' \qquad (A6.6b)$$

as a result of eq. (A6.3b).

What is the meaning of eq. (A6.6b)? It is simply that *the slope of the trade indifference curve is equal to the slope of the corresponding social indifference curve and the slope of the production-possibilities frontier at the corresponding point.*

Consider now the second derivative of $E_Y$ with respect to $E_X$. Differentiating $dE_Y/dE_X$ as given by eq. (A6.6b), we get

$$\frac{d^2E_Y}{dE_X^2} = \frac{d[U'(E_X + X_p)]}{dE_X} = [U''(E_X + X_p)]\left(1 + \frac{dX_p}{dE_X}\right) \qquad (A6.7)$$

To make any progress, we need to evaluate the derivative $dX_p/dE_X$. For this purpose, take the total differential of eq. (A6.3b). We have $U'' \, dX_c = F'' \, dX_p$, or

$$\frac{dX_c}{dX_p} = \frac{F''}{U''} \qquad (A6.8)$$

From eq. (A6.4) it follows that

$$dE_X = dX_c - dX_p$$

or

$$\frac{dE_X}{dX_p} = \frac{dX_c}{dX_p} - 1 = \frac{F''}{U''} - 1 = \frac{F'' - U''}{U''} \qquad (A6.9)$$

(where use has been made of eq. (A.6.8)). Therefore,

$$\frac{dX_p}{dE_X} = \frac{U''}{F'' - U''} \qquad (A6.10)$$

Finally, introducing this result into eq. (A6.7), we get

$$\frac{d^2E_Y}{dE_X^2} = U''\left(1 + \frac{U''}{F'' - U''}\right) = \frac{U''F''}{F'' - U''} \qquad (A6.11)$$

where the arguments of the functions $U$ and $F$ have been omitted for simplicity.

What is the significance of eq. (A6.11)? It gives information about the curvature of the trade indifference curve. If the right-hand side of equation (A6.11) is positive, then the trade indifference curve is convex: it has the same curvature as the social indifference curves. If it is negative, the trade indifference curve is concave.

By assumption, the social indifference curves are convex to the origin. This means that $U'' > 0$. If the production-possibilities frontier is concave to the origin, we must have $F'' < 0$. In this case, the trade indifference curve is convex, that is, it has the same curvature as the social indifference curve.

What if the production-possibilities frontier is convex to the origin? Here $F'' > 0$, and we can distinguish between the following two cases:

1. When $F'' > U'' > 0$, $d^2 E_Y/dE_X^2 > 0$ and the trade indifference curve is convex, just like the social indifference curve. That is, when the production-possibilities frontier is convex like the social indifference curves, but its slope (in absolute terms) decreases faster than the slope of the social indifference curve, then the trade indifference curve is convex.
2. When $0 < F'' < U''$, $d^2 E_Y/dE_X^2 < 0$ and the trade indifference curve is concave.

## SELECTED BIBLIOGRAPHY

Chipman, J. S. (1965). "A Survey of the Theory of International Trade: Part 2, The Neoclassical Theory." *Econometrica*, vol. 33, pp. 685–760.

Edgeworth, F. Y. (1894). "The Theory of International Values." *Economical Journal*, vol. 4, pp. 35–50, 424–443, and 606–638. Reprinted in F. Y. Edgeworth, *Papers Relating to Political Economy.* Macmillan and Company, London, 1925.

——— (1905). "Review of Henry Cunynghame's *A Geometrical Political Economy.*" *Economic Journal*, vol. 15, pp. 62–71.

Heller, H. R. (1968). *International Trade.* Prentice-Hall, Inc., Englewood Cliffs, N.J., chaps. 3, 4, and 5.

Leontief, W. W. (1933). "The Use of Indifference Curves in the Analysis of Foreign Trade." *Quarterly Journal of Economics*, vol. 47, pp. 493–503.

Lerner, A. P. (1934). "The Diagrammatical Representation of Demand Conditions in International Trade." *Economica*, N.S. 1, pp. 319–334. Reprinted in A. P. Lerner, *Essays in Economic Analysis.* Macmillan and Company, London, 1953.

Marshall, A. (1879). *The Pure Theory of Foreign Trade.* (Printed for private circulation in 1879; reprinted in 1930.) London School of Economics and Political Science, London.

——— (1923). *Money, Credit, and Commerce.* Macmillan and Company, London.

Meade, J. E. (1952). *A Geometry of International Trade.* George Allen and Unwin, Ltd., London, chaps. 1 to 4.

Samuelson, P. A. (1947). *Foundations of Economic Analysis.* Harvard University Press, Cambridge, Mass.

# SEVEN

## INCREASING RETURNS

The analysis so far has been based on the assumption of constant returns to scale. When this assumption is dropped, several difficulties arise, in particular, the problems created by the phenomenon of increasing returns to scale.†

Increasing returns to scale are an indisputable fact of life. However, the treatment of increasing returns in the field of international trade theory has been scanty and unsatisfactory, because of the enormous difficulties encountered in incorporating the phenomenon of increasing returns in a general-equilibrium model. The problem is essentially the resultant divergence between private and social costs—but stability also.

Increasing returns are usually attributed to certain "economies"—economies which are reflected in cost reductions. These economies may be *internal* or *external* to the *firm*. Our discussion of constant returns to scale is not inconsistent with the existence of economies which are internal to the firm. Thus, despite the fact that the production function of the industry is characterized by constant returns to scale, the production function of the firm is permitted to exhibit successively increasing, constant, and decreasing returns to scale, giving rise to the usual U-shaped average-cost curve. The first phase of increasing returns in the firm's production function is due to *internal economies*, such as division of labor within the firm. Sooner or later, these internal economies come to an end. They are succeeded by constant and decreasing returns to scale, largely because of the increasing difficulties of supervision.

If the internal economies to the firm were to continue indefinitely, perfect

---

† This chapter is slightly more technical than the rest of the book. It can be skipped, for the analysis of the rest of the book does not depend on it.

competition would break down because eventually one firm would become so large that it would be able to supply the whole industry output. Recall that the supply curve of a purely competitive firm does not exist in the region of decreasing average cost. When the internal economies of a firm continue indefinitely and thus the average-cost curve slopes downward throughout, the firm finds it profitable to increase output beyond all bounds, provided that its average-cost curve dips below the average-revenue curve after a certain point. Thus, the firm eventually becomes so large that it is able to affect the price of its product, i.e., it stops being a perfect competitor. Accordingly, unlimited increasing returns due to internal economies are incompatible with perfect competition.

The compatibility of increasing returns with perfectly competitive conditions is saved by the concept of *external economies*—a concept introduced into the literature by Marshall in 1890 and later refined by Edgeworth, Haberler, Knight, Viner, Kemp, Meade, and others. The basic idea behind this concept is that the cost curves of individual firms shift downward as the industry's output expands. The lower costs can be attributed to either (*a*) lower factor prices or (*b*) increased efficiency of each firm. The first type of external economies, i.e., those which are due to lower factor prices, are called *pecuniary;* the second, i.e., those which are due to increased efficiency, are called *technological.* The pecuniary external economies present no new difficulties, whereas the technological external economies do.

*Pecuniary external economies* cannot be observed in the case of primary factors. They can only be observed in the case of intermediate goods when the supplying industry is either a monopoly or a decreasing-cost industry subject to *technological external economies.* In the former case, perfect competition is ruled out; in the latter, the pecuniary economies arise because of the existence of the second species of external economies, i.e., those of the technological variety.

The introduction of *technological external economies* gives rise to two major difficulties. First, the economy may not produce on the production-possibilities frontier under perfectly competitive conditions. Second, even if it does, the slope of the production-possibilities frontier no longer gives the ratio of commodity prices, except under certain specific circumstances. Both of these complications have been ignored in the pure theory of trade by means of several simplifying assumptions.

It is usually assumed that the technological external economies are such that they do not prevent the economy from producing on its production-possibilities frontier, and that the slope of the frontier is equal to the ratio of commodity prices. The latter assumption is justified in several ways. Meade (1952, p. 33) assumes "either that the economies of scale are external to the individual firms and that there is a system of taxes and subsidies which equates price to marginal social cost in each competitive industry, or that the economies of scale are internal to large monopolistic firms and that the State controls each industry in such a way that it produces up to the point at which the price is equal to the marginal social cost of production." On the other hand, Kemp (1964, p. 111) assumes "that all external economies to the firm are . . . of equal severity in both industries, in the sense that the ratio of marginal private cost to marginal social cost is the same in both industries." Essentially the same assumption is also made by Matthews (1950).

When the preceding complications are assumed away, increasing returns to scale present new problems only to the extent that the production-possibilities frontier is convex to the origin—and not concave, as in the case of constant returns to scale. In other words, when the production-possibilities frontier maintains the concave-to-the-origin shape, the formal analysis of increasing returns to scale does not differ at all from the analysis of constant returns to scale. However, *this is the result of the specific assumption that relative prices are given by the marginal rate of transformation and is totally unrelated to the shape of the production-possibilities frontier.* In general, the price ratio is different from the slope of the production-possibilities frontier, and the geometrical analysis of constant returns to scale has to be amended. The appendix at the end of this chapter gives an example where, in the presence of external economies, a perfectly competitive economy may not be able to produce on its production-possibilities frontier.

The rest of the analysis of this chapter incorporates increasing returns rigorously within the context of an admittedly simple model. The assumption that the marginal rate of transformation reflects relative prices is dropped.

## 7.1 A SIMPLE MODEL OF A CLOSED ECONOMY

### The Model

Consider a closed economy producing two commodities, $X$ and $Y$, by means of an inelastically supplied primary factor of production, called labor ($L$). Industry $Y$ is subject to constant returns to scale. In particular, assume that the production of 1 unit of $Y$ requires exactly 1 unit of labor. On the other hand, industry $X$ is subject to increasing returns to scale which are the result of technological external economies—a necessary assumption for the existence of pure competition.

Figure 7.1 summarizes these assumptions. Consider the first quadrant only for the moment. Measure labor along the horizontal axis, and $Y$ along the vertical axis. The total amount of labor available to the economy ($\bar{L}$) is given by the horizontal distance $O\bar{L}$. The 45° line in this quadrant shows the production function of industry $Y$. Obviously, the maximum amount of $Y$ which the economy can produce is given by the distance $OB$, which is necessarily equal to the distance $O\bar{L}$.

Because 1 unit of $Y$ always requires 1 unit of labor, we can measure the amount of labor which is not employed in the production of $Y$, and therefore is employed in industry $X$, by the difference between the maximum and the actual amount of $Y$ produced. For instance, when $L_1$ units of labor are used to produce $OA$ units of $Y$, the vertical distance $BA(= L_1 \bar{L})$ shows the quantity of labor used in the production of $X$.

In general, then, we can measure labor on the vertical axis also. The total amount of labor is, of course, given by the vertical distance $OB$. Any point between $O$ and $B$ gives the allocation of labor between the two industries. For instance, point $A$ divides the total amount of labor into $OA$ and $BA$. The former ($OA$) is allocated to industry $Y$, and the latter ($BA$) to industry $X$.

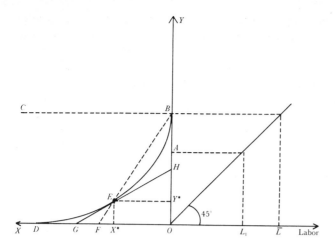

**Figure 7.1** The production functions of $X$ and $Y$, and the production-possibilities frontier.

The second quadrant shows the production function of $X$ as well as the production-possibilities frontier for the economy. Consider point $B$ as the origin for the production function of $X$ and measure along the vertical axis, moving from $B$ to $A$, the amount of labor used in the production of $X$ and along the horizontal line $BC$ the output of $X$. Then, the curve $BD$ is the production function of $X$, characterized by increasing returns. This same curve, considered from the viewpoint of the origin $O$, is the production-possibilities frontier.

## Some Formal Relationships

Let us consider now some formal relationships. Note that the real wage rate expressed in terms of $Y$ is equal to unity. Further, assuming that $q$ units of $X$ are equivalent to 1 unit of $Y$ in the market-place when the quantities $X^*$ and $Y^*$ are produced (that is, $1/q = p_x/p_y = p$), we have

$$\text{Labor used in the production of } Y^* = Y^*$$

$$\text{Labor used in the production of } X^* = \bar{L} - Y^*$$

$$\text{Wage bill expressed in terms of } Y = \bar{L}$$

$$\text{Wage bill expressed in terms of } X = q\bar{L}$$

$$\text{Value of output expressed in terms of } Y = pX^* + Y^*$$

$$\text{Value of output expressed in terms of } X = X^* + qY^*$$

Since prices are equal to their respective average costs of production, the value of output must equal the wage bill, that is,

$$\bar{L} = pX^* + Y^* \tag{7.1}$$

Geometrically, eq. (7.1) is shown by the straight line passing through points $B$ and $E$ of fig. 7.1, and represents the community budget line. Therefore, if the economy happens to be in equilibrium at point $E$, it necessarily follows that $p \neq \mathrm{MRT}$, as illustrated in fig. 7.1, where $\mathrm{MRT} = $ marginal rate of transformation, or the opportunity cost of $X$ in terms of $Y$. Obviously, the relative market price of the commodity whose production function is subject to increasing returns to scale ($X$ in our case) is necessarily higher than its opportunity cost, that is, $p > \mathrm{MRT}$.

Actually, the equality $p = \mathrm{MRT}$ implies losses to the producers of $X$. Thus, assuming that the money wage rate is unity, we have

$$\text{Total cost of production} = \$\bar{L}$$

$$p_y = \$1$$

and

$$p_y Y^* = \$Y^*$$

If $p = \mathrm{MRT}$, then $p_x = p = \mathrm{MRT}$. Therefore, the market value of $X^*$ would be equal to $(\mathrm{MRT})X^*$, which geometrically is equal to the distance $Y^*H$. Since the total cost of production of $X^*$ is equal to $Y^*B$, such pricing would necessarily involve losses to the producers of $X$ equal to the distance $HB$. This state of affairs cannot be viable in the long run.

## Introduction of Demand

Let us now introduce demand by means of the neoclassical device of the social indifference map. Figure 7.2 reproduces the production-possibilities frontier of fig. 7.1, but with the direction of the horizontal axis reversed and with some additional information about demand. The community budget line must necessarily start at the vertical-axis intercept of the production-possibilities frontier,

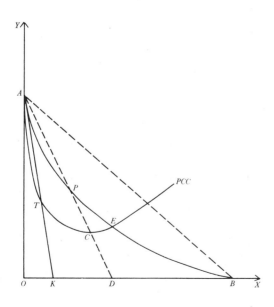

**Figure 7.2** Autarkic equilibrium and a useful breakdown of the range of value of $p$ into three regions.

point $A$. In addition to the production-possibilities frontier, fig. 7.2 shows the Hicksian price-consumption curve (PCC), starting at point $A$. This is all that is needed for our purposes.

Production takes place on the production-possibilities frontier ($AB$) by assumption. Consumption takes place on the PCC. Therefore, general equilibrium occurs at the intersection of the two curves, point $E$.

At the equilibrium point $E$, the marginal rate of substitution in consumption (MRS $= p$), that is, the slope of the line $AE$ (not drawn), is higher than the MRT, that is, the slope of the production-possibilities frontier at $E$. Therefore, one of the Pareto-optimality conditions is not satisfied and the economy is unable to maximize its welfare. This can be achieved only through appropriate economic policy measures (see chaps. 20 and 21 below).

It is usually said that, under conditions of increasing returns, competitive equilibrium exists if the indifference curves are "more convex" than the production-possibilities frontier (see Chipman, 1965; Matthews, 1950; and Young, 1928). This condition is also considered necessary for stability (see Meade, 1952, pp. 33–34). However, these conclusions are based on the incorrect assumption that $p =$ MRT. In the general case examined here, this condition is irrelevant.

## 7.2 THE OFFER CURVE

### Consumption and Production Equilibria

Let us derive a country's offer curve. Since the "offers" are given by the differences between domestic consumption and production, our analysis has to start with a discussion of consumption and production equilibria.

Consumption occurs at the point where the budget line touches the highest social indifference curve. The price-consumption curve (PCC) of fig. 7.2 summarizes the situation when the budget line passes through point $A$. When trade opens up, the budget line need not necessarily pass through $A$. We return to this point later. The problem is much more difficult for the production equilibria, where the possibility of multiple equilibria arises. (For an excellent discussion along the same lines, see Kemp, 1964.)

It is convenient to break down the range of values of $p$ into three regions. Consider the budget lines $AK$ (that is, the tangent to the production-possibilities frontier at point $A$) and $AB$ (that is, the straight line joining the two axis intercepts of the production-possibilities frontier). Region $a$ corresponds to that range of values of $p$ which implies steeper budget lines than $AK$, region $b$ corresponds to values of $p$ which lie between those implied by the budget lines $AK$ and $AB$; and region $c$ corresponds to that range of values of $p$ which implies flatter budget lines than $AB$.

In region $a$, the relative price of $X$ is higher than the limit of the ratio of average costs of production at point $A$, as shown by the slope of $AK$. Therefore, in region $a$, the production of $X$ is profitable, and it becomes even more so as the output of $X$ increases. Consequently, the economy produces at $B$.

If $p$ is equal to the slope of $AB$, production can take place at either $A$ or $B$. However, the production equilibrium is stable at $A$ and unstable at $B$, because at $A$ the average cost of production of $X$ is higher than its price. Despite the fact that it falls as $X$ expands, the average cost of production of $X$ continues to remain higher than its price. Only at point $B$ are the producers of $X$ able to cover their costs. Hence, point $B$ can be considered as a production equilibrium point. It is unstable, though, in the sense that any movement away from $B$ generates forces which put the economy back to point $A$.

If $p$ is equal to the slope of $AK$, equilibrium can again take place at either $A$ or $B$. However, point $B$ is now stable and $A$ unstable.

If the price ratio lies in region $c$, the economy, in the absence of permanent subsidization, specializes in the production of $Y$.

The most interesting possibility is when the price ratio lies in region $b$. Here there are three possible production equilibria. To illustrate, consider a price ratio equal to the slope of the budget line $APCD$. The three possible production equilibria are $A$, $P$, and $B$. Points $A$ and $B$ are stable while the middle point, $P$, is unstable, as can easily be verified.

To summarize: for price ratios in regions $a$ and $c$, unique production equilibria exist at points $B$ and $A$, respectively. For the limiting price ratios shown by the slopes of $AK$ and $AB$, there are two production equilibria at points $A$ and $B$, with point $B$ stable in the former case and $A$ in the latter. For price ratios in region $b$, there are three production equilibria at points $A$ and $B$ and at the intersection between the budget line through $A$ and the production-possibilities frontier.

## The Production Equilibria in Terms of the Average-Cost Schedule

Perhaps the preceding discussion of production equilibria can be clarified further by means of the average-cost schedule for commodity $X$, as illustrated in fig. 7.3. For simplicity, assume that the wage rate is $1, which implies that the average cost (AC) of $Y$ is $1 also.

The average-cost schedule for $X$ (fig. 7.3) is derived from the production-possibilities frontier (fig. 7.2). Thus, as we move from $A$ to $B$ on the production-possibilities frontier, we also move from $A$ to $B$ on the average-cost schedule. The three regions of $p$ discussed earlier can be read off the vertical axis as shown in fig. 7.3.

When the market price of $X$ ($p_x$) is less than $OC$, the production of $X$ ceases completely—the producers cannot cover their costs. In the limiting case where $p_x$ is equal to $OC$ ($X$'s lowest possible average cost of production), production may occur at $B$. However, for any output level which is less than the maximum ($X_0$), the average cost of $X$ is higher than its price and the tendency is for the production of $X$ to drop to zero—not increase. Hence, when $p_x = OC$, the production equilibrium at $B$ (figs. 7.2 and 7.3) is unstable.

When $p_x$ is higher than $OA$, production necessarily occurs at $B$. At *all* output levels profits are positive. In the limiting case $p_x = OA$, profits are zero at $A$ but become positive and tend to increase as soon as the output of $X$ increases above

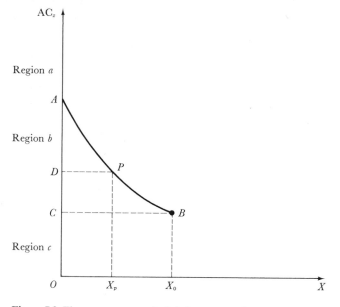

**Figure 7.3** The average-cost schedule for commodity $X$.

zero. Hence, while $A$ is an equilibrium point because $p_x = AC_x$, it is an unstable equilibrium—as soon as $X > 0$, positive profits push the economy toward complete specialization in commodity $X$ at $B$.

When $OC < p_x < OA$, as illustrated in fig. 7.3 by $p_x = OD$, production can occur at three points: $A$, $P$, and $B$. The production equilibria $A$ and $B$ are stable. Thus, for any output between $O$ and $X_p$ (that is, $0 < X < X_p$), the tendency (because of losses) is for the production of $X$ to drop to zero. On the other hand, for any output between $X_p$ and $X_0$ (that is, $X_p < X < X_0$), the tendency (because of profits) is for the production of $X$ to increase to its maximum $X_0$. This also explains why the production-equilibrium point $P$ is unstable: when $X$ is slightly different from $X_p$, the tendency is to return to either $A$ or $B$, not $P$.

The careful reader must note that presently the Marshallian stability analysis is applied—not the Walrasian.

## Derivation of the Offer Curve

The offer curve is derived in fig. 7.4. The production-possibilities frontier and the price-consumption curve (PCC) as well as the two limiting budget lines have been drawn in the fourth quadrant. Point $A$ of fig. 7.2 coincides now with the origin of the diagram, through which are drawn the two limiting price ratios.

For terms of trade in region $c$, our economy specializes in the production of $Y$ and consumes along the PCC to the right of point $C$. Therefore, the economy exports $Y$ and imports $X$. In particular, the offer curve for this range of relative

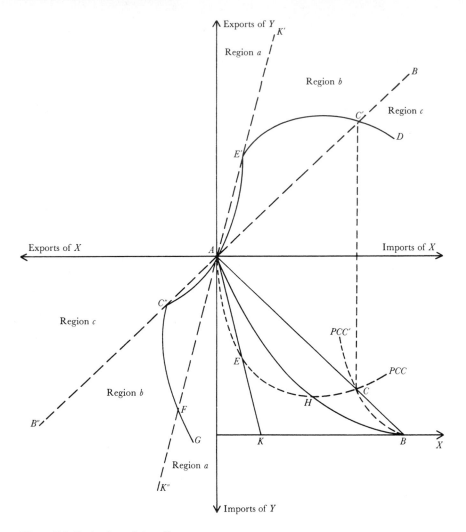

**Figure 7.4** Derivation of the offer curve.

prices lies in the first quadrant (actually, it is the mirror image of that part of the PCC to the right of $C$). This is shown in fig. 7.4 by the curve $C'D$.

When the terms of trade coincide with the slope of $AB$, there are two production equilibria ($A$ and $B$) and a single consumption equilibrium ($C$). Therefore, two offers arise as shown by points $C'$ (in the first quadrant) and $C''$ (in the third quadrant).

For terms of trade in region $a$, our economy specializes in the production of $X$ and consumes along the PCC'. The portion of the offer curve which corresponds to this range is given by the curve $FG$ in the third quadrant. Since this part coincides with the offer curve under Ricardian assumptions (with $AB$ being the

Ricardian production-possibilities frontier), the various steps in its derivation have been omitted.

When the terms of trade coincide with the slope of $AK$, there are two production equilibria (points $A$ and $B$) and two offers. One is shown by point $F$ in the third quadrant (implying production at point $B$) and the other shown by point $E'$ in the first quadrant (corresponding to consumption at $E$, in the fourth quadrant, and implying production at $A$).

When the terms of trade lie in region $b$, there are three possible production equilibria which necessarily give rise to three offers. If production takes place at point $A$, consumption takes place along the PCC between points $E$ and $C$. The offers that arise in this case are shown by the curve $E'C'$ in the first quadrant, which is the mirror image of the part $EC$ of the PCC in the fourth quadrant. If production takes place at $B$, consumption takes place on the PCC′ from point $C$ upward. This gives rise to the part of the offer curve $C''F$, which appears in the third quadrant. It is derived in precisely the same way as the part $FG$ was derived. If production takes place at the intersection of a budget line drawn from point $A$ and the production-possibilities frontier, then we can distinguish among the following cases:

1. If the terms of trade are equal to the slope of the budget line $AH$ (not drawn), then consumption coincides with production and the corresponding point on the offer curve coincides with the origin of the diagram (i.e., point $A$).
2. If the terms of trade lie between the slopes of $AK$ and $AH$, $X$ is imported and $Y$ exported. Curve $AE'$ in the first quadrant is the part of the offer curve which describes the present case.
3. If the terms of trade lie between the slopes of $AH$ and $AB$, then $X$ is exported and $Y$ imported. The part of the offer curve which corresponds to this particular case is the part $AC''$ in the third quadrant.

In summary, the offer curve is shown by the curve $GFC''AE'C'D$. The portion $E'C'D$ implies specialization in the production of $Y$, whereas the portion $C''FG$ implies specialization in $X$. The middle portion, $C''AE'$, corresponds to incomplete specialization.†

## 7.3 INTERNATIONAL EQUILIBRIUM

### A Simple Open Economy

Consider, first, a simple open economy, i.e., an economy which is a price taker in the international market. The behavior of our economy can be summarized in fig. 7.5, which reproduces the offer curve of fig. 7.4. Note that the slope of the tangent ($PP'$) to the offer curve at the origin shows the pretrade price ratio in our economy. (The proof given earlier in relation to constant returns to scale to the

---

† For a brief discussion of the problems involved for the generalization of the preceding analysis when the number of factors is increased to two, see Chacholiades (1970).

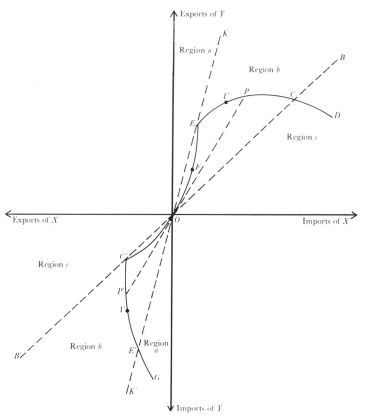

**Figure 7.5** The offer curve summarizes the behavior of the simple open economy.

effect that the slope of the offer curve at the origin shows pretrade relative prices is valid for the present case as well. That proof did not depend upon the characteristics of production functions.)

If the international price ratio lies in region $c$, our economy definitely specializes in the production of $Y$ and imports $X$. The terms-of-trade line necessarily intersects the offer curve in the first quadrant and in the region $CD$ only. Similarly, if the international price ratio lies in region $a$, the terms-of-trade line necessarily intersects the offer curve in the third quadrant in the region $E'G$ only. Thus, our economy specializes completely in the production of $X$, and exports $X$ and imports $Y$. Finally, for any price ratio in region $b$, the direction of trade of our economy as well as its specialization in production remain indeterminate. In this region there are always three offers.

If the international price ratio is equal to the domestic pretrade price ratio, our economy can do one of three things.

1. It can continue to produce and consume exactly as before trade, with the origin on the diagram being the equilibrium trade point. However, this offer is unstable and, in addition, less preferable to the third alternative.

2. It can specialize in the production of $Y$, with the equilibrium offer given by point $P$ in the first quadrant.
3. It can specialize in the production of $X$, with the equilibrium offer given by point $P'$ in the third quadrant.

Both offers $P$ and $P'$ are stable. However, the last offer $(P')$ is preferred because the implied income of the economy expressed in terms of any commodity is higher in this case than the other two, as can be seen from the fact that the consumption-possibilities frontiers implied by the first two alternatives are identical and lie inside the consumption-possibilities frontier implied by the last alternative. In general, *it is to the advantage of a country to specialize in the production of the commodity whose production function is characterized by increasing returns to scale.*

For any international price ratio giving rise to a terms-of-trade line steeper than $PP'$ but flatter than $KK'$, there are again three offers as illustrated by points $U$, $F$, and $V$ (the line $UFV$ has been omitted for simplicity). Points $U$ and $F$ lie in the first quadrant, while $V$ lies in the third. This same pattern is necessarily observed for all terms-of-trade lines lying between $KK'$ and $PP'$. The offers $U$ and $V$, implying complete specialization in $Y$ and $X$, respectively, are stable, while the offer $F$, implying incomplete specialization, is unstable. Nevertheless, social welfare is higher at $V$ than either $U$ or $F$. Actually, points $U$ and $F$ are inferior to the autarkic equilibrium.

For terms-of-trade lines lying between $PP'$ and $CC'$, there are again three offers: one in the first quadrant along the region $PC$ of the offer curve and two in the third quadrant lying, respectively, along the regions $OC'$ and $C'P'$ of the offer curve. The middle offer along the region $OC'$ is again unstable, while the other two are stable. Again, complete specialization in $X$ (that is, the offer along $C'P'$) produces maximum welfare.

A major difference between the present case of increasing returns and the case of constant returns to scale is that in the latter case, when the international terms of trade coincide with the pretrade price ratio, our economy cannot participate (profitably) in international trade. This is not so under increasing returns to scale. Whether or not the international price ratio coincides with the pretrade price ratio, our economy will always participate in international trade. Another major difference between constant and increasing returns to scale is the existence of multiple offers in the latter but not in the former case, with the resulting instability of the offer implying incomplete specialization and the indeterminacy in the structure of production.

## A Two-Country Model

Once the preceding analysis is well understood, the introduction of a second country (or the rest of the world) with a similarly shaped offer curve presents no additional problems. In general, there are multiple equilibria and, what is more, the direction of trade cannot be decided a priori, except in a special case. Figure 7.6 illustrates the general case of three equilibria: $E_1$, $E_2$, and $E_3$. At point $E_1$,

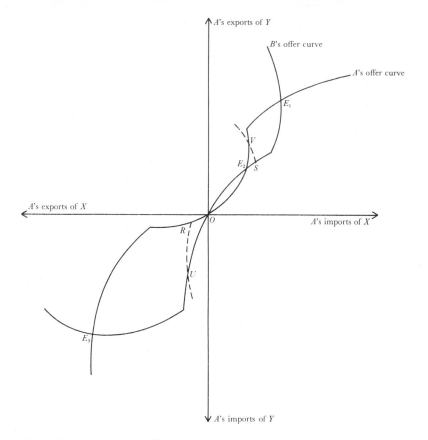

**Figure 7.6** International equilibrium.

country $A$ is completely specializing in the production of $Y$, and $B$ in $X$; thus, $A$ exports $Y$ and $B$ exports $X$. At $E_3$, the pattern of production specialization is opposite that at $E_1$. However, at $E_2$, both countries produce both commodities, with $A$ exporting $Y$ and $B$ exporting $X$. From the preceding analysis, points $E_1$ and $E_3$ are stable while $E_2$ is unstable. In general, an equilibrium point implying incomplete specialization in both countries (such as $E_2$) is unstable.

No attempt is made here to provide an explicit dynamic adjustment mechanism according to which the world economy behaves when it happens to be out of equilibrium. It seems sufficient to point out that the Walrasian stability conditions are satisfied at points $E_1$ and $E_3$. However, it should be emphasized that this characterization of stable equilibria is not sufficient to explain where the world economy would move if it happened to be at $E_2$ and a minor shock threw it out of equilibrium. Would it move toward $E_1$ or $E_3$? Whether the terms-of-trade line becomes steeper or flatter than $OE_2$ after the shock, both $E_1$ and $E_3$ pass the Walrasian stability test. Without the introduction of more specific assumptions about the dynamic adjustment mechanism at work, it is impossible to say whether the world economy will settle at $E_1$ or $E_3$. The outcome would seem to depend on chance.

To illustrate the possibility alluded to earlier, namely, that, in the presence of increasing returns, profitable trade can take place even if the pretrade prices of the two countries are identical, imagine $B$'s (or $A$'s) offer curve in fig. 7.6 rotating through the origin until it becomes tangent to $A$'s ($B$'s) offer curve at the origin. Then, point $E_2$ will coincide with the origin while points $E_1$ and $E_3$ will continue to exhibit the same properties as in fig. 7.6.

Figure 7.6 illustrates the case where the stable equilibria $E_1$ and $E_3$ imply complete specialization in both countries. However, this is not necessary, as illustrated by the broken curves $RU$ and $SV$, implying stable equilibria at $U$ and $V$, respectively. At $U$, country $A$ specializes completely in $X$ while $B$ produces both commodities. At $V$, country $B$ specializes in $X$ while $A$ produces both $X$ and $Y$.

As noted earlier, the direction of trade is indeterminate except in a special case. Thus, in terms of the terminology of fig. 7.5, the direction of trade can be predicted only if $A$'s region $b$ does not overlap with $B$'s region $b$. In particular, if $B$'s region $b$ lies above and to the left of $A$'s in the first quadrant, equilibrium necessarily occurs in the third quadrant, with $A$ exporting $X$ and importing $Y$. On the other hand, if $B$'s region $b$ lies below and to the right of $A$'s in the first quadrant, equilibrium necessarily occurs in the first quadrant, with $A$ exporting $Y$ and importing $X$.

There is no requirement, as in the case of constant returns to scale (barring multiple pretrade equilibria), for the equilibrium terms of trade to lie between the pretrade price ratios. This can be seen in the case where the pretrade prices are identical in the two countries and yet trade takes place at prices that are in general different from the common pretrade price ratio.

Note that there is no necessity for the terms of trade to be different at the three equilibrium points $E_1$, $E_2$, and $E_3$. In other words, it is quite possible for all three points $(E_1, E_2,$ and $E_3)$ to lie on a straight line through the origin. This is illustrated in fig. 7.7, which is similar to fig. 7.2 except that now the production-possibilities frontier, shown here by the curve $KPM$, is common to both countries $A$ and $B$. At the international terms of trade, $p = p_0$, given by the absolute slope of either $KC_BPC_AR$ or $DC'_BC'_AM$, either country can produce at any of the three points $K$, $P$, or $M$. When production occurs at $M$, the consumption-possibilities frontier is given by $DC'_BC'_AM$, and when production occurs either at $K$ or $P$, the consumption-possibilities frontier is given by $KC_BPC_AR$. Further, when $A$'s consumption-possibilities frontier is given by $KC_BPC_AR$, country $A$ consumes at $C_A$, and when it is given by $DC'_BC'_AM$, then $A$ consumes at $C'_A$. The corresponding consumption points for country $B$ are, respectively, $C_B$ and $C'_B$. The triangle $C_BGP$ is identical to $PFC_A$, the triangle $KSC_B$ is identical to $C'_AHM$, and the triangle $KEC_A$ is identical to $C'_BNM$. Therefore, there are three equilibrium points as follows:

1. Both countries produce at $P$, with $A$ consuming at $C_A$ and $B$ at $C_B$. Thus, $B$ exports $GP = FC_A$ units of $X$ to country $A$ in exchange for $FP = GC_B$ units of $Y$. Note that, in this particular case, *country A consumes inside its production-*

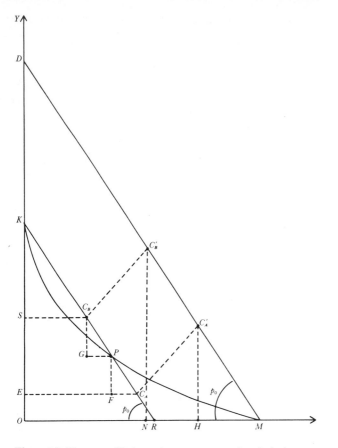

**Figure 7.7** Three equilibria at the same terms of trade ($p_0$).

*possibilities frontier.* Hence, country $A$ becomes worse off (in this particular case) after the introduction of trade. However, country $B$ benefits, mostly at the expense of country $A$.

2. Country $B$ produces at $K$ (that is, $B$ specializes completely in $Y$) and consumes at $C_B$, while $A$ produces at $M$ (that is, $A$ specializes completely in $X$) and consumes at $C'_A$. Thus, $A$ exports $HM = SC_B$ units of $X$ to $B$ in exchange for $KS = HC'_A$ units of $Y$. In this case, while $B$ continues to consume at $C_B$, as in the first case, country $A$'s consumption of both commodities increases: $A$ moves from $C_A$ to $C'_A$. Compared with the pretrade position, both countries clearly gain after the introduction of trade, although $A$ gets the lion's share.

3. Country $A$ produces at $K$ and consumes at $C_A$, and $B$ produces at $M$ and consumes at $C'_B$. Thus, $A$ specializes in $Y$ and $B$ in $X$. In particular, $A$ exports $KE = NC'_B$ units of $Y$ to country $B$ in exchange for $NM = EC_A$ units of $X$. As in case 1, $A$ *becomes worse off with trade.* Country $B$'s gains are much higher in this case than in the previous two.

It is apparent that a country gains most when it specializes in the production of that commodity $(X)$ whose production function is characterized by increasing returns to scale. Therefore, it is in the interest of a country to pursue a trade policy that eventually enables the country to specialize in the production of $X$. But what happens when both countries pursue such a policy? $(a)$ One of the two countries may be satisfied with the meager gains of specialization in the "wrong" commodity, until finally stable equilibrium is reached. $(b)$ Both countries might interfere with the free flow of goods to the point where the latter is actually shrunk to zero. $(c)$ The governments of the two countries may get together and agree upon an equitable distribution of the gains between them. Thus, the country which eventually specializes completely in the production of $X$ (that is, the commodity whose production function is characterized by increasing returns to scale) might agree to make an income transfer (annually) to the other country, which agrees to specialize completely in $Y$ (that is, the commodity whose production function is characterized by constant returns to scale).

# APPENDIX TO CHAPTER SEVEN. EXAMPLES OF EXTERNAL ECONOMIES

This appendix gives an example of external economies which may prevent a perfectly competitive economy from producing on its production-possibilities frontier.

Let the output of commodity $X$ depend on labor $(L_x)$ and land $(T_x)$ used in industry $X$ and on the amount of labor $(L_y)$ used in the production of commodity $Y$. Further, assume that the output of commodity $Y$ depends on the amounts of labor $(L_y)$ and land $(T_y)$ used directly in the production of $Y$. The production functions take the form

$$X = X(L_x, T_x, L_0 - L_x) \tag{A7.1}$$

$$Y = Y(L_y, T_y) \tag{A7.2}$$

since $L_y = L_0 - L_x$, where $L_0 \equiv$ total amount of labor available to the economy. The marginal rate of substitution of labor for land in industry $X$ is given by

$$\text{MRS}_{LT}^X = -\frac{dT_x}{dL_x} = \frac{dX/dL_x}{dX/dT_x} = \frac{(\partial X/\partial L_x) - (\partial X/\partial L_y)}{\partial X/\partial T_x} \tag{A7.3}$$

Similarly, the marginal rate of substitution of $L$ for $T$ in industry $Y$ is given by

$$\text{MRS}_{LT}^Y = -\frac{dT_y}{dL_y} = \frac{\partial Y/\partial L_y}{\partial Y/\partial T_y} \tag{A7.4}$$

The economy will be allocating its resources along the contract curve of the box diagram if the following condition is satisfied:

$$\text{MRS}_{LT}^X = \text{MRS}_{LT}^Y \tag{A7.5}$$

However, perfect competition will bring about the following equality:

$$\frac{\partial X/\partial L_x}{\partial X/\partial T_x} = \mathrm{MRS}^Y_{LT} = \frac{w}{r} \qquad (A7.6)$$

where $w/r$ is the factor-price ratio. Therefore, unless the partial derivative $\partial X/\partial L_y$ is zero, eq. (A7.5) cannot be satisfied and the economy will end up producing inside its production-possibilities frontier. In the present case, where by assumption $\partial X/\partial L_y > 0$, eq. (A7.5) is indeed not satisfied and the economy will indeed be producing inside its frontier.

The above illustration is based on an interaction between the output of one industry and the factors employed by the other. In the terminology of Kemp (1955, 1964), this is the case of a *factor-generated* externality. On the other hand, an externality is called *output-generated* by Kemp when it is based on an interaction between the output of one industry and the output of another.

An output-generated externality cannot prevent a competitive economy from producing on its production-possibilities frontier. For instance, assume that the production functions take the form

$$X = X(L_x, T_x, Y) \qquad (A7.7)$$

$$Y = Y(L_y, T_y) \qquad (A7.8)$$

Equation (A7.8) is the same as (A7.2). Thus, the marginal rate of substitution of $L$ for $T$ in industry $Y$ continues to be given by eq. (A7.4). The marginal rate of substitution of $L$ for $T$ in industry $X$ is now given by

$$\mathrm{MRS}^X_{LT} = -\frac{dT_x}{dL_x} = \frac{(dX/dL_x)}{(dX/dT_x)} = \frac{(\partial X/\partial L_x) - (\partial X/\partial Y)(\partial Y/\partial L_y)}{(\partial X/\partial T_x) - (\partial X/\partial Y)(\partial Y/\partial T_y)} \qquad (A7.9)$$

Again, perfect competition gives rise to eq. (A7.6). Resources, however, are allocated along the contract curve only when eq. (A7.5) holds. Does perfect competition lead to eq. (A7.5) also? The answer is "Yes." To confirm this conclusion, merely substitute from eqs. (A7.4) and (A7.6) into eq. (A7.9) to obtain

$$\mathrm{MRS}^X_{LT} = \frac{(w/r)(\partial X/\partial T_x) - (\partial X/\partial Y)(w/r)(\partial Y/\partial T_y)}{(\partial X/\partial T_x) - (\partial X/\partial Y)(\partial Y/\partial T_y)} = \frac{w}{r} \qquad (A7.10)$$

Even if the economy does produce on its production-possibilities frontier, the equilibrium price ratio, measuring the marginal rate of substitution in consumption, is in general different from the slope of the production-possibilities frontier, because the latter measures the ratio of marginal social costs whereas the former measures the ratio of marginal private costs—and social costs are lower than private costs when technological external economies exist. This difficulty has been circumvented in the literature quite expeditiously by means of several simplifying assumptions.

# SELECTED BIBLIOGRAPHY

Chacholiades, M. (1970). "Increasing Returns and the Theory of Comparative Advantage." *Southern Economic Journal*, vol. 37, pp. 157–162.

Chipman, J. S. (1965). "A Survey of the Theory of International Trade: Part 2, The Neoclassical Theory." *Econometrica*, vol. 33, pp. 685–760.

Herberg, H., and M. C. Kemp (1969). "Some Implications of Variable Returns to Scale." *Canadian Journal of Economics and Political Science*, vol. 2, no. 3 (August), pp. 401–415.

Kemp, M. C. (1955). "The Efficiency of Competition as an Allocator of Resources: I. External Economies of Production." *Canadian Journal of Economics and Political Science*, vol. XXI, no. 1 (February), pp. 30–42.

——— (1964). *The Pure Theory of International Trade*. Prentice-Hall, Inc., Englewood Cliffs, N.J., chap. 8.

Lerner, A. P. (1932). "The Diagrammatical Representation of Cost Conditions in International Trade." *Economica*, vol. 12, pp. 346–356. Reprinted in A. P. Lerner, *Essays in Economic Analysis*. Macmillan and Company, London, 1953.

Matthews, R. C. O. (1950). "Reciprocal Demand and Increasing Returns." *Review of Economic Studies*, vol. 17, pp. 149–158.

Meade, J. E. (1951). "External Economies and Diseconomies in a Competitive Situation." *Economic Journal*, vol. LXII, no. 1 (March), pp. 54–67.

——— (1952). *A Geometry of International Trade*. George Allen and Unwin, Ltd., London, chaps. 1 to 4.

Melvin, J. R. (1969). "Increasing Returns to Scale as a Determinant of Trade." *Canadian Journal of Economics and Political Science*, vol. 2, no. 3 (August), pp. 389–402.

Young, A. A. (1928). "Increasing Returns and Economic Progress." *Economic Journal*, vol. 38, pp. 527–542. Reprinted in R. V. Clemence (Ed.), AEA *Readings in Economic Analysis*, vol. 1. Addison-Wesley Press, Cambridge, Mass., 1950.

# FOUR

## THE MODERN THEORY

# EIGHT

## FACTOR INTENSITY AND FACTOR ABUNDANCE

The preceding chapters show that the direction of trade is determined by the pretrade equilibrium price ratios, ignoring, of course, the cases of pretrade multiple equilibria and increasing returns to scale. Further, these pretrade price ratios depend upon the production-possibilities frontiers of the trading countries, as well as their respective demand conditions.† Therefore, the factors which determine the structure of trade can be traced back to differences in (*a*) the production-possibilities frontiers of the countries involved and (*b*) their demand conditions.

The neoclassical theory, contrary to the classical theory, does not attempt to go beyond these generalizations and, thus, offers no hypothesis as to why the pretrade price ratios differ between countries. (These comments should not be misconstrued to mean that the neoclassical theory is useless. Its value springs from the fact that, in addition to being a great pedagogical tool, it serves as an introduction to the modern theory.) The modern theory, on the other hand, makes a heroic attempt to predict the pattern of trade on the basis of the observable characteristics of the pretrade autarkic equilibria. In a sense, the modern theory begins where the neoclassical theory leaves off.

The modern theory may be broken down into the following two propositions:

1. The *cause* of international trade is to be found largely in differences between the factor endowments of different countries. In particular, a country has a com-

---

† The Ricardian doctrine of comparative advantage seems to have been developed on the basis of labor coefficients alone. However, the doctrine, for its logical validity, requires some demand restrictions. This creeps into the analysis through the implicit assumption that both commodities are produced and consumed in both countries in their respective pretrade equilibrium positions. In other words, any corner solutions in the pretrade situation are ruled out. In the absence of such restrictions on demand, the opening up of trade need not necessarily result in any change in consumption or production in either country. For further details, see chaps. 2 and 3.

parative advantage in the production of that commodity which uses more intensively the country's more abundant factor. This proposition is known as the *Heckscher–Ohlin theorem*.

2. The *effect* of international trade is to tend to equalize factor prices between countries, and thus serve to some extent as a substitute for factor mobility. This proposition is known as the *factor-price equalization theorem*.

As it turns out, neither proposition is generally true. Their validity depends on certain factual assumptions to be analyzed.†

Some preliminary work needs to be done before the two important theorems (i.e., the Heckscher–Ohlin theorem and the factor-price equalization theorem) of the modern theory are discussed. This is the purpose of this and the following chapter. In particular, this chapter deals with the concepts of factor intensity and factor abundance. The following chapter deals with the relationship between factor proportions, factor prices, and commodity prices.

Our discussion in this chapter is divided into four parts. The first three parts deal with the concept of factor intensity while the last (part D) deals with the concept of factor abundance. In particular, part A deals with the *standard model* of the modern theory; i.e., the Heckscher–Ohlin–Samuelson–Lerner model in which primary factors are used to produce directly final goods. Part B extends the analysis to Vanek's *model of interindustry flows*. Finally, part C considers briefly the problem of *pure intermediate commodities* (i.e., commodities which are produced solely for use in the production of final goods).

## PART A. THE STANDARD MODEL

### 8.1 SOME BASIC ASSUMPTIONS OF THE STANDARD MODEL

The Heckscher–Ohlin–Samuelson–Lerner model of international trade assumes that final commodities, say $X$ and $Y$, are produced directly by two homogeneous primary factors of production, say labor ($L$) and land ($T$), under constant returns to scale. The outputs of commodities depend only on inputs of primary factors which enter into their respective production processes. Factors are indifferent between uses and of the same quality in all countries. Pure competition prevails in both product and factor markets.

---

† The founders of the modern theory are Heckscher (1919) and his student Ohlin (1933). Ohlin was greatly influenced by Heckscher. The latter, whose work was not made available in English until 1949, acknowledged Wicksell's influence on his thought. Heckscher stated forthrightly that trade equalizes factor rewards completely. Ohlin, on the other hand, asserted that there is only a *tendency* toward factor-price equalization as a result of free trade. The partial-equalization argument was later made rigorous by Stolper and Samuelson (1941). A few years later, Samuelson (1948, 1949, 1953) extended the argument to establish the case for complete equalization. It should be noted that Samuelson's work prompted Robbins to rediscover a seminar paper which Lerner (1953) wrote in 1933 as a student at the LSE in which he demonstrated in a rigorous fashion the conditions for complete equalization.

The modern theory also makes the assumption that tastes are largely similar between countries. To simplify, assume initially that demand conditions in all countries are identical and homothetic. In particular, assume that there exists a single, homothetic social indifference map which summarizes the tastes of all countries. (The importance of homotheticity becomes evident in chap. 10.) Under these circumstances, any differences in the pretrade equilibrium price ratios must be attributed to differences in the production-possibilities frontiers of the countries involved. What factors, then, are responsible for any differences in the shapes of the production-possibilities frontiers between countries?

As we saw in chap. 4, the production-possibilities frontier of a country depends on: (*a*) its factor endowments and (*b*) the production functions of the various commodities. Consequently, any differences in the shape of the production-possibilities frontiers of, say, two countries must necessarily be attributed either to differences in their production functions or to differences in their factor endowments, or both.

The phrase "differences in their production functions" requires careful interpretation. Consider two countries (*A* and *B*), each endowed with two factors of production (labor and land) and each producing two commodities (*X* and *Y*). When we say that "any differences in the shape of the production-possibilities frontiers of the two countries must necessarily be attributed to . . . *differences in their production functions*," we do not mean differences in the production function of commodity *X* versus the production function of commodity *Y*. Rather, we mean differences in the production function of each commodity separately between countries. In other words, we mean differences in the production function of *X* between countries *A* and *B* and, similarly, differences in the production function of *Y* between *A* and *B*.

Should the production function of *X* be identical with that of *Y*, then from a purely economic point of view the model essentially reduces to a *single*-commodity economy (despite the difference in appearance and even the use of *X* and *Y*), since, with an appropriate choice of units of measurement, 1 unit of *X* can be made to consist of exactly the same factors (or inputs) as 1 unit of *Y*. The implications of this, first noted by Robinson (see Lerner, 1953, pp. 73, 76), will become apparent later in chap. 10.

The modern theory, in contrast to the classical theory, postulates the existence of linear homogeneous production functions which are also *identical between countries*. Thus, following the illustration given in the preceding paragraph, we can say that the modern theory postulates that the production function of commodity *X* is the same in both countries (*A* and *B*). The same, of course, holds for commodity *Y* as well. On the other hand, the production function of commodity *X* must necessarily be different from that of *Y*. On the basis of these assumptions, the modern theory concludes that any differences in the shapes of the production-possibilities frontiers of two countries must be found in differences in factor endowments, and advances the hypothesis that the cause of trade lies with differences in factor endowments. In other words, a country tends to have a comparative advantage in those commodities which use more intensively the country's more abundant factors.

## 8.2 THE MEANING OF "FACTOR INTENSITY"

Before the cause and effect of international trade are analyzed in detail, it is important to understand the meaning of *labor-intensive* or *land-intensive commodities*, as well as the meaning of *labor-abundant* or *land-abundant countries*. The purpose of this section is to clarify the concept of *factor intensity*. Part D below clarifies the concept of *factor abundance*.

   Under the assumption of constant returns to scale, the whole isoquant map is a blown-up version of the unit isoquant. Once the unit isoquant is given, the whole production function (or isoquant map) is simultaneously determined. Further, the expansion paths (or scale lines) are straight lines passing through the origin (for further details, see chap. 4). As a result, this discussion is conveniently restricted to the unit isoquants.

### Fixed Coefficients of Production

Figure 8.1 illustrates the concept of *factor intensity* under the simplifying assumption of fixed coefficients of production. The two L-shaped isoquants, $XX'$ and $YY'$, are assumed to be the unit isoquants for commodities $X$ and $Y$, respectively. The two broken lines, $OR$ and $OS$, represent the expansion paths for $X$ and $Y$, respectively. The slopes of the expansion paths $OR$ and $OS$ show the proportions

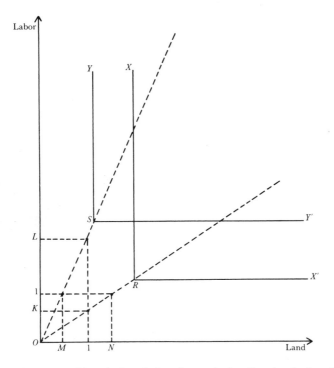

**Figure 8.1** With a single technique for producing $X$ and a single technique for producing $Y$, the two commodities are always classified into labor intensive and land intensive unambiguously.

in which the factors labor and land are used in the production of $X$ and $Y$, respectively. More precisely, the slope of the vector $OR$ shows the number of units of labor per unit of land that are required in the production of commodity $X$; and the slope of the vector $OS$ shows the number of units of labor per unit of land that are required in the production of $Y$. Since the vector $OS$ is steeper than the vector $OR$, it is obvious that commodity $Y$ requires more labor per unit of land than commodity $X$. Thus fig. 8.1 shows that, per unit of land, commodity $X$ requires $OK$ units of labor, whereas commodity $Y$ requires $OL$ units of labor, with $OL > OK$. This is expressed by saying that *commodity $Y$ is labor intensive relative to commodity $X$.*

When the problem is considered from the point of view of the number of units of land per unit of labor, it is obvious that commodity $X$ requires more units of land per unit of labor than commodity $Y$. Thus, fig. 8.1 shows that, per unit of labor, commodity $X$ requires $ON$, and commodity $Y$ requires $OM$, units of land, with $ON > OM$. Again, this can be expressed by saying that *commodity $X$ is land intensive relative to commodity $Y$.* This does not contradict the previous statement, namely, that commodity $Y$ is labor intensive relative to commodity $X$. In fact, the two statements represent two different ways of expressing the same thing. In other words, when we say that commodity $X$ is land intensive relative to commodity $Y$, we necessarily imply that commodity $Y$ is labor intensive relative to commodity $X$, and vice versa. Factor intensity, like comparative advantage, is a relative concept.

## Two Production Techniques for Each Commodity

With a single technique for producing $X$ and a single technique for producing $Y$, it is obvious that the two commodities can always be classified unambiguously into labor intensive and land intensive. The only exception to this general conclusion is the case where the two expansion paths coincide, a case which, as indicated previously, degenerates into the single-commodity economy (from our point of view), and we exclude it by assumption, at least for the time being. (The generalization of this conclusion to the case of more than two commodities is straightforward.) Usually, however, many production techniques for producing each commodity are known. Can we still classify unambiguously the two commodities in terms of factor intensity in this general case? Not always. There are some cases where this is true, of course.

Figure 8.2 illustrates a simple case where it is still possible to rank commodities in terms of factor ratios. Figure 8.2(a) illustrates the case where only two techniques are known for each commodity. (Figure 8.2(b) illustrates the same point when the isoquants are smoothly continuous.) Thus, the two techniques for producing 1 unit of $X$ are given by the coordinates of points $E$ and $F$, and the two techniques for producing 1 unit of $Y$ are given by the coordinates of points $C$ and $D$. On the assumption that the techniques $E$ and $F$ can be combined (without any interaction between them) to produce 1 unit of $X$, it must be clear that 1 unit of commodity $X$ can be produced by any one combination of labor and land that lies on the straight-line segment $EF$. Similarly, 1 unit of commodity $Y$ can be

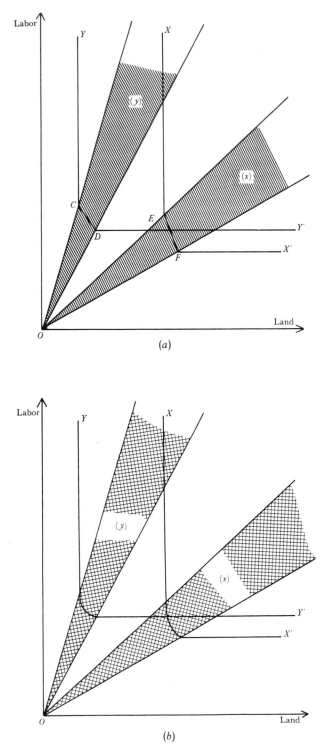

**Figure 8.2** (*a*) Two production techniques for each commodity with nonoverlapping cones of efficient expansion paths. (*b*) Smoothly continuous isoquants with nonoverlapping cones of efficient expansion paths.

produced by any one combination of labor and land that lies on the straight-line segment *CD*. Thus, the expansion path for *X* must necessarily lie in the shaded cone *x*, and the expansion path for *Y* in the shaded cone *y*. (This is also true for the corresponding case of smoothly continuous isoquants, illustrated in fig. 8.2(*b*).)

Figure 8.2 shows that commodity *Y* is labor intensive relative to commodity *X* or, what is the same thing, commodity *X* is land intensive relative to commodity *Y*. This follows from the fact that the shaded cones *x* and *y*, that is, the regions of efficient input ratios, do not overlap.

## Overlapping Cones of Efficient Expansion Paths

Figure 8.3 illustrates a more difficult case. The expansion path for industry *X* can lie in either cone *a* or cone *c*, and the expansion path for industry *Y* can lie in either cone *b* or cone *c*. Since cone *c* is common to both industries, it seems impossible to rank the two commodities unambiguously in terms of factor intensities. But this need not be so. The problem hinges on the way the optimum expansion paths of *X* and *Y* are selected. How is this selection performed under perfectly competitive conditions?

As we have already seen in chap. 4, the selection of the optimum expansion path for an industry depends upon factor prices. In particular, given the factor-price ratio *w/r*, the optimum expansion path is determined by the condition that the marginal rate of substitution of labor for land be equal to the given factor-

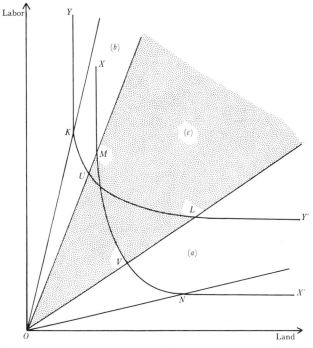

**Figure 8.3** Overlapping cones of efficient expansion paths. Commodity *Y* is labor intensive relative to *X*.

price ratio. Assuming both industries pay identical factor prices, it follows that the optimum expansion paths of the two industries—to be used for purposes of ranking the commodities in terms of factor intensities—must necessarily correspond to identical marginal rates of substitution of labor for land. But since factor prices are not given to begin with, how can we decide which commodity is labor intensive and which land intensive? Put differently, how can we exclude the possibility that one commodity is considered labor intensive for some factor-price ratios but land intensive for other factor-price ratios?

Commodities can be unambiguously ranked in terms of factor intensities if, and only if, prior knowledge of factor prices is unnecessary. Hence, commodity $Y$ is defined to be labor intensive relative to another commodity $X$ if commodity $Y$ uses more units of labor per unit of land than commodity $X$ *for all factor-price ratios*. This definition is illustrated in fig. 8.3, where, for any factor-price ratio, the optimum expansion path for industry $Y$ is steeper than the corresponding optimum expansion path for industry $X$. Observe that the slope of the isoquant $XX'$ at $V$ is steeper than the slope of $YY'$ at $U$. Therefore, for any factor-price ratio for which the optimum expansion path for industry $Y$ falls in the shaded cone $c$, the optimum expansion path for industry $X$ necessarily lies in cone $a$; and for any factor-price ratio for which the optimum expansion path for industry $X$ falls in the shaded cone $c$, the optimum expansion path for industry $Y$ necessarily lies in cone $b$.

The condition that the slope of $XX'$ at $V$ be steeper than the slope of $YY'$ at $U$ is sufficient but not necessary for the ranking of commodities $X$ and $Y$. It should be clear that *a necessary condition for $Y$ to be labor intensive is that any ray through the origin, and within the efficient cones, should cut the two unit isoquants at points such that $Y$'s isoquant is flatter than $X$'s*. For instance, the tangent to $XX'$ at $M$ should by necessity be steeper than the tangent to $YY'$ at $U$. Thus, for the factor-price ratio for which $X$'s expansion path coincides with the vector $OM$, $Y$'s expansion path must by necessity be steeper than $OM$. The point on $YY'$ where the slope is equal to the slope of $XX'$ at $M$ necessarily lies in the region $KU$. Conversely, for the factor-price ratio for which $Y$'s expansion path coincides with the vector $OU$, $X$'s expansion must by necessity be flatter than $OU$.

## Cobb–Douglas Production Functions

When the production functions of commodities $X$ and $Y$ are different and of the Cobb–Douglas type, commodities $X$ and $Y$ can be classified unequivocally into labor intensive and land intensive.

Consider the following Cobb–Douglas production function of commodity $X$:

$$X = AL_x^{\alpha} T_x^{(1-\alpha)} \tag{8.1}$$

where $A > 0$ and the parameter $\alpha$ satisfies the inequalities $0 < \alpha < 1$. The marginal physical products of labor and land are given respectively by

$$\text{MPP}_{LX} \equiv \frac{\partial X}{\partial L_x} = \alpha A L_x^{-(1-\alpha)} T_x^{(1-\alpha)} = \alpha A \left(\frac{1}{\rho_x}\right)^{(1-\alpha)} \tag{8.2}$$

$$\text{MPP}_{TX} \equiv \frac{\partial X}{\partial T_x} = (1 - \alpha)AL_x^\alpha T_x^{-\alpha} = (1 - \alpha)A\rho_x^\alpha \tag{8.3}$$

where $\rho_x \equiv L_x / T_x$. The marginal rate of substitution of labor for land is, of course, given by the ratio of marginal products:

$$\text{MRS}_{LT}^X = \frac{\text{MPP}_{LX}}{\text{MPP}_{TX}} = \frac{\alpha}{1 - \alpha} \frac{1}{\rho_x} \tag{8.4}$$

Similarly, consider the Cobb–Douglas production function of commodity $Y$:

$$Y = BL_y^\beta T_y^{(1 - \beta)} \tag{8.5}$$

where $B > 0$ and $0 < \beta < 1$. Assume that the parameter $\beta$ is different from $\alpha$; otherwise the model reduces to the one-commodity case referred to earlier. (This is precisely what is meant by the two Cobb–Douglas production functions being different: $\alpha \neq \beta$.) The marginal rate of substitution of labor for land in industry $Y$ is given by

$$\text{MRS}_{LT}^Y = \frac{\text{MPP}_{LY}}{\text{MPP}_{TY}} = \frac{\beta}{1 - \beta} \frac{1}{\rho_y} \tag{8.6}$$

When both industries face the same factor-price ratio, the factor proportions ($\rho_x$ and $\rho_y$) must be such that $\text{MRS}_{LT}^X = \text{MRS}_{LT}^Y$, that is,

$$\frac{\alpha}{1 - \alpha} \frac{1}{\rho_x} = \frac{\beta}{1 - \beta} \frac{1}{\rho_y} \tag{8.7}$$

or

$$\frac{\rho_x}{\rho_y} = \frac{(1/\beta) - 1}{(1/\alpha) - 1} \equiv \gamma \tag{8.8}$$

Equation (8.8) shows that, irrespective of the factor-price ratio, the ratio of factor proportions, that is, $\rho_x / \rho_y$, is always equal to a constant, $\gamma$. In particular, when $\alpha > \beta$, $\gamma > 1$ and $\rho_x > \rho_y$; and when $\alpha < \beta$, $\gamma < 1$ and $\rho_x < \rho_y$. In other words, when $\alpha > \beta$, commodity $X$ is labor intensive relative to $Y$ ($\rho_x > \rho_y$); and when $\alpha < \beta$, commodity $Y$ is labor intensive relative to $X$ ($\rho_x < \rho_y$). Obviously, when $\alpha = \beta$, $\gamma = 1$ and $\rho_x = \rho_y$, that is, the model degenerates into the one-commodity case.

## Factor-Intensity Reversals

Unfortunately, there exist particular pairs of isoquants for which commodities $X$ and $Y$ cannot be unambiguously ranked in terms of factor intensity and the Heckscher–Ohlin requirements cannot be met. Figure 8.4 illustrates this case, which has come to be known in the literature as the case of factor-intensity reversals.

Figure 8.4($a$) illustrates the case where $Y$'s unit isoquant is L-shaped whereas $X$'s unit isoquant is smoothly continuous. Commodity $Y$'s isoquant has been so constructed that it touches $X$'s isoquant at point $S$ only. (Since the units of measurement for $X$ and $Y$ can be arbitrarily selected, the unit isoquants can be made to have at least one common point always.) Commodity $Y$'s expansion path

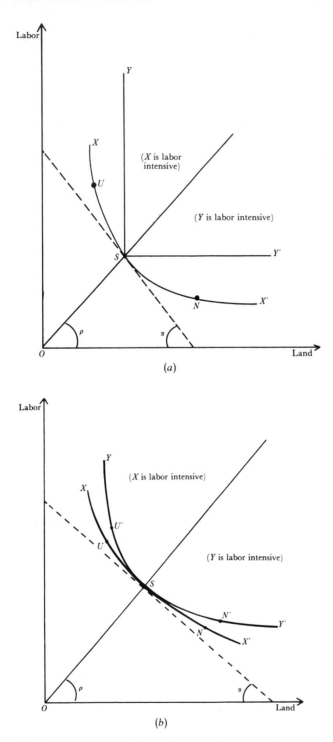

(a)

(b)

**Figure 8.4** A single factor-intensity reversal occurs at S.

is uniquely given by the vector $OS$. However, $X$'s expansion path is not uniquely given; it depends upon the factor-price ratio. When the factor-price ratio is given by the absolute value of the slope $\alpha$ of $X$'s isoquant at point $S$, commodity $X$'s expansion path coincides with $Y$'s. However, for any factor-price ratio lower than $\alpha$ (such as that given by the absolute value of the slope of $XX'$ at point $N$), $X$'s expansion path becomes flatter than $Y$'s. This implies that $Y$ is labor intensive relative to $X$. On the other hand, for any factor-price ratio higher than $\alpha$ (such as that given by the absolute value of the slope of $XX'$ at point $U$), $X$'s expansion path becomes steeper than $Y$'s. This implies that $X$ is labor intensive relative to $Y$. Therefore, in this particular case, an unequivocal classification of commodities by factor intensity is impossible.

Figure 8.4(*b*) is similar to fig. 8.4(*a*) except that now $Y$'s isoquant also has been drawn as a smoothly continuous curve. The basic assumption that characterizes the construction of this diagram is this: any ray through the origin and flatter than $OS$ will intersect the two-unit isoquants at points where the marginal rate of substitution of land for labor is higher in industry $X$ than in $Y$; and any ray steeper than $OS$ will cut the two unit isoquants at points where the marginal rate of substitution of land for labor is higher in $Y$ than in $X$. This is a necessary and sufficient condition for the existence of a single factor-intensity reversal. In general, when more than one reversal is admitted, the preceding condition will not be met.

The conclusion reached earlier with regard to fig. 8.4(*a*) applies equally to fig. 8.4(*b*). Consider a factor-price ratio lower than $\alpha$ (where $\alpha$ is the absolute value of the slope of either isoquant at point $S$), such as the slope of $XX'$ at point $N$. Commodity $X$'s expansion path would then be given by the vector $ON$ (not drawn). To see whether $Y$'s expansion path is steeper or flatter than $X$'s at this factor-price ratio, simply consider the marginal rate of substitution of land for labor in industry $Y$ along the expansion path $ON$. By assumption, it must be lower than that of industry $X$ along $ON$. Therefore, for the specific value of the factor-price ratio we have chosen, $Y$'s expansion path must necessarily be steeper than $ON$ and, in particular, it will be given by a vector lying between $OS$ and $ON$. Thus, for values of the factor-price ratio lower than $\alpha$, $Y$ is labor intensive relative to $X$. In the same way, it can be shown that for values of the factor-price ratio higher than $\alpha$, $Y$'s expansion path is necessarily flatter than $X$'s and, therefore, $X$ is labor intensive relative to $Y$. It is impossible to classify commodities unequivocally by factor intensity.

## CES Production Functions†

Minhas (1962, 1963) has shown that when the production functions for commodities $X$ and $Y$ are of the constant-elasticity-of-substitution (CES) variety, and when the elasticity of substitution is different between the two industries, there exists a factor-intensity reversal.

---

† This subsection may be skipped.

Consider the following CES production function† for commodity $X$:

$$X = [A_1 L_x^{-\alpha} + A_2 T_x^{-\alpha}]^{-(1/\alpha)} \tag{8.9}$$

where $A_1 > 0$, $A_2 > 0$, and $1 + \alpha > 0$ ($\alpha \neq 0$). The limit of this function as $\alpha \to 0$ is the Cobb–Douglas function.

The marginal physical products of labor and land are given by

$$\text{MPP}_{LX} = \frac{\partial X}{\partial L_x}$$

$$= -\frac{1}{\alpha}[A_1 L_x^{-\alpha} + A_2 T_x^{-\alpha}]^{-[(1/\alpha) + 1]}(-\alpha)A_1 L_x^{-(1 + \alpha)}$$

$$= A_1[A_1 L_x^{-\alpha} + A_2 T_x^{-\alpha}]^{-[(1 + \alpha)/\alpha]}L_x^{-(1 + \alpha)} \tag{8.10}$$

$$\text{MPP}_{TX} = \frac{\partial X}{\partial T_x}$$

$$= -\frac{1}{\alpha}[A_1 L_x^{-\alpha} + A_2 T_x^{-\alpha}]^{-[(1 + \alpha)/\alpha]}(-\alpha)A_2 T_x^{-(1 + \alpha)}$$

$$= A_2[A_1 L_x^{-\alpha} + A_2 T_x^{-\alpha}]^{-[(1 + \alpha)/\alpha]}T_x^{-(1 + \alpha)} \tag{8.11}$$

The marginal rate of substitution of labor for land is again given by the ratio of the marginal physical products, that is,

$$\text{MRS}_{LT}^X = \frac{\text{MPP}_{LX}}{\text{MPP}_{TX}} = \frac{A_1}{A_2}\rho_x^{-(1 + \alpha)} \tag{8.12}$$

The elasticity of substitution in industry $X$ ($\sigma_x$) is, by definition, given by

$$\sigma_x \equiv -\frac{d\rho_x}{d\text{MRS}_{LT}^X} \frac{\text{MRS}_{LT}^X}{\rho_x}$$

$$= -\frac{1}{-(1 + \alpha)(A_1/A_2)\rho_x^{-(2 + \alpha)}} \frac{(A_1/A_2)\rho_x^{-(1 + \alpha)}}{\rho_x} = \frac{1}{1 + \alpha} \tag{8.13}$$

Solving eq. (8.13) for $(1 + \alpha)$ and then substituting into eq. (8.12), we finally obtain

$$\text{MRS}_{LT}^X = \frac{A_1}{A_2}\rho_x^{-(1/\sigma_x)} \tag{8.14}$$

Similarly, consider the following CES production function for commodity $Y$:

$$Y = [B_1 L_y^{-\beta} + B_2 T_y^{-\beta}]^{-(1/\beta)} \tag{8.15}$$

where $B_1 > 0$, $B_2 > 0$, and $1 + \beta > 0$ ($\beta \neq 0$). The marginal rate of substitution of labor for land in industry $Y$ is given by

$$\text{MRS}_{LT}^Y = \frac{B_1}{B_2}\rho_y^{-(1/\sigma_y)} \tag{8.16}$$

---

† The CES production function was introduced into the literature by Arrow and coauthors (1961). See also Allen (1968, chap. 3) and Henderson and Quandt (1971, chap. 3).

where $\sigma_y$ is the elasticity of substitution in industry $Y$.

For any given factor-price ratio, the following equations are satisfied:

$$\frac{w}{r} = \frac{A_1}{A_2} \rho_x^{-(1/\sigma_x)} \tag{8.17}$$

$$\frac{w}{r} = \frac{B_1}{B_2} \rho_y^{-(1/\sigma_y)} \tag{8.18}$$

These equations can be solved for $\rho_x$ and $\rho_y$, respectively:

$$\rho_x = \left(\frac{w}{r} \frac{A_2}{A_1}\right)^{-\sigma_x} \tag{8.19}$$

$$\rho_y = \left(\frac{w}{r} \frac{B_2}{B_1}\right)^{-\sigma_y} \tag{8.20}$$

Consider now the ratio of factor proportions:

$$\frac{\rho_x}{\rho_y} = C\left(\frac{w}{r}\right)^{\sigma_y - \sigma_x} \tag{8.21}$$

where the positive constant $C$ is given by $C \equiv (A_2/A_1)^{-\sigma_x}(B_2/B_1)^{\sigma_y}$. When $\sigma_x = \sigma_y$, eq. (8.21) reduces to $\rho_x/\rho_y = C$, and $X$ is unambiguously labor intensive ($\rho_x > \rho_y$) or land intensive ($\rho_x < \rho_y$) according as $C > 1$ or $C < 1$. The Cobb–Douglas production functions studied earlier are a special instance of the present case, since both elasticities of substitution are unity.

When $\sigma_x \neq \sigma_y$, the ratio of factor proportions (that is, $\rho_x/\rho_y$) is not independent of the factor-price ratio. In particular, the ratio $\rho_x/\rho_y$ is either a strictly increasing function of $w/r$ (when $\sigma_y > \sigma_x$), or a strictly decreasing function of $w/r$ (when $\sigma_y < \sigma_x$), with its values (for positive factor prices) ranging from zero to infinity. Obviously, a factor-intensity reversal necessarily occurs at the specific value of $w/r$ for which $\rho_x/\rho_y = 1$.

## The Heckscher–Ohlin Theorem in the Presence of Factor-Intensity Reversals

What meaning could possibly be attached to the Heckscher–Ohlin theorem in the presence of factor-intensity reversals? When commodities cannot be unambiguously classified into labor and land intensive, the Heckscher–Ohlin theorem becomes very difficult to follow, since it is based on the implicit assumption that commodities can indeed be classified a priori in terms of factor intensity. When this implicit assumption is not met, the structure of trade need not coincide with the Heckscher–Ohlin theorem. But does this imply that factor-intensity reversals necessarily render the Heckscher–Ohlin theorem invalid? Not at all. It all depends upon the overall factor proportions (i.e., the ratios of labor to land) in the two countries. Presently, we illustrate the problem for the case of a single factor-intensity reversal. Multiple reversals are considered later in chap. 10.

As we saw in chap. 4, under constant returns to scale, the contract curve in the Edgeworth–Bowley box diagram must necessarily lie on one side of the diagonal:

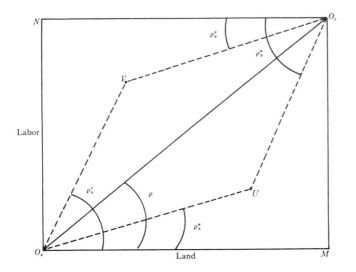

**Figure 8.5** Factor-intensity reversals cannot be observed in a single country.

it can never cross it. This necessarily implies that no matter what type of isoquants we are dealing with, the two commodities can unequivocally be classified by factor intensity once the overall factor proportions are given. This is illustrated in fig. 8.5. The sides of the box diagram (that is, $O_x N$ and $O_x M$) show the aggregate endowments of labor and land for the economy in question. The slope of the diagonal $(\rho)$ shows the overall factor proportions. When resources are allocated with reference to the coordinates of a point below and to the right of the diagonal, such as $U$, commodity $X$ is necessarily land intensive relative to $Y$ ($\rho_x^u < \rho_y^u$). On the other hand, when resources are allocated in accordance with the coordinates of any point above and to the left of the diagonal, such as $V$, commodity $X$ is necessarily labor intensive relative to $Y$ ($\rho_x^v > \rho_y^v$). Accordingly, when the contract curve lies on one side of the diagonal, one commodity is always labor intensive relative to the other for all admissible efficient resource allocations.

Does the preceding argument mean that the phenomenon of factor-intensity reversals cannot be damaging to the Heckscher–Ohlin theorem? Not at all. All we know is that, given the overall factor endowments of, say, country $A$, we can rank commodities $X$ and $Y$ in terms of factor intensity, but from the point of view of country $A$. The same experiment can be repeated for a second country, $B$, of course, but there is no guarantee that the two rankings will not be contradictory. For instance, while we are absolutely sure that commodity $X$ is always labor intensive relative to $Y$ in country $A$, we cannot possibly be absolutely sure that commodity $X$ is also labor intensive in country $B$ as well. It may very well be land intensive in $B$. In other words, in the presence of factor-intensity reversals, it is possible (but not necessary) that commodity $X$ may be labor intensive relative to $Y$ in one country, but land intensive relative to $Y$ in the other country. Under what circumstances would $A$'s ranking of $X$ and $Y$ be consistent with, or contradictory to, $B$'s?

Consider again fig. 8.4. If the overall ratio of labor to land in a particular country were given by the slope of the vector $OS$, the contract curve in the box diagram would necessarily coincide with the diagonal. The production-possibilities frontier would be a straight line, and $X$ and $Y$ would have identical factor intensities. On the other hand, if the overall labor-land ratio were given by a vector flatter than $OS$, such as $ON$, then commodity $Y$ would be labor intensive relative to $X$. Finally, if the overall labor-land ratio were given by a vector steeper than $OS$, such as $OU$, then commodity $X$ would be labor intensive relative to $Y$. Accordingly, if the overall labor-land ratios of both countries were given by vectors lying on the same side of $OS$, the commodity rankings in terms of factor ratios of the two countries would be consistent; otherwise, they would be contradictory. How are these conclusions established?

Consider fig. 8.6. It is a combination of three box diagrams. The vectors $OS$, $ON_1$, and $OU_1$ (which are simply the diagonals of the three box diagrams) correspond to the vectors $OS$, $ON$, and $OU$, respectively, of fig. 8.4. Thus, when the overall labor-land ratio is given by the slope of $OS$ (as shown by the box diagram $ORY_3 M$), the marginal rates of substitution of land for labor in $X$ and $Y$ are necessarily equal along the diagonal of the box diagram—the unit isoquants are by assumption tangent to each other at $S$ (fig. 8.4). Hence, the contract curve coincides with the diagonal and the labor-land ratios used in the two industries are equal to each other and also to the overall labor-land ratio of the economy in general.

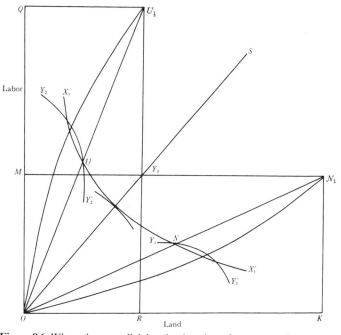

**Figure 8.6** When the overall labor-land ratios of two countries are separated by a factor-intensity reversal (vector $OS$), the two countries' rankings of commodities in terms of factor intensity are contradictory.

On the other hand, when the labor-land ratio is lower than the slope of $OS$ (as shown by the box diagram $OKN_1M$), the contract curve must lie below the diagonal if $Y$ is to be labor intensive relative to $X$. Is there any reason why the contract curve should lie below and to the right of the diagonal of the box diagram $OKN_1M$? The answer lies in the assumption that any ray through the origin and flatter than $OS$ (fig. 8.4($b$)) intersects the two unit isoquants at points where the marginal rate of substitution of land for labor is higher in industry $X$ than in $Y$. What this means is that for any pair of isoquants passing through a point lying on the diagonal $ON_1$ (fig. 8.6), such as $X_1X_1'$ and $Y_1Y_1'$ passing through $N$, industry $Y$'s isoquant is flatter than $X$'s at $N$. But as explained in chap. 4, this necessarily implies that the contract curve lies below and to the right of the diagonal $ON_1$.

When the overall labor-land ratio is higher than the slope of $OS$ (as shown by the box diagram $ORU_1Q$), the contract curve lies above the diagonal and $X$ becomes labor intensive relative to $Y$—$X$'s isoquants along the diagonal $OU_1$ are flatter than $Y$'s. This is illustrated in fig. 8.6 by the typical pair $X_1X_1'$ and $Y_2Y_2'$—the former being flatter than the latter at $U$. Again, this relationship, which follows from the assumption that any ray steeper than $OS$ (fig. 8.4) cuts the two one-unit isoquants at points where the marginal rate of substitution of land for labor is higher in $Y$ than $X$, implies that the contract curve necessarily lies above and to the left of the diagonal $OU_1$ and, therefore, that $X$ is labor intensive relative to $Y$.

It is interesting to note that, when the overall labor-land ratios in both countries are equal to the slope of the vector $OS$ (figs. 8.4 and 8.6), then ($a$) the production-possibilities frontiers become straight lines with equal slope (whose numerical value is quite arbitrary, depending on the units of measurement for $X$ and $Y$), and ($b$) assuming that both commodities are being consumed in both countries in the autarkic state, the pretrade relative prices are equal and thus no trade takes place.

The same conclusions follow when the production functions of $X$ and $Y$ are identical. Thus, by an appropriate choice of units of measurement for $X$ and $Y$, the two one-unit isoquants can be made to coincide. Accordingly, the commodity-price ratio is necessarily equal to unity irrespective of factor prices. Thus, we end up again with the classical equal-costs case.

To summarize, the vector $OS$ (figs. 8.4 and 8.6) divides the diagram into two nonoverlapping cones. If the overall factor proportions of both countries fall in the same cone, then a unique classification of commodities in terms of factor intensity holds for both countries. On the other hand, if the overall factor proportions of the two countries lie in different cones, the ranking of commodities is contradictory between countries.

When the ranking of commodities is contradictory between countries, the logic of the Heckscher–Ohlin theorem breaks down because it is impossible for both countries to export the commodity which uses more intensively their abundant factor. For instance, suppose that the factor proportions of country $A$ are lower, and those of country $B$ higher, than the slope of the vector $OS$ (fig. 8.6). Country $B$ classifies $X$ as labor intensive relative to $Y$, while country $A$ classifies $X$ as land intensive relative to $Y$. If country $A$ is considered labor abundant and country $B$ land abundant, the Heckscher–Ohlin theorem would predict that both countries will export commodity $Y$, which, as we saw in chaps. 2 to 7, is impossible. The situation does not improve if $A$ were considered land abundant relative to $B$. (Indeed, as part D shows, $A$ should be classified as land abundant relative to $B$ under all acceptable definitions.)

# PART B. INTERINDUSTRY FLOWS

We now extend the analysis of part A to Vanek's (1963) model of interindustry flows. Vanek did not allow for any substitutability in production between primary factors and intermediate products, but his analysis can be easily generalized.

## 8.3 SAMUELSON'S SWEEPING THEOREM ON INTERMEDIATE PRODUCTS

Samuelson (1965, pp. 50–52) enunciated a sweeping theorem according to which, in the absence of joint production of any outputs, *net* production functions always exist giving each final good in terms of *total* primary inputs used directly and indirectly for it alone.

Consider again the following linear homogeneous production functions:

$$X = F(L_x, T_x, Y_x) - X_y \tag{8.22a}$$

$$Y = G(L_y, T_y, X_y) - Y_x \tag{8.23a}$$

These production functions were introduced earlier in chap. 4—see eqs. (4.44) and (4.45). Samuelson's theorem tells us that these functions can be reduced to

$$X = f(L_x^*, T_x^*) \tag{8.24a}$$

$$Y = g(L_y^*, T_y^*) \tag{8.25a}$$

where $L_i^*$, $T_i^*$ show the *total* amounts of labor and land, respectively, which go directly and indirectly into the production of the $i$th commodity.†

Samuelson suggests that we imagine the economy described by the production functions (8.22a) and (8.23a) inside a black box; and then observe only the primary factors going into the box and the final goods coming out of the box. By putting $Y = 0$ and thus requiring the economy to produce only *net* amounts of $X$, we can generate a new production function for industry $X$ as given by eq. (8.24a). In effect, industry $X$ can be thought of as organized in one corner of the black box producing for itself all of the unseen intermediate $Y_x$.

Similarly, by putting $X = 0$ and thus requiring the economy to produce only *net* amounts of $Y$, we can generate a new production function for industry $Y$ as

---

† Asterisks are used to indicate *total* primary-factor requirements.

given by eq. (8.25a). Again industry $Y$ can be thought of as organized in another corner of the black box producing for itself all of the unseen intermediate $X_y$.

The new production functions given by eqs. (8.24a) and (8.25a) have all the homogeneity and concavity properties of the neoclassical production functions. (For further details, see the appendix at the end of this chapter.) Therefore, everything that was said earlier about the standard model holds also for the model described by eqs. (8.24a) and (8.25a).

## 8.4 DIRECT (OR NET) VERSUS TOTAL (OR GROSS) FACTOR INTENSITIES

When one industry's output is employed as input in the other industry, a distinction must be drawn between net and gross factor intensities.

Because of constant returns to scale, eqs. (8.22a) to (8.25a) can also be written as follows:

$$1 = F(a_{Lx}, a_{Tx}, a_{yx}) \tag{8.22b}$$

$$1 = G(a_{Ly}, a_{Ty}, a_{xy}) \tag{8.23b}$$

$$1 = f(a_{Lx}^*, a_{Tx}^*) \tag{8.24b}$$

$$1 = g(a_{Ly}^*, a_{Ty}^*) \tag{8.25b}$$

where
$a_{Lx} = L_x/(X + X_y)$, $a_{Tx} = T_x/(X + X_y)$, $a_{yx} = Y_x/(X + X_y)$, $a_{Ly} = L_y/(Y + Y_x)$, $a_{Ty} = T_y/(Y + Y_x)$, $a_{xy} = X_y/(Y + Y_x)$, $a_{Lx}^* = L_x^*/X$, $a_{Tx}^* = T_x^*/X$, $a_{Ly}^* = L_y^*/Y$, and $a_{Ty}^* = T_y^*/Y$. Obviously, the ratios $a_{ij}$ are the *direct unit* coefficients of production. The ratios $a_{ij}^*$ give the *total* (i.e., *direct plus indirect*) labor and land requirements for the production of 1 unit (net) of $X$ or $Y$, as the case may be.

The direct (or net) labor-land ratios of industries $X$ and $Y$ are given by $\rho_x = a_{Lx}/a_{Tx}$ and $\rho_y = a_{Ly}/a_{Ty}$, respectively. Similarly, the total (or gross) labor-land ratios are given by $\rho_x^* = a_{Lx}^*/a_{Tx}^*$ and $\rho_y^* = a_{Ly}^*/a_{Ty}^*$.

What is the relationship between the net and gross factor intensities? In particular, is it possible for a commodity to be, say, labor intensive according to the net factor intensities but capital intensive according to the gross factor intensities? As shown below, *interindustry flows cannot reverse the factor intensity of commodities as revealed by their direct labor and land coefficients of production.*

Consider the full-employment equations:

$$a_{Lx}(X + X_y) + a_{Ly}(Y + Y_x) = \bar{L} \tag{8.26}$$

$$a_{Tx}(X + X_y) + a_{Ty}(Y + Y_x) = \bar{T} \tag{8.27}$$

We also know from the assumed structure of production that

$$a_{yx}(X + X_y) = Y_x \tag{8.28}$$

$$a_{xy}(Y + Y_x) = X_y \tag{8.29}$$

Solving eqs. (8.28) and (8.29) for $X_y$ and $Y_x$ we obtain

$$X_y = \frac{a_{xy}a_{yx}}{\Delta} X + \frac{a_{xy}}{\Delta} Y \tag{8.30}$$

$$Y_x = \frac{a_{yx}}{\Delta} X + \frac{a_{xy}a_{yx}}{\Delta} Y \tag{8.31}$$

where

$$\Delta = 1 - a_{xy}a_{yx} > 0 \tag{8.32}$$

(The determinant $\Delta$ is always positive for a productive economy.†) Finally, substituting eqs. (8.30) and (8.31) into eqs. (8.26) and (8.27), and simplifying, we obtain

$$a^*_{Lx} X + a^*_{Ly} Y = \bar{L} \tag{8.33}$$

$$a^*_{Tx} X + a^*_{Ty} Y = \bar{T} \tag{8.34}$$

where the *gross* production coefficients $a^*_{ij}$ are given by

$$a^*_{Lx} = \frac{a_{Lx} + a_{Ly}a_{yx}}{1 - a_{xy}a_{yx}} \tag{8.35}$$

$$a^*_{Ly} = \frac{a_{Ly} + a_{Lx}a_{xy}}{1 - a_{xy}a_{yx}} \tag{8.36}$$

$$a^*_{Tx} = \frac{a_{Tx} + a_{Ty}a_{yx}}{1 - a_{xy}a_{yx}} \tag{8.37}$$

$$a^*_{Ty} = \frac{a_{Ty} + a_{Tx}a_{xy}}{1 - a_{xy}a_{yx}} \tag{8.38}$$

Consider, finally, the gross labor-land ratios $\rho^*_x$ and $\rho^*_y$. Commodity $X$ can be said to be truly labor intensive when $\rho^*_x > \rho^*_y$, that is, when

$$\frac{a^*_{Lx}}{a^*_{Tx}} = \frac{a_{Lx} + a_{Ly}a_{yx}}{a_{Tx} + a_{Ty}a_{yx}} > \frac{a_{Ly} + a_{Lx}a_{xy}}{a_{Ty} + a_{Tx}a_{xy}} = \frac{a^*_{Ly}}{a^*_{Ty}} \tag{8.39}$$

As it turns out, inequality (8.39) holds if, and only if,

$$\rho_x = \frac{a_{Lx}}{a_{Tx}} > \frac{a_{Ly}}{a_{Ty}} = \rho_y \tag{8.40}$$

---

† The meaning of the product $a_{xy}a_{yx}$ is simple. To produce 1 unit of $X$ we need $a_{yx}$ units of $Y$, while to produce 1 unit of $Y$ we need $a_{xy}$ units of $X$. Thus, the product $a_{xy}a_{yx}$ shows the amount of $X$ which goes indirectly into the production of 1 unit of $X$. This amount (that is, $a_{xy}a_{yx}$) must obviously be less than 1 for a productive economy—if it takes more than 1 unit of $X$ to produce 1 unit of $X$ the economy cannot be viable.

Alternatively, the product $a_{xy}a_{yx}$ can be viewed as the amount of $Y$ which goes into the production of 1 unit of $Y$. Thus, to produce 1 unit of $Y$ we need $a_{xy}$ units of $X$, and each unit of $X$ requires $a_{yx}$ units of $Y$. Again, we must have $a_{xy}a_{yx} < 1$.

That is, in the present case, *the net and gross factor intensities are equivalent.*

To prove the preceding proposition, simplify inequality (8.39) to obtain

$$\rho_x(1 - a_{xy}a_{xy}) > \rho_y(1 - a_{xy}a_{yx}) \tag{8.41}$$

For a productive economy (i.e., an economy capable of producing positive net outputs of $X$ and $Y$), it is necessary that $a_{xy}a_{yx} < 1$. Accordingly, $(1 - a_{xy}a_{yx}) > 0$, and inequality (8.41), and thus (8.39), reduces to inequality (8.40).

## PART C. PURE INTERMEDIATE PRODUCTS

Recently, Batra and Casas (1973) developed a model in which they introduced a "pure" intermediate commodity—one that is produced solely for use in the production of final goods. They reached the obvious conclusion that the Heckscher–Ohlin theorem as well as other related theorems, such as the Stolper–Samuelson theorem and the Rybczynski theorem,† remain valid only if factor intensities are interpreted in terms of *total* primary input requirements. Additional contributions in this area have been made by Ray (1972, 1975), Riedel (1976), and Schweinberger (1975). Chacholiades (1970, 1971) discussed, in relation to balance-of-payments equilibrium, the case in which intermediate products, not available at home, must be imported from the rest of the world.

This part of the present chapter then discusses briefly the case of "pure" intermediate commodities.

## 8.5 STRUCTURE OF PRODUCTION

Consider a model of three commodities ($X$, $Y$, and $Z$) and two primary factors of production, labor ($L$) and land ($T$). The first two commodities ($X$ and $Y$) are final goods while the third ($Z$) is an intermediate good produced solely for use in the production of $X$ and $Y$. The primary factors of production ($L$ and $T$) enter into the production process of all three commodities. Constant returns to scale characterize all production functions. This model is summarized by the following production functions:‡

$$X = F(L_x, T_x, Z_x) \tag{8.42a}$$

$$Y = G(L_y, T_y, Z_y) \tag{8.43a}$$

$$Z = H(L_z, T_z) = Z_x + Z_y \tag{8.44a}$$

---

† The Stolper–Samuelson theorem is discussed later in chap. 19. The Rybczynski theorem is discussed in chap. 13.

‡ Batra and Casas (1973) followed Vanek and excluded the possibility of substitution between the primary factors and the intermediate good in the production of the final goods $X$ and $Y$. Such restriction is not necessary.

Because of constant returns to scale, eqs. (8.42a) to (8.44a) can also be written as

$$1 = F(a_{Lx}, a_{Tx}, a_{zx}) \tag{8.42b}$$

$$1 = G(a_{Ly}, a_{Ty}, a_{zy}) \tag{8.43b}$$

$$1 = H(a_{Lz}, a_{Tz}) = \lambda + (1 - \lambda) \tag{8.44b}$$

where $a_{Lx} \equiv L_x/X$, $a_{Tx} \equiv T_x/X$, $a_{zx} \equiv Z_x/X$, $a_{Ly} \equiv L_y/Y$, $a_{Ty} \equiv T_y/Y$, $a_{zy} \equiv Z_y/Y$, $a_{Lz} \equiv L_z/Z$, $a_{Tz} \equiv T_z/Z$, $\lambda \equiv Z_x/Z$, and $(1 - \lambda) \equiv Z_y/Z$.

For the reader who understood well Samuelson's (1965) sweeping theorem on intermediate products, it must be clear that the preceding production structure reduces to the conventional model of two final goods and two factors of production with no intermediate goods. Thus, as Samuelson suggests, we could imagine that the preceding economy is put inside a black box and observe only the primary factors going into the box and the final goods coming out of the box. By putting $Y = 0$ and thus requiring the economy to produce only $X$ (and, of course, $Z$ as well *inside* the black box), we can generate a new production function for industry $X$ giving the maximum output of $X$ attainable from given amounts of $L$ and $T$. (Industry $X$ can be organized in one corner of the black box producing for itself all the unseen intermediate $Z_x$.) Alternatively, we can set $X = 0$ and generate in a similar fashion a new production function for industry $Y$. These new production functions will also have all the homogeneity and concavity properties of the neoclassical production functions (see the appendix at the end of this chapter). When we concentrate on these new production functions, the Heckscher–Ohlin theorem, as well as the other theorems mentioned earlier, necessarily remain valid.

For the benefit of the reader, the above model is pursued a little further.

## 8.6 FULL EMPLOYMENT EQUATIONS

For full employment, it is required that the following equations be satisfied:

$$a_{Lx} X + a_{Ly} Y + a_{Lz} Z = \bar{L} \tag{8.45}$$

$$a_{Tx} X + a_{Ty} Y + a_{Tz} Z = \bar{T} \tag{8.46}$$

$$a_{zx} X + a_{zy} Y = Z \tag{8.47}$$

Substituting eq. (8.47) into eqs. (8.45) and (8.46) and rearranging, we obtain

$$a_{Lx}^* X + a_{Ly}^* Y = \bar{L} \tag{8.48}$$

$$a_{Tx}^* X + a_{Ty}^* Y = \bar{T} \tag{8.49}$$

where $a_{Lx}^* \equiv a_{Lx} + a_{Lz} a_{zx}$, $a_{Ly}^* \equiv a_{Ly} + a_{Lz} a_{zy}$, $a_{Tx}^* \equiv a_{Tx} + a_{Tz} a_{zx}$, and $a_{Ty}^* \equiv a_{Ty} + a_{Tz} a_{zy}$. Obviously the coefficients $a_{Lx}^*$ and $a_{Tx}^*$ give the *total* (direct plus indirect) amounts of labor and land which go into the production of 1 unit of output of $X$. Similarly, the coefficients $a_{Ly}^*$ and $a_{Ty}^*$ give the *total* amounts of labor and land that go into the production of 1 unit of $Y$. These are the coefficients, of course, which could be obtained directly from Samuelson's new production functions, referred to earlier.

## 8.7 NET AND GROSS FACTOR INTENSITIES

As with Vanek's model of interindustry flows, we have to distinguish again between the net and gross factor intensities. The net factor intensities are given by: $\rho_x \equiv a_{Lx}/a_{Tx}$, $\rho_y \equiv a_{Ly}/a_{Ty}$, and $\rho_z \equiv a_{Lz}/a_{Tz}$. On the other hand, the gross factor intensities are given by: $\rho_x^* \equiv a_{Lx}^*/a_{Tx}^*$ and $\rho_y^* \equiv a_{Ly}^*/a_{Ty}^*$. (No distinction between net and gross factor intensity is needed for the pure intermediate good $Z$ because it is produced directly by the primary factors only.)

The gross factor intensity of industry $X$, that is, $\rho_x^*$, is a weighted average of the net factor intensities $\rho_x$ and $\rho_z$. Thus

$$\rho_x^* \equiv \frac{a_{Lx}^*}{a_{Tx}^*} = \frac{a_{Lx} + a_{Lz}a_{zx}}{a_{Tx} + a_{Tz}a_{zx}} = (1 - \phi)\rho_x + \phi\rho_z \tag{8.50}$$

where

$$\phi \equiv \frac{a_{Tz}a_{zx}}{a_{Tx} + a_{Tz}a_{zx}} \tag{8.51}$$

Similarly, the gross factor intensity of industry $Y$, that is, $\rho_y^*$, is a weighted average of the net factor intensities $\rho_y$ and $\rho_z$. Thus,

$$\rho_y^* \equiv \frac{a_{Ly}^*}{a_{Ty}^*} = \frac{a_{Ly} + a_{Lz}a_{zy}}{a_{Ty} + a_{Tz}a_{zy}} = (1 - \gamma)\rho_y + \gamma\rho_z \tag{8.52}$$

where

$$\gamma \equiv \frac{a_{Tz}a_{zy}}{a_{Ty} + a_{Tz}a_{zy}} \tag{8.53}$$

When the factor intensity of the intermediate good $Z$ (that is, $\rho_z$) lies in between the *net* factor intensities of the two final goods $X$ and $Y$ (that is, $\rho_x$ and $\rho_y$), then the gross factor intensities of $X$ and $Y$ coincide with their corresponding net factor intensities. This follows immediately from the properties of weighted averages. Thus, $\rho_x^*$ lies always between $\rho_x$ and $\rho_z$. Similarly, $\rho_y^*$ lies between $\rho_y$ and $\rho_z$. If, for instance, $\rho_x > \rho_z > \rho_y$, it must also be true that $\rho_x^* > \rho_z > \rho_y^*$.

What happens when $\rho_z$ does not lie between $\rho_x$ and $\rho_y$? A conflict may arise between the net and gross factor intensities. Nevertheless, conditions may be specified to guarantee the correspondence between the net and gross factor intensities. For instance, assume that $\rho_z > \rho_x > \rho_y$. Here we shall also have $\rho_x^* > \rho_y^*$ (that is, commodity $X$ will be truly labor intensive) if the weight of $\rho_z$ in $\rho_x^*$ (that is, $\phi$) is not smaller than the weight of $\rho_z$ in $\rho_y^*$ (that is, $\gamma$). In other words, the net and gross factor intensities will correspond in the present case when $\phi \geq \gamma$, which reduces to $a_{zx}/a_{Tx} \geq a_{zy}/a_{Ty}$.

Similarly, when $\rho_x > \rho_y > \rho_z$, the net and gross factor intensities of $X$ and $Y$ will correspond (that is, $\rho_x^* > \rho_y^*$) if $\phi \leq \gamma$, which again reduces to $a_{zx}/a_{Tx} \leq a_{zy}/a_{Ty}$.

# PART D. DEFINITIONS OF RELATIVE FACTOR ABUNDANCE

Turn now to the concept of factor abundance. As we shall see, there are various (often contradictory) criteria which can be used to classify countries into labor abundant and land abundant.

Consider a model of two countries, $A$ and $B$, with each country endowed with two homogeneous factors of production called labor and land. In particular, assume that $A$ is endowed with $L_A$ units of labor and $T_A$ units of land, and $B$ with $L_B$ units of labor and $T_B$ units of land. Under what circumstances would it be reasonable to say that country $A$ is labor abundant relative to country $B$? The first definition of relative factor abundance is as follows.

**Definition 1 (physical definition)** Country $A$ is said to be labor abundant relative to country $B$ if country $A$ is endowed with more units of labor per unit of land relative to $B$, that is, if the following inequality holds:

$$\frac{L_A}{T_A} > \frac{L_B}{T_B} \tag{8.54}$$

Observe that "factor abundance" is a relative concept. When $A$ is labor abundant relative to $B$, then $B$ is necessarily land abundant relative to $A$. This follows directly from equality (8.54), which can be rearranged as

$$\frac{T_B}{L_B} > \frac{T_A}{L_A} \tag{8.55}$$

Inequality (8.55) tells us that $B$ has more units of land per unit of labor relative to $A$, that is, $B$ is land abundant relative to $A$.

This definition of relative factor abundance is called the *physical definition*, because factor abundance is decided on the basis of the physical quantities of factor endowments. It has been used in the literature by Samuelson, Leontief, and others. But despite its great simplicity in a simplified model, serious conceptual difficulties arise in empirical investigations because of the implied *homogeneity* of factors of production. The traditional trichotomy of factors into capital, labor, and land is useful for some purposes. However, one should never forget that each of these three major classes of factors of production consists of rather heterogeneous as opposed to homogeneous objects. The factor "capital" should be understood to include all kinds of *produced means of production*, such as buildings, machinery of all sorts, buses, airplanes, and so on. In the same way, labor cannot be considered a homogeneous factor, in view of differences in the educational background, motivation, health, nutrition, and other qualities of workers. Similarly, two different parcels of land cannot be expected to be identical in all respects. In view of these (and many other) differences between the Heckscher–Ohlin model and the real world, great care should be exercised in applying the theory to any real-world situation. These comments point to the necessity of a many-factor, many-commodity model, but then no simple hypothesis about the structure of trade can be made.

The physical definition of factor abundance is based on the relative physical abundance of the two factors of production. However, Ohlin himself was concerned not with physical but with *economic* abundance as it is reflected by relative factor prices in the autarkic state. In particular, he defined factor abundance as follows.

**Definition 2 (price definition)** Country $A$ is said to be labor abundant relative to country $B$ if, at the pretrade autarkic equilibrium state, labor is relatively cheaper in $A$ than in $B$. More precisely, $A$ is said to be labor abundant relative to $B$ if, at the pretrade autarkic equilibrium state, the following inequality holds:

$$\frac{w_A}{r_A} < \frac{w_B}{r_B} \tag{8.56}$$

where $w$ and $r$ stand for the money wage rate and rent, respectively, with the subscripts indicating the country.

Are the two definitions of factor abundance, namely, the physical and price definitions, equivalent? In other words, is it necessarily true that, in the autarkic pretrade equilibrium state, labor is relatively cheaper in that country which is endowed with relatively more units of labor? More precisely, does the inequality $L_A/T_A > L_B/T_B$ necessarily imply the inequality $(w/r)_A < (w/r)_B$, where $(w/r)_A$ and $(w/r)_B$ are the pretrade equilibrium factor-price ratios in countries $A$ and $B$, respectively? Unfortunately, the answer turns out to be negative.

As already mentioned, the price definition reflects relative *economic* abundance while the physical definition reflects merely relative *physical* abundance. What is the difference between physical versus economic abundance? The former is based on the absolute quantities of factors that exist in each country. The latter is based on the same factor quantities but relative to demand. Factor prices at the autarkic equilibrium are, like commodity prices, determined by both supply and demand. Thus, while the price definition is based on both supply and demand influences, the physical definition is based solely on supply, ignoring completely the influence of demand.

Demand conditions may outweigh supply conditions with the result that the two definitions of factor abundance may give rise to contradictory classifications of the countries involved. For instance, assume that $A$ is labor abundant relative to $B$ on the basis of the physical definition. Further, assume that $A$'s consumers have a stronger bias toward consuming labor-intensive commodities than $B$'s consumers. Under these circumstances, it is not impossible for labor to be relatively more expensive in $A$ before trade. Then $A$ would be classified as labor abundant according to the physical definition but land abundant according to the price definition. This point becomes clearer as we proceed (see chap. 10, part C).

For completeness, it should be mentioned that a third definition of factor abundance has been proposed by Lancaster (1957) as follows.

> **Definition 3 (Lancaster's definition)** A country is said to be abundant in that factor which is used intensively by the country's exported commodity.

Is Lancaster's definition of factor abundance appropriate for the Heckscher–Ohlin theorem? Not at all. On the basis of this definition, the Heckscher–Ohlin theorem is by necessity tautologically true. The Heckscher–Ohlin theorem asserts that a country exports that commodity which uses relatively more intensively its abundant factor, while Lancaster's definition calls abundant that factor which is being used more intensively by the exported commodity. On the basis of Lancaster's definition, the Heckscher–Ohlin theorem is by definition true—and it can never be refuted. Tautologies cannot help us explain the observed structure of trade. In this connection, one is reminded of Samuelson's (1948, p. 182) observation that "the tropics grow tropical fruits because of the relative abundance there of tropical conditions."

It is interesting to note that, on the basis of Lancaster's definition and when the ranking of commodities in terms of factor intensity is contradictory between countries, both countries are considered abundant in the same factor, which is a nonsensical conclusion, because factor abundance, like comparative advantage, is a relative concept.

# APPENDIX TO CHAPTER EIGHT. INTERMEDIATE PRODUCTS AND THE PRODUCTION FUNCTION OF AN INTEGRATED INDUSTRY

This appendix pursues further Samuelson's (1965) idea that even in the presence of intermediate products, industry production functions always exist, giving each final good in terms of *total* primary inputs used directly and indirectly for it alone.

## A8.1 THE MODEL OF INTERINDUSTRY FLOWS

Return again to the model of interindustry flows discussed in part B of chap. 8. Consider each of the two industries as an *integrated industry* producing for itself all of the unseen intermediate products needed for its net output. Consider only one such integrated industry, say $X$, since the same analysis applies for all.

The production function of the integrated industry $X$ is, in the first instance, given by the following equation:

$$X = F[L_x, T_x, Y(L - L_x, T - T_x, X_y)] - X_y \tag{A8.1}$$

where $L$ and $T$ are the total amounts of labor and land used by the integrated industry $X$; $L_x$ and $T_x$ are the amounts of labor and land used directly in the production of $X$; $L_y = L - L_x$, $T_y = T - T_x$, and $X_y$ are the amounts of labor, land, and $X$ used in the production of the intermediate product $Y$. All $Y$ is used up in the production of $X$.

Equation (A8.1) is linear homogeneous by assumption. Therefore, it may be written as follows:

$$X = LF\left[\frac{L_x}{L}, \frac{T_x}{L}, Y\left(\frac{L - L_x}{L}, \frac{T - T_x}{L}, \frac{X_y}{L}\right)\right] - X_y \tag{A8.2}$$

Equation (A8.2), or (A8.1), corresponds to Samuelson's black box: given the *total* amounts $L$ and $T$, and some optimization conditions to be specified below, eq. (A8.2) gives the *net* output $X$. As Samuelson suggested, eq. (A8.2) can be reduced to the linear homogeneous production function

$$X = H(L, T) \tag{A8.3}$$

which gives $X$ directly in terms of the totals $L$ and $T$. Our objective is to study the properties of eq. (A8.3) and its relationship to (A8.2).

## A8.2 OUTPUT MAXIMIZATION

Adam Smith's invisible hand necessarily leads to a maximization of net output $(X)$ for any given totals $L$ and $T$. What necessary conditions must be satisfied for $X$ to be at a maximum? Setting the first partial derivatives of (A8.2) equal to zero, we obtain

$$\frac{\partial X}{\partial L_x} = F_L - F_Y Y_L = 0 \tag{A8.4}$$

$$\frac{\partial X}{\partial T_x} = F_T - F_Y Y_T = 0 \tag{A8.5}$$

$$\frac{\partial X}{\partial X_y} = F_Y Y_X - 1 = 0 \tag{A8.6}$$

The subscripts $L$, $T$, $X$, and $Y$ indicate partial differention. In particular, $F_L$ is the partial derivative of $F$ with respect to $L_x/L$; $F_T$ is the partial of $F$ with respect to $T_x/L$; $F_Y$ is the partial of $F$ with respect to $Y$; $Y_L$ is the partial of $Y$ with respect to $(L - L_x)/L$; $Y_T$ is the partial of $Y$ with respect to $(T - T_x)/L$; and $Y_X$ is the partial of $Y$ with respect to $X_y/L$. This convention is followed throughout this appendix.

Equations (A8.4) to (A8.6) give the necessary conditions for maximization of $X$. Their interpretation is simple: (a) the marginal physical product of each primary factor ($L$ and $T$) must be the same whether the factor is used directly in the production of $X$ or indirectly through the production of $Y$ first; and (b) the marginal physical product of $X$ (that is, for $X$ used first to produce $Y$ which is later used to produce $X$) must be unity. These conditions explain how the totals $L$ and $T$ must be allocated (i.e., how $L$ is divided into $L_x$ and $L_y$, and $T$ into $T_x$ and $T_y$) in order to maximize $X$.

## A8.3 THE MARGINAL PRODUCTS OF LABOR AND LAND, AND THE MARGINAL RATE OF SUBSTITUTION

The production activity of the integrated industry $X$ is fully described by eqs. (A8.2) and (A8.4) to (A8.6). This is a system of four equations in six unknowns: $X, L, T, L_x, T_x, X_y$. Equations (A8.4) to (A8.6) can be used to eliminate the three unknowns: $L_x$, $T_x$, and $X_y$. When this is done the system reduces to eq. (A8.3). We wish to study now the properties of eq. (A8.3).

Take the total differential of eq. (A8.2) as follows:

$$dX = F\, dL + L\, dF - dX_y \tag{A8.7}$$

where

$$dF = F_L \frac{L\, dL_x - L_x\, dL}{L^2} + F_T \frac{L\, dT_x - T_x\, dL}{L^2} + F_Y\, dY \tag{A8.8}$$

and

$$dY = Y_L \frac{L_x\, dL - L\, dL_x}{L^2} + Y_T \frac{L(dT - dT_x) - (T - T_x)\, dL}{L^2}$$

$$+ Y_X \frac{L\, dX_y - X_y\, dL}{L^2} \tag{A8.9}$$

Substituting eqs. (A8.8) and (A8.9) into eq. (A8.7) and making use of eqs. (A8.4) to (A8.6), eq. (A8.7) is finally simplified to

$$dX = \left( F - F_T \frac{T}{L} - \frac{X_y}{L} \right) dL + F_T\, dT$$

$$= \left( \frac{X}{L} - \frac{T}{L} F_T \right) dL + F_T\, dT \tag{A8.10}$$

Equation (A8.10) is equivalent to

$$dX = H_L\, dL + H_T\, dT \tag{A8.11}$$

which is the total differential of eq. (A8.3). Therefore,

$$H_L = \frac{X}{L} - \frac{T}{L} F_T \tag{A8.12}$$

$$H_T = F_T \tag{A8.13}$$

The partial derivatives $H_L$ and $H_T$ are obviously the marginal physical products of labor and land, respectively.

The marginal rate of substitution of labor for land is given by

$$\text{MRS}^X_{LT} = -\frac{dT}{dL} = \frac{H_L}{H_T} = \frac{(X/L) - (T/L)F_T}{F_T} \tag{A8.14}$$

Because of the linear homogeneity of eq. (A8.2), eq. (A8.3) is also linear homogeneous. Thus, doubling $L$, $T$, $L_x$, $T_x$, and $X_y$ necessarily doubles $X$ (and $Y$). In general, doubling $L$ and $T$, assuming that eqs. (A8.4) to (A8.6) are always satisfied, doubles $X$. This follows from the fact that the partial derivatives $F_L$, $F_T$, $F_Y$, $Y_X$ depend on the proportions $L_x/L$, $T_x/L$, and $X_y/L$ only; and as $L$ and $T$ double, eqs. (A8.4) to (A8.6) continue to be satisfied when the ratios $L_x/L$, $T_x/L$, and $X_y/L$ remain constant, i.e., when $L_x$, $T_x$, and $X_y$ increase at the same rate as $L$ and $T$.

We therefore conclude that eq. (A8.3), which condenses the information given by eqs. (A8.2) and (A8.4) to (A8.6), is the production function for the integrated industry $X$. This production function is linear homogeneous and its partial derivatives (marginal physical products) are given by eqs. (A8.12) and (A8.13).

## A8.4 COST MINIMIZATION

Cost minimization is dual to output maximization. Equations (A8.4) to (A8.6) must also be satisfied for cost minimization. By proving this proposition not only do we show that the integrated industry $X$ behaves as if its production function were given directly by eq. (A8.3) but perhaps we also strengthen the earlier proposition that perfect competition does indeed maximize net output.

The problem of cost minimization can be formalized as follows. Given $X$, $w$, and $r$, minimize

$$C = wL + rT \tag{A8.15}$$

subject to eq. (A8.2).

Form the lagrangian

$$Z \equiv wL + rT + \lambda(X - LF + X_y) \tag{A8.16}$$

where $\lambda$ is the lagrangian multiplier. The arguments of the function $F$ are eliminated for simplicity. Set equal to zero the partial derivatives of $Z$ with respect to $L_x$, $T_x$, $X_y$, $L$, and $T$:

$$\frac{\partial Z}{\partial L_x} = -\lambda(F_L - F_Y Y_L) = 0 \tag{A8.17}$$

$$\text{(or } F_L - F_Y Y_L = 0)$$

$$\frac{\partial Z}{\partial T_x} = -\lambda(F_T - F_Y Y_T) = 0 \tag{A8.18}$$

$$\text{(or } F_T - F_Y Y_T = 0)$$

$$\frac{\partial Z}{\partial X_y} = -\lambda(F_Y Y_X - 1) = 0 \tag{A8.19}$$

$$(\text{or } F_Y Y_X - 1 = 0)$$

$$\frac{\partial Z}{\partial L} = w - \lambda \left[ F + L \left( -F_L \frac{L_x}{L^2} - F_T \frac{T_x}{L^2} + F_Y Y_L \frac{L_x}{L^2} \right. \right.$$

$$\left. \left. - F_Y Y_T \frac{T - T_x}{L^2} - F_Y Y_X \frac{X_y}{L^2} \right) \right] = 0 \tag{A8.20}$$

$$\frac{\partial Z}{\partial T} = r - \lambda F_Y Y_T = 0 \tag{A8.21a}$$

$$\text{or} \qquad r = \lambda F_Y Y_T \tag{A8.21b}$$

Equations (A8.17) to (A8.19) are equivalent to eqs. (A8.4) to (A8.6). They tell us that if $L$ and $T$ were constant, the way to minimize $C$ is to maximize $X$. Substituting eqs. (A8.17) to (A8.19) into eq. (A8.20), we obtain

$$\frac{\partial Z}{\partial L} = w - \lambda \left( F - F_Y Y_X \frac{X_y}{L} - F_Y Y_T \frac{T}{L} \right) = 0 \tag{A8.22a}$$

$$\text{or} \qquad w = \lambda \left( F - F_Y Y_X \frac{X_y}{L} - F_Y Y_T \frac{T}{L} \right) = \lambda \left( \frac{X}{L} - \frac{T}{L} F_T \right) \tag{A8.22b}$$

Recall eqs. (A8.12) and (A8.13), and observe that eqs. (A8.21b) and (A8.22b) reduce to

$$r = \lambda H_T \tag{A8.23}$$

$$w = \lambda H_L \tag{A8.24}$$

Finally, take the ratio of the last two equations to obtain the familiar condition

$$\frac{w}{r} = \frac{H_L}{H_T} = \text{MRS}_{LT}^X \tag{A8.25}$$

We therefore conclude that the integrated industry $X$ does indeed behave as if intermediate products did not exist and its production function were given by eq. (A8.3).

## SELECTED BIBLIOGRAPHY

Allen, R. G. D. (1968). *Macro-Economic Theory*. St. Martin's Press, New York.

Arrow, K. J., H. B. Chenery, B. S. Minhas, and R. M. Solow (1961). "Capital-Labor Substitution and Economic Efficiency." *Review of Economics and Statistics*, vol. 43 (August), pp. 225–251.

Batra, R. N., and F. R. Casas (1973). "Intermediate Products and the Pure Theory of International Trade: A Neo-Heckscher–Ohlin Framework." *American Economic Review*, vol. LXIII, no. 3 (June), pp. 297–311.

Chacholiades, M. (1970). " Balance-of-Payments Equilibrium with Imports as a Factor of Production." *Oxford Economic Papers*, vol. 22, no. 2 (July), pp. 173–193.

——— (1971). " Imported Inputs under Variable Proportions." *Oxford Economic Papers*, vol. 23, no. 2 (July), pp. 169–181.

Heckscher, E. (1919). "The Effect of Foreign Trade on the Distribution of Income." *Ekonomisk Tidskrift*, vol. 21, pp. 1–32. Reprinted in H. S. Ellis and L. A. Metzler (Eds.), *Readings in the Theory of International Trade*, Richard D. Irwin, Inc., Homewood, Ill., 1950.

Henderson, J. M., and R. E. Quandt (1971). *Microeconomic Theory*, 2d ed. McGraw-Hill Book Company, New York.

Kemp, M. C. (1969). *The Pure Theory of International Trade and Investment*. Prentice-Hall, Inc., Englewood Cliffs, N.J., chap. 7.

Lancaster, K. (1957). "The Heckscher–Ohlin Trade Model: A Geometric Treatment." *Economica*, vol. 24, pp. 19–39.

Lerner, A. P. (1953). *Essays in Economics Analysis*. Macmillan and Company, Ltd., London, pp. 67–100.

Minhas, B. S. (1962). "The Homohypallagic Production Function, Factor-Intensity Reversals, and the Heckscher–Ohlin Theorem." *Journal of Political Economy*, vol. 60 (April), pp. 138–156.

——— (1963). *An International Comparison of Factor Costs and Factor Use*. North-Holland Publishing Company, Amsterdam.

Ohlin, B. (1933). *Interregional and International Trade*. Harvard University Press, Cambridge, Mass., chaps. 1 to 5 and app. III.

Ray, A. (1972). "Traded and Non-traded Intermediate Inputs and Rybczynski Theorem." *International Economic Review*, vol. 13, no. 3 (October), pp. 523–530.

——— (1975). "Traded and Non-traded Intermediate Inputs and Some Aspects of the Pure Theory of International Trade." *Quarterly Journal of Economics*, vol. 89 (May), pp. 331–340.

Riedel, J. (1976). "Intermediate Products and the Theory of International Trade: A Generalization of the Pure Intermediate Good Case." *American Economic Review*, vol. 66, no. 3 (June), pp. 441–447.

Samuelson, P. A. (1948). "International Trade and the Equalization of Factor Prices." *Economic Journal*, vol. 58, pp. 165–184.

——— (1949). "International Factor Price Equalization Once Again." *Economic Journal*, vol. LIX, no. 234 (June), pp. 181–197.

——— (1952). "A Comment on Factor Price Equalization." *The Review of Economic Studies*, vol. XIX (2), no. 49 (February), pp. 121–122.

——— (1953). " Prices of Factors and Goods in General Equilibrium." *Review of Economic Studies*, vol. 21, pp. 1–20.

——— (1965). "Equalization by Trade of the Interest Rate Along with the Real Wage." In R. E. Baldwin et al. (Eds.), *Trade, Growth, and the Balance of Payments*. Rand-McNally and Company, Chicago, Ill.

Schweinberger, A. G. (1975). " Pure Traded Intermediate Products and the Heckscher–Ohlin Theorem." *American Economic Review*, vol. LXV, no. 4 (September), pp. 634–643.

Stolper, W. F., and P. A. Samuelson (1941). " Protection and Real Wages." *Review of Economic Studies*, vol. 9, pp. 58–73.

Vanek, J. (1963). " Variable Factor Proportions and Interindustry Flows in the Theory of International Trade." *Quarterly Journal of Economics*, vol. 80 (November), pp. 129–142.

(Additional references may be found in "Selected Bibliography" at the end of chap. 10.)

# CHAPTER NINE

# FACTOR PROPORTIONS, FACTOR PRICES, AND COMMODITY PRICES

This chapter considers the fundamental relationships between factor proportions, factor prices, and commodity prices. The discussion is divided into four parts. Part A deals with the relationship between factor prices and factor intensities, and part B with the relationship between factor prices and commodity prices. Part C introduces the overall factor endowment ratio and considers the range of factor prices and commodity prices in a closed economy. Finally, part D considers briefly the general-equilibrium configuration of a closed economy.

The appendix at the end of chap. 8 proved an important proposition, namely, that intermediate products cannot prevent us from postulating a linear homogeneous production function for each integrated industry giving final output in terms of the *total* primary inputs used both directly and indirectly in its production. As a result of this theorem, the present discussion is confined to the standard Heckscher–Ohlin–Samuelson–Lerner model, with the understanding that the amounts of primary factors used in the production of each commodity represent *total* amounts used directly and indirectly, and the corresponding factor intensities are total or gross—not net (even though in Vanek's model of interindustry flows there cannot be any conflict between net and gross factor intensities).

## PART A. FACTOR PRICES AND FACTOR INTENSITIES

The given technical possibilities of production, as summarized by the production functions, imply a definite relationship between relative factor prices (that is, $w/r$), optimum factor proportions in the two industries, and relative costs of production of commodities—which under the assumption of pure competition are equal to the relative commodity prices (that is, $p_x/p_y$). This part analyzes the relationship between $w/r$ and factor proportions only. The following part considers the relationship between factor proportions, factor prices, and commodity prices.

## 9.1 THE OPTIMUM COEFFICIENTS OF PRODUCTION

For any given factor-price ratio (that is, $w/r$) the optimum coefficients of production of both commodities are determined by the coordinates of the points on the unit isoquants of commodities $X$ and $Y$ where the marginal rate of substitution of labor for land is equal to the given factor-price ratio $w/r$. The equality between the marginal rate of substitution of labor for land and the factor-price ratio $w/r$, that is,

$$\text{MRS}_{LT} = \frac{w}{r} \tag{9.1}$$

is required for cost minimization. The ratio of the optimum coefficients of each commodity shows, of course, the proportion in which the factors labor and land are used in the production of these commodities.

Figure 9.1 illustrates the case for commodity $X$. The isoquant $XX'$ is the unit isoquant. The factor-price ratio $w/r$ is assumed to be given by the ratio $OM/ON$. The slope of the isoquant at point $E$ is equal to the given $w/r$. The coordinates of point $E$ (that is, $a^0_{Lx}$, $a^0_{Tx}$) are the optimum coefficients of production for the given factor-price ratio. The slope of the vector $OE$ with respect to the vertical axis shows the labor-land ratio in the production of $X$ (that is, $\rho_x$) for the given factor-price ratio.

## 9.2 THE EFFECT OF FACTOR-PRICE VARIATIONS ON OPTIMUM FACTOR PROPORTIONS

What happens to the labor-land ratios of both industries when the factor-price ratio varies? As $w/r$ falls, both factor ratios, $\rho_x$ and $\rho_y$, tend to rise. Geometrically, as $w/r$ falls, we move southeast on each unit isoquant as illustrated by the movement from $E$ to $E'$ in fig. 9.1. This implies that the labor coefficient increases (from $a^0_{Lx}$ to $a'_{Lx}$) while the land coefficient decreases (from $a^0_{Tx}$ to $a'_{Tx}$), and therefore the ratio $\rho_x = a_{Lx}/a_{Tx}$ necessarily rises. What is the basic economic reason for this? As $w/r$ falls, costs can be reduced by substituting the relatively cheaper factor, labor, for the more expensive factor, land. Therefore, as $w/r$ falls, both industries tend to become more labor intensive (i.e., both $\rho_x$ and $\rho_y$ rise) in an attempt to continue minimizing costs. On the other hand, as $w/r$ rises, both industries tend to become more land intensive.

Figure 9.2 illustrates the relationship between factor prices and factor proportions, on the assumption that commodity $X$ is labor intensive relative to $Y$ for all factor-price ratios. The curve $XX'$ represents the relationship between $w/r$ and $\rho_x$, while the curve $YY'$ represents the relationship between $w/r$ and $\rho_y$. Both curves have been drawn downward sloping, which implies that, as the factor-price ratio $w/r$ falls, both industries become more labor intensive (i.e., both $\rho_x$ and $\rho_y$

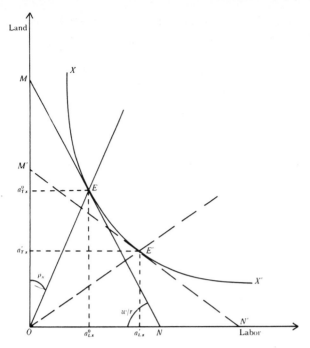

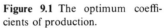

**Figure 9.1** The optimum coefficients of production.

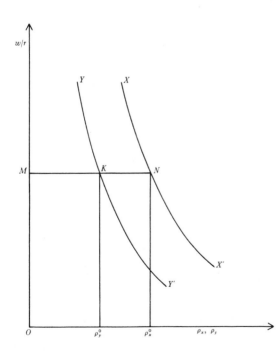

**Figure 9.2** Factor intensities of industries $X$ and $Y$.

increase). Further, the curve $XX'$ lies totally to the right of the curve $YY'$, implying that commodity $X$ is labor intensive relative to $Y$ for all factor-price ratios.
Figure 9.2 summarizes the relationship between $w/r$ and $\rho_x$ and $\rho_y$. Thus, for any
given factor-price ratio, we can quickly determine the optimum factor proportions
in the two industries without having to refer back to fig. 9.1. For instance, assuming that the factor-price ratio is given by the distance $OM$, the optimum factor
proportions for industries $X$ and $Y$ are $\rho_x^0$ and $\rho_y^0$, respectively.

## 9.3 THE OVERALL FACTOR-ENDOWMENT RATIO AS A WEIGHTED AVERAGE OF $\rho_x$ AND $\rho_y$

It follows, from the general principles of production, that both industries tend
to become more labor intensive as labor becomes relatively cheaper (i.e., as the
factor-price ratio $w/r$ falls). But is the increase in both $\rho_x$ and $\rho_y$ consistent with the
assumption of *fixed overall factor supplies?* And, if so, how can the two statements
be reconciled?

The overall factor-endowment ratio $\rho$ in a country is a weighted average of
the factor proportions of the two industries. More precisely,

$$\rho \equiv \frac{L}{T} = \frac{L_x}{T} + \frac{L_y}{T} = \frac{T_x}{T}\frac{L_x}{T_x} + \frac{T_y}{T}\frac{L_y}{T_y} = \frac{T_x}{T}\rho_x + \frac{T_y}{T}\rho_y \tag{9.2}$$

Since we have been assuming that $X$ is labor intensive relative to $Y$, we must
necessarily have

$$\rho_y < \rho < \rho_x \tag{9.3}$$

Now start from a position where eq. (9.2) is satisfied and assume that the
factor-price ratio $w/r$ falls. Both $\rho_x$ and $\rho_y$ tend to increase, and eq. (9.2) is violated
when the original allocation of land between $X$ and $Y$ is maintained (that is,
eq. (9.2) is not satisfied if $\rho_x$ and $\rho_y$ increase while $T_x$ and $T_y$ remain constant).
However, if a heavier weight is given to $\rho_y$ than to $\rho_x$ (that is, if $T_y$ increases and $T_x$
falls sufficiently), then eq. (9.2) is reestablished. This is illustrated below by means
of the box diagram. In the meantime, we must discuss an important lemma.

## 9.4 AN IMPORTANT LEMMA

**Lemma** Given the optimum factor proportions in the two industries and
assuming that the outputs of $X$ and $Y$ are always selected in such a way as to
keep land fully employed, an increase in the output of the labor-intensive
commodity at the expense of the land-intensive commodity necessarily increases the aggregate demand for labor; and an increase in the output of the
land-intensive commodity at the expense of the labor-intensive commodity
necessarily decreases the aggregate demand for labor.

That this is true follows from the fact that, per unit of land, the labor-intensive
industry employs more labor than the land-intensive industry. Thus, if $X$ changes
by $\Delta X$ and $Y$ by $\Delta Y$ subject to the condition that

$$a_{Tx}\,\Delta X + a_{Ty}\,\Delta Y = 0 \tag{9.4}$$

(that is, subject to the condition that the aggregate employment of land remains constant), the total demand for labor will change by

$$\Delta L = a_{Lx} \, \Delta X + a_{Ly} \, \Delta Y = a_{Tx} \rho_x \, \Delta X + a_{Ty} \rho_y \, \Delta Y \tag{9.5}$$

Solving (9.4) for $\Delta Y$ and substituting into (9.5), we get

$$\Delta L = a_{Tx} \rho_x \, \Delta X + a_{Ty} \rho_y \left(-\frac{a_{Tx}}{a_{Ty}}\right) \Delta X = a_{Tx}(\rho_x - \rho_y) \, \Delta X \tag{9.6}$$

Hence, if $\rho_x > \rho_y$, the sign of $\Delta L$ will be the same as the sign of $\Delta X$. That is, an increase in the output of the labor-intensive commodity (and therefore a fall in $Y$) will cause the aggregate demand for labor to increase; and a decrease in the output of the labor-intensive commodity $X$ will cause the aggregate demand for labor to fall—assuming, of course, that land remains fully employed and the same techniques of production remain in use.

Interchanging the roles of labor and land, it becomes obvious that as the output of the labor-intensive commodity increases at the expense of the land-intensive commodity in such a way that labor remains fully employed, the aggregate demand for land decreases; and when the output of the land-intensive commodity increases at the expense of the labor-intensive commodity, the aggregate demand for land increases.

## Graphical Illustration of the Lemma

The preceding lemma can be illustrated graphically as follows. Given the land coefficients, $a_{Tx}$ and $a_{Ty}$, determine the full-employment equation for land

$$T = a_{Tx} X + a_{Ty} Y \tag{9.7}$$

Graphically, eq. (9.7) gives the linear *land frontier* as shown in fig. 9.3 by the curve $UV$. The absolute slope of $UV$ is $a_{Tx}/a_{Ty}$.

At each and every point on the land frontier there exists an aggregate need for labor ($L_d$), given by the equation

$$L_d = a_{Lx} X + a_{Ly} Y \tag{9.8}$$

Alternatively, for any given $L_d$, eq. (9.8) can be illustrated by a linear contour line whose absolute slope is given by the ratio $a_{Lx}/a_{Ly}$. Draw the whole family of these labor-contour lines, as illustrated in fig. 9.3 by $L_1, L_2, L_3$.

When the labor-contour lines are steeper than the land frontier ($a_{Lx}/a_{Ly} > a_{Tx}/a_{Ty}$), as illustrated in fig. 9.3, a movement along the land frontier from $U$ toward $V$ shifts the economy to higher and higher labor-contour lines. On the other hand, when the labor-contour lines are flatter than the land frontier ($a_{Lx}/a_{Ly} < a_{Tx}/a_{Ty}$), a movement from $U$ toward $V$ shifts the economy to lower and lower labor-contour lines. The lemma is proved when it is realized that in the former case ($a_{Lx}/a_{Ly} > a_{Tx}/a_{Ty}$) commodity $X$ is labor intensive, and in the latter case ($a_{Lx}/a_{Ly} < a_{Tx}/a_{Ty}$) land intensive, relative to commodity $Y$. This is so because the inequalities $a_{Lx}/a_{Ly} \gtrless a_{Tx}/a_{Ty}$ are equivalent to the inequalities $a_{Lx}/a_{Tx} \gtrless a_{Ly}/a_{Ty}$.

**Figure 9.3** The labor requirements along the land frontier UV.

The reader can now interchange the roles of labor and land and consider instead a labor frontier along with a family of land-contour lines.

## 9.5 RECONCILIATION BETWEEN THE VARIABLES $\rho_x$ AND $\rho_y$ AND THE FIXED OVERALL FACTOR-ENDOWMENT RATIO $\rho$

Consider now fig. 9.4. The sides of the box diagram show the overall factor endowments. The amounts of $L$ and $T$ used in industry $X$ ($L_x$ and $T_x$, respectively) are measured from the origin $O_x$. Similarly, the amounts of $L$ and $T$ used in industry $Y$ ($L_y$ and $T_y$) are measured from the origin $O_y$. Assume that commodity $X$ is labor intensive relative to $Y$ and suppose that the factor-price ratio is such that the economy happens to be initially at point $E_1$ on the contract curve. Thus, $O_x C$ units of labor and $O_x M$ units of land are used in the production of $X$. The slope of the vector $O_x E_1$ with respect to the $T_x$ axis shows the labor-land ratio used in industry $X$ ($\rho_x^1$). Similarly, $O_y H$ units of labor and $O_y F$ units of land are used in the production of $Y$. The slope of the vector $O_y E_1$ with respect to the $T_y$ axis shows the labor-land ratio used in industry $Y$ ($\rho_y^1$).

Assume now that the factor-price ratio $w/r$ falls. An explanation for this is given in the following section. As $w/r$ falls, both industries become more labor intensive. In particular, assume that $\rho_x$ increases from $\rho_x^1$ to $\rho_x^2$ and $\rho_y$ increases from $\rho_y^1$ to $\rho_y^2$. How can both industries become more labor intensive, given that the same totals of labor and land continue to be employed by the economy as a whole? Figure 9.4 shows that this is possible because the output of the labor-intensive industry ($X$) contracts while the output of the land-intensive industry ($Y$) expands. Thus, the maintenance of full employment at the higher labor-land

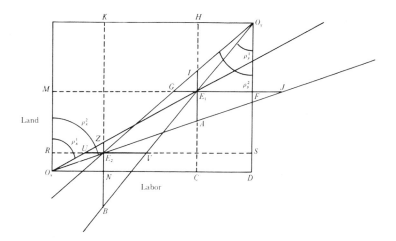

**Figure 9.4** As labor becomes cheaper relative to land, both commodities become more labor intensive. Full employment is maintained by an increase in the production of the land-intensive commodity and a decrease in the production of the labor-intensive commodity.

ratios causes the economy to move from $E_1$ to $E_2$. The necessity for this movement can be justified in several ways.

1. Consider the initial position at $E_1$. What would the total labor requirements be if, as both $\rho_x$ and $\rho_y$ increase, both industries were to continue employing the same amounts of land they were employing before the increase in the labor-land ratios? They would be $MJ$ for $X$ and $FG$ for $Y$. The aggregate demand for labor by both industries would be $MJ + FG = MG + FG + GJ$. Since the total supply of labor is only $MG + GF$, an excess demand for labor would emerge, given by the horizontal distance $GJ$. How could this excess demand for labor be eliminated if both industries continue to maintain the factor ratios $\rho_x^2$ and $\rho_y^2$? According to the lemma, this can be accomplished by allowing the labor-intensive industry to contract and the land-intensive industry to expand. Imagine that the horizontal line $MGFJ$ shifts downward continuously (in a parallel fashion), intersecting the two expansion paths $O_x J$ and $O_y G$ at points such as $J$ and $G$, respectively. The horizontal distance $JG$ gives the excess demand for labor under the assumption that all the available land is always employed. As the line $MGFJ$ shifts downward, i.e., as land is transferred from $X$ to $Y$ and therefore $X$ contracts while $Y$ expands, the excess demand for labor decreases. The latter shrinks to zero when the horizontal line $MGFJ$ coincides with $RUVS$. Thus, when $RM$ units of land are transferred from $X$ to $Y$, the aggregate demand for labor equals the aggregate supply.

2. Consider again the initial position at $E_1$. What would the total land requirements be if, as both $\rho_x$ and $\rho_y$ increase, both industries were to continue employing the same amounts of labor they were employing before the increase in the labor-land ratios? The aggregate demand for land would obviously be $CA + HI$, which falls short of the aggregate supply of land by $AI$. What can be

done to eliminate this excess supply of land, assuming that $X$ and $Y$ maintain the ratios $\rho_x^2$ and $\rho_y^2$, respectively? Again, according to the lemma, the output of the land-intensive industry $(Y)$ should expand and the output of the labor-intensive industry $(X)$ should contract. As the vertical line $HIAC$ moves leftward in a parallel fashion, i.e., as labor is transferred from $X$ to $Y$, the excess supply of land (given by the vertical distances between the vectors $E_2 A$ and $E_2 I$) necessarily shrinks. In particular, the excess supply of land shrinks to zero when $NC$ units of labor are transferred from $X$ to $Y$.

3. Assume that the optimum factor ratios in $X$ and $Y$ are $\rho_x^1$ and $\rho_y^1$, respectively, and the economy happens to be at $E_1$. What would happen to the aggregate demand for labor if we let $X$ contract and $Y$ expand while keeping land fully employed? Again, on the basis of the lemma, there will emerge an excess supply of labor. In particular, if $RM$ units of land are transferred from $X$ to $Y$, the aggregate demand for labor would be $RU + VS$. Thus, an excess supply of labor would emerge, given by the distance $UV$. It is precisely this excess supply of labor which enables both industries to become more labor intensive as the factor-price ratio $w/r$ falls. At the higher factor ratios, $\rho_x^2$ and $\rho_y^2$, industry $X$ would be able to employ an additional amount of labor given by the distance $UE_2$; and industry $Y$ would be able to employ $E_2 V$ extra units of labor.

4. Assume again that the optimum factor ratios in $X$ and $Y$ are $\rho_x^1$ and $\rho_y^1$, respectively, and allow $X$ to contract and $Y$ to expand from their respective levels at $E_1$. What happens to the aggregate demand for land, assuming that labor is always fully employed? It definitely increases because the expanding industry is the land-intensive industry. In particular, when $NC$ units of labor are transferred from $X$ to $Y$, the aggregate demand for land is given by the sum $KB + NZ$, which is larger than the aggregate supply $(KN)$ by the amount $ZB$. This excess demand for land is eliminated, of course, when both industries become more labor intensive, which is another way of saying that they become less land intensive.

The preceding analysis—in particular, the conclusion that as $w/r$ falls both $\rho_x$ and $\rho_y$ increase—is valid whether factor-intensity reversals are absent or not. The complications of factor-intensity reversals are studied in the next chapter.

## PART B. FACTOR PRICES AND COMMODITY PRICES

It has already been said that the production functions imply a definite relationship between the optimum labor-land ratios in the two industries, the relative factor prices, and the relative costs of production of commodities. Part A analyzed the relationship between factor prices and the optimum labor-land ratios. This part analyzes the relationship between factor prices and commodity prices.

The basic proposition is that, as the factor-price ratio $w/r$ falls, i.e., as *labor becomes relatively cheaper, the labor-intensive commodity becomes cheaper relative to the land-intensive commodity.* In our example where $X$ is the labor-intensive commodity, as $w/r$ falls the commodity-price ratio $p_x/p_y$ also falls.

A heuristic proof of this proposition follows.

## 9.6 A HEURISTIC PROOF $k$ $h$

If the factor proportions, $\rho_x$ and $\rho_y$, in industries $X$ and $Y$, respectively, remain constant as the factor-price ratio $w/r$ falls (as, for instance, in the case of fixed coefficients of production), then obviously the relative cost of the labor-intensive commodity would also fall, that is, $p_x/p_y$ would fall. (A rigorous proof is given below.) A difficulty arises in the case of variable proportions where, as $w/r$ falls, labor is being substituted for land in both industries. Could this substitution of labor for land reverse the direction of change of the relative commodity-price ratio? In other words, is it possible that $p_x/p_y$ might increase as $w/r$ falls? The answer is definitely "No." Let us see why.

In fig. 9.5, the production-possibilities frontier corresponds to the box diagram of fig. 9.4. As shown in chap. 4, the production-possibilities frontier (under the present assumptions of constant returns to scale and differing factor intensities between commodities $X$ and $Y$) is necessarily concave to the origin. Points $E_1$ and $E_2$ on the frontier correspond to the synonymous points on the contract curve of fig. 9.4. Under these circumstances, as the factor-price ratio $w/r$ falls and the economy moves from point $E_1$ to point $E_2$, commodity $X$ becomes cheaper relative to $Y$, as indicated by the fact that the production-possibilities frontier is flatter at point $E_2$ compared with point $E_1$.

This can be summarized as follows. *As the factor-price ratio $w/r$ falls, both industries tend to become more labor intensive* (or less land intensive) *in order to minimize costs.* That is, both industries tend to substitute the cheaper factor (labor) for the more expensive factor (land). In the context of general equilibrium, *this substitution of labor for land in both industries is possible if, and only if, the output of the land-intensive industry expands at the expense of the output of the*

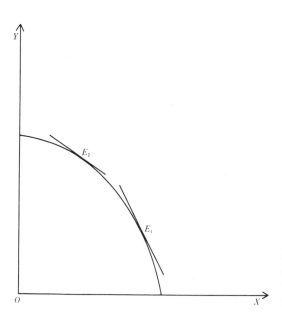

**Figure 9.5** As $w/r$ falls, the output of the land-intensive commodity ($Y$) increases while the output of the labor-intensive commodity ($X$) decreases. Because of increasing opportunity costs, the price ratio $p_x/p_y$ falls.

*labor-intensive industry. As a result, the labor-intensive commodity tends to become cheaper relative to the land-intensive commodity because of the underlying increasing opportunity costs.*

### Reversing the Sequence of Events

Perhaps it seems unusual to consider the factor-price ratio as the independent variable and the commodity-price ratio as the dependent variable. In static analysis this is immaterial. But what would a probable dynamic sequence of events be? A dynamic sequence of events would probably proceed along opposite lines, with the commodity-price ratio playing the role of the independent variable and the factor-price ratio being the dependent variable. This is also illustrated in figs. 9.4 and 9.5. Assume that the economy is originally in equilibrium at point $E_1$ but moves to $E_2$ as a result of a change in tastes. The first impact of the change in tastes is reflected immediately in a lower price of commodity $X$ (whose demand has fallen) relative to $Y$. What does this change in commodity prices imply for the active producers of $X$ and $Y$? Obviously, the producers of $Y$ enjoy positive profits and the producers of $X$ suffer losses. The ensuing profits in industry $Y$ and losses in industry $X$ attract resources from industry $X$ to industry $Y$. But since, by assumption, industry $X$ is labor intensive relative to $Y$, the proportion in which labor and land are released by industry $X$ is not the same as the proportion in which industry $Y$ is willing to absorb the two factors. In particular, there emerges an excess demand for land and/or an excess supply of labor; and both of these forces cause the factor-price ratio $w/r$ to fall. As $w/r$ falls, of course, both industries substitute labor for land (i.e., both industries become more labor intensive or less land intensive), and this process continues until a new equilibrium is established.

This sequence of events is no doubt more appealing than the original exposition. However, for our purposes, whatever reasons are given for the relationship between factor prices and commodity prices are immaterial, although it must be admitted that the second version approximates the actual sequence of events better than the first. Our main purpose is to establish a one-to-one correspondence between factor prices and commodity prices. Put differently, our analysis is basically static.

## 9.7 A RIGOROUS PROOF

We now provide a rigorous proof of the proposition that the price ratio $p_x/p_y$ is a strictly increasing function of the factor-price ratio $w/r$ (assuming, of course, that $X$ is the labor-intensive commodity).

### Fixed Coefficients of Production

Consider the case of fixed coefficients of production first. The commodity-price ratio is given by

$$\frac{p_x}{p_y} = \frac{(w/r)a_{Lx} + a_{Tx}}{(w/r)a_{Ly} + a_{Ty}} \tag{9.9}$$

Equation (9.9) can be rewritten as

$$\frac{p_x}{p_y} = c\,\frac{(w/r)\rho_x + 1}{(w/r)\rho_y + 1} \tag{9.10}$$

where $c$ is a constant defined by the ratio $a_{Tx}/a_{Ty}$.

Differentiating $p_x/p_y$ as given by eq. (9.10) with respect to $w/r$, we get

$$\frac{d(p_x/p_y)}{d(w/r)} = c\,\frac{\rho_x - \rho_y}{[(w/r)\rho_y + 1]^2} > 0 \tag{9.11}$$

which is positive, since, by assumption, $\rho_x > \rho_y$. This shows that the commodity-price ratio $p_x/p_y$ is a strictly increasing function of the factor-price ratio $w/r$.

For completeness, it should be pointed out that, should commodity $Y$ be the labor-intensive commodity (that is, $\rho_y > \rho_x$), the ratio $p_x/p_y$ will be a strictly decreasing function of $w/r$.

## Variable Coefficients of Production

The case of variable coefficients is slightly more complicated. The coefficients $a_{Lx}$, $a_{Tx}$, $a_{Ly}$, and $a_{Ty}$ are themselves functions of the factor-price ratio $w/r$. This is important in the following differentiations. For simplicity, the convention of using primes is adopted in differentiating the coefficients $a_{Lx}$, $a_{Tx}$, $a_{Ly}$, and $a_{Ty}$ with respect to the ratio $w/r$.

Differentiating $p_x/p_y$ as given by eq. (9.9) with respect to $w/r$, we get

$$\frac{d(p_x/p_y)}{d(w/r)} = \frac{1}{[a_{Ly}(w/r) + a_{Ty}]^2}\left[\left(a_{Lx} + a'_{Tx} + \frac{w}{r}a'_{Lx}\right)\left(\frac{w}{r}a_{Ly} + a_{Ty}\right)\right.$$
$$\left. - \left(a_{Ly} + \frac{w}{r}a'_{Ly} + a'_{Ty}\right)\left(\frac{w}{r}a_{Lx} + a_{Tx}\right)\right] \tag{9.12}$$

Equation (9.12) can be greatly simplified by making use of the marginal conditions which have to be satisfied for cost minimization. Thus, the marginal rate of substitution of labor for land should be equal to the factor-price ratio $w/r$ in each industry; that is,

$$\mathrm{MRS}^X_{LT} = -\frac{da_{Tx}}{da_{Lx}} = -\frac{a'_{Tx}}{a'_{Lx}} = \frac{w}{r} \tag{9.13a}$$

$$\mathrm{MRS}^Y_{LT} = -\frac{da_{Ty}}{da_{Ly}} = -\frac{a'_{Ty}}{a'_{Ly}} = \frac{w}{r} \tag{9.14a}$$

where $\mathrm{MRS}^i_{LT}$ stands for the marginal rate of substitution of labor for land in the $i$th industry.

From eqs. (9.13a) and (9.14a) it follows that

$$a'_{Tx} + \frac{w}{r}a'_{Lx} = 0 \tag{9.13b}$$

$$a'_{Ty} + \frac{w}{r}a'_{Ly} = 0 \tag{9.14b}$$

Using eqs. (9.13$b$) and (9.14$b$), we can simplify eq. (9.12) as follows:

$$\frac{d(p_x/p_y)}{d(w/r)} = \frac{a_{Lx}a_{Ty} - a_{Ly}a_{Tx}}{[a_{Ly}(w/r) + a_{Ty}]^2} = c\frac{\rho_x - \rho_y}{[(w/r)\rho_y + 1]^2} \qquad (9.15)$$

Now eq. (9.15) is identical to eq. (9.11), and therefore, the conclusion must be the same as the conclusion reached under the simplified assumption of fixed coefficients of production; i.e., the commodity-price ratio $p_x/p_y$ is a strictly increasing function of $w/r$ (assuming, of course, $\rho_x > \rho_y$).

## PART C. THE RANGE OF FACTOR PRICES AND COMMODITY PRICES IN A CLOSED ECONOMY

### 9.8 SUMMARY OF PARTS A AND B

Parts A and B are conveniently summarized in fig. 9.6. The first quadrant contains the information in fig. 9.2. The fact that both curves (that is, $XX'$ and $YY'$) are drawn downward sloping indicates that, as the factor-price ratio $w/r$ falls (rises), both commodities tend to become more (less) labor intensive. Further, the curve $XX'$ lies totally to the right of curve $YY'$, indicating our assumption that commodity $X$ is labor intensive relative to $Y$ for all factor-price ratios.

In the second quadrant, the commodity-price ratio $p_x/p_y$ is measured along the horizontal axis and in the negative direction. The curve $PP'$ shows the relationship between the factor-price ratio $w/r$ and the commodity-price ratio $p_x/p_y$. As can be easily verified, the curve $PP'$ implies that, as the factor-price ratio $w/r$ falls (rises),

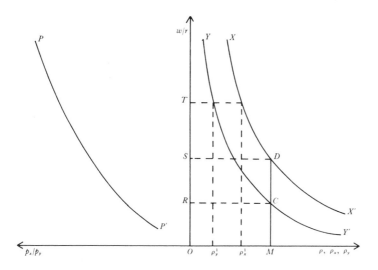

**Figure 9.6** The relationship between optimum factor proportions, factor prices, and commodity prices.

the commodity-price ratio also falls (rises), and vice versa. The reason why this relationship should hold between the factor-price ratio $w/r$ and the commodity-price ratio $p_x/p_y$ has already been explained in part B.

## 9.9 THE OVERALL FACTOR-ENDOWMENT RATIO AND THE POSSIBLE RANGE OF THE FACTOR-PRICE RATIO

The analysis so far, as summarized in fig. 9.6, has been concerned with the relationships between optimum factor proportions, factor prices, and commodity prices implicit in the given technological possibilities of production. In a particular economy, however, with a given factor endowment, only a limited range of the techniques available can actually be used efficiently. How do we know this? Remember that the contract curve lies on one side of the diagonal. Therefore, the techniques implied by the opposite side (i.e., the area in which the contract curve does not lie) are never used. What is the possible range of factor prices, commodity prices, and optimum factor proportions after the introduction of the overall factor-endowment ratio?

Consider a country whose factor endowment of labor relative to land (that is, $L/T$) is given by the distance $OM$ of fig. 9.6. We can be sure that, when both commodities are being produced, a labor-land ratio greater than $OM$ must be used in industry $X$ and a labor-land ratio smaller than $OM$ must be used in industry $Y$. This follows directly from the assumption that, at uniform factor prices, industry $X$ is using a higher labor-land ratio than industry $Y$ (that is, $\rho_x > \rho_y$) and the observation that the overall factor-endowment ratio (total labor/total land = $OM$) is a weighted average of the proportions used in the two industries, the exact weights being the relative proportions of total land applied to each use (see eq. (9.2)). In the limiting case where only $X$ is being produced, industry $X$ necessarily uses the two factors in the same proportion as the overall factor proportion $OM$; and when only $Y$ is being produced, industry $Y$ necessarily uses the two factors in the existing overall proportion $OM$.

What is the possible range of the factor-price ratio? Clearly, if something of both goods is to be produced, the factor-price ratio can only range between points $S$ and $R$ (that is, $OR < w/r < OS$). This can best be seen by noting that, for any factor-price ratio higher than the distance $OS$, such as $OT$, both industries tend to use the factors labor and land in proportions smaller than the overall labor-land ratio, $OM$. In particular, for $w/r = OT$, we have $\rho_x = \rho_x^1 < OM$ and $\rho_y = \rho_y^1 < OM$. Under these circumstances, the full-employment assumption cannot be fulfilled. No matter what the outputs of $X$ and $Y$ are, there is always a surplus of labor (i.e., positive excess supply of labor) and/or a deficit of land (i.e., positive excess demand for land). The former causes the wage rate to fall, while the latter causes the rent for the services of land to rise, and both of these forces cause the factor-price ratio $w/r$ to fall.

Similarly, when the factor-price ratio is smaller than $OR$, both industries tend to use the factors labor and land in proportions higher than the overall labor-land ratio (that is, $OM$). Under these circumstances, there is always a deficit of labor (i.e., positive excess demand for labor) and/or a surplus of land (i.e., positive excess supply of land). Again, the former causes the wage rate to rise, while the latter causes the rent to fall, and both of these forces cause the factor-price ratio $w/r$ to rise.

When the factor-price ratio equals $OR$, industry $Y$ uses labor and land in the same proportion as that in which these factors exist in the economy (that is, $OM$), while industry $X$ uses a labor-land ratio higher than $OM$. Under these circumstances, only $Y$ is produced. The output of $X$ has to be zero for full employment.

Similarly, when the factor-price ratio equals $OS$, industry $X$ uses a labor-land ratio equal to $OM$ while industry $Y$ uses a ratio smaller than $OM$. Again, the economy specializes completely in the production of $X$. Any positive production of $Y$ necessarily violates the full-employment assumption.

For any factor-price ratio in the range $OR < w/r < OS$, both commodities must necessarily be produced if full employment is to be preserved. In this range, neither commodity is using a labor-land ratio equal to $OM$. Therefore, specialization in the production of only one commodity necessarily violates the full-employment assumption. However, since in this range $\rho_y < OM < \rho_x$, a proper combination of outputs of $X$ and $Y$ can be found to satisfy the full-employment assumption. Further, as the factor-price ratio falls continuously from the value $OS$ to the value $OR$, the output of commodity $X$ falls while the output of commodity $Y$ increases. This proposition has already been established in part A, and no additional discussion is necessary.

Observe that in the extreme case of fixed coefficients of production, the two curves $XX'$ and $YY'$ become vertical, with the range of variation of the factor-price ratio becoming infinite. On the other hand, when the production functions of $X$ and $Y$ are identical, except for a scale factor, the curves $XX'$ and $YY'$ coincide and the range of variation of $w/r$ necessarily shrinks to a single point. In this special case, the equilibrium factor-price ratio depends only on the overall factor-endowment ratio: it is independent of demand conditions.

## 9.10 THE OUTPUTS OF $X$ AND $Y$

Can we determine the precise amounts of $X$ and $Y$ produced for factor-price ratios in the range $OR < w/r < OS$? Unfortunately, this cannot be done on the basis of the information given in fig. 9.6. For this, we have to know the land coefficients, $a_{Tx}$ and $a_{Ty}$, as well as the total amount of land available. Thus, the full-employment equations are

$$a_{Lx} X + a_{Ly} Y = L \qquad (9.16a)$$

$$a_{Tx} X + a_{Ty} Y = T \qquad (9.17)$$

Since by definition

$$a_{Lx} = \rho_x a_{Tx} \qquad a_{Ly} = \rho_y a_{Ty} \qquad L = \rho T$$

eq. (9.16a) can be rewritten as follows:

$$\rho_x a_{Tx} X + \rho_y a_{Ty} Y = \rho T \qquad (9.16b)$$

If, in addition to $\rho_x$, $\rho_y$, and $\rho$, we also know the coefficients $a_{Tx}$ and $a_{Ty}$ as well as the total quantity of land $T$, we can solve eqs. (9.16$b$) and (9.17) for $X$ and $Y$ to get

$$X = \frac{T a_{Ty}}{\Delta} (\rho - \rho_y) \tag{9.18}$$

$$Y = \frac{T a_{Tx}}{\Delta} (\rho_x - \rho) \tag{9.19}$$

where $\Delta = a_{Tx} a_{Ty} (\rho_x - \rho_y)$.

## 9.11 THE ALLOCATION OF LABOR AND LAND

However, despite the fact that we cannot determine the outputs of $X$ and $Y$ unless we know $a_{Tx}$, $a_{Ty}$, and $T$, in addition to $\rho$, $\rho_x$, and $\rho_y$, we can nevertheless determine the proportion in which $L$ and $T$ is allocated in the production of $X$ and $Y$ for full employment. Thus, taking the ratio of $X$ and $Y$ as given, respectively, by eqs. (9.18) and (9.19), we get

$$\frac{X}{Y} = \frac{a_{Ty}}{a_{Tx}} \frac{\rho - \rho_y}{\rho_x - \rho} \tag{9.20}$$

Equation (9.20) can also be rearranged as follows:

$$\frac{\rho - \rho_y}{\rho_x - \rho} = \frac{a_{Tx} X}{a_{Ty} Y} = \frac{T_x}{T_y} \tag{9.21}$$

where $T_x$ is the total amount of $T$ used in the production of $X$ and $T_y$ is the total amount of $T$ used in the production of $Y$. Equation (9.21) shows that the ratio $T_x/T_y$ depends only on the ratios $\rho$, $\rho_y$, and $\rho_x$.

It should be noted that, as long as $\rho$ lies between $\rho_x$ and $\rho_y$, the ratio $T_x/T_y$ is necessarily positive. On the other hand, should $\rho$ become smaller (or higher) than $\rho_x$ and $\rho_y$, the ratio $T_x/T_y$ would become negative. Since negative production is not possible, such an arrangement has to be ruled out, which explains once more why the only possible range for the factor-price ratio is $OR \le w/r \le OS$ (see fig. 9.6). Finally, if $\rho = \rho_y$, then $T_x/T_y = 0$, that is, $T_x = 0$ and $T_y = T$; and if $\rho = \rho_x$, $T_x/T_y \to \infty$, that is, $T_x = T$ and $T_y = 0$.

The allocation of labor, of course, is given by $L_x = \rho_x T_x$ and $L_y = \rho_y T_y$, or

$$\frac{L_x}{L_y} = \frac{\rho_x(\rho - \rho_y)}{\rho_y(\rho_x - \rho)} \tag{9.22}$$

## 9.12 TECHNICAL CHANGE AND THE RANGE OF VARIATION OF FACTOR PRICES

How does technical change affect the range of variation of $w/r$? In particular, suppose that, as a result of a technical innovation, *the labor-intensive industry* $(X)$ *becomes more labor intensive* at every value of $w/r$. How does this change affect the range of variation of $w/r$? Figure 9.6 shows that the range of variation of $w/r$ necessarily increases in this case because the curve $XX'$ shifts totally to the right. Essentially the same conclusion follows when, as a result of a technical innovation, *the land-intensive industry becomes more land intensive* at every value of $w/r$. Here, the curve $YY'$ shifts totally to the left and the vertical distances between $XX'$ and $YY'$ increase.

On the other hand, when technical change causes either the labor-intensive commodity to become *less* labor intensive, or the land-intensive commodity *less* land intensive, at all factor-price ratios, the range of variation of $w/r$ necessarily decreases. (It is assumed that $X$ continues to be labor intensive relative to $Y$ after the innovation.)

## 9.13 THE RANGE OF VARIATION OF COMMODITY PRICES IN GENERAL

We have just seen that the permissible range of variation of both the factor-price ratio and the labor-land ratios in the two industries are rather limited once the overall labor-land ratio is given. But what about the commodity-price ratio? Is it reasonable to expect that the commodity-price ratio will necessarily vary within narrow limits, too? Not at all.

After the introduction of the overall factor-endowment ratio, the curve $PP'$ of fig. 9.6 is necessarily distorted. This is illustrated in fig. 9.7, which reproduces only the second quadrant of fig. 9.6. The solid curve $PP'$ of fig. 9.7 corresponds to the curve $PP'$ of fig. 9.6. However, the curve showing the relationship between the commodity-price ratio and the factor-price ratio is $KS'R'R$. For factor prices in

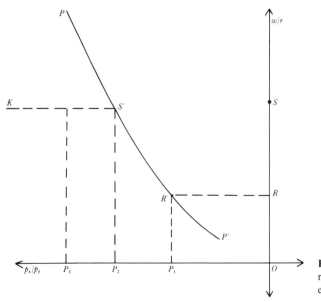

**Figure 9.7** The commodity-price ratio after the overall factor-endowment ratio is introduced.

the admissible range ($OR$ and $OS$), the relationship between factor prices and commodity prices corresponds to that originally given by the curve $PP'$.

Now consider points $S$ and $R$. At $w/r = OS$, the economy is specializing entirely in the production of commodity $X$. The distance $SS'$ (or $OP_2$) shows the ratio

$$\frac{\text{Marginal cost of commodity } X}{\text{Marginal cost of commodity } Y} = \frac{\text{MC}_x}{\text{MC}_y}$$

But the ratio of marginal costs may or may not be equal to the ratio of commodity prices, since the economy is completely specializing in the production of $X$. As shown in chap. 4, the slope of the production-possibilities frontier shows the ratio of marginal costs rather than the ratio of commodity prices. With pure competition prevailing in the commodity markets, marginal costs are equal to prices, provided that both commodities are produced. If, however, a commodity is not produced, we must allow for the possibility that its price is lower than its marginal cost, i.e., price < marginal cost. Thus, when commodity $Y$ is not produced, we must have $\text{MC}_y \geq p_y$. Since commodity $X$ is produced, and thus $\text{MC}_x = p_x$, we must also have $\text{MC}_x/\text{MC}_y \leq p_x/p_y$. This is exactly what is allowed for by the horizontal broken line $KS'$ of fig. 9.7. Similar arguments can be provided for the justification of the broken line $R'R$ of fig. 9.7, where we allow for the possibility that $p_x \leq \text{MC}_x$.

To understand better what is involved, assume that our economy is a small open economy which takes international prices as given. Assume initially that the international-price ratio is given by $OP_2$ and thus our country specializes in the production of commodity $X$. The factor-price ratio is given by $OS$, which is simply the marginal rate of substitution of labor for land in the production of commodity $X$ when all available land and labor are used in the production of $X$. In this case, the ratio of marginal costs equals the ratio of commodity prices. Now suppose that the demand for commodity $X$ increases in the international market, causing the international-price ratio to rise to $OP_3$. Since by assumption our economy is small and cannot affect international prices, the commodity-price ratio $OP_3$ must necessarily prevail in our economy as well. However, since our economy is already specializing in the production of $X$, its allocation of resources cannot be affected: the factor ratio used in industry $X$ (that is, $\rho_x$) and the factor-price ratio $w/r$ remain at their original levels (that is, $\rho_x = OM$ and $w/r = OS$, as shown in fig. 9.6). Thus, while the commodity-price ratio is free to rise above $OP_2$, the factor-price ratio continues to be given by $OS$. This explains the horizontal part $KS'$ of fig. 9.7. A similar argument can be provided for the horizontal part $R'R$.

## 9.14 THE RANGE OF VARIATION OF COMMODITY PRICES WHEN BOTH COMMODITIES ARE PRODUCED

While the possible range of variation of the commodity-price ratio is in general infinite, the permissible range when both commodities are produced is drastically limited. For instance, in fig. 9.7 the range of variation of $p_x/p_y$ when both commodities are produced is limited to $OP_1 < p_x/p_y < OP_2$. Two factors determine this limited range of the commodity-price ratio: the permissible range of variation of the factor-price ratio and the elasticity of the curve $PP'$. Thus, for any given range of $w/r$, the more elastic the $PP'$ curve is, the larger is the range of variation of $p_x/p_y$. What actually determines the elasticity of the curve $PP'$?

The elasticity $e$ of the $PP'$ curve is given by

$$
\begin{aligned}
e &\equiv \frac{d(p_x/p_y)}{d(w/r)} \frac{(w/r)}{(p_x/p_y)} \\
&= c \frac{\rho_x - \rho_y}{[(w/r)\rho_y + 1]^2} \frac{(w/r)[(w/r)\rho_y + 1]}{c[(w/r)\rho_x + 1]} \\
&= \frac{(w/r)(\rho_x - \rho_y)}{[(w/r)\rho_y + 1][(w/r)\rho_x + 1]} \\
&= \frac{1}{(w/r)\rho_y + 1} - \frac{1}{(w/r)\rho_x + 1}
\end{aligned} \tag{9.23}
$$

where use was made of eqs. (9.10) and (9.15).

The ratio

$$
\frac{1}{(w/r)\rho_i + 1} = \frac{1}{(w/r)(L_i/T_i) + 1} = \frac{rT_i}{wL_i + rT_i} \tag{9.24}
$$

gives the share of land in the $i$th industry. Therefore, *the elasticity of the PP' curve, as given by eq. (9.23), is equal to the difference between the land shares in the two industries.*

Obviously, when $\rho_x > \rho_y$, the land share in industry $Y$ is larger than the land share in industry $X$, and the $PP'$ is upward sloping ($e > 0$). On the other hand, when $\rho_x < \rho_y$, the land share in industry $X$ is larger than the land share in industry $Y$, and the $PP'$ curve is downward sloping ($e < 0$).

The $PP'$ curve becomes more elastic when the difference between the land shares in the two industries becomes larger. Nevertheless, an increase in the difference between land shares is *not* equivalent to an increase in the difference between factor intensities (that is, $\rho_x - \rho_y$), even though an increase in $\rho_x$ (given $\rho_y$) and a decrease in $\rho_y$ (given $\rho_x$) lead to an increase in both the difference $\rho_x - \rho_y$ and the difference between land shares. In other words, it is quite possible for the difference $\rho_x - \rho_y$ to decrease while the difference between land shares actually increases.

For instance, suppose that both $\rho_x$ and $\rho_y$ increase by the same amount so that their difference $\rho_x - \rho_y$ remains constant. As the reader can verify directly from eq. (9.23), the difference between land shares (and $e$) increases. Had $\rho_x$ increased by a little less (or, what is the same thing, had $\rho_y$ increased by a little more), the difference $\rho_x - \rho_y$ would have been smaller but the difference in land shares and the elasticity of the $PP'$ curve would have been larger.

## PART D. EQUILIBRIUM IN A CLOSED ECONOMY

Within the range of variation permitted by technology and factor endowment, the equilibrium factor-price ratio and the equilibrium commodity-price ratio is determined by the forces of demand. In particular, the equilibrium $w/r$ and $p_x/p_y$ is determined by the condition that the marginal rate of transformation of $X$ for $Y$ (given by the absolute value of the slope of the production-possibilities frontier, which in turn is equal to the ratio of the marginal cost of $X$ to the marginal cost of $Y$) be just equal to the marginal rate of substitution of $X$ for $Y$ in consumption (which is given by the ratio of the marginal utility of $X$ to the marginal utility of $Y$).

Assuming, for simplicity, that demand conditions are given by a social indifference map, the complete general-equilibrium solution can be summarized as follows. In fig. 9.8, the production-possibilities frontier $(Y_0 E X_0)$ is superimposed on the social indifference map. Equilibrium occurs at point $E$. The quantities $OX_1$ and $OY_1$ of commodities $X$ and $Y$, respectively, are produced and consumed. From fig. 9.8 read off the commodity-price ratio $p_x/p_y$ as the absolute value of the common slope of the production-possibilities frontier and the social indifference curve $I_2$ at point $E$, as shown by the slope of the broken line through $E$. Call this equilibrium commodity-price ratio $p^*$. With this information, read directly from fig. 9.9 (which is a combination of figs. 9.6 and 9.7) the equilibrium factor-price ratio $w^*$ and the equilibrium factor ratios in the two industries, namely, $\rho_x^*$ and $\rho_y^*$. The absolute equilibrium values of labor and land used in the two industries can be easily recovered from the box diagram (not reproduced here) by simply drawing the expansion paths of the two industries with slopes (with respect to the land

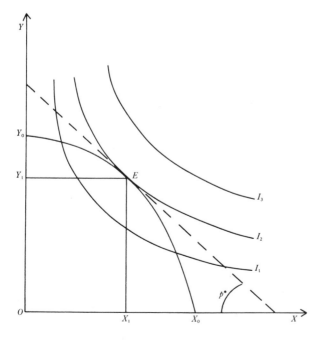

**Figure 9.8** Determination of the equilibrium price ratio in a closed economy.

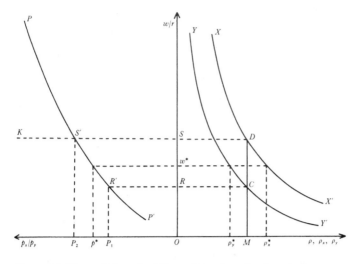

**Figure 9.9** Given $p^*$ from fig. 9.8, we determine $w^*$, $\rho_x^*$, and $\rho_y^*$.

axis) equal to $\rho_x^*$ and $\rho_y^*$, respectively. These expansion paths necessarily intersect each other somewhere on the contract curve. (Why?) The coordinates of the point of their intersection with respect to the origin $O_x$ show the total quantities of labor and land used in the production of commodity $X$; the coordinates of the same point with respect to the origin $O_y$ show the total quantities of labor and land used in the production of commodity $Y$.

As a result of the assumption that demand conditions are given by a social indifference map, the possibility of multiple equilibria is necessarily ruled out.

## SELECTED BIBLIOGRAPHY

Heckscher, E. (1919). "The Effect of Foreign Trade on the Distribution of Income." *Ekonomisk Tidskrift*, vol. 21, pp. 1–32. Reprinted in AEA *Readings in the Theory of International Trade*. Richard D. Irwin, Inc., Homewood, Ill., 1950.

Lerner, A. P. (1953). *Essays in Economics Analysis*. Macmillan and Company, Ltd., London. pp. 67–100.

Ohlin, B. (1933). *Interregional and International Trade*. Harvard University Press, Cambridge, Mass. chaps. 1 to 6 and app. 3.

Samuelson, P. A. (1948). "International Trade and the Equilization of Factor Prices." *Economic Journal*, vol. 58, pp. 165–184.

———— (1949). "International Factor Price Equalization Once Again." *Economic Journal*, vol. 59, pp. 181–197.

Stolper, W. F., and P. A. Samuelson (1941). "Protection and Real Wages." *Review of Economic Studies*, vol. 9, pp. 50–73. Reprinted in AEA *Readings in the Theory of International Trade*. Richard D. Irwin, Inc., Homewood, Ill., 1950.

(Additional references may be found in "Selected Bibliography" at the end of chap. 10.)

# CHAPTER TEN

# THE CAUSE AND EFFECT OF INTERNATIONAL TRADE

We are now ready to consider the main propositions of the modern theory:

(a) *the Heckscher–Ohlin theorem*, i.e., the hypothesis that a country has a comparative advantage in the production of that commodity which uses more intensively the country's relatively abundant factor; and

(b) the *factor-price equalization theorem*, i.e., the hypothesis that the effect of trade is to tend to equalize factor prices between countries, thus serving to some extent as a substitute for factor mobility.

This chapter is divided into three parts. Part A deals with the factor-price equalization theorem proper. Part B considers the Heckscher–Ohlin theorem—whether factor abundance is decided on the basis of the price or the physical definition. Finally, part C considers some of the implications of the assumptions made by the modern theory and also points out some fundamental differences between the classical and the Heckscher–Ohlin theories. Some of the problems which arise in the context of many countries and many commodities are considered in the appendix at the end of this chapter.

## PART A. THE FACTOR-PRICE EQUALIZATION THEOREM

This part deals with the conditions under which free international trade leads to complete factor-price equalization.

## 10.1 INTRODUCTION

The factor-price equalization theorem has attracted the attention of many distinguished trade theorists. Heckscher (1919) stated that free trade equalizes factor rewards completely. Ohlin (1933), on the other hand, cited several reasons why full factor-price equalization cannot occur in practice, and asserted that partial factor-price equalization is more likely in the sense that free trade brings about a tendency (but only a tendency) toward factor-price equalization. The partial-equalization argument was later made rigorous by Stolper and Samuelson (1941). Uzawa (1959) also developed a model which leads to partial equalization. More recently, Samuelson (1971c) set forth a Ricardo–Viner, pure-rent model, with which he attempts to vindicate Ohlin's partial equalization hypothesis.

The case for complete equalization was established by Samuelson (1948, 1949, 1953). As noted in chap. 8, Samuelson's work prompted Robbins to rediscover a seminar paper which Lerner (1953) wrote in 1933 as a student at the London School of Economics. In this paper, Lerner demonstrates rigorously the conditions for complete factor-price equalization.

It appears that, as far as the two-country, two-factor, two-commodity case is concerned, Samuelson stated everything that has ever been said subsequently. Since this book is mainly confined to the restrictive case of two factors and two commodities, Samuelson's analysis will be followed rather closely.

It should be emphasized that "factor prices" in this context does not mean prices of the factors of production themselves (i.e., the price of a piece of land, and so on). It means, rather, the *rentals* for the *services* of these factors, such as the wage rate for the services of labor and the rent for the services of land, per unit of time. The equalization of factor rentals is neither necessary nor sufficient for the equalization of the prices of the factors of production. This follows directly from the fact that the relation between a factor's rental and its price is determined, among other things, by the rate of interest, and the rate of interest is equalized between countries only in special circumstances (see Samuelson, 1965). Thus, it is entirely possible for, say, one acre of homogeneous land to earn the same real rental in both countries and yet command substantially different market prices in the two countries. The confusing use in the literature of the term "factor prices" instead of "factor rentals" is unfortunate.

## 10.2 THE BASIC MODEL

We continue now with the description of the two-country, two-factor, two-commodity model which forms the basis for this chapter's discussion of both the factor-price equalization theorem and the Heckscher–Ohlin theorem.

Consider two countries ($A$ and $B$). Each country uses two homogeneous primary factors of production called labor ($L$) and land ($T$) to produce two commodities ($X$ and $Y$). In addition, assume the following:

  (i) pure competition in both product and factor markets

(ii) nonreversible and different factor intensities of the two commodities at all factor prices
(iii) identical production functions for each commodity between countries
(iv) linear homogeneous production functions (i.e., constant returns to scale in the production of each commodity)
(v) absence of production externalities (i.e., the output of each commodity depends only on inputs of factors which enter into the production process of that commodity alone), factor indifference between uses, and identical factor quality between countries

The argument is usually simplified further by assuming initially that the two homogeneous factors (labor and land) are inelastically supplied in both countries. In other words, the available quantities of labor and land are independent of their prices.

This is our basic model. In the following section we use it to demonstrate that free trade leads to complete factor-price equalization.

## 10.3 FACTOR-PRICE EQUALIZATION

Given the basic model of sec. 10.2, we can enunciate the following important theorem.

**Theorem 10.1: Factor-price equalization theorem** When the assumptions enumerated in sec. 10.2 above are satisfied and, in addition, free trade leads to (a) commodity-price equalization and (b) incomplete specialization in production in each country, then both relative and absolute factor prices are completely equalized between countries.

The heart of the factor-price equalization theorem is to show that, as a result of assumptions (i) to (v) plus the assumption of incomplete specialization in production in each country, there exists the same one-to-one correspondence between the equilibrium commodity-price ratio and the factor-price ratio in both countries. In the absence of trade impediments (such as tariffs, quotas, etc.) and transportation costs, commodity trade equalizes commodity prices. Because of the one-to-one correspondence between commodity prices and factor prices, international trade equalizes factor prices also.

PROOF As we have seen in chap. 9, the given technical possibilities of production (summarized by the production functions) imply a definite relationship between relative factor prices (that is, $w/r$), factor proportions in the two industries (that is, $\rho_x$ and $\rho_y$), and relative commodity prices (that is, $p_x/p_y$). Since by assumption production functions are identical between countries, this basic relationship, as illustrated in fig. 9.6, is necessarily the same in both countries.

What is, then, the difference, if any, between the two countries? Factor endowments. Different factor endowments necessarily imply different regions for autarkic equilibrium factor-price ratios and factor proportions in the two industries. In other words, different factor endowments force the two countries to operate in different regions of the same curves. Therefore, in general, the relationship between relative factor prices and relative commodity prices (the curve $KS'R'R$ of fig. 9.9) is necessarily different between the two countries. How, then, are factor prices equalized?

For any commodity-price ratio at which a country specializes incompletely in production (i.e., produces positive amounts of both commodities), the corresponding factor-price ratio is always read off the $PP'$ curve (fig. 9.9), which by assumption is common to both countries. Therefore, when in the final equilibrium configuration both countries produce both commodities, and commodity prices are everywhere the same, the factor-price ratio must be equalized between countries—the two countries must operate at the same point on the $PP'$ curve of fig. 9.9.

Does the equalization of the factor-price ratio between countries lead to the equalization of the *individual factor rentals* (i.e., *absolute* factor prices) expressed in terms of either commodity? It most certainly does. As we saw in chap. 4, we can always move from the relative factor prices to the absolute marginal productivities of labor and land in both industries because of the assumption of constant returns to scale. Recall that all marginal physical productivities are functions of the relevant labor-land ratios only—not the absolute quantities of labor and land used; and the labor-land ratios are perfectly determined when the factor-price ratio $w/r$ is given. We therefore conclude that commodity trade equalizes factor prices both relatively and absolutely.

The proof of the factor-price equalization theorem is now complete. For further clarifications and extensions, see part C below (and also the appendix to this chapter).

## PART B. THE HECKSCHER–OHLIN THEOREM

We proceed now with the Heckscher–Ohlin theorem. In fact, we consider two versions of the Heckscher–Ohlin theorem: (*a*) when the price definition of factor abundance is adopted and (*b*) when the physical definition of factor abundance is adopted. The scenario is again that of the basic model described in sec. 10.2 above.

## 10.4 THE HECKSCHER–OHLIN THEOREM WHEN THE PRICE DEFINITION OF FACTOR ABUNDANCE IS ADOPTED

Consider again two countries, $A$ and $B$, endowed with fixed quantities of two inelastically supplied factors of production, labor ($L$) and land ($T$). Each economy produces under constant returns to scale two commodities, $X$ and $Y$. The production functions are identical between countries, commodity $X$ is labor intensive relative to $Y$ for all factor-price ratios, and perfect competition rules throughout.

Assume that the respective autarkic equilibria in countries $A$ and $B$ are unique. Then, in general, to show that the Heckscher–Ohlin theorem is true, we must demonstrate that, in the autarkic equilibrium state, the labor-abundant country produces the labor-intensive commodity $(X)$ more cheaply than the land-abundant country. When the price definition of factor abundance is adopted, this means that we must show that the country with the lowest pretrade commodity-price ratio $p_x/p_y$ is also the country with the lowest pretrade factor-price ratio $w/r$. That this proposition is, in general, true follows from what we have said so far.

Make the reasonable assumption that, before trade, both commodities are produced and consumed in both countries. (Part C below shows that if this assumption is not satisfied and one country actually produces only one commodity before trade, the Heckscher–Ohlin conclusion may be reversed.) Then, before trade, both countries operate at two (in general, different) points on the $PP'$ curve of fig. 9.9. Because factor-intensity reversals are excluded by assumption, the $PP'$ curve slopes downward throughout, and a lower factor-price ratio $w/r$ along this curve necessarily implies a lower commodity-price ratio $p_x/p_y$. Accordingly, the labor-intensive commodity must be cheaper, before trade, in the labor-abundant country, i.e., the country with the lower factor-price ratio $w/r$. This completes the proof.

Nowhere in the preceding proof was it assumed that consumption patterns were identical between countries. Consequently, in the absence of factor-intensity reversals and when the price definition of factor abundance is used, the Heckscher–Ohlin theorem is necessarily true irrespective of any differences in tastes in the two countries.

## Factor-Intensity Reversals

Does the Heckscher–Ohlin theorem remain valid when factor-intensity reversals are allowed? Not in general. This follows from the fact that the price ratio $p_x/p_y$ is no longer a monotonic function of the factor-price ratio $w/r$. For the simple case of a single factor-intensity reversal, the following conclusions pertain.

1. If the overall factor proportions of the two countries are such that a unique classification of $X$ and $Y$ in terms of factor intensity holds in both countries, the preceding analysis can be applied step by step to show that, before trade, the labor-intensive commodity is relatively cheaper in the labor-abundant country (i.e., the country with the lower $w/r$ ratio).
2. If the overall factor proportions of the two countries are such that a contradictory classification of $X$ and $Y$ in terms of factor intensity is adopted by the two countries, the Heckscher–Ohlin theorem cannot possibly be correct for both countries simultaneously, although it is always true for one of the two countries.

If the number of factor-intensity reversals is greater than one, conclusion 2 continues to be correct but conclusion 1 can no longer be maintained. This is considered below in part C.

## 10.5 THE HECKSCHER–OHLIN THEOREM WHEN THE PHYSICAL DEFINITION OF FACTOR ABUNDANCE IS ADOPTED

Turn now to the validity of the Heckscher–Ohlin theorem when factor abundance is decided on the basis of the physical definition. To show now that the Heckscher–Ohlin theorem is true, we must demonstrate that, in the autarkic state, the labor-intensive commodity $(X)$ is produced more cheaply in the country (say, $A$) with the higher overall labor-land ratio. As we shall see, some assumption about tastes is now necessary for the validity of the Heckscher–Ohlin theorem.

Central to the current version of the Heckscher–Ohlin theorem is the following important lemma.

**Lemma** Assume that $\rho_A > \rho_B$ (that is, $A$ is labor abundant relative to $B$). When the two countries produce the two commodities in the same proportion, the marginal rate of transformation of $X$ for $Y$ is lower in $A$ than in $B$. That is, when $X_A^P/Y_A^P = X_B^P/Y_B^P$, then $\mathrm{MRT}_{xy}^A < \mathrm{MRT}_{xy}^B$ (that is, the opportunity cost of $X$ in terms of $Y$ is lower in $A$ than in $B$).

The truth of the above lemma can be established easily. We saw in chap. 9 that, given the production functions and the overall labor-land ratio of a country, the factor-price ratio must vary within certain limits if full employment is to be preserved (see fig. 9.6). Within these limits, the proportion in which $X$ and $Y$ are produced by the economy is given by eq. (9.20), which can be rearranged as follows:

$$\frac{X}{Y} = \frac{a_{Ty}\,\rho - \rho_y}{a_{Tx}\,\rho_x - \rho} = \frac{a_{Ty}\rho - a_{Ly}}{a_{Lx} - \rho a_{Tx}} \tag{10.1}$$

Chapter 9 showed that as the factor-price ratio decreases continuously from its maximum permissible value to its minimum, both commodities tend to become relatively more labor intensive, and the output of the labor-intensive commodity $(X)$ decreases while the output of the land-intensive commodity $(Y)$ increases, continuously. That is, as $w/r$ falls, the ratio $X/Y$ falls also. This, of course, establishes a one-to-one correspondence between the factor-price ratio $w/r$ and the output ratio $X/Y$.

What we now wish to show is this. Suppose we allow the overall labor-land ratio $\rho$ to increase while we keep the output ratio $X/Y$ constant. What happens to the corresponding factor-price ratio? It follows from eq. (10.1) that if the factor-price ratio is kept constant as $\rho$ increases, the output ratio $X/Y$ increases also (i.e., the output of the labor-intensive commodity increases relative to the output of the land-intensive commodity). To reduce $X/Y$ to its original value, we must allow labor to become cheaper relative to land, i.e., allow $w/r$ to fall. (As $w/r$ falls, both land coefficients, $a_{Tx}$ and $a_{Ty}$, also fall, while both labor coefficients, $a_{Lx}$ and $a_{Ly}$, rise; therefore, the numerator of the last ratio in eq. (10.1) falls, while the denominator rises.)

A rigorous proof of the lemma is not difficult to establish. Solve eq. (10.1) for $\rho$ as follows:

$$\rho = \frac{a_{Lx}(X/Y) + a_{Ly}}{a_{Tx}(X/Y) + a_{Ty}} \tag{10.2}$$

Assume that $X/Y$ remains constant, and differentiate $\rho$ with respect to $w/r$ to obtain (after some simplification):

$$\frac{d\rho}{d(w/r)} = \frac{[(X/Y)a'_{Lx} + a'_{Ly}]\{(w/r)[(X/Y)a_{Lx} + a_{Ly}] + [(X/Y)a_{Tx} + a_{Ty})]\}}{[(X/Y)a_{Tx} + a_{Ty}]^2} < 0 \tag{10.3}$$

where use was made of eqs. (9.13) and (9.14). Equation (10.3) proves that, when $X/Y$ is kept constant and $\rho$ increases, $w/r$ falls.

From the analysis of chap. 9, we also know that as the factor-price ratio $w/r$ falls, the labor-intensive commodity becomes cheaper relative to the land-intensive commodity. We therefore conclude that, when the output ratio $X/Y$ is kept fixed, the labor-intensive commodity becomes cheaper relative to the land-intensive commodity (i.e., the $\mathrm{MRT}_{xy}$ falls) as labor becomes more abundant relative to land (i.e., as $\rho$ increases). Since country $A$ is assumed to be labor-abundant relative to $B$ (that is, $\rho_A > \rho_B$), it follows that, for any given output ratio $X/Y$ common to both countries, the opportunity cost of $X$ in terms of $Y$ is lower in $A$ than in $B$, that is, $\mathrm{MRT}_{xy}^A < \mathrm{MRT}_{xy}^B$. This completes the proof of the lemma.

Figure 10.1 illustrates the preceding proposition. Any vector through the origin (such as $OM$) intersects the two production-possibilities frontiers at points (such as $S$ and $T$) such that $A$'s slope is flatter than $B$'s. This means that when both countries produce the two commodities in the same proportion, $X$ (the labor-intensive commodity) is relatively cheaper in $A$.

## Proof of the Heckscher–Ohlin Theorem

We proceed now to use the preceding lemma and prove the Heckscher–Ohlin theorem, i.e., that country $A$ necessarily has a comparative advantage in the production of $X$ (which is the commodity which uses more intensively $A$'s abundant factor), and $B$ in $Y$. For this purpose, we must make the additional assumption that tastes are similar *and* homothetic between countries. In particular, assume that tastes in $A$ and $B$ are given by a common homothetic social indifference map. This is, no doubt, a much stronger assumption than similarity of tastes. What is actually required is not only similarity of tastes between $A$ and $B$ but

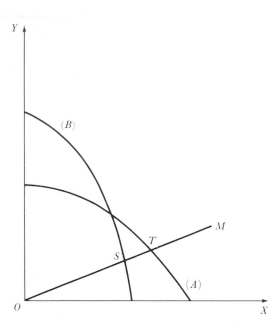

**Figure 10.1** For any given output ratio $X/Y$ common to both countries, the labor-intensive commodity $(X)$ is cheaper in the labor-abundant country $(A)$.

similarity of tastes between income levels as well (i.e., the income-consumption curves must be straight lines through the origin).

Figure 10.2 illustrates the problem for the simple case where in the autarkic state both countries reach the same social indifference curve $II'$. Before trade, country $A$ is in equilibrium at point $E_A$ and country $B$ at $E_B$. Because of the law of diminishing marginal rate of substitution, the slope of the indifference curve $II'$ at $E_A$ is flatter than its slope at $E_B$. Therefore, in autarkic equilibrium, $X$ is relatively cheaper in $A$ than in $B$. Consequently, $A$ has a comparative advantage in $X$ (that is, the commodity which uses more intensively $A$'s abundant factor), and $B$ in $Y$ (that is, the commodity which uses more intensively $B$'s abundant factor). In this special case, the assumption of homotheticity of tastes is not necessary for the Heckscher–Ohlin theorem—similarity of tastes seems to be sufficient.

So far so good. But what if the two countries reach *different* social indifference curves at their respective pretrade equilibrium positions? Can we still prove that $A$ has a comparative advantage in $X$ and $B$ in $Y$? Yes, if the common social indifference map is also homothetic. This more difficult case is illustrated in fig. 10.3, where country $B$ is small and country $A$ is large.

Before trade is opened up, country $A$ is in equilibrium at point $E_A$. The common slope of $A$'s production-possibilities frontier and social indifference curve $I_3$ at point $E_A$ (in absolute terms) shows $A$'s pretrade equilibrium-price ratio. Let us call this price ratio $p_A$. As was previously shown, $B$'s production-possibilities frontier at point $N$ must be steeper than $A$'s at point $E_A$. However, because of the assumption of homotheticity of tastes, the slope of the social indifference curve $I_1$ at $N$ must be the same as the slope of the social indifference curve $I_3$ at point $E_A$. Therefore, the social indifference curve passing through

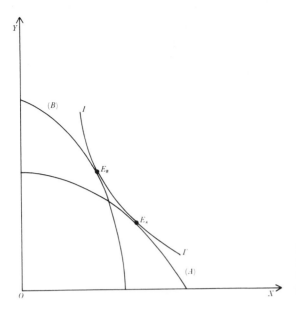

**Figure 10.2** The Heckscher–Ohlin theorem when, in the autarkic state, both countries reach the same social indifference curve.

$N(I_1)$ must necessarily intersect $B$'s production-possibilities frontier from left to right, indicating that pretrade equilibrium in $B$ must necessarily occur somewhere in the region $MN$ of $B$'s production-possibilities frontier, say at point $E_B$. Let $p_B$ stand for $B$'s pretrade equilibrium price ratio (as given by the common slope of $B$'s production-possibilities frontier and the broken social indifference curve $I_2$ at point $E_B$). What remains to be shown is that $p_B > p_A$, implying that $A$ has a comparative advantage in $X$ and $B$ in $Y$.

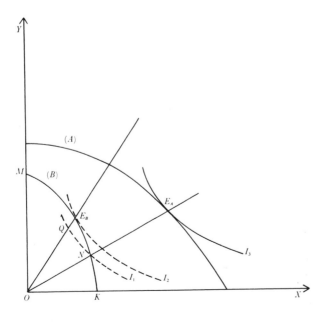

**Figure 10.3** The Heckscher–Ohlin theorem when, in the autarkic state, the two countries reach different social indifference curves.

Because of the assumed homotheticity of tastes, the slope of the broken indifference curve $I_2$ at $E_B$ is equal to the slope of the broken indifference curve $I_1$ at $Q$. Therefore, the pretrade equilibrium-price ratios of both countries can be read off the social indifference curve $I_1$. Thus, $p_B$ is given by the absolute value of the slope of $I_1$ at point $Q$, and $p_A$ is given by the absolute value of the slope of $I_1$ at point $N$. Because of the law of diminishing marginal rate of substitution, we must conclude that $p_A < p_B$, which is exactly what we set out to prove.

## The Importance of Similarity of Tastes Between Countries and Income Levels

It is important to emphasize once more the role of the homotheticity assumption and show where it crucially enters into the proof of the Heckscher–Ohlin theorem. Remember that the homotheticity assumption was used twice: first, to show that the indifference curves $I_3$ and $I_1$ have the same slope at points $E_A$ and $N$, respectively, and second, to show that the indifference curves $I_2$ and $I_1$ have the same slope at points $E_B$ and $Q$, respectively. The first step seems to eliminate the region $NK$ of $B$'s production-possibilities frontier as a possible candidate for pretrade equilibrium in $B$. However, this is not crucial to the argument. In fact, if pretrade equilibrium in $B$ occurs in the region $NK$, the Heckscher–Ohlin conclusion follows immediately, since all points in this region have an absolute slope steeper than the slope of $A$'s production-possibilities frontier at point $E_A$. The importance of the first step is that it eliminates the possibility of the slope of $I_1$ at $N$ being smaller than the slope of $I_3$ at $E_A$. In the same way, it can be shown that the importance of the second step in the use of the homotheticity assumption is that it eliminates the possibility of the slope of $I_2$ at $E_B$ being smaller than the slope of $I_1$ at $Q$.

More precisely, our proof establishes that $p_A = $ slope of $I_3$ at $E_A = $ slope of $I_1$ at $N < $ slope of $I_1$ at $Q = $ slope of $I_2$ at $E_B = p_B$. The homotheticity assumption is used twice: first, to eliminate the possibility of having slope of $I_3$ at $E_A > $ slope of $I_1$ at $N$, and second, to eliminate the possibility of having slope of $I_2$ at $E_B < $ slope of $I_1$ at $Q$.

Similarity of tastes and homotheticity are sufficient for the Heckscher–Ohlin theorem. They are not necessary, however. In other words, the Heckscher–Ohlin theorem could be true even in the absence of these assumptions on demand conditions. What *is* necessary is that the slope of $A$'s production-possibilities frontier at $E_A$ be smaller (in absolute terms) than the slope of $B$'s production-possibilities frontier at point $E_B$.

Nevertheless, without any restrictions on demand, the direction of trade might be opposite to what the Heckscher–Ohlin theorem would predict, even though all other assumptions regarding production functions and so on are actually met.

As chap. 5 shows, the existence of pretrade multiple equilibria in one or both countries makes it virtually impossible to predict the direction of trade by simply comparing the pretrade equilibrium-price ratios. Thus, even if we were told that

$p_A < p_B$ in the pretrade position, we could not possibly conclude that $A$ has a comparative advantage in $X$ and $B$ in $Y$. Pretrade multiple equilibria are presently excluded because of the assumption that tastes are given by a social indifference map.

## Factor-Intensity Reversals

Finally, the preceding analysis is based on the assumption that commodity $X$ is labor intensive relative to $Y$ for all factor-price ratios. In other words, the phenomenon of factor-intensity reversals has been excluded by assumption. How should the preceding conclusions be amended in the presence of factor-intensity reversals? Without going into any detail, we can easily reach the following conclusions for the simple case where only one factor-intensity reversal exists.

1. If the overall factor proportions of the two countries (that is, $\rho_A$ and $\rho_B$) are such that a unique classification of $X$ and $Y$ in terms of factor intensity holds in both countries (see sec. 8.2), then the preceding analysis can be applied step by step to show that, under the rest of the assumptions, the labor-abundant country has a comparative advantage in the production of the labor-intensive commodity, and the land-abundant country in the land-intensive commodity. The proof of this statement is similar to the proof given above, where the phenomenon of factor-intensity reversals was assumed away.
2. If the overall factor proportions of the two countries are such that a contradictory classification of $X$ and $Y$ in terms of factor intensity is adopted in the two countries, the Heckscher–Ohlin theorem cannot possibly be correct for both countries simultaneously. However, it is always correct for one of the two countries. This does not mean that the Heckscher–Ohlin theorem does not entirely lose its validity in the present case, however, for we cannot predict a priori the country for which the theorem remains valid.

## 10.6 THE HECKSCHER–OHLIN THEOREM: SUMMARY

1. In the absence of factor-intensity reversals, the Heckscher–Ohlin theorem is necessarily true on the basis of the price definition of factor abundance. The identity of tastes between countries is unnecessary to assume in the present case. But incomplete specialization before trade is in general required.
2. In the absence of factor-intensity reversals, the Heckscher–Ohlin theorem is true on the basis of the physical definition of factor abundance if tastes are homothetic and similar between countries. The latter assumption is sufficient but not necessary for the validity of the theorem.
3. In the presence of factor-intensity reversals, the Heckscher–Ohlin theorem is not true in general.

# PART C. CLARIFICATIONS, EXTENSIONS, AND QUALIFICATIONS

In this last part of the chapter we proceed to clarify and extend further the analysis of the first two parts. In addition, we take a hard look at the empirical relevance of the assumptions of the modern theory.

## 10.7 THE MODERN THEORY IN THE ABSENCE OF FACTOR-INTENSITY REVERSALS

This section considers the importance of some of the assumptions of the basic model (sec. 10.2 above) for the rigorous proof of both the factor-price equalization theorem and the Heckscher–Ohlin theorem.

Consider fig. 10.4. Assume that $A$'s overall factor proportions are given by the distance $OK$. Therefore, country $A$'s relative factor-price region, permitted by the factor-endowment ratio $OK$, is given by $RS$, and its relative commodity-price region with incomplete specialization is given by $P_1 P_2$. Distinguish between two cases: ($a$) country $B$'s overall factor-endowment ratio lies in the region $MN$; and ($b$) country $B$'s overall factor-endowment ratio lies outside the region $MN$. It must be obvious that complete factor-price equalization cannot occur in the second case, because the range of variation of $w/r$ in country $A$ does not overlap the range of variation of $w/r$ in country $B$. These two regions overlap only in case ($a$), and this is the only case where factor-price equalization is possible. We consider each of the two cases in turn.

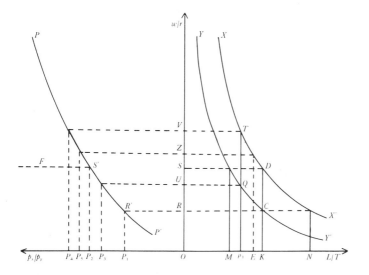

**Figure 10.4** Overlapping factor-price regions. Factor-price equalization is possible.

## Case (*a*) Country *B*'s Overall Labor-Land Ratio Lies in the Region *MN*

This case can be decomposed into three subcases:

(i) *B*'s overall factor-endowment ratio equals *A*'s (that is, it is also given by the distance *OK*).
(ii) *B*'s overall factor-endowment ratio lies in the region *MK*.
(iii) *B*'s overall factor-endowment ratio lies in the region *KN*.

In case (i), where the overall factor-endowment ratios of the two countries coincide, both the relative factor-price region and the relative commodity-price region are given, respectively, by *RS* and $P_1 P_2$ (assuming incomplete specialization) for both countries. Is factor-price equalization possible? Not only is it possible, but it is a necessity. Given any commodity-price ratio, we can uniquely determine the factor-price ratio for *both* countries, since the distorted *PP'* curves of *A* and *B* in the second quadrant of fig. 10.4 coincide completely. The equalization of commodity prices through commodity trade necessarily brings about (in the present case) complete equalization of factor prices.

If we could be assured unequivocally that tastes are indeed identical in the two countries and, in particular, that they are given by the same social indifference map, would it be reasonable to conclude that profitable trade will not take place between the two countries? Not at all, for while we know that the overall factor-endowment ratio of the two countries is the same, we know nothing about the relative sizes of the two countries. Put differently, the identity of factor proportions does not imply that the production-possibilities frontiers of the two countries coincide. It simply means that any ray through the origin cuts the two frontiers at points of equal slope. Under these conditions, similarity of tastes[†] between countries is sufficient to eliminate profitable trade only in the special case where the two countries happen to be of equal size with identical production-possibilities frontiers. In general, when the two countries are of unequal size, similarity of tastes has to be supplemented by homotheticity of tastes if all profitable trade is to be ruled out. However, as explained in part B above, while these two assumptions are sufficient to eliminate all profitable trade, neither assumption is by itself necessary.

In the present case, the Heckscher–Ohlin theorem is correct (i.e., the labor-abundant country will export the labor-intensive commodity and the land-abundant country will export the land-intensive commodity) only when the price definition of factor abundance is used. On the basis of the physical definition, the Heckscher–Ohlin theorem would predict no trade, but the outcome would obviously depend on tastes.

Consider now case (ii). Country *B*'s overall factor-endowment ratio lies somewhere in the region *MK*. Assume that it is actually equal to the distance $O\rho_1$. Note

---

† Recall that "similarity of tastes between countries" means that the *same* social indifference map portrays tastes in each and every country. The common social indifference map need not be homothetic. Homotheticity is always stated separately because it is an additional condition.

that, on the basis of the physical definition of factor abundance, country $B$ is $T$ abundant relative to $A$ (or $A$ is $L$ abundant relative to $B$). Country $B$'s relevant region of relative commodity prices (when both commodities are produced) is given by $P_3 P_4$. Is factor-price equalization possible now? Yes, because, while the relevant regions of relative factor and commodity prices of the two countries do not completely coincide, they do overlap. In particular, the two regions of relative factor prices overlap in the area $US$, while the two regions of relative commodity prices overlap in the area $P_3 P_2$. If demand conditions in the two countries are such as to cause the pretrade equilibrium relative commodity prices in the two countries to lie in the region $P_3 P_2$, then the posttrade equilibrium relative commodity prices will also lie in the same region (that is, $P_3 P_2$), and factor-price equalization will be complete. But this is not the only possibility. The posttrade equilibrium commodity-price ratio may very well lie in the region $P_2 P_4$, or in the region $P_1 P_3$ (as can be verified); and then factor-price equalization cannot possibly be complete.

If the posttrade equilibrium commodity-price ratio lies in the region $P_2 P_4$, country $A$ will definitely specialize completely in the production of $X$. Accordingly, factor prices cannot be equalized (either relatively or absolutely), except in the limiting case where the posttrade equilibrium commodity-price ratio happens to be equal to $OP_2$. This is illustrated by the commodity-price ratio $OP_5$, which causes the factor-price ratio $w/r$ to be equal to $OS$ in country $A$ (because $A$ necessarily specializes in the production of $X$) and $OZ$ in country $B$, with $OZ > OS$.

The failure of complete factor-price equalization in this case is due to the fact that one of the two countries (country $A$) specializes completely in the production of only one of the two commodities (commodity $X$). But this implies that a basic assumption of the factor-price equalization theorem is violated. Since all other assumptions are not violated, only a limited migration of labor from $A$ (the country with low wages) to $B$ (the country with high wages) is necessary to bring about complete factor-price equalization. In particular, sufficient amounts of labor should migrate from $A$ to $B$ to reduce $A$'s factor-endowment ratio from $OK$ to $OE$.

If factor prices are not equalized completely in the present case, is there any *tendency* toward factor-price equalization? Yes. Assuming that the posttrade equilibrium commodity-price ratio is given by $OP_5$, we must necessarily infer, on the assumption that both countries produce both commodities before trade, that $B$'s pretrade commodity-price ratio must be higher than $OP_5$, and $A$'s lower than $OP_2$. Hence, $B$'s pretrade equilibrium factor-price ratio must be higher than $OZ$, and $A$'s lower than $OS$. Free commodity trade, therefore, causes factor prices in the two countries to move closer together.

If the posttrade equilibrium-price ratio lies in the region $P_1 P_3$, country $B$ will specialize completely in the production of $Y$ and factor-price equalization cannot be complete, although there will be a tendency toward equalization. The posttrade equilibrium factor-price ratio $w/r$ will necessarily be higher in country $B$ relative to country $A$. Again, only limited labor migration from $A$ to $B$ will completely eliminate any gap between factor prices in the two countries.

The failure of complete factor-price equalization witnessed thus far has been attributed to the fact that one of the two countries is completely specializing in the production of only one commodity. In *all* cases, we have seen that complete factor-price equalization could be brought about if a sufficient amount of labor migrated from $A$ to $B$. *The fundamental reason for the failure of complete factor-price equalization is the great disparity between factor proportions in the two countries.* This disparity in factor proportions is evident in the complete specialization in production of at least one of the two countries. Thus, if sufficient labor were to migrate from $A$ to $B$ (thus causing $\rho_A$ to fall and $\rho_B$ to rise and, therefore, causing the difference $\rho_A - \rho_B$ to shrink), the great dissimilarity in overall factor proportions would be eliminated and factor prices would be completely equalized, with neither country specializing completely in production. Finally, note that in all of the preceding cases there is always a tendency toward factor-price equalization.

Is the Heckscher–Ohlin theorem correct in case (ii)? Part B above proves that the Heckscher–Ohlin theorem is always true on the basis of the price definition of factor abundance *and* in the absence of factor-intensity reversals. Since factor-intensity reversals are absent in the present case, the Heckscher–Ohlin theorem must necessarily be true on the basis of the price definition. Difficulties arise only when the physical definition of factor abundance is used. When does the Heckscher–Ohlin theorem become incorrect on the basis of the physical definition?

In case (ii), country $A$ is labor abundant relative to country $B$ and commodity $X$ is labor intensive relative to commodity $Y$. According to the Heckscher–Ohlin theorem, country $A$ must be exporting to $B$ commodity $X$ and it must be importing from $B$ commodity $Y$. Accordingly, the Heckscher–Ohlin theorem will be valid if, and only if, the pretrade commodity-price ratio $p_x/p_y$ is lower in $A$ than in $B$. Is the latter condition necessarily satisfied in the present case? No. If $A$'s pretrade commodity-price ratio lies in the region $P_1 P_3$, or if $B$'s pretrade commodity-price ratio lies in the region $P_2 P_4$, then the Heckscher–Ohlin theorem will be correct. But when both pretrade commodity-price ratios lie in the region $P_2 P_3$, the Heckscher–Ohlin theorem is not necessarily correct. In the latter case, demand conditions may be such as to render commodity $X$ relatively cheaper in $B$ than in $A$ before trade. In this case, the factor-price equalization theorem will necessarily be correct.

Case (iii) is similar to case (ii), except that the roles of the two countries are now interchanged; this case will not be discussed here.

## Case (*b*) Country *B*'s Overall Labor-Land Ratio Lies Outside the Region *MN*

When country $B$'s overall factor-endowment ratio $\rho_B$ lies outside the region $MN$, the permissible ranges of variation of relative factor prices in the two countries do not overlap at all, and thus complete factor-price equalization is ruled out. This is illustrated in fig. 10.5, which is similar to fig. 10.4. Again, $A$'s factor-endowment ratio is given by the distance $OK$, $A$'s permitted range of variation of relative

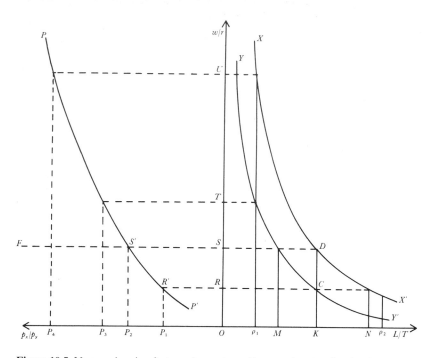

**Figure 10.5** Nonoverlapping factor-price regions. Factor-price equalization is not possible.

factor prices is given by $RS$, and $A$'s permitted range of variation of relative commodity prices with incomplete specialization is given by $P_1 P_2$.

Assume that country $B$'s factor-endowment ratio lies in the region $OM$ (that is, country $B$ is land abundant relative to country $A$, or $A$ is labor abundant relative to $B$, on the basis of the physical definition). In particular, assume that $B$'s factor-endowment ratio is given by $\rho_1$. The permitted range of variation of $B$'s relative factor prices is then given by $TU$, while the permitted range of variation of its relative commodity prices is given by $P_3 P_4$. Under these circumstances, the following conclusions can be derived:

1. Both the pretrade factor-price ratio $w/r$ and the pretrade commodity-price ratio $p_x/p_y$ of country $B$ are necessarily higher than the corresponding pretrade equilibrium relative prices in country $A$.
2. Country $A$ is labor abundant relative to country $B$ on the basis of the price definition of factor abundance, irrespective of tastes.
3. Country $A$ must export commodity $X$ and country $B$ must export commodity $Y$, which is in line with the Heckscher–Ohlin theorem (on the basis of both the price definition and the physical definition of factor abundance).
4. The equilibrium terms of trade must lie somewhere in the region $P_1 P_4$. If they lie in the region $P_1 P_2$, country $A$ will produce both commodities while country $B$ will specialize completely in the production of commodity $Y$; if they lie in the

region $P_3 P_4$, country $B$ will produce both commodities while country $A$ will specialize completely in the production of commodity $X$; and if they lie in the region $P_2 P_3$, country $A$ will specialize completely in the production of commodity $X$ and country $B$ will specialize completely in the production of commodity $Y$. *In all cases, at least one country specializes completely in the production of only one commodity.* This violates one of the assumptions of the factor-price equalization theorem.

5. After trade, the factor-price ratio $w/r$ necessarily continues to be higher in country $B$ than in $A$. However, the pretrade divergence between factor prices in the two countries tends to become smaller. In other words, despite the fact that complete factor-price equalization is impossible (because the regions $RS$ and $TU$ do not overlap), there is nevertheless a *tendency* toward factor-price equalization.

When country $B$'s factor-endowment ratio is higher than $ON$ (for example, $\rho_B = \rho_2$), the conclusions are the same except that the roles of the two countries are reversed.

The failure of complete factor-price equalization in the present case is due to the fact that one of the fundamental assumptions of the factor-price equalization theorem, namely, incomplete specialization in both countries, is violated. But again, the violation of the assumption of incomplete specialization is due to the fact that the factor-endowment ratios of the two countries are very dissimilar. Only a limited migration of labor from the labor-abundant country to the land-abundant country (with factor abundance decided on the basis of the physical definition) is all that is necessary to eliminate the possibility of complete specialization and thus permit commodity trade to establish complete factor-price equalization.

## Price Versus Physical Definition of Factor Abundance

Under what conditions do the two definitions of factor abundance give rise to contradictory classifications? In the absence of factor-intensity reversals, the two definitions give rise to identical results when the possible ranges of variation of factor prices do not overlap. The first condition necessary for a possible divergence between the two definitions is that the ranges of variation of factor prices in the two countries overlap. In terms of figs. 10.4 and 10.5, $B$'s factor-endowment ratio must lie in the region $MN$. The second condition is that the pretrade relative commodity prices must lie in the region where the possible ranges of variation of relative commodity prices with incomplete specialization overlap. This is illustrated in fig. 10.4 by the region $P_3 P_2$, assuming that $\rho_B = \rho_1$. Third, each country must have a very strong preference for the commodity which uses intensively its abundant factor, with factor abundance decided on the basis of the physical definition.

Refer back to fig. 10.4 and assume that $\rho_B = \rho_1$. A divergence between the two definitions arises when the pretrade relative commodity prices lie in the region $P_3 P_2$ and, in addition, commodity $X$ is relatively more expensive in $A$ than in $B$. For commodity $X$ to be relatively more expensive in $A$ than in $B$, country $A$ (the $L$-abundant country) must have a strong preference for commodity $X$ (that is, the $L$-intensive commodity), and $B$ (the $T$-abundant country) for commodity $Y$ (that is, the $T$-intensive commodity).

While these three conditions are necessary they are not sufficient. The sufficient condition, of course, is that, before trade, the $L$-intensive commodity must be relatively cheaper in the $T$-abundant country.

## Variable Factor Supplies

Let us consider briefly the case of variable factor supplies. Does the preceding analysis of the factor-price equalization theorem apply equally to the case where the factor supplies are not perfectly inelastic? Yes. The only difference now is that the overall factor-endowment ratio is not rigidly fixed; it is, rather, a function of the factor-price ratio $w/r$. Thus, in determining the possible range of variation of the factor-price ratio, we have to draw, in the first quadrant of fig. 10.5, a curve showing the behavior of the overall factor-endowment ratio as a function of the factor-price ratio, instead of a vertical line at the given overall factor-endowment ratio. The intersection of this factor-endowment curve with the curves $XX'$ and $YY'$ determines the range of variation of $w/r$. Once this is done, the analysis can proceed along lines similar to the analysis of the case of perfectly inelastic factor supplies.

Is the above conclusion also true for the Heckscher–Ohlin theorem? Unfortunately, variable factor supplies can conceivably give rise to additional difficulties for the Heckscher–Ohlin theorem, for it may not be possible to uniquely classify countries into labor abundant and land abundant on the basis of the physical definition *for all factor-price ratios*. In other words, the factor-endowment curves of the two countries in the first quadrant of figs. 10.4 and 10.5 may intersect each other any number of times. Then, one country will be classified as labor abundant for some factor-price ratios but land abundant for some others. Would the difficulties disappear if we were to base our classification of countries into labor and land abundant on the pretrade equilibrium factor-endowment ratios? Certainly not, for we still cannot exclude the possibility that the so-defined labor-abundant country may export the land-intensive commodity.

## Summary

In the absence of factor-intensity reversals, we have been able to derive the following conclusions:

1. A *tendency* toward factor-price equalization exists.
2. Factor prices are equalized between countries provided that the divergence between the factor proportions of the two countries is not too large. Put

differently, the failure of complete factor-price equalization is necessarily due to a large disparity between the factor proportions of the two countries.
3. The Heckscher–Ohlin theorem is necessarily true on the basis of the price definition of factor abundance.
4. The Heckscher–Ohlin theorem is *not* necessarily true on the basis of the physical definition of factor abundance.

## 10.8 FACTOR-INTENSITY REVERSALS†

How does the phenomenon of factor-intensity reversals affect the conclusions of the preceding section? This is the question we wish to analyze in the present section. First, we consider the case of a single factor-intensity reversal and then generalize the discussion to multiple reversals.

### A Single Factor-Intensity Reversal

Figure 10.6 illustrates the case of a single factor-intensity reversal. In particular, commodity $X$ is assumed to be labor intensive for relative factor prices smaller than $W_N$; land intensive for relative factor prices higher than $W_N$; and, for the

† Particular attention to factor-intensity reversals has been given by Brown (1957), Harrod (1958), Johnson (1957), Jones (1956), Lancaster (1957), Pearce (1952), Robinson (1956), and others.

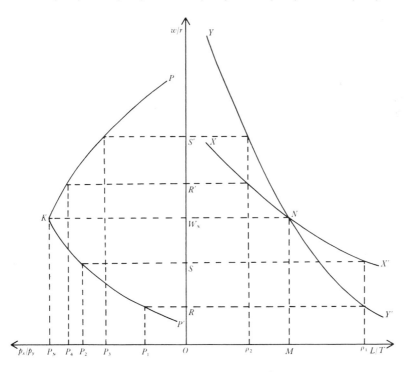

**Figure 10.6** The case of a single factor-intensity reversal.

specific factor-price ratio $W_N$, as labor intensive as commodity $Y$. These assumptions are reflected in the properties of the curves $XX'$ and $YY'$ (in the first quadrant). The curve $XX'$ lies to the right of $YY'$ for $w/r < W_N$; it lies to the left of $YY'$ for $w/r > W_N$; and it intersects $YY'$ at $w/r = W_N$, that is, at point $N$.

How is the $PP'$ curve in the second quadrant affected by the factor-intensity reversal at $N$? According to eq. (9.15), the commodity-price ratio $p_x/p_y$ is an increasing function of the factor-price ratio $w/r$ only when commodity $X$ is labor intensive relative to $Y$. If $X$ is land intensive relative to $Y$, the ratio $p_x/p_y$ becomes a decreasing function of $w/r$. If $X$ is as labor intensive as $Y$, the ratio $p_x/p_y$ becomes a constant—its precise value depends on the arbitrarily chosen units of measurement of $X$ and $Y$. Accordingly, the $PP'$ curve (in the second quadrant) is drawn upward sloping in the region $0 < w/r < W_N$, where $X$ is labor intensive; backward bending in the region $w/r > W_N$, where $X$ is land intensive; and vertical at the specific value $w/r = W_N$, where both $X$ and $Y$ have identical labor-land ratios.

What are the implications of the nonmonotonicity of the $PP'$ curve† of fig. 10.6? The immediate consequence is that the one-to-one correspondence between relative commodity prices and relative factor prices is lost. To be sure, given a factor-price ratio, we can uniquely determine a commodity-price ratio, as can be verified by the fact that *any* horizontal line will cut the $PP'$ curve only once. However, the converse is no longer true. In other words, given a commodity-price ratio, we have two factor-price ratios consistent with the originally given commodity-price ratio, as can be verified by the fact that any vertical line that cuts the $PP'$ curve (with the exception of $P_N K$) will cut it twice.

Why is it important that, after the introduction of factor-intensity reversals, the one-to-one correspondence between relative commodity prices and relative factor prices is lost? Because even with incomplete specialization in both countries, the equality of commodity prices between countries (through free commodity trade) need not necessarily imply equality of factor prices between countries as well. The outcome depends upon additional information regarding factor proportions in the two countries.

The new problems created by factor-intensity reversals are discussed in terms of the following three cases.

**Case ($a$)** The factor-endowment ratios of both countries are either larger or smaller than $OM$ (see fig. 10.6), where $OM$ is the optimum labor-land ratio for both $X$ and $Y$ when the factor-price ratio is equal to $W_N$. This case presents no new problems besides those already discussed in the preceding section. Although commodities $X$ and $Y$ cannot be uniquely classified into labor intensive and land intensive on the basis of their respective production functions alone (as illustrated by the fact that the curves $XX'$ and $YY'$ in the first quadrant of fig. 10.6 intersect each other at point $N$), the additional condition on factor endowments, namely, that both $\rho_A$ and $\rho_B$ are either smaller or larger than $OM$, restricts the area of substitutability in a way that prevents the factor-intensity reversal from being

---

† By which we mean that the $PP'$ curve is neither upward sloping throughout nor downward sloping throughout.

actually observed. In other words, factor proportions are such that the contract curves of both countries lie on the same side of the diagonal of their respective box diagrams. Therefore, in the absence of complete specialization, factor prices are completely equalized between countries. The Heckscher–Ohlin theorem is also true on the basis of the price definition of factor abundance. However, on the basis of the physical definition, the Heckscher–Ohlin theorem is true only if tastes are largely similar (and homothetic) between countries.

**Case (b)** The factor-endowment ratio of one of the two countries is equal to $OM$. Assume that it is $A$'s factor-endowment ratio that is equal to $OM$ (that is, $\rho_A = OM$). This case can be conveniently subdivided into the following three subcases:

(i) $\rho_A = \rho_B = OM$. This corresponds to the classical case of equal comparative costs. In other words, the production-possibilities frontiers of both countries are parallel straight lines, and their common slope is equal to $P_N$ (see fig. 10.6). As we have seen in chap. 3, no trade takes place in this case. However, factor prices are equal in both countries in the autarkic state, and they continue to remain equal after the possibility of trade is allowed.

   The assumption that the two commodities have different factor intensities is an important one. As noted earlier, when the factor intensities of the two commodities are actually the same, the curves $XX'$ and $YY'$ coincide and the range of variation of factor prices in each country shrinks to a single point. Under these circumstances, differing factor-endowment ratios between countries necessarily imply different factor prices between countries—both before and after trade. Factor prices can only be equal if, and only if, the factor-endowment ratios of the two countries are equal. However, this leads to the equal comparative-costs case with no trade—and factor prices are equal between countries in the autarkic equilibrium state to begin with. In the present case where the curves $XX'$ and $YY'$ do not coincide but intersect each other at $N$, the conclusion must be the same, because, when $\rho_A = \rho_B = OM$, the only observable production techniques are those implied by point $N$. The rest of the curves become irrelevant.

(ii) $\rho_A = OM$ but $\rho_B > OM$, and, in particular, $\rho_B = \rho_1$. In this case, $A$'s production-possibilities frontier is again a straight line. Its absolute slope is equal to $P_N$, as in case (i) above. The only factor-price ratio consistent with full employment in $A$ is still $W_N$. However, the possible range of variation of the factor-price ratio in $B$ is now given by $RS$, while the range of variation of the commodity-price ratio (with incomplete specialization) is given by $P_1 P_2$. Thus, before trade, $X$ is relatively cheaper in $B$ than in $A$, and the posttrade equilibrium commodity-price ratio definitely lies in the region $P_1 P_N$. Thus, country $A$ specializes in the production of commodity $Y$. However, country $B$ either specializes in the production of commodity $X$ (when the commodity-price ratio lies in the region $P_2 P_N$) or produces both commodities (when the commodity-price ratio lies in the region $P_1 P_2$). Factor-price equalization cannot possibly take place, since $A$'s equilibrium factor-price ratio $W_N$ does not lie in the region $RS$ (that is, $B$'s permissible range of variation of relative factor prices). However, there is a tendency toward factor-price equalization. In this case, the Heckscher–Ohlin theorem seems to be correct from the point of view of country $B$, which is exporting that commodity ($X$) which uses intensively its abundant factor ($L$). This is true on the basis of both the price and the physical definitions of factor abundance: they both give rise to the same classification of countries. From the point of view of country $A$, the Heckscher–Ohlin theorem cannot be applied, because in this country the two commodities have equal factor intensities. But if we were to use the classification of country $B$, the Heckscher–Ohlin theorem would also hold from the point of view of country $A$ as well.

(iii) $\rho_A = OM$ but $\rho_B < OM$, and, in particular, $\rho_B = \rho_2$. As in the preceding case, in the autarkic equilibrium state $X$ is relatively cheaper in $B$ than in $A$. Country $B$, which is the land-abundant country now on the basis of both the price and the quantity definitions, exports commodity $X$. But $X$ is also the land-intensive commodity now. Hence, the Heckscher–Ohlin theorem is again correct, subject to the qualification made in the preceding case in relation to country $A$. Complete factor-price equalization is again impossible, because $W_N$ (that is, $A$'s equilibrium factor-price ratio) does not lie in the region $R'S'$ (that is, $B$'s permissible range of variation of relative factor prices). However, there is definitely a tendency toward factor-price equalization.

It should be pointed out that in case (ii) a limited migration of labor from $B$ to $A$, and in case (iii) a limited migration of labor from $A$ to $B$, would bring about complete factor-price equalization between the two countries.

**Case ($c$)** The factor-endowment ratio of one country is higher than $OM$, while the factor-endowment ratio of the other country is lower than $OM$. Assume that $\rho_A > OM$ and $\rho_B < OM$. This is the case of factor-intensity reversals proper. This important case is illustrated in fig. 10.7, which reproduces the basic relationships exhibited in fig. 10.6. To facilitate the exposition, assume that $A$'s factor-endowment ratio remains fixed at $\rho_1$ and allow $B$'s factor-endowment ratio to vary in the region $OM$. This enables us to cover all the important subcases of this important case.

Is factor-price equalization possible? Is there a tendency toward equalization? Is the Heckscher–Ohlin theorem correct? These are the important questions, but the answers are rather disappointing.

Given that $\rho_A = \rho_1$, the range of variation of $A$'s relative factor prices is given by $RS$ while its range of variation of relative commodity prices (with incomplete specialization) is given by $P_1 P_2$. As long as $\rho_B < OM$, the range of variation of $B$'s relative factor prices necessarily lies above $A$'s range (that is, $RS$). Therefore,

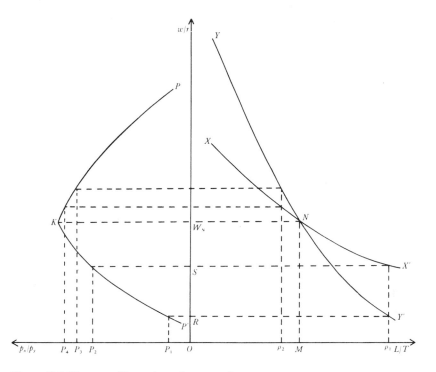

**Figure 10.7** The case of factor-intensity reversal proper.

complete factor-price equalization is ruled out. What is even more disappointing in this case is that even a tendency toward factor-price equalization need not exist. More precisely, in this case free trade in commodities necessarily causes factor prices to move in the same direction in both countries, and the difference between them may either narrow or widen according to circumstances. Why is this so?

Observe that commodity $X$ is labor intensive in $A$ but land intensive in $B$. Therefore, if $A$ exports $X$ and $B$ exports $Y$, the factor-price ratio $w/r$ will tend to rise in both countries because both countries export their labor-intensive commodity. On the other hand, if $A$ exports $Y$ and $B$ exports $X$, the factor-price ratio $w/r$ will fall in both countries because both countries export their land-intensive commodity. Under these circumstances, the disparity between factor prices may expand or contract, depending on which factor-price ratio changes faster.

In the present case, country $A$ is classified as labor abundant relative to $B$, from the point of view of both the price and the quantity definition of factor abundance. Notice also that this conclusion holds *irrespective of any differences in tastes between countries*. However, because commodity $X$ is labor intensive relative to $Y$ in country $A$ but land intensive relative to $Y$ in country $B$, the Heckscher–Ohlin theorem cannot possibly be correct from the point of view of both countries. (The Heckscher–Ohlin theorem requires that both countries export commodity $X$!)

Is it possible to predict, in the present case, the pattern of trade—even though the Heckscher–Ohlin theorem cannot be correct for both countries—from the knowledge that $\rho_A > OM$ and $\rho_B < OM$? Definitely not. Remember that the direction of trade depends on the pretrade equilibrium relative commodity prices. Keeping $\rho_A = \rho_1$ and letting $\rho_B$ fall from $OM$ toward zero, we can see that, even without any information on tastes in the two countries, the pattern of trade is necessarily reversed. Thus, when $\rho_B = \rho_2$, the range of variation of $B$'s commodity-price ratio (with incomplete specialization) is given by $P_3 P_4$. Therefore, $X$ is relatively cheaper in $A$, so that $A$ exports $X$ and $B$ exports $Y$. On the other hand, when $\rho_B$ is reduced sufficiently below $\rho_2$, the range of variation of $B$'s commodity-price ratio can be made to lie totally to the right of $P_1 P_2$. In this case, $X$ is relatively cheaper in $B$ than in $A$, and therefore $B$ exports commodity $X$ and $A$ exports $Y$.

## Multiple Reversals

The preceding analysis is based on the assumption that only one reversal separates the factor-endowment ratios of the two countries. However, the analysis can be easily generalized to the case where $n$ $(n > 1)$ reversals separate $\rho_A$ from $\rho_B$. In particular, if $n$ is *odd*, none of the preceding conclusions are affected. Thus, countries can be uniquely classified into labor abundant and land abundant on the basis of either the price or the physical definition. However, $A$'s classification of commodities is contradictory to $B$'s, so that the Heckscher–Ohlin theorem cannot be correct. Complete factor-price equalization is also ruled out because the permissible factor-price ranges of the two countries do not overlap. As a result of the contradictory classification of commodities, even a tendency toward equalization may not exist.

On the other hand, if $n$ is *even*, a commodity is unequivocally classified into labor intensive, or land intensive, in both countries. But the direction of trade is indeterminate. Thus, the labor-abundant country may export either the labor-intensive or the land-intensive commodity. When the labor-abundant country exports the labor-intensive commodity (and thus the land-abundant country exports the land-intensive commodity), factor prices in the two countries move toward each other, despite the fact that complete factor-price equalization is impossible. But when the pattern of trade is the opposite, i.e., when the labor-abundant country exports the land-intensive commodity and the land-abundant country exports the labor-intensive commodity, there is a tendency for factor prices in the two countries *to move away from each other*.

Figure 10.8 illustrates this analysis of multiple reversals. It is similar to fig. 10.7, except that now there are four reversals as the curves $XX'$ and $YY'$ (in the first quadrant) intersect each other four times at points $R_1, R_2, R_3$, and $R_4$. As a result, the $PP'$ curve assumes the twisted shape shown in the second quadrant. Assume now that $\rho_A$ is equal to $\rho_A^0$, as shown in fig. 10.8. Then $A$'s range of variation of the factor-price ratio is given by $W_0 W_1$ and its range of variation of the commodity-price ratio by $P_0 P_1$.

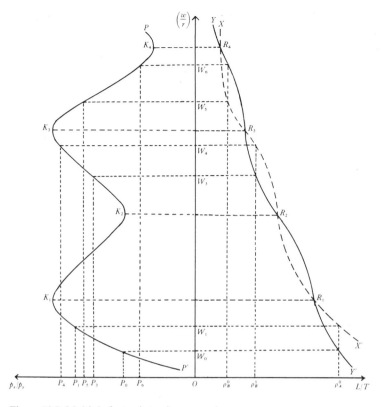

**Figure 10.8** Multiple factor-intensity reversals.

If $\rho_B$ were equal to $\rho_B^0$, then $\rho_A$ would be separated from $\rho_B$ by three (i.e., an *odd* number of) reversals. Country $B$'s range of variation of $w/r$ would be given by $W_5 W_6$, and its range of variation of $p_x/p_y$ would be given by $P_5 P_6$. Several things are obvious.

1. Since $\rho_A^0 > \rho_B^0$ and the factor-price ratio $w/r$ assumes higher values in the range $W_5 W_6$ than in the range $W_0 W_1$, that is, $(w/r)_A < (w/r)_B$, $A$ will be classified as labor abundant relative to $B$ on the basis of either the price or the physical definition of factor abundance.
2. Since it is always (i.e., before and after trade) true that $(w/r)_A < (w/r)_B$ (because the region $W_0 W_1$ is uniformly lower than the region $W_5 W_6$), complete factor-price equalization is ruled out.
3. Commodity $X$ is labor intensive relative to $Y$ in country $A$ but land intensive relative to $Y$ in country $B$. Hence, the Heckscher–Ohlin theorem cannot be correct.
4. Any pattern of trade is possible. If $A$ exports $X$ and $B$ exports $Y$, then both $A$'s and $B$'s posttrade factor-price ratios will be higher than their respective pretrade levels. On the other hand, if $A$ exports $Y$ and $B$ exports $X$, then both $A$'s

and $B$'s posttrade factor-price ratios will be lower than their respective pretrade levels. Hence, in neither case is there reason to believe that there exists a tendency toward factor-price equalization.

Suppose now that $\rho_B$ is equal to $\rho_B^1$, as shown in fig. 10.8. In this case $\rho_A$ is separated from $\rho_B$ by only two (i.e., an *even* number of) reversals. What difference does this make to conclusions 1 to 4? It is obvious that $A$ is still labor abundant relative to $B$ on the basis of both the price and the quantity definition of factor abundance, and that complete factor-price equalization is ruled out because it is always true that $(w/r)_A < (w/r)_B$. Commodity $X$ is labor intensive relative to $Y$ in both countries. But the direction of trade need not be that predicted by the Heckscher–Ohlin theorem (that is, $A$ may export $Y$ and $B$ may export $X$). This conclusion does not necessarily depend on differences in tastes between $A$ and $B$. Imagine that the curves and factor-endowment ratios have been drawn in such a way as to make the region $P_3 P_4$ (that is, $B$'s range of variation of the commodity-price ratio) lie uniformly to the right of $P_0 P_1$. Under these circumstances, $B$ will necessarily be exporting $X$ and $A$ will be exporting $Y$ *irrespective of tastes*. Note that if $A$ exports $X$ and $B$ exports $Y$, factor prices in the two countries will be moving toward each other, i.e., there will be a tendency toward factor-price equalization. On the other hand, if $A$ exports $Y$ and $B$ exports $X$, factor prices in the two countries will be moving away from each other.

## Summary

This section can be summarized thus:

1. The Heckscher–Ohlin theorem is not generally true whether the price definition or the quantity definition of factor abundance is used. However, in the absence of factor-intensity reversals between the factor-endowment ratios of the two countries, the Heckscher–Ohlin theorem is true only on the basis of the price definition; on the basis of the physical definition, the outcome depends on tastes.
2. Commodity trade equalizes factor prices completely only in the absence of factor-intensity reversals between the factor-endowment ratios of the two countries and provided that neither country specializes completely in the production of one commodity. In the presence of factor-intensity reversals between $\rho_A$ and $\rho_B$, commodity trade may have any effect whatsoever on factor prices. Incomplete specialization in both countries *is* consistent with widely differing factor prices between countries.

## 10.9 THE IDENTITY OF PRODUCTION FUNCTIONS BETWEEN COUNTRIES

One of the crucial assumptions of the Heckscher–Ohlin theorem is that production functions are identical between countries. In fact, Ohlin appears to have taken it for granted that production functions are the same everywhere. He based his conclusion on the observation that, at any time, the same causes everywhere produce the same results. In Ohlin's (1933, p. 14) words, "the physical conditions of production . . . are everywhere the same." This assumption seems necessary for the Heckscher–Ohlin theorem. Otherwise, any empirical evidence contrary to that indicated by factor proportions could always be explained by arbitrary differences in production functions. But such an explanation would contribute nothing to our understanding of the causes of trade.

The assumption that production functions are identical between countries raises the fundamental question of the proper definition of two concepts, namely, production functions and factors of production. As Samuelson (1948, pp. 181–182) noted, the concept "factor of production" can be used in at least three different senses: ($a$) as a concrete input item (such as raw materials) purchasable in the market-place; ($b$) as a nonappropriable factor (such as weather conditions) that is free (in the sense that its price is zero) though not available in unlimited quantities; and ($c$) as a condition bearing on production (such as technological knowledge). By including all three categories under "factors of production," we can no doubt make the production functions identical between countries.

Ricardo's production functions illustrate the point. He specifically assumed the following relationships between labor input ($L$) and cloth output ($C$):

$$\text{Portugal:} \quad C = \frac{L}{90}$$

$$\text{England:} \quad C = \frac{L}{100}$$

If labor, of course, were considered the only "factor of production," it would be obvious that England and Portugal would indeed have different production functions. However, the two countries may be regarded as sharing a common production function, $C = f(L, W_1, W_2, \ldots, W_n)$, where $W_i$ signifies one aspect of "the peculiar powers bestowed by nature" (Ricardo's phrase), such as temperature, humidity, and so on, that are considered relevant for the production of cloth. It could be said that England and Portugal share the same production function but that they operate in different regions of the production function. In other words, considering the factors $W_i$ as parameters, we can rewrite the common production function as follows:

$$C = f(L, W_1, W_2, \ldots, W_n) = g(L)$$

Since the parameters $W_1, \ldots, W_n$ take different values in the two countries, the function $g(L)$ is necessarily different, despite the fact that the function $f(L, W_1, \ldots, W_n)$ is common to both countries.

By considering every conceivable circumstance affecting output as a separate factor, we can no doubt make the production functions identical between countries. However, this seems to be a useless tautology. It would be more appropriate to include in the concept "factor of production" only the concrete input items purchasable in the market-place. But, then, we can no longer pretend on the basis of a priori reasoning alone that the production functions are identical between countries. Under these circumstances, the Heckscher–Ohlin theorem cannot be a sufficient explanation of the pattern of trade. With different production functions, trade can take place between any two countries with similar factor endowments and similar consumption patterns. Serious problems arise after the assumption is dropped that production functions are identical between countries. It is then required to explain when and how production functions come to differ—a necessary prerequisite for the use of the theory of comparative advantage to predict (ex ante) the pattern of trade.

## 10.10 SOME DIFFERENCES BETWEEN THE CLASSICAL AND THE HECKSCHER–OHLIN THEORIES

The classical and the Heckscher–Ohlin theories constitute two different hypotheses in relation to the structure of trade. First, the classical doctrine is based on the labor theory of value, while the Heckscher–Ohlin theorem is necessarily based on a more general theory of production, postulating at least two factors of production. (It should be noted that when the number of factors is greater than two, the concept of "factor intensity" is very difficult to interpret.)

Second, the classical theory emphasizes the gains from trade. That is, the classical theory is a contribution to welfare economics. On the other hand, the modern theory is a contribution to positive economics.

Third, if we restrict our comments to the two-commodity case, the classical theory requires only that demand conditions in the two countries be such that both commodities are produced and consumed in both countries in the autarkic equilibrium state. On the other hand, the Heckscher–Ohlin theorem assumes that tastes are homothetic and largely similar between countries, which appears to be a stronger assumption.

Fourth, in the classical theory, the distribution of income necessarily remains the same after as before trade, because of the existence of a single factor of production. Further, the derivation of the offer curves can proceed directly from the indifference maps of individuals (as explained in chaps. 2 to 6) instead of having to postulate the existence of social indifference maps, as we were practically forced to do with the neoclassical and modern theories. To be sure, the Heckscher–Ohlin theorem could proceed from the indifference maps of individuals, but this approach has the disadvantage that it cannot be easily handled with simple analytical tools. Another consequence of the constancy of the income distribution in the classical theory as opposed to the Heckscher–Ohlin theorem is that, in the classical theory, the welfare of every individual unequivocally improves with trade; or, in the limiting case where a large country trades with a small one and the equilibrium terms of trade coincide with the large country's pretrade equilibrium-price ratio, the welfare of each individual citizen of the large country necessarily remains at the same level as it was before trade. Thus, in the classical theory the introduction of trade does not make anybody worse off. The same unqualified statement cannot be made about the Heckscher–Ohlin theorem.

Fifth, multiple pretrade equilibria can be easily ruled out in the case of the classical theory. The only requirement is that both commodities are produced and consumed in both countries in the autarkic equilibrium state. (Note that the latter condition does not require every individual to consume both commodities.) But again, the same statement cannot be made about the Heckscher–Ohlin theorem. Thus, comparative advantage can be decided on the basis of pretrade price ratios with certainty only in the classical theory.

Finally, and perhaps most importantly, the classical theory attributes comparative advantage to arbitrary differences in production functions. On the other hand, the Heckscher–Ohlin theorem postulates the identity of production functions between countries and attributes comparative advantage to differences in factor proportions.

## 10.11 THE EMPIRICAL RELEVANCE OF THE ASSUMPTIONS OF THE FACTOR-PRICE EQUALIZATION THEOREM

No logical objections can be raised against the factor-price equalization theorem. If the assumptions enumerated earlier are correct, factor prices will be completely equalized between countries via free trade in commodities. But how far are these assumptions correct in the real world, and what conclusions can be reached in analyzing any actual situation?

It goes without saying that the assumption of perfect competition cannot be relaxed. The introduction of oligopolistic market structures, wage, and price rigidities, and so on, necessarily impede the equalization of factor prices via commodity movements, because under these circumstances, commodity prices are not equal to the costs of production. Therefore, knowing factor prices (and thus costs of production), we cannot uniquely determine commodity prices, let alone the reverse proposition of going from commodity prices to factor prices.

Whether factor-intensity reversals may or may not impede factor-price equalization depends on the factor endowments of the two countries, as explained in the preceding section. Minhas (1962) first noted that, if the production functions of the two commodities are characterized by a constant elasticity of substitution† and if the elasticity coefficient is different between the two industries, then factor-intensity reversals necessarily occur (see chap. 8). This is an important objection to the factor-price equalization theorem from an empirical point of view if, in addition, the factor-endowment ratios of the two countries are actually separated by factor-intensity reversals. Otherwise, the existence of factor-intensity reversals as such need not impede factor-price equalization.

The assumption of identical production functions for each commodity between countries has already been discussed in sec. 10.9 above. For the present, if production functions are different between countries, factor prices cannot be equalized. However, if the differences are of the sort attributed to neutral technical

† Minhas calls this form of production function "homohypallagic."

progress, *relative* factor prices will still be equalized, although no equality of *absolute* factor prices can take place. This topic is discussed in part five of the book.

The assumption of constant returns to scale cannot be relaxed either. With variable returns to scale, whether increasing or decreasing, and even with the assumption that the production functions are homogeneous (of a degree different from unity), absolute factor prices do not depend only on the labor-land ratios used in the two industries; they depend, in addition, on the scales of output. Under these circumstances, the most that can be expected is relative factor-price equalization. Finally, with increasing returns due to economies internal to the firm, perfect competition breaks down, which, as we have seen, necessarily impedes factor-price equalization.

Differences in the quality of factors have been particularly emphasized by Harrod and Viner (see Viner, 1952, pp. 29, 131). Differences in the educational background, motivation, health and nutrition, and other sociological characteristics of workers should prevent us from describing labor as a homogeneous factor. The wide heterogeneity of capital goods (specialized production and transportation equipment) and the well-known difficulties connected with this heterogeneity should also prevent us from regarding "capital" as a single homogeneous factor of production. The same can also be said for the factor "land." The fact is, in the real world, it is not two homogeneous factors of production (in the two countries) we must contend with, but many. However, new problems are created for the factor-price equalization theorem when the number of factors of production is increased ($n > 2$). Unfortunately, this more general case is beyond the scope of this book (see the appendix at the end of this chapter).

The consequences of complete specialization—and the impact of differences in factor endowments between the two countries as well as the impact of differences in factor intensities of the two commodities on specialization in production—were examined in secs. 10.7 and 10.8 above.

It is obvious that trade restrictions and transportation costs exist in the real world, which means that commodity trade does not really equalize relative commodity prices in the real world. Even if there were a one-to-one correspondence between factor prices and commodity prices, complete factor-price equalization would still not occur in the real world, because of the absence of complete commodity-price equalization. The most we can hope for is a *tendency* toward equalization.

The general conclusion that one can derive from these comments is that the conditions for factor-price equalization through commodity trade are so restrictive that they are unlikely to be fulfilled, even approximately, in the real world. Haberler (1961, p. 19) expressed the opinion that "we must thus conclude that the Lerner–Samuelson theory, though formally correct, rests on such restrictive and unrealistic assumptions that it can hardly be regarded as a valuable contribution to economic theory." Harrod (1973, p. 37) described the factor-price equalization theorem as a *curiosum* in economics. Chipman (1965, p. 479), on the other hand, expressed the opinion that the modern theory "represents probably the most complex and impressive theoretical structure that has yet been developed in economic thought." Both of these positions are extremes. The truth probably lies somewhere in between. It can be argued that, although the assumptions of the factor-price equalization theorem are violated in the real world, the importance of the theorem itself springs mainly from the fact that it directs our attention toward the examination of the relevant variables that determine the impact on factor prices of free trade in commodities. The factor-price equalization theorem can tell us how far we can hope to go toward world efficiency, while maintaining barriers to factor movements, through free commodity trade plus technical assistance plus, possibly, capital movements (the latter two being "foreign aid").

# APPENDIX TO CHAPTER TEN. MANY COUNTRIES, MANY COMMODITIES, AND MANY FACTORS

This appendix deals with the generalization of the modern theory to many countries, many commodities, and many factors. The discussion is divided into two parts. Part A deals with the generalization of the factor-price equalization theorem and part B with the generalization of the Heckscher–Ohlin theorem.

# PART A. GENERALIZATION OF THE FACTOR-PRICE EQUALIZATION THEOREM

Attempts have been made to generalize the factor-price equalization theorem to many commodities and many factors. The purpose of this part is (a) to point out some straightforward generalizations of the conclusions reached in chap. 10 and (b) refer the reader to the relevant literature.

## A10.1 TWO FACTORS AND MANY COMMODITIES

Samuelson (1949, p. 192) had already pointed out that adding more commodities to the model discussed in chap. 10 does not alter the analysis much. As long as trade equalizes the prices of any two commodities which are unequivocally classified into labor intensive and land intensive for all factor prices and which are produced by both countries in the final free-trade equilibrium configuration, factor prices must be equalized between countries relatively and absolutely. This much must be obvious from the discussion in chap. 10.

The additional commodities introduced into the model may very well be *domestic* (or *nontraded*), i.e., commodities which are not traded internationally but are produced and consumed domestically by each country. The only requirement for the validity of the factor-price equalization theorem when only two factors exist is that any two commodities (unequivocally classified into labor intensive and land intensive for all factor-price ratios, and whose prices are equalized between countries by trade) are produced by all countries in the final equilibrium.

Samuelson (1949, p. 192) also made the additional claim that the addition of a third commodity (or more) "increases the likelihood of complete factor-price equalization." What Samuelson meant by this statement was that the introduction of additional commodities cannot reduce the permissible range of variation of the factor-price ratio in any country—on the contrary, the likelihood is that the introduction of additional commodities will enlarge it. Hence, if factor-price equalization is possible with two commodities, it is more so when the number of commodities increases. In addition, one may add, if with two commodities factor-price equalization is not possible because of a large disparity between the overall factor-endowment ratios of countries, the addition of more commodities with extreme factor intensities may make complete factor-price equalization possible!

Land (1959) produced an example in which free trade, after the introduction of a third commodity, causes factor prices to diverge from their autarkic values rather than converge. She also concluded (Land, 1959, p. 142) that "in general the denser is the spectrum of commodities in terms of their factor intensities . . . the less meaningful is it to speak of factor prices being equalized by trade in commodities." Johnson (1967) argued that Land's analysis and conclusions are incorrect because her example is subject to certain inconsistencies. Bertrand (1970) argued that both Johnson's and Land's arguments are not valid, while more recently Stewart (1976) argued that Johnson's argument on the possibility of diverging factor rewards is incorrect and that Land's example does not suffer from any inconsistencies.

While demand conditions may indeed be such that the introduction of more commodities causes factor prices to diverge from their autarkic levels, the Johnson–Samuelson thesis is necessarily valid. The peculiarities created by demand should be treated as exceptions to the general rule since as Johnson (1970) observes:

> It has always been well known that any analysis of the factor-price equalization problem conducted in terms of differences in factor endowments only, without explicit treatment of demand conditions, can only deal with necessary conditions for equalization, in the sense that factor endowments may make equalization possible or impossible, but if they make it possible it may nevertheless not occur because demand conditions lead one country to specialize (p. 89).

## A10.2 MANY FACTORS AND MANY COMMODITIES

The case of many factors and many commodities was discussed by Samuelson (1953), whose main theorem on factor-price equalization was later proved to be false by Nikaido. The correct theorem in the present context is due to Gale (see Chipman, 1966, pp. 19–35, especially p. 30). This topic is beyond the scope of the present book, however, and the interested reader is referred to Chipman (1966),

Kemp (1969), and Samuelson (1953, 1967) for further discussion. See also the 1965 postscript by Samuelson in *The Collected Scientific Papers of Paul A. Samuelson*, vol. 2, p. 908; and the recent contributions of Ethier (1974) and Kuga (1972).

# PART B. GENERALIZATION OF THE HECKSCHER–OHLIN THEOREM

Turn now to the generalization of the Heckscher–Ohlin theorem to many countries, many commodities, and many factors.

## A10.3 MANY COUNTRIES

The conclusions of part B of chap. 10 can easily be generalized to the case of many countries. Assume that there are $n > 2$ countries which can be classified in the order of factor abundance on the basis of either the price or the physical definition. In particular, assume that

$$\frac{L_1}{T_1} < \frac{L_2}{T_2} < \cdots < \frac{L_n}{T_n}$$

where $L_i$ = total labor endowment of the $i$th country and $T_i$ = total land endowment of the $i$th country. On the basis of the physical definition of factor abundance, the first country is land abundant relative to the second, the second country is land abundant relative to the third, and so on down the line to the $n$th country.

Without any loss of generality, also assume that tastes are similar and homothetic between countries and that commodity $X$ is land intensive relative to $Y$ for all factor-price ratios. Therefore, the preceding classification of countries in the order of factor abundance holds also under the price definition.

On the basis of the analysis of part B of chap. 10, the following inequalities necessarily hold before trade opens up:

$$p_1 < p_2 < \cdots < p_n$$

where $p_i$ = the pretrade equilibrium price ratio (i.e., price of $X$/price of $Y$) of the $i$th country. That is, considering any pair of countries, we can definitely say that the land-abundant country is producing $X$ relatively more cheaply than the labor-abundant country before trade. Does this conclusion enable us to determine a priori the direction of trade for all $n$ countries? Not at all. All we can be sure of is that the first country will be exporting commodity $X$ in exchange for $Y$ and that the $n$th country will be exporting commodity $Y$ in exchange for $X$. The direction of trade of the countries in between (countries $2, 3, \ldots, n - 1$) cannot be predicted without introducing demand into the picture. However, this much can be said. Demand conditions can be introduced to "break the chain" into exporters of $X$ and exporters of $Y$. If, for instance, the third country exports commodity $X$ and imports $Y$, then the preceding countries (the first and second) must also export $X$ and import $Y$. This is very similar to the appendix to chap. 3 in relation to the classical theory. Therefore, no further discussion is necessary.

## A10.4 MANY COMMODITIES AND TWO FACTORS†

Let us now turn to the case of two countries ($A$ and $B$) but many ($m > 2$) commodities. Some economists‡ have contended that the introduction of more commodities into the analysis does not destroy the conclusions reached in part B of chap. 10. In particular, these economists contend that, ignoring the possibility of factor-intensity reversals, it is still possible to rank the commodities (from technological data and factor supply data) in terms of factor ratios and *thereby uniquely rank them in terms of comparative advantage as in the classical system.* Demand conditions will then "break the chain" into exports and imports. Unfortunately, this proposition is false. There is no need to give rigorous proof; a counterexample should be sufficient.

### A Counterexample

Assume that there are three commodities, $X$, $Y$, and $Z$, and that $X$ is labor intensive relative to $Y$ and $Y$ is labor intensive relative to $Z$ (and therefore $X$ is also labor intensive relative to $Z$) for all factor-price ratios. Assume also that country $A$ is endowed with 350 units of labor and 600 units of land, and $B$ with 300 units of labor and 600 units of land. Assume, further, that international commodity trade equalizes factor prices between countries.

Consider now a general-equilibrium situation. In particular, assume that the optimum coefficients of production (in both countries) at the observed equilibrium point are as follows: 1 unit of $X$ requires 1 unit of labor and 1 unit of land; 1 unit of $Y$ requires 1 unit of labor and 2 units of land; and 1 unit of $Z$ requires 1 unit of labor and 3 units of land. On the basis of these assumptions and the factor endowments of $A$ and $B$, we can formulate the following full-employment equations:

$$X_A^P + Y_A^P + Z_A^P = 350 \tag{A10.1}$$

$$X_A^P + 2Y_A^P + 3Z_A^P = 600 \tag{A10.2}$$

$$X_B^P + Y_B^P + Z_B^P = 300 \tag{A10.3}$$

$$X_B^P + 2Y_B^P + 3Z_B^P = 600 \tag{A10.4}$$

The term $X_A^P \equiv$ amount of $X$ produced in country $A$, and so on.

---

† This section was originally written in 1969 and published later in Chacholiades (1973, pp. 216–224). The author discovered subsequently that essentially the same ideas were formulated in an elegant paper by Vanek (1968), and also by Travis (1964, pp. 94–99). Additional contributions in this area have been made by Bertrand (1972), Hong (1970), Horiba (1971, 1974), and Vanek (1971).

‡ See Jones (1956) and Bhagwati (1964). The latter has changed his mind on this point. See Bhagwati (1972).

We have four equations in six unknowns; therefore, we cannot, without further information, determine the equilibrium values for all variables. Note that *this situation is created by the fact that there are more commodities than factors of production.*† For the moment, treat the output of the third commodity as a parameter and solve eqs. (A10.1) and (A10.2) for $X_A^P$ and $Y_A^P$ and eqs. (A10.3) and (A10.4) for $X_B^P$ and $Y_B^P$. The solutions are

$$X_A^P = 100 + Z_A^P \tag{A10.5}$$

$$Y_A^P = 250 - 2Z_A^P \tag{A10.6}$$

$$X_B^P = Z_B^P \tag{A10.7}$$

$$Y_B^P = 300 - 2Z_B^P \tag{A10.8}$$

Since only nonnegative solutions are acceptable, eq. (A10.6) restricts·the value of $Z_A$ to less than 125; that is,

$$0 \le Z_A^P \le 125 \tag{A10.9}$$

Similarly, eq. (A10.8) restricts the value of $Z_B^P$ to

$$0 \le Z_B^P \le 150 \tag{A10.10}$$

Let us introduce another piece of exogenous information about the general-equilibrium situation we are assuming exists. In particular, suppose that the total production and consumption of $Z$ in both countries is 100 units. Can we also determine the aggregate production of $X$ and $Y$? The answer is "Yes." Thus,

$$X_W^P \equiv X_A^P + X_B^P = 100 + Z_A^P + Z_B^P = 100 + Z_W^P \tag{A10.11}$$

$$Y_W^P \equiv Y_A^P + Y_B^P = 250 - 2Z_A^P + 300 - 2Z_B^P = 550 - 2Z_W^P \tag{A10.12}$$

where the subscript $W$ indicates the total "world output." Since, by assumption, $Z_W^P = 100$, it must also be true that $X_W^P = 200$ and $Y_W^P = 350$.

What is the direction of trade? Can we determine it uniquely? If so, does it correspond to what the Heckscher–Ohlin theorem would predict? Unfortunately, the answers are all negative, mainly because, although we know the combined outputs of countries $A$ and $B$ for each one of the three commodities—and thus we know a point on the world production-possibilities frontier—we cannot determine *uniquely* the individual outputs of $A$ and $B$. That is, the structure of production is indeterminate as in the classical equal-costs case.

To illustrate the implications of the indeterminacy of the structure of production, let us first introduce demand into the picture. We can follow the Heckscher–Ohlin tradition and suppose that tastes are homothetic and similar between countries. Therefore, irrespective of prices, both countries will be consuming the three commodities in the same proportion. Since we already know the aggregate production of $X$, $Y$, and $Z$ (200, 350, and 100, respectively), we can infer that the

---

† The indeterminacy of this case was pointed out by Samuelson (1953). See also Melvin (1968).

three commodities must be consumed in the proportion $4X : 7Y : 2Z$ in both countries.

What are the precise amounts of $X$, $Y$, and $Z$ consumed in $A$ and $B$? That depends on the division of income between $A$ and $B$, which in turn depends upon the equilibrium factor prices. Even without knowing the equilibrium factor prices, we can still determine upper and lower limits for the ratio $Q_A/Q_B$, where $Q_i \equiv$ income of the $i$th country. Thus,

$$\frac{Q_A}{Q_B} = \frac{(w/r)350 + 600}{(w/r)300 + 600} \tag{A10.13a}$$

or, dividing both numerator and denominator by $w/r$,

$$\frac{Q_A}{Q_B} = \frac{350 + (r/w)600}{300 + (r/w)600} \tag{A10.13b}$$

The factor-price ratio $w/r$ can vary from 0 to $\infty$. When $w/r = 0$, it follows from eq. (A10.13a) that $Q_A/Q_B = 1$, and when $w/r = \infty$, or $r/w = 0$, it follows from (A10.13b) that $Q_A/Q_B = \frac{7}{6}$. That is, the income ratio can only vary between 1 and $\frac{7}{6}$, or

$$1 < \frac{Q_A}{Q_B} < \frac{7}{6} \tag{A10.14}$$

Assume that, at the particular equilibrium we are interested in, the income ratio is $Q_A/Q_B = \frac{13}{12}$. Therefore, the outputs of $X$, $Y$, and $Z$ must be absorbed by countries $A$ and $B$ in the proportion $13 : 12$. The equilibrium consumption levels are

$$X_A^c = 104 \qquad Y_A^c = 182 \qquad Z_A^c = 52$$
$$X_B^c = 96 \qquad Y_B^c = 168 \qquad Z_B^c = 48$$

where the superscript $c$ indicates consumption.

As long as $A$ produces only 3 units of $Z$ or less, it will definitely export $Y$ and import $X$ and $Z$. For instance, suppose that $A$ produces only 2 units of $Z$. The pattern of production of both countries will then be

$$X_A^p = 102 \qquad Y_A^p = 246 \qquad Z_A^p = 2$$
$$X_B^p = 98 \qquad Y_B^p = 104 \qquad Z_B^p = 98$$
$$X_W^p = 200 \qquad Y_W^p = 350 \qquad Z_W^p = 100$$

Therefore, $A$ must be exporting 64 units of $Y$ to $B$ in exchange for 2 units of $X$ and 50 units of $Z$. But this pattern of trade is precisely what some economists thought could never occur, for $Y$ is labor intensive relative to $Z$ but land intensive relative to $X$. This clearly shows that commodities cannot be uniquely ranked in terms of comparative advantage as in the classical system—whether the price or the quantity definition of factor abundance is used.

## A Reformulation of the Heckscher–Ohlin Theorem

If (as the preceding analysis shows) commodities cannot be uniquely ranked in terms of comparative advantage, is there any way in which the Heckscher–Ohlin theorem can be reformulated and be logically consistent in the presence of more than two commodities? Probably, because in a deeper sense the Heckscher–Ohlin (or the factor-proportions) theory points to an indirect exchange of factors between countries—an exchange which tends to equalize the proportion in which the two factors are indirectly (through commodities) absorbed despite the fact that the labor-land ratios differ between countries. It is this fundamental property of the Heckscher–Ohlin model which is not lost even when the number of commodities is allowed to increase.

Assume that countries $A$ and $B$ have identical and homothetic tastes. On the basis of this assumption alone, the consumption levels of all commodities in country $A$ will necessarily be proportional to the corresponding consumption levels in country $B$. In other words,

$$C_i^A = \lambda C_i^B \tag{A10.15}$$

where $C_i^A = A$'s consumption level of the $i$th good, $C_i^B = B$'s consumption level of the $i$th good, and $\lambda =$ factor of proportionality. The factor of proportionality $\lambda$ depends on the precise equilibrium value of the factor-price ratio. In what follows, $\lambda$ will be treated as a constant because it will be assumed that the world economy is already in equilibrium. Our job is to study the properties of this equilibrium.

Let us now follow the Heckscher–Ohlin theorem and assume that the techniques of production at the observed international equilibrium are identical between countries. Let the symbols $a_{Li}$ and $a_{Ti}$ denote the amounts of labor and land, respectively, required for the production of 1 unit of the $i$th commodity in either country. The total amounts of labor and land absorbed by countries $A$ and $B$ are calculated as follows:

$$L_A^D \equiv \sum_{i=1}^{n} a_{Li} C_i^A \tag{A10.16}$$

$$T_A^D \equiv \sum_{i=1}^{n} a_{Ti} C_i^A \tag{A10.17}$$

$$L_B^D \equiv \sum_{i=1}^{n} a_{Li} C_i^B \tag{A10.18}$$

$$T_B^D \equiv \sum_{i=1}^{n} a_{Ti} C_i^B \tag{A10.19}$$

The new symbols are self-evident. For instance, $L_A^D$ denotes the total amount of labor absorbed (or demanded) by country $A$, and so on.

Applying eq. (A10.15) to eqs. (A10.16) to (A10.19) gives

$$L_A^D \equiv \sum_{i=1}^{n} a_{Li} C_i^A = \lambda \sum_{i=1}^{n} a_{Li} C_i^B = \lambda L_B^D \tag{A10.20}$$

$$T_A^D \equiv \sum_{i=1}^{n} a_{Ti} C_i^A = \lambda \sum_{i=1}^{n} a_{Ti} C_i^B = \lambda T_B^D \tag{A10.21}$$

That is, the amounts of labor and land absorbed by $A$ are proportional to the respective amounts absorbed by $B$, with $\lambda$ being the factor of proportionality.

Let $\bar{L}_A$ and $\bar{T}_A$ denote $A$'s endowments of labor and land, respectively. Similarly, let $\bar{L}_B$ and $\bar{T}_B$ denote the corresponding endowments for $B$. It is further convenient to define the following:

$$\bar{L} \equiv \bar{L}_A + \bar{L}_B \tag{A10.22}$$

$$\bar{T} \equiv \bar{T}_A + \bar{T}_B \tag{A10.23}$$

That is, $\bar{L}$ and $\bar{T}$ show the aggregate amounts of labor and land, respectively, which exist in both countries together.

Full employment in both countries requires that the following equations be satisfied:

$$\bar{L} = L_A^D + L_B^D = \lambda L_B^D + L_B^D = (1 + \lambda)L_B^D \tag{A10.24a}$$

$$\bar{T} = T_A^D + T_B^D = \lambda T_B^D + T_B^D = (1 + \lambda)T_B^D \tag{A10.25a}$$

It is clear from eqs. (A10.20), (A10.21), (A10.24a) and (A10.25a) that

$$\frac{L_A^D}{T_A^D} = \frac{L_B^D}{T_B^D} = \frac{\bar{L}}{\bar{T}} \tag{A10.26}$$

Consider now the budget equations of countries $A$ and $B$:

$$w\bar{L}_A + r\bar{T}_A = wL_A^D + rT_A^D \tag{A10.27a}$$

$$w\bar{L}_B + r\bar{T}_B = wL_B^D + rT_B^D \tag{A10.28a}$$

or

$$w(L_A^D - \bar{L}_A) + r(T_A^D - \bar{T}_A) = 0 \tag{A10.27b}$$

$$w(L_B^D - \bar{L}_B) + r(T_B^D - \bar{T}_B) = 0 \tag{A10.28b}$$

Also, from eqs. (A10.24a) and (A10.25a) it follows that

$$(L_A^D - \bar{L}_A) + (L_B^D - \bar{L}_B) = 0 \tag{A10.24b}$$

$$(T_A^D - \bar{T}_A) + (T_B^D - \bar{T}_B) = 0 \tag{A10.25b}$$

Hence, when $(L_A^D - \bar{L}_A)$ is positive, $(T_A^D - \bar{T}_A)$ must be negative, $(L_B^D - \bar{L}_B)$ must be negative, and $(T_B^D - \bar{T}_B)$ must be positive. In other words, when country $A$ is importing labor indirectly, it must be exporting land, and country $B$ must be exporting labor and importing land.

The above conclusions are illustrated in fig. A10.1. The sides of the box show the aggregate amounts of labor and land ($\bar{L}$ and $\bar{T}$). The coordinates of point $Z$ show, with respect to the $O_A$ origin, $A$'s factor endowments, and with respect to the $O_B$ origin, $B$'s factor endowments. Equilibrium will occur somewhere along the diagonal $O_A O_B$ (eq. (A10.26)). In particular, equilibrium will occur somewhere in the region $UV$ because the equilibrium factor prices ($w$ and $r$) are positive. This is illustrated by point $E$. Therefore, $A$ must be exporting $GZ$ units of land to $B$ in exchange for $ZH$ units of labor. It is important to note that the quantities $GZ$ and

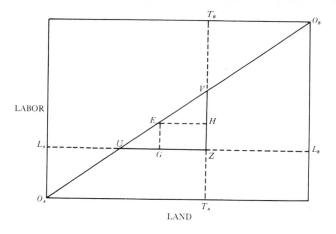

**Figure A10.1** Indirect exchange of factor services between countries.

$ZH$ are the net (not the gross) exports and imports of labor and land. Finally, note that the precise position of the equilibrium point $E$ depends on the equilibrium value of the factor-price ratio: we must have $(w/r)ZH = GZ$.

Consider now the case illustrated in fig. A10.1 where $A$ will necessarily be exporting land to $B$ in exchange for labor. We can classify the $n$ commodities into two categories: $A$'s exportables (those commodities exported by $A$ to $B$) and $A$'s importables (those imported by $A$ from $B$). (We know that we cannot uniquely classify commodities in this fashion, but we are only interested in the general properties of any feasible classification, i.e., a classification which is consistent with general equilibrium.) Let us adopt the following symbols: $X_i$ = amount of $i$th commodity exported from $A$ to $B$ $(i = 1, 2, \ldots, s)$ and $M_j$ = amount of $j$th commodity exported from $B$ to $A$ $(j = s + 1, s + 2, \ldots, n)$. Then the quantities $(L_A^D - \bar{L}_A)$, $(T_A^D - \bar{T}_A)$, $(L_B^D - \bar{L}_B)$, and $(T_B^D - \bar{T}_B)$ can be defined directly in terms of quantities of $A$'s exportables and importables. Thus,

$$L_A^D - \bar{L}_A = \sum_{j=s+1}^{n} a_{Lj} M_j - \sum_{i=1}^{s} a_{Li} X_i > 0 \qquad (A10.29a)$$

$$T_A^D - \bar{T}_A = \sum_{j=s+1}^{n} a_{Tj} M_j - \sum_{i=1}^{s} a_{Ti} X_i < 0 \qquad (A10.30a)$$

Since $L_B^D - \bar{L}_B = -(L_A^D - \bar{L}_A)$ and $(T_B^D - \bar{T}_B) = -(T_A^D - \bar{T}_A)$, these are the only equations we need.

Inequalities (A10.29a) and (A10.30a) can be simplified by introducing the optimum labor-land ratios $\rho_i \equiv a_{Li}/a_{Ti}$ for $i = 1, 2, \ldots, n$, which gives us

$$\sum_{j=s+1}^{n} \rho_j(a_{Tj} M_j) > \sum_{i=1}^{s} \rho_i(a_{Ti} X_i) \qquad (A10.29b)$$

$$\sum_{j=s+1}^{n} a_{Tj} M_j < \sum_{i=1}^{s} a_{Ti} X_i \qquad (A10.30b)$$

Dividing the left-hand side of (A10.29$b$) by the left-hand side of (A10.30$b$) and the right-hand side of (A10.29$b$) by the right-hand side of (A10.30$b$), we get the fundamental inequality

$$\frac{\sum\limits_{j=s+1}^{n} \rho_j(a_{Tj}M_j)}{\sum\limits_{j=s+1}^{n} a_{Tj}M_j} > \frac{\sum\limits_{i=1}^{s} \rho_i(a_{Ti}X_i)}{\sum\limits_{i=1}^{s} a_{Ti}X_i} \tag{A10.31a}$$

or, defining

$$z_i \equiv \frac{a_{Ti}X_i}{\sum\limits_{i=1}^{s} a_{Ti}X_i} \qquad z_j \equiv \frac{a_{Tj}M_j}{\sum\limits_{j=s+1}^{n} a_{Tj}M_j}$$

$$\left( \text{thus } \sum_{i=1}^{s} z_i = 1 \qquad \text{and} \qquad \sum_{j=s+1}^{n} z_j = 1 \right)$$

and substituting into (A10.31$a$), we finally get

$$\sum_{j=s+1}^{n} \rho_j z_j > \sum_{i=1}^{s} \rho_i z_i \tag{A10.31b}$$

That is, *the weighted average of the labor-land ratios of A's imported commodities must be higher than the weighted average of the labor-land ratios of A's exported commodities, with the weights being given by the relative amounts of land absorbed by each commodity within each group.*

Therefore, although it cannot be said that every commodity exported by $A$ (that is, the land-abundant country) must be land intensive relative to every commodity imported by $A$, it can be said that *A's exportables as a group are necessarily land intensive relative to A's importables as a group*, with "factor intensity" defined in terms of the weighted averages as shown by inequality (A10.31$b$).

In conclusion, note that the familiar case of two commodities is a special case of this more general formulation. Then the land-abundant country can export land in exchange for labor only by exporting the land-intensive commodity in exchange for the labor-intensive commodity.

The above formulation of the Heckscher–Ohlin theorem is implicit in Leontief's (1953) empirical work on the structure of the U.S. trade (see chap. 11 below).

## A10.5 MANY FACTORS AND MANY COMMODITIES

The preceding discussion generalizes easily to many factors as well. However, this complication is not pursued here and the reader is referred to Vanek's (1968) elegant treatment and the additional references given earlier in sec. A10.4.

# SELECTED BIBLIOGRAPHY

Acheson, K. (1970). "The Aggregation of Heterogeneous Capital Goods and Various Trade Theorems." *Journal of Political Economy*, vol. 78 (May), pp. 565–571.

American Economic Association (1968). *Readings in International Economics*. Edited by Caves and Johnson. Richard D. Irwin, Inc., Homewood, Ill., chaps. 1 to 6, 30.

—— (1950). *Readings in the Theory of International Trade*. Edited by Ellis and Metzler. Richard D. Irwin, Inc., Homewood, Ill., chap. 13.

Balassa, B. (1961). "The Factor-Price Equalization Controversy." *Weltwirtschaftliches Archiv.*, vol. 87, pp. 111–123.

Bertrand, T. J. (1970). "On Factor Price Equalization When Commodities Outnumber Factors: A Note." *Economica*, vol. 37 (February), pp. 86–88.

—— (1972). "An Extension of the *N*-Factor Case of Factor Proportions Theory." *Kyklos*, vol. 25 (3), pp. 592–596.

Bhagwati, J. (1964). "The Pure Theory of International Trade." *Economic Journal*, vol. 74, pp. 1–78.

—— (1972). "The Heckscher–Ohlin Theorem in the Multi-Commodity Case." *Journal of Political Economy*, vol. 80 (5), pp. 1052–1055.

Brown, A. J. (1957). "Professor Leontief and the Pattern of World Trade." *Yorkshire Bulletin of Economic and Social Research*, vol. 9, pp. 63–75.

Chacholiades, M. (1972). "Multiple Pre-trade Equilibria and the Theory of Comparative Advantage." *Metroeconomica*, vol. XXIV, fasc. II, pp. 128–139.

—— (1973). *The Pure Theory of International Trade*. Aldine Publishing Company, Chicago, Ill.

Chipman, J. S. (1965). "A Survey of the Theory of International Trade: Part 1, The Classical Theory." *Econometrica*, vol. 33, pp. 477–519.

—— (1965). "A Survey of the Theory of International Trade: Part 2, The Neo-classical Theory." *Econometrica*, vol. 33, pp. 685–760.

—— (1966). "A Survey of the Theory of International Trade: Part 3, The Modern Theory." *Econometrica*, vol. 34, pp. 18–76.

Clement, M. O., R. L. Pfister, and K. J. Rothwell (1967). *Theoretical Issues in International Economics*. Houghton-Mifflin Company, Boston, Mass., chaps. 1 and 2.

Corden, W. M. (1965). *Recent Developments in the Theory of International Trade*. Princeton University Special Papers in International Economics, no. 7, Princeton, N.J.

Ethier, W. (1972). "Nontraded Goods and the Heckscher–Ohlin Model." *International Economic Review*, vol. 13, no. 1 (February), pp. 132–147.

—— (1974). "Some of the Theorems of International Trade with Many Goods and Factors." *Journal of International Economics*, vol. 4, pp. 199–206.

Flatters, F. (1972). "Commodity Price Equalization: A Note on Factor Mobility and Trade." *American Economic Review*, vol. LXII, no. 3 (June), pp. 473–476.

Gale, D., and H. Nikaido (1965). "The Jacobian Matrix and Global Univalence of Mappings." *Mathematische Annalen*, vol. 159, pp. 81–93.

Haberler, G. (1961). *A Survey of International Trade Theory*. Princeton University Special Papers in International Economics, no. 1, 2d ed., Princeton, N.J.

Harrod, R. F. (1958). "Factor-Price Relations under Free Trade." *Economic Journal*, vol. 68 (June), pp. 245–255.

—— (1973). *International Economics*, 5th ed. Cambridge University Press, Cambridge.

Heckscher, E. (1919). "The Effect of Foreign Trade on the Distribution of Income." *Ekonomisk Tidskrift*, vol. 21, pp. 1–32. Reprinted in AEA *Readings in the Theory of International Trade*. Richard D. Irwin, Inc., Homewood, Ill., 1950.

Hong, W. (1970). "The Heckscher–Ohlin Theory of Factor-Price Equalization and the Indeterminacy in International Specialization." *International Economic Review*, vol. 11, no. 2 (June), pp. 328–333.

Horiba, Y. (1971). "A Note on the Factor Proportions Theory in the *N*-Factor Case." *Kyklos*, vol. 24 (2), pp. 339–343.

——— (1974). "General Equilibrium and the Heckscher–Ohlin Theory of Trade: The Multi-Country Case." *International Economic Review*, vol. 15, no. 2 (June), pp. 440–449.

Inada, K. (1967). "A Note on the Heckscher–Ohlin Theorem." *Economic Record*, vol. 43 (September), pp. 88–96.

Johnson, H. G. (1957). "Factor Endowments, International Trade and Factor Prices." *Manchester School of Economics and Social Studies*, vol. 25 (September), pp. 270–283. Reprinted in H. G. Johnson, *International Trade and Economic Growth*, George Allen and Unwin, Ltd., London, 1958.

——— (1967). "The Possibility of Factor-Price Equalization When Commodities Outnumber Factors." *Economica*, vol. 34 (August), pp. 282–288.

——— (1970). "On Factor Price Equalization When Commodities Outnumber Factors: A Comment." *Economica*, vol. 37 (February), pp. 89–90.

Jones, R. W. (1956). "Factor Proportions and the Heckscher–Ohlin Theorem." *Review of Economic Studies*, vol. 24, pp. 1–10.

Kemp, M. C. (1969). *The Pure Theory of International Trade and Investment*. Prentice-Hall, Inc., Englewood Cliffs, N.J., pt. I.

Khang, C. (1969). "A Dynamic Model of Trade Between the Final and the Intermediate Products." *Journal of Economic Theory*, vol. 1, pp. 416–437.

Komiya, R. (1967). "Non-Traded Goods and the Pure Theory of International Trade." *International Economic Review*, vol. 8, no. 2 (June), pp. 132–152.

Kuga, K. (1972). "The Factor-Price Equalization Theorem." *Econometrica*, vol. 40, no. 4 (July), pp. 723–736.

Lancaster, K. (1957). "The Heckscher–Ohlin Trade Model: A Geometric Treatment." *Economica*, vol. 24, pp. 19–39.

Land, A. H. (1959). "Factor Endowments and Factor Prices." *Economica*, N.S., vol. 26 (May), pp. 137–142.

Leontief, W. W. (1953). "Domestic Production and Foreign Trade: The American Capital Position Reexamined." *Proceedings of the American Philosophical Society*, vol. 97, pp. 332–349. Reprinted in R. E. Caves and H. G. Johnson (Eds.), AEA *Readings in International Economics*. Richard D. Irwin, Inc., Homewood, Ill., 1968.

——— (1956). "Factor Proportions and the Structure of American Trade." *Review of Economics and Statistics*, vol. 38, pp. 386–407.

Lerner, A. P. (1953). *Essays in Economics Analysis*. Macmillan and Company, Ltd., London, pp. 67–100.

Meade, J. E. (1950). "The Equalization of Factor Prices: The Two Country Two Factor Three Product Case." *Metroeconomica*, vol. 2 (December), pp. 129–133.

——— (1955). *The Theory of International Economic Policy*. vol. 2: *Trade and Welfare*. Oxford University Press, Oxford, chaps. 19 to 23.

Melvin, J. R. (1968). "Production and Trade with Two Factors and Three Goods." *American Economic Review*, vol. 58, pp. 1249–1268.

——— (1971). "Production Indeterminacy with Three Goods and Two Factors: Reply." *American Economic Review*, vol. LXI, no. 1 (March), pp. 245–246.

Metzler, L. A. (1948). "The Theory of International Trade." In H. S. Ellis (Ed.), *Survey of Contemporary Economics*. The Blakiston Company, Philadelphia, Pa.

Michaely, M. (1964). "Factor Proportions in International Trade: Current State of the Theory." *Kyklos*, vol. 17, fasc. 4.

Minhas, B. (1962). "The Homohypallagic Production Function, Factor Intensity Reversals, and the Heckscher–Ohlin Theorem." *Journal of Political Economy*, vol. 70, pp. 138–156.

Mundell, R. A. (1960). "The Pure Theory of International Trade." *American Economic Review*, vol. 40, pp. 301–322.

Ohlin, B. (1933). *Interregional and International Trade*. Harvard University Press, Cambridge, Mass., chaps. 1 to 6, app. 3.

Pearce, I. F. (1952). "The Factor Price Equalization Myth." *Review of Economic Studies*, vol. 19, pp. 111–120.

Robinson, R. (1956). "Factor Proportions and Comparative Advantage." *Quarterly Journal of Economics*, vol. 70, pt. I (May), pp. 169–192; and pt. II (August), pp. 246–263.

Rodriguez, C. A. (1975). "International Factor Mobility, Nontraded Goods, and the International Equalization of Prices of Goods and Factors." *Econometrica*, vol. 43, no. 1 (January), pp. 115–124.

Samuelson, P. A. (1948). "International Trade and the Equalization of Factor Prices." *Economic Journal*, vol. 58, pp. 165–184.

——— (1949). "International Factor Price Equalization Once Again." *Economic Journal*, vol. 59, pp. 181–197.

——— (1953). "Prices of Factors and Goods in General Equilibrium." *Review of Economic Studies*, vol. 21, pp. 1–20.

——— (1965). "Equalization by Trade of the Interest Rate Along with the Real Wage." In R. E. Baldwin et al. (Eds.), *Trade, Growth, and the Balance of Payments*. Rand-McNally and Company, Chicago, Ill.

——— (1967). "Summary on Factor Price Equalization." *International Economic Review*, vol. 8, pp. 286–295.

——— (1971a). "An Exact Hume–Ricardo–Marshall Model of International Trade." *Journal of International Economics*, vol. 1, pp. 1–18.

——— (1971b). "On the Trail of Conventional Beliefs about the Transfer Problem." In J. N. Bhagwati et al. (Eds.), *Trade, Balance of Payments, and Growth: Papers in International Economics in Honor of Charles P. Kindleberger*. North-Holland Publishers, Amsterdam.

——— (1971c). "Ohlin was Right." *The Swedish Journal of Economics*, vol. 73 (4), pp. 365–384.

Stewart, D. B. (1971). "Production Indeterminacy with Three Goods and Two Factors: A Comment on the Pattern of Trade." *American Economic Review*, vol. LXI, no. 1 (March), pp. 241–244.

——— (1976). "Can Trade Widen the Difference Between Factor Rewards? Another Look at the More-Goods-Than-Factors Case." *American Economic Review*, vol. 66, no. 4 (September), pp. 671–674.

Stiglitz, J. E. (Ed.) (1965). *The Collected Scientific Papers of Paul A. Samuelson*, vol. 2. The MIT Press, Cambridge, Mass.

Stolper, W. F., and P. A. Samuelson (1941). "Protection and Real Wages." *Review of Economic Studies*, vol. 9, pp. 58–73.

Tinbergen, J. (1949). "The Equalization of Factor Prices Between Free Trade Areas." *Metroeconomica*, vol. 1 (April), pp. 39–47.

Travis, W. P. (1964). *The Theory of Trade and Protection*. Harvard University Press, Cambridge, Mass.

Uzawa, H. (1959). "Prices of the Factors of Production in International Trade." *Econometrica*, vol. 27, pp. 448–468.

Vanek, J. (1960). "An Alternative Proof of the Factor Price Equalization Theorem." *Quarterly Journal of Economics*, vol. 74, pp. 633–640.

——— (1968). "The Factor Proportions Theory: The *N*-Factor Case." *Kyklos*, vol. 21 (4), pp. 749–755.

——— (1971). "Rejoinder, Clarification and Further Extension." *Kyklos*, vol. 24 (2), pp. 344–345.

———, and T. J. Bertrand (1971). "Trade and Factor Prices in a Multi-Commodity World." In J. Bhagwati et al. (Eds.), *Trade, Balance of Payments and Growth: Papers in International Economics in Honor of Charles P. Kindleberger*. North-Holland Publishers, Amsterdam.

Viner, J. (1953). *International Trade and Economic Development*. Free Press, New York.

Warne, R. D. (1973). "Factor Intensity and the Heckscher–Ohlin Theorem in a Three-Factor, Three-Good Model." *Canadian Journal of Economics and Political Science*, vol. 6 (August), pp. 369–375.

Yeh, Y. (1968). "A Note on Consumer Preferences in the Heckscher–Ohlin Trade Model." *Economic Record*, vol. 44 (December), pp. 516–519.

# ELEVEN

## THE LEONTIEF PARADOX

Having discussed the theoretical foundations of the Heckscher–Ohlin theory, we now turn to its empirical verification.

## 11.1 INTRODUCTION

After its reformulation by Bertil Ohlin (1933), the Heckscher–Ohlin theory (i.e., the proposition that each country exports those commodities which use more intensively its abundant factor) was generally accepted on the basis of casual empiricism. The first serious attempt to test the theory empirically was made by Wassily W. Leontief (1953). Leontief reached the paradoxical conclusion that the United States, the most capital-abundant country in the world by any criterion, exported labor-intensive, and imported capital-intensive, commodities.† This result, which came to be known in the literature as Leontief's paradox, took the profession by surprise and stimulated an enormous amount of empirical and theoretical research.‡ Useful surveys of the literature on the Leontief paradox have been provided by Baldwin (1971), Bhagwati (1964), Brown (1957), Chipman (1966, pp. 44–57), and Stern (1975).

---

† If Leontief's empirical findings are actually correct, then not only is the Heckscher–Ohlin theorem refuted, but also certain important policy implications follow immediately. For instance, U.S. tariff protection would appear to be detrimental rather than beneficial to U.S. labor. See the discussion of the Stolper–Samuelson theorem in chap. 19.

‡ Two other studies by MacDougall (1951) and Kravis (1956b), much less elaborate than Leontief's study, also failed to verify the Heckscher–Ohlin theory. On the other hand, Tarshis (1959) provided some relief by discovering that capital-intensive commodities were cheaper in the United States than in other countries (Great Britain, Soviet Union, and Japan) relative to labor-intensive commodities.

This chapter summarizes the main empirical findings and then reviews the main explanations of the Leontief paradox which are found in the literature.

## 11.2 EMPIRICAL FINDINGS: THE PATTERN OF U.S. TRADE

To perform his test, Leontief (1953) used the 1947 input-output table of the U.S. economy. He aggregated industries into 50 sectors (38 of which traded their products directly on the international market) and factors into two categories—labor and capital. Then he estimated the capital and labor requirements for the production of a representative bundle (one million dollars' worth) of U.S. exports and a representative bundle of U.S. import-competing commodities (also one million dollars' worth).† He surprised himself (and the rest of the profession) with the discovery that U.S. import replacements required 30 percent *more* capital per worker than U.S. exports.

Leontief was criticized on methodological and statistical grounds. Thus, on methodological matters he was criticized by Valavanis-Vail (1954) and Ellsworth (1954). The former (Valavanis-Vail) erroneously asserted that Leontief's input-output approach was logically incompatible with international trade.‡ The latter (Ellsworth) objected that it was not appropriate for Leontief to use the U.S. capital-labor ratio for "import" production. Ellsworth claimed that the capital-labor ratio prevailing in the rest of the world for the actual production of such U.S. imports, which according to Ellsworth was substantially lower than the corresponding U.S. ratio, is the appropriate figure to compare with the capital-labor ratio for U.S. exports. Ellsworth's argument rests on the existence of either different production functions between countries, or factor-intensity reversals.

On statistical matters Leontief was criticized by Swerling (1954), Buchanan (1955, pp. 793–794), and Diab (1956). In particular, Swerling complained that 1947 was not a typical year: the postwar disorganization of production overseas had not been corrected by that time, and the results were biased both by the capital-labor ratios of a few industries (such as agriculture and fisheries) with significant export or import positions and by the way in which transport, commercial services, and wholesale trade were incorporated into the analysis.

Leontief (1956) repeated the test using the average composition of U.S. exports and imports which prevailed in 1951. In this later study, he retained the 1947 U.S. production structure but disaggregated into 192 sectors of commodity groups. He found that U.S. import replacements were still more capital intensive relative to U.S. exports, even though their capital intensity over U.S. exports was reduced to only 6 percent. In a more recent test, Baldwin (1971), using the 1958

---

† For his computations, Leontief assumed that the level of noncompetitive imports (i.e., products which are not produced in the United States—mainly coffee, tea, and jute) remained unchanged.

‡ For further discussion of the Valavanis-Vail argument, see Caves (1960), Chipman (1966, pp. 46–48), and Robinson (1956).

U.S. production structure but the 1962 composition of U.S. exports and imports, found that the U.S. import-competing sector was 27 percent more capital intensive relative to the U.S. export sector. The paradox continues.

Buchanan's main criticism was that the capital coefficients used by Leontief were essentially "investment-requirements coefficients" and did not really account for the difference in the durability of capital in the various industries. Diab made a similar criticism. In repeating his test, Leontief (1956, p. 397, computation A) included capital replacement in the input-output coefficients and showed that the U.S. import-competing sector remained 17.57 percent more capital intensive relative to the U.S. export sector.

## 11.3 TRADE PATTERNS OF OTHER COUNTRIES

Leontief's methodology was used by a number of economists to study the trade patterns of other countries as well. Thus, Tatemoto and Ichimura (1959) studied Japan's trade pattern and discovered another paradox: Japan, a labor-abundant country, exports capital-intensive, and imports labor-intensive, commodities. Tatemoto and Ichimura attributed this result to the fact that Japan's place in the world economy is somewhere between the advanced and the underdeveloped countries. They found that 25 percent of Japanese exports went to advanced and 75 percent to underdeveloped countries, and argued that Japan may be expected to have a comparative advantage in labor-intensive commodities when trading with the advanced countries, and in capital-intensive commodities when trading with the underdeveloped countries.

To substantiate their conjecture, Tatemoto and Ichimura computed the capital-labor ratio of Japanese exports to the U.S. and found that it was much lower than the capital-labor ratio of Japan's total exports. They also computed the capital-labor ratio of U.S. exports to Japan and found that it was larger than the capital-labor ratio of both the U.S. total exports and U.S. competitive imports. They took these findings to mean two things: (a) that Japan's foreign trade is indeed two-sided as they had thought; and (b) the Leontief paradox is reversed when the U.S.–Japanese trade is considered.

Stolper and Roskamp (1961) applied Leontief's methods to the trade pattern of East Germany and found that East German exports are capital intensive relative to East German imports. Since about three-quarters of East German trade is with the communist block within which East Germany is considered to be capital abundant, Stolper and Roskamp find their empirical result consistent with the Heckscher–Ohlin theory.

Wahl (1961) studied Canada's pattern of trade and found that Canadian exports are capital intensive relative to Canadian imports. Since most Canadian trade is with the United States, Wahl's result apparently runs against the Heckscher–Ohlin theory.

Finally, Bharadwaj (1962a) studied India's trade pattern and found that Indian exports are labor intensive relative to Indian imports. This is, of course, apparently consistent with the Heckscher–Ohlin hypothesis. Nevertheless, when Bharadwaj (1962b) considered the Indian trade with the United States, he found that Indian exports to the United States are capital intensive relative to Indian imports from the United States.

Before turning to the various explanations of the Leontief paradox, perhaps we should note that there is no theoretical necessity for the Heckscher–Ohlin relationship to hold bilaterally. For further thoughts on this point, see Baldwin (1971, pp. 143–144) and Horiba (1974).

## 11.4 EXPLANATIONS OF THE LEONTIEF PARADOX

The empirical evidence which has been accumulated so far does not dispel the Leontief paradox. How then are the empirical findings reconciled with the Heckscher–Ohlin theory? Several explanations of the paradox have been provided in the literature. Some of them attempt to bring about a reconciliation within the Heckscher–Ohlin model itself. Others attempt to go beyond the Heckscher–Ohlin model and provide new theories which are basically dynamic in character and deal with technical progress and the product cycle. These alternative explanations of the Leontief paradox are summarized below.

### Effectiveness of U.S. Labor

The first unsuccessful attempt to explain Leontief's paradox was made by Leontief himself. He asserted that the apparent higher abundance of capital per worker in the United States relative to that of other countries is actually an illusion. The United States, Leontief argued, is instead a labor-abundant country because American workers are much more productive than foreign workers. In particular, he suggested that 1 man-year of American labor is equivalent to 3 man-years of foreign labor—the number of American workers must be multiplied by 3. Leontief attributed the higher productivity of American labor not to the employment of a larger amount of capital per worker, but rather to American entrepreneurship, superior organization, and favorable environment.

Unfortunately, it is very difficult to accept Leontief's explanation. American entrepreneurship, superior organization, and favorable environment may indeed raise the productivity of American labor. Nevertheless, they also raise the productivity of American capital. Leontief's argument may be admissible only to the extent that the preceding factors raise the productivity of U.S. labor much more than they raise the productivity of U.S. capital. For if they raise the productivity of U.S. capital by the same amount by which they raise the productivity of U.S. labor, then the greater abundance of capital in the United States relative to other countries remains intact.

To test empirically Leontief's conjecture, Kreinin (1965) conducted a survey of managers and engineers familiar with production conditions in the United States and abroad. The results of the survey confirmed that U.S. labor is indeed superior to its foreign counterpart, although such superiority amounts perhaps to 20 or 25 percent (not 300 percent as Leontief claimed), and is not sufficient to convert the United States into a labor-abundant country.

## Consumption Patterns

As noted earlier in chap. 10, the capital-abundant country need not export the capital-intensive commodity if her tastes are strongly biased toward the capital-intensive commodity. Accordingly, Leontief's paradox could be easily explained if it were shown that the United States has a strong consumption bias toward capital-intensive goods. Leontief (1933) himself was already aware of this possibility. Several other writers, e.g., Brown (1957), Jones (1956), Robinson (1956), Travis (1964), and Valavanis-Vail (1954), pointed this out also. Nevertheless, no writer has argued strongly that consumption bias is the major explanation of the Leontief paradox. For one thing, Houthakker's (1957, 1960, 1963) studies suggest that there is considerable similarity in demand functions among countries. For another, as per capita incomes rise, people tend to spend more on labor-intensive goods (such as services) rather than capital-intensive goods. Hence, if there is indeed a consumption bias in the United States, the bias must be toward labor-intensive rather than capital-intensive goods—that is the opposite of what is actually needed to explain Leontief's paradox.

## Factor-Intensity Reversals

We have seen earlier in chap. 10 that in the presence of factor-intensity reversals, and when the overall factor proportions of two countries are such that a contradictory classification of commodities in terms of factor intensity occurs in the two countries, the Heckscher–Ohlin theorem cannot possibly be correct for both countries simultaneously; i.e., one of the two countries must show a Leontief paradox. Factor-intensity reversals as a possible explanation of the Leontief paradox were emphasized by Brown (1957), Jones (1956), Johnson (1957), Lancaster (1957), and Robinson (1956).

The first systematic study of factor-intensity reversals was performed by Minhas (1962, 1963), who concluded that such reversals occur extensively in the real world. Leontief (1964) and others questioned seriously the validity of Minhas' conclusions. Subsequent studies by Lary (1968), Yahr (1968), and Philpot (1970) did not support the Minhas empirical findings either. All one can say at this stage is that the matter of factor-intensity reversals remains unresolved.

## Tariffs and Other Distortions

Travis (1964, 1972) has argued that tariff and nontariff barriers to trade may have been responsible for the Leontief paradox in as much as they restricted U.S. imports of labor-intensive commodities. (Tariffs alone cannot reverse the pattern of trade, of course.) Baldwin (1971) showed that there is a grain of truth in the

Travis thesis in the sense that tariffs and nontariff barriers operate in the direction of, but are not responsible for, the Leontief paradox. According to Baldwin, if all tariff and nontariff barriers were removed, the capital-labor ratio of U.S. imports would fall by only 5 percent, and this is not enough to explain the Leontief paradox.

In connection with market imperfections, Diab (1956, pp. 53–56) made the interesting suggestion that perhaps production abroad by American corporations or their subsidiaries (aided by American capital, technology, and labor and managerial skills) should be considered an extension of the American economy. Thus, Diab argued that once these "American economic colonies" are structurally incorporated in the "mother economy of the United States," their (highly capital-intensive) shipments to the United States would be regarded as part of the U.S. internal trade rather than U.S. imports. In turn, such a procedure may reverse the capital intensity of the American trade with the rest of the world, and thus explain the Leontief paradox.

## Natural Resources

Leontief was criticized by Diab (1956) and Vanek (1959, 1963) for ignoring natural resources.† In particular, Diab (1956, pp. 46–56) divided the products traded by the United States on the international market into two groups: manufacturing (i.e., those products whose production does not depend crucially on natural resources) and nonmanufacturing (i.e., those products whose production depends crucially on natural resources). He then observed that: (a) the nonmanufacturing group was relatively more predominant in U.S. competitive imports (where they constituted 65 percent) than in U.S. exports (where they constituted only 15 percent); and (b) the capital-labor ratio of the nonmanufacturing group was higher than the capital-labor ratio of the manufacturing group, while the corresponding capital-labor ratios of the two groups were practically the same in U.S. exports and U.S. competitive imports. Given this information, Diab (1956, p. 50) concluded that the Leontief paradox was due to the fact that "the highly capital-intensive non-manufacturing group of industries enjoys, percentage-wise, a higher weighting in import replacements than in exports. . . ." He attributed the high percentage of nonmanufacturing industries in U.S. imports to the relative scarcity and poor quality of U.S. natural resources, and also to the fact that, because of the vast U.S. territory, U.S. producers often import their raw materials from neighboring countries than from other parts of the United States.

Vanek (1963, pp. 132–135) provided additional support to Diab's contention. Specifically, he found that the ratios between U.S. export and competitive import requirements of labor, capital, and natural resources are, respectively, 1.07, 0.83, and 0.54. He inferred from this evidence that labor is relatively abundant and

---

† On the role of natural resources in relation to the composition of U.S. trade and the Leontief paradox, see also the interesting discussion by Kravis (1956b).

natural resources are relatively scarce in the United States, while capital occupies an intermediate position. Vanek then assumed that capital is strongly complementary to natural resources and concluded that, although capital may well be a relatively abundant factor in the United States, U.S. imports are capital-intensive relative to U.S. exports because natural resources, the scarce factor, enter efficient production only in conjunction with large amounts of capital.[†]

In his subsequent work, Leontief (1956, p. 398, computation D) made allowance for the natural-resource factor. In particular, by eliminating 19 natural-resource products from his matrix (i.e., by treating them as noncompetitive imports), he succeeded in eliminating the paradox that the United States is exporting labor-intensive commodities. On the other hand, Baldwin (1971) found that when natural-resource products are eliminated from the factor-content calculations, the capital intensity of U.S. import replacements drops substantially but U.S. imports remain more capital intensive than U.S. exports by 4 percent—the paradox continues. Perhaps it must be pointed out that in all such calculations the precise definition of natural-resource industries is both arbitrary and critical to the outcome.

## Human Capital

Another important factor which must be taken into account in evaluating the Leontief paradox is *human capital*. The idea is simple: human capital is created by "investing" in education. Education, like investment in physical capital, requires time and uses resources. The skills and expertise which education and training create last a long time and tend to increase the productivity of the labor force substantially. The view of education as capital creation has assumed a predominant role in the economics of education. See the recent survey by Blaug (1976).

There are two alternative ways in which the concept of human capital may be used to explain the Leontief paradox. One way is to argue that countries, like the United States, which are relatively abundant in highly trained labor will have a comparative advantage in, and export, skill-intensive commodities. Alternatively, it may be argued that the value of human capital must be added to the value of physical capital as done, for instance, by Kenen (1965), as explained below.

Leontief (1956, pp. 398–399) did not include the value of human capital in his calculations although he recognized its significance and stressed that the U.S. export industries employed more skilled labor than U.S. import-competing industries. This conclusion, which was later confirmed by Baldwin (1971), was consistent with the findings of Kravis (1956a), who observed that wages in U.S. export industries tend to be higher than wages in import-competing industries—a tendency which seems to exist in most countries. In this connection, see the additional contributions made by Keesing (1965, 1966, 1968, 1971), Kenen (1965, 1970), Waehrer (1968), and Yahr (1968).

---

† For a criticism of the Diab–Vanek thesis, see Travis (1964, pp. 94–99).

Using a 9 percent rate of discount, Kenen (1965) estimated the value of human capital involved in U.S. exports and import-competing products by capitalizing the excess income of skilled over unskilled workers. He then added the estimates of human capital to Leontief's physical capital estimates and found that the Leontief paradox was reversed. (Kenen also showed that the Leontief paradox is reversed only when the rate of discount used in the capitalization process is less than 12.7 percent.) Baldwin (1971), on the other hand, used the costs of education plus foregone earnings to obtain a crude measure of the human capital involved in U.S. export and import-competing production, and concluded that the addition of such a measure of human capital to the estimates of physical capital was not sufficient to reverse the paradox except when the natural-resource products were excluded.

## Technological Gap and Product Cycle

The Heckscher–Ohlin theory is static. Several distinguished economists have argued recently that perhaps the composition of trade depends on dynamic factors such as technical change. In particular, it has been argued that what gives the United States its ability to compete in world markets is its ability to supply a steady flow of new products.

The *technological-gap theory* makes use of the sequence of innovation and imitation, particularly as they affect exports. As a new product is developed in a country and becomes profitable in the domestic market, the innovating firm, which enjoys a temporary monopoly, has initially an easy access to foreign markets.† Initially, the country's exports grow. Later on, however, the profits of the innovating firm prompt imitation in other countries which may actually prove to have a comparative advantage in the production of the new commodity after the innovation is disseminated. (In this connection, see also the discussion of the infant-industry argument in chap. 21.) But as the innovating country loses, through imitation, its absolute advantage in one commodity, a new cycle of innovation imitation begins in another. Thus, the innovating country may continue to develop new products and may continue to have a temporary absolute advantage in products which are eventually more efficiently produced by other countries.

A couple of decades ago Irving Kravis (1956b) argued that a country's exports are determined by *availability*. He did not give a precise definition to the term "availability." He took it to mean that the domestic supply of exports is "elastic" (perhaps relative to the corresponding foreign supply). Kravis claimed that availability is a reflection of a country's relative abundance of natural resources and temporary superiority in technology which innovation confers upon the country.

---

† Catering for the domestic market first before expanding into foreign markets is an idea which was first stressed by Linder (1961). He specifically claimed that exports start out as goods produced for the domestic market, and that a necessary condition for manufactures to become eventually exports is the existence of sufficient domestic demand for them. Exceptions do exist, as illustrated by the exports of Christmas trees by Japan, a non-Christian country.

The technological-gap theory fails to explain why the gap is what it is, and why it is not larger or smaller. Raymond Vernon (1966) generalized the theory into the *product cycle* which stresses the standardization of products. In particular, the product-cycle theory suggests three product stages: new product, maturing product, and standardized product. In addition, the input requirements change over the life-cycle of a new product. For instance, at the new-product stage, production requires much highly skilled labor for the development and improvement of the product. As the product matures, marketing and capital costs become dominant. Finally, at the standardized-product stage, the technology stabilizes and the product enjoys general consumer acceptance. This leads to mass production which largely requires raw materials, capital, and unskilled labor. Accordingly, as the product matures and becomes standardized, comparative advantage may shift from a country relatively abundant in skilled labor to a country which is abundant in unskilled labor.

Keesing (1967), Gruber, Mehta, and Vernon (1967), and others, have taken research and development (R&D) expenditures as a proxy for temporary, comparative-cost advantages created by the development of new products, and found a strong correlation between the intensity of R&D activity and export performance.†

Why does the United States have a comparative advantage based on technology and innovation? Several factors are usually cited for this phenomenon. First, the United States has a per capita income which is high by international standards—a fact which creates unique consumption patterns and a favorable market for new or improved products. Second, the development of new or improved products requires much skilled labor which is relatively abundant in the United States. Third, because of the high U.S. labor costs and the alleged tendency of innovations to be labor saving, there is a greater incentive to innovate in the United States. (See, however, the discussion of technical progress in chap. 13.) Finally, the development and marketing of new or improved products may be associated with economies of scale which tend to be realizable in large, high-income markets such as that of the United States. This last point is, of course, closely related to the first.

## SELECTED BIBLIOGRAPHY

Adler, F. M. (1970). "The Relationship Between the Income and Price Elasticities of Demand for United States Exports." *Review of Economics and Statistics*, vol. 52 (August), pp. 313–319.

Baldwin, R. E. (1971). "Determinants of the Commodity Structure of U.S. Trade." *American Economic Review*, vol. LXI, no. 1 (March), pp. 126–146.

——— (1972). "Determinants of the Commodity Structure of U.S. Trade: Reply." *American Economic Review*, vol. LXII, no. 3 (June), p. 465.

† See also the studies by Adler (1970), Gruber and Vernon (1970), Hufbauer (1970), and Wells (1968, 1969).

—— and J. D. Richardson (Eds.), (1974). *International Trade and Finance*. Little, Brown and Company, Boston, Mass., pt. I.

Bhagwati, J. (1964). "The Pure Theory of International Trade." *Economic Journal*, vol. 74, pp. 1–78.

Bharadwaj, R. (1962a). *Structural Basis of India's Foreign Trade*. Series in Monetary and International Economics, no. 6, University of Bombay, Bombay.

—— (1962b). "Factor Proportions and the Structure of Indo–U.S. Trade." *Indian Economic Journal*, vol. 10 (October), pp. 105–116.

Blaug, M. (1976). "The Empirical Status of Human Capital Theory: A Slightly Jaundiced Survey." *Journal of Economic Literature*, vol. XIV, no. 3 (September), pp. 827–855.

Brown, A. J. (1957). "Professor Leontief and the Pattern of World Trade." *Yorkshire Bulletin of Economic and Social Research*, vol. 9 (November), pp. 63–75.

Buchanan, N. S. (1955). "Lines on the Leontief Paradox." *Economia Internazionale*, vol. 8 (November), pp. 791–794.

Caves, R. E. (1960). *Trade and Economic Structure*. Harvard University Press, Cambridge, Mass.

Chipman, J. S. (1966). "A Survey of the Theory of International Trade: Part 3, The Modern Theory." *Econometrica*, vol. 34, no. 1 (January), pp. 18–76.

Diab, M. A. (1956). *The United States Capital Position and the Structure of its Foreign Trade*. North-Holland Publishing Company, Amsterdam.

Ellsworth, P. T. (1954). "The Structure of American Foreign Trade: A New View Examined." *Review of Economics and Statistics*, vol. 36 (August), pp. 279–285.

Gruber, W., D. Mehta, and R. Vernon (1967). "The R&D Factor in International Trade and Investment of United States Industries." *Journal of Political Economy*, vol. 75 (February), pp. 20–37. Reprinted (with footnotes and references omitted) in R. E. Baldwin and J. D. Richardson (Eds.), *International Trade and Finance*. Little, Brown and Company, Boston, Mass., 1974.

Gruber, W. H., and R. Vernon (1970). "The Technology Factor in a World Trade Matrix." In R. Vernon (Ed.), *The Technology Factor in International Trade*. Columbia University Press, New York.

Hodd, M. (1967). "An Empirical Investigation of the Heckscher–Ohlin Theory." *Economica*, vol. 34 (February), pp. 20–29.

Horiba, Y. (1974). "General Equilibrium and the Heckscher–Ohlin Theory of Trade: The Multi-Country Case." *International Economic Review*, vol. 15, no. 2 (June), pp. 440–449.

Houthakker, H. S. (1957). "An International Comparison of Household Expenditure Patterns, Commemorating the Centenary of Engel's Law." *Econometrica*, vol. 25 (October), pp. 532–551.

—— (1960). "The Influence of Prices and Incomes on Household Expenditures." *Bulletin de l'Institut International de Statistique*, vol. 37, pp. 9–22.

—— (1963). "Some Problems in the International Comparison of Consumption Patterns." In R. Mossé (Ed.), *L'Evaluation et le Rôle des Besoins de Biens de Consommation dans les Divers Régimes Economiques*. Centre National de la Recherche Scientifique, Paris.

Hufbauer, G. C. (1970). "The Impact of National Characteristics and Technology on the Commodity Composition of Trade in Manufactured Goods." In R. Vernon (Ed.), *The Technology Factor in International Trade*. Columbia University Press, New York.

Johnson, H. G. (1957). "Factor Endowments, International Trade and Factor Prices." *Manchester School of Economics and Social Studies*, vol. 25 (September), pp. 270–283. Reprinted in R. E. Caves and H. G. Johnson (Eds.), *Readings in International Economics*. Richard D. Irwin, Inc., Homewood, Ill., 1968.

Jones, R. W. (1956). "Factor Proportions and the Heckscher–Ohlin Theorem." *Review of Economic Studies*, vol. 24, pp. 1–10.

Keesing, D. B. (1965). "Labor Skills and International Trade: Evaluating Many Trade Flows with a Single Measuring Device." *Review of Economics and Statistics*, vol. 47 (August), pp. 287–294.

—— (1966). "Labor Skills and Comparative Advantage." *American Economic Review*, vol. 56 (May), pp. 249–258. Reprinted in R. E. Baldwin and J. D. Richardson (Eds.), *International Trade and Finance*. Little, Brown and Company, Boston, Mass., 1974.

—— (1967). "The Impact of Research and Development on the United States Trade." *Journal of Political Economy*, vol. 75, no. 1, pp. 38–48. Reprinted in P. B. Kenen and R. Lawrence (Eds.), *The Open Economy*. Columbia University Press, New York, 1968.

—— (1968). "Labor Skills and the Structure of Trade in Manufactures." In P. B. Kenen and R. Lawrence (Eds.), *The Open Economy*. Columbia University Press, New York.

—— (1971). "Different Countries' Labor Skill Coefficients and the Skill Intensity of International Trade Flows." *Journal of International Economics*, vol. 1 (November), pp. 453–460.

Kenen, P. B. (1965). "Nature, Capital and Trade." *Journal of Political Economy*, vol. 73 (October), pp. 437–460.

—— (1970). "Skills, Human Capital, and Comparative Advantage." In W. L. Hansen (Ed.), *Education, Income and Human Capital*. Conference on Research in Income and Wealth, Studies in Income and Wealth, vol. 35, Columbia University Press, New York.

——, and R. Lawrence (1968). *The Open Economy*. Columbia University Press, New York. pts. I and II.

Kravis, I. B. (1956a). "Wages and Foreign Trade." *Review of Economics and Statistics*, vol. 38 (February), pp. 14–30.

—— (1956b). "Availability and Other Influences on the Commodity Composition of Trade." *Journal of Political Economy*, vol. 64 (April), pp. 143–155.

Kreinin, M. E. (1965). "Comparative Labor Effectiveness and the Leontief Scarce Factor Paradox." *American Economic Review*, vol. 55 (March), pp. 131–140.

Lancaster, K. (1957). "The Heckscher–Ohlin Trade Model: A Geometric Treatment." *Economica*, vol. 24, pp. 19–39.

Lary, H. B. (1968). *Imports of Manufactures from Less Developed Countries*. National Bureau of Economic Research, New York.

Leontief, W. W. (1933). "The Use of Indifference Curves in the Analysis of Foreign Trade." *Quarterly Journal of Economics*, vol. 47 (May), pp. 493–503. Reprinted in H. S. Ellis and L. A. Metzler (Eds.), *Readings in the Theory of International Trade*. R. D. Irwin, Inc., Homewood, Ill., 1950.

—— (1953). "Domestic Production and Foreign Trade; the American Positioned Re-examined." *Proceedings of the American Philosophical Society*, vol. 97 (September), pp. 332–349. Reprinted in H. G. Johnson and R. E. Caves (Eds.), *Readings in International Economics*. Richard D. Irwin, Inc., Homewood, Ill., 1968.

—— (1956). "Factor Proportions and the Structure of American Trade: Further Theoretical and Empirical Analysis." *Review of Economics and Statistics*, vol. 38 (November), pp. 386–407.

—— (1964). "An International Comparison of Factor Costs and Factor Use." *American Economic Review*, vol. 54 (June), pp. 335–345.

Linder, S. B. (1961). *An Essay on Trade and Transformation*. Almqvist and Wiksell, Stockholm.

MacDougall, G. D. A. (1951). "British and American Exports: A Study Suggested by the Theory of Comparative Costs." *Economic Journal*, vol. 61, pp. 697–724. Reprinted in H. G. Johnson and R. E. Caves (Eds.), *Readings in International Economics*. Richard D. Irwin, Inc., Homewood, Ill., 1968.

Minhas, B. S. (1962). "The Homohypallagic Production Function, Factor-Intensity Reversals, and the Heckscher–Ohlin Theorem." *Journal of Political Economy*, vol. 60 (April), pp. 138–156.

—— (1963). *An International Comparison of Factor Costs and Factor Use*. North-Holland Publishing Company, Amsterdam.

Ohlin, B. (1933). *Interregional and International Trade*. Harvard University Press, Cambridge, Mass.

Philpot, G. (1970). "Labor Quality, Returns to Scale and the Elasticity of Factor Substitution." *Review of Economics and Statistics*, vol. 52 (May), pp. 194–199.

Robinson, R. (1956). "Factor Proportions and Comparative Advantage." *Quarterly Journal of Economics*, vol. LXX, no. 2 (May), pp. 169–192. Reprinted in H. G. Johnson and R. E. Caves (Eds.), *Readings in International Economics*. Richard D. Irwin, Inc., Homewood, Ill., 1968.

Stern, R. M. (1975). "Testing Trade Theories." In P. B. Kenen (Ed.), *International Trade and Finance*. Cambridge University Press, New York.

Stolper, W., and K. Roskamp (1961). "Input-Output Table for East Germany with Applications to Foreign Trade." *Bulletin of the Oxford University Institute of Statistics*, vol. 23 (November), pp. 379–392.

Swerling, B. C. (1954). "Capital Shortage and Labor Surplus in the United States?" *Review of Economics and Statistics*, vol. 36 (August), pp. 286–289.

Tarshis, L. (1959). "Factor Inputs and International Price Comparison." In M. Abramovitz et al. (Eds.), *Allocation of Economic Resources*. Stanford University Press, Stanford, Calif., pp. 236–244.

Tatemoto, M., and S. Ichimura (1959). "Factor Proportions and Foreign Trade: The Case of Japan." *Review of Economics and Statistics*, vol. 41 (November), pp. 442–446.

Travis, W. P. (1964). *The Theory of Trade and Protection*. Harvard University Press, Cambridge, Mass.

———— (1972). "Production, Trade, and Protection When There Are Many Commodities and Two Factors." *American Economic Review*, vol. LXII, no. 1 (March), pp. 87–106.

Valavanis-Vail, S. (1954). "Leontief's Scarce Factor Paradox." *Journal of Political Economy*, vol. 52 (December), pp. 523–528.

Vanek, J. (1959). "The Natural Resource Content of Foreign Trade, 1870–1955, and the Relative Abundance of Natural Resources in the United States." *Review of Economics and Statistics*, vol. 41 (May), pp. 146–153.

———— (1963). *The Natural Resource Content of United States Foreign Trade 1870–1955*. The MIT Press, Cambridge, Mass.

Vernon, R. (1966). "International Investment and International Trade in the Product Cycle." *Quarterly Journal of Economics*, vol. 80, (May), pp. 190–207.

———— (Ed.) (1970). *The Technology Factor in International Trade*. Columbia University Press, New York.

Waehrer, H. (1968). "Wage Rates, Labor Skills, and United States Foreign Trade." In P. B. Kenen and R. Lawrence (Eds.), *The Open Economy*. Columbia University Press, New York.

Wahl, D. F. (1961). "Capital and Labour Requirements for Canada's Foreign Trade." *Canadian Journal of Economics and Political Science*, vol. 27 (August), pp. 349–358.

Weiser, L., and K. Jay (1972). "Determinants of the Commodity Structure of U.S. Trade: Comment." *American Economic Review*, vol. LXII, no. 3 (June), pp. 459–464.

Wells, L. T., Jr. (1968). "A Product Life Cycle for International Trade?" *Journal of Marketing*, vol. 32 (July), pp. 1–6. Reprinted (with footnotes omitted) in R. E. Baldwin and J. D. Richardson (Eds.), *International Trade and Finance*. Little, Brown and Company, Boston, 1974.

———— (1969). "Test of a Product Cycle Model of International Trade: U.S. Exports of Consumer Durables." *Quarterly Journal of Economics*, vol. 82 (February), pp. 152–162.

Yahr, M. I. (1968). "Human Capital and Factor Substitution in the CES Production Function." In P. B. Kenen and R. Lawrence (Eds.), *The Open Economy*. Columbia University Press, New York.

# PART FIVE

ECONOMIC GROWTH
AND TRADE

# TWELVE

# THE EFFECTS OF ECONOMIC GROWTH ON TRADE

The preceding chapters are limited by the assumption that the two fundamental data which delimit the production-possibilities frontier, namely, factor endowments and technology, are given. But in the real world, neither factor endowments nor technology remain static. With the passage of time, factor endowments grow and new and more efficient methods of production replace old and inefficient ones. Factor-endowment growth and technical progress give rise to some interesting economic problems, the study of which forms the *theory of the effects of economic growth on trade.*

We shall now be concerned with the *comparative static analysis* of the effects of labor growth and capital accumulation, on the one hand, and technical progress, on the other, on the growing country's consumption, production, demand for imports, supply of exports, terms of trade, factor prices, and social welfare. The major architect of this analysis is Johnson (1958), though the idea of export and import bias originated with Hicks' (1953) article on the long-run dollar problem. In addition, contributions have been made by Bhagwati (1958), Corden (1956), Findlay and Grubert (1959), and Rybczynski (1955).

This chapter deals with the effects of economic growth. It is divided into two parts. Part A discusses the effects of growth on the small country, and part B generalizes the analysis to the large country. The discussion is rather general in the sense that it does not distinguish among the three main sources of economic growth: labor growth, capital accumulation, and technical progress.

## PART A. THE EFFECTS OF GROWTH ON THE SMALL COUNTRY

Let us begin our analysis with a discussion of the effects of economic growth on a small country which is a price taker in the international market. To simplify, assume that the units of measurement of commodities $X$ and $Y$ are such that the given international price ratio, $p_x/p_y$, is unity. Needless to say, this is not a crucial assumption—it is merely convenient.

## 12.1 DEFINITIONS

The main sources of economic growth are labor growth, capital accumulation, and technical progress. Their common characteristic is that they cause the production-possibilities frontier of the growing economy to shift outward through time. In the next chapter, we have to distinguish among these three sources of economic growth. For present purposes, it suffices to concentrate on the resultant outward shift of the production-possibilities frontier and study its effects on the consumption and production patterns of the growing economy, as well as its volume of trade, at the initial terms of trade.

### Average Propensities

Assume that our simple economy is in long-run equilibrium. In particular, assume that at this initial equilibrium our economy produces $X_p$ units of $X$ (exportables) and $Y_p$ units of $Y$ (importables), consumes $X_c$ units of $X$ and $Y_c$ units of $Y$, and exports $Z \equiv X_p - X_c$ units of $X$ in exchange for $M \equiv Y_c - Y_p$ units of $Y$. Therefore, the real national income, $Q$, of our economy (expressed in terms of either commodity) is given by

$$Q = X_p + Y_p = X_c + Y_c \tag{12.1}$$

and the volume of trade, $V$, by

$$V = M = Y_c - Y_p = Z = X_p - X_c \tag{12.2}$$

Let us now introduce the following definitions:

$$\text{Average propensity to produce exportables} \equiv \frac{X_p}{Q} \equiv \theta_x^p$$

$$\text{Average propensity to produce importables} \equiv \frac{Y_p}{Q} \equiv \theta_y^p$$

$$\text{Average propensity to consume exportables} \equiv \frac{X_c}{Q} \equiv \theta_x^c$$

$$\text{Average propensity to consume importables} \equiv \frac{Y_c}{Q} \equiv \theta_y^c$$

$$\text{Average propensity to import importables} \equiv \frac{M}{Q} \equiv \theta_m$$

$$\text{Average propensity to export exportables} \equiv \frac{Z}{Q} \equiv \theta_z$$

$$\text{Average propensity to trade} \equiv \frac{V}{Q} \equiv \theta_v$$

The meaning of subscripts and superscripts is as follows: $\theta$ = average propensity, $p$ = production, $c$ = consumption, $x$ = exportables, $y$ = importables, $m$ = imports, $z$ = exports, and $v$ = volume of trade.

Given the above definitions and eqs. (12.1) and (12.2), we can easily formulate the following relationships:

$$\theta_x^p + \theta_y^p \equiv \theta_x^c + \theta_y^c \equiv 1 \tag{12.3}$$

(by dividing all terms in eqs. (12.1) by $Q$) and

$$\theta_v \equiv \theta_m \equiv \theta_y^c - \theta_y^p \equiv \theta_z \equiv \theta_x^p - \theta_x^c \tag{12.4}$$

(by dividing all terms in eqs. (12.2) by $Q$).

## Marginal Propensities

Suppose now that our economy's production-possibilities frontier shifts outward. Given sufficient time, our economy will reach a new equilibrium. At the new equilibrium, our economy will produce, consume, export, and import different amounts from the corresponding amounts at the initial equilibrium. What follows concerns the differences between the new and the old quantities. Using the operator $\Delta$ to indicate the difference between the value of a certain variable at the new equilibrium and its value at the initial equilibrium, we can write $\Delta X_p$ for the "difference in $X_p$," $\Delta X_c$ for the "difference in $X_c$," and so on. (Assume that at the new equilibrium our economy continues to export $X$ and import $Y$.) Thus, using the superscripts 0 and 1 to indicate the values at the initial equilibrium and the new one, respectively, we have

$$\Delta Q = Q^1 - Q^0 \qquad \Delta X_p = X_p^1 - X_p^0$$

$$\Delta Y_p = Y_p^1 - Y_p^0 \qquad \Delta X_c = X_c^1 - X_c^0$$

$$\Delta Y_c = Y_c^1 - Y_c^0 \qquad \Delta V = V^1 - V^0$$

$$\Delta M = M^1 - M^0 \qquad \Delta Z = Z^1 - Z^0$$

Since eqs. (12.1) and (12.2) must hold at both equilibria, the following equations must be true:

$$\Delta Q = \Delta X_p + \Delta Y_p = \Delta X_c + \Delta Y_c \tag{12.5}$$

$$\Delta V = \Delta M = \Delta Y_c - \Delta Y_p = \Delta Z = \Delta X_p - \Delta X_c \tag{12.6}$$

Let us now introduce the following definitions:

$$\text{Marginal propensity to produce exportables} \equiv \frac{\Delta X_p}{\Delta Q} \equiv \xi_x^p$$

$$\text{Marginal propensity to produce importables} \equiv \frac{\Delta Y_p}{\Delta Q} \equiv \xi_y^p$$

$$\text{Marginal propensity to consume exportables} \equiv \frac{\Delta X_c}{\Delta Q} \equiv \xi_x^c$$

$$\text{Marginal propensity to consume importables} \equiv \frac{\Delta Y_c}{\Delta Q} \equiv \xi_y^c$$

$$\text{Marginal propensity to import importables} \equiv \frac{\Delta M}{\Delta Q} \equiv \xi_m$$

$$\text{Marginal propensity to export exportables} \equiv \frac{\Delta Z}{\Delta Q} \equiv \xi_z$$

$$\text{Marginal propensity to trade} \equiv \frac{\Delta V}{\Delta Q} \equiv \xi_v$$

The Greek letter $\xi$ stands for marginal propensity.

Dividing all terms of eqs. (12.5) by $\Delta Q$ and applying the preceding definitions, we get

$$\xi_x^p + \xi_y^p = \xi_x^c + \xi_y^c = 1 \tag{12.7}$$

Dividing all terms of eqs. (12.6) by $\Delta Q$ and applying the preceding definitions, we get

$$\xi_v = \xi_m = \xi_y^c - \xi_y^p = \xi_z = \xi_x^p - \xi_x^c \tag{12.8}$$

## Rates of Growth†

The literature on growth makes use of some additional concepts, namely, "rates of growth" and "output elasticities." The various rates of growth are defined as follows:

$$\text{Rate of growth of output} \equiv \frac{\Delta Q}{Q^0} \equiv \lambda_q$$

$$\text{Rate of growth of production of exportables} \equiv \frac{\Delta X_p}{X_p^0} \equiv \lambda_x^p$$

$$\text{Rate of growth of production of importables} \equiv \frac{\Delta Y_p}{Y_p^0} \equiv \lambda_y^p$$

---

† This subsection, and also the following two, may be omitted.

$$\text{Rate of growth of consumption of exportables} \equiv \frac{\Delta X_c}{X_c^0} \equiv \lambda_x^c$$

$$\text{Rate of growth of consumption of importables} \equiv \frac{\Delta Y_c}{Y_c^0} \equiv \lambda_y^c$$

$$\text{Rate of growth of imports (of importables)} \equiv \frac{\Delta M}{M^0} \equiv \lambda_m$$

$$\text{Rate of growth of exports (of exportables)} \equiv \frac{\Delta Z}{Z^0} \equiv \lambda_z$$

$$\text{Rate of growth of (the volume of) trade} \equiv \frac{\Delta V}{V^0} \equiv \lambda_v$$

The Greek letter $\lambda$ stands for rate of growth.

Given eqs. (12.2) and (12.6) and applying the preceding definitions, we get

$$\lambda_v \equiv \lambda_m \equiv \lambda_z \tag{12.9}$$

## Output Elasticities†

The definitions of output elasticities are as follows:

$$\text{Output elasticity of supply of exportables} \equiv \frac{\Delta X_p}{\Delta Q}\frac{Q^0}{X_p^0} \equiv \eta_x^p$$

$$\text{Output elasticity of supply of importables} \equiv \frac{\Delta Y_p}{\Delta Q}\frac{Q^0}{Y_p^0} \equiv \eta_y^p$$

$$\text{Output elasticity of demand for exportables} \equiv \frac{\Delta X_c}{\Delta Q}\frac{Q^0}{X_c^0} \equiv \eta_x^c$$

$$\text{Output elasticity of demand for importables} \equiv \frac{\Delta Y_c}{\Delta Q}\frac{Q^0}{Y_c^0} \equiv \eta_y^c$$

$$\text{Output elasticity of demand for imports} \equiv \frac{\Delta M}{\Delta Q}\frac{Q^0}{M^0} \equiv \eta_m$$

$$\text{Output elasticity of supply of exports} \equiv \frac{\Delta Z}{\Delta Q}\frac{Q^0}{Z^0} \equiv \eta_z$$

$$\text{Output elasticity of (the volume of) trade} \equiv \frac{\Delta V}{\Delta Q}\frac{Q^0}{V^0} \equiv \eta_v$$

The Greek letter $\eta$ stands for output elasticity.

We now have

$$\eta_v = \eta_m = \eta_z \tag{12.10}$$

which corresponds to eq. (12.9).

† This subsection may be omitted.

### Some Important Relationships†

The relationships among marginal propensities, average propensities, rates of growth, and output elasticities are simple and can be summarized as follows:

$$\frac{\text{Marginal propensity}}{\text{Average propensity}} = \frac{\text{rate of growth}}{\text{rate of growth of output}} = \text{output elasticity}$$

This equation follows directly from the definitions. Thus,

$$\lambda_x^p \equiv \frac{\Delta X_p}{X_p^0} = \frac{\Delta X_p}{\Delta Q} \frac{Q^0}{X_p^0} \frac{\Delta Q}{Q^0} = \frac{\xi_x^p}{\theta_x^p} \lambda_q = \eta_x^p \lambda_q \tag{12.11}$$

$$\lambda_x^c \equiv \frac{\Delta X_c}{X_c^0} = \frac{\Delta X_c}{\Delta Q} \frac{Q^0}{X_c^0} \frac{\Delta Q}{Q^0} = \frac{\xi_x^c}{\theta_x^c} \lambda_q = \eta_x^c \lambda_q \tag{12.12}$$

$$\lambda_y^p \equiv \frac{\Delta Y_p}{Y_p^0} = \frac{\Delta Y_p}{\Delta Q} \frac{Q^0}{Y_p^0} \frac{\Delta Q}{Q^0} = \frac{\xi_y^p}{\theta_y^p} \lambda_q = \eta_y^p \lambda_q \tag{12.13}$$

$$\lambda_y^c \equiv \frac{\Delta Y_c}{Y_c^0} = \frac{\Delta Y_c}{\Delta Q} \frac{Q^0}{Y_c^0} \frac{\Delta Q}{Q^0} = \frac{\xi_y^c}{\theta_y^c} \lambda_q = \eta_y^c \lambda_q \tag{12.14}$$

$$\lambda_m \equiv \frac{\Delta M}{M^0} = \frac{\Delta M}{\Delta Q} \frac{Q^0}{M^0} \frac{\Delta Q}{Q^0} = \frac{\xi_m}{\theta_m} \lambda_q = \eta_m \lambda_q \tag{12.15}$$

$$\lambda_z \equiv \frac{\Delta Z}{Z^0} = \frac{\Delta Z}{\Delta Q} \frac{Q^0}{Z^0} \frac{\Delta Q}{Q^0} = \frac{\xi_z}{\theta_z} \lambda_q = \eta_z \lambda_q \tag{12.16}$$

$$\lambda_v \equiv \frac{\Delta V}{V^0} = \frac{\Delta V}{\Delta Q} \frac{Q^0}{V^0} \frac{\Delta Q}{Q^0} = \frac{\xi_v}{\theta_v} \lambda_q = \eta_v \lambda_q \tag{12.17}$$

The rate of growth of output $\lambda_q$ is a weighted average of the rate of growth of production of exportables $\lambda_x^p$ and the rate of growth of production of importables $\lambda_y^p$. In addition, $\lambda_q$ is a weighted average of the rate of growth of consumption of exportables $\lambda_x^c$ and the rate of growth of consumption of importables $\lambda_y^c$. These statements can be proved as follows:

$$\lambda_q \equiv \frac{\Delta Q}{Q^0} = \frac{\Delta X_p + \Delta Y_p}{Q^0} = \frac{X_p^0}{Q^0} \frac{\Delta X_p}{X_p^0} + \frac{Y_p^0}{Q^0} \frac{\Delta Y_p}{Y_p^0} = \theta_x^p \lambda_x^p + \theta_y^p \lambda_y^p \tag{12.18}$$

$$\lambda_q \equiv \frac{\Delta Q}{Q^0} = \frac{\Delta X_c + \Delta Y_c}{Q^0} = \frac{X_c^0}{Q^0} \frac{\Delta X_c}{X_c^0} + \frac{Y_c^0}{Q^0} \frac{\Delta Y_c}{Y_c^0} = \theta_x^c \lambda_x^c + \theta_y^c \lambda_y^c \tag{12.19}$$

Since all average propensities are positive and less than unity, it follows from eqs. (12.3) and (12.18) that $\lambda_q$ is a weighted average of $\lambda_x^p$ and $\lambda_y^p$, and from eqs. (12.3) and (12.19) that $\lambda_q$ is a weighted average of $\lambda_x^c$ and $\lambda_y^c$. Hence, $\lambda_q$ must always lie between $\lambda_x^p$ and $\lambda_y^p$, and between $\lambda_x^c$ and $\lambda_y^c$.

---

† This subsection may be omitted.

The rate of growth of production of exportables $\lambda_x^p$ is a weighted average of the rate of growth of the volume of trade $\lambda_v$ and the rate of growth of consumption of exportables $\lambda_x^c$. This is proved as follows:

$$\lambda_v = \lambda_z = \frac{\Delta Z}{Z^0} = \frac{\Delta X_p - \Delta X_c}{X_p^0 - X_c^0} = \frac{(\Delta X_p / X_p^0) - [(\Delta X_c / X_c^0)(X_c^0 / X_p^0)]}{1 - (X_c^0 / X_p^0)}$$

$$= \frac{\lambda_x^p - \lambda_x^c (X_c^0 / X_p^0)}{1 - (X_c^0 / X_p^0)}$$

or
$$\lambda_x^p = \left(1 - \frac{X_c^0}{X_p^0}\right)\lambda_v + \frac{X_c^0}{X_p^0}\lambda_x^c \qquad (12.20)$$

Since $0 < X_c^0 / X_p^0 < 1$, $\lambda_x^p$ is a weighted average of $\lambda_v$ and $\lambda_x^c$, and its value must always lie between $\lambda_v$ and $\lambda_x^c$.

The rate of growth of consumption of importables $\lambda_y^c$ is a weighted average of the rate of growth of the volume of trade $\lambda_v$ and the rate of growth of production of importables $\lambda_y^p$. Therefore, $\lambda_y^c$ must always lie between $\lambda_v$ and $\lambda_y^p$. This can be proved as follows:

$$\lambda_v = \lambda_m = \frac{\Delta M}{M^0} = \frac{\Delta Y_c - \Delta Y_p}{Y_c^0 - Y_p^0} = \frac{(\Delta Y_c / Y_c^0) - [(\Delta Y_p / Y_p^0)(Y_p^0 / Y_c^0)]}{1 - (Y_p^0 / Y_c^0)}$$

$$= \frac{\lambda_y^c - \lambda_y^p (Y_p^0 / Y_c^0)}{1 - (Y_p^0 / Y_c^0)}$$

or
$$\lambda_y^c = \left(1 - \frac{Y_p^0}{Y_c^0}\right)\lambda_v + \frac{Y_p^0}{Y_c^0}\lambda_y^p \qquad (12.21)$$

Our statement follows when we observe that $0 < Y_p^0 / Y_c^0 < 1$.

## 12.2 GROWTH UNDER CLASSICAL ASSUMPTIONS (COMPLETE SPECIALIZATION)

Turn now to the effects of economic growth on the growing country's consumption, production, demand for imports, and supply of exports. Recall that our growing economy is a simple open economy, i.e., it can trade unlimited amounts of $X$ and $Y$ at given international prices. Again, assume for convenience that the given international price ratio is unity. Even in this simple case, it is useful to distinguish between the classical theory, where the production-possibilities frontier is linear and our economy specializes completely in the production of exportables, and the neoclassical and modern theories, where the production-possibilities frontier is concave to the origin (implying increasing opportunity costs) and our economy produces both commodities before and after growth. This section considers the classical case (or the case of complete specialization) and the following section the neoclassical-modern case (or the case of incomplete specialization).

## The Initial Equilibrium

Figure 12.1 illustrates the general nature of the effects of growth on production, consumption, demand for imports, and supply of exports in the classical case. The 45° straight line $P_1 K_1$ is the original consumption-possibilities frontier, with production taking place at point $P_1$ and consumption at $C_1$. Therefore, our economy is assumed to be specializing in the production of $X$, exporting $X_1 P_1$ units of $X$ in exchange for $X_1 C_1$ units of $Y$. The absolute slope of the consumption-possibilities frontier $K_1 P_1$ is unity, which is consistent with our assumption that the given international price ratio is unity.

At the initial, pregrowth equilibrium, the average propensity to produce exportables, and so on, can be measured as follows:

$$\theta_x^p = \frac{OP_1}{OP_1} = 1 \qquad\qquad \theta_x^c = \frac{OX_1}{OP_1} < 1$$

$$\theta_y^p = \frac{\text{zero}}{OP_1} = 0 \qquad\qquad \theta_y^c = \frac{OY_1}{OK_1} = \frac{X_1 P_1}{OP_1} < 1$$

$$\theta_m = \theta_z = \theta_v = \frac{X_1 P_1}{OP_1} = \frac{OY_1}{OK_1}$$

In addition, we can verify eqs. (12.3) and (12.4) thus:

$$\theta_x^p + \theta_y^p = 1 + 0 = 1$$

$$\theta_x^c + \theta_y^c = \frac{OX_1}{OP_1} + \frac{X_1 P_1}{OP_1} = \frac{OP_1}{OP_1} = 1$$

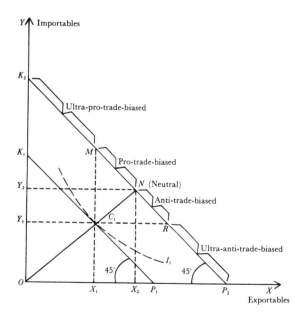

Exportables    **Figure 12.1** The effects of growth.

$$\theta_y^c - \theta_y^p = \frac{X_1 P_1}{O P_1} - 0 = \frac{X_1 P_1}{O P_1} = \theta_v$$

$$\theta_x^p - \theta_x^c = 1 - \frac{O X_1}{O P_1} = \frac{O P_1 - O X_1}{O P_1} = \frac{X_1 P_1}{O P_1} = \theta_v$$

## The Outward Shift of the Production-Possibilities Frontier

With economic growth the production-possibilities frontier (not drawn) shifts outward. What happens to the optimum production point depends on exactly how the production-possibilities frontier shifts outward. Figure 12.1 is based on the implicit assumption that, after the production-possibilities frontier shifts outward, the country continues to enjoy a comparative advantage in the production of commodity $X$. In the classical theory, this is always the case when economic growth is due to labor growth. However, if growth is due to technical progress, this need not be so. Thus, if technical progress is heavily biased in favor of commodity $Y$ (that is, if $Y$'s labor coefficient, $a_y$, falls faster than $X$'s labor coefficient, $a_x$, through time), the comparative advantage of the country may very well shift from $X$ to $Y$. To simplify, disregard the latter possibility.

Since, by assumption, the country continues to enjoy a comparative advantage in the production of $X$ after the production-possibilities frontier shifts outward, it must continue to specialize completely in the production of $X$. Accordingly, the optimum production point shifts to the right along the horizontal axis. This is illustrated in fig. 12.1 by the shift of the production point from $P_1$ to $P_2$. As a result, the new consumption-possibilities frontier is given by the straight line $K_2 P_2$, which is parallel to $K_1 P_1$ because of the assumed constancy of the international price ratio. With no further information about demand, the only statement that can be made about the new consumption point is that it will lie somewhere on the postgrowth consumption-possibilities frontier, $K_2 P_2$. However, the region $K_2 M$ implies "inferiority" in $X$, and the region $R P_2$, "inferiority" in $Y$. If we wish to exclude inferiority by assumption, we can restrict the consumption point to the region $MNR$. We shall return to this point shortly.

## Marginal Propensities and Rates of Growth

Even with no further information on the postgrowth position of the optimum consumption point, several propensities and rates of growth can be determined merely with the information that the production point shifts from $P_1$ to $P_2$. Thus, we can determine the marginal propensity to produce exportables $\xi_x^p$, the marginal propensity to produce importables $\xi_y^p$, the rate of growth of output $\lambda_q$, the output elasticity of supply of exportables $\eta_x^p$, and the rate of growth of production of exportables $\lambda_x^p$ as follows:

$$\xi_x^p \equiv \frac{\Delta X_p}{\Delta Q} = \frac{P_1 P_2}{P_1 P_2} = 1$$

$$\xi_y^p \equiv \frac{\Delta Y_p}{\Delta Q} = \frac{\text{zero}}{P_1 P_2} = 0$$

$$\lambda_q \equiv \frac{\Delta Q}{Q^0} = \frac{P_1 P_2}{OP_1} = \frac{K_1 K_2}{OK_1} = \frac{C_1 N}{OC_1}$$

$$\eta_x^p \equiv \frac{\Delta X_p}{\Delta Q} \frac{Q^0}{X_p^0} = \frac{P_1 P_2}{P_1 P_2} \frac{OP_1}{OP_1} = 1$$

$$\lambda_x^p \equiv \frac{\Delta X_p}{X_p^0} = \frac{P_1 P_2}{OP_1}$$

We can verify eq. (12.11) as follows:

$$\eta_x^p \lambda_q = 1 \frac{P_1 P_2}{OP_1} = \lambda_x^p$$

## Types of Growth

What is the effect of economic growth on the growing country's relative dependency on trade as revealed by the average propensity to trade? In other words, does growth tend to increase or decrease the average propensity to trade $\theta_v$?

When growth does not affect the average propensity to trade (i.e., when the average propensity to trade remains constant), the growth is *neutral*. When the average propensity to trade tends to increase with growth, the growth is *protrade biased*. When the average propensity to trade tends to fall, the growth is *antitrade biased*. We can predict whether the average propensity to trade increases, decreases, or remains constant with growth by comparing the pregrowth *average* propensity to trade $\theta_v$ with the *marginal* propensity to trade $\xi_v$. Thus, if $\xi_v > \theta_v$, then $\theta_v$ must be increasing; if $\xi_v < \theta_v$, then $\theta_v$ must be decreasing; and if $\xi_v = \theta_v$, then $\theta_v$ must remain constant. Accordingly, neutral growth occurs when $\xi_v = \theta_v$; protrade-biased growth occurs when $\xi_v > \theta_v$; and antitrade-biased growth occurs when $\xi_v < \theta_v$.

Two extreme cases of growth can be distinguished: *ultra-protrade-biased growth*, in which $\xi_v > 1$ (implying that the absolute increase in the volume of trade, $\Delta V$, is larger than the absolute increase in national income, $\Delta Q$, so that the growing country becomes absolutely less self-sufficient); and *ultra-antitrade-biased growth*, in which $\xi_v < 0$ (implying that the absolute volume of trade actually falls, that is, $\Delta V < 0$, so that the growing country becomes absolutely more self-sufficient).

## Graphical Illustration

Figure 12.2 (a) and (b) illustrate the five types of growth. Figure 12.2(a) measures horizontally the value of output produced ($Q$), and vertically the value of the volume of trade ($V$). At any equilibrium state, the equilibrium values of $Q$ and $V$ are represented by the coordinates of a point below and to the right of the 45° line ($OR$). At the pregrowth equilibrium state, our economy's position is at point $E$. The average propensity to trade is shown by the slope of the vector $OE$. Assume now that the economy grows and its national income increases from $Q^0$ to $Q^1$. If point $E$ moves along the vector $ON$, then growth is neutral ($N$); if $E$ moves to the

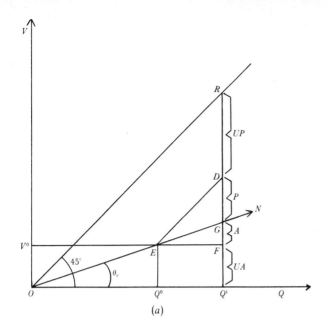

(a)

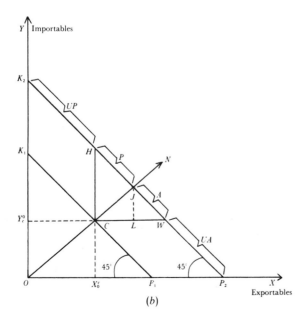

(b)

**Figure 12.2** (a) The five types of growth. (b) The five types of growth and the classification of the consumption effect.

**Table 12.1 Classification of growth**

| Type of growth | Range of the marginal propensity to trade $\xi_v$ (1) | Range of the rate of growth of the volume of trade $\lambda_v$ $\lambda_v = (\xi_v/\theta_v)\lambda_q$ (2) | Range of the output elasticity of the volume of trade $\eta_v$ $\eta_v = \xi_v/\theta_v$ (3) |
|---|---|---|---|
| Neutral | $\xi_v = \theta_v$ | $\lambda_v = \lambda_q$ | $\eta_v = 1$ |
| Protrade biased | $\theta_v < \xi_v < 1$ | $\lambda_q < \lambda_v < (1/\theta_v)\lambda_q$ | $1 < \eta_v < 1/\theta_v$ |
| Ultra-protrade biased | $\xi_v > 1 > \theta_v$ | $\lambda_v > (1/\theta_v)\lambda_q$ | $1/\theta_v < \eta_v$ |
| Antitrade biased | $0 < \xi_v < \theta_v$ | $0 < \lambda_v < \lambda_q$ | $0 < \eta_v < 1$ |
| Ultra-antitrade biased | $\xi_v < 0 < \theta_v$ | $\lambda_v < 0 < \lambda_q$ | $\eta_v < 0$ |

region $GD$ (where the line $ED$ is parallel to $OR$), then growth is protrade biased ($P$); if $E$ moves to the region $DR$, then growth is ultra-protrade biased ($UP$); if $E$ moves to the region $FG$, then growth is antitrade biased ($A$); and if $E$ moves to the region $Q^1F$, growth is ultra-antitrade biased ($UA$).

Figure 12.2($b$), similar to fig. 12.1, illustrates the five types of growth in terms of the familiar diagram of the consumption-possibilities frontier. Before growth, the economy produces at $P_1$ and consumes at $C$; after growth, the economy produces at $P_2$ and the consumption point can lie, in general, anywhere on the new consumption-possibilities frontier, $K_2 P_2$. If $C$ moves along the vector $ON$, growth is neutral; if $C$ moves to the region $HJ$, growth is protrade biased; if $C$ moves to the region $K_2 H$, growth is ultra-protrade biased; if $C$ moves to the region $JW$, growth is antitrade biased; and if $C$ moves to the region $WP_2$, growth is ultra-antitrade biased. These conclusions follow when we note that $\Delta X_p = \Delta Q = P_1 P_2 = CW = CH$, $V^0 = OY_c^0 = X_c^0 C$, and $\Delta V$ is given by the vertical distance from the postgrowth consumption point to the horizontal line $Y_c^0 CW$. Thus, in the region $K_2 H$, $\Delta V > \Delta Q$ (or $\xi_v > 1$); and in the region $WP_2$, $\Delta V < 0$ (or $\xi_v < 0$). Further, if $C$ moves to $J$, we have

$$\xi_v \equiv \frac{\Delta V}{\Delta Q} = \frac{LJ}{CW} = \frac{X_c^0 C}{OP_1} = \frac{V_0}{Q^0} = \theta_v$$

From this, it follows that if $C$ moves to the region $HJ$, we have $1 > \xi_v > \theta_v$ (because $LJ < \Delta V < \Delta Q = CH$); and if $C$ moves to the region $JW$, we have $0 < \xi_v < \theta_v$ (because $LJ > \Delta V > 0$). The preceding conclusions are conveniently summarized in table 12.1.

## Classification of Growth in Terms of the Rate of Growth and the Output Elasticity of the Volume of Trade†

Because of the strict relationship which exists between the marginal and average propensities to trade and the rates of growth of the volume of trade and output,

---

† This subsection may be omitted. If the reader omitted the definitions of rates of growth and output elasticities given in sec. 12.1 above, he must omit this subsection also.

the classification of growth into five types can be accomplished in terms of the rate of growth of the volume of trade. Accordingly, column (2) of table 12.1 gives the appropriate range of the rate of growth of the volume of trade for each type of growth. This follows from the entries in column (1) and from eq. (12.17), which is partially reproduced in the heading of column (2) for convenience. Similarly, column (3) gives the range of the output elasticity of the volume of trade $\eta_v$ for each type of growth. Again, the results follow from either column (1) or column (2) and the equation $\eta_v = \xi_v/\theta_v$. The three alternate ways of classifying growth into its five types, as given in table 12.1, can be used in any particular situation.

It is interesting to note that, in the classical case of complete specialization in exportables before and after trade, where $\theta_y^p = \xi_y^p = 0$, we necessarily have $\xi_v = \xi_y^c - \xi_y^p = \xi_y^c$ and $\theta_v = \theta_y^c - \theta_y^p = \theta_y^c$, where eqs. (12.8) and (12.4), respectively, are used. Accordingly, growth can be classified, in this case, in terms of the marginal propensity and the average propensity to consume importables. The same classification can be made in terms of the output elasticity of demand for importables $\eta_y^c$, since $\eta_y^c = \xi_y^c/\theta_y^c = \eta_v$, and in terms of the rate of growth of consumption of importables $\lambda_y^c$, since $\lambda_y^c = \eta_y^c \lambda_q = \eta_v \lambda_q = \lambda_v$.

## 12.3 NEOCLASSICAL AND MODERN THEORIES (INCOMPLETE SPECIALIZATION)

Within the context of the classical theory, the growing country necessarily specializes completely in the production of exportables before and after trade. In other words, economic growth causes the optimum production point to slide along the axis of exportables. As we have seen, this implies that $\theta_y^p = \xi_y^p = 0$, $\xi_v = \xi_y^c - \xi_y^p = \xi_y^c$, and $\theta_v = \theta_y^c - \theta_y^p = \theta_y^c$. As a result, growth can be classified (within the context of complete specialization) in terms of the marginal propensity to consume importables $\xi_y^c$ and the average propensity to consume importables $\theta_y^c$, that is, in terms only of the consumption behavior of the growing country.

However, when the assumption of constant opportunity costs is replaced by the assumption of increasing costs, the classification of growth becomes more difficult. For, in general, increasing opportunity costs imply incomplete specialization, and the classification of growth necessarily depends on the behavior of both the optimum consumption point and the optimum production point. Put differently, the marginal propensity to trade $\xi_v$ is given by the difference $(\xi_y^c - \xi_y^p)$. Unlike the classical case of complete specialization where $\xi_y^p = 0$, in the present case $\xi_y^p \neq 0$ in general. Therefore, the value of $\xi_v$ (and thus the type of growth) cannot be predicted from the knowledge of the marginal propensity to consume importables $\xi_y^c$ alone. We need to know, in addition to $\xi_y^c$, the value of the marginal propensity to produce importables $\xi_y^p$. Therefore, in the case of incomplete specialization, the effect of growth on the volume of trade (and thus the classification of growth) depends on the combined behavior of consumption and production. For analytical purposes, it is convenient to consider separately the effects on the country's volume of trade of the consumption and production shifts associated with growth, before considering their combined effect.

As explained earlier, economic growth results in an outward shift of the production-possibilities frontier. This causes the consumption-possibilities frontier to shift outward in a parallel fashion. Since consumption necessarily takes place on the consumption-possibilities frontier and the latter is also tangent to the production-possibilities frontier at the equilibrium production point, only the pregrowth and postgrowth consumption-possibilities frontiers are needed for the classification of the consumption and production effects.

## The Consumption Effect

The consumption effect is *neutral* when growth leaves the average propensity to consume importables $\theta_y^c$ constant; when the average propensity to consume importables $\theta_y^c$ tends to increase with growth, the consumption effect is *protrade biased*; and when $\theta_y^c$ tends to fall with growth, the consumption effect is *antitrade biased*. Accordingly, when $\xi_y^c = \theta_y^c$, the consumption effect is neutral; when $\xi_y^c > \theta_y^c$, it is protrade biased; and when $\xi_y^c < \theta_y^c$, it is antitrade biased. In addition, there are two extreme cases: *ultra-protrade biased* (consumption effect), in which $\xi_y^c > 1$ (implying that the absolute increase in the consumption of importables, $\Delta Y_c$, is larger than the absolute increase in national income, $\Delta Q$); and *ultra-antitrade biased* (consumption effect), in which $\xi_y^c < 0$ (implying that the domestic consumption of importables falls absolutely, that is, $\Delta Y_c < 0$).

The above classification of the consumption effect coincides with the classification of growth (or, what is the same thing, the classification of the combined effect of the production and consumption shifts) in the case of complete specialization, for in the latter case, $\xi_v = \xi_y^c$ and $\theta_v = \theta_y^c$. Hence, fig. 12.2(b) can be used to illustrate the classification of the consumption effect in general.

Because of eqs. (12.3) and (12.7), the consumption effect can also be classified in terms of the behavior of the domestic consumption of exportables. Table 12.2 summarizes the classification.

## Table 12.2 Classification of the consumption effect

| Type of consumption effect | Range of the marginal propensity to consume importables $\xi_y^c$ <br> (1) | Range of the marginal propensity to consume exportables $\xi_x^c$ <br> $\xi_x^c \equiv 1 - \xi_y^c$ <br> $\theta_x^c \equiv 1 - \theta_y^c$ <br> (2) |
|---|---|---|
| Neutral | $\xi_y^c = \theta_y^c$ | $\xi_x^c = \theta_x^c$ |
| Protrade biased | $\theta_y^c < \xi_y^c < 1$ | $0 < \xi_x^c < \theta_x^c$ |
| Ultra-protrade biased | $+\infty > \xi_y^c > 1$ | $-\infty < \xi_x^c < 0$ |
| Antitrade biased | $0 < \xi_y^c < \theta_y^c$ | $\theta_x^c < \xi_x^c < 1$ |
| Ultra-antitrade biased | $-\infty < \xi_y^c < 0$ | $+\infty > \xi_x^c > 1$ |

## The Production Effect

The production effect can be similarly classified. Thus, when growth leaves unchanged the average propensity to produce exportables $\theta_x^p$, that is, $\xi_x^p = \theta_x^p$, the production effect is *neutral*. When the average propensity to produce exportables $\theta_x^p$ tends to increase with growth, that is, $\xi_x^p > \theta_x^p$, the production effect is *protrade biased;* and when $\theta_x^p$ tends to fall with growth, that is, $\xi_x^p < \theta_x^p$, the production effect is *antitrade biased*. Again, there are the two extreme cases: *ultra-protrade biased* (production effect), in which $\xi_x^p > 1$ (implying that the absolute increase in the production of exportables, $\Delta X_p$, is larger than the absolute increase in national income, $\Delta Q$); and *ultra-antitrade biased* (production effect), in which case $\xi_x^p < 0$ (implying that the domestic production of exportables falls absolutely). As before, because of eqs. (12.3) and (12.7), the production effect can be classified, alternatively, in terms of the behavior of the production of importables. The classification is summarized in table 12.3.

A comparison of tables 12.2 and 12.3 reveals that largely similar inequalities are used to classify both the production effect and the consumption effect, except for one major difference: the consumption effect emphasizes (initially) the behavior of the domestic consumption of importables, whereas the production effect emphasizes the behavior of the domestic production of exportables. The roles of the two commodities are reversed as we move from the classification of the consumption effect to the classification of the production effect because, other things being equal, increased consumption of importables tends to increase the volume of trade while increased consumption of exportables tends to decrease the volume of trade. On the other hand, increased production of exportables, like increased consumption of importables, tends to increase the volume of trade; and increased production of importables, like increased consumption of exportables, tends to decrease the volume of trade.

Figure 12.3 illustrates the five types of production effect. Production before growth occurs at $P$. The straight line $MPF$ is the economy's pregrowth consumption-possibilities frontier, and shifts (in a parallel fashion) to $NRSUV$ after growth. If the postgrowth optimum production point coincides with point $S$,

**Table 12.3 Classification of the production effect**

| Type of production effect | Range of the marginal propensity to produce exportables $\xi_x^p$ (1) | Range of the marginal propensity to produce importables $\xi_y^p$ $\xi_y^p = 1 - \xi_x^p$ $\theta_y^p = 1 - \theta_x^p$ (2) |
|---|---|---|
| Neutral | $\xi_x^p = \theta_x^p$ | $\xi_y^p = \theta_y^p$ |
| Protrade biased | $\theta_x^p < \xi_x^p < 1$ | $0 < \xi_y^p < \theta_y^p$ |
| Ultra-protrade biased | $+\infty > \xi_x^p > 1$ | $-\infty < \xi_y^p < 0$ |
| Antitrade biased | $0 < \xi_x^p < \theta_x^p$ | $\theta_y^p < \xi_y^p < 1$ |
| Ultra-antitrade biased | $-\infty < \xi_x^p < 0$ | $+\infty > \xi_y^p > 1$ |

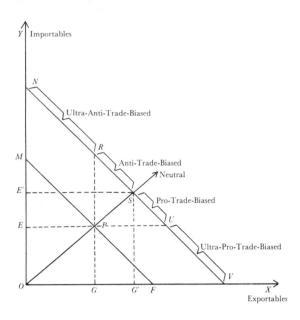

Figure 12.3 The five types of production effect.

the production effect is neutral; if it shifts to the region $SU$, it is protrade biased; if it shifts to the region $UV$, it is ultra-protrade biased; if it shifts to the region $RS$, it is antitrade biased; and if it shifts to the region $NR$, it is ultra-antitrade biased.

## The Addition of the Consumption and Production Effects

The overall effect of growth on the average propensity to trade depends on the sum of the consumption and production effects. These two effects can be added simply by determining in each case the range of variation of the marginal propensity to trade $\xi_v$. That is, we need only determine the upper and the lower limits of $\xi_v$. We can do this by using eqs. (12.4) and (12.8) and the inequalities given in tables 12.2 and 12.3. For example, if the consumption effect is neutral (that is, $\xi_x^c = \theta_x^c$) while the production effect is protrade biased (that is, $\theta_x^p < \xi_x^p < 1$), the upper limit of $\xi_v$ is given by

$$(\xi_v)^U = (\xi_x^p)^U - (\xi_x^c)^L = 1 - \theta_x^c$$

and the lower limit by

$$(\xi_v)^L = (\xi_x^p)^L - (\xi_x^c)^U = \theta_x^p - \theta_x^c = \theta_v$$

where the superscripts $U$ and $L$ stand for the upper limit and the lower limit, respectively. Hence, $\theta_v < \xi_v < 1 - \theta_x^c < 1$.

The limits of $\xi_v$ in all other cases have been similarly calculated, and the results are summarized in table 12.4. Note that when both effects are biased in the same direction, the total effect is similarly biased, and when one effect is neutral, the bias of the total effect is in the same direction as the bias of the other effect. If, however, the two effects are biased in opposite directions, the total effect cannot be easily predicted. When the production effect is ultra-antitrade biased, the total

**Table 12.4 The addition of the consumption and production effects**

| Production effect $\xi_v = \xi_x^p - \xi_x^c$ $\theta_v = \theta_x^p - \theta_x^c$ | Consumption effect | | | | |
|---|---|---|---|---|---|
| | Neutral $\xi_x^c = \theta_x^c$ | Protrade biased $0 < \xi_x^c < \theta_x^c$ | Ultra-protrade biased $-\infty < \xi_x^c < 0$ | Antitrade biased $\theta_x^c < \xi_x^c < 1$ | Ultra-antitrade biased $1 < \xi_x^c < +\infty$ |
| **Neutral** $\xi_x^p = \theta_x^p$ | $\xi_v = \xi_x^p - \xi_x^c$ $= \theta_x^p - \theta_x^c = \theta_v$ (N) | $\theta_v = \theta_x^p - \theta_x^c$ $= (\xi_v)^L < \xi_v < (\xi_v)^U$ $= \theta_x^p < 1$ (P) | $\theta_v < \theta_x^p = (\xi_v)^L$ $< \xi_v < (\xi_v)^U$ $= +\infty$ (P or UP) | $0 > \theta_x^p - 1 = (\xi_v)^L$ $< \xi_v < (\xi_v)^U$ $= \theta_x^p - \theta_x^c = \theta_v$ (A or UA) | $-\infty = (\xi_v)^L$ $< \xi_v < (\xi_v)^U$ $= \theta_x^p - 1 < 0$ (UA) |
| **Protrade biased** $\theta_x^p < \xi_x^p < 1$ | $\theta_v = \theta_x^p - \theta_x^c = (\xi_v)^L$ $< \xi_v < (\xi_v)^U$ $= 1 - \theta_x^c < 1$ (P) | $\theta_v = \theta_x^p - \theta_x^c = (\xi_v)^L$ $< \xi_v < (\xi_v)^U = 1$ (P) | $\theta_v < \theta_x^p = (\xi_v)^L < \xi_v$ $< (\xi_v)^U = +\infty$ (P or UP) | $0 > \theta_x^p - 1 = (\xi_v)^L$ $< \xi_v < (\xi_v)^U$ $= 1 - \theta_x^c$ with $\theta_v < 1 - \theta_x^c < 1$ (Not UP) | $-\infty = (\xi_v)^L < \xi_v$ $< (\xi_v)^U = 0$ (UA) |
| **Ultra-protrade biased** $1 < \xi_x^p < +\infty$ | $\theta_v < 1 - \theta_x^c = (\xi_v)^L$ $< \xi_v < (\xi_v)^U$ $= +\infty$ (P or UP) | $\theta_v < 1 - \theta_x^c = (\xi_v)^L$ $< \xi_v < (\xi_v)^U$ $= +\infty$ (P or UP) | $1 = (\xi_v)^L < \xi_v$ $< (\xi_v)^U = +\infty$ (UP) | $0 = (\xi_v)^L < \xi_v$ $< (\xi_v)^U = +\infty$ (Not UA) | $-\infty = (\xi_v)^L < \xi_v$ $< (\xi_v)^U = +\infty$ (All types possible) |
| **Antitrade biased** $0 < \xi_x^p < \theta_x^p$ | $-\theta_x^c = (\xi_v)^L < \xi_v$ $< (\xi_v)^U$ $= \theta_x^p - \theta_x^c = \theta_v$ (A or UA) | $-\theta_x^c = (\xi_v)^L < \xi_v$ $< (\xi_v)^U = \theta_x^p < 1$ (Not UP) | $0 = (\xi_v)^L < \xi_v$ $< (\xi_v)^U = +\infty$ (Not UA) | $-1 = (\xi_v)^L < \xi_v$ $< (\xi_v)^U$ $= \theta_x^p - \theta_x^c = \theta_v$ (A or UA) | $-\infty = (\xi_v)^L < \xi_v$ $< (\xi_v)^U$ $= \theta_x^p - 1 < 0$ (UA) |
| **Ultra-antitrade biased** $-\infty < \xi_x^p < 0$ | $-\infty = (\xi_v)^L < \xi_v$ $< (\xi_v)^U$ $= -\theta_x^c < 0$ (UA) | $-\infty = (\xi_v)^L < \xi_v$ $< (\xi_v)^U = 0$ (UA) | $-\infty = (\xi_v)^L < \xi_v$ $< (\xi_v)^U = +\infty$ (All types possible) | $-\infty = (\xi_v)^L < \xi_v$ $< (\xi_v)^U$ $= -\theta_x^c < 0$ (UA) | $-\infty = (\xi_v)^L < \xi_v$ $< (\xi_v)^U = -1$ (UA) |

*Note:* Parenthetical material beneath equations refers to type of growth ($N$ = neutral, $P$ = protrade biased, $UP$ = ultra-protrade biased, $A$ = antitrade biased, $UA$ = ultra-antitrade biased). $(\xi_v)^U$ = upper limit of $\xi_v$; $(\xi_v)^L$ = lower limit of $\xi_v$.

effect is also ultra-antitrade biased, except when the consumption effect is ultra-protrade biased, and then the total effect can be anything. Similarly, when the consumption effect is ultra-antitrade biased, the total effect is also ultra-antitrade biased, except when the production effect is ultra-protrade biased, and then the total effect can be anything.

## The Types of Growth and the Offer Curve

Figure 12.4 illustrates the various types of growth in terms of shifts of the offer curve of the growing country. The given international terms of trade are shown by the slope of the terms-of-trade line TOT. Our country's original offer curve is the solid curve $OE_0K$; equilibrium, before growth, occurs at $E_0$. The broken curves $UP$, $P$, $N$, $A$, and $UA$ show how the growing country's offer curve tends to shift with growth that is ultra-protrade biased, protrade biased, neutral, antitrade biased, and ultra-antitrade biased, respectively. The analysis of the present section enables us to identify the points $E_{UP}$, $E_P$, $E_N$, $E_A$, and $E_{UA}$ only—not the whole new offer curves. The implicit assumption made in fig. 12.4 is that the type of growth is independent of the specific value of the terms of trade, but this is not correct in general. As concerns the case of the small country which is a price taker in the international market, the only relevant points on the new offer curves are $E_{UP}$, $E_P$, $E_N$, $E_A$, and $E_{UA}$; therefore, the behavior of the offer curves elsewhere is irrelevant. However, when the assumption of the small country is dropped, this is no longer true. How, then, can the analysis of the present section be applied to the case of a large country whose purchases and sales of commodities $X$ and $Y$ in the international market affect the terms of trade?

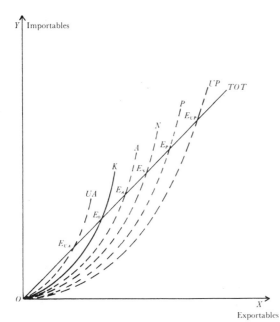

**Figure 12.4** The five types of growth in terms of shifts of the offer curve of the growing country.

# PART B. THE EFFECTS OF GROWTH ON THE LARGE COUNTRY

Assume that there are two countries, $A$ and $B$, producing two commodities, $X$ and $Y$. At the original equilibrium position, assume that $A$ is exporting commodity $X$ and $B$ is exporting commodity $Y$. Their general-equilibrium positions can be shown in terms of the familiar offer curves. Assume that only country $A$ grows. Thus, only $A$'s offer curve shifts through time while $B$'s remains the same, although the equilibrium point on $B$'s offer curve shifts because $A$'s offer curve shifts. How does $A$'s growth affect the terms of trade?

Using the analysis of part A, we can predict how $A$'s offer curve at the *initial* equilibrium terms of trade shifts. But in the present case, by assumption, the terms of trade do not remain constant. Nevertheless, the preceding analysis becomes sufficient for the determination of the effect of $A$'s growth on the terms of trade when we make the additional assumption that international equilibrium is unique and stable before and after growth.

## 12.4 COMPLETE SPECIALIZATION

Let us now proceed with the simple case of the classical theory where the production-possibilities frontier is linear and at least one country specializes completely in the production of only one commodity.

Consider fig. 12.5. The production block $B_0 K_1 B_1$ is $B$'s (linear) production-possibilities frontier, which is assumed to remain constant throughout. The production block $A_0 A_1 K_1$ is $A$'s pregrowth production-possibilities frontier. Accordingly, the pregrowth world production-possibilities frontier is given by $A_1 K_1 B_1$. Tastes are assumed given by a world social indifference map, illustrated in fig. 12.5 by the indifference curves $I_1 I_1'$ and $I_2 I_2'$. Equilibrium occurs initially at point $K_1$, with the equilibrium price ratio $p_x/p_y$ given by the absolute slope of the indifference curve $I_1 I_1'$ at $K_1$.

Assume now that $A$'s production-possibilities frontier shifts outward in a parallel fashion, as illustrated by the production block $A_0 A_2 K_2$ (fig. 12.5). This shift of $A$'s production-possibilities frontier may be due to either *labor growth* (labor being the only factor of production) or *neutral technical progress*, causing both labor coefficients, $a_x$ and $a_y$, to fall by the same percentage. How does the shift of $A$'s production-possibilities frontier affect (*a*) the world production-possibilities frontier and (*b*) $A$'s terms of trade? The world production-possibilities frontier shifts to $A_2 K_2 B_3$. Postgrowth equilibrium occurs somewhere along $A_2 K_2 B_3$, the precise equilibrium point being determined by tastes. In the example given in fig. 12.5, equilibrium occurs at $E$, with the postgrowth equilibrium price ratio given by $A$'s domestic price ratio. Thus, in fig. 12.5, $A$'s terms of trade deteriorate with growth, i.e., the price ratio $p_x/p_y$ falls. But this need not be the case, for, depending on tastes, postgrowth equilibrium may occur at $K_2$ or

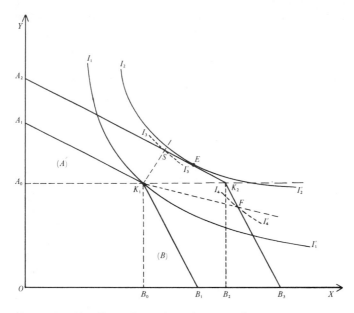

**Figure 12.5** The effects of growth on the terms of trade.

even in the region $K_2 B_3$. In the latter case, $A$'s terms of trade definitely improve. Under what conditions do $A$'s terms of trade deteriorate with growth? Under what conditions do they improve?

## The Effect of Growth on the Terms of Trade

Concentrating for the moment on the geometry of fig. 12.5, we can prove that, if commodity $Y$ is neutral (i.e., if the consumption of $Y$ remains constant as income changes), the relative price of $X$ remains constant; if $Y$ is superior or normal (i.e., if the consumption of $Y$ tends to increase as income increases), $p_x/p_y$ falls; and if $Y$ is inferior (i.e., if the consumption of $Y$ tends to decrease as income increases), $p_x/p_y$ increases with growth. To prove this, note that, when $Y$ is neutral, the income-consumption curve is horizontal, as illustrated by the broken line $A_0 K_1 K_2$. Hence, at $K_2$ all curves maintain the same slopes they originally had at $K_1$, equilibrium shifts from $K_1$ to $K_2$, and the marginal rate of substitution of $X$ for $Y$ (and thus the relative price of $X$) remains constant.

On the other hand, when commodity $Y$ is a superior good, the income-consumption curve through $K_1$ is upward sloping, as illustrated by the broken curve $K_1 S$. Therefore, the indifference curve $I_3 I_3'$ passing through $S$ intersects the world production-possibilities frontier at $S$ from above, with equilibrium occurring somewhere in the region $SK_2$, implying a lower relative price for $X$. When commodity $Y$ is inferior, the income-consumption curve through $K_1$ is negatively sloped, as illustrated by the broken curve $K_1 F$. Accordingly, the indifference curve $I_4 I'_4$ passing through $F$ intersects the world production-possibilities frontier at $F$ from left to right, with equilibrium occurring somewhere in the region $FK_2$ and implying a higher relative price for $X$.

The conclusion that $A$'s terms of trade can change in either direction with $A$'s growth is reached also when each country's tastes are represented separately by a social indifference map. Thus, we can easily identify the effect of $A$'s growth on $A$'s terms of trade by determining the type of growth experienced by $A$, which in the present, classical, complete-specialization case coincides with the type of $A$'s consumption effect. If $A$'s consumption effect (and therefore $A$'s growth) is anything but ultra-antitrade biased, $A$'s demand for imports (or supply of exports) becomes absolutely larger with growth at the pregrowth terms of trade. If international equilibrium is unique and stable before and after growth, $A$'s terms of trade, $p_x/p_y$, deteriorate with growth. However, if $A$'s consumption effect is ultra-antitrade biased, $A$'s growth is definitely ultra-antitrade biased and its terms of trade, $p_x/p_y$, improve with growth, i.e., the ratio $p_x/p_y$ increases.

That $A$'s growth can affect $A$'s terms of trade either favorably or unfavorably appears inescapable. But is it not possible to eliminate certain types of consumption behavior and, thus, narrow down the range of possible outcomes? In particular, can we not eliminate the possibility that $A$'s consumption effect may be ultra-antitrade biased? If $A$'s growth is the result of technical progress, the ultra-antitrade-biased consumption effect cannot be excluded on the basis of a priori reasoning, but when $A$'s growth is the result of sheer labor growth, the exclusion of the ultra-antitrade-biased consumption effect is inevitable.

Suppose that $A$'s citizens have identical tastes and factor endowments. Then $A$'s demand for $Y$ at the pregrowth terms of trade increases *pari passu* with $A$'s labor and output. That is, $A$'s consumption effect is *neutral:* all residents of country $A$ are doing after growth exactly the same thing they were doing before growth. The consumption effect is also neutral when $A$'s residents are assumed to have identical and homothetic tastes. But what if neither of these assumptions is made? Again the possibility of an ultra-antitrade-biased consumption effect must be excluded: as $A$'s workers, and therefore consumers, increase, it is impossible for $A$'s demand for any commodity to fall at the pregrowth terms of trade. Country $A$'s old consumers continue to consume the same quantities after growth as before, and $A$'s new consumers cannot have a negative demand for any commodity. Accordingly, in the absence of any shift in tastes, and with the growth of labor, $A$'s consumption effect cannot possibly be ultra-antitrade biased; therefore, *A's terms of trade definitely deteriorate.*

## The Effect of Growth on Social Welfare

How does $A$'s labor growth affect the level of social welfare in $A$ and in $B$? To simplify, assume that $A$'s citizens have identical tastes and factor endowments. The same goes for $B$'s citizens. Therefore, we can determine the effect of $A$'s labor growth on the level of social welfare in $A$ by determining its effect on the welfare of

$A$'s "representative citizen." Similarly, we can determine the effect of $A$'s labor growth on the level of social welfare in $B$ by determining its effect on the welfare of $B$'s representative citizen.

Consider country $B$ first. How does $A$'s labor growth affect the welfare of $B$'s representative citizen? Remember that $B$'s production-possibilities frontier can be scaled down in proportion to its representative citizen. Under these circumstances, it should be clear that *the welfare of $B$'s representative citizen necessarily improves with $A$'s labor growth*, because, on the one hand, $B$'s representative citizen specializes completely in the production of $Y$ and, on the other hand, $A$'s increased (net) supply of $X$ and demand for $Y$ cause the commodity-price ratio $p_x/p_y$ to fall, and, therefore, the budget line of $B$'s representative citizen rotates outward through the $Y$-axis intercept of his (scaled-down) production-possibilities frontier.

Observe that when $A$'s growth is the result of technical progress, $B$'s representative citizen may become either better off (when $A$'s growth is not ultra-antitrade biased and the price ratio $p_x/p_y$ falls) or worse off (when $A$'s growth is ultra-antitrade biased and the price ratio $p_x/p_y$ rises).

When $A$'s growth is the result of sheer labor growth, $A$'s representative citizen necessarily becomes worse off, for, given his uniquely determined (scaled-down) production-possibilities frontier, his budget line rotates inward through the $X$-axis intercept of his (scaled-down) production-possibilities frontier, thus reaching equilibrium at a lower indifference curve. When we say that $A$'s growth makes $A$'s representative citizen worse off, we do not mean that free trade is not beneficial to $A$ but, rather, that *its citizens are forced to give up part of the gains they used to enjoy from trade before growth*. Eventually, as $A$'s growth proceeds, $A$'s citizens may be forced back to the level of welfare they enjoyed under autarky.

What happens to the welfare of $A$'s representative citizen when $A$'s growth is the result of technical progress? We have to distinguish between the *terms-of-trade effect*, which is due to the favorable or unfavorable change in the commodity-price ratio $p_x/p_y$, and the *wealth effect*, which is due to the outward shift of $A$'s production-possibilities frontier, implying a corresponding outward shift of the production-possibilities frontier of $A$'s representative citizen. The wealth effect is always favorable to the welfare of $A$'s representative citizen, but the terms-of-trade effect can go either way. Accordingly, when the terms-of-trade effect is also favorable (when $A$'s growth is ultra-antitrade biased), $A$'s representative citizen definitely becomes better off with growth. When the terms-of-trade effect is unfavorable, the outcome obviously depends on whether the unfavorable terms-of-trade effect outweighs the favorable wealth effect, or vice versa.

The case of technical progress is illustrated in fig. 12.6. The curve $SK$ is $A$'s production-possibilities frontier before growth. Since $A$ is specializing completely in the production of $X$, consider $K$ as a new origin and draw $A$'s offer curve through $K$, as shown by $KGE$ (in the manner of chap. 6, part A). In addition, superimpose $B$'s offer curve, $KHE$. The two offer curves intersect each other at $E$. Hence, before growth, $A$ exports $DK$ units of $X$ to $B$ in exchange for $DE$ units of $Y$, with the equilibrium terms of trade given by the ratio $DE/DK$ or the absolute slope of $MEK$. Line $MEK$ is $A$'s pregrowth consumption-possibilities frontier. Observe that, before growth, $A$ reaches the social indifference curve $I_1 I_1'$.

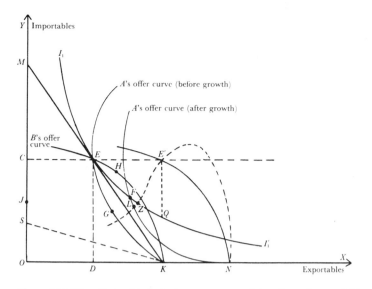

**Figure 12.6** The effects of technical progress on social welfare: the possibility of immiserizing growth.

Suppose now that, as a result of neutral technical progress, $A$'s production-possibilities frontier shifts outward in a parallel fashion, as illustrated by the broken curve $JN$ (not drawn). How does this shift affect $A$'s social welfare? (Note that the social indifference map in the present case describes social welfare; i.e., a movement from a lower to a higher social indifference curve necessarily implies that $A$'s social welfare increases. Figure 12.6 could be scaled down in proportion to $A$'s representative citizen, thus directly showing the effect of growth on the economic welfare of $A$'s representative citizen.) If $A$'s production-possibilities frontier is allowed to shift outward sufficiently, it can be made tangent to the social indifference curve $I_1 I_1'$ or a higher one; then $A$'s social welfare cannot possibly deteriorate with growth. The paradoxical reduction in $A$'s level of social welfare arises only when $A$'s postgrowth production-possibilities frontier $JN$ cannot reach the social indifference curve $I_1 I_1'$. Further, if $A$'s terms of trade $(p_x / p_y)$ do not deteriorate with growth, $A$'s social welfare definitely increases with growth, for then $A$'s consumption-possibilities frontier would start at $N$ and be at least as steep as its pregrowth consumption-possibilities frontier $MEK$. But if $A$'s postgrowth production-possibilities frontier does not reach the indifference curve $I_1 I_1'$ and if $A$'s terms of trade deteriorate (that is, $p_x / p_y$ falls), the possibility that $A$'s social welfare may deteriorate with growth cannot be ruled out. This possibility is illustrated in fig. 12.6.

Consider $A$'s postgrowth production point $N$ and draw $B$'s offer curve through $N$. The horizontal distances between $B$'s offer curve through $K$ and the new one through $N$ must always be equal to $KN$; in particular, $EE' = KN$. To complete the picture, draw $A$'s new offer curve through $N$. If $A$'s offer curve intersects $B$'s in the region $E'N$ (as is the case when $A$'s growth is ultra-antitrade biased), then $A$'s terms of trade and social welfare improve. Thus, a necessary condition for $A$ to become worse off with growth is that its offer curve intersect $B$'s at a point which lies beyond point $E'$. In addition, the new equilibrium point should lie below the indifference curve $I_1 I'_1$. How can this happen? Observe that $A$'s postgrowth offer curve necessarily intersects the indifference curve $I_1 I'_1$ to the right and below the initial equilibrium point $E$. Another condition necessary for the paradoxical reduction in $A$'s level of social welfare is that the latter intersection should occur somewhere in the region $EQ$ (point $F$ in fig. 12.6). Equilibrium should occur on $A$'s postgrowth offer curve somewhere in the region $FN$ (point $L$ in fig. 12.6). This requires that $B$'s offer curve be backward bending, as illustrated by the broken curve $NE'ZL$. A final necessary (but not sufficient) condition for $A$'s social welfare to decrease with technical progress is that $B$'s demand for imports be inelastic.

There are some important differences between the present case of technical progress and the previous case of labor growth. In the latter case $A$'s social welfare always deteriorates, but in the former case the outcome can go either way. In fact, in the presence of large technical progress, the growing country always benefits from growth. In the case of technical progress, the growing country can pursue an optimum tariff policy (to be discussed in chap. 19) and always gain from growth; i.e., the growing country, $A$, can use a tariff to force the other country, $B$, to trade anywhere on its (that is, $B$'s) offer curve. Since $B$'s offer curve through $N$ (fig. 12.6) lies beyond $B$'s offer curve through $K$, $A$'s social welfare will always improve with technical progress when an optimum tariff policy is being pursued.† However, even an optimum tariff policy cannot prevent the deterioration of $A$'s social welfare when $A$'s growth is the result of sheer labor growth, in which case the production-possibilities frontier of $A$'s representative citizen remains the same after growth as before, but the offer curve of $B$ *scaled down in proportion to $A$'s representative citizen* shifts unfavorably (it shrinks), because, by assumption, the number of $A$'s citizens increases.

The paradox that a growing country can become worse off with growth was first noted by Edgeworth (1894, pp. 40–42). More recently, Bhagwati (1958) has dealt with this phenomenon, which he calls "immiserizing growth."

## 12.5 INCOMPLETE SPECIALIZATION

Turn now to the case of incomplete specialization. What are the effects of growth on the terms of trade, the volume of exports, and the volume of imports of the growing country?

---

† In the terminology of chap. 19, this means that technical progress causes the Baldwin frontier to shift outward always.

## The Terms-of-Trade Effect

The analysis of part A can be used to predict the effect of growth on the terms of trade of the growing country when international equilibrium is unique and stable. In particular, only ultra-antitrade-biased growth improves the growing country's terms of trade: all other types of growth tend to deteriorate them. At the original equilibrium terms of trade, all types of growth, except ultra-antitrade biased, tend to increase the growing country's *absolute* demand for imports and supply of exports. Since the other country's (i.e., the rest of the world's) demand for imports and supply of exports remain the same, it follows that, at the pregrowth equilibrium terms of trade, there emerges a positive excess demand for $A$'s importables $(Y)$ and a positive excess supply of $A$'s exportables $(X)$, causing the relative price of $A$'s exportables (that is, $p_x/p_y$) to fall. On the other hand, if the growth is ultra-antitrade biased, the growing country's demand for imports and supply of exports, at the pregrowth equilibrium terms of trade, fall absolutely with growth. Consequently, there emerges a positive excess demand for $A$'s exportables $(X)$ and a positive excess supply of $A$'s importables $(Y)$, causing $A$'s terms of trade to improve with growth (i.e., causing the commodity-price ratio $p_x/p_y$ to rise).

## The Effect of Growth on the Volume of Imports and Exports

When $A$'s growth is not ultra-antitrade biased and $B$'s demand for imports is elastic (that is, $B$'s offer curve is upward sloping), the physical quantity of both $A$'s exports of $X$ and imports of $Y$ increase with growth. But when $A$'s growth is ultra-antitrade biased and $B$'s demand for imports is elastic, both $A$'s imports of $Y$ and exports of $X$ fall. On the other hand, when $B$'s demand for imports is inelastic, the physical quantity of $A$'s imports of $Y$ falls and the quantity of its exports of $X$

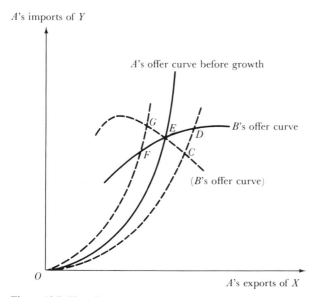

**Figure 12.7** The effects of growth on the volume of exports and the volume of imports.

rises for all types of growth except ultra-antitrade biased. When $A$'s growth is ultra-antitrade biased, $A$'s imports rise while its exports fall.

The above conclusions are illustrated in fig. 12.7. Before growth, equilibrium occurs at $E$. With $A$'s ultra-antitrade-biased growth, $A$'s offer curve shifts to $OFG$, with equilibrium occurring either at $F$ (when $B$'s demand for imports is elastic) or at $G$ (when $B$'s demand for imports is inelastic). With any other type of growth besides ultra-antitrade biased, $A$'s offer curve shifts to the right, as illustrated by the broken curve $OCD$. Equilibrium occurs either at $D$ (when $B$'s demand for imports is elastic) or at $C$ (when $B$'s demand for imports is inelastic).

## SELECTED BIBLIOGRAPHY

Bhagwati, J. (1958). "Immiserizing Growth: A Geometrical Note." *Review of Economic Studies*, vol. 25, pp. 201–205. Reprinted in R. E. Caves and H. G. Johnson (Eds.), AEA *Readings in International Economics*. Richard D. Irwin, Inc., Homewood, Ill., 1968.

Corden, W. M. (1956). "Economic Expansion and International Trade: A Geometric Approach." *Oxford Economic Papers*, vol. 8, pp. 223–228.

Edgeworth, F. Y. (1894). "The Theory of International Values." *Economic Journal*, vol. 4, pp. 35–50.

Findlay, R., and H. Grubert (1959). "Factor Intensities, Technological Progress and the Terms of Trade." *Oxford Economic Papers*, vol. 11, pp. 111–121.

Hicks, J. R. (1953). "An Inaugural Lecture." *Oxford Economic Papers*, vol. 5, pp. 117–135.

Ikema, M. (1969). "The Effect of Economic Growth on the Demand for Imports: A Simple Diagram." *Oxford Economic Papers*, vol. 21 (March), pp. 66–69.

Johnson, H. G. (1958). *International Trade and Economic Growth*. George Allen and Unwin, Ltd., London, chap. 3.

Rybczynski, T. M. (1955). "Factor Endowment and Relative Commodity Prices." *Economica*, vol. 22, pp. 336–341.

# THIRTEEN

## THE SOURCES OF ECONOMIC GROWTH AND INTERNATIONAL TRADE

When we know $A$'s type of growth, we can predict whether $A$'s terms of trade tend to improve or deteriorate with growth. But can we predict the type of growth if we know the factors responsible for the outward shift of $A$'s production-possibilities frontier? In particular, can we predict the type of $A$'s growth if we know, for instance, that it is the result of sheer labor growth, or sheer capital accumulation, or a combination of labor growth and capital accumulation, or technical progress? Further, how does $A$'s growth affect the level of social welfare in $A$? This chapter takes a closer look at the factors that work behind the scenes, so to speak, and cause the growing country's production-possibilities frontier to shift outward. The discussion is divided into two parts. Part A deals with labor growth and capital accumulation. Part B deals with technical progress.

## PART A. FACTOR GROWTH

Assume again that there are two countries, $A$ and $B$, endowed with two factors of production, labor, $L$, and capital, $K$, and producing two commodities, $X$ and $Y$. Both commodities are produced under constant returns to scale, and commodity $X$ is labor intensive relative to commodity $Y$. Assume, further, that $B$'s factor endowments and technology, as well as tastes, remain constant throughout. Thus, $B$'s behavior can be represented conveniently by its offer curve, which remains constant throughout. The system is in long-run equilibrium to begin with, but we need not specify, at this stage, the structure of trade.

How does an increase in $A$'s factor endowments affect $A$'s demand for imports and supply of exports at the pregrowth terms of trade? We must first determine what type of production effect $A$ will experience (at the pregrowth terms of trade) and then draw on the analysis of chap. 12 to determine $A$'s type of growth.

## 13.1 THE PRODUCTION EFFECT AT CONSTANT TERMS OF TRADE

Consider the familiar box diagram of country $A$, as illustrated in fig. 13.1. Assume that, at the pregrowth international equilibrium position, country $A$ is producing at point $E$ on the contract curve, $O_x E O_y$. Because of constant returns to scale, the absolute quantities of $X$ and $Y$ produced by $A$ can be made equal to the distances $O_x E$ and $O_y E$, respectively, by an appropriate choice of units of measurement. Accordingly, $X_p^0 = O_x E$ and $Y_p^0 = O_y E$, where $X_p^0$ and $Y_p^0$ stand for $A$'s pregrowth production levels of $X$ and $Y$, respectively.

### The Effect of Factor Growth on Production

When $A$'s factor endowments grow, $A$'s box diagram expands. In particular, an increase in $A$'s factor endowments can be represented in fig. 13.1 either by a shift of the origin for commodity $Y$ into the region $MO_y N$, while $X$'s origin remains constant at $O_x$, or by a shift of the origin for commodity $X$ into the region $HO_x D$, while $Y$'s origin remains constant at $O_y$. For present purposes, let us shift $Y$'s origin. The type of $A$'s production effect depends crucially on the exact location of the new origin for commodity $Y$.

We already know that, as $A$'s factor endowments grow, the type of $A$'s production effect depends on what happens to the outputs of commodities $X$ and $Y$. In order to determine the type of production effect which country $A$ experiences, we must first determine the differences $\Delta X_p$ and $\Delta Y_p$ *under the assumption that the commodity prices remain constant at their pregrowth level.* Because of the one-to-one correspondence which exists between commodity prices and factor prices, on the one hand, and between factor prices and the optimum capital-labor ratio, on the other, we can determine the differences $\Delta X_p$ and $\Delta Y_p$ by assuming that the pregrowth optimum capital-labor ratios $\mu_x^0$ and $\mu_y^0$ in industries $X$ and $Y$, respectively, continue to be optimum after growth. The ratios $\mu_x^0$ and $\mu_y^0$ are illustrated in fig. 13.1 by the slopes of the pregrowth expansion paths of industries $X$ and $Y$, respectively. After growth, industry $X$ produces somewhere along its pregrowth expansion path, $O_x ER$, and industry $Y$ along an expansion path which starts at $Y$'s new origin (i.e., a point in the region $MO_y N$) and is parallel to $Y$'s pregrowth expansion path, $O_y E$. The postgrowth equilibrium point occurs at the intersection

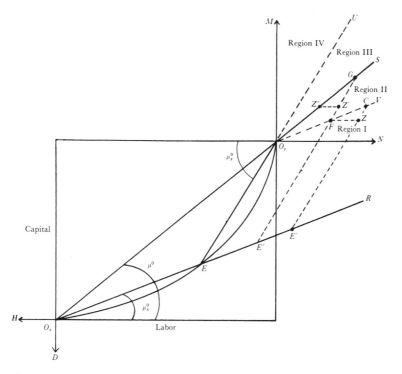

**Figure 13.1** The production effect of factor increases at constant terms of trade.

of $Y$'s postgrowth expansion path with $X$'s. (The implicit assumption in the present construction is that, after growth, country $A$ continues to specialize incompletely in the production of $X$ and $Y$ at the pregrowth factor prices.)

In fig. 13.1, draw through the pregrowth origin, $O_y$, for commodity $Y$ three straight lines: $O_y S$, $O_y V$, and $O_y U$, with $O_y S$ being merely an extension of the diagonal $O_x O_y$; $O_y V$ being parallel to $X$'s expansion path $O_x ER$; and $O_y U$ being an extension of $Y$'s expansion path, $O_y E$. These three lines divide the quadrant $MO_y N$ into four regions (or cones). Now consider the *incremental capital-labor ratio*, $\Delta K/\Delta L$. When $\Delta K/\Delta L$ is equal to the pregrowth overall capital-labor ratio $\mu^0$, that is, the slope of the diagonal $O_x O_y$, $Y$'s origin shifts to a point on the line $O_y S$; when $\Delta K/\Delta L = \mu_x^0$, $Y$'s origin shifts to a point on the line $O_y V$; when $\Delta K/\Delta L = \mu_y^0$, $Y$'s origin shifts to a point on the line $O_y U$; when $\Delta K/\Delta L < \mu_x^0$, $Y$'s origin shifts to a point in region I; when $\mu_x^0 < \Delta K/\Delta L < \mu^0$, $Y$'s origin shifts to a point in region II; when $\mu^0 < \Delta K/\Delta L < \mu_y^0$, $Y$'s origin shifts to a point in region III; and, finally, when $\Delta K/\Delta L > \mu_y^0$, $Y$'s origin shifts to a point in region IV.

**Theorem 13.1** Assume that $\mu_x^0 < \mu_y^0$ and that prices remain constant at their pregrowth levels. As $A$'s capital and labor increase by $\Delta K$ and $\Delta L$, respectively, $X_p$ and $Y_p$ change as follows:

(a) When $\Delta K/\Delta L = \mu^0$, $X_p$ and $Y_p$ grow at the same rate, that is, $\lambda_x^p = \lambda_y^p$. Further, $\xi_y^p = \theta_y^p$ and $\xi_x^p = \theta_x^p$. Hence, $A$'s production effect is neutral.

(b) When $\Delta K/\Delta L < \mu_x^0$, we necessarily have $\Delta X_p > 0$ and $\Delta Y_p < 0$. Hence, $\xi_y^p < 0$ and $\xi_x^p > 1$.

(c) When $\mu_x^0 < \Delta K/\Delta L < \mu^0$, we necessarily have $\Delta X_p > 0$ and $\Delta Y_p > 0$. In addition, we have $\lambda_x^p > \lambda_y^p$; $1 > \xi_x^p > \theta_x^p$; and $0 < \xi_y^p < \theta_y^p$.

(d) When $\mu^0 < \Delta K/\Delta L < \mu_y^0$, we necessarily have $\Delta X_p > 0$ and $\Delta Y_p > 0$. In addition, we have $\lambda_y^p > \lambda_x^p$; $1 > \xi_y^p > \theta_y^p$; and $0 < \xi_x^p < \theta_x^p$.

(e) Finally, when $\Delta K/\Delta L > \mu_y^0$, we necessarily have $\Delta X_p < 0$ and $\Delta Y_p > 0$. Hence, $\xi_x^p < 0$ and $\xi_y^p > 1$.

PROOF The truth of part (a) follows directly from the analysis of chaps. 9 and 10. For a given factor-price ratio, the ratio $X_p/Y_p$ depends only on the overall factor-endowment ratio $\mu$. When the latter remains constant, so does the ratio $X_p/Y_p$. Accordingly, when $\Delta K > 0$, $\Delta L > 0$, and $\Delta K/\Delta L = \mu^0$, $X_p$ and $Y_p$ must be growing at the same rate (that is, $\lambda_x^p = \lambda_y^p$). Since the rate of growth of output $\lambda_q$ is a weighted average of the rate of growth of $X_p(\lambda_x^p)$ and the rate of growth of $Y_p(\lambda_y^p)$, it follows that $\lambda_q = \lambda_x^p = \lambda_y^p$, implying that the production effect is neutral.

This argument can be verified geometrically. Assume that $Y$'s origin shifts to point $G$ (fig. 13.1). Postgrowth equilibrium must occur at $E''$, where the broken line $GE''$ is parallel to $O_yE$. Since we measure $X_p$ and $Y_p$ by the distances from the equilibrium point on the contract curve to the origins for $X$ and $Y$, respectively, we have $\Delta X_p = EE''$ and $\Delta Y_p = FG$. Note that the triangles $O_xEO_y$ and $O_yFG$ are similar. Consequently,

$$\lambda_x^p \equiv \frac{\Delta X_p}{X_p^0} = \frac{EE''}{O_xE} = \frac{FG}{O_yE} = \frac{\Delta Y_p}{Y_p^0} \equiv \lambda_y^p \tag{13.1}$$

Thus, the outputs of $X$ and $Y$ increase at the same rate. Recalling eq. (12.18), we have

$$\lambda_x^p = \lambda_y^p = \lambda_q \tag{13.2}$$

Substituting from (13.2) into eqs. (12.11) and (12.13), we get

$$\xi_x^p = \theta_x^p \quad \text{and} \quad \xi_y^p = \theta_y^p$$

In words, the marginal propensity to produce $X$ ($\xi_x^p$) is equal to the average propensity to produce $X$ ($\theta_x^p$), and the marginal propensity to produce $Y$ ($\xi_y^p$) is equal to the average propensity to produce $Y$ ($\theta_y^p$).

To prove part (b), note that, for any point along the vector $O_yV$ (implying $\Delta K/\Delta L = \mu_x^0$), such as points $F$ and $C$, the change in $Y_p$ is zero (that is, $\Delta Y_p = 0$). Consider point $Z$ in region I and the line $CZE'$, which is parallel to $O_yE$. Obviously, $ZE' < CE'$; hence $\Delta Y_p < 0$. However, $\Delta X_p = EE' > 0$.

The interpretation of the above result is simple. In fact, it follows from the important lemma of chap. 9. Thus, when $\Delta K/\Delta L = \mu_x^0$, then $X_p$ can increase and absorb all $\Delta K$ and $\Delta L$, with $Y_p$ remaining constant. But when $\Delta K/\Delta L < \mu_x^0$, this is not possible, for all $\Delta K$ is used up before all $\Delta L$ is employed (see fig. 13.1). Suppose that $\Delta L$ and $\Delta K$ are given by the coordinates of point $Z$ with respect to $O_y$. The total amounts of $L$ and $K$ are then given by the coordinates of $Z$ with respect to $O_x$. If we keep $Y_p$ constant at $Y_p^0 = O_y E$ and allow $X_p$ to expand to $O_x E''$, the total amounts of $L$ and $K$ employed in both industries will be given by the coordinates of point $F$ with respect to $O_x$. Under the circumstances, $K$ will be fully employed, but there will still be a certain amount of unemployment of $L$, as shown by the horizontal distance $FZ$. This unemployment of labor can be removed, as we saw in chap. 9, by allowing the output of the labor-intensive commodity $(X)$ to expand and the output of the capital-intensive commodity $(Y)$ to contract. Accordingly, $X_p$ must expand beyond $O_x E''$ and $Y_p$ must fall below $O_y E$. In particular, $X_p$ must change to $O_x E'$ and $Y_p$ to $ZE'$. Hence, $\Delta X_p > 0$ and $\Delta Y_p < 0$, and therefore $\xi_x^p > 1$ and $\xi_y^p < 0$.

Given the preceding analysis, an increase in factor endowments that causes $Y$'s origin to shift to some point in region I, such as the shift from $O_y$ to $Z$, can be decomposed into the following two shifts: $(\alpha)$ a shift from $O_y$ to $F$ (on the vector $O_y V$), implying that $\Delta X_p^\alpha > 0$ and $\Delta Y_p^\alpha = 0$, and $(\beta)$ a shift from $F$ to $Z$ (corresponding to a sheer labor increase), implying that $\Delta X_p^\beta > 0$ and $\Delta Y_p^\beta < 0$, where the superscripts $\alpha$ and $\beta$ indicate the changes which correspond to the shifts $(\alpha)$ and $(\beta)$, respectively. The total change in $X_p$ is given by $\Delta X_p = \Delta X_p^\alpha + \Delta X_p^\beta > 0$, and the total change in $Y_p$ is given by $\Delta Y_p = \Delta Y_p^\alpha + \Delta Y_p^\beta < 0$.

A corollary to the above conclusion is what is known in the literature as the *Rybczynski theorem: when only one factor grows, the output of the commodity which uses intensively the increased factor expands, and the output of the other commodity contracts.* For instance, when only labor grows, the output of the labor-intensive commodity expands and the output of the capital-intensive commodity contracts. On the other hand, when only capital grows, the output of the capital-intensive commodity expands and the output of the labor-intensive commodity contracts.†

Part $(c)$ is proved as follows. Assume that $\Delta L$ and $\Delta K$ are given by the coordinates of point $Z'$ with respect to $O_y$. Shifting $Y$'s origin to $Z'$ implies that both $X_p$ and $Y_p$ necessarily increase, because $O_x E'' > O_x E$ and $Z'E'' > FE'' = O_y E$. In addition, as we saw earlier (eq. (13.1)), $EE''/O_x E = FG/O_y E$. Since $FG > FZ'$, we necessarily have $\lambda_x^p = EE''/O_x E = FG/O_y E >$

---

† Given Samuelson's sweeping theorem on intermediate products (see the appendix to chap. 8), it is evident that the Rybczynski theorem holds in the presence of intermediate goods as well. On this point, see also the references to intermediate products given in chap. 9. Komiya (1967) has shown that the Rybczynski theorem holds also in the presence of nontraded goods, provided only that the marginal propensity to consume nontraded goods is between zero and unity. For instance, add a third, nontraded good $Z$, and allow capital to increase while keeping the terms of trade constant. The economy's income increases and so does the consumption and production of the nontraded good $Z$. Nevertheless, the increase in the output of $Z$ falls short of the increase in national income because, by assumption, the marginal propensity to consume $Z$ is less than unity. To increase the output of $Z$, the economy must use part of the additional $K$ and some $L$ which must be withdrawn from the production of $X$ and $Y$. Therefore, for the production of the internationally traded goods $X$ and $Y$, the economy (after $K$ increases) has more $K$ but less $L$. As a result, the output of the $K$-intensive commodity (say $Y$) increases and the output of the $L$-intensive commodity (say $X$) decreases. For further details see Ethier (1972), Kemp (1969, chap. 6), and Komiya (1967).

$FZ'/O_yE = \lambda_y^p$. Since $\lambda_q$ is a weighted average of $\lambda_x^p$ and $\lambda_y^p$ (see eq. (12.18)), we necessarily have $\lambda_x^p > \lambda_q > \lambda_y^p$. Combining the inequality $\lambda_x^p > \lambda_q$ with eq. (12.11), we get $\xi_x^p > \theta_x^p$. Similarly, combining the inequality $\lambda_q > \lambda_y^p$ with eq. (12.13), we get $\xi_y^p < \theta_y^p$. Recalling that $\Delta Y_p > 0$, we conclude that $0 < \xi_y^p < \theta_y^p$ and $1 > \xi_x^p > \theta_x^p$.

Again, the shift of $Y$'s origin from $O_y$ to $Z'$ can be decomposed into a shift from $O_y$ to $Z''$, implying an equiproportional increase in factors and outputs, and a shift from $Z''$ to $Z'$, implying an increase in labor only, causing $X_p$ to increase further and $Y_p$ to fall. Since $Z'$ lies above and to the left of the vector $O_y V$, the overall change in $Y_p$ is positive. Hence, both $X_p$ and $Y_p$ increase, with $X_p$ increasing faster than $Y_p$.

Part (d) is similar to part (c), and part (e) is similar to part (b), except that the roles of the two commodities are reversed.

## The Type of the Production Effect

What type of production effect does $A$ experience in each of cases (a) to (e)? With the exception of case (a), where the production effect is always neutral, we cannot predict the type of $A$'s production effect in the last four cases on the basis of the information we have thus far. We need to know, in addition, which commodity is being exported by $A$ (see table 13.1).

## 13.2 THE IMPORTANCE OF THE INITIAL FACTOR-PRICE RATIO

The four regions of fig. 13.1, which are used as the basis for classifying $A$'s production effect (as shown in table 13.1), depend on the pregrowth prices. If we start with a different set of pregrowth prices (and thus a point on the contract curve different from $E$), the same factor increases may give rise to different results. This

### Table 13.1 Classification of $A$'s production effect

| | | | Type of production effect | |
|---|---|---|---|---|
| Incremental capital-labor ratio, $\Delta K/\Delta L$ | Marginal propensity to produce $X$, $\xi_x^p$ (1) | Marginal propensity to produce $Y$, $\xi_y^p$ (2) | When $A$ exports the labor-intensive commodity $(X)$ (3) | When $A$ exports the capital-intensive commodity $(Y)$ (4) |
| (a) $\mu_x^0 < \Delta K/\Delta L = \mu^0 < \mu_y^0$ | $\xi_x^p = \theta_x^p$ | $\xi_y^p = \theta_y^p$ | N | N |
| (b) $\Delta K/\Delta L < \mu_x^0 < \mu_y^0$ | $\xi_x^p > 1$ | $\xi_y^p < 0$ | UP | UA |
| (c) $\mu_x^0 < \Delta K/\Delta L < \mu^0 < \mu_y^0$ | $\theta_x^p < \xi_x^p < 1$ | $0 < \xi_y^p < \theta_y^p$ | P | A |
| (d) $\mu_x^0 < \mu^0 < \Delta K/\Delta L < \mu_y^0$ | $0 < \xi_x^p < \theta_x^p$ | $\theta_y^p < \xi_y^p < 1$ | A | P |
| (e) $\Delta K/\Delta L > \mu_y^0 > \mu_x^0$ | $\xi_x^p < 0$ | $\xi_y^p > 1$ | UA | UP |

*Note:* $N$ = neutral, $P$ = protrade biased, $UP$ = ultra-protrade biased, $A$ = antitrade biased, $UA$ = ultra-antitrade biased.

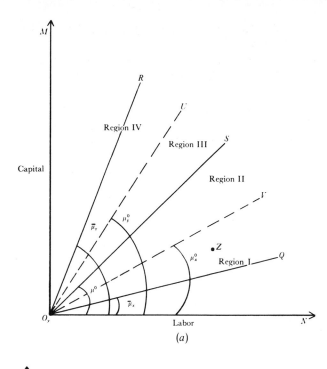

(a)

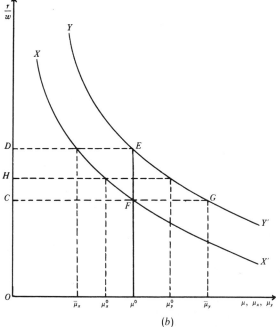

(b)

**Figure 13.2** (*a*) The production effects of factor growth depend on the pregrowth factor prices and overall endowment ratio. (*b*) Given the overall capital-labor ratio $\mu^0$, the ratio $r/w$ can vary between $OC$ and $OD$ only. Hence, $\bar{\mu}_x < \mu_x \leq \mu^0$ and $\mu^0 \leq \mu_y < \bar{\mu}_y$.

is illustrated in fig. 13.2. Figure 13.2($a$) partially reproduces fig. 13.1 (in particular, the area $MO_yN$). Capital is measured vertically and labor horizontally. The slope of the vector $O_yS$ shows the pregrowth overall capital-labor ratio which exists in $A$. Figure 13.2($b$) is similar to fig. 9.6. The capital-labor ratios $\mu$, $\mu_x$, and $\mu_y$ are measured horizontally; the factor-price ratio $r/w$ is measured vertically. The curves $XX'$ and $YY'$ give the optimum values of $\mu_x$ and $\mu_y$, respectively, for given values of $r/w$. Given the overall capital-labor ratio $\mu^0$, the ratio $r/w$ can vary between $OC$ and $OD$ only. Hence, $\bar{\mu}_x < \mu_x \le \mu^0$ and $\mu^0 \le \mu_y < \bar{\mu}_y$. Given $\bar{\mu}_x$ and $\bar{\mu}_y$, we can draw two vectors in fig. 13.2($a$), $O_yQ$ and $O_yR$, with slopes equal to $\bar{\mu}_x$ and $\bar{\mu}_y$, respectively. For any value of $r/w$ between the limits $OC$ and $OD$, such as $OH$, we can determine the optimum values of $\mu_x$ and $\mu_y$, as illustrated by the values $\mu_x^0$ and $\mu_y^0$, respectively.

Assume that the pregrowth factor-price ratio is actually given by $OH$. Then the four regions of fig. 13.1 are given by the synonymous regions in fig. 13.2($a$). Consider a point, such as $Z$, lying in region I. If $\Delta L$ and $\Delta K$ were given by the coordinates of $Z$ with respect to $O_y$, then $X_p$ would expand and $Y_p$ would contract with growth. But this necessarily depends on the particular pregrowth prices we have chosen. If the factor-price ratio were sufficiently higher than $OH$, the vector $O_yV$ could have been flatter than the vector $O_yZ$ (not drawn); then both $X_p$ and $Y_p$ would increase with growth, with $X_p$ increasing faster than $Y_p$. *We therefore conclude that when the factor increases, $\Delta L$ and $\Delta K$, determine a point in the cone $RO_yQ$, the type of $A$'s production effect cannot be predicted without further information about the pregrowth factor-price ratio. On the other hand, if the factor increases, $\Delta L$ and $\Delta K$, determine a point in the cone $QO_yN$, then $X_p$ increases and $Y_p$ falls with growth, irrespective of the pregrowth value of the factor-price ratio. Similarly, if the factor increases, $\Delta L$ and $\Delta K$, determine a point in the cone $MO_yR$, then $X_p$ falls and $Y_p$ increases with growth, irrespective again of the pregrowth factor-price ratio.* Note, finally, that the cones $MO_yR$ and $QO_yN$ depend on the pregrowth capital-labor ratio $\mu^0$.

## 13.3 THE TYPE OF OVERALL GROWTH

What type of growth would country $A$ experience in each of the preceding five cases of factor increases we have studied? That depends, in addition to the production effect, on the consumption effect. (Note that when only one factor increases, the extra income goes to the augmented factor and the consumption effect is a pure income effect of demand. On the other hand, if both factors increase, the incomes of both factors increase and the consumption effect becomes a weighted sum of income effects on demand.) The classification of $A$'s production effect (summarized in table 13.1) can be used to determine the resultant type of overall growth, under the various types of consumption behavior, directly from table 12.4. Further, given the type of overall growth, the effect of factor-endowment growth on $A$'s terms of trade can be predicted. Finally, making use of the one-to-one correspondence between the commodity-price ratio and the factor-price ratio, the effect of growth on factor prices can be inferred also.

## 13.4 THE EFFECT ON SOCIAL WELFARE

Let us consider the effect of overall growth on the level of social welfare in the growing country, $A$. Assume that country $A$ consists of identical individuals with respect to tastes (which are also homothetic) and factor endowments both before and after growth. What is the effect of $A$'s growth on the welfare of its representative citizen?

First distinguish between the *terms-of-trade effect*, which is due to the change in the commodity-price ratio, and the *wealth effect*, which is due to the shift of the production-possibilities frontier of $A$'s representative citizen. Other things being equal, $A$'s representative citizen tends to become better off when $A$'s terms of trade improve (this occurs only with ultra-antitrade-biased growth); he tends to become worse off when $A$'s terms of trade deteriorate; and he is indifferent when $A$'s terms of trade remain constant. Other things being equal, $A$'s representative citizen tends to become better off with an outward shift of his (scaled-down) production-possibilities frontier, which occurs when he has more capital to work with, i.e., when the overall capital-labor ratio $\mu$ increases; he tends to become worse off when his production-possibilities frontier shifts inward, which occurs when $\mu$ falls; and he is indifferent when his production-possibilities frontier remains constant, which occurs when $\mu$ remains constant.

The total effect on the welfare of $A$'s representative citizen depends on the combined effect of both the wealth effect and the terms-of-trade effect. When neither effect is unfavorable, $A$'s representative citizen definitely becomes better off with growth; and when neither effect is favorable, he definitely becomes worse off. But when one effect is favorable while the other is unfavorable, the total effect on the welfare of $A$'s representative citizen is indeterminate, the outcome depending on which of the two effects outweighs the other. Can we go beyond these generalizations and predict the total effect of growth on the welfare of $A$'s representative citizen in each of the five cases of factor increases?

Table 13.2 shows the nature of the wealth effect, the terms-of-trade effect, and the overall effect on the welfare of $A$'s representative citizen. Column (1) shows the nature of the wealth effect, which depends on the relationship between $\mu^0$ and $\Delta K/\Delta L$. Thus, when $\Delta K/\Delta L > \mu^0$, the wealth effect is necessarily favorable; when $\mu^0 > \Delta K/\Delta L$, the wealth effect is unfavorable; and when $\mu^0 = \Delta K/\Delta L$, the wealth effect is zero (or neutral). Columns (2) and (3) reproduce columns (3) and (4) of table 13.1. Column (4) shows the nature of the consumption effect, which is neutral, because all citizens have, by assumption, identical and homothetic tastes and factor endowments. Columns (5) and (6) show the type of overall growth. The information in columns (2) to (4), along with table 12.4, is used to determine the overall growth (columns (5) and (6)). Columns (7) and (8) show the terms-of-trade effect, which depends on the nature of the overall growth, given in columns (5) and (6). Columns (9) and (10) show the *total* effect of growth on the welfare of $A$'s representative citizen by combining the entries in column (1) with the corresponding entries in columns (7) and (8). It is clear from columns (9) and (10) that, *when country A exports the labor-intensive commodity* $(X)$, *A's representative citizen becomes worse off with growth when the incremental capital-labor ratio* $\Delta K/\Delta L$ *is*

# Table 13.2 The effects of factor increases

| Incremental capital-labor ratio $\Delta K/\Delta L$ | Production effect | | | Consumption effect (4) | Overall growth | | A's terms-of-trade effect | | Total effect on the welfare of A's representative citizen | |
|---|---|---|---|---|---|---|---|---|---|---|
| | Wealth effect on A's representative citizen (1) | When A exports the L-intensive commodity (X) (2) | When A exports the K-intensive commodity (Y) (3) | | When A exports the L-intensive commodity (X) (5) | When A exports the K-intensive commodity (Y) (6) | When A exports the L-intensive commodity (X) (A's terms of trade $= p_x/p_y$) (7) | When A exports the K-intensive commodity (Y) (A's terms of trade $= p_y/p_x$) (8) | When A exports the L-intensive commodity (X) (9) | When A exports the K-intensive commodity (Y) (10) |
| (a) $\mu_x^0 < \Delta K/\Delta L = \mu^0 < \mu_y^0$ | Neutral (production-possibilities frontier remains constant) | N | N | N | N | N | Unfavorable (deteriorate) | Unfavorable (deteriorate) | Unfavorable (worse off) | Unfavorable (worse off) |
| (b) $\Delta K/\Delta L < \mu_x^0 < \mu_y^0$ | Unfavorable (production-possibilities frontier shifts inward) | UP | UA | N | P or UP | UA | Unfavorable (deteriorate) | Favorable (improve) | Unfavorable (worse off) | Indeterminate (may become better off, worse off, or remain indifferent) |
| (c) $\mu_x^0 < \Delta K/\Delta L < \mu^0 < \mu_y^0$ | Unfavorable (production-possibilities frontier shifts inward) | P | A | N | P | A or UA | Unfavorable (deteriorate) | Indeterminate (may, improve, deteriorate or remain constant) | Unfavorable (worse off) | Indeterminate (may become better off, worse off, or remain indifferent) |
| (d) $\mu_x^0 < \mu^0 < \Delta K/\Delta L < \mu_y^0$ | Favorable (production-possibilities frontier shifts outward) | A | P | N | A or UA | P | Indeterminate (may improve, deteriorate, or remain constant) | Unfavorable (deteriorate) | Indeterminate (may become better off, worse off, or remain indifferent) | Indeterminate (may become better off, worse off, or remain indifferent) |
| (e) $\Delta K/\Delta L > \mu_y^0 > \mu_x^0$ | Favorable (production-possibilities frontier shifts outward) | UA | UP | N | UA | P or UP | Favorable (improve) | Unfavorable (deteriorate) | Favorable (better off) | Indeterminate (may become better off, worse off, or remain indifferent) |

*Note:* $N$ = neutral, $P$ = protrade biased, $UP$ = ultra-protrade biased, $A$ = antitrade biased, $UA$ = ultra-antitrade biased.

*either equal to or less than the pregrowth overall capital-labor ratio* $\mu^0$. Then $A$'s representative citizen has less capital to work with after growth, on the one hand, and $A$'s terms of trade deteriorate, on the other. Further, when $A$ exports the labor-intensive commodity $X$, $A$'s representative citizen becomes definitely better off only when $\Delta K/\Delta L > \mu_y^0$; when $\mu^0 < \Delta K/\Delta L < \mu_y^0$, the outcome is indeterminate. On the other hand, when $A$ exports the capital-intensive commodity $Y$, $A$'s representative citizen becomes worse off only when $\Delta K/\Delta L = \mu_0$; in all other cases, the outcome is indeterminate.

## PART B. TECHNICAL PROGRESS

Technical progress is an important factor of growth. It occurs when increased output can be obtained over time from given resources of capital and labor. It can take a variety of forms. Before we study its effects, we must define some of the simpler varieties.

## 13.5 EMBODIED VERSUS DISEMBODIED TECHNICAL PROGRESS

*Embodied technical progress* occurs when progress is *embodied* in *new* capital goods; it becomes effective after the installation of the new capital goods (usually machines) in which it is embodied. Since, with the passage of time, new and more productive capital goods come into existence, capital can no longer be assumed to be homogeneous. On the contrary, capital becomes essentially a mixed stock of capital goods of different "vintages." Capital goods of one vintage are different from those of another; because of embodied technical progress, capital goods of a more recent vintage are more productive than capital goods of an earlier vintage, other things being equal.

Labor can also be treated in a similar fashion. Thus, other things being equal, the workers of the most recent "vintage" (i.e., those who have had their training most recently) are more productive than those of earlier vintages.

*Disembodied technical progress* applies equally to all workers and capital goods. In other words, disembodied technical progress implies that increased output can be obtained over time from given quantities of labor and capital. This occurs irrespective of the "vintage" of workers and capital goods. In fact, labor and capital are assumed to be two homogeneous factors, with no two units of the same factor being in any way different with respect to productivity. Disembodied technical progress in general can be viewed as an inward shift of all isoquants of an industry undergoing technical progress.

In what follows, we are primarily interested in the various types of disembodied technical progress. We assume throughout that constant returns to scale prevail before and after the occurrence of technical progress and that technical progress occurs in a once-and-for-all fashion.

# 13.6 CLASSIFICATION OF DISEMBODIED TECHNICAL PROGRESS

Disembodied technical progress is usually classified into neutral, labor saving, and capital saving, but in the literature there exist several sets of definitions of neutral, labor-saving, and capital-saving technical progress. In general, the different definitions give rise to different classifications of otherwise similar phenomena. Needless to say, each particular set of definitions is adapted to a certain purpose. We shall adopt the Hicksian definitions (Hicks, 1964), which are the most appropriate for our purposes.

## Neutral Technical Progress

*Neutral technical progress* occurs in an industry when increased output is obtained from given quantities of labor and capital and, in addition, when the same factor ratio, $K/L$, is optimal before and after the change for each and every value of the factor-price ratio. In other words, the isoquants of the industry undergoing technical progress shift inward and, in addition, the marginal rate of substitution of labor for capital is the same before and after the technical change for all possible values of the capital-labor ratio in the industry. This type of disembodied technical progress amounts to a mere renumbering of the isoquants of the industry undergoing change.

Mathematically, this type of technical progress can be expressed as follows. Assume that $Q = Q(K, L)$ is a production function characterized by constant returns to scale. Then neutral technical progress implies that $Q^* = \lambda Q(K, L)$, where $\lambda > 1$ and $Q^* = $ the new amount of output produced with $K$ and $L$. Thus, $Q^* = \lambda Q$, with $Q$ the maximum amount of output which was obtained from the employment of $K$ and $L$ before the technical progress took place. Since $\partial Q^*/\partial L = \lambda(\partial Q/\partial L)$ and $\partial Q^*/\partial K = \lambda(\partial Q/\partial K)$, it follows that $(\partial Q^*/\partial L)/(\partial Q^*/\partial K) = (\partial Q/\partial L)/(\partial Q/\partial K)$. The renumbering of isoquants follows directly from the equation $Q^* = \lambda Q$.

## Labor-Saving Technical Progress

*Labor-saving technical progress* occurs in an industry when increased output is obtained from given quantities of labor and capital and, in addition, for any factor-price ratio, a smaller amount of labor per unit of capital (i.e., a smaller labor-capital ratio) is optimally employed after the change than before. Thus, labor is being saved per unit of capital employed. But this does not mean that only the labor factor is saved while the other factor, capital, is not. Whatever combination of $L$ and $K$ was originally used to produce a specified amount of output, there is at least one new combination of smaller $L$ and $K$ capable of producing that same amount of output after the change, since each isoquant shifts inward.

The case of labor-saving technical progress is illustrated in fig. 13.3, where the curve *bb* is the unit isoquant before the change and the curve *aa* is the unit

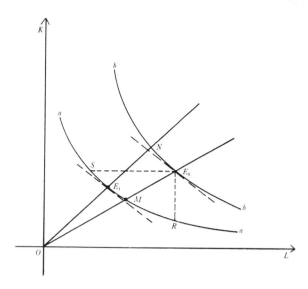

**Figure 13.3** Labor-saving technical progress.

isoquant after the change. Note that the new isoquant lies totally inside the old isoquant. For any factor-price ratio, such as that shown by the slope of $bb$ at $E_0$, the ratio $K/L$ used after the change is higher than that used before the change. Thus the vector $OE_1$ is steeper than the vector $OE_0$, where the slope of the $aa$ isoquant at point $E_1$ is equal to the slope of the $bb$ isoquant at $E_0$. This same relationship must hold for all factor prices.

Labor-saving technical progress in a certain industry tends to make that industry capital intensive relative to what the industry was before the change. *When the industry uses labor and capital in the same proportion before and after the change, the marginal rate of substitution of labor for capital is smaller after the change than before.* This is illustrated in fig. 13.3 where the slope at $E_0$ is steeper than the slope at $M$. Accordingly, an industry which experiences labor-saving technical change employs labor and capital in the same proportion after as before the change if, and only if, labor becomes, after the change, sufficiently cheaper relative to capital.

## Capital-Saving Technical Progress

*Capital-saving technical progress* occurs in an industry when increased output is obtained from given quantities of labor and capital and, in addition, at any factor prices, a smaller amount of capital per unit of labor (i.e., a smaller capital-labor ratio) is optimally employed after the change than before. Therefore, capital is being saved per unit of labor employed. Again, this does not mean that only the capital factor is saved.

The case of capital-saving technical progress is illustrated in fig. 13.4. Again, the curves $bb$ and $aa$ are the unit isoquants before and after the change, respectively. For any given value of the factor-price ratio, such as that implied by the

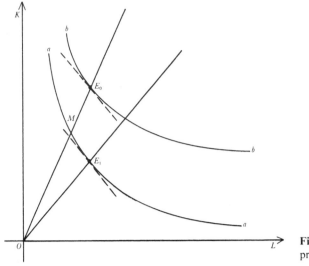
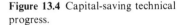

**Figure 13.4** Capital-saving technical progress.

slopes at points $E_0$ and $E_1$, the factor ratio $K/L$ is lower after the change, as illustrated by the fact that the vector $OE_1$ is flatter than the vector $OE_0$.

Capital-saving technical progress in a certain industry tends to make that industry labor intensive relative to what the industry was before the change. *For the same capital-labor ratio, the marginal rate of substitution of labor for capital is therefore higher after the change than before.* This is illustrated in fig. 13.4, where the slope at $M$ is steeper than the slope at $E_0$. Accordingly, an industry which experiences capital-saving technical change employs labor and capital in the same proportion after as before the change if, and only if, capital becomes, after the change, sufficiently cheaper relative to labor.

## The Original Hicksian Definitions

The original Hicksian definitions are worded differently. Hicks (1964) says that:

> . . . we can classify inventions according as their initial effects are to increase, leave unchanged, or diminish the ratio of the marginal product of capital to that of labour. We may call these inventions "labour-saving," "neutral," and "capital-saving" respectively. "Labor-saving" inventions increase the marginal product of capital more than they increase the marginal product of labour, "capital-saving" inventions increase the marginal product of labour more than that of capital, "neutral" inventions increase both in the same proportion (pp. 121–122).

In other words, Hicks compares the slopes of the unit isoquants of figs. 13.3 and 13.4 at points $E_0$ and $M$, that is, the *marginal rates of substitution at the original factor proportions used by the industry*. On the other hand, our definitions center on the comparison between the slopes of the vectors $OE_0$ and $OE_1$, under the assumption that the slope of the isoquant $bb$ at $E_0$ is equal to the slope of the isoquant $aa$ at $E_1$.

## Factor-Augmenting Technical Progress

*Factor-augmenting technical progress* is a fruitful formulation of disembodied technical progress which is used in the literature quite frequently. The idea is rather simple.

In general, disembodied technical progress is represented by a production function which includes time as a parameter. For instance, we may postulate the following production function:

$$Q = F(K, L; t) \tag{13.3}$$

with $\partial F/\partial t \geq 0$. As time $t$ increases, the function shifts so that increased $Q$ can be obtained from any given $K$ and $L$.

The formulation of factor-augmenting technical progress assumes that eq. (13.3) takes the more specific form

$$Q = F[\alpha(t)K, \beta(t)L] \tag{13.4}$$

where $\alpha(t)$ and $\beta(t)$ are increasing functions of time. In eq. (13.4) output $Q$ is a function of the *effective* amounts of capital and labor, that is, $\alpha(t)K$ and $\beta(t)L$—not just the *natural* amounts, $K$ and $L$. Even though the natural amounts $K$ and $L$ may remain constant, with the passage of time the effective amounts $\alpha(t)K$ and $\beta(t)L$ are augmented, and therefore output increases.

How is factor-augmenting technical progress related to the Hicksian classification of disembodied technical progress into neutral, labor saving, and capital saving? Consider two distinct points in time, say $t_0$ and $t_1$. Assume that at the initial point $(t_0)$, the parameters $\alpha$ and $\beta$ are unity, that is, $\alpha(t_0) = \beta(t_0) = 1$. As time moves to $t_1$, the parameters change to, say, $\alpha_1 = \alpha(t_1) \geq 1$ and $\beta_1 = \beta(t_1) \geq 1$, respectively. The classification into neutral, labor saving, and capital saving depends on whether $\alpha_1 = \beta_1$, $\alpha_1 > \beta_1$, or $\alpha_1 < \beta_1$, respectively.

When $\alpha_1 > 1$ and $\beta_1 = 1$, the technical change is said to be *purely capital augmenting*. On the other hand, when $\alpha_1 = 1$ and $\beta_1 > 1$, the technical change is said to be *purely labor augmenting*.

Consider the marginal physical products of labor and capital at $t_0$ and $t_1$ as follows:

$$\text{MPP}_L^1 = \beta_1 \frac{\partial F}{\partial L} = \beta_1 \text{MPP}_L^0 \tag{13.5}$$

$$\text{MPP}_K^1 = \alpha_1 \frac{\partial F}{\partial K} = \alpha_1 \text{MPP}_K^0 \tag{13.6}$$

where the superscripts 0 and 1 refer to the two points in time, $t_0$ and $t_1$, respectively. Take the ratio of eqs. (13.5) and (13.6) to establish the following relationship between the marginal rates of substitution of labor for capital at $t_0$ and $t_1$:

$$\text{MRS}_{LK}^1 = \frac{\text{MPP}_L^1}{\text{MPP}_K^1} = \frac{\beta_1 \text{MPP}_L^0}{\alpha_1 \text{MPP}_K^0} = \frac{\beta_1}{\alpha_1} \text{MRS}_{LK}^0 \tag{13.7}$$

Therefore, $\text{MRS}_{LK}^1 \gtrless \text{MRS}_{LK}^0$ according as $\beta_1/\alpha_1 \gtrless 1$, or $\beta_1 \gtrless \alpha_1$. If both factors are augmented at the same rate $(\alpha_1 = \beta_1)$, the technical progress is neutral; if capital is augmented at a higher rate than labor ($\alpha_1 > \beta_1$), technical progress is labor saving; and if labor is augmented at a higher rate than capital ($\alpha_1 < \beta_1$), technical progress is capital saving.

Labor-saving technical progress ($\alpha_1 > \beta_1$) can now be decomposed into *neutral* technical progress (where both factors are augmented by $\beta_1$) plus purely capital-augmenting technical progress (where capital is further augmented by the factor $\alpha_1 - \beta_1$). On the other hand, capital-saving technical progress ($\alpha_1 < \beta_1$) can be decomposed into neutral plus purely labor-augmenting technical progress.

## 13.7 TECHNICAL PROGRESS IN THE LABOR-INTENSIVE INDUSTRY ($X$)

Assume for the moment that $A$ is a small country which can buy and sell unlimited amounts of commodities $X$ and $Y$ in the international market at given prices. Assume further that $X$ and $Y$ are produced with two factors (labor, $L$, and capital, $K$) and that $X$ is labor intensive relative to $Y$. How does technical progress in each of the two industries of country $A$ affect $A$'s demand for imports and supply of exports, that is, $A$'s volume of trade at the pregrowth prices? We must first determine the type of production effect $A$ will experience by analyzing the behavior of $X_p$ ($A$'s output of $X$) and $Y_p$ ($A$'s output of $Y$) with the occurrence of one or another type of disembodied technical progress either in industry $X$ or in $Y$.

A simple but important proposition is that the relative price of the commodity undergoing technical progress is necessarily lower after the change for any given factor prices because, with technical progress, the unit isoquant for the said commodity necessarily shifts inward, closer to the origin. Irrespective of the type of technical progress, a lower isocost line is tangent to it after the change than before, and hence, the average cost of production, which is equal to the price of the commodity, is necessarily lower after the change for any given factor prices. For any given factor prices, the price of the other commodity whose production function does not shift (by assumption) necessarily remains the same. Accordingly, the relative price of the first commodity (which undergoes technical progress) necessarily falls. For instance, if, by assumption, technical progress occurs in industry $X$ only, the price ratio $p_x/p_y$ is necessarily lower after technical progress for any given factor prices.

### Neutral Technical Progress in Industry $X$

How does neutral technical progress in industry $X$ affect $A$'s box diagram and its production-possibilities frontier? As noted earlier, neutral technical progress in any industry results in a mere renumbering of that industry's isoquants, with each isoquant corresponding to a higher output after the change than before. From a purely geometrical point of view, as industry $X$ experiences neutral technical progress, its isoquants (inside the box diagram), and therefore the contract curve, remain the same after the change as before. Does this mean that the country's production-possibilities frontier also remains the same? No, for despite the fact

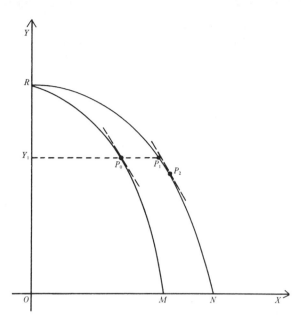

**Figure 13.5** Neutral technical progress in industry $X$.

that the isoquants and the contract curve do not appear to change with neutral technical progress, the renumbering of $X$'s isoquants necessarily causes the production-possibilities frontier to shift outward. This is illustrated in figure 13.5.

The curve $RP_0 M$ is $A$'s production-possibilities frontier. With neutral technical progress in industry $X$, $A$'s production-possibilities frontier shifts to $RP_1 P_2 N$ because, for any point on the contract curve (not shown), the output of $Y$ is the same before and after the change while the output of $X$ is necessarily higher after the change. For instance, when $OY_1$ units of commodity $Y$ are produced (as implied by a certain point on the contract curve), the output of commodity $X$ increases from $Y_1 P_0$ to $Y_1 P_1$.

The production-possibilities frontier necessarily has the same $Y$-axis intercept, $R$, after the change as before. The distance $OR$ shows the maximum output of $Y$ which could be obtained if all resources were employed in the production of $Y$. Since industry $Y$ does not undergo any change, $A$'s production-possibilities frontier must necessarily start at the same point, $R$, after industry $X$ experiences technical progress (neutral or any other type).

Assume now that the international price ratio $p_x/p_y$ is given by the absolute slope of $A$'s pregrowth production-possibilities frontier at $P_0$. The latter $(P_0)$ is $A$'s optimum production point before the change. Given that $p_x/p_y$ remains constant, where does $A$ produce after the change? Observe that each and every point on the (constant) contract curve implies the same marginal rate of substitution of labor for capital in both industries after as well as before the change. Hence, each and every point on the contract curve implies the same factor-price ratio after as well as before the change. In addition, each point on the contract curve implies the same output for $Y$. If the factor-price ratio were kept constant at the pregrowth level, $A$'s production point would therefore shift from $P_0$ to $P_1$. But at $P_1$, the slope of $A$'s production-possibilities frontier is necessarily flatter than the slope at $P_0$—for any given factor prices, commodity $X$ becomes relatively cheaper after industry $X$ experiences technical progress. Accordingly, at the pregrowth commodity prices, $A$ must be producing somewhere in the region $P_1 N$, as illustrated by point $P_2$.

To summarize, the slope at $P_1$ is flatter than the slope at $P_0$. Therefore, the point on $RP_1 P_2 N$ where the slope is equal to the slope at $P_0$ must lie in the region $P_1 N$, as shown by the point $P_2$. After the occurrence of neutral technical progress in industry $X$, the output of commodity $Y$ necessarily falls absolutely while the output of $X$ increases at given commodity prices.

## Labor-Saving Technical Progress in the Labor-Intensive Industry $X$

What happens to the output of $X$ $(X_p)$ and the output of $Y$ $(Y_p)$ at the internationally given commodity prices if industry $X$'s technical progress is not neutral but labor saving?

Consider first the effect (of labor-saving technical progress in industry $X$) on $X_p$ and $Y_p$ at the pregrowth equilibrium factor prices. Recall that industry $X$ necessarily tends to become less labor intensive (or more capital intensive) relative to its pre-technical-change status. In particular, if we assume that factor prices remain at their pregrowth equilibrium level, then $X$'s expansion path after the change becomes steeper than its expansion path before the change. This is illustrated in fig. 13.6.

The expansion path of industry $X$ before the change is given by the vector $O_x E_0$, and after the change by the steeper vector $O_x E_1$. Observe that, at the pregrowth factor prices, $Y$'s expansion path remains the same, as illustrated in fig. 13.6 by the straight line $O_y E_1 E_0$. Accordingly, the equilibrium point in the box diagram shifts from $E_0$ (before) to $E_1$ (after), and $Y$'s output falls from $O_y E_0$ to $O_y E_1$. Commodity $X$'s output increases for two reasons: (a) at $E_0$, $X$'s output is higher after the change, because with (any type of) technical progress increased output can be obtained from the same amounts of labor and capital; and (b) the shift from $E_0$ to $E_1$ necessarily implies a movement from a lower to a higher isoquant for industry $X$.

These changes in $X_p$ and $Y_p$ (that is, $\Delta X_p > 0$ and $\Delta Y_p < 0$) assume that *factor* prices are kept constant at their pregrowth level. We are actually interested in the changes in $X_p$ and $Y_p$ when *commodity* prices remain constant at their pregrowth level. Recall that, for the same factor prices (before and after the change), the commodity-price ratio $p_x/p_y$ is necessarily lower after the occurrence of technical progress in industry $X$. Because of increasing opportunity costs, as $p_x/p_y$ is allowed to increase to the pregrowth level, $X_p$ tends to increase further and $Y_p$ tends to fall further, from their respective levels at point $E_1$. These changes in $X_p$ and $Y_p$ reinforce the initial changes corresponding to the shift from $E_0$ to $E_1$ (fig. 13.6). Accordingly, the direction of total change in $X_p$ and $Y_p$ is a fortiori the same as in the preceding case of neutral technical change.

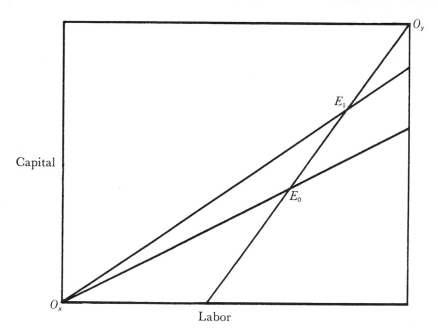

**Figure 13.6** Labor-saving and capital-saving technical progress in the labor-intensive industry ($X$).

## Capital-Saving Technical Progress in the Labor-Intensive Industry $X$

Figure 13.6 can also be used to illustrate the case of capital-saving technical change in industry $X$. Now the original expansion paths for $X$ and $Y$ are given by the vectors $O_x E_1$ and $O_y E_1 E_0$, respectively. Consider what happens to $X_p$ and $Y_p$ at the pregrowth equilibrium factor prices. With capital-saving technical progress, industry $X$ becomes less capital intensive (or more labor intensive), with its expansion path shifting from $O_x E_1$ to $O_x E_0$. Equilibrium shifts from $E_1$ to $E_0$, with $Y$'s output greater at $E_0$ than at $E_1$. Nothing, of course, can be said about the change in $X_p$—the outcome depends on the strength of the inward shift of $X$'s isoquants. For instance, if the isoquant passing originally through $E_1$ shifts to the isoquant that now passes through $E_0$, then the output of industry $X$ is the same at the two points; if the isoquant passing originally through $E_1$ shifts to a position below point $E_0$, the output of industry $X$ is higher at $E_0$ (after the change) than at $E_1$ (before the change); and if the isoquant passing originally through $E_1$ shifts to a position above point $E_0$, the output of industry $X$ is lower at $E_0$ (after the change) than at $E_1$ (before the change). In general, therefore, the sign of $\Delta X_p$ (at given factor prices) is indeterminate.

We also have to consider the changes that occur in $X_p$ and $Y_p$ as the commodity-price ratio $p_x/p_y$ is allowed to rise to its pregrowth level. Again, because of increasing opportunity costs, $Y_p$ falls and $X_p$ increases.

The total change in $X_p$ and $Y_p$ at the pregrowth equilibrium commodity prices is indeterminate. This is left as an exercise for the reader.

**Table 13.3 The effect of technical progress on $X_p$ and $Y_p$**

| | | | Production effect | |
|---|---|---|---|---|
| Technical progress | Sign of $\Delta X_p$ | Sign of $\Delta Y_p$ | When $A$ exports the labor-intensive commodity ($X$) | When $A$ exports the capital-intensive commodity ($Y$) |
| In industry $X$: | | | | |
|   Neutral | $\Delta X_p > 0$ | $\Delta Y_p < 0$ | $UP$ | $UA$ |
|   Labor saving | $\Delta X_p > 0$ | $\Delta Y_p < 0$ | $UP$ | $UA$ |
|   Capital saving | ? | ? | All types possible | All types possible |
| In industry $Y$: | | | | |
|   Neutral | $\Delta X_p < 0$ | $\Delta Y_p > 0$ | $UA$ | $UP$ |
|   Labor saving | ? | ? | All types possible | All types possible |
|   Capital saving | $\Delta X_p < 0$ | $\Delta Y_p > 0$ | $UA$ | $UP$ |

## 13.8 TECHNICAL PROGRESS IN THE CAPITAL-INTENSIVE INDUSTRY ($Y$)

There is no need to analyze the effects on $X_p$ and $Y_p$ of technical progress in industry $Y$. To do so, merely reverse the roles of the two factors and proceed as above. The results are summarized in table 13.3, where the last two columns show the nature of the production effect depending on whether $A$ is exporting commodity $X$ or $Y$.

## 13.9 THE EFFECT OF TECHNICAL PROGRESS ON THE TERMS OF TRADE

Drop the assumption that the commodity prices are fixed in the international market. What is the effect of the various types of technical progress on $A$'s terms of trade? First determine the type of overall growth that $A$ experiences with technical progress. As we have seen, $A$'s type of overall growth depends, in addition to the production effect, on the consumption effect. Using the information in part A of chap. 12, especially table 12.4, determine $A$'s type of overall growth as well as the effect on $A$'s terms of trade (see table 13.4). Note that $A$'s terms of trade are given by the ratio (price of $A$'s exportables)/(price of $A$'s importables). An increase in the latter ratio implies that $A$'s terms of trade improve, and a decrease implies that they deteriorate.

## 13.10 THE EFFECT OF TECHNICAL PROGRESS ON SOCIAL WELFARE

What is the effect of technical progress on the level of social welfare in $A$? Assume again that $A$'s citizens are identical with respect to tastes and factor endowments. Assume also that tastes are homothetic, which implies that the consumption effect is neutral. As before, distinguish between two effects on the welfare of $A$'s rep-

# Table 13.4 The effect of technical progress on A's terms of trade

| Technical progress | A exports the L-intensive commodity (X) | | | | | | A exports the K-intensive commodity (Y) | | | | | |
|---|---|---|---|---|---|---|---|---|---|---|---|---|
| | Production effect | Consumption effect | | | | | Production effect | Consumption effect | | | | |
| | | N | P | UP | A | UA | | N | P | UP | A | UA |
| **In the labor-intensive industry X:** | | | | | | | | | | | | |
| Neutral | UP | G: P or UP TOT: deteriorate | G: P or UP TOT: deteriorate | G: UP TOT: deteriorate | G: Not UA TOT: deteriorate | ? | UA | G: UA TOT: improve | G: UA TOT: improve | ? | G: UA TOT: improve | G: UA TOT: improve |
| Labor-saving | UP | G: P or UP TOT: deteriorate | G: P or UP TOT: deteriorate | G: UP TOT: deteriorate | G: not UA TOT: deteriorate | ? | UA | G: UA TOT: improve | G: UA TOT: improve | ? | G: UA TOT: improve | G: UA TOT: improve |
| Capital-saving | ? | ? | ? | ? | ? | ? | ? | ? | ? | ? | ? | ? |
| **In the capital-intensive industry Y:** | | | | | | | | | | | | |
| Neutral | UA | G: UA TOT: improve | G: UA TOT: improve | ? | G: UA TOT: improve | G: UA TOT: improve | UP | G: P or UP TOT: deteriorate | G: P or UP TOT: deteriorate | G: UP TOT: deteriorate | G: not UA TOT: deteriorate | ? |
| Labor-saving | ? | ? | ? | ? | ? | ? | ? | ? | ? | ? | ? | ? |
| Capital-saving | UA | G: UA TOT: improve | G: UA TOT: improve | ? | G: UA TOT: improve | G: UA TOT: improve | UP | G: P or UP TOT: deteriorate | G: P or UP TOT: deteriorate | G: UP TOT: deteriorate | G: not UA TOT: deteriorate | ? |

Note: G = type of overall growth, TOT = terms of trade, N = neutral, P = protrade biased, UP = ultra-protrade biased, A = antitrade biased, UA = ultra-antitrade biased.

resentative citizen: a *terms-of-trade effect*, which has already been determined in table 13.4, and a *wealth effect*, which corresponds to the outward shift of the production-possibilities frontier of $A$'s representative citizen. The wealth effect is always favorable: the production-possibilities frontier of $A$'s representative citizen always shifts outward with technical progress. However, as shown in table 13.4, the terms-of-trade effect may go either way. When it is favorable (i.e., when $A$'s terms of trade improve), $A$'s representative citizen becomes better off with growth. This occurs with certainty in only two cases: (a) when $A$ exports the labor-intensive commodity and either neutral or capital-saving technical progress occurs in the capital-intensive industry; and (b) when $A$ exports the capital-intensive commodity and either neutral or labor-saving technical progress occurs in the labor-intensive industry.

When either neutral or capital-saving technical progress occurs in the capital-intensive industry and, in addition, country $A$ exports the capital-intensive commodity, $A$'s terms of trade deteriorate. Similarly, when $A$ exports the labor-intensive commodity and, in addition, either neutral or labor-saving technical progress occurs in the labor-intensive industry, $A$'s terms of trade deteriorate. In these two cases, the total effect on the welfare of $A$'s representative citizen depends on which of the two effects outweighs the other—the wealth effect or the terms-of-trade effect.

The effect on $A$'s terms of trade is indeterminate in the following two cases: (a) when capital-saving technical progress occurs in the labor-intensive industry; and (b) when labor-saving technical progress occurs in the capital-intensive industry. As a result, in these two cases the total effect on the welfare of $A$'s representative citizen is, in general, indeterminate. If $A$'s terms of trade do not deteriorate, $A$'s representative citizen becomes better off; if they do deteriorate, $A$'s representative citizen may become better off (when the favorable wealth effect outweighs the unfavorable terms-of-trade effect) or worse off (when the unfavorable terms-of-trade effect outweighs the favorable wealth effect).

Two final comments are in order.

1. When technical progress of whatever type and in whichever industry is large enough to cause the production-possibilities frontier of $A$'s representative citizen to shift sufficiently outward and at least touch the indifference curve where $A$'s representative citizen is consuming in the pregrowth equilibrium state, $A$'s representative citizen definitely becomes better off with growth, irrespective of what happens to $A$'s terms of trade. Thus, the phenomenon of "immiserizing growth" occurs only when technical progress is rather small.
2. If country $A$ pursues an optimum tariff policy (discussed in chap. 19), then technical progress always makes $A$'s representative citizen better off.

## SELECTED BIBLIOGRAPHY

Bhagwati, J. (1958). "Immiserizing Growth: A Geometrical Note." *Review of Economic Studies*, vol. 25, pp. 201–205. Reprinted in R. E. Caves and H. G. Johnson (Eds.), AEA *Readings in International Economics*. Richard D. Irwin, Homewood, Ill., Inc., 1968.

Clement, M. O., R. L. Pfister, and K. J. Rothwell (1967). *Theoretical Issues in International Economics.* Houghton Mifflin Company, Boston, Mass., chap. 3.

Corden, W. M. (1956). "Economic Expansion and International Trade: A Geometric Approach." *Oxford Economic Papers*, vol. 8, pp. 223–228.

Edgeworth, F. Y. (1894). "The Theory of International Values." *Economic Journal*, vol. 4, pp. 35–50.

Ethier, W. (1972). "Nontraded Goods and the Heckscher–Ohlin Model." *International Economic Review*, vol. 13, no. 1 (February), pp. 132–147.

Findlay, R., and H. Grubert (1959). "Factor Intensities, Technological Progress and the Terms of Trade." *Oxford Economic Papers*, vol. 11, pp. 111–121.

Heller, H. R. (1968). *International Trade.* Prentice-Hall, Inc., Englewood Cliffs, N.J., chap. 7.

Hicks, J. R. (1964). *The Theory of Wages*, 2d ed. Macmillan and Company, Ltd., London.

——— (1953). "An Inaugural Lecture." *Oxford Economic Papers*, vol. 5, pp. 117–135.

Johnson, H. G. (1958). *International Trade and Economic Growth.* George Allen and Unwin, Ltd., London, chap. 3.

——— (1962). *Money, Trade and Economic Growth.* Harvard University Press, Cambridge, Mass., chap. 4. Reprinted in R. E. Caves and H. G. Johnson (Eds.), AEA *Readings in International Economics.* Richard D. Irwin, Inc., Homewood, Ill., 1968.

Kemp, M. C. (1964). *The Pure Theory of International Trade.* Prentice-Hall, Inc., Englewood Cliffs, N.J.

——— (1969). *The Pure Theory of International Trade and Investment.* Prentice-Hall, Inc., Englewood Cliffs, N.J.

Komiya, R. (1967). "Non-traded Goods and the Pure Theory of International Trade." *International Economic Review*, vol. 8, no. 2 (June), pp. 132–152.

Meier, G. M. (1963). *International Trade and Development.* Harper and Row, New York, chaps. 2 and 3.

Rybczynski, T. M. (1955). "Factor Endowment and Relative Commodity Prices." *Economica*, vol. 22, pp. 336–341.

Samuelson, P. A. (1956). "Social Indifference Curves." *Quarterly Journal of Economics*, vol. 70, pp. 1–22.

# FOURTEEN

## GROWTH IN A SIMPLE OPEN ECONOMY

The modern theory of international trade is basically a long-run *static* theory. It postulates the existence of two homogeneous factors of production which are usually assumed to remain in fixed supply throughout. Johnson (1962, chap. 4), among others, has developed a useful comparative-statics framework within which the assumptions of given technology and factor endowments can be relaxed. In fact, chaps. 12 and 13 are largely based on Johnson's work. But even though a comparative-statics analysis is useful, it leaves much to be desired, for it considers all changes in factor endowments as totally exogenous phenomena. Even though modern economists take, with some justification, the rate of growth of the labor force as given exogenously by demographic factors, the same claim cannot be made for capital, because the capital factor should be understood to mean "produced means of production," e.g., machines. How do these capital goods (i.e., machines) get to be produced, and how does their stock change through time? Is it legitimate to assume that the stock of machines as well as its changes through time are given exogenously? To answer these questions, the model of chaps. 8 to 10 has to be amended to include explicitly the capital-goods sector.

When the capital-goods sector is introduced into the model explicitly, the current stock of capital (machines) will be the integral of net saving and investment from the beginning of time until the current period. The current change of the stock of capital will be equal to the net saving and investment of the current period. Since the acts of saving and investment form an integral part of the economic process, the stock of capital and its growth cannot be taken as exogenous; they are, rather, endogenous, with their respective equilibrium values determined by the behavior of the economic system itself. Thus, contrary to the labor ratio will not be a variable whose value is being determined by factors which lie totally outside the scope of the economic system; i.e., it will not be an exogenous variable. It will, rather, be an endogenous variable, at least partially, with its long-run equilibrium value, if it exists, determined by the general-equilibrium solution of the system. For this purpose, a truly dynamic model must be developed. This is the purpose of the present chapter. A dynamic model of a simple open economy will be set up to show how the long-run equilibrium capital-labor ratio, and therefore the pattern of specialization, is determined.

This dynamic model can be considered as an integration of the one-sector and two-sector growth models developed by Solow (1956) and Uzawa (1961), respectively, because, on the one hand, relative prices will be held constant by assumption (and this makes our model akin to Solow's one-sector growth model) and, on the other hand, two sectors (a consumption-goods sector plus a capital-goods sector) will be explicitly considered (and this makes our model akin to Uzawa's two-sector growth model).

Recent important contributions in this field have been made by Bertrand (1973), Deardorff (1973, 1974a, 1974b, 1974c), Findlay (1970), Inada (1968), Johnson (1971a, 1971b, 1972), Kemp (1968, 1969, 1970), Khang (1971), Oniki and Uzawa (1965), and Vanek (1971).

## 14.1 THE ASSUMPTIONS

Let us start the discussion by enumerating the assumptions on which the analysis is based.

1. There are two factors of production, machines ($K$) and labor ($L$).
2. There are two products, newly produced machines ($Q_k$) and consumption goods ($Q_c$). (Note that both $Q_k$ and $K$ refer to machines; the former is the current output of machines and the latter is the stock of machines at a point in time.)
3. The production functions of both machines and consumption goods ($Q_k$ and $Q_c$) are characterized by constant returns to scale. Therefore, these production functions can be written in the following form:

$$Q_k = F_k(K_k, L_k) = L_k F_k\left(\frac{K_k}{L_k}, 1\right) = L_k f_k(\mu_k) \tag{14.1}$$

$$Q_c = F_c(K_c, L_c) = L_c F_c\left(\frac{K_c}{L_c}, 1\right) = L_c f_c(\mu_c) \tag{14.2}$$

where $K_k \equiv$ machines used in the production of machines; $L_k \equiv$ labor used in the production of machines; $K_c \equiv$ machines used in the production of consumption goods; $L_c \equiv$ labor used in the production of consumption goods; $\mu_k \equiv K_k/L_k$; $\mu_c \equiv K_c/L_c$; $f_k(\mu_k) \equiv F_k[(K_k/L_k), 1] =$ per capita output in the capital-goods industry; and $f_c(\mu_c) \equiv F_c[(K_c/L_c), 1] =$ per capita output in the consumption-goods industry.

4. Machines do not depreciate.†
5. The price of machines $(p_k)$ and the price of the consumption good $(p_c)$ are given in the international market.
6. Saving $(S)$ is proportional to income $(Y)$; that is,

$$S = sY \tag{14.3}$$

where $s \equiv$ marginal (and average) propensity to save and

$$Y \equiv Q_c + \frac{p_k}{p_c} Q_k \tag{14.4}$$

7. All saving is invested in newly produced machines. In other words, the possibility of a Keynesian inconsistency between saving and investment at full employment is ruled out.
8. Labor grows exponentially at the natural rate $n$. In other words,

$$L = L_0 e^{nt} \tag{14.5}$$

where $L =$ labor supply at time $t$ and $L_0 =$ labor supply at time 0.

## 14.2 EQUILIBRIUM IN THE SHORT RUN

Given these assumptions, we can draw upon the analyses of chaps. 5 to 10 to determine the short-run equilibrium of the model, i.e., the equilibrium of the model during a single time period. Thus, at the beginning of the period, the economy will be endowed with a certain amount of labor (which is historically determined) and a certain stock of machines (which is the result of capital accumulation in the past and, therefore, perfectly determined). On the basis of the historically given supply of labor $(L_0)$ and the stock of machines $(K_0)$, we can determine the production-possibilities frontier of the economy. Further, the equilibrium production point is that point where the production-possibilities frontier becomes tangent to the highest income-contour line, with slope equal to the given international price ratio, as explained in chap. 5. Finally, once the equilibrium production point is determined, the equilibrium absorption point‡ can be

---

† Exponential depreciation can be easily substituted for zero depreciation. The latter assumption is maintained throughout for simplicity.

‡ The term "absorption point" is substituted for "consumption point" used earlier in the book, because "consumption point" implies that both commodities are consumed, which is not the case now. The term "absorption point" seems to describe the present situation better.

determined by the condition that saving (which is assumed to be proportional to income) is being used to purchase newly produced machines.

## Graphical Solution

The preceding description of the short-run equilibrium process is illustrated in fig. 14.1. The output of consumption goods $Q_c$ and income $Y$ are measured along the horizontal axis, while the output of machines $Q_k$ is measured along the vertical axis. The curve $MPN$ is the economy's production-possibilities frontier for the time period under consideration. Where should the economy produce? As explained earlier in the book, the economy should produce at that point where income is being maximized. Imagine that the family of income contour lines with common absolute slope equal to the internationally given price ratio $p_c/p_k$ is superimposed on fig. 14.1. The economy will then produce at that point where the production-possibilities frontier is tangent to the highest income contour line. This is illustrated by point $P$, where the production-possibilities frontier is tangent to the straight line $ZPT$, this being the highest income contour line. Having determined the optimum production point, we can measure the economy's maximum income in terms either of the consumption good or of the capital good. In the former case, the economy's maximum income will be given by the horizontal distance $OT$, and in the latter case, by the vertical distance $OZ$.

    The equilibrium absorption point must lie on the highest income contour line $ZPT$. But how can it be determined? For this purpose, we can concentrate on

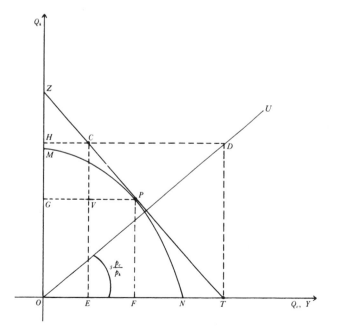

**Figure 14.1** Determination of equilibrium production, consumption, and trade in the short run.

either the demand for $Q_c$ or the demand for $Q_k$. Let us choose the latter. The demand for $Q_k$ ($Z_k$) is obviously equal to the value of saving expressed in terms of the capital good. In other words,

$$Z_k = \frac{p_c}{p_k} S = s \frac{p_c}{p_k} Y \tag{14.6}$$

Equation (14.6) is represented graphically by the vector $OU$ whose slope is given by $s(p_c/p_k)$. Since $Y$ is given by the distance $OT$, the economy must be saving and investing in newly produced machines in the amount $TD$. Thus, the equilibrium absorption point must lie on the income contour line $ZPT$, and the absolute quantity of capital goods demanded must be equal to the vertical distance $TD$. Obviously, the equilibrium absorption point occurs at the intersection of the horizontal line through point $D$ (that is, $DC$) and the income contour line $ZPT$ (that is, point $C$).

How do we know that the horizontal line through $D$ will intersect the income contour line $ZPT$ in the first quadrant? Put differently, how do we know that the distance $TD$ will not be larger than the distance $OZ$? Aggregate expenditure on both $Q_c$ and $Q_k$ is equal to the value of output produced. Since the value of output produced expressed in terms of the capital good is given by $OZ$, the economy can never demand a larger quantity of capital goods than $OZ$. In other words, the average propensity to save can never be larger than unity. In fact, it is less than unity, since the economy is assumed to spend part of its income on $Q_c$. Thus, $0 < s < 1$, and $TD = s(OZ)$; that is, $TD < OZ$.

Having determined the equilibrium production and absorption points, we can determine the quantities of $Q_c$ and $Q_k$ traded by the economy in the international market as the differences between the levels of production and consumption of each commodity. Therefore, in the example of fig. 14.1, the economy must be exporting $EF = VP$ units of the consumption good in exchange for $GH = VC$ units of the capital good.

## Mathematical Solution

The graphical solution can be clarified by setting up the problem in the form of a system of simultaneous equations. This is a necessary step for the determination of the long-run equilibrium solution. The system of equations is

$$Q_k = L_k \, f_k(\mu_k) \tag{14.1}$$

$$Q_c = L_c \, f_c(\mu_c) \tag{14.2}$$

$$K = K_k + K_c \tag{14.7}$$

$$L = L_k + L_c \tag{14.8}$$

$$p_k \frac{\partial Q_k}{\partial K} = p_k \, f'_k = r$$

or

$$f'_k = \frac{r}{p_k} \tag{14.9}$$

$$p_c \frac{\partial Q_c}{\partial K} = p_c\, f'_c = r$$

or
$$f'_c = \frac{r}{p_c} \tag{14.10}$$

$$p_k \frac{\partial Q_k}{\partial L} = p_k(f_k - \mu_k\, f'_k) = w$$

or
$$f_k - \mu_k\, f'_k = \frac{w}{p_k} \tag{14.11}$$

$$p_c \frac{\partial Q_c}{\partial L} = p_c(f_c - \mu_c\, f'_c) = w$$

or
$$f_c - \mu_c\, f'_c = \frac{w}{p_c} \tag{14.12}$$

$$\frac{f_c - \mu_c\, f'_c}{f'_c} = \frac{f_k - \mu_k\, f'_k}{f'_k} = \frac{w}{r} \tag{14.13}$$

$$Y = Q_c + \frac{p_k}{p_c} Q_k = L_c\, f_c + p L_k\, f_k \tag{14.14}$$

$$Z_k = \frac{S}{p} = \frac{sY}{p} \tag{14.6}$$

$$Z_c = (1 - s)Y \tag{14.15}$$

where the additional symbols in the above equations are $p \equiv p_k/p_c$, $r =$ money rental per unit of capital, $w =$ money wage rate, $Z_k =$ absolute quantity of new capital goods demanded (i.e., current investment evaluated in terms of the capital good), and $Z_c =$ absolute quantity of consumption goods demanded (i.e., current consumption evaluated in terms of the consumption good).

What is the interpretation of these equations? Equations (14.1) and (14.2) are the two production functions discussed earlier. Equations (14.7) and (14.8) are the full-employment conditions. Equations (14.9) to (14.12) are the familiar marginal productivity conditions. Equation (14.13), which follows from eqs. (14.9) to (14.12), is the condition that the marginal rate of substitution of labor for capital in the two industries must be equal. This is the condition which guarantees that the economy will allocate its resources according to the coordinates of some point on the contract curve in the box diagram and produce somewhere along the production-possibilities frontier. In fact, eqs. (14.1), (14.2), (14.7), (14.8), and (14.13) can be used to derive a relationship between $Q_k$ and $Q_c$ which is simply the mathematical expression for the economy's production-possibilities frontier.†

† Note that we have five equations in six unknowns: $Q_k$, $Q_c$, $L_k$, $L_c$, $K_k$, and $K_c$. Thus, four equations can be used to eliminate the four unknowns $L_k$, $L_c$, $K_k$, and $K_c$. The last equation, i.e., the production-possibilities frontier equation, will simply be an equation in $Q_k$ and $Q_c$.

Equation (14.14) expresses national income $Y$ as the value of output produced, while eqs. (14.6) and (14.15) show the aggregate demand for capital goods and consumption goods, respectively.

Let us write the equation for the economy's production-possibilities frontier as

$$G(Q_k, Q_c) = 0 \qquad (14.16)$$

It is impossible to derive an explicit expression for the production-possibilities frontier. Note, too, that the equilibrium production point (on the production-possibilities frontier) is determined by the condition

$$-\frac{dQ_c}{dQ_k} = \frac{dG/dQ_k}{dG/dQ_c} = p \qquad (14.17)$$

Thus, starting with eq. (14.17), we can determine the optimum production point $(Q_k^*, Q_c^*)$ and work backwards, with the system of five equations we have formulated, to determine the equilibrium values of all other variables in the system, that is, $L_k^*$, $L_c^*$, $K_k^*$, and $K_c^*$, where the asterisks are used to indicate equilibrium quantities. We can also determine the ratios

$$\mu_k^* = \frac{K_k^*}{L_k^*} \qquad \text{and} \qquad \mu_c^* = \frac{K_c^*}{L_c^*}$$

When $Q_k^*$ and $Q_c^*$ are known, eq. (14.14) can be used to determine the equilibrium value of output produced, $Y^*$. Equations (14.6) and (14.15) can be used to determine the equilibrium quantities $Z_k^*$ and $Z_c^*$. The differences $(Z_k^* - Q_k^*)$ and $(Z_c^* - Q_c^*)$ are the economy's excess demand for capital goods and consumption goods, respectively, and they must satisfy the equation

$$p(Z_k^* - Q_k^*) + (Z_c^* - Q_c^*) = 0$$

Thus far, we have worked with the aggregate variables $Y$, $Z_k$, and $Z_c$. Consider now the per capita version of these variables, defined as

$$y \equiv \frac{Y}{L} = \frac{L_c}{L}f_c + p\frac{L_k}{L}f_k \qquad (14.18)$$

$$z_k \equiv \frac{Z_k}{L} = \frac{sy}{p} \qquad (14.19)$$

$$z_c \equiv \frac{Z_c}{L} = (1 - s)y \qquad (14.20)$$

## The Per Capita Income

The per capita income $y$ turns out to be of crucial importance to the analysis of long-run equilibrium. For this reason, let us devote the rest of this section to refining eq. (14.18).

Note the following relationship:

$$\mu \equiv \frac{K}{L} = \frac{K_k + K_c}{L} = \frac{K_k}{L_k}\frac{L_k}{L} + \frac{K_c}{L_c}\frac{L_c}{L} = \frac{L_k}{L}\mu_k + \frac{L_c}{L}\mu_c \qquad (14.21)$$

Equation (14.21) can be solved simultaneously with the equation

$$\frac{L_k}{L} + \frac{L_c}{L} = \frac{L}{L} = 1$$

for the ratios $L_k/L$ and $L_c/L$. Thus,

$$\frac{L_k}{L} = \frac{\mu - \mu_c}{\mu_k - \mu_c} \tag{14.22}$$

$$\frac{L_c}{L} = \frac{\mu_k - \mu}{\mu_k - \mu_c} \tag{14.23}$$

Substituting eqs. (14.22) and (14.23) into eq. (14.18) gives us

$$y = \frac{\mu_k - \mu}{\mu_k - \mu_c} f_c + p \frac{\mu - \mu_c}{\mu_k - \mu_c} f_k \tag{14.24a}$$

Equation (14.24a) expresses the per capita income in terms of the ratios $\mu$, $\mu_k$, and $\mu_c$ and the price ratio $p$. Now $p$ is given in the international market and the ratios $\mu_c$ and $\mu_k$ are uniquely determined when $p$ and $\mu$ are known. Thus, given $p$, we can determine the corresponding factor-price ratio $w/r$ on the basis of which we can determine the optimum ratios $\mu_c^*$ and $\mu_k^*$. The latter ratios will actually be observed if and only if $\mu$ falls between these ratios, for $\mu$ is always a weighted average of the *observed* ratios $\mu_c$ and $\mu_k$. Thus, if $\mu_c^* < \mu_k^*$ and $\mu$ lies outside the region $(\mu_c^*, \mu_k^*)$, the country will be specializing completely in the production of one commodity only, as is shown in chaps. 8 to 10. In particular, if $\mu < \mu_c^* < \mu_k^*$, the economy will be specializing in the production of $Q_c$, with $\mu_c = \mu$ and $L_k = K_k = 0$. On the other hand, if $\mu_c^* < \mu_k^* < \mu$, the economy will be specializing in $Q_k$, with $\mu_k = \mu$ and $L_c = K_c = 0$. With this understanding, we can state that $y$ is a function of $\mu$. In particular, when both commodities are produced, $y$ is given by eq. (14.24a), with $\mu_c = \mu_c^*$ and $\mu_k = \mu_k^*$; when the economy is specializing in $Q_c$, $y$ is given by eq. (14.25); and when the economy is specializing in $Q_k$, $y$ is given by eq. (14.26):

$$y = f_c(\mu) \qquad \text{(specialization in } Q_c\text{)} \tag{14.25}$$

$$y = p f_k(\mu) \qquad \text{(specialization in } Q_k\text{)} \tag{14.26}$$

In the short run, $\mu$ is of course given. With the passage of time, however, $\mu$ will in general change as $K$ and $L$ grow until long-run equilibrium is established. It is interesting to see how changes in $\mu$ affect $y$.

If the economy is specializing completely in one or the other commodity, it should be obvious from eqs. (14.25) and (14.26) that $y$ changes in the same direction as $\mu$, because $f_c' > 0$ and $f_k' > 0$. But what if the economy is producing both commodities? Is it still true that $y$ changes in the same direction as $\mu$? Differentiating $y$ (as given by eq. (14.24a)) with respect to $\mu$, and remembering that $\mu_c = \mu_c^*$ and $\mu_k = \mu_k^*$, we get

$$\frac{dy}{d\mu} = \frac{f_c - p f_k}{\mu_c^* - \mu_k^*} \tag{14.27}$$

What is the sign of the derivative $dy/d\mu$ in this case? Is it still positive? Although it may not be obvious, it is necessarily positive, for an increase in $\mu$ implies that the amount of capital allocated to the representative citizen increases. Thus, his production-possibilities frontier shifts outward, resulting in an increase of his income $y$, however measured, at the original prices. Even though this intuitive reasoning shows that $dy/d\mu$ must be positive, we have to show that this is so by proving that the right-hand side of eq. (14.27) is necessarily positive. How can this be done?

Observe that the value of output produced in the consumption-good industry (expressed in terms of the consumption good) per unit of labor employed in the consumption-good industry is given by $f_c$ and that the value of output produced in the capital-good industry (expressed in terms of the consumption good) per unit of labor employed in the capital-good industry is given by $pf_k$. Further, the value of output produced in either industry is necessarily equal to the total cost of production of that output. Since factor prices are assumed identical for both industries, when one industry uses absolutely more labor and capital than the other industry, the value of output produced by the first industry must necessarily be higher than the value of output produced by the second. Now $f_c$ and $pf_k$ in eq. (14.27) show the value of output produced in the consumption-good industry and the capital-good industry, respectively, per unit of labor employed in each industry. Since labor is only one of two factors, whether $f_c \gtreqless pf_k$ depends upon the amount of capital per unit of labor used in each industry, that is, $\mu_c$ and $\mu_k$. Thus, if $\mu_c > \mu_k$, $f_c$ must necessarily be higher than $pf_k$, and if $\mu_c < \mu_k$, $f_c$ must be lower than $pf_k$. That is,

$$\mu_c \gtreqless \mu_k \leftrightarrow f_c \gtreqless pf_k$$

which necessarily implies that the right-hand side of eq. (14.27) is positive.

A more direct mathematical proof of the conclusion that the right-hand side of eq. (14.27) is positive can be given in several ways. The following is not the easiest, but it is a by-product of a further simplification of eq. (14.24a) that will be quite useful to our future investigations. Let us rewrite eq. (14.24a) as

$$y = \frac{1}{\mu_k - \mu_c} [\mu_k\, f_c - p\mu_c\, f_k + \mu(pf_k - f_c)] \tag{14.24b}$$

Before the expression in brackets on the right-hand side of eq. (14.24b) can be simplified, observe that from eqs. (14.11) and (14.12) it follows that

$$p(f_k - \mu_k\, f'_k) = f_c - \mu_c\, f'_c$$

or

$$pf_k - f_c = p\mu_k\, f'_k - \mu_c\, f'_c = f'_c(\mu_k - \mu_c) \tag{14.28}$$

because $p = f'_c/f'_k$. The latter follows from eqs. (14.9) and (14.10). From eqs. (14.13) we have

$$\mu_k\, f_c = \frac{w}{r}\, \mu_k\, f'_c + \mu_k\mu_c\, f'_c$$

$$p\mu_c\, f_k = \frac{w}{r}\, \mu_c\, f'_k p + \mu_c\mu_k\, f'_k p = \frac{w}{r}\, \mu_c\, f'_c + \mu_c\mu_k\, f'_c$$

Thus,

$$\mu_k f_c - p\mu_c f_k = \frac{w}{r}\mu_k f'_c + \mu_k\mu_c f'_c - \frac{w}{r}\mu_c f'_c - \mu_c\mu_k f'_c$$

$$= \frac{w}{r}f'_c(\mu_k - \mu_c) \tag{14.29}$$

Substituting eqs. (14.28) and (14.29) into eq. (14.24b) and simplifying, we get

$$y = \left(\frac{w}{r} + \mu\right)f'_c = \left(\frac{w}{r} + \mu\right)pf'_k \tag{14.30}$$

Thus, $dy/d\mu = f'_c > 0$.

For completeness, note that

$$\frac{dz_k}{d\mu} = \frac{s}{p}\frac{dy}{d\mu} > 0 \tag{14.31}$$

$$\frac{dz_c}{d\mu} = (1 - s)\frac{dy}{d\mu} > 0 \tag{14.32}$$

## 14.3 EQUILIBRIUM IN THE LONG RUN

The problem of long-run equilibrium is an interesting one. The short-run equilibrium considered in the preceding section is based on the assumption that the overall capital-labor ratio $\mu$ is historically given. The analysis is deliberately limited to the short run, where the system does not have the time to react on the given value of $\mu$. In the long run, however, this assumption has to be dropped, and the system will be allowed to react on the overall capital-labor ratio. As long as $\mu$ changes through time, the short-run equilibrium solution will change continuously. Only when the value of $\mu$ is stabilized at some level will the short-run equilibrium solution be repeated continuously. This long-run equilibrium state of affairs is called *steady-state growth*. When steady-state growth is achieved, both labor and capital, as well as aggregate income, consumption, investment, exports, and imports, will all grow at the natural rate $n$. Only the per capita counterparts of these variables will remain constant. The major task in this section is to determine the long-run equilibrium value of $\mu$ and show whether or not a system will be driven automatically to that value, i.e., whether or not a system will be stable.

### A Methodological Problem

Let us first consider a methodological problem. In a real economy, not only does $\mu$ change with the passage of time but other short-run parameters change as well. Thus, shifts in international supply and demand relations affect $p$, which in turn affects $\mu_c^*$ and $\mu_k^*$; and technical progress causes the functions $f_k$ and $f_c$ to shift upward through time, and so on. Why then does our long-run analysis consider only the changes in the overall capital-labor ratio? The importance of changes in the various parameters of a system should not be underestimated, and certainly it would be foolish to imply that the changes of $\mu$ through time are somehow more important than the changes of any other short-run parameters. However, all other changes except those of the overall capital-labor ratio are *exogenous* in the sense that they cannot be determined by the equations of our model. They represent phenomena which our system takes as given. In other words, we lack the information necessary to predict the behavior of these short-run parameters through time. As a result, we make the easiest assumption, namely, that they remain constant. On the other hand, $\mu$ changes through time as a result of labor growth and capital accumulation. But whereas labor growth is also considered exogenous, capital accumulation is not. Therefore, despite the fact that at any point in time $\mu$ can be considered as given, its behavior through time as well as its long-run equilibrium value can be *endogenously* determined.

## The Condition for Long-Run Equilibrium

Let us now return to the analysis of the long-run equilibrium of our simple model. From eq. (14.5), we have

$$\frac{dL}{dt} \equiv \dot{L} = nL_0 e^{nt} = nL$$

or

$$\frac{\dot{L}}{L} = n \tag{14.33}$$

The rate of increase of the capital stock $dK/dt$, or $\dot{K}$, is given by $\dot{K} = Z_k = sY/p$. Thus,

$$\frac{\dot{K}}{L} = z_k = s\frac{y}{p} \tag{14.34}$$

Differentiating the ratio $\mu \equiv K/L$ with respect to time $t$ and substituting from eqs. (14.33) and (14.34), we get

$$\frac{d\mu}{dt} \equiv \dot{\mu} = \frac{L\dot{K} - K\dot{L}}{L^2} = \frac{\dot{K}}{L} - \frac{K}{L}\frac{\dot{L}}{L} = \frac{sy}{p} - \mu n \tag{14.35}$$

Steady-state growth occurs when $\dot{\mu} = 0$, that is, when $s(y/p) - \mu n = 0$, or

$$\frac{y}{p} = \mu\frac{n}{s} \tag{14.36a}$$

Equation (14.36a), which is the condition for steady-state growth, can also be cast in terms of the natural rate of growth of labor $n$, the marginal propensity to save, and the capital-output ratio $v$. Thus, rewrite eq. (14.36a) as

$$n = \frac{ys}{p\mu} = \frac{(Y/L)s}{p(K/L)} = \frac{s}{p(K/Y)} = \frac{s}{v} \tag{14.36b}$$

Note that $v \equiv pK/Y$, that is, capital has to be measured in the same units as income.

Let us introduce the variables

$$\phi \equiv \phi(\mu; p) = \frac{y}{p} \tag{14.37}$$

$$\psi \equiv \psi(\mu; n, s) = \mu \frac{n}{s} \tag{14.38}$$

The long-run equilibrium condition (14.36$a$) can now be rewritten as

$$\phi(\mu; p) = \psi(\mu; n, s) \tag{14.36c}$$

Both $\phi$ and $\psi$ are functions of $\mu$. In addition, changes in $p$ affect only the function $\phi$, whereas changes in either $n$ or $s$ affect only the function $\psi$. Let us attempt the solution of eq. (14.36c) graphically.

## A Graphical Solution

In fig. 14.2, the ratios $\mu$, $\mu_c$, and $\mu_k$ are measured along the horizontal axis, moving rightward from the origin; the variables $f_c$, $f_k$, $\phi$, and $\psi$ are measured along the vertical axis, moving upward from the origin. The functions $f_c$, $f_k$, and $\psi$ are given by the synonymous curves in the first quadrant. The function $\psi = \mu(n/s)$ is given by a vector through the origin with slope equal to the ratio $n/s$. The functions $f_c(\mu_c)$ and $f_k(\mu_k)$ start from the origin, by assumption, and they are both strictly concave in the sense that the tangent to either curve at any point will lie totally above the curve except at the point of tangency itself.[†] The strict concavity of the functions $f_c$ and $f_k$ is the result of diminishing returns to capital. In particular, the slope of the $f_c$ curve ($f'_c$) at any point gives the marginal physical product of capital in the consumption-goods industry. The slope of the $f_k$ curve ($f'_k$) at any point gives the marginal physical product of capital in the capital-goods industry. Since $f''_c < 0$ and $f''_k < 0$ (because of the assumption that the marginal physical product of capital is diminishing in both industries), both the $f_c$ curve and the $f_k$ curve are strictly concave.

To determine the long-run equilibrium value of $\mu$, the function $\phi = y/p$ must be represented graphically. As noted earlier, $y$ is a function of $\mu$. In particular, it is given by eq. (14.25), (14.26), and (14.30). But how can the variable $y/p$ or $\phi$ be represented graphically?

Consider the third quadrant of fig. 14.2 Along the horizontal axis, we measure, moving leftward from the origin, the factor-price ratio $w/r$, and along the vertical axis, moving downward from the origin, we measure the commodity-price ratio $p = p_k/p_c$. The curve $JMS$ in the third quadrant shows the familiar one-directional relation of commodity prices to factor prices. Thus, starting with the

---

[†] A function $f(x)$ is said to be concave in a certain region if, for any two points $x_1$ and $x_2$ in the specified region, the following relationship holds:

$$f[\lambda x_1 + (1 - \lambda)x_2] \geq \lambda f(x_1) + (1 - \lambda)f(x_2) \qquad 0 \leq \lambda \leq 1$$

It is *strictly* concave if the strict inequality holds for all $\lambda$ such that $0 < \lambda < 1$ and $x_1 \neq x_2$.

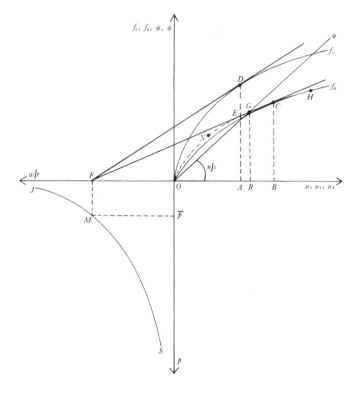

**Figure 14.2** Steady-state growth.

commodity-price ratio $\bar{p}$ given in the international market, we determine the corresponding factor-price ratio $OF$ which will prevail in the country, in the absence of complete specialization.

Given any value of the factor-price ratio, such as $OF$, we can determine the optimum capital-labor ratios of both industries as follows. Draw from point $F$ the tangents to the curves $f_c$ and $f_k$ as shown by $FD$ and $FEC$, respectively. Then project the tangency points $D$ and $C$ on the horizontal axis as shown by the broken lines $DA$ and $CB$. The horizontal distance $OA$ is the optimum capital-labor ratio in the consumption-goods industry, and the distance $OB$ is the optimum capital-labor ratio in the capital-goods industry. It should be noted that in fig. 14.2 it is implicitly assumed that the capital good is capital intensive relative to the consumption good for all factor prices. This is confirmed by the fact that $OB > OA$. The real question, however, concerns the logic behind this construction. Why can the optimum capital-labor ratios $\mu_c^*$ and $\mu_k^*$ be determined in the fashion just described? The answer is implicit in the analysis of short-run equilibrium.

Consider any point on the $f_c$ curve, such as point $D$. At $D$, the average physical product of labor in the $Q_c$ industry is given by the vertical distance $AD$, the capital-labor ratio $\mu_c$ by the horizontal distance $OA$, and the marginal physical product of capital $f'_c$ by the slope of the $f_c$ curve at $D$, that is, $AD/FA$. What is the marginal rate of substitution of labor for capital at point $D$? By definition, we must have

$$\text{MRS}^c_{LK} = \frac{\text{MPP}^c_L}{\text{MPP}^c_K} = \frac{f_c - \mu_c f'_c}{f'_c} = \frac{f_c}{f'_c} - \mu_c$$

$$= \frac{AD}{AD/FA} - OA = FA - OA = FO \qquad (14.39)$$

That is, the marginal rate of substitution of labor for capital at $D$ is given by the distance $FO$, that is, the intercept of the tangent to the $f_c$ curve at $D$ with the $w/r$ axis. Repeating the same exercise for the capital-good industry, we can easily establish a similar relationship. We already know that when both commodities are produced, the marginal rate of substitution of labor for capital in either industry has to be equal to the common factor-price ratio $w/r$—hence the technique of fig. 14.2.

Let us derive the $\phi = y/p$ curve in the first quadrant of fig. 14.2. All we have to do is apply eqs. (14.25), (14.26), and (14.30), after dividing both sides of these equations by $p$. Thus, if the overall capital-labor ratio $\mu$ is larger than $OB$ (that is, the optimum capital-labor ratio of the capital-intensive industry), $\phi = y/p$ will be given by the $f_k$ curve because the economy will be specializing in the production of the capital good. Further, for $OA \le \mu \le OB$, $\phi = y/p$ will be given by the straight-line segment $EC$. Finally, for $\mu < OA$, $\phi = y/p$ will be given by $f_c/p$, as shown by the broken curve $OE$, because the country will be specializing in the production of the consumption good.

Note that the broken curve $OE$ has been drawn to lie totally above the $f_k$ curve in the region $\mu \le OA$, except at the origin, where the two curves coincide. Is this necessary, or is it because the curve has simply been drawn that way? The broken curve $OE$ must necessarily lie totally above the $f_k$ curve. This follows from the fact that, in this region, the economy specializes in the production of the consumption good. This pattern of specialization necessarily implies that the per capita income, however measured, is at a maximum. In other words, the income contour line lies farther from the origin when the economy produces at the intercept of the production-possibilities frontier with the $Q_c$ axis, as compared with any other point, on the frontier, and, in particular, as compared with the intercept of the frontier with the $Q_k$ axis.

Steady-state growth occurs at the intersection of the $\phi$ curve (that is, $ONEGCH$) with the $\psi$ curve (i.e., the vector $OG$). That is, long-run equilibrium occurs at point $G$, with the overall capital-labor ratio given by the distance $OR$.

In this illustration, the economy necessarily produces both commodities, since $OA < OR < OB$. But this is not always so. For instance, if the natural rate of growth of labor were a little higher, so that the $\psi$ curve were a little steeper than the vector $OE$ (not drawn), such as the vector $ON$ (not drawn), the economy's long-run equilibrium capital-labor ratio would be smaller than $OA$ and the economy would specialize completely in the production of the consumption good which is the labor-intensive commodity. On the other hand, if $n$ were a little smaller, so that the $\psi$ curve were flatter than the vector $OC$ (not drawn), such as the vector $OH$ (not drawn), the overall long-run equilibrium capital-labor ratio would be higher than $OB$ and the economy would specialize completely in the production of the capital-intensive commodity, that is, $Q_k$.

## Existence, Uniqueness, and Stability of Long-Run Equilibrium

The equilibrium point $G$ in fig. 14.2 is globally stable. That is, if the economy starts with a capital-labor ratio different from $OR$, there will be a continuous change through time until $\mu = OR$. Why? For one thing, $G$ is the only intersection of the $\phi$ curve with the $\psi$ curve. In addition, for values of $\mu$ in the region $\mu < OR$, $\phi - \psi > 0$ or $y/p - (\mu n)/s = \dot{\mu}/s > 0$, that is, $\dot{\mu} > 0$. But a *positive* $\dot{\mu}$ means that $\mu$ *increases* through time. On the other hand, for values of $\mu$ in the region $\mu > OR$, $\phi - \psi < 0$ or $y/p - (\mu n)/s = \dot{\mu}/s < 0$, that is, $\dot{\mu} < 0$, and a *negative* $\dot{\mu}$ means that $\mu$ *decreases* through time. Accordingly, irrespective of the initial capital-labor ratio, the economy will sooner or later attain and maintain the equilibrium capital-labor ratio $OR$; that is, it will attain the steady-state growth path which, as fig. 14.2 shows, is uniquely determined.

The long-run equilibrium portrayed in fig. 14.2 is unique. But is this an inherent property of our model, or is it something accidental? A closer look at fig. 14.2 will show that, if a long-run equilibrium exists at all, it will have to be unique and globally stable. Why? Because the $\psi$ curve is a vector through the origin, while the $\phi$ curve is concave. In particular, the $\phi$ curve is concave in the region $EC$ but strictly concave elsewhere. Equilibrium can occur in the concave region $EC$ if, and only if, the $\psi$ curve is steeper than $EC$, that is, if, and only if, $n/s > (1/p)f'_c(\mu^*_c) = f'_k(\mu^*_k)$. Put differently, equilibrium cannot occur in the region $EC$ when the $\psi$ curve is parallel to $EC$. Therefore, if equilibrium exists, it has to be unique because the $\psi$ curve cannot intersect the $\phi$ curve more than once.

Another important question arises in relation to the existence of a steady-state growth path. Does it always exist? Or better, what are the necessary and sufficient conditions for its existence? From fig. 14.2, it should be clear that two conditions are necessary and sufficient: (a) the tangent to the $\phi$ curve at the origin must be steeper than the $\psi$ curve; and (b) the $\phi$ curve must become flatter than the $\psi$ curve past a certain point. Each condition is necessary, and together they are sufficient for the existence of a steady-state growth path. Thus, if the $\psi$ curve (or vector) is steeper than the tangent to the $\phi$ curve at the origin, no intersection will ever occur between the two curves other than the origin. The overall capital-labor ratio will fall continuously through time. This case would arise if the natural rate of growth of labor $n$ is exceedingly high and the average propensity to save $s$ is exceedingly low. Eventually, the economy disappears, and thus this case is uninteresting. On the other hand, if the economy is so productive that the marginal physical product of capital in the capital-goods industry (that is, the slope of the $f_k$ curve) never falls below the ratio $n/s$, again no intersection would occur between the two curves ($\phi$ and $\psi$), but this time the overall capital-labor ratio would tend to rise continuously. This would certainly be the case if $n$ were zero and $f'_k$ remained nonnegative throughout. In what follows, assume that a unique, globally stable, long-run equilibrium exists.

The first condition, namely, that the tangent to the $\phi$ curve at the origin be steeper than the $\psi$ curve, can be stated as $(1/p)f'_c(0) > n/s$. But this condition seems to depend on $p$. Can we reformulate it so that it is independent of $p$? We can do so with a slightly stronger condition. Recall that the broken curve $OE$ must necessarily lie above the $f_k$ curve in the region $\mu < OA$. In general, the $\phi$ curve will not lie below the $f_k$ curve irrespective of $p$, if we assume, of course, that $Q_k$ is capital intensive relative to $Q_c$. Therefore, a stronger condition would be for the $\psi$ curve to be flatter than the slope of the $f_k$ curve at the origin, that is, $f'_k(0) > n/s$. This condition also holds in the case where $Q_c$ is capital intensive relative to $Q_k$.

## The Pattern of Specialization

Although the pattern of specialization is perfectly determined once the steady-state growth path is attained, nothing can be said about the pattern of specialization during the transitional period when the system is moving toward long-run equilibrium. Any pattern of specialization is possible during this transitional period, as can be verified from fig. 14.2. But even when the steady-state growth path is attained, we cannot be sure, from the construction of fig. 14.2, which commodity is exported and which imported, unless the economy is completely specialized in the production of a single commodity. This does not mean, of course, that at point $G$ the pattern of specialization is indeterminate. On the contrary, it is perfectly determinate, but it is not obvious from fig. 14.2 which is the exported and which the imported commodity. However, all the information is available for the determination of the pattern of specialization at point $G$. Thus, the per capita demand for newly produced capital goods is given by $z_k = s(RG)$. On the other hand, the per capita output of capital goods, say $y_k$, is given by

$$y_k = \frac{L_k}{L} f_k(\mu_k^*) = \frac{\mu - \mu_c^*}{\mu_k^* - \mu_c^*} f_k(\mu_k^*) = \frac{OR - OA}{OB - OA} BC = \frac{AR}{AB} BC$$

In addition, applying eq. (14.24a) directly gives us

$$RG = \frac{RB}{AB} AE + \frac{AR}{AB} BC$$

or

$$z_k = s(RG) = s\left(\frac{RB}{AB} AE + \frac{AR}{AB} BC\right)$$

The imports of capital goods will be zero if $z_k = y_k$, that is,

$$s = \frac{(AR)(BC)}{(RB)(AE) + (AR)(BC)} \equiv s_0 < 1 \tag{14.40}$$

On the other hand, if $s > s_0$, the capital good will be imported (that is, $z_k > y_k$), and if $s < s_0$, the capital good will be exported (that is, $z_k < y_k$). It should be clear now why the pattern of specialization is not obvious from fig. 14.2. We do not know what the value of $s$ is, because an infinite number of values of $s$ is consistent with equilibrium at point $G$.

The assumption that the capital good is capital intensive relative to the consumption good can be reversed and the long-run equilibrium of the system determined along the lines of the analysis of this section.

## 14.4 COMPARATIVE DYNAMICS

So far, the discussion has been limited to the problems of uniqueness, existence, and stability of long-run equilibrium under the assumption that the parameters $p$, $n$, and $s$ assume certain specific values. It would be interesting to consider the effects of changes in these parameters on the long-run equilibrium values of the variables in our model. For instance, how would the long-run equilibrium capital-labor ratio (or the rate of growth, or per capita consumption, or per capita income, and so on) be affected by a change in $p$, or $n$, or $s$? All these are questions of *comparative dynamics*. Despite the fact that there are not enough equations to determine the behavior of these parameters through time, changes in these parameters will nevertheless occur. In addition, from the point of view of policy, if the government could somehow affect these parameters, what would be the best policy?

Any changes in $n$ or $s$ affect the $\psi$ curve only, and any changes in $p$ affect the $\phi$ curve only. Let us start with the effects of a once-and-for-all change in the natural rate of growth of labor $n$.

### The Effects of a Change in the Natural Rate of Growth

Suppose that $n$ increases from, say, $n_0$ to $n_1$. How does the new steady-state growth path compare with the old? In terms of fig. 14.2, as $n$ increases, the $\psi$ curve tends to become steeper. This implies that the equilibrium capital-labor ratio and thus per capita income will necessarily fall; and since per capita income falls, per capita consumption and per capita investment also fall. In addition, the per capita output of the consumption-goods industry (i.e., the labor-intensive commodity) will tend to rise and the per capita output of the capital-goods industry will tend to fall. In other words, $y_c \equiv (L_c/L)f_c(\mu_c^*)$ rises and $y_k \equiv (L_k/L)f_k(\mu_k^*)$ falls. This follows from the Rybczynski theorem studied in chap. 13, but we can also see this directly from fig. 14.2.

If $n$ increases so much that the $\psi$ curve becomes steeper than the vector $OE$ (not drawn), the economy will specialize completely in the production of $Q_c$. But what if the new equilibrium falls in the region $EG$, where the country continues to produce both commodities? As we saw earlier, $y_k = (AR)(BC)/AB$, and as equilibrium moves closer to point $E$, the distance $AR$ shrinks (while $BC$ and $AB$ remain constant), causing $y_k$ to fall. In a similar fashion, it can be shown that

$$y_c = \frac{\mu_k^* - \mu^*}{\mu_k^* - \mu_c^*} f_c(\mu_c^*) = \frac{RB}{AB} AD$$

Thus, as $\mu$ falls, $RB$ rises while $AB$ and $AD$ remain the same; hence, $y_c$ rises.

Note that if the new equilibrium occurs in the region $EG$ of the $\phi$ curve, the economy will continue to produce both commodities and the factor-price ratio will continue to be given by $OF$. But what if the new equilibrium occurs in the region $ONE$ and the economy specializes in the production of $Q_c$? Will the factor-price ratio remain constant in this case, too? Obviously not. The economy will be producing somewhere along the region $OD$ of the $f_c$ curve, and the tangent to the $f_c$ curve in this region will necessarily intersect the $(w/r)$ axis to the right of $F$. Therefore, the factor-price ratio will necessarily fall. Note, too, that all aggregates in the system $(K, \dot{K}, Z_c, Y, Q_c, Q_k$, and imports and exports) will now grow at the faster rate $n_1$.

## The Effects of a Change in the Average Propensity to Save

Let us turn now to the parameter $s$. How does a once-and-for-all change in $s$ affect the long-run equilibrium of the system? From fig. 14.2, it can be shown that an increase in $s$ will cause the overall capital-labor ratio to rise, and a decrease in $s$ will cause it to fall. Therefore, when $s$ falls, the per capita income also falls, and when $s$ rises, the per capita income rises. We know this from the fact that the $\phi$ curve is upward sloping, implying a higher per capita income in terms of the capital good as $\mu$ rises. Does this also mean that the per capita consumption falls when $s$ falls and it rises when $s$ rises? Not necessarily. As $s$ changes, per capita consumption can go either way, despite the fact that the per capita income will change in the same direction as $s$.

In particular, per capita consumption is given by eq. (14.20), or

$$z_c = (1 - s)y = (1 - s)p\phi \tag{14.41}$$

Steady-state growth requires that eq. (14.36a) be satisfied. But eq. (14.36a) can be solved for $s$. Thus,

$$s = \frac{n\mu}{\phi} \tag{14.42}$$

Substituting eq. (14.42) into eq. (14.41), we get

$$z_c = (1 - s)p\phi = \left(1 - \frac{n\mu}{\phi}\right)p\phi = (\phi - n\mu)p$$

Since $p$ is assumed constant, by an appropriate choice of the units of measurement we can make it equal to unity. Thus,

$$z_c = \phi - n\mu \tag{14.43}$$

Equation (14.43) is given graphically in fig. 14.3. The $\phi$ curve is the familiar curve derived in fig. 14.2. A vector is drawn through the origin with slope equal to $n$. In fig. 14.3a, the straight-line segment $RH$ is flatter than the vector $n\mu$; in fig. 14.3b, they are parallel. The per capita consumption is now given by the vertical distances between the $\phi$ curve and the vector $n\mu$. Draw another curve $(z_c)$ which shows directly the vertical differences between the $\phi$ curve and the vector $n\mu$

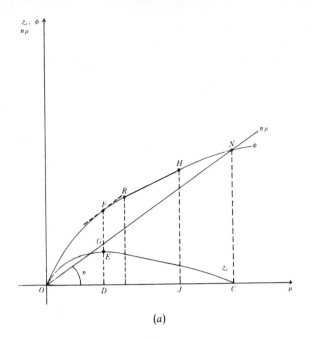

(a)

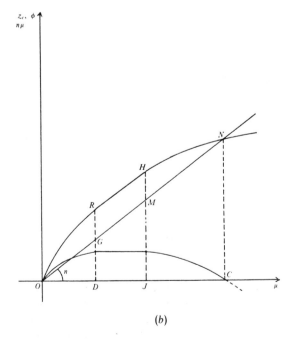

(b)

**Figure 14.3** Per capita consumption. (a) The vector $ON$ is steeper than $RH$. Here maximization of per capita consumption implies complete specialization and occurs at a unique value of $\mu$ (and $s$). (b) The vector $ON$ is parallel to $RH$. Here maximization of per capita consumption implies incomplete specialization and occurs over a range of $\mu$ (and $s$).

(that is, per capita consumption) for all values of $\mu$. Observe that $z_c$ is initially rising, because for the existence of long-run equilibrium it is required that the slope of the $\phi$ curve at the origin be greater than $n/s$. Since $s < 1$, the slope to the $\phi$ curve at the origin will definitely be greater than $n$ if it is already greater than $n/s$ ($> n$). Beyond a certain point, the $z_c$ curve becomes downward sloping. In fact, beyond a certain point, per capita consumption becomes negative. Nevertheless, this part of the curve is totally irrelevant, because equilibrium will certainly take place in the region where $z_c$ is positive. Graphically, $z_c$ becomes negative for values of $\mu$ beyond the intersection of the $\phi$ curve with the vector $n\mu$.

Given the value of $s$, we can determine the long-run equilibrium of the system by rotating the vector $n\mu$ upward until its slope becomes equal to $n/s$. This will be the $\psi$ curve of fig. 14.2, so equilibrium can be determined as before. As $s$ increases, the $\psi$ curve becomes flatter and the equilibrium capital-labor ratio as well as the per capita income necessarily rise. On the other hand, as $s$ falls, the $\psi$ curve becomes steeper and the equilibrium capital-labor ratio as well as the per capita income necessarily fall. However, per capita consumption does not behave in this fashion. If the initial equilibrium capital-labor ratio is smaller than $OD$, per capita consumption will tend to move in the same direction as $s$. But if the initial equilibrium capital-labor ratio is larger than $OD$, as $s$ increases per capita consumption will either fall immediately (fig. 14.3($a$)) or remain constant for a while and then fall (fig. 14.3($b$)).

From the preceding discussion, it follows that per capita consumption is maximized at a specific value of $\mu$ (as shown in fig. 14.3($a$)) or over a certain region of values of $\mu$ (as illustrated in fig. 14.3($b$)). Since there is a one-to-one correspondence between $\mu$ and $s$, there will be a certain value (or region of values) of $s$ at which per capita consumption is maximized. How can we determine the value(s) of the average propensity to save for which per capita consumption is maximized? In fig. 14.3($a$), per capita consumption is maximized when $\mu = OD$. At that point, we have $\phi = DF$. Long-run equilibrium will now occur at point $F$ (where $\mu = OD$) if, and only if, the vector $\psi$ coincides with the vector $OF$ (not drawn), i.e., if $n/s = DF/OD$ or $s = n(OD)/DF$. But $n = DG/OD$. Therefore,

$$s = \frac{DG}{OD} \frac{OD}{DF} = \frac{DG}{DF} < 1$$

Figure 14.3($b$) illustrates the case where per capita consumption is maximized over a range of values of $\mu$ and $s$. In this case, per capita consumption is maximized for any value of $\mu$ in the region $OD \leq \mu \leq OJ$. The corresponding range of $s$ is, of course, $DG/DR \leq s \leq JM/JH$.

The optimum value of $s$ is uniquely determined only when maximization of per capita consumption implies complete specialization in one or the other commodity. If both commodities are produced, there will be an infinite number of values of $s$ and $\mu$ that will be compatible with that maximum level of per capita consumption. In particular, per capita consumption is maximized when $dz_c/d\mu = \phi' - n = 0$, or

$$\phi' = n \tag{14.44}$$

That is, per capita consumption is maximized when the slope of the $\phi$ curve is equal to the rate of growth of labor. If the slope of the straight-line segment $(RH)$ of the $\phi$ curve, where the economy is actually producing both commodities, is equal to $n$, as in fig. 14.3($b$), the $z_c$ curve will become horizontal over that region. Thus, maximal per capita consumption occurs over this whole range of values of $\mu$ and a corresponding range of values of $s$.

Why should there be this important difference between the case of complete specialization and the case of complete diversification (i.e., the case where both commodities are produced)? Let us first attempt a common-sense interpretation of eq. (14.44). Assume that the economy has been on a steady-state growth path—not necessarily the maximum per capita consumption path. Had $\mu$ been higher all along, per capita income would have been higher. How much higher depends on the marginal product of capital expressed in terms of the consumption good $(\text{MPP}_k)$, since per capita income is measured in terms of the consumption good. Therefore, when the economy is specializing in the consumption good, we have $\text{MPP}_k = f'_c(\mu_c)$; when it is specializing in the capital good, we have $\text{MPP}_k = pf'_k(\mu_k)$; and when it is producing both commodities, we have $\text{MPP}_k = f'_c(\mu_c) = pf'_k(\mu_k)$. Thus, having a bit more capital per unit of labor, that is, $\Delta\mu$, at this time would yield $\text{MPP}_k \Delta\mu$ more per capita output. But not all of this is available for consumption. Having a bit more capital per unit of labor now commits the economy (under the steady-state growth rules of the game) to some additional investment now and in the future, to keep the slightly higher $\mu$ constant: $K$ and $L$ must grow at the fixed rate $n$ in long-run equilibrium. In particular, an extra bit of capital per unit of labor $(\Delta\mu)$ now means that an output of $n \Delta\mu$ of capital goods (or $np \Delta\mu$ of consumption goods) per unit of labor is required simply to maintain $\mu$ at its higher level. Clearly, if $\text{MPP}_k \Delta\mu > np \Delta\mu$ or $\text{MPP}_k > np$, a larger $\mu$ will yield some extra per capita consumption now and forever. If $\text{MPP}_k < np$, a larger $\mu$ now will imply a smaller per capita consumption now and forever. Thus, per capita consumption is at a maximum when $\text{MPP}_k = np$. Note that $\text{MPP}_k = dy/d\mu$; hence, the equation $\text{MPP}_k = np$ is equivalent to eq. (14.44).

Suppose the economy specializes completely in the production of one commodity only. As $\mu$ increases, $\text{MPP}_k$ falls continuously; therefore, there exists one, and only one, value of $\mu$ at which eq. (14.44) is satisfied. However, when the country is producing both commodities, $\text{MPP}_k$ does not necessarily fall as $\mu$ increases. This is because $\mu$ is a weighted average of $\mu_c$ and $\mu_k$; and as $\mu$ changes, the weights of $\mu_c$ and $\mu_k$ change, leaving $\mu_c$ and $\mu_k$ themselves unchanged. Thus, $\text{MPP}_k$ remains constant in this range, as evidenced by the linear segment $RH$ of fig. 14.3. If this constant value of $\text{MPP}_k$ (along the straight-line segment $RH$) coincides with the product $np$ (which is constant by assumption), there will be a whole range of values of $\mu$ giving rise to the same maximum per capita consumption.

The condition for maximum per capita consumption is described in the literature as the "golden rule" condition (or as the "neo-neoclassical growth theorem"). It should be noted, however, that it is a technical condition and not a normative rule. Thus, if the economy's actual capital-labor ratio were larger than the "golden rule" capital-labor ratio, per capita consumption could be raised both immediately and in the future by reducing the average propensity to save to the " golden rule" level. In this case, the " golden rule" is a normative prescription for increasing welfare, unless the economy derives utility from the mere possession of capital in addition to the utility it derives from consumption. But if the economy's actual capital-labor ratio $\bar{\mu}$ is smaller than the "golden rule" capital-labor ratio $\mu_g$, the increase in the average propensity to save required to raise $\bar{\mu}$ to $\mu_g$ would entail a sacrifice of immediate consumption for the sake of higher future consumption. This would involve an intertemporal choice between present and future consumption, the basis for which is not provided by the model.

These comments hold not only for the case where per capita consumption is maximized at a specific value of $\mu$ (as shown in fig. 14.3($a$)) but also for the case where it is maximized over a certain region of values of $\mu$ (as shown in fig. 14.3($b$)). But in the latter case the argument is slightly more complicated. Thus, in fig. 14.3($b$), per capita consumption is maximized for any value of $\mu$ in the region $OD \leq \mu \leq OJ$. As noted earlier, the corresponding range of $s$ is $DG/DR \leq s \leq JM/JH$. If the actual value of $s$ is smaller than $DG/DR$, per capita consumption can increase in the future only if immediate consumption is sacrificed; therefore, in this case the "golden rule" cannot serve as a normative prescription for increasing welfare because the model does not provide for the required intertemporal choice between present and future consumption. Now assume that the actual average propensity to save is higher than $JM/JH$. Per capita consumption could increase now and in the future if the average propensity to save were allowed to fall to $JM/JH$. But should $s$ be allowed to fall below $JM/JH$? Yes, it should be allowed to fall to $DG/DR$, the smallest value of $s$ which maximizes per capita consumption, for as $s$ falls from $JM/JH$ to $DG/DR$, current consumption increases without any sacrifice of future consumption. This is clearly a welfare gain, under the proviso given in the preceding paragraph.

To summarize, as $s$ increases, the overall capital-labor ratio $\mu$ and per capita income $y$ increase. Per capita consumption $z_c$ may increase, decrease, or remain constant, and it is actually maximized when $\phi' = n$.

Suppose now that, as the average propensity to save $s$ increases, the per capita consumption $z_c$ increases also. Is it possible for the rate of growth of $z_c$ to be higher than the rate of growth of $y$? Observe that the rate of growth of $y$ is a weighted average of the rate of growth of $z_c$ and $z_k$, because

$$y = z_c + pz_k \tag{14.45}$$

$$\Delta y = \Delta z_c + p\,\Delta z_k \tag{14.46}$$

$$\frac{\Delta y}{y} = \frac{\Delta z_c}{y} + p\frac{\Delta z_k}{y} = \left(\frac{\Delta z_c}{z_c}\right)\left(\frac{z_c}{y}\right) + \left(\frac{\Delta z_k}{z_k}\right)\left(\frac{pz_k}{y}\right) \tag{14.47}$$

From eq. (14.19) it is clear that $z_k$ increases faster than $y$, since both $s$ and $y$ increase. Accordingly, the rate of growth of $y$ must be smaller than the rate of growth of $z_k$ but higher than the rate of growth of $z_c$. This is sensible because, as $s$ and thus $\mu$ increase, a larger amount of saving will be needed to maintain $\mu$ at the higher level. This makes the rate of growth of $z_c$ fall short of the rate of growth of $y$.

How does a change in $s$ affect the long-run equilibrium volume of trade? Contrary to the comparative-static analysis of the preceding chapter, where the long-run equilibrium volume of trade was uniquely determined before and after growth, in the present case the aggregate volume of trade is growing before and after the change in $s$ at the natural rate of growth $n$. Accordingly, we must either compare the aggregate volume of trade before with the aggregate volume of trade after the change in $s$ at a single point in time or, better, compare the per capita volume of trade before with the per capita volume of trade after the change in $s$, because the per capita volume of trade is indeed uniquely determined. How does a change in $s$, then, affect the per capita volume of trade? To illustrate, assume that $s$ increases. We distinguish among the following three cases.

**Case (a)** Assume that our economy is specializing in the production of $Q_c$ before and after the increase in $s$. Then $\mu_c = \mu$. As $s$ increases, $\mu = \mu_c$ increases, too. Therefore, $y = f_c(\mu_c)$ increases. Since $Q_c$ is exported by assumption, the per capita volume of trade, measured by the difference $(f_c - z_c)$, will definitely increase, because $f_c \ (= y)$ increases faster than $z_c$. In fact, $z_c$ might even decrease.

In terms of the terminology adopted in chap. 12, in the present case the production effect is neutral while the consumption effect is either protrade biased or ultra-protrade biased. Hence, the overall effect of the increase in $s$ on the per capita volume of trade is either protrade biased or ultra-protrade biased.

**Case (b)** Assume that our economy is specializing in the production of $Q_k$ before and after the increase in $s$. Then $\mu_k = \mu$. As $s$ increases, $\mu = \mu_k$ increases, too. Therefore, $f_k \ (= y/p)$ increases. Now the volume of trade, measured by the amount of $Q_c$ imported, may increase or decrease. But if the volume of trade actually increases, it cannot increase as fast as $y$.

Here again, in terms of the terminology adopted in chap. 12, the production effect is necessarily neutral while the consumption effect is either antitrade biased or ultra-antitrade biased. Accordingly, the overall effect of the increase in $s$ on the per capita volume of trade is either antitrade biased or ultra-antitrade biased.

**Case (c)** Assume that both commodities (that is, $Q_c$ and $Q_k$) are being produced before and after the increase in $s$. Here, an increase in $s$ will cause $\mu$ and $y$ to increase. However, the per capita output of the consumption-goods industry $(L_c f_c / L)$ will fall and the per capita output of the capital-goods industry $(L_k f_k / L)$ will rise. But what happens to the per capita volume of trade? It appears that anything is possible, except in the case where $Q_c$ is exported and $z_c$ increases with $s$. Then the per capita volume of trade will definitely fall. This is so because the per capita volume of trade is given by the difference $(L_c f_c / L) - z_c$; or, if we apply the terminology of chap. 12, because in this special case the production effect is ultra-antitrade biased while the consumption effect is protrade biased. In all other cases, the outcome cannot be determined by a prior analysis.

## The Effects of a Change in the Terms of Trade

Consider now the parameter $p$. How do changes in $p$ affect the $\phi$ curve? Consider fig. 14.4. When $p = p_0$, the $\phi$ curve is given by $OE'C'H$. When $p$ increases to

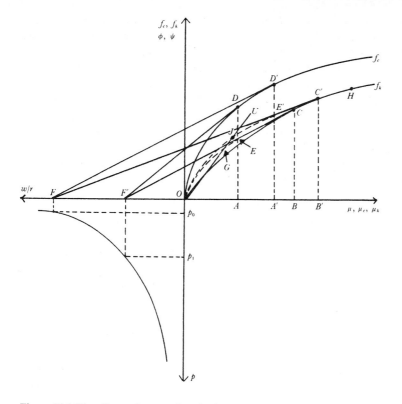

**Figure 14.4** The effects of terms-of-trade changes.

$p = p_1$, the corresponding factor-price ratio falls from $OF$ to $OF'$ and points $A'$, $B'$, $C'$, $D'$, and $E'$ shift to $A$, $B$, $C$, $D$, and $E$, respectively. The new $\phi$ curve at $p = p_1$ is given by $OECH$. That is, as $p$ rises, the $\phi$ curve shifts downward and to the right in the region $\mu < OB'$; it remains stable in the region $\mu \geq OB'$.

Reversing the procedure, we can also find out how the $\phi$ curve shifts when $p$ falls. Thus, if $p$ were initially at $p_1$ and fell to $p_0$, the $\phi$ curve would shift from $OECH$ to $OE'C'H$. In other words, as $p$ falls, the $\phi$ curve shifts upward and to the left in the region $\mu < OB'$; it remains stable in the region $\mu \geq OB'$. Point $B'$ is not fixed; it depends on the lower of the two values of $p$ considered.

The limit of the $\phi$ curve as $p$ increases beyond bounds is the $f_k$ curve itself. Thus, as $p$ increases, point $C$ travels along the $f_k$ curve toward the origin; its limiting position is surely the origin. The broken part ($OE$ or $OE'$) of the $\phi$ curve disappears completely as $p$ increases beyond a certain point.

Suppose now that the economy has been on a steady-state growth path for some time and then $p$ changes. The system, given sufficient time, will move to another steady-state growth path. How does the new path compare with the old? If the economy was originally specializing in the production of $Q_k$, an increase in $p$ will leave the intersection between the $\phi$ curve and the vector $\psi$ totally unaffected. This is so because, in terms of fig. 14.4, if $p = p_0$ and the economy is specializing in

$Q_k$, equilibrium would occur, on the $\phi$ curve, to the right of point $C'$, such as point $H$. But as we have seen, when $p$ increases, the $\phi$ curve remains stable in the region $\mu > OB'$, that is, beyond point $C'$. Hence, the intersection at $H$ will not be affected. Does this mean that the new steady-state growth path will be identical to the old? Not in every respect. The long-run equilibrium capital-labor ratio and $\phi$ (that is, $y/p$) will, of course, remain the same. But the per capita income expressed in $Q_c$ (that is, $y$) and the per capita consumption $z_c$ will rise in proportion to $p$. This follows from the fact that the ratio $y/p$ remains constant while $p$ rises. The per capita investment, however, given by $z_k = s\phi$, will necessarily remain the same. Therefore, under these circumstances, an increase in $p$ (that is, an improvement in the terms of trade) will simply raise the per capita consumption and hence the per capita imports of $Q_c$ in proportion to $p$ and $y$. Note that since $\mu$ remains constant, the production-possibilities frontier of the representative citizen will necessarily remain the same before and after the increase in $p$. His consumption-possibilities frontier will change, though, because of the change in $p$. In particular, the production point will remain the same. However, the absorption point will imply higher consumption of $Q_c$ but the same investment in $Q_k$ compared with the initial steady-state growth path. The preceding argument can be reversed for moderate decreases in $p$—moderate in the sense that the economy continues to specialize completely in $Q_k$ after the reduction in $p$.

Suppose now that at the initial steady-state growth path the economy is specializing in the production of the consumption good. How does a change in $p$ affect this path in the long run? That is, how does the new path compare with the old? In this case, the initial equilibrium occurs somewhere in the region $OE$ or $OE'$ (fig. 14.4), as the case may be. This part of the $\phi$ curve shifts when $p$ changes. Therefore, even the equilibrium capital-labor ratio will have to change in this case. Suppose that the vector $OU$ in fig. 14.4 is the $\psi$ vector. When $p = p_0$, equilibrium occurs at point $J$. On the other hand, when $p = p_1$, equilibrium occurs at point $G$. It follows that, as $p$ rises, $\mu$ falls; and as $p$ falls, $\mu$ rises. That is, $p$ and the equilibrium capital-labor ratio move, in this case, in opposite directions. What happens to the per capita income $y$, per capita consumption $z_c$, and per capita investment $z_k$ as $p$ changes in this case? Recall that the economy is assumed to specialize completely in the production of $Q_c$ before and after the change in $p$. Accordingly, $y$ is identical with $f_c(\mu)$. As $p$ falls (i.e., as the terms of trade improve), $\mu$ increases and thus $f_c$ increases. Per capita consumption necessarily increases proportionally to per capita income, since $z_c = (1 - s)y$. On the other hand, per capita investment rises more than proportionally to per capita income, because $z_k = sy/p$ and $y/p$ rises faster than $y$ because $p$ falls. Finally, since the economy is specializing in $Q_c$, it must be importing $Q_k$. Hence, $z_k$ shows per capita imports of the economy. Per capita imports therefore increase more than proportionally to per capita income. But how can this be so? Since per capita exports are given by $y - z_c = sy$, per capita exports must be increasing proportionally to $y$. These two conclusions can be reconciled in the presence of balanced trade because $z_k$ is not measured in the same units as $y$ and $z_c$. Thus, measuring $z_k$ in terms of $Q_c$ gives us $pz_k = sy$, and $pz_k$ does increase proportionally to $y$. The volume of trade therefore increases proportionally to per capita income. This discussion can be reversed for moderate increases in $p$, that is, increases in $p$ which do not make it profitable for the economy to produce both commodities.

Let us analyze the effects of a once-and-for-all change in $p$ when the economy is producing both commodities before and after the change. Can we still predict the changes in $\mu$, $y$, $z_c$, $z_k$, and per capita exports and imports? Suppose that $p = p_1$ initially, as shown in fig. 14.4. In this case, the $\psi$ vector (not drawn) must intersect the $\phi$ curve somewhere along the straight-line segment $EC$. Let $p$ fall to $p_0$ and assume that at the new steady-state growth path the economy continues to produce both commodities; i.e., the $\psi$ vector intersects the new $\phi$ curve somewhere in the region $E'C'$. Two things are obvious from fig. 14.4: (a) the new equilibrium capital-labor ratio must necessarily be larger than the old, and (b) $f_c$, $f_k$, and $\phi$ are necessarily larger at the new steady state. The first conclusion follows directly from the fact that, as $p$ falls, the $\phi$ curve shifts upward in the region $\mu < OB'$. This also shows that the equilibrium value of $\phi$ (that is, $y/p$) must necessarily be larger at the new equilibrium for two reasons: the $\phi$ curve shifts upward and $\mu$ increases. Finally, $f_c$ and $f_k$ increase, because, as $p$ falls, both industries tend to become more capital intensive. In particular, $\mu_c$ increases from $OA$ to $OA'$, and $\mu_k$ increases from $OB$ to $OB'$. Since $z_k$ is proportional to $y/p$, it must necessarily increase proportionally to $y/p$. But it will increase more than proportionally to $y$ because $p$ is lower at the new equilibrium and, therefore, the rate of increase of $y/p$ must be higher than the rate of increase in $y$. Does $y$ necessarily increase? No. Note that there is a minimum $p$, say $p_m$, at which the economy is specializing completely in the production of $Q_c$ but the marginal rate of transformation (i.e., the slope of the production-possibilities frontier at the $Q_c$-axis intercept) is equal to $p_m$. Further, there is a maximum $p$, say $p_M$, at which the economy is completely specializing in the production of $Q_k$ and with MRT $= p_M$. Assume that $p > p_M$ and let it decrease continuously to $p_m$. In the region $p \geq p_M$, the economy will continue to maintain the same capital-labor ratio and specialize completely in $Q_k$. Since $y = pf_k$ in this region, $y$ will fall proportionally to $p$. The moment $p$ falls below $p_M$, $\mu$ tends to increase and the economy produces both commodities. The reduction in $p$ and the increase in $\mu$ affect $y$ in diametrically opposite ways. For a given $\mu$, $y$ falls as $p$ falls, and for a given $p$, $y$ increases as $\mu$ increases. The outcome, of course, depends upon which of these two forces is stronger. While nothing can be said a priori, the following general statement is probably correct. For values of $p$ immediately lower than $p_M$, the effect of the reduction in $p$ will be stronger than the effect of the increase in $\mu$, and for values of $p$ immediately higher than $p_m$, the effect of $p$ is weaker than the effect of $\mu$. This follows from the observation that, for $p \geq p_M$, $y$ falls as $p$ falls and, for $p \leq p_m$, $y$ increases as $p$ falls. Because of continuity, therefore, we must expect the order of importance of $p$ and $\mu$ to change at least once somewhere in the region $p_m < p < p_M$. In general, the reversal of importance of $p$ and $\mu$ might occur an odd number of times. But what is more important than this pathological phenomenon is the fact that, as $p$ falls, $y$ and, therefore, per capita consumption might fall while the country is exporting $Q_c$ and importing $Q_k$. In other words, it is possible that an improvement of the terms of trade of a small country might cause such a change in the capital-labor ratio as to make the per capita income and per capita consumption of the country actually fall after the terms-of-trade improvement. Alternatively, a deterioration of the terms of trade might cause a change in the capital-labor ratio that will make the per capita income and per capita consumption higher. It should be noted that these conclusions are independent of the classification of commodities according to factor intensities.

The effect on the volume of trade cannot be decided a priori. Thus, concentrating on the difference between $z_k$ and domestic per capita production of $Q_k$, we observe that, as $p$ falls, $z_k$ increases but the outcome on the per capita output of $Q_k(q_K)$ is indeterminate. For as $\mu$ increases, $q_K$ increases at the same $p$. But $p$ falls as well, and it has an adverse effect on $q_K$.

## The Secondary Burden of a Unilateral Transfer†

We finally consider briefly the problem of unilateral transfers within the context of our simple growing economy. As we shall see, in this context a secondary burden of a unilateral transfer can take the form of a reduction in the consumption per head over and above the reduction due to the transfer itself and any possible terms-of-trade deterioration. As it turns out, such reduction in the consumption per head of the paying country occurs when the paying country's equilibrium capital-labor ratio $\mu^*$ is lower than the golden-rule capital-labor ratio $\mu_g$, that is, that which maximizes the country's per capita consumption. Since most societies can be assumed to fall short of the golden-rule position—rates of return on capital typically exceed growth rates of gross national product—the suggested secondary burden is no doubt an important one.

Suppose that our small open economy makes a unilateral transfer to the rest of the world. Since long-run equilibrium in the present context is cast in per capita terms, assume that the transfer is fixed in per capita terms also. Thus, the aggregate amount of the transfer will increase at the annual rate $n$. In particular, assume that the aggregate transfer $U$ expressed in terms of the consumption good is equal to $U = Lu$ where the constant $u$ is the fixed amount of the transfer per head.

If the pretransfer equilibrium capital-labor ratio $\mu^*$ remained the same, the per capita income $y$ would exactly fall by the amount of the transfer per head $u$. But, unfortunately, the capital-labor ratio cannot stay at the pretransfer level. Why? Simply because the disposable per capita income in terms of the capital good, that is, $(y - u)/p$, is now smaller than $n\mu^*/s$ at $\mu = \mu^*$. Hence, $K$ will be growing less rapidly than $L$ and thus the ratio $K/L$ will fall. Accordingly, the first adverse effect of the transfer is a reduction in the capital-labor ratio, and, as a result, a reduction in the per capita disposable income by an amount which is necessarily bigger than the amount of the per capita transfer.

The preceding conclusion can be verified graphically by shifting the curve $ONEGCH$ (fig. 14.2) downward uniformly by the amount $u$. Then, the equilibrium point will slide down toward the origin along the $\psi$ curve and the per capita

† For a general introduction to the transfer problem and review of the literature, see Chacholiades (1978, chap. 12).

disposable income will be smaller than what it was originally at $G$ by an amount bigger than $u/p$ simply because the curve $ONEGCH$ is upward sloping.

If per capita disposable income (expressed in terms of the capital good) falls by more than $u/p$, does it follow that per capita consumption necessarily falls by more than $u$ also? No. It may, and it may not. As is well known,[†] per capita consumption is not a monotonic function of the equilibrium $\mu^*$. Thus, there exists a golden-rule value of $\mu$, say $\mu_g$, at which per capita consumption is maximized. For $\mu^* \leq \mu_g$, per capita consumption falls as $\mu^*$ falls. On the other hand, if $\mu^* > \mu_g$, per capita consumption *increases* as $\mu^*$ falls. Accordingly, if our economy happens to have, before the transfer, an equilibrium $\mu^* > \mu_g$, the transfer would cause $\mu^*$ to fall, and contrary to the necessary fall of the per capita income, per capita consumption (before the transfer is subtracted) would rise. Therefore, in this case, per capita consumption would fall by less than $u$, even though per capita income falls by more than $u$. In the more realistic case, however, where $\mu^* < \mu_g$, the transfer causes $\mu^*$ to fall, pulling with it not only gross[‡] per capita income but also gross[‡] per capita consumption. Accordingly, in this typical case, in addition to the reduction in per capita income $y/p$ by more than $u/p$, per capita consumption $z_c$ is also reduced by more than $u$. These propositions can be made rigorous very easily.

Let $p$ be the relative price of the capital good in terms of the consumption good in the international market; and let $u$ be expressed in terms of the consumption good. Then

$$z_c = (1 - s)(y - u) \tag{14.48}$$

In addition, in the presence of the transfer, eq. (14.36a) becomes

$$\frac{y - u}{p} = \mu \frac{n}{s} \tag{14.49}$$

Remembering that $y$ is a function of $\mu$, and differentiating eq. (14.49) totally with respect to $u$ for $u = 0$, we obtain

$$\frac{d\mu}{du} = \frac{1/p}{(1/p)(dy/d\mu) - (n/s)} < 0 \tag{14.50}$$

For stability, it is necessary that $(1/p)(dy/d\mu) < n/s$ at the long-run equilibrium point. Therefore, $d\mu/du < 0$. This verifies our earlier conclusion that the transfer reduces the capital-labor ratio of the paying country. Further, since $dy/d\mu > 0$, it follows that $dy/du = (dy/d\mu)(d\mu/du) < 0$, which again verifies our earlier conclusion that the transfer reduces the "gross" per capita income of the paying country.

To study the effect of the transfer on the per capita consumption, solve eq. (14.49) for $s$ and substitute into eq. (14.48) to obtain

$$z_c = y - \mu np - u \tag{14.51}$$

---

[†] See Black (1963), Chapernowne (1962), Meade (1962), Robinson (1962), Solow (1962), and fig. 14.3 above.

[‡] The word "gross" is used here to indicate the magnitude of $y$ or $z_c$ before $u$ is subtracted.

Differentiating eq. (14.51) with respect to $u$, we obtain

$$\frac{dz_c}{du} = \left(\frac{dy}{d\mu} - np\right)\frac{d\mu}{du} - 1 \tag{14.52}$$

We can now formulate the following important theorem.

**Theorem 14.1**
(a) If $dy/d\mu = np$ (that is, if $\mu^* = \mu_g$) at the pretransfer equilibrium, then $dz_c/du = -1$; that is, the consumption per head of the paying country will fall exactly by the amount of the transfer expressed in terms of $Q_c$ (that is, $u$).
(b) If $dy/d\mu > np$ (that is, if $\mu^* < \mu_g$), then $dz_c/du < -1$; and consumption per head will fall by more than the per head transfer.
(c) If $dy/d\mu < np$ (that is, if $\mu^* > \mu_g$), then $0 > dz_c/du > -1$; that is, the transfer causes the per head consumption to fall by a smaller amount than the transfer.

PROOF The proof of the theorem follows directly from eqs. (14.52) and (14.50). Thus, substitute eq. (14.50) into eq. (14.52) to obtain (after some elementary manipulation)

$$\frac{dz_c}{du} = \frac{\dfrac{dy}{d\mu} - np}{\dfrac{dy}{d\mu} - \dfrac{np}{s}} - 1 < 0 \tag{14.53}$$

Obviously, when $dy/d\mu = np$, then $dz_c/du = -1$, since the first term on the right-hand side of eq. (14.53) becomes zero. On the other hand, when $np/s > dy/d\mu > np$ ($dy/d\mu < np$), then the first term on the right-hand side of eq. (14.53) becomes negative (positive, but less than unity) and thus $dz_c/du < -1$ ($0 > dz_c/du > -1$). This proves the theorem.

In most societies we observe $dy/d\mu > n$, and the equilibrium $\mu^*$ falls short of the golden rule $\mu_g$. In this important case, a transfer would impose a "secondary burden" on the paying country in the form of a reduction in the per head consumption over and above the per head transfer.

## SELECTED BIBLIOGRAPHY

Bardhan, P. K. (1970). *Economic Growth, Development, and Foreign Trade*. Wiley-Interscience, New York.

Bertrand, T. J. (1973). "Trade and Growth: A Comment." *Journal of International Economics*, vol. 3, pp. 193–195.

Black, J. (1962). "Technical Progress and Optimum Savings." *Review of Economic Studies*, vol. 29 (June), pp. 238–240.

Chacholiades, M. (1972). "Short-Run Equilibrium and Stability in the Two-Sector Growth Model." *Econometrica*, vol. 42, no. 6 (November), pp. 1081–1091.

——— (1978). *International Monetary Theory and Policy*. McGraw-Hill Book Company, New York.

Champernowne, D. G. (1962). "Some Implications of Golden Age Conditions When Savings Equal Profits." *Review of Economic Studies*, vol. 29 (June), pp. 235–237.

Deardorff, A. V. (1973). "The Gains from Trade in and out of Steady-State Growth." *Oxford Economic Papers*, vol. 25, no. 2 (July), pp. 173–191.

—— (1974a). "Trade Reversals and Growth Stability." *Journal of International Economics*, vol. 4 (April), pp. 83–90.

—— (1974b). "A Geometry of Growth and Trade." *Canadian Journal of Economics and Political Science*, vol. 7 (May), pp. 295–306.

—— (1974c). "Factor Proportions and Comparative Advantage in the Long-Run: Comment." *Journal of Political Economy*, vol. 82, no. 4 (July), pp. 829–833.

Findlay, R. (1970). "Factor Proportions and Comparative Advantage in the Long Run." *Journal of Political Economy*, vol. 78, no. 1 (January), pp. 27–34.

Inada, K. (1968). "Free Trade, Capital Accumulation and Factor-Price Equalization." *Economic Record*, vol. 44, no. 107 (September), pp. 322–341.

Johnson, H. G. (1962). *Money, Trade and Economic Growth*. Harvard University Press, Cambridge, Mass., chap. 4. Reprinted in R. E. Caves and H. G. Johnson (Eds.), AEA *Readings in International Economics*. R. D. Irwin, Inc., Homewood, Ill., 1968.

—— (1971a). "Trade and Growth: A Geometrical Exposition." *Journal of International Economics*, vol. 1, pp. 83–101.

—— (1971b). "The Theory of Trade and Growth: A Diagrammatic Analysis." In J. Bhagwati, R. Jones, R. A. Mundell, and J. Vanek (Eds.), *Trade, Balance of Payments, and Growth, Essays in Honor of Charles P. Kindleberger*. American Elsevier Publishing Company, New York.

—— (1972). "Trade and Growth: A Correction." *Journal of International Economics*, vol. 2, pp. 87–88.

Kemp, M. C. (1968). "International Trade and Investment in a Context of Growth." *Economic Record*, vol. 44, no. 106 (June), pp. 211–223.

—— (1969). *The Pure Theory of International Trade and Investment*. Prentice-Hall, Inc., Englewood Cliffs, N.J., chaps. 10 and 11.

—— (1970). "International Trade between Countries with Different Natural Rates of Growth." *Economic Record*, vol. 46, no. 116 (December), pp. 467–481.

Khang, C. (1971). "Equilibrium Growth in the International Economy: The Case of Unequal Natural Rates of Growth." *International Economic Review*, vol. 12, no. 2 (June), pp. 239–249.

Meade, J. (1962). "The Effect of Savings on Consumption in a State of Steady Growth." *Review of Economic Studies*, vol. 29 (June), pp. 227–234.

Oniki, H., and H. Uzawa (1965). "Patterns of Trade and Investment in a Dynamic Model of International Trade." *Review of Economic Studies*, vol. XXXII (January), pp. 15–38.

Robinson, J. (1962). "A Neo-Classical Theorem." *Review of Economic Studies*, vol. 29 (June) pp. 219–226.

Solow, R. M. (1956). "A Contribution to the Theory of Economic Growth." *Quarterly Journal of Economics*, vol. 70, pp. 65–94. Reprinted in J. E. Stiglitz and H. Uzawa (Eds.), *Readings in the Modern Theory of Economic Growth*. The MIT Press, Cambridge, Mass., 1969.

—— (1962). "Comment on the Golden Rule." *Review of Economic Studies*, vol. 29 (June), pp. 255–257.

Stiglitz, J. E. (1970). "Factor Price Equalization in a Dynamic Economy." *Journal of Political Economy*, vol. 78, pp. 456–488.

Swan, T. W. (1956). "Economic Growth and Capital Accumulation." *Economic Record*, vol. 32, pp. 334–361. Reprinted in J. E. Stiglitz and H. Uzawa (Eds.), *Readings in the Modern Theory of Economic Growth*. The MIT Press, Cambridge, Mass., 1969.

Uzawa, H. (1961). "On a Two-Sector Model of Economic Growth." *Review of Economic Studies*, vol. 29, pp. 40–47.

—— (1963). "On a Two-Sector Model of Economic Growth II." *Review of Economic Studies*, vol. 30, pp. 105–118. Reprinted in J. E. Stiglitz and H. Uzawa (Eds.), *Readings in the Modern Theory of Economic Growth*. The MIT Press, Cambridge, Mass., 1969.

Vanek, J. (1971). "Economic Growth and International Trade in Pure Theory." *Quarterly Journal of Economics*, vol. 85, no. 3 (August), pp. 377–390.

# SIX

# TRADE AND WELFARE

# CHAPTER FIFTEEN

# TRADE AND THE WELFARE OF INDIVIDUALS

Do countries benefit from international trade? This issue was intentionally avoided in earlier chapters despite the fact that our starting point, the Ricardo–Torrens theory of comparative advantage, purported to show that free international trade is beneficial to all trading countries—or, in the limiting case, international trade does not hurt any country. It was pointed out then that the concept of social welfare is rather subtle.

A more careful examination of the doctrine that trade is better than no trade is now in order. This is done in this chapter and the following. In particular, the present chapter deals with the effect of international trade on the welfare of the citizens of the trading countries. Chapter 16 considers the more fundamental question of whether free international trade increases social welfare.

This chapter is divided into three parts. Part A is a short, but necessary, introduction to the problem of welfare. Part B deals with certain cases in which the introduction of international trade improves the welfare of everybody. Finally, part C deals with certain cases in which the introduction of international trade may hurt some individuals.

## PART A. INTRODUCTION

As is shown below in part C, the introduction of international trade usually makes some individuals worse off. This fact creates enormous difficulties in evaluating the contribution of free trade to economic welfare.

## 15.1 THE TWO APPROACHES

As mentioned in chap. 1, it can be postulated that social welfare depends on the welfare of the individuals comprising the society, and on nothing else. The mathematical expression of this statement is the Bergson–Samuelson social welfare function in its general form, discussed in the following chapter. This function is usually made a little more specific by attributing to it an ethical property, namely, that social welfare increases when one individual becomes better off with no one else being worse off. Now if the introduction of international trade were to make everybody better off, we could conclude that the introduction of international trade increases social welfare. Unfortunately, however, some individuals become worse off after the introduction of international trade; and ethical neutrality prevents us from passing judgement on cases where some individuals lose. How, then, can we evaluate the effect of international trade on social welfare when some people lose?

Two possibilities are open to us: we can either assume that society has a specific social welfare function and implements it consistently in the manner of chap. 5 to achieve maximum welfare always, or we have to use the so-called *compensation principle* and talk about what the society could potentially do. The former approach leads to a single social indifference map (as explained in chap. 5) which portrays both positive behavior and economic welfare. Excluding increasing returns, the earlier analysis of this book (see especially chap. 6) shows conclusively that free international trade is indeed beneficial to all trading countries—free trade causes each economy to move from a lower to a higher social indifference curve. The latter approach (compensation principle) is studied below in chap. 16.

Essentially, the compensation-principle approach boils down to this: even though some individuals become worse off with trade, it is always possible for those who gain to compensate those who lose, with the result that all *could* be made better off. To be ethically neutral, we have to show that such a compensation scheme is indeed possible for *all* possible income distributions. This is done in the following chapter. The central idea is this. As we have seen, the consumption-possibilities frontier lies beyond the boundaries of the production-possibilities frontier, except at the optimum production point where the two frontiers coincide. As a result, *the cum-trade utility frontier can be shown to lie, in general, beyond the autarkic utility frontier*, except at one or more points where the two utility frontiers may be tangent to each other. Accordingly, irrespective of the initial equilibrium point on the autarkic utility frontier, there are points on the cum-trade utility frontier which imply higher utility for all citizens relative to the autarkic equilibrium; and thus, potentially at least, international trade could make everyone better off.

## 15.2 PSEUDOARGUMENTS FOR FREE TRADE

It is usually taken for granted, especially in public debate over commercial policy, that international trade and specialization is beneficial to all participating countries. This is mainly due to the fact that classical and neoclassical writers have always felt that in some sense perfect competition represents an optimal situation. There are various explanations for this belief, but the following two seem to be the most common and interesting: (a) free international trade is better than no trade simply because trade is voluntary; and (b) free international trade maximizes the sum of total satisfactions. We dispense with these pseudoarguments in turn.

### The Voluntary Nature of International Trade

A market transaction is voluntary; hence, no party can be hurt by a voluntary transaction, because he can always refuse to trade. For example, a worker might choose to work for what might appear to be a relatively low wage only because in the end he can consume more as compared with the extreme case where he himself would have to produce everything. He may resent the fact that his wage is low, but he nevertheless accepts it because he is better off with it than without it.

It is thought that a similar argument can show that international trade is beneficial to all participating countries. Thus, it may be argued, participation in international trade is free. If countries participate in international trade, they do so voluntarily. Hence, international trade (and specialization) is mutually beneficial—one party does not gain what the other loses—and, therefore, free trade is better than no trade.

What is wrong with the above argument? It suggests that with the opening up of trade, all members of all countries become better off because their participation is voluntary. But voluntary in what sense? Does a single individual in a certain country have a choice between his pretrade and posttrade equilibrium positions? In other words, can a single individual refuse to participate in international trade and be no worse off than in his pretrade position? Not necessarily. With the opening up of trade, the consumption-possibilities frontier (or the equilibrium budget line) of each consumer is different from what it used to be in the pretrade equilibrium position. Despite the fact that some consumers definitely become better off after the introduction of trade, we cannot rule out the possibility that some consumers may become worse off.

Actually, an individual consumer can refuse the exchange of the services of the factors of production he owns for the commodities and services he can get in the market—but then he would have to produce, with the factors he owns, everything he consumes. The fact that no individual does that is proof that participation in production and exchange, even after the introduction of trade, is still beneficial to all. This does not mean that every individual becomes better off after the introduction of trade; it means, rather, that, even if international trade hurts some individuals, these individuals are still better off than if each were to produce everything he consumed.

## Maximization of the Sum Total of Satisfactions

A second, more sophisticated argument attempts to show not that each individual is made better off after the introduction of international trade but that in some sense the sum total of satisfactions is maximized. This involves the notion of adding the utilities of different individuals. That is, it is assumed that it is possible to compare and weight the utilities of different individuals. To many modern economists, interpersonal comparisons of well-being are both impossible and "unscientific," although the preceding generation of economists used to make interpersonal comparisons of well-being almost without question. Today, the welfare of an economy is clearly considered to be no more than a heterogeneous collection of individual welfares.

## PART B. SOME CASES IN WHICH THE INTRODUCTION OF INTERNATIONAL TRADE IMPROVES THE WELFARE OF EVERYBODY

In earlier chapters, several simple cases are discussed in which international trade improves the welfare of all individuals of all trading countries or—in the limiting case where the posttrade equilibrium prices are equal to the pretrade equilibrium prices of an economy—it does not *hurt* anybody. Let us review some of these cases briefly.

## 15.3 THE CLASSICAL THEORY AGAIN

First, consider the classical theory where it is assumed that there exists one factor of production, labor, and all commodities are produced under constant returns to scale. The introduction of trade cannot hurt anybody in this case. The worst that could happen is for every individual to enjoy the same level of welfare after as before the introduction of international trade. This occurs in the limiting case where the pretrade domestic price ratio coincides with the posttrade international price ratio. How can this proposition be proved?

Consider again the simple case of two commodities, $X$ and $Y$, with $a_x$ and $a_y$ being the respective labor coefficients. We know that the domestic price ratio $p_x/p_y$ before trade is given by the ratio $a_x/a_y$. Further, if the international price ratio $p$ ($\equiv p_x/p_y$) is larger than $a_x/a_y$, our economy specializes in the production of $X$; if $p < a_x/a_y$, our economy specializes in the production of $Y$; and if $p = a_x/a_y$, the production point is indeterminate—any pattern of specialization is possible.

## The Budget Equation in the Autarkic State

Consider now an individual endowed with $L_0$ units of labor. His budget equation in the autarkic state is

$$wL_0 = p_x X + p_y Y \qquad (15.1)$$

However,

$$p_x = wa_x \quad \text{and} \quad p_y = wa_y \qquad (15.2)$$

Substituting eqs. (15.2) into eq. (15.1) and simplifying, we get

$$L_0 = a_x X + a_y Y \qquad (15.3)$$

Equation (15.3) is the individual's budget line in the autarkic state. The individual chooses that bundle of $X$ and $Y$ which maximizes his welfare, as illustrated by fig. 15.1. The straight line $MN$ is the individual's budget line as given by eq. (15.3). The individual maximizes his welfare at point $E_1$, where his budget line touches the highest indifference curve, $I_1$.

## The Budget Equation with Free Trade

Suppose now that our economy can buy and sell unlimited quantities of $X$ and $Y$ in the international market at the relative price $p_0 > a_x/a_y$. What happens to the welfare of our typical individual with this new development? Refer to eq. (15.1). What are the prices $p_x$ and $p_y$ equal to now? Since our economy specializes

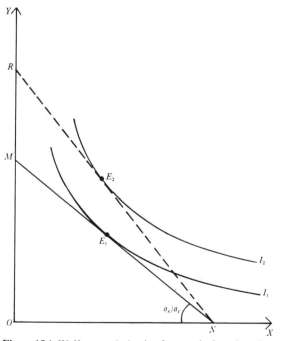

**Figure 15.1** Welfare maximization for a typical worker. Free trade causes the budget line to shift from $MN$ to $RN$.

completely in the production of $X$ (because $p_0 > a_x/a_y$), $p_x$ continues to be given by the domestic average cost of production $wa_x$. But what about $p_y$? This cannot be determined by the domestic average cost, because $Y$ cannot profitably be produced at home. As we saw in chap. 2, we must necessarily have: $p_y <$ domestic average cost of production $= wa_y$. How is $p_y$ determined then?

By definition, $p_0 = p_x/p_y$. Thus,

$$p_y = \frac{p_x}{p_0} = w\frac{a_x}{p_0} \tag{15.4}$$

Substituting again $p_x$ and $p_y$ into eq. (15.1) and simplifying, we get

$$L_0 = a_x X + \frac{a_x}{p_0} Y \tag{15.5}$$

Equation (15.5) is the new budget equation of our typical consumer. How does this equation compare with eq. (15.3)? They are both linear and they both have the same $X$-axis intercept: $L_0/a_x$. Which is steeper? The slope of the autarkic budget line, as given by eq. (15.3), is given by $a_x/a_y$; and the slope of the free-trade budget line, as given by eq. (15.5), is given by $a_x/(a_x/p_0) = p_0$. Since $p_0 > a_x/a_y$ by assumption, the free-trade budget line must be steeper, as shown in fig. 15.1 by the broken line $NR$. Therefore, after the introduction of international trade, the consumer reaches equilibrium at point $E_2$ on the higher indifference curve $I_2$. Accordingly, free trade makes our typical individual—and thus all individuals—better off.

It can be shown, following the same line of reasoning, that when the international price ratio is smaller than $a_x/a_y$, the free-trade budget line of the typical individual starts at $M$ and is flatter than the autarkic budget line $MN$. Hence, the free-trade budget line again lies totally outside the autarkic budget line, except at the singular point $M$. Therefore, the typical individual (and thus all individuals) again become better off with trade. In the limiting case where $p = a_x/a_y$, the free-trade budget line coincides with the autarkic budget line, and the typical individual remains as well off after the introduction of trade as in the autarkic state.

## 15.4 TWO FACTORS BUT CONSTANT OPPORTUNITY COSTS

Essentially the same analysis holds in the case in which the economy is endowed not with one but with two primary factors of production, labor ($L$) and land ($T$), and the production-possibilities frontier of the economy is a straight line.

The production-possibilities frontier becomes a straight line if, and only if, at the given overall labor-land ratio, the marginal rate of substitution of labor for land is the same in both $X$ and $Y$. The two industries may have the same marginal rate of substitution of labor for land either for all values of the overall labor-land ratio or for only the specific value of the overall labor-land ratio that our economy happens to be endowed with. The reason why the production-possibilities frontier is linear is immaterial. The only requirement is that it is linear, and both industries always use the two factors in the overall proportion in which they exist in the economy at large. We can easily show that trade improves the welfare of all individuals in this case as well.

## The Budget Equation in the Autarkic State

Consider a typical individual endowed with $L_0$ units of labor and $T_0$ units of land. Note that $L_0$ and $T_0$ are arbitrarily chosen. It is possible for either $L_0$ or $T_0$ to be zero. The budget equation of our typical individual is, in general, given by the equation

$$wL_0 + rT_0 = p_x X + p_y Y \tag{15.6a}$$

In addition, in the autarkic state, the following marginal productivity conditions necessarily hold:

$$w = p_x \, \mathrm{MPP}_L^X = p_y \, \mathrm{MPP}_L^Y \tag{15.7}$$

$$r = p_x \, \mathrm{MPP}_T^X = p_y \, \mathrm{MPP}_T^Y \tag{15.8}$$

The term $\mathrm{MPP}_L^X \equiv$ the marginal physical product of labor in the production of $X$, and so on.

Since, by assumption, the labor-land ratios in the two industries are always equal to the overall labor-land ratio, and since $\mathrm{MPP}_L^X$ and $\mathrm{MPP}_T^X$ are functions of the labor-land ratio used in the $X$ industry while $\mathrm{MPP}_L^Y$ and $\mathrm{MPP}_T^Y$ are functions of the labor-land ratio used in the $Y$ industry, the marginal physical products of both factors in both industries must be uniquely determined and they must necessarily remain constant throughout at the uniquely determined level.

Now rewrite eq. (15.6a) as

$$\frac{w}{r} L_0 + T_0 = \frac{p_x}{r} X + \frac{p_y}{r} Y \tag{15.6b}$$

The factor-price ratio $w/r$ is by assumption uniquely determined. Therefore, we can introduce a new symbol, $I_0$, to represent the income of the typical individual in terms of units of land; that is,

$$I_0 \equiv \frac{w}{r} L_0 + T_0 \tag{15.9}$$

Observe that $I_0$ is a constant. It is independent of the equilibrium production point and, therefore, it remains constant even after the introduction of international trade.

Solving eqs. (15.8) for $p_x/r$ and $p_y/r$, we get

$$\frac{p_x}{r} = \frac{1}{\mathrm{MPP}_T^X} \tag{15.10}$$

$$\frac{p_y}{r} = \frac{1}{\mathrm{MPP}_T^Y} \tag{15.11}$$

Substituting eqs. (15.9) to (15.11) into eq. (15.6$b$), we get

$$I_0 = \frac{1}{\mathrm{MPP}_T^X} X + \frac{1}{\mathrm{MPP}_T^Y} Y \tag{15.12}$$

Equation (15.12) is the typical individual's budget equation in the autarkic state. It is a linear equation and is represented graphically by a straight line whose absolute slope is equal to the ratio $\mathrm{MPP}_T^Y/\mathrm{MPP}_T^X$. By a simple division of eqs. (15.10) and (15.11), it becomes clear that the ratio $\mathrm{MPP}_T^Y/\mathrm{MPP}_T^X$ is simply the domestic price ratio $p_x/p_y$ prevailing in the autarkic state. Qualitatively, this budget equation looks like the straight line $MN$ of fig. 15.1.

## The Budget Equation with Free International Trade

Let us now introduce international trade by assuming that our economy can buy and sell unlimited quantities of $X$ and $Y$ in the international market at the relative price $p_0 > \mathrm{MPP}_T^Y/\mathrm{MPP}_T^X$. Thus, $X$ is assumed to be relatively more expensive in the international market and, therefore, our economy specializes completely in the production of $X$. Such being the case, eq. (15.10) continues to hold after the introduction of international trade. But what about eq. (15.11)? Does it continue to hold, too? No.

By assumption, the international price of $Y$ ($p_y^*$) is lower than the domestic average cost of production of $Y$ ($r/\mathrm{MPP}_T^Y$). In other words, after the introduction of trade, we must have

$$p_y^* < \frac{r}{\mathrm{MPP}_T^Y}$$

How is $p_y^*$ determined? Again, we have $p_0 \equiv p_x/p_y^*$, or

$$p_y^* = \frac{p_x}{p_0} = \frac{r}{p_0 \, \mathrm{MPP}_T^X}$$

Thus,
$$\frac{p_y^*}{r} = \frac{1}{p_0 \, \mathrm{MPP}_T^X} \tag{15.13}$$

Substituting eqs. (15.9), (15.10) and (15.13) into eq. (15.6$b$), we get

$$I_0 = \frac{1}{\mathrm{MPP}_T^X} X + \frac{1}{p_0 \, \mathrm{MPP}_T^X} Y \tag{15.14}$$

Equation (15.14) is simply the budget equation of our typical individual after the introduction of international trade. How does this budget equation compare with the budget equation of the autarkic state, i.e., eq. (15.12)? Again, they are both linear and have the same $X$-axis intercept. Which is steeper? Again, the free-trade budget equation, because the slope of the budget equation in the autarkic state is given by the ratio $\mathrm{MPP}_T^Y/\mathrm{MPP}_T^X$ while the slope of the budget equation after the introduction of free trade is given by $(1/\mathrm{MPP}_T^X)/(1/p_0\,\mathrm{MPP}_T^X) = p_0$, which by assumption is larger than the ratio $\mathrm{MPP}_T^Y/\mathrm{MPP}_T^X$. Therefore, the situation is again similar to that illustrated in fig. 15.1.

Similar reasoning shows that, when the international price ratio is smaller than the ratio $\mathrm{MPP}_T^Y/\mathrm{MPP}_T^X$, the free-trade budget line of the typical individual has the same $Y$-axis intercept as his budget line under autarky, with the latter being steeper than the former. Hence, the free-trade budget line lies totally outside the budget line under autarky, except at their common $Y$-axis intercept, and, therefore, the typical individual (and thus all individuals) again becomes better off with trade. In the limiting case where the international price ratio is equal to the domestic price ratio under autarky, the free-trade budget line coincides with the autarkic budget line and the typical individual continues to enjoy, after the introduction of trade, the same level of welfare he used to enjoy in the autarkic state.

## 15.5 IDENTICAL TASTES AND FACTOR ENDOWMENTS

A third and last case to be considered is when all members of our economy are identical in every respect. That is, they have the same tastes and factor ownership. As before, all production functions are characterized by constant returns to scale.

A great simplification is possible in the present case: *the economy's production-possibilities frontier can be scaled down in proportion to each individual* (i.e., the representative citizen), and then the scaled-down production-possibilities frontier can be used to show the equilibrium production and consumption positions of each individual.

In fig. 15.2, the curve $MP_3 E_1 P_2 N$ is the scaled-down production-possibilities frontier of the typical individual. Before trade, the typical individual is

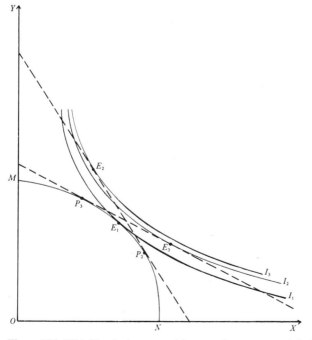

**Figure 15.2** With identical tastes and factor endowments, each individual is self-sufficient before trade (see point $E_1$). Trade makes everybody better off (see points $E_2$ and $E_3$).

in equilibrium at point $E_1$. Now assume that our economy can buy and sell unlimited quantities of $X$ and $Y$ at given international prices. Whether the international price ratio $p_x/p_y$ is higher, as shown by the broken line $E_2 P_2$, or smaller, as shown by the broken line $E_3 P_3$, than the domestic price ratio under autarky, the introduction of international trade definitely improves the welfare of the typical individual, except in the limiting case where the international price ratio is equal to the domestic price ratio under autarky, in which case the introduction of trade neither hurts nor benefits the typical individual.

# PART C. INTERNATIONAL TRADE MAY HURT SOME INDIVIDUALS

International trade takes place because the relative pretrade equilibrium commodity prices differ between countries. With the opening up of trade, these relative commodity prices tend, in the absence of transportation costs, toward complete equality. What effect, if any, does this change in relative commodity prices have on the income distribution of the trading countries? And what is the effect on the welfare of each individual? The answers to these questions necessarily depend on factor ownership and tastes.

## 15.6 UNIFORM FACTOR OWNERSHIP BUT DIFFERENT TASTES

When factor ownership is uniform, the distribution of income is independent of factor prices. For instance, suppose that, in an economy composed of $n$ individuals,

$$\frac{L_i}{T_i} = \frac{\bar{L}}{\bar{T}} \qquad (i = 1, 2, \ldots, n)$$

where $L_i \equiv$ labor owned by the $i$th individual, $T_i \equiv$ land owned by the $i$th individual. Further,

$$\bar{L} \equiv \sum_{i=1}^{n} L_i$$

$$\bar{T} \equiv \sum_{i=1}^{n} T_i$$

The proportion of the $i$th individual's income $(I_i)$ to total income $(I)$ is given by

$$\frac{I_i}{I} = \frac{wL_i + rT_i}{w\bar{L} + r\bar{T}} = \frac{T_i[w(L_i/T_i) + r]}{\bar{T}[w(\bar{L}/\bar{T}) + r]} = \frac{T_i}{\bar{T}} = \frac{L_i}{\bar{L}} \tag{15.15}$$

which is constant and independent of factor prices. Therefore, the introduction of international trade does not affect the distribution of income in the present case. But what about the welfare of each individual? Can we reasonably expect that the introduction of international trade makes everybody better off? Or does trade make some people better off without making others worse off? In other words, can we eliminate the possibility that the introduction of international trade hurts some individuals?

First, a way must be found to determine the general equilibrium of the economy before and after the introduction of international trade in terms of the excess-demand functions of all individuals. Then, we can see whether or not all individuals move to higher indifference curves after the introduction of international trade. How can this be done without getting involved in an unmanageable number of equations?

## General Equilibrium

When factor ownership is uniform (in the sense that each individual owns the two factors of production in the same proportion as the economy's overall factor-endowment ratio), general equilibrium can easily be determined by considering each individual as an island. Then, on the basis of his factor endowments and tastes, we can determine his excess-demand curves as in the case of countries. In other words, we have to determine each individual's production-possibilities frontier, superimpose the latter on the individual's indifference map, and so on. Of course, when the excess-demand curves are so derived, they have to be summed laterally for the determination of the general equilibrium of the economy—a procedure that must be quite familiar by now.

Is the assumption of uniformity of factor ownership crucial to the suggested procedure? If so, why? The answer is rather simple. When we proceed from the production-possibilities frontier of the individual citizen (not the economy), we necessarily assume that it is always economical for each individual to organize production and employ fully his own factors at all possible factor-price ratios. In other words, no individual ever has the need to exchange one factor for another in the factor market in order to be able to organize production and fully employ the factors available to him by adopting those production techniques that happen to be optimal for the economy as a whole. When factor ownership is uniform, this is no doubt true, since, under constant returns to scale, scale is immaterial. But when factor ownership is not uniform, this need not be so. This is, of course, easily illustrated by the case where some individuals (at least) own only one factor, such as labor, and both commodities require both factors, labor and land. Therefore, we conclude that uniformity of factor ownership is both necessary and sufficient for the suggested procedure of solving the general-equilibrium problem.

## Three Categories of Individuals

Let us assume now that we have been able to determine the equilibrium commodity-price ratio $p_x/p_y$ of the economy. We can then classify all individuals into the following three categories: ($a$) those who produce exactly as much as they need for their personal consumption; these people are self-sufficient—not only do they not have to exchange factors of production (which is ruled out by the

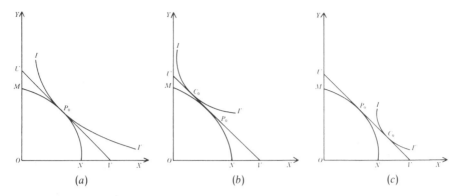

**Figure 15.3** With uniform factor ownership but different tastes, all individuals can be classified into three categories, as shown by the three panels according to their pretrade equilibria. In panel (a), Mr. A is self-sufficient; in panel (b), Mr. B exchanges $X$ for $Y$; and in panel (c), Mr. C exchanges $Y$ for $X$.

assumption that factor ownership is uniform), but also they need not exchange commodities; (b) those who, in the general-equilibrium situation, exchange commodity $X$ for commodity $Y$; that is, they produce more $X$ and less $Y$ than what they consume; (c) and those who, in the general-equilibrium situation, exchange commodity $Y$ for commodity $X$; in other words, they produce less $X$ and more $Y$ than what they actually consume.

These categories are illustrated in fig. 15.3. Figure 15.3(a) illustrates the case of a typical individual, Mr. A, who belongs to the first category; part (b) illustrates the case of a typical individual, Mr. B, who belongs to the second category; and part (c) illustrates the case of a typical individual, Mr. C, who belongs to the third category. In all panels, the curve $MN$ is the individual's production-possibilities frontier, $UV$ is the individual's consumption-possibilities frontier, $II'$ is the indifference curve that the individual can reach at the autarkic general-equilibrium situation, $P_0$ is the optimum production point, and $C_0$ is the optimum consumption point. In part (a), illustrating the case of self-sufficient individuals, the consumption point coincides, of course, with the production point. In the other two cases, the consumption point is different from the production point. How does the introduction of international trade affect the welfare of each individual?

## The Effect of Trade on Each Category of Individuals

Consider first the self-sufficient Mr. A. The introduction of international trade cannot possibly hurt him. He is self-sufficient, and he can always reach the pre-trade level of satisfaction by continuing to produce and consume at $P_0$. But is this what he will actually do? No—unless the international price ratio is equal to the economy's pretrade price ratio. When the international price ratio is different from $(p_x/p_y)_0$, Mr. A can definitely improve his welfare by participating in international trade. Thus, any budget line (other than $UV$) tangent to Mr. A's production-possibilities frontier necessarily intersects the indifference curve $II'$.

This means that Mr. A can reach a higher indifference curve after the introduction of international trade.

Mr. A's total gain from trade can be decomposed into a consumption gain and a production gain in the manner discussed in part B of chap. 5. Thus, with the same production (point), he can do better through exchange (consumption gain), but he can do still better by shifting his production point (production gain).

Can we infer from this that the introduction of international trade makes Mr. B and Mr. C better off as well? No. In fact, we can show that when the international price ratio is different from $(p_x/p_y)_0$, that is, the pretrade price ratio, one individual becomes better off and the other worse off. Suppose that commodity $X$ is relatively cheaper in the international market. Mr. C can reach a higher indifference curve than $II'$, since any budget line tangent to his production-possibilities frontier and flatter than $UV$ necessarily intersects $II'$. What about Mr. B? Can he improve his welfare, or at least maintain the same level, after the introduction of international trade? No, because any budget line tangent to Mr. B's production-possibilities frontier and flatter than $UV$ fails to reach $II'$.

Why is it not possible for Mr. B to maintain at least the same level of welfare he used to enjoy before trade? Why is he different from Mr. A, who can at least maintain his pretrade level of welfare by refusing to trade? In other words, why is it not possible for Mr. B to refuse to participate in international trade and at the same time maintain his pretrade level of well-being? The crucial difference between Mr. A and Mr. B is that, while the former does not need any cooperation from the rest of the economy to reach the indifference curve $II'$, the latter does. In other words, while Mr. A is self-sufficient, Mr. B has to exchange $X$ for $Y$ in the commodity market. Still better, Mr. A is consuming along his production-possibilities frontier while Mr. B is consuming beyond his production-possibilities frontier. After the introduction of international trade, those individuals (like Mr. C) who want to exchange $Y$ for $X$ at $(p_x/p_y)_0$ simply refuse transactions with Mr. B at the pretrade terms: they demand more units of $X$ per unit of $Y$. What this means is that Mr. B is unable, after the introduction of international trade, to reach the indifference curve $II'$.

Another way of looking at this problem is to regard Mr. C as a net supplier of the good whose price goes up; hence, he benefits. On the other hand, Mr. B is a net demander of the good whose price goes up; hence he loses.

Do Mr. B's losses account fully for Mr. C's gains? This is an important question, and is answered satisfactorily later in the next chapter. Briefly, the gainers could compensate the losers for their losses so that in the end some individuals are better off without anybody being worse off.

## 15.7 WORKERS VERSUS LANDLORDS

Let us now discuss another important case where the introduction of international trade hurts some individuals. Drop the assumption that factor ownership is uniform. Once this is done, there are an infinite number of alternative assumptions that could be made with regard to factor ownership. Since our main interest lies in the demonstration that trade may actually hurt some individuals, let us adopt the simplifying assumption that in our economy there are two classes of people: workers and landlords. The landlords own all the land, but they do not offer any labor services. The latter are being offered by the workers, who do not own any land at all. Of course, in any real world situation, workers own some land and landlords offer some labor services. However, our assumption brings out quite sharply the consequences of nonuniformity in factor ownership.

Assume that our economy produces two commodities, $X$ and $Y$, under constant returns to scale. For the given overall labor-land ratio in our economy, commodity $Y$ is assumed to be land intensive relative to $X$. Note that the complication of factor-intensity reversals is of no consequence to this classification, because, as demonstrated in chap. 8, the two commodities can *always* be classified uniquely into labor intensive and land intensive when the overall labor-land ratio is given. Assume that our economy can buy and sell unlimited quantities of $X$ and $Y$ in the international market at fixed prices $p_0$. In particular, assume that the international price ratio $p_x/p_y$ is smaller than the pretrade domestic price ratio. That is, $X$ is cheaper (and $Y$ more expensive) in the international market. What happens when trade opens up?

### The Effect of Trade on Relative and Absolute Income Shares

Since, by assumption, $X$ is relatively cheaper in the international market, our economy will be exporting $Y$ in exchange for $X$. Thus, the domestic production of $Y$, that is, the land-intensive commodity, will rise and the domestic production of $X$ will fall. What happens to factor prices? As a result of the shift toward increased production of the land-intensive commodity, both commodities will tend to become more labor intensive and the marginal physical product of labor will fall while the marginal physical product of land will rise in both industries. Thus, the factor-price ratio $w/r$ (see eqs. (15.7) and (15.8)) will definitely fall. What happens to the workers' and landlords' *relative* share in real national income?

National income is the sum of the income of workers ($w\bar{L}$) plus the income of landlords ($r\bar{T}$), or $w\bar{L} + r\bar{T}$. Therefore, the relative income of workers is given by $w\bar{L}/(w\bar{L} + r\bar{T})$, and equals (using eqs. (15.7) and (15.8) and simplifying)

$$\frac{\text{MPP}_L^{\cdot}\bar{L}}{\text{MPP}_L^{\cdot}\bar{L} + \text{MPP}_T^{\cdot}\bar{T}} = \frac{\bar{L}}{\bar{L} + (\text{MPP}_T^{\cdot}/\text{MPP}_L^{\cdot})\bar{T}} \tag{15.16}$$

Note that a superior dot has replaced the superscripts $X$ and $Y$ from the symbols $\text{MPP}_T$ and $\text{MPP}_L$, because we can use the marginal productivities of both factors in either of the two industries. Thus, we can use either the pair $(\text{MPP}_L^X, \text{MPP}_T^X)$ or the pair $(\text{MPP}_L^Y, \text{MPP}_T^Y)$. An examination of eq. (15.16) reveals that, as the production of $Y$ increases at the expense of $X$ and therefore the ratio $\text{MPP}_T^{\cdot}/\text{MPP}_L^{\cdot}$ increases, the *relative income of workers falls*.

Similar reasoning shows that, as resources are being transferred from industry $X$ to industry $Y$, the *relative income of landlords rises*. Thus, the relative income of landlords is

$$\frac{\text{MPP}_T^{\cdot}\bar{T}}{\text{MPP}_L^{\cdot}\bar{L} + \text{MPP}_T^{\cdot}\bar{T}} = \frac{\bar{T}}{(\text{MPP}_L^{\cdot}/\text{MPP}_T^{\cdot})\bar{L} + \bar{T}} \tag{15.17}$$

Accordingly, when $\mathrm{MPP}_L/\mathrm{MPP}_T$ falls, the relative income of landlords rises.

We cannot conclude from the preceding analysis that the introduction of trade necessarily makes the workers worse off and the landlords better off. All we have proved so far is that the *relative* income of workers falls and the *relative* income of landlords rises. In order to conclude anything about the welfare of each group, we must first determine what happens to the *absolute* income of each group. If international trade actually increases national income, the absolute income of workers might still increase, even though their relative income falls: a smaller share from a large pie may very well be bigger than a larger share from a small pie. However, with the introduction of trade, all prices change, which presents a dilemma: do we evaluate income at the pretrade or posttrade prices? We seem to be heading toward an index number problem, which, fortunately, can be avoided.

## The Effect of Trade on the Welfare of a Typical Worker

In principle, it is possible to determine whether an individual's welfare has increased or decreased only if it can be shown that that individual has moved to a higher or a lower indifference curve. This presupposes a detailed knowledge of the indifference map of the individual. But is it possible to predict the effect of international trade on the welfare of each worker and landlord without such information? Yes indeed, as we can demonstrate that, with the introduction of international trade, each worker becomes worse off while each landlord becomes better off irrespective of the peculiarities of each individual's indifference map.

Consider the budget line of the $i$th worker as given by the equation

$$wL_i = p_x X + p_y Y$$

or
$$L_i = \frac{p_x}{w} X + \frac{p_y}{w} Y \tag{15.18}$$

As long as both commodities are domestically produced, eqs. (15.7) and (15.8) are satisfied. Solving eqs. (15.7) for $p_x/w$ and $p_y/w$, we get

$$\frac{p_x}{w} = \frac{1}{\mathrm{MPP}_L^X} \tag{15.19}$$

$$\frac{p_y}{w} = \frac{1}{\mathrm{MPP}_L^Y} \tag{15.20}$$

Substituting eqs. (15.19) and (15.20) into eq. (15.18), we get

$$L_i = \frac{1}{\mathrm{MPP}_L^X} X + \frac{1}{\mathrm{MPP}_L^Y} Y \tag{15.21}$$

Equation (15.21) is the budget equation of the $i$th worker. It depends only on the marginal physical product of labor in the two industries. Assuming that the introduction of international trade does not cause our country to specialize completely in the production of $Y$ (and that something of both commodities is being produced both before and after trade), we can use eq. (15.21) to show how the budget line of the $i$th worker shifts with the opening up of trade. For this purpose, it is only necessary to find out how trade affects the marginal physical product of labor in both industries.

As we saw earlier, with the introduction of trade the production of $Y$ (that is, the land-intensive commodity) expands while the production of $X$ (that is, the labor-intensive commodity) contracts, and both commodities tend to become more labor intensive. As a result of diminishing returns to factor proportions, the marginal physical product of labor falls in both industries after the introduction of international trade, because more units of labor are combined with each unit of land in both industries. In other words, with the introduction of international trade, both $MPP_L^X$ and $MPP_L^Y$ fall.

What happens to the budget equation of the $i$th worker? First, it becomes flatter because the international price ratio $p_x/p_y$ is by assumption lower than the domestic pretrade price ratio. But second, and more important, it shifts totally toward the origin; i.e., the posttrade budget line of the $i$th worker lies completely inside the corresponding pretrade budget line. How can this important proposition be proved?

Observe that all budget lines are straight lines. To find out whether the pretrade budget line of an individual lies beyond his posttrade budget line, we have only to compare the corresponding intercepts of the two budget lines with the two axes. Thus, the $X$-axis intercept of the $i$th worker's budget line is given by the product $L_i MPP_L^X$ and the $Y$-axis intercept by the product $L_i MPP_L^Y$.† Since both $MPP_L^X$ and $MPP_L^Y$ fall with the opening up of trade, both intercepts are smaller after trade. Therefore, the posttrade budget line of the $i$th worker lies totally inside his pretrade budget line, although their slopes differ.

What happens, then, to the welfare of the $i$th worker? Since, with the introduction of trade, the budget line of the $i$th worker shifts totally toward the origin, he must necessarily be consuming on a lower indifference curve after trade compared with his pretrade position. Hence, the $i$th worker is definitely hurt by the introduction of international trade. This conclusion does not depend on the details of his indifference map. The effect of international trade on the welfare of the $i$th worker is a general conclusion; it holds for each and every worker.

### The Effect of Trade on the Welfare of a Typical Landlord

Similar reasoning shows that trade makes every landlord better off. Thus, the budget equation of the $j$th landlord is given by

$$rT_j = p_x X + p_y Y$$

or
$$T_j = \frac{p_x}{r} X + \frac{p_y}{r} Y \qquad (15.22)$$

---

† Given a budget equation $M = aX + bY$, where $M$, $a$, and $b$ are parameters, we can determine the $X$-axis intercept by putting $Y = 0$ and solving the budget equation for $X$. Similarly, the $Y$-axis intercept is determined by putting $X = 0$ into the budget equation and solving for $Y$. Thus: $X$-axis intercept $= M/a$ and $Y$-axis intercept $= M/b$.

Substituting $p_x/r$ and $p_y/r$ as given by eqs. (15.10) and (15.11), respectively, into eq. (15.22), we get

$$T_j = \frac{1}{\mathrm{MPP}_T^X} X + \frac{1}{\mathrm{MPP}_T^Y} Y \qquad (15.23)$$

Equation (15.23) is the budget equation of the $j$th landlord. It depends only on the marginal physical product of land in the two industries. Assuming again that our economy produces something of both commodities before and after the introduction of trade, we can use eq. (15.23) to show how the budget line of the $j$th landlord shifts with the opening up of trade.

As we saw earlier, with the opening up of trade, both industries tend to become more labor intensive or less land intensive. As a result, both $\mathrm{MPP}_T^X$ and $\mathrm{MPP}_T^Y$ rise, and both intercepts of the $j$th landlord's budget line (that is, $T_j \mathrm{MPP}_T^X$ and $T_j \mathrm{MPP}_T^Y$) increase. The budget line of the $j$th landlord shifts totally outward, and irrespective of the details of his indifference map, the $j$th landlord definitely becomes better off after trade. The same conclusion holds, of course, for all landlords.

## Summary of the Effects of Trade on the Welfare of Workers and Landlords

To summarize, when the introduction of international trade renders the land-intensive commodity more expensive, the production of the land-intensive commodity expands while the production of the labor-intensive commodity contracts. Both industries tend to become more labor intensive, thus causing the marginal physical product of labor to fall everywhere (i.e., both $\mathrm{MPP}_L^X$ and $\mathrm{MPP}_L^Y$ fall) and the marginal physical product of land to rise everywhere (i.e., both $\mathrm{MPP}_T^X$ and $\mathrm{MPP}_T^Y$ rise).

The $X$-axis and $Y$-axis intercepts of the $i$th worker's budget line are given, respectively, by $L_i \mathrm{MPP}_L^X$ and $L_i \mathrm{MPP}_L^Y$, and the corresponding intercepts of the $j$th landlord's budget line are given by $T_j \mathrm{MPP}_T^X$ and $T_j \mathrm{MPP}_T^Y$. Hence, each worker's budget line shifts unequivocally inward and each landlord's budget line shifts unequivocally outward after the introduction of trade.[†] As a result, each worker becomes worse off and each landlord becomes better off with trade.

This conclusion depends only on the direction of change of the commodity-price ratio after the introduction of trade, and nothing else. In particular, it does not depend on the validity of the Heckscher–Ohlin theorem. Whether or not factor prices are completely equalized through commodity trade is also immaterial. Also, factor-intensity reversals do not affect our conclusion that *the factor used intensively in the commodity whose price rises after the introduction of trade benefits positively from trade while the other factor is definitely hurt.*

---

† Can it be proved that, when the introduction of international trade renders the land-intensive commodity cheaper, the budget line of each worker shifts outward and the budget line of each landlord shifts inward?

## The Effect of Trade on Aggregate Welfare

What is the effect of international trade on our economy's welfare? This is a very difficult question, because some people benefit from trade while others are hurt by it. To judge the effect of trade on welfare, we need either a means of weighing losses versus gains or a policy that compensates for losses. We shall return to this important question later in the next chapter.

What happens to our economy's welfare when, as a result of a shift in international demand from $X$ to $Y$, the terms of trade of our economy improve (i.e., the international price ratio $p_x/p_y$ falls)? Does the welfare of our economy improve as well? Again, we cannot be sure, because from the preceding analysis, each worker must be hurt while each landlord must benefit from the terms-of-trade improvement. Since interpersonal comparisons of well-being are both impossible and "unscientific," we must reserve judgement on the question of whether welfare improves when the terms of trade improve.

It can be similarly shown that a deterioration in the terms of trade benefits every worker and hurts every landlord. But we cannot tell at this stage whether welfare improves or deteriorates.

## Complete Specialization

So far, we have been assuming that the introduction of international trade does not bring about complete specialization. In other words, after the introduction of trade, our economy continues to produce both commodities. What happens if this assumption is dropped? Can we still conclude that one factor is definitely injured by the introduction of trade while the other definitely benefits from it? No.

Consider the case where both commodities are produced and the international price ratio $p_x/p_y$ starts falling continuously. As long as the economy continues to produce both commodities, the preceding analysis holds. That is, the factor $(L)$ used intensively in the production of the commodity whose price falls $(X)$ is hurt while the factor $(T)$ used intensively in the production of the commodity whose price rises $(Y)$ benefits from trade. But beyond a crucial price ratio—corresponding to the slope of the economy's production-possibilities frontier at the $Y$-axis intercept—the production of $X$ ceases completely. Further reductions in the commodity-price ratio $p_x/p_y$ alter neither the production point nor the marginal physical productivities of the two factors in the production of $Y$.

The budget eqs. (15.18) and (15.22), beyond the critical value of $p_x/p_y$ at which the country specializes completely in the production of $Y$, become

$$L_i = \frac{p_x}{w} X + \frac{p_y}{w} Y = \frac{p_y}{w} \frac{p_x}{p_y} X + \frac{p_y}{w} Y$$

$$= \frac{p_x/p_y}{\mathrm{MPP}_L^Y} X + \frac{1}{\mathrm{MPP}_L^Y} Y \tag{15.24}$$

$$T_j = \frac{p_x}{r} X + \frac{p_y}{r} Y = \frac{p_y}{r} \frac{p_x}{p_y} X + \frac{p_y}{r} Y$$

$$= \frac{p_x/p_y}{\mathrm{MPP}_T^Y} X + \frac{1}{\mathrm{MPP}_T^Y} Y \tag{15.25}$$

Remember that after $p_x/p_y$ falls below its critical value, the marginal physical products of labor and land in the $Y$ industry, that is, $\text{MPP}_L^Y$ and $\text{MPP}_T^Y$, remain constant. Therefore, when $p_x/p_y$ falls below its critical value, the $Y$-axis intercepts of both budget lines, $L_i \text{MPP}_L^Y$ and $T_j \text{MPP}_T^Y$, remain constant, while both $X$-axis intercepts, $L_i \text{MPP}_L^Y/(p_x/p_y)$ and $T_j \text{MPP}_T^Y/(p_x/p_y)$, tend to increase. (Both of these cases are similar to the case of a consumer who is endowed with a fixed income and consumes two commodities $X$ and $Y$, with the price of $Y$ held constant and the price of $X$ allowed to fall continuously.)

After the commodity-price ratio $p_x/p_y$ falls below its critical value, both workers and landlords tend to become better off compared with their positions at the critical value of $p_x/p_y$. Under these circumstances, a terms-of-trade improvement definitely implies an improvement in the welfare of the country as a whole. But how does the posttrade welfare positions of workers and landlords compare with their pretrade positions?

One thing is clear: the welfare of each landlord increases definitely because it increases continuously as $p_x/p_y$ falls. We cannot tell what happens to the welfare of the workers though, for as $p_x/p_y$ falls, each worker individually (and as a group) becomes continuously worse off, until $p_x/p_y$ reaches its critical value. Beyond that point, as $p_x/p_y$ continues to fall, each worker (and the group as a whole) tends to become better off. Thus, the outcome is necessarily indeterminate.

## Diagrammatic Illustration

The above conclusions are illustrated diagrammatically in fig. 15.4. Panel (a) reproduces the information contained in fig. 10.4. The curve $PP'$ in the second quadrant shows the relationship between the commodity-price ratio $p_x/p_y$ and the factor-price ratio $w/r$; the curve $XX'$ in the first quadrant shows the relationship between the marginal rate of substitution of labor for land in the production of $X$ and the labor-land ratio $\rho_x$ used in the production of $X$; and the curve $YY'$ shows the relationship between the marginal rate of substitution of labor for land in $Y$ and the labor-land ratio $\rho_y$ used in $Y$. The overall labor-land ratio is given by the distance $OM$. The factor-price ratio can vary from $OR$ to $OS$ depending on the commodity-price ratio; $\rho_y$ can vary from $ON$ to $OM$; and $\rho_x$ can vary from $OM$ to $OG$. Recall that, after the introduction of the overall labor-land ratio, the relationship between commodity prices and factor prices is given by the solid curve $KS'R'R$.

Figure 15.4($b$) shows, in the first quadrant, the curves of the marginal physical product of labor, $\text{MPP}_L^X$ and $\text{MPP}_L^Y$, as functions of $\rho_x$ and $\rho_y$, respectively. Both of these curves are necessarily downward sloping because of diminishing returns. Note that only the solid parts of these curves are relevant to this discussion, because the following inequalities must necessarily be satisfied: $OM \leq \rho_x \leq OG$ (or $OM' \leq \rho_x \leq OG'$) and $ON \leq \rho_y \leq OM$ (or $ON' \leq \rho_y \leq OM'$). Note, also, that the two marginal productivity curves may intersect each other, but this complication is of no significance to this discussion.

In the first quadrant of fig. 15.4($c$) are drawn two curves ($\text{MPP}_T^X$ and $\text{MPP}_T^Y$) showing the marginal physical product of land in the production of $X$ and $Y$ as functions of $\rho_x$ and $\rho_y$, respectively. These two curves are upward sloping, because

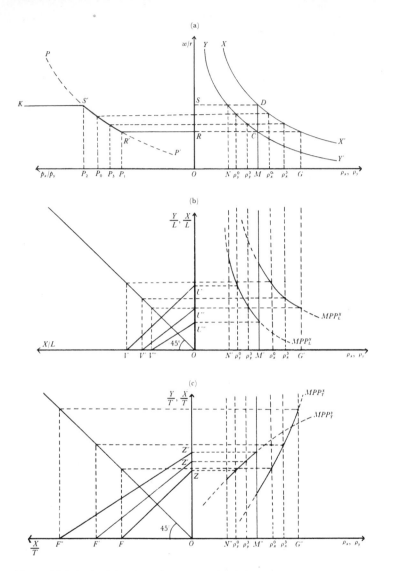

**Figure 15.4** As the labor-intensive commodity ($X$) becomes cheaper, and before the economy specializes completely in $Y$, the budget line of each worker shifts inward and that of each landlord outward. When $X$ becomes cheaper after complete specialization in $Y$, both budget lines rotate through their respective $Y$-axis intercepts ($U''$ and $Z''$), becoming flatter.

when the labor-land ratio increases in any industry, the marginal physical product of land necessarily increases. Again, only the solid parts of these two curves are relevant. Let us now derive the budget line of a worker endowed with 1 unit of labor and the budget line of a landlord endowed with 1 unit of land, for any commodity-price ratio.

Assume that the pretrade price ratio is equal to $OP_0$. The optimum labor-land ratios in the production of $X$ and $Y$ are $\rho_x^0$ and $\rho_y^0$, respectively. Hence, the marginal physical product of labor in $X$ is given by $OV$ and in $Y$ by $OU$, and the budget line of our worker is given by the straight line $VU$ in the second quadrant of fig. 15.4($b$). Similarly, the marginal physical product of land in $X$ is given by $OF$ and in $Y$ by $OZ$. Thus, the budget line of our landlord is given by the straight line $FZ$ in the second quadrant of fig. 15.4($c$). Note that $FZ$ is parallel to $VU$ and their common slope is equal to $OP_0$.

Now suppose that the country participates in international trade and that the international price ratio $p_x/p_y$, considered a constant by our economy, is given by $OP_3$. The domestic price ratio necessarily falls from $OP_0$ to $OP_3$, and both labor-land ratios, $\rho_x$ and $\rho_y$, increase from $\rho_x^0$ and $\rho_y^0$ to $\rho_x^3$ and $\rho_y^3$, respectively. The marginal physical product of labor falls in $Y$ from $OU$ to $OU'$ and in $X$ from $OV$ to $OV'$, and the budget line of our worker shifts *inward* from $UV$ to $U'V'$. The budget line of our landlord shifts *outward* from $ZF$ to $Z'F'$. Again, $Z'F'$ is parallel to $U'V'$ and their common slope is equal to $OP_3$. Thus, $Z'F'$ and $U'V'$ are flatter than $ZF$ and $UV$. Note that, without any knowledge of the indifference curves of landlords and workers, we can conclude that, with the introduction of trade, landlords become better off and workers become worse off.

Now assume that the international price ratio falls to $OP_1$. This is the critical value of the price ratio $p_x/p_y$ referred to earlier. At this commodity-price ratio, the budget line of a typical worker is given by $U''V''$ and the budget line of a typical landlord by $Z''F''$. Our economy specializes completely in the production of $Y$. What happens when the international price ratio falls below its critical value $OP_1$? How do the two budget lines shift? They simply rotate through their respective $Y$-axis intercepts, becoming flatter and flatter. Thus, starting from a position where $p_x/p_y = OP_1$ and allowing $p_x/p_y$ to fall, we can see that both workers and landlords tend to become better off. Can we compare their pretrade with their posttrade positions? The budget line of a typical landlord lies definitely farther from the origin in the posttrade position, but the posttrade budget line of a typical worker may lie totally inside the corresponding pretrade budget line or it may intersect it. In the former case, the introduction of trade definitely hurts the workers. In the latter case, the result is in general indeterminate: the indifference map of each worker is necessarily needed for such evaluation, and the outcome can go either way.

## SELECTED BIBLIOGRAPHY

References will be found in "Selected Bibliography" at the end of chap. 16.

# SIXTEEN

## THE GAINS FROM INTERNATIONAL TRADE

This chapter considers the fundamental question of whether free international trade increases welfare. The emphasis is on the compensation principle and potential welfare. The classic contribution in this field was made by Samuelson (1939). Over two decades later, Kemp (1962) and Samuelson (1962) extended significantly Samuelson's original contribution. Additional contributions were made by Baldwin (1952), Bhagwati (1968), and others.

## 16.1 THE SOCIAL WELFARE FUNCTION

The preceding chapter makes clear that the introduction of international trade can be expected to make some people better off and others worse off. In what sense, then, can we claim that international trade increases the welfare of all trading countries? As noted earlier, the difficulty arises essentially because of the impossibility of making interpersonal comparisons of well-being. We saw that the introduction of international trade hurt the workers and benefited the landlords in our model, but we could not say whether trade increased or decreased social welfare. For this purpose, we need either a policy that compensates for losses or a means of somehow weighing the losses of the workers against the gains of the landlords. The latter method requires a judgement of an essentially ethical nature—and no two observers can be counted on to agree that a country benefits or suffers from international trade.

Ethical judgements have nothing to do with economics. But if we are willing to make them explicit, we can determine definitely whether or not the introduction of international trade improves social welfare.

Ethical judgements can be formalized in the shape of a Bergson–Samuelson social welfare function: $W(U_1, U_2, \ldots, U_n)$, where $U_i \equiv$ utility indicator of the $i$th individual in the economy. The social welfare function is supposed to characterize some ethical belief: yours, mine, the State's, God's, and so on. It is only required "that the belief be such as to admit of an unequivocal answer as to whether one configuration of the economic system is 'better' or 'worse' than any other or 'indifferent,' and that these relationships are transitive; i.e., $A$ better than $B$, $B$ better than $C$, implies $A$ better than $C$, etc." (Samuelson 1947, p. 221). It is important to remember that the social welfare function is intrinsically ascientific: it either summarizes or implies a detailed set of ethical judgements regarding the way in which one man's welfare is to be "added" to another's.

No two observers can be counted on to make identical judgements. If we had to wait until we were given a specific social welfare function before we could say anything about the effect of trade on social welfare, we would not get very far. What we really want to do is to say as much as can be said that will be true on the basis of ethical propositions of a broad and commonly accepted kind. So we shall confine ourselves to those social welfare functions for which an increase in one person's welfare—the welfare of all other members of the society remaining the same—leads to an increase in social welfare. The totality of such functions is usually referred to as the *Paretian class*. This class of social welfare functions requires only the very broad ethical judgement that *it is a good thing to make one man better off if nobody else is made worse off*. No statement made on this basis requires the making of any interpersonal comparisons.

It seems that any statements made about the effect of international trade on social welfare on the basis of the Paretian class of social welfare functions (i.e., statements that are true for *all* social welfare functions which belong to the Paretian class) will meet a negligible amount of objection, because only a very broad ethical judgement ("that it is a good thing . . .") is required and nothing else. But can we really get very far with the Paretian class of social welfare functions?

Assume that our economy consists only of two individuals, $A$ and $B$. In fig. 16.1, the utility of $A$ $(U_A)$ is measured along the horizontal axis and the utility of $B$ $(U_B)$ is measured along the vertical axis. Consider point $E$. At $E$ the utility enjoyed by $A$ is given by the horizontal distance $OM$ and the utility of $B$ is given by the vertical distance $ON$. (The construction of fig. 16.1 does not imply that utility is measurable; $U_A$ and $U_B$ are assumed to be arbitrarily chosen ordinal utility indicators.) If the economy before trade happens to be at $E$, the introduction of trade actually increases social welfare if the economy moves to a point northeast of $E$, such as point $R$. On the other hand, if the economy moves to a point southwest of $E$, such as $Q$, social welfare decreases after trade. Both of these conclusions are true for any Paretian social welfare function. It should be noted, however, that both of these cases imply that both individuals become either better off (point $R$) or worse off (point $Q$) with the introduction of trade.

What about the case where one individual becomes better off while the other becomes worse off, as illustrated by points $S$ and $Z$? Unless we know precisely the shape of the social welfare contour line passing through $E$, we cannot possibly say whether social welfare increases with the opening up of trade. Yet this is precisely

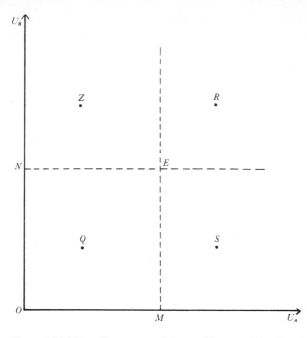

**Figure 16.1** The utility space and the need for a social welfare function when one individual becomes worse off and the other better off.

the problem we want to avoid. If we are forced to conclude that nothing can be said in these cases unless a social welfare function is completely specified, our results cannot claim generality. Is there a way around this difficulty? This question can be answered after the concept of the utility-possibility frontier, or, for short, the utility frontier, is mastered.

## 16.2 THE UTILITY-POSSIBILITY FRONTIER

Continue to assume that our economy consists of two individuals, $A$ and $B$. The utility frontier shows the maximum level of well-being that $B$ can enjoy, given the level of well-being enjoyed by $A$—or the maximum level of well-being that $A$ can enjoy, given the level of well-being enjoyed by $B$. In chap. 5, the utility frontier is derived for the simple case where the economy happens to be endowed with fixed quantities of two commodities, $X$ and $Y$. But how can the utility frontier be derived when the economy is endowed with fixed quantities of two factors of production, $L$ and $T$, and produces, under constant returns to scale, two commodities, $X$ and $Y$?

### The True Utility Frontier as an Outer Envelope

Consider fig. 16.2. The curve $MSN$ is the economy's production-possibilities frontier. Choose any point, $S$, on this frontier. The coordinates of $S$ denote a specific quantity of $X$ and $Y$. From $S$, drop lines parallel to the axes and form the

Edgeworth–Bowley box $OCSD$. Now draw in the $OCSD$ box the indifference maps of $A$ and $B$, with $O$ as $A$'s origin and $S$ as $B$'s. Every point in the box fixes six variables: $X_A$, $X_B$, $Y_A$, $Y_B$, $U_A$, and $U_B$, where $X_A \equiv$ amount of $X$ allocated to $A$; $X_B \equiv$ amount of $X$ allocated to $B$; $Y_A \equiv$ amount of $Y$ allocated to $A$; $Y_B \equiv$ amount of $Y$ allocated to $B$; $U_A \equiv U_A(X_A, Y_A) \equiv$ ordinal level of satisfaction of $A$; and $U_B \equiv U_B(X_B, Y_B) \equiv$ ordinal level of satisfaction of $B$. Now determine the locus of tangencies between the two sets of indifference curves, as shown by the contract curve $OS$. Note that only points on the contract curve $OS$ are Pareto optimal. That is, starting from any point not lying on the contract curve, such as $E$, we can always make at least one consumer better off without making the other worse off. Thus, a movement from $E$ to $H$ makes $B$ better off, with $A$ remaining on the same indifference curve; a movement from $E$ to $G$ makes $A$ better off, with $B$ remaining on the same indifference curve; and a movement from $E$ to any point in the shaded area bounded by the two indifference curves through $E$ makes both consumers better off. This is not possible when we start off from a point on the contract curve. Thus, starting at $H$, any movement which makes $A$ better off necessarily makes $B$ worse off, and any movement which makes $B$ better off makes $A$ worse off. Hence, all points on the contract curve are Pareto optimal.

From the contract curve $OS$, which is associated with the single production point $S$, we can read off the maximal combinations of $U_A$ and $U_B$ and plot them in the utility space $(U_A, U_B)$ as shown by the downward-sloping curve $S'S'$ in fig. 16.3. For each point $S$ on the production-possibilities frontier, we therefore

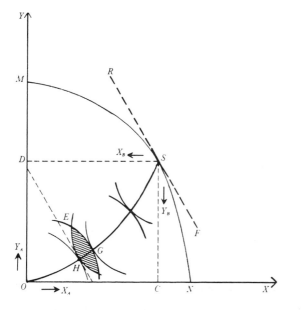

**Figure 16.2** For any point on the production-possibilities frontier draw the Edgeworth–Bowley box (such as $OCSD$) and the contract curve $(OHGS)$. The latter gives rise to a utility curve in the utility space. Only points (such as $H$) where MRT = MRS correspond to points on the true utility frontier.

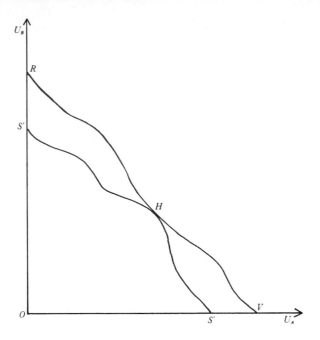

**Figure 16.3** The true utility frontier as an outer envelope of utility curves derived with respect to each and every point on the production-possibilities frontier.

determine a utility curve $(S'S')$ in the utility space. Repeating the same experiment for each and every point on the production-possibilities frontier, we shall thus be able to derive an infinite number of such utility curves. What is the true (or grand) utility-possibility frontier for the economy? It is the *outer envelope* of these individual utility curves.

## An Optimality Rule for Direct Derivation of the True Utility Frontier

There is a possible shortcut in the derivation of the utility frontier which enables us to see some important relationships between the production-possibilities frontier and the true utility frontier.

We can use an efficiency relationship to choose the point or points that belong to the true utility frontier from each contract curve $OS$ associated with every output point $S$. Pareto-optimality, which exists only along the true utility frontier, requires that *it should be impossible by any shift in production cum exchange to make one consumer better off without making the other worse off. This criterion is met only when the marginal rate of transformation in production (i.e., the slope of the production-possibilities frontier at the specified point) is equal to the marginal rate of substitution in consumption.*

The above criterion is illustrated in fig. 16.2 by points $S$ and $H$. Production takes place at $S$, and the marginal rate of transformation is indicated by the absolute slope of the tangent to the production-possibilities frontier at $S$, that is, the slope of the broken line $RSF$. The marginal rate of substitution (along the contract curve $OS$) equals the slope at $S$ only at point $H$. Hence, point $H$ is a point along the contract curve $OS$ which belongs to the true utility-possibilities frontier. In fact, it corresponds to point $H$ in fig. 16.3.

What is the rationale behind the optimality rule that the marginal rate of substitution ($MRS_{XY}$) must be equal to the marginal rate of transformation ($MRT_{XY}$)? Suppose that $MRS_{XY} = 3$ and $MRT_{XY} = 2$. How can we prove that the point on the contract curve, where $MRS_{XY} = 3$, cannot possibly belong to the true utility frontier? The equality $MRT_{XY} = 2$ implies that the economy can increase the output of $X$ by 1 unit by transferring resources from $Y$ to $X$ and reducing the output of $Y$ by 2 units. Assume that we do just that. We have 1 extra unit of $X$ and 2 less units of $Y$. Leaving $A$ undisturbed, take away 3 units of $Y$ from $B$ and replace them by 1 unit of $X$. Since $MRS_{XY} = 3$, $B$ is left indifferent. But we have an extra unit of $Y$ left over. Since, by allocating this extra $Y$ arbitrarily between $A$ and $B$, we can make either $A$ or $B$ or both better off, the initial situation could not have been Pareto optimal, i.e., the original point in the utility space could not have been on the true utility frontier.

Repetition of this process for each point on the production-possibilities frontier yields the true utility frontier. In fig. 16.3, the true utility frontier is illustrated by the curve $RHV$. Note that the curve $S'HS'$ must be tangent to $RHV$ at point $H$.

## Correspondence Between Points on the Production-Possibilities Frontier and the True Utility Frontier

Is there a one-to-one correspondence between points on the production-possibilities frontier and the true utility frontier? Not necessarily. In fact, in general, a point on the production-possibilities frontier can correspond to none, one, two, or any number of points on the true utility frontier. However, a point on the true utility frontier necessarily corresponds to a single point on the production-possibilities frontier. How can we prove these propositions?

We already know that a point on a contract curve gives rise to a point on the true utility frontier if $MRT = MRS$. In turn, the condition $MRT = MRS$ is satisfied at the point(s) where the income-consumption curves of $A$ (emanating from $O$) and $B$ (emanating from $S$) for $p_x/p_y = MRT = $ slope of the production-possibilities frontier at $S$ intersect each other. Figure 16.4($a$) illustrates the possibility that the condition $MRT = MRS$ is not satisfied along the contract curve $OS$; fig. 16.4($b$) illustrates the possibility that the condition $MRT = MRS$ is satisfied only once along the contract curve; and fig. 16.4($c$) illustrates the possibility that the condition $MRT = MRS$ is satisfied at two different points ($S_1'$ and $S_2'$) on the contract curve.

There are other examples where the two income-consumption curves intersect each other any number of times. In the limiting case where the indifference maps of $A$ and $B$ are identical and homothetic, there is a point on the production-possibilities frontier for which the two income-consumption curves coincide throughout (this point is simply the pretrade equilibrium point). In this case, no other point on the production-possibilities frontier corresponds to any point on the true utility frontier, the latter being generated totally by that unique point on the production-possibilities frontier.

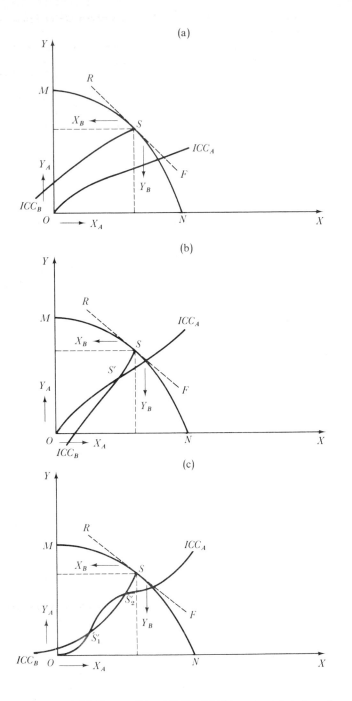

**Figure 16.4** (*a*) The condition MRT = MRS is not satisfied along the contract curve *OS* (not drawn). (*b*) The condition MRT = MRS is satisfied only once, i.e., at *S'*. (*c*) The condition MRT = MRS is satisfied twice (i.e., at points $S'_1$ and $S'_2$).

How do we know that a point on the true utility frontier corresponds to a unique point on the production-possibilities frontier? This is implicit in the discussion of Scitovsky's social indifference curves in chap. 5. Consider fig. 16.5, which is similar to fig. 16.4. The indifference curves of $A$ and $B$ are drawn tangentially through the optimum point $S'$. The corresponding Scitovsky social indifference curve is drawn tangent to the production-possibilities frontier at $S$. The slope of the Scitovsky social indifference curve at a certain point is necessarily equal to the slope of the corresponding point of either individual's indifference curve. Therefore, it is obvious from fig. 16.5 that the Scitovsky indifference curve must be tangent to the production-possibility frontier at $S$ and it must lie beyond the production-possibility frontier elsewhere. This implies that, if $A$ remains on his indifference curve $I_A$ through $S'$, any point on the production-possibilities frontier $MSN$ other than $S$ necessarily puts $B$ on a lower indifference curve than $I_B$. Hence, point $S$ on the production-possibilities frontier is the only point where $B$'s utility is maximized for a given level of utility for $A$ implied by the indifference curve $I_A$. Thus, when $A$'s utility level is held constant, there is one and only one point on the production-possibilities frontier where $B$'s utility is maximized, which is another way of saying that a point on the utility frontier corresponds to a unique point on the production-possibilities frontier.

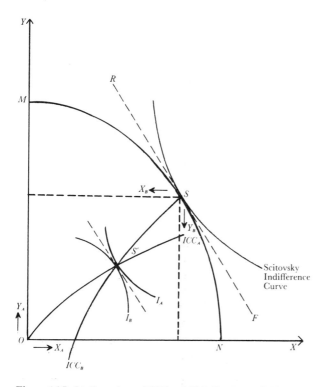

**Figure 16.5** At $S'$ we have MRT = MRS. Because of this, the corresponding Scitovsky indifference curve is tangent to the production-possibilities frontier at $S$. Hence, no other point on the production-possibilities frontier can put $A$ and $B$ on their respective indifference curves through $S'$.

## The Shape of the Utility Frontier

The shape, curvature, and position of the utility-possibility frontier depend on the particular indices selected to represent individual levels of well-being. But the direction of slope is invariant. Normally, it slopes downward: $A$ can be made better off if, and only if, $B$ becomes worse off. However, in the presence of externalities (economies or diseconomies) in consumption, the utility frontier may, in certain regions, slope upward. If we confine ourselves to the Paretian class of social welfare functions, it becomes obvious that all those parts which slope upward can be ruled out as positions of maximum welfare: everybody can be made better off if the economy happens to be at an upward-sloping section of the utility frontier. The following discussion ignores the possibility that the utility frontier may, in certain regions, slope upward.

## Significance of the Utility Frontier

What is the significance of the true utility frontier? First of all, no point outside the true utility frontier is attainable by our economy. Further, social welfare measured in terms of any Paretian social welfare function can never be maximized at a point lying inside the utility frontier. If we start from any point inside the utility frontier, it is always possible to reorganize production and exchange and make everybody better off. Social welfare is therefore at a maximum at some point on the true utility frontier. Does this conclusion imply that a movement from a point inside the utility frontier to a point on the utility frontier always represents an increase in social welfare? No. The economy may very well move from a higher to a lower social welfare contour line, and social welfare may thus decrease.

Does the economy always operate on its true utility frontier? No. The economy necessarily operates on its true utility frontier if it produces on its production-possibilities frontier and, further, if the marginal rate of transformation is equal to the marginal rate of substitution. But both of these conditions can be violated, as we saw in earlier chapters. Under our simplified assumptions of constant returns to scale, perfect competition, and complete absence of external effects, both conditions are met and the economy indeed operates somewhere on the utility frontier. Exactly where on the frontier depends on the distribution of income, which in turn depends on factor ownership. Since factor ownership, at least in the context of our model, is considered exogenous, the final equilibrium point on the true utility frontier is arbitrarily determined. In fact, by arbitrarily changing the factor ownership, we can make the economy operate on any point on the true utility frontier.

## Perfect Competition and Welfare Maximization

Perfect competition, under several assumptions, puts the economy on its true utility frontier. On the other hand, social welfare is maximized at some point on the true utility frontier. Does the solution attained under perfect competition necessarily maximize social welfare? No. Many great economists have fallen into the trap of believing that perfect competition necessarily maximizes social welfare. But this need not be so. The equilibrium point attained under perfect competition necessarily depends on factor ownership. To say that perfect competition puts the economy on the best or optimum point on the true utility frontier is to assert that the initial factor ownership is somehow optimum, and this need not be true.

The point on the utility frontier where social welfare is maximized—the bliss point—can be determined only with reference to a social welfare function that is completely specified. Without complete specification of the social welfare function, it is absolutely impossible to determine the bliss point. We are sure only that it lies somewhere on the utility frontier.

Figure 16.6 illustrates the determination of the bliss point. The curve $REV$ is the economy's true utility frontier. The curves $W_1$, $W_2$, and $W_3$ are only three social welfare contour (or indifference) lines. The contour lines are necessarily downward sloping, because our social welfare function is Paretian. A movement from a lower to a higher social welfare contour line causes social welfare to increase. Social welfare is seen to be maximized at point $E$, where the true utility frontier touches the highest contour of the welfare function.

Remember that *the bliss point, E, is the point of maximum welfare only in relation to the family of social welfare contours drawn.* For a different set of contours, another point on the utility frontier $REV$ becomes the bliss point.

As noted earlier, perfect competition puts our economy on the utility frontier. But there is no guarantee that perfect competition puts the economy at point $E$, assuming that a social welfare function is completely specified and thus the bliss

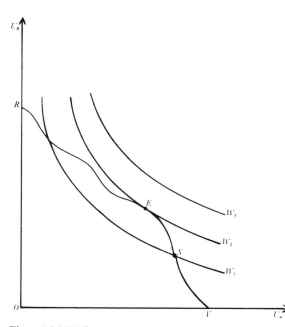

**Figure 16.6** Welfare maximization always occurs on the utility frontier. The precise point (such as $E$), however, depends on the particular social welfare function used.

point $E$ is perfectly determined. If perfect competition does not put the economy at $E$, how is it possible for social welfare to be maximized? For instance, suppose that perfect competition puts the economy at point $N$. How is it possible to secure a movement *along* the utility frontier from $N$ to $E$? This can be accomplished by a proper redistribution of wealth in the form of lump-sum transfers which destroy none of the conditions necessary for the economy to operate on its true utility frontier.

## 16.3 THE GAINS FROM INTERNATIONAL TRADE: THE CASE OF THE SMALL COUNTRY

The preceding section is intentionally confined to a closed economy. But the tools we have developed can be effectively used to enlighten our discussion of the gains from trade. Let us begin with the simple case of a country that is too small to affect its terms of trade. Section 16.4 deals with the more general case of a country that is large enough to affect its terms of trade.

Given the international terms of trade $(p \equiv p_x/p_y)$ and the production-possibilities frontier, we can determine a consumption-possibilities frontier which is simply the highest income contour line generated by the equation

$$\text{Income} = pX_p + Y_p$$

which the production-possibilities frontier can reach. The consumption-possibilities frontier lies beyond the production-possibilities frontier, except at the optimum production point $(X_p, Y_p)$, where the two frontiers coincide (i.e., they are tangential). Using the technique of the preceding section, we can determine, on the basis of the consumption-possibilities frontier, what may be called society's *cum-trade true utility frontier*. The relationship between the cum-trade true utility frontier and the true utility frontier under autarky is crucial, because in the end the gains from trade depend on it.

### The Cum-Trade Utility Frontier

Let us first derive the cum-trade utility frontier. Again, assume for simplicity that our economy consists of two individuals, $A$ and $B$. Given their indifference maps and the international price ratio $p$, we can determine uniquely the income-consumption curve for each individual.

Consider fig. 16.7. The straight line $UV$ is assumed to be the consumption-possibilities frontier. With respect to the origin of the diagram, draw the income-consumption curve of $A$ as shown by $\text{ICC}_A$. Now rotate by 180° $B$'s diagram of the income-consumption curve and place its corner at $U$, as shown by $\text{ICC}_B$. Then slide the origin of $B$'s income-consumption curve along the consumption-possibilities frontier and determine the region $RN$ on the consumption-possibilities frontier where the two income-consumption curves intersect each other at least once in the first quadrant, or they are tangential. The region $RN$ on the consumption-possibilities frontier is the only region where the condition $\text{MRS} = \text{MRT} = p$ is satisfied for some income distribution. The cum-trade utility

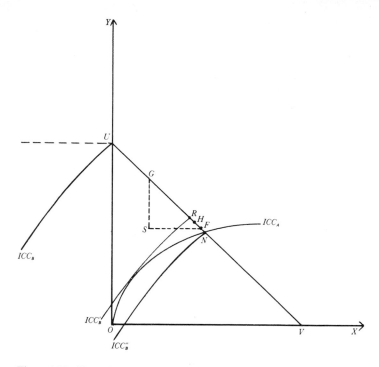

**Figure 16.7** Given the consumption-possibilities frontier $UV$, we can determine the region $RN$ where the condition MRS = MRT = $p$ is satisfied. The region $RN$ is superior to $UR$ and $NV$.

frontier corresponds to this region $(RN)$ only. The regions $UR$ and $NV$ have no counterpart on the cum-trade utility frontier.

The region $RN$ is definitely superior to the regions $UR$ and $NV$ in the sense that, for any distribution of utilities (that is, $U_A$ and $U_B$) corresponding to a point in either region $UR$ or $NV$, there is always at least one point in the region $RN$ which yields higher utilities for both $A$ and $B$. The truth of this proposition follows directly from the analysis of the preceding section and, in particular, from the construction of fig. 16.5.

## The Relationship Between the Autarkic and Cum-Trade Utility Frontiers

Figure 16.8 shows the cum-trade utility frontier $CD$, derived on the basis of the consumption-possibilities frontier of fig. 16.7. What is the relationship between this and the autarkic utility frontier?

One thing is certain: the autarkic utility frontier cannot lie beyond the cum-trade utility frontier $CD$, because the autarkic production-possibilities frontier cannot lie beyond the consumption-possibilities frontier. Thus, for any point $(S)$ on the production-possibilities frontier that lies inside the consumption-possibilities frontier $UV$, there corresponds a utility curve $(S'S'')$ in the utility space (fig. 16.8) that lies totally inside the cum-trade utility frontier. This is because, for any point $S$ that lies inside the consumption-possibilities frontier,

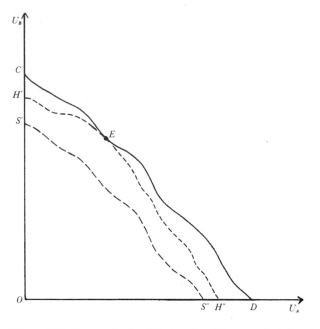

**Figure 16.8** The cum-trade utility frontier $CD$ cannot lie below the autarkic utility frontier.

there are points on the frontier (i.e., region $FG$) implying larger quantities of $X$ and $Y$; and any of these points yields a utility curve in fig. 16.8 which lies totally beyond the $S'S''$ curve. For instance, point $H$ in fig. 16.7 gives rise to the utility curve $H'H''$ in fig. 16.8, which necessarily lies uniformly beyond $S'S''$.

The curve $H'H''$ is tangent to the cum-trade utility frontier at point $E$, because we selected point $H$ to lie in the region $RN$. Had we picked a point in the region $GR$ of fig. 16.7, we would have ended up with a utility curve in fig. 16.8 lying between $S'S''$ and $CD$ without touching either of them. Does this argument prove that the autarkic utility frontier lies completely inside the cum-trade utility frontier? No.

All we have proved is that all points on the production-possibilities frontier which lie inside the consumption-possibilities frontier yield utility curves which lie inside the cum-trade utility frontier. But what about the equilibrium production point, i.e., the point where the consumption-possibilities frontier is tangent to the production-possibilities frontier? Does not this point at least yield a utility curve in fig. 16.8 that is tangent to the cum-trade utility frontier at one or more points? That depends on the position of the production point. If it lies in the region $RN$ (fig. 16.7), it necessarily yields a utility curve in fig. 16.8 that is tangent to the cum-trade utility frontier at one or more points. However, if it lies in the regions $UR$ or $NV$, it yields a utility curve that lies totally inside the cum-trade utility frontier.

It is therefore appropriate to distinguish clearly between these two cases: (*a*) when the equilibrium production point lies in the regions $UR$ or $NV$, the cum-trade utility frontier lies totally beyond the autarkic utility frontier; and (*b*) when the equilibrium production point lies in the region $RN$, the cum-trade utility frontier normally lies outside the autarkic utility frontier but with the two frontiers being tangent to each other at one or more points. Of course, when the region $RN$ shrinks to a single point—as in the case of identical and homothetic tastes—which actually happens to coincide with the equilibrium production point before and after trade, the two utility frontiers coincide completely.

## The Effect of Trade on Social Welfare: Case ($a$) When the Cum-Trade Utility Frontier Lies Uniformly Beyond the Autarkic Utility Frontier

What can be said about the effect of trade on social welfare? Does the opening up of trade necessarily improve social welfare?

Consider fig. 16.9, which is similar to fig. 16.8. The curve $CD$ is the cum-trade utility frontier, while the curve $FG$ is the autarkic frontier. By assumption, $FG$ lies uniformly inside $CD$. Before trade, the economy is somewhere on $FG$, such as point $M$. With the opening up of trade, the economy moves to some point on $CD$. Does this movement necessarily imply an increase in social welfare? In other words, does the country become better off with trade?

If we knew that the economy moved from $M$ to a point on $CD$ in the region $RS$ where both $A$ and $B$ become better off with trade, we could unequivocally claim that trade improved social welfare, because, for *any* Paretian welfare func-

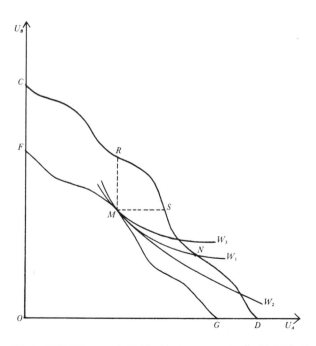

**Figure 16.9** When one individual becomes worse off with trade, the effect on *actual* welfare depends on the specific social welfare function adopted.

tion, the country can reach a higher welfare contour line with trade. This is so because all Paretian welfare functions give rise to welfare contour lines that are strictly negatively sloped; and higher welfare contour lines imply higher social welfare. Thus, the welfare contour line passing through $M$ cannot cross $CD$ in the region $RS$; and any point in the region $RS$ definitely lies on a higher welfare contour line. This conclusion is true for all Paretian welfare functions. It is also independent of whether or not social welfare before trade is actually maximized at $M$. To put it differently, it is immaterial to our conclusion (that all points in the region $RS$ are superior to $M$) whether the welfare contour line through $M$ is or is not tangent to the autarkic utility frontier $FG$ at $M$.

What if one individual becomes worse off with trade, i.e., what if the economy moves from $M$ to some point in the region $CR$ or the region $SD$? Can we still claim that our economy becomes better off with trade? Unfortunately, nothing can be said about this important case. Suppose that the economy moves from $M$ to $N$. Now $A$ becomes better off (that is, $U_A$ increases) and $B$ becomes worse off (that is, $U_B$ decreases) with trade. What happens to social welfare depends on the specific social welfare function we happen to adopt. For instance, the welfare contour line passing through $M$ may pass through $N$ (as illustrated by $W_1$), or below $N$ (as illustrated by $W_2$), or above $N$ (as illustrated by $W_3$). If the actual welfare contour line is $W_1$, then social welfare remains the same; if it is $W_2$, social welfare improves; and if it is $W_3$, social welfare deteriorates.

We therefore conclude that when one individual becomes worse off with trade, the effect on *actual* welfare depends on the specific social welfare function adopted. Some people will pass the ethical judgement that $N$ is superior to $M$; others will prefer $M$ to $N$; and still others will be indifferent between the two points. This is a sad conclusion, because if there is nothing we can say in general— i.e., for *all* Paretian social welfare functions—we cannot possibly claim that trade is unquestionably superior to no trade. How can this difficulty be resolved?

Consider again fig. 16.9. We have already seen that, if the economy moves from $M$ to any point in the region $RS$ (including points $R$ and $S$), social welfare definitely improves. But perfect competition cannot be expected to shift the economy from $M$ to a point in the region $RS$. However, recall that we can make the economy move along its utility frontier through a system of lump-sum transfers. Hence, irrespective of the actual posttrade equilibrium point on the cum-trade utility frontier, say point $N$, the economy could be made to move to some point in the region $RS$ where everybody becomes better off and thus social welfare unquestionably improves.

We can therefore say that trade is *potentially* superior to no trade, because for *any* Paretian welfare function, our country, through a system of lump-sum transfers, can be made to reach a higher welfare contour line after trade. Does this conclusion depend on the initial position of $M$? Not at all. The same can be said of any point on the autarkic utility frontier, because the cum-trade utility frontier lies uniformly outside the autarkic frontier.

Therefore, potentially, everybody can be made better off with trade, because no matter what the original equilibrium point on the autarkic utility frontier is, there is always a region on the cum-trade utility frontier which implies that everybody is better off with trade. In other words, *compensated free trade is better than no trade for all income distributions.* As Samuelson (1939) put it:

> Although it cannot be shown that every individual *is* made better off by the introduction of trade, it can be shown that through trade every individual *could* be made better off (or in the limiting case, no worse off). In other words, if a unanimous decision were required in order for trade to be permitted, it would always be possible for those who desired trade to buy off those opposed to trade, with the result that all could be made better off (p. 204).

Conversely, it is impossible under autarky to make everyone better off than at the free-trade equilibrium point, because the autarkic utility frontier cannot lie beyond the cum-trade utility frontier. Thus, given any point on the cum-trade utility frontier, it is impossible to find a point on the autarkic utility frontier where *everybody* is better off under autarky.

When the production-possibilities frontier is linear, the equilibrium production point coincides, in general, with either point $U$ or point $V$ of fig. 16.7. Since neither $U$ nor $V$ can be expected to lie in the region $RN$ (both consumers usually want to consume something of both commodities), trade is general potentially better than no trade. In the limiting case where the international price ratio happens to coincide with the slope of the linear production-possibilities frontier, the consumption-possibilities frontier coincides with the production-possibilities frontier and the cum-trade utility frontier coincides with the autarkic utility frontier. In this case, trade need not take place, but even if it does—because the production point is indeterminate—it need not affect the welfare of anybody. In this limiting case, we can thus safely say that trade is not potentially inferior to no trade.

## The Effect of Trade on Welfare: (*b*) When the Cum-Trade Utility Frontier Is Tangent to the Autarkic Utility Frontier at One or More Points

Turn now to the case where the cum-trade utility frontier is tangent to the autarkic utility frontier at one or more points. This occurs in general when the production-possibilities frontier is curvilinear rather than linear. As noted earlier, the two utility frontiers are tangent to each other at one or more points if, and only if, the posttrade equilibrium production point lies in the region $RN$ (fig. 16.7). Assuming that this is actually the case, can we still assert that trade is potentially better than no trade? This cannot possibly be true for *all* Paretian welfare functions and *all* income distributions.

In particular, for those welfare functions for which social welfare is maximized at a point of tangency between the autarkic and the cum-trade utility frontiers—and there is an infinite number of such Paretian welfare functions—social welfare does not increase after the introduction of international trade, assuming that the pretrade income distribution is optimum. But social welfare need not decrease either in the present case.

We therefore conclude that, even though the introduction of trade could not make everybody better off for *all* income distributions and *all* Paretian welfare functions, it need not make anybody worse off (potentially) either.

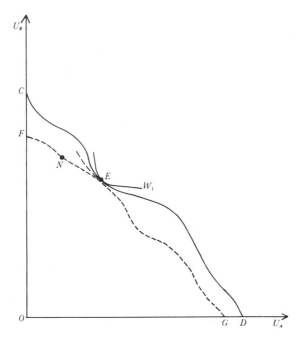

**Figure 16.10** The autarkic utility frontier *FG* is tangent to the cum-trade utility frontier *CD* at *E*. Trade may increase potential welfare but it does not reduce it.

Figure 16.10 illustrates the point. The curve *CD* is the cum-trade utility frontier and the broken curve *FG* is the autarkic utility frontier. The two utility frontiers are tangent at *E*, which corresponds to the posttrade equilibrium production point on the production-possibilities frontier (point *H*, say, of fig. 16.7). If social welfare happens to be maximized at *E*, we cannot claim that free trade makes everybody better off (potentially), for the economy could reach point *E* even without trade. However, and this is important, free trade need not make anybody worse off in a potential sense. This is obvious because the autarkic utility frontier cannot possibly lie beyond the cum-trade utility frontier. Finally, note that even in the present case a slightly modified welfare contour line (as shown by the broken contour line through $E_1$) could imply increased social welfare after the introduction of trade.

## 16.4 THE GAINS FROM INTERNATIONAL TRADE: THE CASE OF THE LARGE COUNTRY

The preceding analysis depends on the assumption that our country is too small to affect the international price ratio. Do the same conclusions hold for a country that is large enough to affect the international price ratio? To answer this question, we have to find out how free trade affects the utility frontier of the economy. As a first step, we have to determine the economy's consumption-possibilities frontier. But the trading opportunities of the large country cannot be represented by a linear offer curve of the rest of the world; therefore, a way must be found to represent the commodity combinations attainable by trade.

## The Free-Trade Consumption-Possibilities Frontier

Figure 16.11 shows the offer curve of the rest of the world. The curve $MN$ in figure 16.12 is our economy's production-possibilities frontier. For any international price ratio $p_x/p_y$, we can determine two things: (a) the optimum production point on our economy's production-possibilities frontier by the condition $\mathrm{MRT} = p_x/p_y$; and (b) the equilibrium trade point on the offer curve of the rest of the world by drawing a vector with slope equal to the given international price ratio through the origin of fig. 16.11 until it intersects the offer curve—the intersection being the equilibrium trade point.

For the international price ratio given by the slope of $\mathrm{TOT}_1$ (fig. 16.11) or the slope of $UV$ (fig. 16.12), the equilibrium trade point for the rest of the world is $T_1$ (fig. 16.11) and the optimum production point for our economy is $P_1$ (fig. 16.12). If our economy were small, the straight line $UP_1V$ (fig. 16.12) would be its consumption-possibilities frontier. What happens now that the rest of the world is

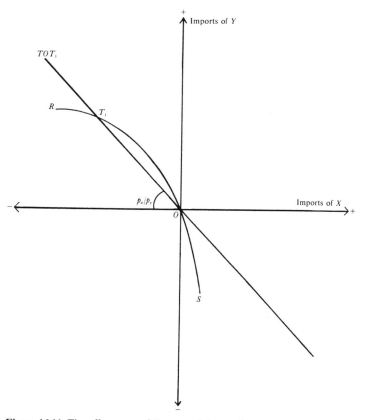

**Figure 16.11** The offer curve of the rest of the world.

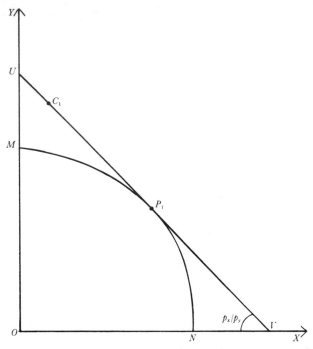

**Figure 16.12** Derivation of points (such as $C_1$) on the consumption-possibilities frontier.

willing to trade at point $T_1$ only? Our economy can produce at $P_1$ and consume at $C_1$ only where the distance $P_1 C_1$ (fig. 16.12) is equal to the distance $OT_1$ (fig. 16.11). Point $C_1$ is a point on our economy's consumption-possibilities frontier.

Repetition of the above process for all values of $p_x/p_y$ yields our country's free-trade consumption-possibilities frontier, which definitely lies beyond our economy's production-possibilities frontier except at one point—the point where the slope of the production-possibilities frontier is equal to the slope of the offer curve of the rest of the world at the origin.

Note that not all points on the production-possibilities frontier are acceptable candidates as production points under free trade. Point $C_1$ (fig. 16.12) has to lie in the first quadrant; but for some values of $p_x/p_y$, and hence for some points on the production-possibilities frontier, point $C_1$ will lie in the second or fourth quadrants. These points are simply not relevant.

## The Effect of Trade on Welfare

Figure 16.13 shows the consumption-possibilities frontier $CD$ and the production-possibilities frontier $MN$. The two frontiers are tangential at point $R$. Elsewhere, the consumption-possibilities frontier $CD$ lies beyond the production-possibilities frontier $MN$.

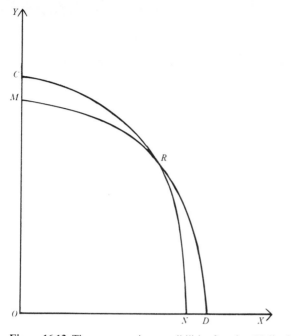

**Figure 16.13** The consumption-possibilities frontier $CD$ lies beyond the production-possibilities frontier $MN$ except at their common tangency ($R$).

What about the corresponding utility-possibilities frontiers? From the preceding analysis, it follows that the autarkic utility frontier cannot lie beyond the cum-trade utility frontier and the cum-trade utility frontier cannot lie inside the autarkic utility frontier. Nevertheless, the two frontiers can be tangent to each other at one or more points, depending on the number of intersections between the income-consumption curve of $A$ drawn with respect to $O$ and the income-consumption curve of $B$ drawn with respect to $R$ (as in fig. 16.4) for a price ratio equal to the common slope of the two frontiers at $R$ (fig. 16.13).

If no intersection between the two income-consumption curves just described exists, then the cum-trade utility frontier lies totally outside the autarkic utility frontier, and compensated free trade (i.e., free trade accompanied by optimal transfers) is definitely better than no trade at all. But what if the two utility frontiers are tangent to each other at one or more points? Can we still assert that compensated free trade is superior to no trade? As is pointed out in sec. 16.3, such a statement cannot be made for *all* Paretian welfare functions and all income distributions. Even in this limiting case, however, trade cannot be proved potentially inferior to no trade.

In summary, compensated free trade is superior to no trade, or, in the limiting case, compensated free trade is not inferior to no trade. This conclusion remains valid for all countries. Chapter 19 considers the proposition that restricted trade is better than free trade.

## 16.5 THE GAINS FROM TRADE: THE WORLD AS A WHOLE

So far, we have been dealing with the effect of international trade on a single country's welfare. Let us now demonstrate that international trade improves the potential welfare of all trading countries.

Chapter 2 shows (*a*) how the world production-possibilities frontier can be constructed when the production-possibilities frontiers of the individual countries are linear; (*b*) that under autarky the world is in general producing *inside* the world frontier; and (*c*) that free trade enables the world to produce *on* the world frontier. We can now show that these conclusions hold even in the case where the production-possibilities frontiers of the individual countries are curvilinear and argue that compensated free international trade is superior to no trade, or, in the limiting case, compensated free trade is not inferior to no trade, for the world as a whole.

How can the world production-possibilities frontier be derived in the presence of increasing opportunity costs in individual countries? Assume that we have two countries, *A* and *B*. In fig. 16.14, *A*'s production-possibilities frontier is given by the curve *MN*. Country *A*'s production block (*ONEM*) remains in this position throughout. Now rotate *B*'s production block by 180° and place it tangent to *A*'s production block, as shown by *HCED*. Let *B*'s production block slide along *A*'s

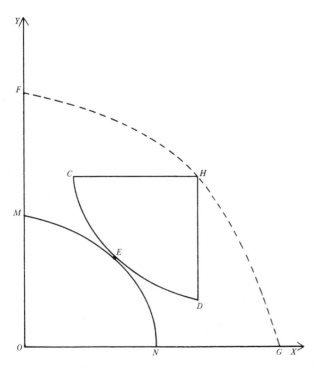

**Figure 16.14** The world production-possibilities frontier.

production block in such a way that the curve $CED$ remains tangent to $MEN$, $CH$ remains parallel to the horizontal axis, and $HD$ remains parallel to the vertical axis. The corner of $B$'s production block now traces out the broken curve $FHG$, which is simply the world production-possibilities frontier. It shows the maximum amount of one commodity that the world as a whole can produce given the amount of production of the other.

What condition must be satisfied if the world is to produce on the world frontier $FHG$ and not inside it? From the construction of fig. 16.14, the two countries must be producing at points on their individual production-possibilities frontiers where their respective opportunity costs are the same, since the two production frontiers in fig. 16.14 are required to be tangential. What is the commonsense meaning of this condition?

Suppose that $A$'s marginal rate of transformation $(\text{MRT}_{XY}^A)$ is 3 and $B$'s $(\text{MRT}_{XY}^B)$ 2. How can we show that the world is not producing on the world frontier? Assume that $A$ reduces its production of $X$ by 1 unit while $B$ increases its production of $X$ by 1 unit. The total world production of $X$ remains constant. What happens to the world output of $Y$? Since $\text{MRT}_{XY}^A = 3$, $A$'s output of $Y$ increases by 3 units; and since $\text{MRT}_{XY}^B = 2$, $B$'s output of $Y$ falls by only 2 units. Therefore, the world output of $Y$ increases by $3 - 2 = 1$ unit. By the suggested reallocation of resources, the world can increase the output of $Y$ without reducing the output of $X$. Thus, the initial allocation could not have been optimal, i.e., the world could not have been producing on the world frontier. Only when $\text{MRT}_{XY}^A = \text{MRT}_{XY}^B$ is it impossible to increase the output of one commodity without reducing the output of the other.

As we have seen, international trade takes place when the pretrade price ratios of the two countries differ. But the pretrade price ratios merely reflect the equilibrium marginal rates of transformation under autarky. Hence, international trade takes place when the pretrade marginal rates of transformation differ between countries. In other words, international trade takes place when the world is not producing on the world production-possibilities frontier. But free trade equalizes relative prices (and hence marginal rates of transformation) between countries. Free trade thus makes it possible for the world as a whole to produce on the world frontier and not inside it.

Does the world as a whole actually become better off with free international trade? Free trade in general makes some people better off and others worse off. Under these circumstances, nothing can be said in general about the effect of free international trade on actual world welfare. However, free international trade is *potentially* better than no trade from the point of view of the world as a whole.

Starting from any pretrade equilibrium position implying $\text{MRT}_{XY}^A \neq \text{MRT}_{XY}^B$, we can increase the world output of both commodities. Let each individual get what he was consuming before trade. By arbitrarily distributing the excess production—over the pretrade levels—to all individuals around the world, we can make every individual better off, or at least we can make some better off without making others worse off. It is in this sense of *potential welfare* that we conclude that free trade is better than no trade, from the point of view of each individual country and of the world as a whole.

For completeness, the limiting case where in the pretrade equilibrium position $\text{MRT}_{XY}^A = \text{MRT}_{XY}^B$ must be noted. Here, the opening up of international trade is not followed by any international transactions; hence, every individual retains his pretrade status.

## SELECTED BIBLIOGRAPHY

Baldwin, R. (1952). "The New Welfare Economics and Gains in International Trade." *Quarterly Journal of Economics*, vol. 66, pp. 91–101. Reprinted in R. E. Caves and H. G. Johnson (Eds.), AEA *Readings in International Economics*. Richard D. Irwin, Inc., Homewood, Ill., 1968.

Bhagwati, J. (1968). "The Gain from Trade Once Again." *Oxford Economic Papers* (New Series), vol. 20, no. 2 (July), pp. 137–148.

Kemp, M. C. (1961). "Gains and Losses from Trade." *Canadian Journal of Economics and Political Science*, vol. 27, no. 3 (August), pp. 382–383.

—— (1962). "The Gain from International Trade." *Economic Journal*, vol. 72, no. 288 (December), pp. 303–319.

—— (1968). "Some Issues in the Analysis of Trade Gains." *Oxford Economic Papers* (New Series), vol. 20, no. 2 (July), pp. 149–161.

—— (1969). *The Pure Theory of International Trade and Investment*. Prentice-Hall, Inc., Englewood Cliffs, N.J. chap. 12.

Krueger, A. O., and H. Sonnenschein (1967). "The Terms of Trade, the Gains from Trade and Price Divergence." *International Economic Review*, vol. 8, no. 1 (February), pp. 121–127.

Otani, Y. (1972). "Gains from Trade Revisited." *Journal of International Economics*, vol. 2, no. 2 (May), pp. 127–156.

Samuelson, P. A. (1938). "Welfare Economics and International Trade." *American Economic Review*, vol. 28, pp. 261–266. Reprinted in J. Stiglitz (Ed.), *The Collected Scientific Papers of Paul A. Samuelson*. The MIT Press, Cambridge, Mass., 1966.

—— (1939). "The Gains from International Trade." *Canadian Journal of Economics and Political Science*, vol. 5, pp. 195–205. Reprinted in H. Ellis and L. Metzler (Eds.), AEA *Readings in the Theory of International Trade*. Richard D. Irwin, Inc., Homewood, Ill. 1950.

—— (1947). *Foundations of Economic Analysis*. Harvard University Press, Cambridge, Mass.

—— (1950). "Evaluation of Real National Income." *Oxford Economic Papers* (New Series), vol. 2, no. 1 (January), pp. 1–28.

—— (1962). "The Gains from International Trade Once Again." *Economic Journal*, vol. 72, pp. 820–829. Reprinted in J. Stiglitz (Ed.), *The Collected Scientific Papers of Paul A. Samuelson*. The MIT Press, Cambridge, Mass., 1966.

Stolper, W., and P. A. Samuelson (1941). "Protection and Real Wages." *Review of Economic Studies*, vol. 9, pp. 58–73. Reprinted in H. Ellis and L. Metzler (Eds.), AEA *Readings in the Theory of International Trade*. Richard D. Irwin, Inc., Homewood, Ill., 1950.

## INTERNATIONAL TRADE POLICY

# SEVENTEEN

## IMPORT AND EXPORT TAXES: THE CASE OF THE SMALL COUNTRY

Chapter 16 demonstrates that free international trade is potentially better than no trade from the point of view both of the world as a whole and of each individual trading country. This thesis has never been successfully refuted, despite the fact that most arguments for protection are asserted with great conviction. Yet, in the real world, the free flow of trade has been, as a rule, impeded by several trade-control devices, such as tariffs, quotas, and exchange controls. This last part of the book analyzes the effects of these trade-control devices.

Throughout the present discussion we employ a neoclassical model of production. The issues of intermediate products and *effective protection* are ignored.[†]

Chapters 17 to 19 deal mainly with what Johnson (1969) calls the *standard theory of tariffs*. Chapter 20 surveys the theory of *domestic distortions*. Chapter 21 applies the theory of domestic distortions to the infant-industry argument as well as several other noneconomic arguments for protection. Finally, chaps. 22 and 23 deal with the theory of customs unions.

The present chapter deals with the effects of export and import taxes and subsidies in the context of a small country. The discussion is divided into three parts. Part A deals briefly with the forms of trade control; part B deals with the effects of tariffs; and part C extends the analysis of part B to export taxes, and import and export subsidies.

---

[†] The seminal contributions to the theory of effective protection are Corden (1966) and Johnson (1965). Additional contributions have been made by Balassa (1965, 1970a, 1970b, 1971), Batra and Casas (1974), Bertrand and Vanek (1971), Bhagwati and Srinivasan (1973), Corden (1969, 1971), Grubel (1971), Guisinger (1969), Humphrey (1969), Johnson (1972), Kreinin, Ramsey, and Kmenta (1971), Leith (1968, 1971), Lloyd (1970), Massell (1968), Ruffin (1969, 1970), Sendo (1974), Tan (1970), and Travis (1968).

# PART A. CLASSIFICATION OF TRADE CONTROLS

Trade controls can be classified into two major categories: those trade controls that directly influence prices, such as taxes and subsidies, and those that directly influence quantities, such as quotas and exchange controls.† Taxes or subsidies, as well as quotas, may be imposed on exports or imports, so there are really four trade controls operating through prices and two trade controls operating through quantities, as shown in table 17.1.

In general, taxes (whether on imports or exports) can be imposed in any one of the following three ways:

1. *The ad valorem basis.* This tax, or "duty," is legally fixed in the form of a percentage on the value of the commodity imported or exported, inclusive or exclusive of transport cost. For instance, if an ad valorem import duty of 10 percent is fixed on the value of imports, exclusive of transport cost, an importer of commodities valued at $100 is required to pay $10 import duty to the government. In general, if $t_a$ is the ad valorem import duty, the importer is required to pay $(1 + t_a)p_m$ per unit imported, where $p_m$ is the price accruing to the foreign exporter and $t_a p_m$ is the tax revenue per unit imported.
2. *The specific basis.* This tax is legally fixed in the form of an absolute amount of domestic currency per unit imported or exported. For instance, if a tariff of $1 is imposed on every unit of a particular commodity imported irrespective of its price, an importer must pay $\$(p_m + t_s)$ per unit imported, where $p_m$ is the price accruing to the foreign exporter and $t_s$ is the tax revenue per unit imported.
3. *The combined basis.* This is a combination of an ad valorem tax *plus* a specific tax. For instance, if an importer is required to pay to the government $\$t_s$

**Table 17.1 Trade controls**

|  | Controls operating through: | | |
|---|---|---|---|
|  | Prices | | Quantities |
|  | Taxes | Subsidies | Quotas |
| Exports | Export tax | Export subsidy | Export quota |
| Imports | Import tax (or tariff) | Import subsidy | Import quota |

† Such "monetary controls" as exchange controls and multiple exchange rates will not be discussed. However, quotas and exchange controls can be shown to produce the same economic results, and any system of multiple exchange rates can be shown to be equivalent to a system of import and export taxes and subsidies. See also Chacholiades (1978, chap. 14).

(specific duty) plus $t_a \times 100$ percent on the price of the commodity $(p_m)$ per unit imported, the importer will be paying to the government $t_s + t_a p_m$ per unit imported; his per unit cost (inclusive of the tax) will be equal to $t_s + (1 + t_a)p_m$.

Given the price of the commodity exported or imported, as the case may be, there is a one-to-one correspondence between ad valorem rates and specific rates. Consider the case of a commodity imported into the United States whose price in the international market is $\$p_m$. A specific import duty of $\$t_s$ implies that the per unit cost to the U.S. importer is $p_m + t_s$. On the other hand, an ad valorem rate of $t_a$ implies that the per unit cost to the U.S. importer is $(1 + t_a)p_m$. The two import duties will be equivalent if

$$(1 + t_a)p_m = p_m + t_s$$

or
$$t_a p_m = t_s \tag{17.1a}$$

or
$$t_a = \frac{t_s}{p_m} \tag{17.1b}$$

On the assumption that $p_m$ is known, given $t_a$ we can determine $t_s$ directly from eq. (17.1a), and given $t_s$ we can determine $t_a$ directly from eq. (17.1b). In the same way, it can be shown that any tax imposed on the combined basis is equivalent to a uniquely determined ad valorem rate.

The above demonstration does not imply that it is of no consequence whether one or another of the three methods is used to fix the tax rate legally. This analysis assumes that $p_m$ is known, but $p_m$ may or may not be known. If $p_m$ is known to begin with, it may not remain constant through time, even though factor supplies, technology, and tastes remain everywhere the same, for $p_m$ is a "money" (or absolute) price and depends, in addition, on monetary conditions. During an inflationary period when $p_m$ is rising, the ad valorem rate equivalent to a specific rate tends to fall. During a deflationary period when $p_m$ is falling, the ad valorem rate equivalent to a specific rate tends to rise. This can be verified with eq. (17.1b). Given $t_s$, as $p_m$ rises $t_a$ falls, and as $p_m$ falls $t_a$ rises.†

Since subsidies are merely negative taxes, what has been said in relation to export and import taxes necessarily holds for export and import subsidies as well. Thus, subsidies may be imposed on an ad valorem, specific, or combined basis; the equivalence between ad valorem and specific rates holds for subsidies as well.

What follows concerns ad valorem rates only because we will continue to concentrate on relative prices, for which all taxes or subsidies must be expressed in the form of ad valorem rates. Once the equilibrium relative prices are determined, there will be a one-to-one correspondence between the "absolute price level" and the specific rates equivalent to the originally imposed ad valorem rates. Therefore,

---

† Another difference between ad valorem and specific rates occurs where various qualities of a certain commodity exist and a flat ad valorem rate is used for all qualities. Then the absolute per unit tax (i.e., the equivalent specific tax) is lower for cheaper qualities. On the other hand, if a flat specific tax is used, the equivalent ad valorem rate is lower for the more expensive qualities.

the effects of the equivalent specific rates will be identical, in long-run equilibrium, to the effects of the ad valorem rates.

Quotas, as opposed to taxes and subsidies on imports and exports, control the absolute quantities of exports or imports, as the case may be. A government may wish to limit the imports of a particular commodity to a certain maximum quantity (import quota) per unit of time. For this reason, it may issue import licences that it may either sell to importers at a competitive price or just give away as gifts to importers on a first-come, first-served basis. (Alternatively, the government may consider it desirable to limit the *value* of imports by providing the importers with a limited amount of foreign currency for the purchase of a particular commodity.) Observe that, while the government can restrict the quantity of a particular commodity imported into the country, it cannot force importers to import a larger quantity than they would have imported under free-trade conditions.

A government may consider it desirable to restrict the exports of a particular commodity to a certain maximum quantity (export quota) per unit of time. Thus, exporters may be licensed to sell abroad only a certain quota of the product. Again, while the government is capable of directly reducing exports below their free-trade level, it is unable to force the exporters through this kind of quantitative restriction to increase their exports beyond the level where they achieve profit maximization.

## PART B. TARIFFS

This part discusses the various effects of a tariff which is imposed by a small country, i.e., a country which is a price-taker in the international market.

## 17.1 THE SETTING

Consider the case of a small country whose buying and selling in the international market does not have any appreciable effect on international prices. In particular, assume that our economy is endowed with two factors of production, labor ($L$) and land ($T$), and produces under constant returns to scale two commodities, $X$ and $Y$, with $X$ being labor intensive relative to $Y$. Assume that tastes can be summarized by a social indifference map and that our economy can trade commodities $X$ and $Y$ in the international market at the given prices $\bar{p}_x$ and $\bar{p}_y$, respectively. For convenience, the given international price ratio $\bar{p}_x/\bar{p}_y$ will be represented by the symbol $\bar{p}$. (In general, $p$ will indicate the international price ratio and $\bar{p}$ a specific value of $p$.) What is the international equilibrium of our small country?

For our present purposes, we use Meade's geometric technique which was explained in chap. 6. The free-trade, long-run equilibrium position is illustrated in fig. 17.1, which is similar to fig. 6.7 in all essential respects. Thus, the terms-of-trade line is given by TOT whose slope is equal to $\bar{p}$. Our economy's offer curve is

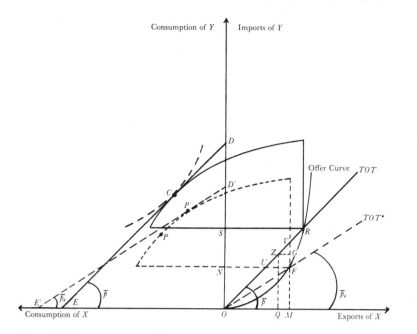

**Figure 17.1** International equilibrium of a small country before and after the imposition of a non-prohibitive tariff. The government spends the tariff revenue on $X$ and $Y$.

given by $OFR$ in the first quadrant. The straight line $ECD$ in the second quadrant, parallel to TOT, is the consumption-possibilities frontier. The economy's production block $RC$ has been placed to be tangent to the consumption-possibilities frontier at the equilibrium consumption point $C$; its corner lies necessarily on the terms-of-trade line TOT, as shown by point $R$.

## 17.2 THE IMPOSITION OF A NONPROHIBITIVE TARIFF

How does the imposition of an ad valorem import duty (i.e., a tariff), $t$, affect the equilibrium position of fig. 17.1? Nothing that our economy does affects the international prices, $\bar{p}_x$ and $\bar{p}_y$. Therefore, the rest of the world continues to trade along the terms-of-trade line TOT. But now the domestic price ratio $p_d$ is no longer equal to the international price ratio. As a result, domestic production, consumption, exports, and imports change, in general, after the imposition of the tariff.

Our object is to determine our small economy's equilibrium trade point at the constant international price ratio $\bar{p}$. As shown below, this equilibrium necessarily depends on how the government of the small country uses the tariff revenue.

In what follows, we distinguish between two cases: ($a$) when the government spends the tariff revenue on commodities $X$ and $Y$ (public consumption); and ($b$) when the government redistributes the tariff revenue to the private consumers. In the former case, some additional and, in general, arbitrary assumption about the tastes of the government must be made. In the latter case, no such arbitrary assumption on tastes is necessary—the social indifference map serves this purpose also.

## The Relationship Between the Domestic and Foreign Price Ratio When the Tariff Is Nonprohibitive

What is the relationship between the domestic price ratio $p_d$ and $\bar{p}$? A full answer is given later in this chapter. For the moment, let us simplify our analysis by assuming that the tariff is *nonprohibitive*. In other words, assume that the ad valorem rate is such that our economy continues, after the imposition of the tariff, to import commodity $Y$ and export commodity $X$.

The imposition of a nonprohibitive tariff $t$ necessarily raises the domestic price of commodity $Y$ $(p_y^d)$ above the international price $\bar{p}_y$. In particular,

$$p_y^d = (1 + t)\bar{p}_y \tag{17.2}$$

The domestic price of commodity $X$ $(p_x^d)$, however, continues to be equal to the international price $\bar{p}_x$. Accordingly, the domestic price ratio, after the imposition of the tariff, is given by

$$\bar{p}_d = \frac{p_x^d}{p_y^d} = \frac{\bar{p}_x}{(1 + t)\bar{p}_y} = \frac{1}{1 + t}\bar{p} < \bar{p} \tag{17.3}$$

The symbol $p_d$ is the domestic price ratio in general and the symbol $\bar{p}_d$ is a specific value of $p_d$. From eq. (17.3), the domestic price ratio $\bar{p}_d$ is definitely lower than the corresponding international price ratio $\bar{p}$.

## The Significance of the Tariff Revenue

Consider, in fig. 17.1, the broken terms-of-trade line TOT*, whose slope is given by $\bar{p}_d$. What would the equilibrium trade point have been in the absence of tariffs if the international price ratio had been equal to $\bar{p}_d$? Equilibrium would have occurred at $F$ (at the point where the terms-of-trade line TOT* intersects our economy's offer curve), $E'P'D'$ would have been the consumption-possibilities frontier, $P'$ with respect to the origin $O$ would have been the equilibrium consumption point, and $P'$ with respect to $F$ would have been the equilibrium production point. But now the situation is slightly different.

While the domestic price ratio is $\bar{p}_d$ and the economy definitely produces on the production block at point $P'$, the international price ratio is $\bar{p}$ and the rest of the world trades in equilibrium somewhere along the terms-of-trade line TOT. If our economy were to consume at $P'$ and trade at $F$, international equilibrium would not exist, for point $F$ does not lie on the terms-of-trade line TOT. Yet we know that, when the domestic price ratio is $\bar{p}_d$, our economy produces at $P'$ on the production block $FP'$, the consumption-possibilities frontier is given by $E'P'D'$, and consumption occurs at $P'$, thus giving rise to the trade point $F$. How can these facts be reconciled?

There is a difference between the case where the international price ratio is $\bar{p}_d$ and the present case, where it is actually $\bar{p}$. The difference is the tariff revenue which in the present case accrues to the government. Thus, in addition to the income accruing to the domestic factors of production, given by $OE'$ in terms of $X$, or by $OD'$ in terms of $Y$, we have the tariff revenue that actually enables the country as a whole (i.e., private consumers and government) to consume beyond point $P'$ and trade northwest of point $F$. In fact, as we shall see, the country will end up trading somewhere along the terms-of-trade line TOT, the precise equilibrium point depending on the way in which the government actually uses the tariff revenue.

## The Magnitude of the Tariff Revenue

What is the tariff revenue equal to? Although it can be measured in either commodity (as we shall see), assume that the government initially collects the tariff revenue in terms of the imported commodity $Y$.

Our economy is exporting $OM$ units of $X$. The rest of the world exports to our economy, in exchange for $OM$ of $X$, $MV$ units of $Y$. The amount $MF$ accrues to the private consumers while the residual $FV$ accrues to the government in the form of tariff revenue—all this from the construction of TOT*. Thus, $\bar{p}_d = MF/OM$ and $\bar{p} = MV/OM$. But $\bar{p} = (1 + t)\bar{p}_d$ (see eq. (17.3)). Hence, $(1 + t)MF/OM = MV/OM$, or

$$(1 + t)MF = MV$$

$$tMF = MV - MF = FV$$

In words, if the private consumers of our economy import $MF$ units of $Y$, the government will collect $t(MF)$ units of $Y$, which is actually given by the vertical distance $FV$.

## The Budget Line of the Government

What alternative combinations of $X$ and $Y$ are available to the government? Since the private consumers of our economy are importing from the rest of the world $MF$ units of $Y$, the tariff revenue of the government in terms of abstract purchasing power is $t\bar{p}_y(MF)$. With this tariff revenue, the government can buy

$$\frac{t\bar{p}_y(MF)}{\bar{p}_y} = t(MF) = FV$$

units of $Y$. Observe that the government is not required to pay any tax; hence it can buy $Y$ at the international price $\bar{p}_y$. The maximum amount of $X$ that the government could buy if it were to spend the whole tariff revenue on $X$ is

$$\frac{t\bar{p}_y(MF)}{\bar{p}_x} = \frac{t(MF)}{\bar{p}} = \frac{FV}{\bar{p}} = UF$$

It is evident that the government can actually purchase any combination along the straight-line segment $UV$, all quantities measured with respect to $F$, of course. The problem is similar to that of a consumer (endowed with a fixed income) facing given market prices. Thus, the straight-line segment $UV$, with $F$ as origin, is simply the budget line of the government. Depending on the way the government actually spends the tariff revenue, equilibrium occurs somewhere on $UV$.

## The Equilibrium Trade Point

The government's equilibrium consumption point on $UV$ (viewed with respect to $F$ as origin) is actually the equilibrium trade point for the economy as a whole (viewed with respect to the origin $O$).

As we have seen, private consumption gives rise to the trade point $F$. The coordinates of $F$ (with respect to the origin $O$) show, respectively, $X$'s excess domestic production over domestic consumption (i.e., private exports of $X = OM$) and $Y$'s excess domestic consumption over domestic production (i.e., private imports of $Y = MF$). Since all domestic production is actually used up in this fashion, the government can consume $X$ or $Y$ only through imports from abroad.

Suppose that the government actually consumes $FG$ of $Y$ and $ZG$ of $X$. The government's equilibrium consumption point is assumed to be given by $Z$. What are the total quantities of $X$ and $Y$ exported and imported, respectively? Private *imports* of $Y$ are $MF$ and government *imports* of $Y$ are $FG$, giving rise to a grand total of imports of $Y$ equal to $MG$ or $QZ$. On the other hand, private *exports* of $X$ are given by $OM$ while government *imports* of $X$ are given by $ZG$ or $QM$. Hence, total exports of $X$ are given by the difference $OM - QM = OQ$. Thus the coordinates of point $Z$ actually give us the total quantities of $X$ and $Y$ exported and imported, respectively.

## Redistribution of the Tariff Revenue

So far we have been assuming that the government spends its tariff revenue to buy $X$ and $Y$ directly for public consumption. What happens when the government, instead of spending its tariff revenue on $X$ and $Y$, decides to redistribute it to the consumers in the form of, say, lump-sum transfers or a general income tax reduction?

In a study of the effects of a tariff imposed for any purpose, except that of raising revenue, it seems more plausible to assume that the government already has a budget financed by other means and that the government can therefore be expected to return to the consumers, in one way or another, the tariff revenue. In addition, by assuming that the government returns the tariff revenue to the consumers, we do not have to introduce an arbitrary assumption about the use of the tariff revenue: the social indifference map can also be used for this purpose. Having introduced this new assumption, how is international equilibrium to be determined?

Given the international price ratio $\bar{p}$, it follows that (*a*) international equilibrium has to occur somewhere along the terms-of-trade line TOT (fig. 17.1) quite irrespective of any trade taxes (or subsidies) imposed by our economy; and (*b*) the domestic price ratio is $\bar{p}_d$, as shown by eq. (17.3). Point $(b)$ follows directly from the logic by which eq. (17.3) was derived. Point $(a)$ is justified by observing that international prices remain constant, by assumption, irrespective of any taxes or subsidies imposed by our economy, and that the value of exports of the rest of the world to our economy must, in equilibrium, be equal to the value of our exports to the rest of the world, *both aggregates being evaluated at international prices.*

It may be helpful to consider the problem from the point of view of our economy. Assume that, at the domestic price ratio $\bar{p}_d$, our economy produces $X_p$ and $Y_p$ units of commodities $X$ and $Y$, respectively. The value of output produced $(I)$ at domestic market prices is

$$I = \bar{p}_d X_p + Y_p$$

In national-income accounting, $I$ is usually called the *net national income at factor cost*, i.e., the income which accrues directly to the factors of production. In the absence of import taxes, $I$ is also equal to the domestic expenditure on $X$ and $Y$. However, under the present circumstances, where a tariff is imposed, the domestic aggregate expenditure $(E)$ is higher than $I$ by the tariff revenue. What is the tariff revenue equal to?

Recall that $I$ is expressed in terms of commodity $Y$ at the domestic price ratio $\bar{p}_d$. Hence, the tariff revenue must be so expressed, too. To demonstrate, let us first evaluate the tariff revenue in terms of abstract purchasing power. Thus,

$$\text{Tariff revenue} = t\bar{p}_y(Y_c - Y_p)$$

where $Y_c = $ total domestic consumption of $Y$. To express the tariff revenue in terms of commodity $Y$ at *domestic prices*, divide the above expression by $p_y^d$ (not $\bar{p}_y$). Thus,

$$\text{Tariff revenue in terms of } Y = t\frac{\bar{p}_y}{p_y^d}(Y_c - Y_p) = \frac{t}{1+t}(Y_c - Y_p)$$

using eq. (17.2). Therefore, the domestic aggregate expenditure is

$$E = \bar{p}_d X_p + Y_p + \frac{t}{1+t}(Y_c - Y_p)$$

The budget line for our economy is given by

$$E = \bar{p}_d X_c + Y_c$$

or

$$\bar{p}_d X_p + Y_p + \frac{t}{1+t}(Y_c - Y_p) = \bar{p}_d X_c + Y_c$$

or

$$\bar{p}_d(X_p - X_c) = \frac{1}{1+t}(Y_c - Y_p) \tag{17.4}$$

or

$$\bar{p}(X_p - X_c) = Y_c - Y_p \tag{17.5}$$

Equation (17.5) states what was concluded earlier: *the value of our exports must be equal to the value of our imports provided both aggregates are evaluated at the international prices.*

If exports and imports are evaluated at domestic prices, they cannot possibly be equal, as eq. (17.4) reveals. In particular, the value of imports, $Y_c - Y_p$, is higher than the value of exports, $\bar{p}_d(X_p - X_c)$.

### International Equilibrium When the Government Redistributes the Tariff Revenue to the Consumers

We have established that, when $p$ is given, the domestic price ratio is determined by eq. (17.3), assuming that the tariff is nonprohibitive. Further, international equilibrium requires that eq. (17.5) be satisfied. How is international equilibrium determined?

Figure 17.2 reproduces all the essential information from fig. 17.1. The straight lines TOT and TOT* are identical to the corresponding lines in fig. 17.1. The curve $OFR$ is again our economy's offer curve. Equilibrium has to occur somewhere along the terms-of-trade line TOT. To determine the precise equilibrium point along TOT, we have to use the conclusion that the domestic price ratio is given by the slope of TOT*. Thus, equilibrium occurs at a point $S$ on TOT where the slope of our economy's trade indifference curve passing through $S$ is equal to $\bar{p}_d$, that is, the slope of TOT*.

To determine precisely the equilibrium point $S$, imagine that the terms-of-trade line TOT* shifts continuously upward in a parallel fashion. Trace out the tangencies between the family of parallel terms-of-trade lines and the trade indifference curves, as shown by the broken curve $FS$. International equilibrium necessarily occurs at the intersection between the broken curve $FS$ and the terms-of-trade line TOT, that is, point $S$.

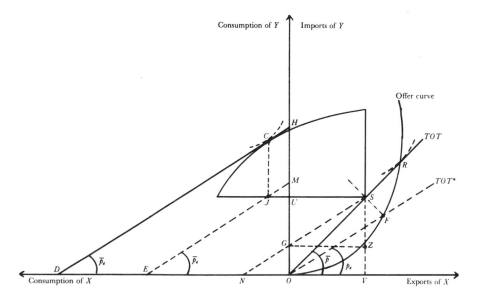

**Figure 17.2** International equilibrium when the government of the small country redistributes the tariff revenue to the consumers.

Point $S$ must lie somewhere along the straight-line segment $OR$; it cannot lie beyond $R$. What is the reason for this? The trade indifference curve passing through $R$ is by assumption tangent to the terms-of-trade line TOT. All other trade indifference curves necessarily intersect the line TOT. But any trade indifference curve passing through any point of TOT beyond $R$ must be steeper than TOT at the point of intersection. Hence, equilibrium can occur only in the region $OR$. This argument also shows that the equilibrium point $S$ must necessarily lie to the left of our country's offer curve.

Note, too, that when the broken line $FS$ is negatively sloped, as shown in fig. 17.2, the total consumption of both commodities increases as we move from $F$ to $S$; hence, both commodities are superior (or normal). On the other hand, if $FS$ is positively sloped, the consumption of one commodity decreases as we move from $F$ to $S$, that is, one commodity is inferior.

Having determined the equilibrium point $S$, let us place our economy's production block in position with its corner at $S$, as shown in fig. 17.2. Draw the tangent to the production block at its tangency point with the highest social indifference curve, point $C$. This is shown by $DCH$, which by necessity is parallel to TOT*. Draw lines ($EJM$ and $NGS$) parallel to TOT* through points $S$ and $J$, where $J$ lies on the horizontal base of the production block and directly below $C$. Thus, $SJ$ = domestic production of $X$, and $JC$ = domestic production of $Y$. The value of output domestically produced and evaluated at factor cost is now given by $ND$ in terms of $X$ and by $GH$ in terms of $Y$. In particular, $EN = JS$ = domestic production of $X$, and $DE = CJ/\bar{p}_a$ = value of domestic production of $Y$ in terms of $X$ at domestic prices. Further, $HM = CJ$ = domestic production of $Y$, and $GM = \bar{p}_a(EN)$ = value of domestic production of $X$ in terms of $Y$ at domestic prices.

While $ND$ and $GH$ measure the value of the net national income in our economy in terms of commodities $X$ and $Y$, respectively, the total expenditure on $X$ and $Y$ by our economy is given by $DO$ in terms of $X$ and by $OH$ in terms of $Y$. Therefore the tariff revenue expressed in terms of $X$ (at domestic prices) is given by the horizontal distance $NO$. Expressed in terms of $Y$, the tariff revenue is given by the vertical distance $OG$.

What is the ad valorem rate of tariff equal to? We saw earlier that the tariff revenue expressed in terms of $Y$ (at the domestic price ratio $\bar{p}_a$) is equal to $(t/1 + t)(Y_c - Y_p)$; but $Y_c - Y_p = OU$. Therefore, we can form the equation $[t/(1 + t)]OU = OG$. Solving for $t$, we get

$$t = \frac{OG}{OU - OG} = \frac{OG}{GU}$$

Observe that the triangles $OGN$ and $ZSG$ are similar. Since $GU = ZS$, by a well-known property of similar triangles it becomes apparent that

$$t = \frac{OG}{GU} = \frac{NO}{OV} = \frac{NG}{GS} \qquad (17.6)$$

These are three convenient measures of the ad valorem tariff rate.

## 17.3 THE EFFECTS OF THE NONPROHIBITIVE TARIFF

The major conclusions of the preceding section plus some additional conclusions are summarized below.

1. *The imported commodity becomes relatively more expensive in the domestic market*, as shown by eq. (17.3). Note that the domestic price ratio can no longer be equal to $\bar{p}$. For $t > 0$, we necessarily have $\bar{p} > \bar{p}_d$.
2. As the domestic price ratio falls below $\bar{p}$, *the domestic output of the imported commodity, Y, expands* at the expense of the output of the exported commodity, $X$. This is usually called the *protective effect* of the tariff.
3. *The imposition of the (nonprohibitive) tariff raises the real wage of the factor used intensively in the production of importables (Y), and lowers the real wage of the other factor, both relatively and absolutely.* In particular, since commodity $Y$ is by assumption land intensive relative to $X$, the tariff raises (both relatively and absolutely) the real wage of the land factor and lowers the real wage of the labor factor. This follows from the analysis of chap. 15 and is usually called the *redistribution effect* of the tariff. (See also the discussion of the Stolper–Samuelson theorem in chap. 19.)
4. *With revenue redistribution the volume of trade, expressed in terms of international prices, falls* after the imposition of the tariff. This follows from the fact that point $S$ lies between the origin and point $R$ (see fig. 17.2).

   The above conclusion does not in general hold when the government spends the tariff revenue on $X$ and $Y$. It holds when the offer curve is not backward bending (i.e., when the demand for imports is not inelastic). When the offer curve is backward bending, conclusion 4 holds when all tariff revenue is spent on exportables ($X$), but is violated when the tariff revenue is spent on importables ($Y$). (For more details, see chap. 18 below.)
5. As a result of the protective effect of the tariff, *the small economy consumes inside the free-trade consumption-possibilities frontier* but outside the production-possibilities frontier. This is illustrated in fig. 17.3.

   The curve $MP_2 P_1 N$ is our economy's production-possibilities frontier. Before the imposition of the tariff, our country produces at $P_1$ and consumes at $C_1$ along the straight-line segment $KP_1$, with $Y$ the imported commodity. The straight line $KP_1 R$ is our economy's free-trade consumption-possibilities frontier. After the imposition of the tariff, the domestic price ratio falls to $\bar{p}_d$ and production shifts from $P_1$ to $P_2$. The slope of the tangent to the production-possibilities frontier at $P_2$, that is, the broken line $CP_2 D$, is equal to $\bar{p}_d$. Where does the economy consume? Certainly not on the straight-line segment $CP_2$, which would neglect the tariff revenue. As we saw earlier, in equilibrium the value of exports equals the value of imports when both aggregates are evaluated at international prices. Hence, our economy must consume somewhere along the straight-line segment $VP_2$ (see point $C_3$), which is parallel to $KP_1 R$. But all points along $VP_2$ lie inside $KP_1 R$. Hence, the cum-tariff equilibrium consumption point must necessarily lie inside the free-trade consumption-possibilities frontier but outside the production-possibilities frontier.

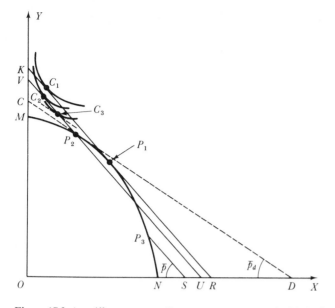

**Figure 17.3** A tariff causes a small economy to consume inside its free-trade consumption-posibilities frontier.

6. The tariff has also an *effect on the consumption levels of both X and Y* (that is, $X_c$ and $Y_c$).

To determine exactly how $X_c$ and $Y_c$ are affected by the tariff, consider fig. 17.4, which reproduces the free-trade consumption-possibilities frontier $KP_1R$ of fig. 17.3 together with the straight line $VP_2U$, which is parallel to $KP_1R$ and passes through $P_2$. Production occurs before the imposition of the tariff at $P_1$, and after at $P_2$. Assume that, before the tariff is imposed, consumption occurs at $C_1$. Consumption after the imposition of the tariff necessarily occurs somewhere along the straight-line segment $VP_2$. The precise posttariff equilibrium consumption point partially depends on how the government chooses to spend the tariff revenue.

If we make the neutral assumption that the government redistributes the tariff revenue to consumers, then the outcome will depend on consumer tastes, i.e., the characteristics of the social indifference map. To determine the effect of the tariff on $X_c$ and $Y_c$, we have to derive the income-consumption curve through $C_1$, on the assumption that the domestic price ratio is $\bar{p}$. When both commodities are superior, this income-consumption curve (not drawn) intersects $VP_2$ somewhere in the region $DE$, say at $Z$. The slope of the social indifference curve passing through $Z$ is equal to $\bar{p}$ in absolute terms. Consumption equilibrium occurs at a point where the slope of the social indifference curve is equal, in absolute terms, to the domestic price ratio $\bar{p}_d$, which is smaller than $\bar{p}$. This necessarily occurs somewhere in the region $ZP_2$. Hence, after the imposition of the tariff and provided that both commodities are superior, $Y_c$ falls definitely while $X_c$ may either increase or decrease.

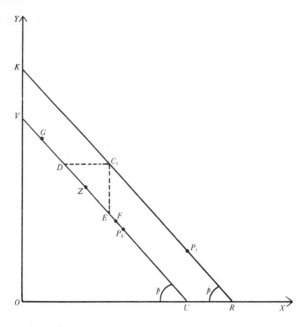

**Figure 17.4** The effects of the tariff on consumption. Unless the imported commodity is inferior, the imposition of a tariff causes its consumption to fall.

When $X$ is inferior, the income-consumption curve through $C_1$ intersects $VP_2$ somewhere in the region $EP_2$, say at $F$, where the absolute slope of the social indifference curve is $\bar{p}$. Hence, consumption equilibrium, after the imposition of the tariff, occurs somewhere in the region $FP_2$. Therefore, $Y_c$ definitely falls after the imposition of the tariff and $X_c$ definitely rises.

When $Y$ is inferior, the income-consumption curve through $C_1$ intersects $VP_2$ somewhere in the region $VD$, say at point $G$. Hence, consumption equilibrium after the imposition of the tariff occurs somewhere in the region $GP_2$. Therefore, $X_c$ may increase or decrease, and $Y_c$ may also increase or decrease. If $Y_c$ increases, however, $X_c$ necessarily falls; and if $X_c$ increases, $Y_c$ necessarily falls. Thus, *unless the imported commodity is inferior, the imposition of the tariff necessarily causes its consumption to fall.*

7. *The tariff on imports of Y can be decomposed into a domestic production subsidy to importables (Y) plus a domestic consumption tax on importables (Y).*

In terms of fig. 17.3, a production subsidy to $Y$ at the ad valorem rate $t/(1 + t)$ shifts the production point from $P_1$ to $P_2$. Without a domestic consumption tax on $Y$, consumption would shift from $C_1$ to $C_2$ where the marginal rate of substitution continues to be equal to $\bar{p}$. However, when a consumption tax on $Y$ (at the ad valorem rate $t$)† is added, consumption shifts from $C_2$ to $C_3$. At $C_3$ the marginal rate of substitution of $X$ for $Y$ is equal to $\bar{p}_d$.

---

† The ad valorem rate of the production subsidy, that is, $t/(1 + t)$, is necessarily lower than the ad valorem rate of the consumption tax $t$ because the latter is estimated on $\bar{p}_y$ while the former is estimated on the domestic average cost of production of $Y$, which is higher than $\bar{p}_y$ by the per unit subsidy.

When the tariff is decomposed into a production subsidy plus a consumption tax, it becomes apparent that the total welfare loss imposed by the tariff can be decomposed into a *production loss* (associated with the production-subsidy element of the tariff) plus a *consumption loss* (associated with the consumption-tax element of the tariff). The production loss is illustrated in fig. 17.3 by the movement from $P_1$ to $P_2$, and the consumption loss by the movement from $C_2$ to $C_3$.

Finally, a production subsidy is preferable (as a protective device) to a tariff because it does not involve any consumption loss. This idea is pursued further in chaps. 20 and 21.

## 17.4 THE CUM-TARIFF CONSUMPTION-POSSIBILITIES FRONTIER, PROHIBITIVE TARIFFS, AND WELFARE LOSS

To evaluate the effect of a tariff (whether prohibitive or nonprohibitive) on potential welfare, we must first derive the cum-tariff consumption-possibilities frontier. Remember that the tariff is imposed on commodity $Y$ only—the commodity which is imported before the imposition of the tariff. After the imposition of the tariff, the domestic price ratio falls from $\bar{p}$ to $\bar{p}_d$ only when $Y$ continues to be imported. Under these circumstances, our economy produces at $P_2$ (see fig. 17.3), i.e., the point where the broken line $CD$ with absolute slope equal to $\bar{p}_d$ becomes tangent to the production-possibilities frontier, and consumes somewhere along the straight-line segment $VP_2$. We can thus see that $VP_2$ is a part of our economy's cum-tariff consumption-possibilities frontier. But where is the rest of the cum-tariff consumption-possibilities frontier?

### The Permissible Range of Variation of the Domestic Price Ratio and the Cum-Tariff Consumption-Possibilities Frontier

First determine the permissible range of variation of the domestic price ratio $p_d$. We know that $p_d$ cannot fall below $\bar{p}_d$. That is, commodity $Y$ cannot become relatively more expensive than $Y$'s international price plus the tariff. But there is no reason why it cannot become cheaper, although it cannot fall below the level set by the international market. Therefore, the domestic price ratio must necessarily satisfy the relationship $\bar{p}_d \leq p_d \leq \bar{p}$. When $p_d = \bar{p}_d$, production occurs at $P_2$; when $p_d = \bar{p}$, production occurs at $P_1$; and when $\bar{p}_d < p_d < \bar{p}$, production occurs somewhere between $P_1$ and $P_2$ at the point where the marginal rate of transformation equals $p_d$.

Observe that when $\bar{p}_d < p_d < \bar{p}$, consumption necessarily coincides with domestic production. Thus, on the one hand, commodity $Y$ cannot be exported, because it is still cheaper in the international market ($p_d < \bar{p}$), and on the other, it cannot be imported either, because the sum of the international price plus the tariff is certainly higher than the domestic price ($\bar{p}_d < p_d$). By the same token, $X$ cannot be exported because $\bar{p}_d < p_d$. Therefore, when $\bar{p}_d < p_d < \bar{p}$, the consumption and production points necessarily coincide and lie on the production-possibilities frontier in the region $P_1 P_2$ (see fig. 17.3). Accordingly, the region $P_1 P_2$ is another part of our economy's cum-tariff consumption-possibilities frontier.

Consider the value $p_d = \bar{p}$. Production necessarily occurs at $P_1$. Consumption can take place anywhere along the straight-line segment $P_1 R$ because now $X$ can be imported and $Y$ exported. Since by assumption there is no tariff on $X$, our economy behaves in this region as if free trade completely existed. The tariff on $Y$ does not interfere because $Y$ is no longer imported.

Therefore, the cum-tariff consumption-possibilities frontier is given by $VP_2 P_1 R$, which is not necessarily concave. It lies inside the free-trade consumption-possibilities frontier except in the region $P_1 R$, where the two frontiers coincide. The straight-line segment $VP_2$ disappears completely when $P_2$ is made to coincide with $M$—or when the absolute slope of the production-possibilities frontier at $M$ is equal to, or higher than, $\bar{p}_d$.

## A Tariff on All Imports

When the tariff is not imposed on $Y$ alone but on all imports, our analysis must be modified slightly. When $Y$ is imported, $p_d = \bar{p}_d < \bar{p}$. On the other hand, when $X$ is imported, $p_d = (1 + t)\bar{p} > \bar{p}$. Thus, $p_d$ can now vary within the limits $\bar{p}_d = \bar{p}/(1 + t)$ and $(1 + t)\bar{p}$, that is, $\bar{p}/(1 + t) \le p_d \le (1 + t)\bar{p}$. When $\bar{p}/(1 + t) < p_d < (1 + t)\bar{p}$, no trade takes place, as before. The cum-tariff consumption-possibilities frontier in this case is given by $VP_2 P_3 S$, where $P_3 S$ is parallel to $KP_1 R$ and point $P_3$ is determined by the requirement that the absolute slope of the production-possibilities frontier be equal to $(1 + t)\bar{p}$. In this case, the cum-tariff consumption-possibilities frontier lies inside the free-trade consumption-possibilities frontier except at the singular point $P_1$. Note that the regions $VP_2$ and $P_3 S$ can be made to disappear by raising the tariff sufficiently. Then the cum-tariff consumption-possibilities frontier coincides completely with our economy's production-possibilities frontier.

Both $VP_2 P_1 R$ and $VP_2 P_3 S$ do not lie inside the production-possibilities frontier; they lie partially outside it while they coincide with it over the regions $P_2 P_1$ and $P_2 P_3$, respectively. Thus, *our economy cannot be forced by a tariff to consume inside its production-possibilities frontier;* it can still consume beyond the production-possibilities frontier, although this possibility is rather restricted relative to the free-trade consumption-possibilities frontier.

## The Prohibitive Tariff Rate

This analysis can be used to determine the minimum rate at which the tariff becomes prohibitive. Consider fig. 17.5. The curve *MEPR* is our economy's production-possibilities frontier. In the autarkic state, equilibrium occurs at $E$, where the production-possibilities frontier becomes tangent to the highest possible social indifference curve (SIC). When trade opens up, our country produces at $P$ and consumes at $C$. An infinitesimal tariff causes the economy to produce somewhere in the region $EP$ and very close to $P$. It continues to import $Y$ and export $X$.

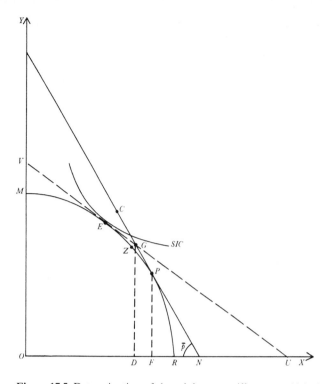

**Figure 17.5** Determination of the minimum tariff rate at which the tariff becomes prohibitive.

Now suppose that the tariff rate is allowed to rise continuously. The production point travels along the production-possibilities frontier from $P$ toward $E$. Trade continues for a while at a continuously diminishing rate, but it stops completely when the tariff rate reaches a certain minimum value. What is this minimum tariff rate equal to?

First observe that trade ceases completely when the tariff rate is raised sufficiently to make the production point coincide with the pretrade equilibrium point $E$. Thus, for any production point in the region $EP$ (but excluding point $E$), such as $Z$, the economy continues to import $Y$, for production occurs at $Z$ if $p_d$ is equal to the slope of the production-possibilities frontier at $Z$, and consumption occurs at $Z$ if $p_d$ is equal to the slope of the social indifference curve passing through $Z$. Since at $Z$ only the first condition is satisfied, it follows that commodity $Y$ continues to be imported. At $E$, however, the marginal rate of substitution in consumption equals the marginal rate of transformation in production. If $p_d$ is made equal to the slope at $E$, trade will cease completely.

Now draw the tangent to the production-possibilities frontier at $E$ and determine the point $(G)$ where it intersects the pretariff consumption-possibilities frontier. The maximum domestic price ratio $p_d^*$ consistent with zero trade is now given by the ratio $DG/DU$. On the other hand, $\bar{p} = DG/DN$. Finally, from eq. (17.3), we have $t = (\bar{p} - p_d^*)/p_d^*$. Therefore, the minimum value of $t$ at which the tariff becomes prohibitive, say $t^*$, is given by

$$t^* = \frac{\bar{p} - p_d^*}{p_d^*} = \frac{(DG/DN) - (DG/DU)}{DG/DU}$$

$$= \frac{(1/DN) - (1/DU)}{1/DU}$$

$$= \frac{DU - DN}{DN} \tag{17.7}$$

The specific value $t^*$ can also be determined in fig. 17.2. There $p_d^*$ is represented by the slope of the offer curve at the origin. The reader can now apply the equation $t^* = (\bar{p} - p_d^*)/p_d^*$ to determine $t^*$ graphically. The tariff is prohibitive when $t \geq t^*$.

## The Effect of the Tariff on Potential Welfare

What is the effect of the tariff on the potential welfare of our small country? We saw in fig. 17.3 that the cum-tariff consumption-possibilities frontier $(VP_2 P_1 R)$ lies mostly inside the free-trade consumption-possibilities frontier, although it coincides with it over the region $P_1 R$. Therefore, if the region $P_1 R$ does not give rise to any points on the free-trade utility-possibilities frontier, restricted trade is potentially inferior to free trade (for the small country) because the cum-tariff utility-possibilities frontier lies uniformly inside the free-trade utility-possibilities frontier. But there is no guarantee that this is the case. The cum-tariff utility-possibilities frontier can in general be expected to coincide with the free-trade utility-possibilities frontier over a certain region. Then, for some Paretian welfare functions, restricted trade will not be shown to be inferior to free trade.

However, free trade will never be shown to be inferior to restricted trade, because the free-trade utility-possibilities frontier cannot lie inside the cum-tariff utility-possibilities frontier. If the tariff is imposed on imports in general and not only imports of commodity $Y$, the cum-tariff consumption-possibilities frontier $(VP_2 P_1 P_3 S$ in fig. 17.3) will lie totally inside the free-trade consumption-possibilities frontier, except for the singular point $P_1$ where the two frontiers become tangential. Then, as in the comparison between free trade and autarky and with the same reservations, free trade is potentially superior to restricted trade. It is emphasized that *these conclusions apply only to the case of the small country.*

## PART C. THE SYMMETRY BETWEEN EXPORT AND IMPORT TAXES AND SUBSIDIES

Lerner (1936) showed that in a long-run, static equilibrium model (ignoring possible transitional difficulties such as unemployment and balance-of-payments disequilibria) a general export tax has the same effect as a general import tax of the same ad valorem percentage. This symmetry is also extended to subsidies. Thus, a general export subsidy has the same effect as a general import subsidy of the same ad valorem percentage. Lerner's symmetry theorem is discussed briefly below.

## 17.5 THE IMPOSITION OF AN EXPORT TAX

What if our country imposes an export tax instead of a tariff? The analysis of the tariff can be applied step by step to the case of the export tax. It does not matter which money price is taxed, because one good is exchanged for another in trade, and hence there is only one relative price. From the point of view of long-run equilibrium analysis, it is immaterial whether a tax is imposed on exports or imports: the outcome is identical. This symmetry is demonstrated as follows.

When a tax $t$ on exports is imposed, the domestic price $p_y^d$ of importables $Y$ continues to be identical with the international price $\bar{p}_y$, while the domestic price of exportables $X$ (that is, $p_x^d$)—on the assumption that $X$ continues to be exported after the imposition of the export tax—satisfies the equation $p_x^d(1 + t) = \bar{p}_x$. Thus,

$$p_x^d = \frac{1}{1 + t} \, \bar{p}_x$$

Accordingly,

$$p_a = \frac{p_x^d}{p_y^d} = \frac{1}{1 + t} \frac{\bar{p}_x}{\bar{p}_y} = \frac{1}{1 + t} \bar{p} = \bar{p}_d$$

This is identical to the result obtained with eq. (17.3). From this point, the analysis of the export tax follows the analysis of the tariff step by step. For this reason, no further discussion of the problem is given.

That the effects of an export tax are identical to the effects of an import tax (provided the tax revenue is spent in the same way) holds only from the point of view of the long-run static theory. With regard to the effects on the balance of payments and the level of employment (i.e., in the short run), a tariff operates in an expansionary, stimulating fashion whereas an export tax operates in a contractive, depressive manner.

## 17.6 IMPORT AND EXPORT SUBSIDIES

Trade subsidies are merely negative trade taxes. There is one difference, however, between the analysis of trade subsidies and that of trade taxes. In the latter case, the government has the choice of spending the tax revenue directly on $X$ and $Y$ in any proportion whatsoever, or distributing it among its private citizens. In the case of trade subsidies, we are practically forced to make the assumption that *the government raises the amount used to subsidize trade through a general income tax on its private citizens.* Otherwise, the government would be required to somehow produce positive quantities of $X$ and $Y$. While it is always possible for the government to consume positive amounts of $X$ and $Y$, as in the case of trade taxes, it is absolutely impossible to produce positive amounts of $X$ and $Y$ (in the case of trade subsidies) when all productive activity is in the hands of its private citizens.

The assumption that the government imposes a general income tax is actually a simplification, because it reduces the number of possibilities.†

A detailed analysis of trade subsidies would be redundant. However, an indication of how trade subsidies modify the offer curve of the country paying the subsidies is in order. Assume that the international price ratio $p_x/p_y$ is $\bar{p}$. If $A$'s government pays an export subsidy of $s \times 100$ percent to $A$'s exporters of $X$, $A$'s domestic price ratio $p_d$ would be

$$\bar{p} = p_d(1 - s) \tag{17.8}$$

Exactly the same relationship between $\bar{p}$ and $p_d$ as given by eq. (17.8) also exists when $A$'s government pays an import subsidy of $s \times 100$ percent to $A$'s importers of $Y$. Therefore, there is no need to distinguish between an export subsidy and an import subsidy.

Consider now fig. 17.6. The terms-of-trade line TOT represents the offer curve of the rest of the world; and $O_A$ is $A$'s free-trade offer curve. Free-trade equilibrium occurs at $E_0$. The slope of the broken line $OE_1$ shows $A$'s domestic price ratio under the assumption that the international price ratio is $\bar{p}$ and $A$'s government pays a trade subsidy of $s \times 100$ percent. At domestic prices given by the slope of $OE_1$, $A$'s consumers would like to trade at $E_1$ provided the government did not impose any income tax on its citizens. However, $A$'s government does impose a general income tax to finance the trade subsidy. Where do $A$'s private consumers

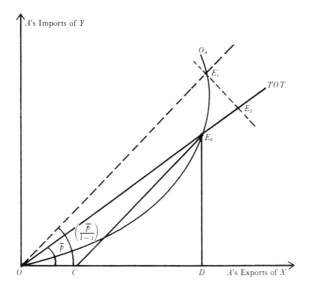

**Figure 17.6** The effect of export and import subsidies.

---

† The assumption in the text is that there is no public consumption (by the government) in the free-trade equilibrium position. Otherwise, a government could always subsidize trade by means of a reduction in the public consumption of $X$ and $Y$.

like to trade when $p_d = \bar{p}/(1-s)$ and $A$'s government imposes the necessary income tax? Imagine the broken line $OE_1$ shifted in a parallel fashion to the right and trace out all tangencies generated by it with $A$'s trade indifference curves, as shown by the broken line $E_1 E_2$. As we have shown in the case of trade taxes, equilibrium can only occur along TOT. Hence the desired trade point must be $E_2$. For reasons explained in the case of trade taxes, point $E_2$ must lie to the right of $A$'s free-trade offer curve.

How can the rate-of-trade subsidy be shown graphically? Draw a line through $E_0$ parallel to $OE_1$, and also draw the vertical line $E_0 D$. Now we have $\bar{p} = DE_0/OD$ and

$$\frac{\bar{p}}{1-s} = \frac{DE_0}{CD}$$

or

$$\bar{p} = \frac{DE_0}{CD}(1-s)$$

Therefore,

$$\frac{DE_0}{OD} = \frac{DE_0}{CD}(1-s)$$

or

$$\frac{CD}{OD} = 1-s$$

or

$$s = 1 - \frac{CD}{OD} = \frac{OD-CD}{OD} = \frac{OC}{OD} \tag{17.9}$$

Having determined a point $(E_2)$ on $A$'s subsidy-distorted offer curve, we can repeat the same experiment as many times as we want and produce the whole subsidy-distorted offer curve. This will necessarily lie to the right of the free-trade offer curve. Once the subsidy-distorted offer curve is completely derived, the analysis can proceed along familiar lines.

## SELECTED BIBLIOGRAPHY

Balassa, B. (1965). "Tariff Protection in Industrial Countries: An Evaluation." *Journal of Political Economy*, vol. LXXIII (December), pp. 573–594.

―――― (1970a). "Tariffs, Intermediate Goods, and Domestic Protection: Comment." *American Economic Review*, vol. LX, no. 5 (December), pp. 959–963.

―――― (1970b). "Tariffs, Intermediate Goods, and Domestic Protection: Further Comment." *American Economic Review*, vol. LX, no. 5 (December), pp. 968–969.

―――― (1971). *The Structure of Protection in Developing Countries*. John Hopkins Press, Baltimore.

Batra, R. N., and F. R. Casas (1974). "Traded and Non-Traded Intermediate Inputs, Real Wages, and Resource Allocation." *Canadian Journal of Economics and Political Science*, vol. 7, no. 2 (May), pp. 225–239.

Bertrand, T. J., and J. Vanek (1971). "The Theory of Tariffs, Taxes and Subsidies: Some Aspects of the Second Best." *American Economic Review*, vol. LXI, no. 5 (December), pp. 925–931.

Bhagwati, J. N., and T. N. Srinivasan (1973). "The General Equilibrium Theory of Effective Protection and Resource Allocation." *Journal of International Economics*, vol. 3, no. 3 (August), pp. 259–281.

Chacholiades, M. (1978). *International Monetary Theory and Policy*. McGraw-Hill Book Company, New York.

Corden, W. M. (1966). "The Structure of a Tariff System and the Effective Protective Rate." *Journal of Political Economy*, vol. LXXIV, no. 3 (June), pp. 221–237.

———— (1969). "Effective Protective Rates in the General Equilibrium Model: A Geometric Note." *Oxford Economic Papers* (N.S.), vol. 21, no. 2 (July), pp. 135–141.

———— (1971). *The Theory of Protection*. Oxford University Press, London.

Grubel, H. G. (1971). "Effective Tariff Protection: A Non-Specialist Introduction to the Theory, Policy Implications, and Controversies." In H. G. Grubel and H. G. Johnson (Eds.), *Effective Tariff Protection*. General Agreement on Tariffs and Trade and Graduate Institute of International Studies, Geneva. Reprinted in R. E. Baldwin and J. D. Richardson (Eds.), *International Trade and Finance*. Little, Brown and Company, Boston, Mass., 1974.

Guisinger, S. E. (1969). "Negative Value Added and the Theory of Effective Protection." *Quarterly Journal of Economics*, vol. 83, no. 3 (August), pp. 415–433.

Humphrey, D. B. (1969). "Measuring the Effective Rate of Protection: Direct and Indirect Effects." *Journal of Political Economy*, vol. 77, no. 5 (September), pp. 834–844.

Johnson, H. G. (1965). "The Theory of Tariff Structure with Special Referrence to World Trade and Development." In H. G. Johnson and P. B. Kenen, *Trade and Development*. Librairie Droz, Geneva.

———— (1969). "The Standard Theory of Tariffs." *Canadian Journal of Economics and Political Science*, vol. II, no. 3 (August), pp. 333–352.

———— (1972). *Aspects of the Theory of Tariffs*. Harvard University Press, Cambridge, Mass.

Kreinin, M. E., J. B. Ramsey, and J. Kmenta (1971). "Factor Substitution and Effective Protection Reconsidered." *American Economic Review*, vol. LXI, no. 5 (December), pp. 891–900.

Leith, J. C. (1968). "Substitution and Supply Elasticities in Calculating the Effective Protective Rate." *Quarterly Journal of Economics*, vol. 82, no. 4 (November), pp. 588–601.

———— (1971). "The Effect of Tariffs on Production, Consumption, and Trade: A Revised Analysis." *American Economic Review*, vol. LXI, no. 1 (March), pp. 74–81.

Lerner, A. P. (1936). "The Symmetry Between Import and Export Taxes." *Economica*, vol. III, no. 11 (August), pp. 306–313. Reprinted in R. E. Caves and H. G. Johnson (Eds.), AEA *Readings in International Economics*. Richard D. Irwin, Inc., Homewood, Ill., 1968.

Lloyd, P. J. (1970). "Effective Protection: A Different View." *Economic Record*, vol. 46, no. 115 (September), pp. 329–340.

Massell, B. F. (1968). "The Resource-Allocative Effects of a Tariff and the Effective Protection of Individual Inputs." *Economic Record*, vol. 44, no. 107 (September), pp. 369–376.

Ruffin, R. J. (1969). "Tariffs, Intermediate Goods, and Domestic Protection." *American Economic Review*, vol. LIX, no. 3 (June), pp. 261–269.

———— (1970). "Tariffs, Intermediate Goods, and Domestic Protection: Reply." *American Economic Review*, vol. LX, no. 5 (December), pp. 964–967.

Sendo, Y. (1974). "The Theory of Effective Protection in General Equilibrium: An Extension of the Bhagwati–Srinivasan Analysis." *Journal of International Economics*, vol. 4, no. 2 (May), pp. 213–215.

Tan, A. H. H. (1970). "Differential Tariffs, Negative Value-Added and the Theory of Effective Protection." *American Economic Review*, vol. LX, no. 1 (March), pp. 107–116.

Travis, W. P. (1968). "The Effective Rate of Protection and the Question of Labor Protection in the United States." *Journal of Political Economy*, vol. 76, no. 3 (May), pp. 443–461.

(Additional references will be found in "Selected Bibliography" at the end of chaps. 18 and 19.)

# EIGHTEEN

# IMPORT AND EXPORT TAXES: THE CASE OF THE LARGE COUNTRY

This chapter is divided into two parts. Part A extends the earlier discussion (chap. 17) of import and export taxes to a two-country model. Part B considers briefly the effects of quantitative restrictions.

## PART A. IMPORT AND EXPORT TAXES

Let us extend the analysis of import and export taxes to a two-country model (*A* and *B*) where either country's actions are substantial enough to affect international prices. Again, international equilibrium is usually portrayed in terms of offer curves, which we can derive under free-trade conditions. But how can offer curves be derived when import and export taxes interfere with the free flow of trade? In what follows, assume that only country *A* imposes trade taxes. The offer curve of country *B* is thus assumed given and invariant.

## 18.1 THE TRADE-TAX-DISTORTED OFFER CURVE

We now have enough information to derive a *trade-tax-distorted offer curve*, i.e., the offer curve that shows the willingness of a country to export and import commodities at world (not domestic) prices. What the preceding chapter actually accomplishes is the derivation of a single point on the trade-tax-distorted offer curve by assuming that the international price ratio is given. By repeating the same exercise for all possible values of the international price ratio, we can thus trace out the whole trade-tax-distorted offer curve. Note that, the *trade-tax-*

distorted offer curve is discussed here, because it is immaterial to the analysis whether an import or export tax is imposed.

There is no need to repeat the analysis for each and every possible value of the international price ratio. We only need to compare the trade-tax-distorted offer curve with the free-trade offer curve in general, and then predict the effect of import and export taxes on the international price ratio, i.e., the *barter terms of trade* of the trade-tax-imposing country.

As we have seen, given the international price ratio $\bar{p}$, the relevant point on the trade-tax-distorted offer curve can be determined only after it has been decided how the government disposes of the tax revenue. In particular, the government may spend the tax revenue on either commodity or on any feasible combination of $X$ and $Y$, or it may redistribute the tax revenue among the private consumers. Let us distinguish among the following three cases: (*a*) the government spends the tax revenue on the exported commodity, $X$; (*b*) the government spends the tax revenue on the imported commodity, $Y$; and (*c*) the government redistributes the tax revenue among the private consumers. If the government actually spends the tax revenue on both $X$ and $Y$ (either in some arbitrary fashion or according to some existing government tastes summarized in a government indifference map), the outcome will, of course, lie somewhere between (*a*) and (*b*).

### The Government Spends the Tax Revenue on the Exported Commodity ($X$)

Consider fig. 18.1. The curve $O_A$ is $A$'s free-trade offer curve. Assume that the international price ratio is equal to the slope of the terms-of-trade line TOT.

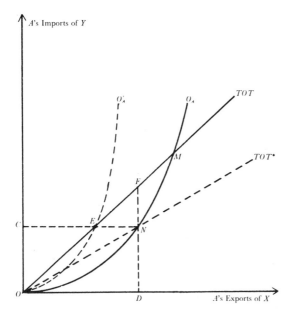

**Figure 18.1** The effects of trade taxes on the offer curve of the tax-imposing country.

Under free-trade conditions, country $A$ trades at point $M$. If a trade tax (i.e., a tariff or an export tax), $t$, is imposed, at what point would country $A$ trade?

Consider the broken terms-of-trade line TOT*, whose slope is equal to the slope of TOT $\times 1/(1 + t)$. If the government does not redistribute the tax revenue to the private consumers, $A$'s private sector will want to import $DN$ of $Y$ and export $OD$ of $X$. If the government spends the tariff revenue on the exported commodity $X$, the relevant point on the trade-tax-distorted offer curve would be $E$. Now point $E$ lies to the left of point $N$, and this is always the case for all values of the international price ratio.

Therefore, given any point on the free-trade offer curve, such as $N$, the corresponding point on the trade-tax-distorted offer curve lies directly to the left of $N$ if the government spends the tax revenue on the exported commodity $X$.

How can point $E$ be precisely determined when $N$ and $t$ are known? Point $E$ lies at the intersection of the terms-of-trade line TOT with the horizontal line $CN$. We already know that

$$\frac{DN}{OD} = \frac{DF}{OD}\left(\frac{1}{1 + t}\right) = \frac{OC}{CE}\left(\frac{1}{1 + t}\right) = \frac{DN}{CE}\left(\frac{1}{1 + t}\right)$$

or

$$\frac{1}{OD} = \left(\frac{1}{1 + t}\right)\frac{1}{CE}$$

or

$$\frac{CE}{CN} = \frac{1}{1 + t}$$

or

$$1 + t = \frac{CN}{CE}$$

or

$$t = \frac{CN - CE}{CE} = \frac{EN}{CE} = \frac{EN}{CN - EN} \tag{18.1}$$

Equation (18.1) has a very simple interpretation. At the international price ratio $p = DF/OD$, the private sector of country $A$ imports $DN$ of $Y$ from country $B$ in exchange for $OD$ of $X$. However, not all $X$ given up by $A$'s private sector accrues to $B$. Country $A$'s government collects $EN$ of $X$, and thus only $CE = CN - EN$ accrues to $B$. It is no wonder, then, that the tax rate is equal to the ratio $EN/CE$. The amount $EN$ is the tax revenue (in terms of $X$ at world prices) that accrues to $A$'s government, while $CE$ is simply $A$'s exports of $X$, or $A$'s imports of $Y$ expressed in terms of $X$ at world prices.

Equation (18.1) can also be solved for $EN$ as follows:

$$EN = \left(\frac{t}{1 + t}\right)CN \tag{18.2}$$

Therefore, point $E$ can be determined as follows. Draw a horizontal line through $N$ and let it intersect the vertical axis at $C$. Point $E$ must now be determined in such a way as to satisfy eq. (18.2) (or eq. (18.1)). For instance, if $t$ is 25 percent, we must have

$$EN = \frac{0.25}{1.25}CN = \frac{1}{5}CN$$

In other words, for $t = 0.25$, point $E$ lies to the left of $N$ one-fifth of the distance $CN$. Therefore, for $t = 0.25$ and assuming that the government spends the tax revenue on $X$, the trade-tax-distorted offer curve lies to the left of the free-trade offer curve. It is easily derived by reducing the original horizontal distances between the free-trade offer curve and the vertical axis by 20 percent (i.e., $\frac{1}{5}$). This is illustrated by the broken curve $O'_A$, which is drawn on the assumption that $t = 0.666$.

In general, *the trade-tax-distorted offer curve can be derived by shifting the free-trade offer curve to the left in such a way that the horizontal distances between the free-trade offer curve and the trade-tax-distorted offer curve are equal to $[t/(1 + t)] \times 100$ percent of the horizontal distances between the free-trade offer curve and the vertical axis.*

## The Government Spends the Tax Revenue on the Imported Commodity $(Y)$

What is the trade-tax-distorted offer curve when the government spends the tax revenue on the imported commodity? Consider again fig. 18.1. For the international price ratio $p = DF/OD$, the private sector of country $A$ wants to trade at $N$, and the tax revenue in terms of commodity $Y$ at world prices is equal to $NF$. Therefore, when the government spends the tax revenue on $Y$, the relevant point on the trade-tax-distorted offer curve is $F$. In other words, country $B$ exports $DF$ of $Y$ in exchange for $OD$ of $X$. However, only $DN$ of $Y$ accrues to $A$'s private sector; the rest (that is, $NF$) accrues to $A$'s government.

The tax rate must be equal to the ratio $NF/ND$. That this is so follows again from the relationship

$$\frac{DN}{OD} = \left(\frac{1}{1 + t}\right)\frac{DF}{OD}$$

or

$$DN = \left(\frac{1}{1 + t}\right)DF$$

or

$$1 + t = \frac{DF}{DN}$$

or

$$t = \frac{DF - DN}{DN} = \frac{NF}{DN} \tag{18.3}$$

Therefore, point $F$ lies directly above $N$, and the vertical distance $NF$ is equal to $t \times 100$ percent of the vertical distance $DN$. The same relationship must necessarily hold between any other point on the free-trade offer curve (i.e., the point where $A$'s private sector would like to trade) and the corresponding point on the trade-tax-distorted offer curve.

We therefore conclude that, *when the government spends the tax revenue on $Y$, the trade-tax-distorted offer curve can be easily derived by shifting the free-trade offer curve upward in such a way that the vertical differences between the two offer* *curves are equal to t × 100 percent of the corresponding vertical distances between the free-trade offer curve and the horizontal axis.*

There is one fundamental difference between the case where A's government spends the tax revenue on the exported commodity, X, and the case where it spends it on the imported commodity, Y. In the former case, the trade-tax-distorted offer curve lies totally to the left of the free-trade offer curve—the two offer curves can never intersect. In the latter case, however, the trade-tax-distorted offer curve will intersect the free-trade offer curve if the latter becomes backward bending (i.e., if A's demand for imports by the private sector becomes inelastic). This can be illustrated in fig. 18.1. Note that point F depends on point N alone. Thus, the behavior of the free-trade offer curve beyond point N is irrelevant as concerns the determination of point F and the rest of the trade-tax-distorted offer curve from the origin to F. Therefore, should the free-trade offer curve become backward bending beyond point N, it will intersect the trade-tax-distorted offer curve. This is shown more clearly in fig. 18.2, where $O_A$ is the free-trade offer curve and $O'_A$ the trade-tax-distorted offer curve.

The intersection of the trade-tax-distorted offer curve with the free-trade offer curve when the government spends the tax revenue on the imported commodity

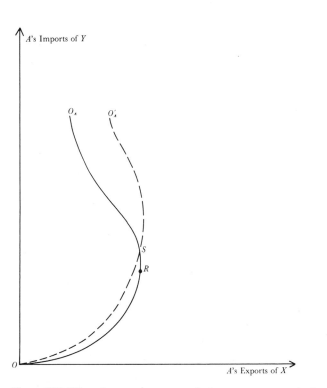

**Figure 18.2** When the government spends the tax revenue on the imported commodity (Y), the trade-tax-distorted offer curve intersects the free-trade offer curve if the latter is backward bending (i.e., if the demand for imports by the private sector is inelastic).

but not on the exported commodity has implications for the analysis of the effects of the trade tax.

## The Government Spends the Tax Revenue on Both Commodities

If the government chooses to spend the tax revenue on both commodities, the trade-tax-distorted offer curve will lie somewhere between the trade-tax-distorted curves just derived under the assumption that the government spends the tax revenue only on $X$ or only on $Y$, its precise position depending on the proportion in which the government allocates the tax revenue between $X$ and $Y$.

## The Government Redistributes the Tax Revenue to the Private Sector

Consider now the case where $A$'s government redistributes the tax revenue among $A$'s consumers. Here it is no longer possible to derive the trade-tax-distorted offer curve in a mechanical fashion. The outcome depends upon the characteristics of the social indifference map. But we can say more than this.

On the basis of the analysis of the preceding section, we can say that *the trade-tax-distorted offer curve lies totally to the left of the free-trade offer curve, except at the origin*, as in the case where the government spends the tax revenue on the exported commodity $X$. This should be obvious from fig. 17.2. Point $S$ is the point on the trade-tax-distorted offer curve corresponding to point $F$ on the free-trade offer curve. As we have seen, point $S$ lies always along the vector $OR$ but never beyond point $R$. By necessity, any ray through the origin cuts the trade-tax-distorted offer curve before it cuts the free-trade offer curve. Accordingly, the trade-tax-distorted offer curve lies closer to the origin than the free-trade offer curve. This necessarily implies that the trade-tax-distorted offer curve lies to the left of the free-trade offer curve.

How can the trade-tax-distorted offer curve be derived under the assumption that $A$'s government redistributes the tax revenue among $A$'s consumers? The answer lies in the construction of fig. 17.2. For convenience, all necessary information is transferred to fig. 18.3. Thus, $O_A$ is $A$'s free-trade offer curve. Consider point $F$ on $O_A$. To find the corresponding point on the trade-tax-distorted offer curve, recall that, under free-trade conditions, $A$'s consumers like to trade at $F$ only when the domestic price ratio is given by the slope of the vector $OF$ (that is, $CF/OC$). When a tax is imposed, however, and the domestic price ratio happens to be given by the slope of the vector $OF$, $A$'s consumers do not actually trade at $F$ because they are subsidized by the government by means of the tax-revenue redistribution, which enables them to spend more on $X$ and $Y$ than under free-trade conditions. Where do they trade then?

We must first determine all combinations of exports of $X$ and imports of $Y$ which have the same value at world prices. These combinations lie on a straight line through the origin (see TOT in fig. 17.2), with slope equal to the international price ratio corresponding to the given domestic price ratio $CF/OC$. This straight line is perfectly determined once another point on it (besides the origin) is found. This is easily done by determining point $N$ directly above $F$ in such a way that the

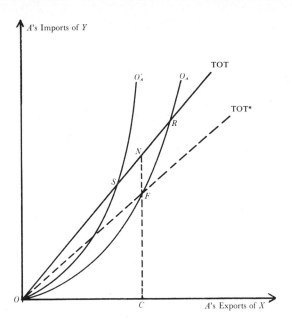

**Figure 18.3** The trade-tax-distorted offer curve when the government redistributes the tax revenue to the private sector.

distance $FN$ is $t \times 100$ percent of the distance $CF$. Therefore, all combinations of exports and imports implying "value of exports = value of imports" estimated at world prices corresponding to the domestic price ratio $CF/OC$ are given by the straight line $ON$. Country $A$'s consumers will, in equilibrium, trade somewhere along $ON$. *The precise trade point, S, is where the slope of the trade indifference curve at its intersection with the line ON is equal to CF/OC.*

Repeating the same experiment for all points on the free-trade offer curve, we can determine the trade-tax-distorted offer curve as shown by $O'_A$ in fig. 18.3.

## 18.2 TRADE TAXES AND THE BARTER TERMS OF TRADE

Consider fig. 18.4. The curves $O_A$ and $O_B$ are the free-trade offer curves of countries $A$ and $B$, respectively. Equilibrium under free-trade conditions occurs at $E$, where $A$ exports $CE$ units of $X$ to $B$ in exchange for $OC$ units of $Y$. The equilibrium terms of trade are given by the slope of the vector $OE$, that is, $OC/CE$. Now suppose that $A$ imposes a trade tax. What happens to $A$'s barter terms of trade? In other words, after the imposition of the trade tax, is $A$ able to exchange 1 unit of $X$ ($A$'s exported commodity) for more or fewer units of $Y$ ($A$'s imported commodity) compared with free-trade equilibrium? That depends on: (*a*) the nature of $B$'s offer curve; (*b*) whether $A$'s government spends the tax revenue (or a substantial amount of it) on the imported commodity; and (*c*) if $A$'s government spends the tax revenue on the imported commodity, whether $A$'s demand for imports at the free-trade equilibrium position is elastic or inelastic.

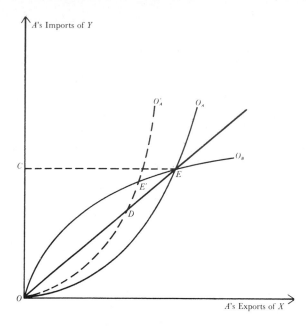

**Figure 18.4** The effect of the tariff on the barter terms of trade when the government spends the tax revenue on the exported commodity, or when it redistributes it among the consumers.

## The Normal Result

International equilibrium occurs always somewhere along $B$'s free-trade offer curve $O_B$: by assumption, $B$ does not impose any trade taxes. Further, $A$'s terms of trade are given by the slope of the vector passing through the origin and the equilibrium point on $B$'s offer curve. When $B$'s offer curve is a straight line through the origin—as it is in the preceding chapter, where $A$ is assumed to be small—$A$'s terms of trade remain the same after the imposition of the trade tax irrespective of how $A$'s government uses the tax revenue and irrespective of whether or not $A$'s demand for imports is elastic at the free-trade equilibrium point $E$.

When $B$'s offer curve is not a straight line, the outcome depends on whether $A$'s demand for imports at free-trade world prices increases or decreases. If it increases, $A$'s terms of trade tend to deteriorate. If it decreases, they tend to improve.

According to the analysis of the preceding section, when $A$'s government spends the tax revenue on the exported commodity, or when it redistributes the tax revenue among $A$'s consumers, the trade-tax-distorted offer curve definitely lies to the left of the free-trade offer curve, as shown by the broken curve $O'_A$ in fig. 18.4. In these two cases, $A$'s demand for imports falls at the free-trade world prices after the imposition of the trade tax (compare points $E$ and $D$), equilibrium shifts from $E$ to $E'$, and $A$'s terms of trade improve (the vector $OE'$ is steeper than the vector $OE$). This is the result that one would normally expect, but it is by no means the only possibility.

## The Lerner Case

When $A$'s government spends the tax revenue on the imported commodity $Y$, $A$'s trade-tax-distorted offer curve lies above and to the right of $A$'s free-trade offer curve over the backward-bending region of $A$'s free-trade offer curve, as can be seen from fig. 18.2. Actually, the trade-tax-distorted offer curve remains to the left of the free-trade offer curve immediately after the latter becomes backward bending. Thus, in fig. 18.2, the free-trade offer curve becomes vertical at $R$ and backward bending beyond $R$; and it is intersected by the trade-tax-distorted offer curve at $S$, which lies beyond $R$ in the backward-bending region of $O_A$.

For world prices such that $A$'s demand for imports is elastic before the imposition of the trade tax, $A$'s trade-tax-distorted offer curve lies to the left of the free-trade offer curve. If free-trade equilibrium occurs in this region of the free-trade offer curve (where $A$'s demand for imports is elastic), the imposition of the trade tax definitely improves $A$'s terms of trade. When point $D$ (fig. 18.4) lies to the left and below point $E$ along the vector $OE$, equilibrium occurs somewhere in the region $OE$ of $B$'s offer curve, which implies that $A$'s terms of trade improve.

If $A$'s demand for imports is inelastic at the free-trade equilibrium point and $A$'s government spends the tariff revenue on the imported commodity, the possibility that $A$'s terms of trade deteriorate after the imposition of the trade tax cannot be ruled out. This can be shown graphically by means of fig. 18.2. Draw $B$'s offer curve in such a way as to intersect $O_A$ at the latter's backward-bending region beyond $S$, and then show that *A's terms of trade deteriorate after the imposition of the trade tax*.

Lerner (1936) showed that $A$'s terms of trade may also deteriorate when $A$'s government spends the tax revenue on both commodities. In particular, Lerner showed that *A's terms of trade deteriorate after the imposition of the trade tax if, and only if, the absolute value of A's elasticity of demand for imports at the free-trade equilibrium point is smaller than the fraction of the tax revenue spent by A's government on the imported good*. This important result is proved rigorously below.

## Mathematical Analysis of Lerner's Case

Assume that the government spends only a fraction, $\lambda$, of the tax revenue on the imported commodity and the rest on the exported commodity. Let the function $Y_c(1/\bar{p}_d)$ stand for the demand for imports of $Y$ by $A$'s consumers, and $Y_g$ the demand for imports of $Y$ by $A$'s government. The domestic price ratio $p_x/p_y$ is given by $\bar{p}_d$ as before, while the international price ratio is given by $\bar{p}$. Given the trade tax $t$, we must have $\bar{p}_d = \bar{p}/(1 + t)$. What is $A$'s tax revenue in terms of commodity $Y$ equal to? Obviously, it must be given by $tY_c$. Since only the fraction $\lambda$ $(0 \leq \lambda \leq 1)$ of this tax revenue is actually spent on $Y$, $A$'s government's demand for imports of $Y$ (that is, $Y_g$) is given by $\lambda t Y_c$. Accordingly, $A$'s total demand for imports of $Y$, say $Z$, is given by

$$Z \equiv Y_c + Y_g = Y_c + \lambda t Y_c = (1 + \lambda t)Y_c \qquad (18.4)$$

To determine how $Z$ changes as $t$ increases from zero to a positive value in the neighborhood of the free-trade equilibrium point (i.e., when $p_d = \bar{p}$), differentiate eq. (18.4) with respect to $t$:

$$\frac{dZ}{dt} = \lambda Y_c + (1 + \lambda t)\frac{dY_c}{dt} \tag{18.5}$$

What is the value of the derivative $dY_c/dt$? The quantity $Y_c$ is a decreasing function of $1/\bar{p}_d$; and given $\bar{p}$, $\bar{p}_d$ is also a function of $t$. Therefore,

$$\frac{dY_c}{dt} = \frac{dY_c}{d(1/\bar{p}_d)}\frac{d(1/\bar{p}_d)}{dt} \tag{18.6a}$$

However,

$$\frac{1}{\bar{p}_d} = \frac{1+t}{\bar{p}}$$

Hence,

$$\frac{d(1/\bar{p}_d)}{dt} = \frac{1}{\bar{p}} \tag{18.7}$$

Substituting eq. (18.7) into eq. (18.6a), we get

$$\frac{dY_c}{dt} = \frac{dY_c}{d(1/\bar{p}_d)}\frac{1}{\bar{p}} \tag{18.6b}$$

Recall that, at the free-trade equilibrium ($t = 0$), $\bar{p}_d = \bar{p}$ and that the elasticity of demand for imports by $A$'s consumers ($e_A$) is given by

$$e_A \equiv \frac{dY_c}{d(1/\bar{p}_d)}\frac{1/\bar{p}_d}{Y_c} \tag{18.8}$$

Therefore, eq. (18.6a) can be simplified to

$$\left(\frac{dY_c}{dt}\right)_{t=0} = e_A Y_c \tag{18.9}$$

Substituting eq. (18.9) into eq. (18.5), and remembering that we are interested in the value of $dZ/dt$ when $t = 0$, we get

$$\left(\frac{dZ}{dt}\right)_{t=0} = \lambda Y_c + \left(\frac{dY_c}{dt}\right)_{t=0} = Y_c(\lambda + e_A) \tag{18.10}$$

Equation (18.10) gives the rate of change of $Z$ with respect to $t$ when $t = 0$. It is obvious that, as $t$ increases, $A$'s total demand for imports increases (and therefore $A$'s terms of trade deteriorate) when the sum $\lambda + e_A$ is positive.

We therefore conclude that the necessary and sufficient condition for the deterioration of $A$'s terms of trade, after $A$'s government imposes an infinitesimal trade tax and spends only the fraction $\lambda$ of the tax revenue on the imported commodity, is $\lambda + e_A > 0$, or

$$\lambda > -e_A \tag{18.11}$$

In words, $A$'s terms of trade deteriorate after the imposition of the trade tax if, and only if, the absolute value of $A$'s elasticity of demand for imports at the free-trade equilibrium position is smaller than the fraction $\lambda$ of the tax revenue spent by $A$'s government on the imported good.

When $A$'s government spends all tax revenue on the exported commodity, then $\lambda = 0$. Since, in general, $e_A < 0$, inequality (18.11) cannot be satisfied and $A$'s terms of trade improve.

On the other hand, when $A$'s government spends the tax revenue on the imported commodity, $\lambda = 1$ and inequality (18.11) is satisfied when $A$'s demand for imports at the free-trade equilibrium point is inelastic. That is, when $A$'s government spends the tax revenue on the imported commodity ($\lambda = 1$) and $A$'s demand for imports is inelastic, $A$'s terms of trade deteriorate.

## Commonsense Explanation of Lerner's Case

For the benefit of the reader, we conclude our discussion of the effect of trade taxes on the barter terms of trade by a commonsense explanation of the preceding mathematical result.

As we have seen, the effect of a trade tax on $A$'s terms of trade depends crucially on what happens to $A$'s demand for imports at the pretariff world prices. How does $A$'s demand change with the trade tax?

There are two effects on $A$'s demand for imports: (a) a *substitution effect* and (b) an *income effect*. The former results usually in a *reduction* in *private* consumption as the *domestic* price ratio falls from $\bar{p}$ (the pretariff world price ratio) to $p_d = \bar{p}/(1 + t)$; it is illustrated by a movement along $A$'s free-trade offer curve. The latter results in an increase in *public* consumption as the government spends the tariff revenue.

The substitution effect depends on the nature of $A$'s offer curve at the free-trade equilibrium point. In particular, the substitution effect is captured by $A$'s elasticity of demand for imports (see eq. (18.9)).

On the other hand, the income effect depends on how the government spends the tax revenue on $X$ and $Y$. In particular, the income effect is captured by the parameter $\lambda$, that is, the government's marginal propensity to spend on $Y$ (see the first term on the right-hand side of eq. (18.5)).

## 18.3 TRADE TAXES AND DOMESTIC PRICES

For problems of domestic resource allocation and income distribution, what is important is not whether the terms of trade of the tax-imposing country improve or deteriorate after the imposition of the trade tax but, rather, whether the domestic price ratio falls below or rises above the free-trade equilibrium price ratio. Do we have $p_d > \bar{p}$, $p_d = \bar{p}$, or $p_d < \bar{p}$ after the imposition of the trade tax (where $\bar{p}$ = the free-trade equilibrium price ratio)?

Note that, since in the case of nonprohibitive trade taxes there exists a one-to-one correspondence between the domestic price ratio $p_d$ and the terms of trade $p$, as shown by eq. (17.3), the preceding comparison between $p_d$ and $\bar{p}$ can easily be turned into a comparison between the equilibrium value of $p$ after the imposition of the trade tax, say $p_e$, and $\bar{p}$. Thus, we shall have to determine which one of the following relations holds:

$$p_d = \frac{1}{1 + t} p_e \gtreqless \bar{p}$$

The issue is not whether $A$'s terms of trade improve, deteriorate, or remain the same after the imposition of the trade tax. The comparison is between $[1/(1 + t)]p_e$ and $\bar{p}$; or, multiplying both by $(1 + t)$, we can say that the comparison is between $p_e$ and $(1 + t)\bar{p}$. If $p_e > (1 + t)\bar{p}$ after the tax, the domestic price ratio will be higher than $\bar{p}$; if $p_e = (1 + t)\bar{p}$, $p_d$ will be equal to $\bar{p}$ after the tax; and if $p_e < (1 + t)\bar{p}$, $p_d$ will be lower than $\bar{p}$. Therefore, if $A$'s barter terms of trade deteriorate after the imposition of the trade tax, $p_d$ will definitely fall below $\bar{p}$, because, if $p_e < \bar{p}$, it must also be true that $p_e < (1 + t)\bar{p}$.

## Metzler's Paradox

Problems arise when $A$'s barter terms of trade improve, which is no doubt the most usual case. Will $A$'s barter terms of trade improve so much that $p_e > (1 + t)\bar{p}$, or will they improve only slightly, so that $p_e < (1 + t)\bar{p}$? In the latter case, $A$'s terms of trade improve but the domestic price ratio falls (that is, $p_d$ and $p$ move in opposite directions). This means that the imported commodity becomes more expensive, after the imposition of the trade tax, in the tax-imposing country while it becomes cheaper in the rest of the world. Thus, the output of $Y$ in $A$ tends to rise, in this case, after the imposition of the trade tax. This is, no doubt, the normal case in which $A$ is able to "protect" its import-competing industries via the trade tax.

However, as Metzler (1949) pointed out, it is not inconceivable that the imposition of a trade tax by $A$ may turn the barter terms of trade so much in $A$'s favor that $p_e > (1 + t)\bar{p}$. In this case, which in the literature is known as Metzler's paradox (or Metzler case)[†], the imposition of the trade tax by $A$ makes commodity $Y$ cheaper everywhere. Therefore, $A$'s production of $Y$ necessarily *falls* after the imposition of the trade tax. This is indeed a paradoxical outcome, because trade taxes (and especially tariffs) are imposed by politicians who want to *protect* the import-competing industries. Under what conditions will Metzler's paradox occur?

---

† Metzler's paradox was recently challenged by Södersten and Vind (1968) who attempted to show via a general-equilibrium model that a tariff on imports can never lower the relative domestic price of the imported commodity. Jones (1969) retaliated by showing that Södersten and Vind are themselves the guilty parties. See also the reply to Jones by Södersten and Vind (1969).

On the extension of Metzler's paradox to nontraded and intermediate commodities, see Jones (1974).

## Mathematical Analysis of Metzler's Paradox

Assume for the moment that $A$'s government spends a fraction $\lambda$ of the tariff proceeds on the imported commodity and a fraction $(1 - \lambda)$ on the exported commodity, with $0 \le \lambda \le 1$. As noted earlier, the general equilibrium of the present model can be formulated in terms of the demand and supply relations of either commodity. Let the function $D(1/p_a)$ denote the demand for imports of $Y$ by $A$'s private consumers and let the function $S(1/p)$ denote $B$'s supply of exports of $Y$. The demand for imports of $Y$ by $A$'s government, as we saw in the preceding section, is given by $\lambda t D$. Therefore, equilibrium occurs when the following condition is satisfied:

$$(1 + \lambda t)D\left(\frac{1}{p_a}\right) = S\left(\frac{1}{p}\right) \tag{18.12}$$

where $p = (1 + t)p_a$.

Equation (18.12) is simply a single equation in two variables, namely, $p_a$ and $t$. Actually, $t$ is a parameter, so eq. (18.12) can be interpreted as giving $p_a$ as a function of the parameter $t$. To find out how $p_a$ changes as $t$ increases from zero, calculate the derivative $dp_a/dt$ and then put $t = 0$. Differentiating eq. (18.12) totally with respect to $t$, we get

$$\lambda D + (1 + \lambda t)D'\frac{d(1/p_a)}{dt} = S'\frac{d(1/p)}{dt} \tag{18.13}$$

where primes indicate differentiation, and the arguments of the functions $D$, $D'$, and $S'$ are eliminated for simplicity.

From the equation $p = (1 + t)p_a$, we also get

$$\frac{1}{p} = \frac{1}{1 + t}\frac{1}{p_a} \tag{18.14}$$

Thus,
$$\frac{d(1/p)}{dt} = \frac{(1 + t)[d(1/p_a)/dt] - (1/p_a)}{(1 + t)^2} \tag{18.15}$$

Substituting eq. (18.15) into eq. (18.13) and solving the latter for $d(1/p_a)/dt$, we get

$$\frac{d(1/p_a)}{dt} = \frac{\lambda D + (1/p_a)[1/(1 + t)]^2 S'}{[1/(1 + t)]S' - (1 + \lambda t)D'} \tag{18.16}$$

Putting $t = 0$ and remembering that, at $t = 0$, $p = p_a = \bar{p}$ and $D = S$, we get

$$\left[\frac{d(1/p_a)}{dt}\right]_{t=0} = \frac{\lambda D + (1/p_a)S'}{S' - D'} = \frac{\lambda + (1/\bar{p})(S'/S)}{(S'/S) - (D'/D)} = \frac{\lambda + \eta_B}{\bar{p}(\eta_B - e_A)} \tag{18.17}$$

where (according to part B of chap. 6)

$$\eta_B \equiv \frac{1}{\bar{p}}\frac{S'}{S} \equiv B\text{'s supply elasticity of exports}$$

$$e_A \equiv \frac{1}{\bar{p}}\frac{D'}{D} \equiv A\text{'s demand elasticity of imports}$$

with both elasticities evaluated at the free-trade equilibrium point.

What is the sign of the right-hand side of eq. (18.17)? We know from chap. 6 (see eq. (6.14)) that, for stability, it is required that $(\eta_B - e_A) > 0$. Therefore, assuming that the free-trade equilibrium is stable, the sign of the right-hand side of eq. (18.17) depends on the sign of the numerator, i.e., the sign of $(\lambda + \eta_B)$. When $(\lambda + \eta_B) > 0$, the derivative $[d(1/p_d)/dt]_{t=0}$ is positive and, therefore, $1/p_d$ tends to rise with the imposition of the trade tax $t$ (or $p_d$ tends to fall). Commodity $Y$ becomes more expensive in the tax-imposing country $A$, and therefore its output rises (in $A$) at the expense of the output of $X$. On the other hand, when $(\lambda + \eta_B) < 0$, $Y$ becomes cheaper in $A$ (after the imposition of the trade tax) and its output contracts, which is the paradoxical outcome noted by Metzler. In the limiting case $\lambda + \eta_B = 0$, $p_d = \bar{p}$ after the tax and the resource allocation in $A$ remains, after the imposition of the tax, as it was under free-trade conditions.

Making use of eq. (6.9), we can rewrite the numerator of eq. (18.17) as $\lambda + \eta_B = \lambda - e_B - 1$. Thus, when $(\lambda - e_B) > 1$, $p_d$ falls (that is, $Y$ becomes more expensive in $A$) after the imposition of the tax; if $(\lambda - e_B) < 1$, $p_d$ rises; and if $\lambda - e_B = 1$, $p_d$ remains the same as before the imposition of the tax. In words, *when the sum of the fraction $\lambda$, which can be interpreted as the marginal propensity to import in $A$, and $B$'s elasticity of demand for imports of $X$ (in absolute terms) is greater than unity, the domestic relative price of imports $1/p_d$ rises in the tax-imposing country, $A$; when it is less than unity, the domestic relative price of imports $1/p_d$ falls in $A$; and if it is unity, domestic prices remain the same as before the tax.*

The paradox of the imported commodity becoming cheaper in the tax-imposing country after the imposition of the trade tax occurs when $(\lambda - e_B) < 1$, or $-e_B < (1 - \lambda)$. That is, the absolute value of $B$'s elasticity of demand for imports at the free-trade equilibrium position must be less than $1 - \lambda$. Since $0 \le \lambda \le 1$, it is required that *$B$'s elasticity of demand for imports be less than unity;* i.e., the free-trade equilibrium must occur somewhere in the backward-bending region of $B$'s offer curve. Thus, when $B$'s demand for imports at the free-trade equilibrium is elastic, the paradox does not arise.

The above conclusion is based solely on the assumption that $A$'s government spends the tax revenue on both commodities $X$ and $Y$. The higher the fraction $(\lambda)$ of the tax revenue that $A$'s government spends on the imported commodity, $Y$, the less likely it is for $Y$ to become cheaper in $A$ after the imposition of the trade tax. In particular, when $\lambda = 1$, the condition that $Y$ becomes cheaper in $A$ after the tax reduces to $-e_B < 0$, or $e_B > 0$. We can dismiss this as a rather unusual case, because commodity $X$ would have to be not only inferior and a Giffen good but also a Giffen good whose demand, in the region where free-trade equilibrium occurs, falls more sharply than $B$'s production of $X$ as the relative price of $X$ falls. On the other hand, when $\lambda = 0$, the condition that $Y$ becomes cheaper in $A$ after the tax reduces to $-e_B < 1$; that is, $B$'s demand for imports of $X$ must be inelastic at the free-trade equilibrium.

## Graphical Illustration

Let us illustrate the preceding conclusions graphically. This will also enable us to extend the analysis to the case where $A$'s government redistributes the tax revenue among its private residents.

Consider fig. 18.5. The curve $O_A$ is $A$'s free-trade offer curve. Assume that free-trade equilibrium occurs at $E$, with the free-trade equilibrium price ratio given by the slope of the vector $OE$. Now consider the terms-of-trade line $OCD$; its slope is, by assumption, equal to $(1 + t)$ times the slope of $OE$. That is, $FD/OF = (1 + t)(FE/OF)$. Country $A$'s domestic price ratio will continue to be given by the ratio $FE/OF$ (that is, the free-trade price ratio) if, and only if, $A$'s barter terms of trade after the imposition of the trade tax are given by the slope of the terms-of-trade line $OCD$. If $A$'s barter terms of trade rise above $FD/OF$, $A$'s domestic price ratio will rise after the imposition of the trade tax; i.e., commodity $Y$ will become cheaper in $A$ after the tax (Metzler's paradox). On the other hand, if $A$'s barter terms of trade are lower than $FD/OF$ after the tax, commodity $Y$ will become more expensive in $A$.

Country $A$'s barter terms of trade after the imposition of the trade tax will be higher than, lower than, or equal to the ratio $FD/OF$ depending on whether, at the barter terms of trade $FD/OF$, the international excess demand for commodity $X$ is positive, negative, or zero, respectively (or the international excess demand for $Y$ is negative, positive, or zero, respectively). Therefore, we have to compare the offers of $A$ and $B$ at $p = FD/OF$. Country $A$'s offer, as we saw earlier, will fall somewhere along the hypotenuse $CD$. Where will $B$'s offer lie? That depends on the nature of $B$'s offer curve.

If $B$'s offer curve is upward sloping (that is, $B$'s demand for imports is elastic) in the neighborhood of the free-trade equilibrium position (i.e., in the neighborhood of $E$) as shown by the broken curve $GE$, $B$'s offer will lie somewhere along the straight-line segment $OC$, as illustrated by point $G$. In this case, the international excess demand for $X$ at $p = FD/OF$ will be negative, and $A$'s domestic price

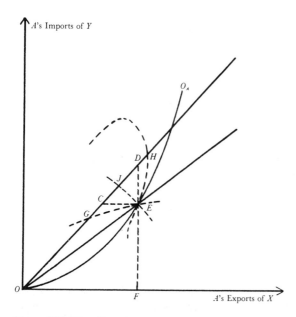

**Figure 18.5** The effect of trade taxes on the domestic price ratio.

ratio will definitely be lower than the free-trade price ratio (that is, $FE/OF$) after the imposition of the trade tax. Country $A$ will shift resources from the production of $X$ to the production of $Y$; this reallocation of resources will have the usual effects on factor prices and the distribution of income. This is the normal case where a trade tax enables the import-competing industry of the tax-imposing country to expand at the expense of the export industry.

At the other end of the spectrum is the case where commodity $X$ is a "relatively strong" Giffen good in $B$ such as to cause $B$'s offer curve to behave like the broken curve $HE$. Note that $B$'s offer curve has a positive slope in this case in the neighborhood of point $E$. Thus, as $X$ becomes cheaper, $B$ wants to import less and less of $X$ and it offers in exchange less and less of $Y$. That is, $e_B > 0$. In this case, $B$'s offer for $p = FD/OF$ will lie on the terms-of-trade line $OCD$ but beyond point $D$, as illustrated by point $H$. Therefore, at $p = FD/OF$, there will be a positive international excess demand for commodity $X$, and $A$'s barter terms of trade will be higher than the free-trade international equilibrium-price ratio $FE/OF$. Commodity $Y$ will become cheaper in $A$ after the imposition of the trade tax, and therefore $A$'s import-competing industry, $Y$, will contract while its export industry, $X$, will expand, with the usual consequences for factor prices and income distribution.

When $B$'s demand for imports is merely inelastic in the neighborhood of point $E$, $B$'s offer curve will intersect the terms-of-trade line $OCD$ somewhere along the hypotenuse $CD$, as illustrated by the broken curve $JE$. Country $B$'s offer at $p = FD/OF$ will lie somewhere along $CD$, as illustrated by point $J$. Whether $A$'s barter terms of trade will be higher or lower than $FD/OF$ after the imposition of the trade tax depends on whether $A$'s offer lies in the region $CJ$ or $JD$. The precise position of $A$'s offer at $p = FD/OF$ is determined by the way in which $A$'s government spends the tax revenue on $X$ and $Y$. If all is spent on the imported commodity $Y$, that is, if $\lambda = 1$, $A$'s offer will coincide with point $D$ and $A$'s barter terms of trade will definitely be lower than $FD/OF$ after the imposition of the trade tax. (The production of $Y$ will expand at the expense of $X$.) On the other hand, if $A$'s government spends all the tax revenue on $X$, $A$'s offer will coincide with point $C$. Commodity $Y$ will become relatively cheaper in $A$ after the imposition of the trade tax, and resources will shift out of the production of $Y$ into the production of $X$. What happens when $0 < \lambda < 1$? According to the preceding algebraic analysis, for a sufficiently small trade tax, $A$'s offer at $p = FD/OF$ will coincide with $B$'s when $\lambda - e_B = 1$; it will lie in the region $JD$ when $(\lambda - e_B) > 1$; and it will lie in the region $CJ$ when $(\lambda - e_B) < 1$.

## Commonsense Explanation of Metzler's Paradox

It is useful to consider a commonsense explanation of the Metzler paradox.

As we have seen, the effect of a trade tax on $A$'s domestic price ratio depends crucially on what happens to the world demand for commodity $Y$ at the world price ratio $(1 + t)\bar{p}$, which corresponds to a domestic price ratio in $A$ equal to the pretariff terms of trade (that is, $\bar{p}$). How does the world demand for $Y$ change as $A$'s domestic price ratio remains at the initial value $\bar{p}$ while the world price ratio increases to $(1 + t)\bar{p}$?

As with the Lerner case, there are two effects: ($a$) a substitution effect and ($b$) an income effect. The former results usually in a reduction in $B$'s supply of exports of $Y$ as the world price ratio increases from $\bar{p}$ to $(1 + t)\bar{p}$; it is illustrated by a movement along $B$'s offer curve. The latter results in an increase in consumption in country $A$ as $A$'s government spends the tariff revenue.

Suppose that, at the free-trade equilibrium, country $A$ exports $X_0$ units of $X$ to $B$ in exchange for $Y_0$ units of $Y$. Surely $\bar{p}X_0 = Y_0$. When, after the tariff, $A$'s domestic price ratio is given by $\bar{p}$, $A$'s private sector continues to import $Y_0$. $A$'s tariff revenue in terms of $Y$ is given by $t Y_0$, and the increase in public consumption of commodity $Y$ is given by $\lambda t Y_0$. The latter increase is the income effect in country $A$.

The substitution effect in country $B$ can be recovered from the definition of $B$'s supply elasticity of exports $\eta_B$. Thus, by definition,

$$\eta_B = \frac{\text{relative change in } B\text{'s exports}}{\text{relative change in } 1/p}$$

We know that $B$'s volume of exports changes from $Y_0$ to $Y_0 + \Delta Y$; and $B$'s relative price of commodity $Y$ falls from $1/\bar{p}$ to $1/p$, where by assumption $1/p = 1/\bar{p}(1 + t)$. What are the relative changes in $B$'s volume of exports and relative price of $Y$ equal to?

As is well known, there is some ambiguity in the estimation of relative changes when the absolute changes are "large." Because of the strict relationship between $\eta_B$ and $e_B$ (that is, $\eta_B + e_B = -1$) and the desire to maintain the relationship between $e_B$ and $B$'s expenditure on $X$, we draw on elementary price theory and estimate the relative change in $B$'s exports with respect to $Y_0$ (that is, $B$'s initial volume of exports), and the relative change in $B$'s relative price of $Y$ with respect to $1/p$ (that is, the new price ratio). Accordingly,

$$\text{Relative change in } B\text{'s exports} \equiv \frac{\Delta Y}{Y_0}$$

$$\text{Relative change in } 1/p \equiv \frac{(1/p) - (1/\bar{p})}{1/p}$$

$$= \frac{(1/p) - (1 + t)(1/p)}{1/p} = -t$$

Substituting these results into the definition of $\eta_B$, and solving for $\Delta Y$, we obtain:

$$\eta_B = \frac{\Delta Y/Y_0}{-t} \quad \text{and} \quad \Delta Y = -\eta_B t Y_0$$

Finally, subtract the change in $B$'s supply of exports of $Y$ from the increase in $A$'s demand for imports of $Y$ to determine the excess demand for $Y$:

$$\lambda t Y_0 + \eta_B t Y_0 = (\lambda + \eta_B)t Y_0$$

When $\lambda + \eta_B = 0$, the excess demand for $Y$ in the international market is zero, and $A$'s domestic price ratio remains at $\bar{p}$; when $\lambda + \eta_B > 0$, the excess demand for $Y$ is positive, and commodity $Y$ tends to become more expensive (that is, $p_d$ falls below $\bar{p}$); and when $\lambda + \eta_B < 0$, the excess demand for $Y$ is negative, and commodity $Y$ tends to become cheaper (that is, $p_d$ tends to rise above $\bar{p}$). The last possibility is, of course, Metzler's paradox.

## Redistribution of the Tax Revenue

What happens when $A$'s government redistributes the tax revenue among its private citizens? We can use the preceding geometric technique to determine what happens to $A$'s domestic price ratio after the imposition of the trade tax. Consider fig. 18.6. The curve $O_B$ is $B$'s offer curve, while the slope of the terms-of-trade line $OE$ shows, as before, $A$'s free-trade equilibrium barter terms of trade. Thus, by assumption, free-trade equilibrium occurs at $E$. To keep the diagram simple, country $A$'s free-trade offer curve is not drawn. It is not actually needed for the present discussion. Our problem now is the condition under which $A$'s domestic price ratio will remain equal to the free-trade barter terms of trade (i.e., the slope of the vector $OE$) if country $A$ should impose an infinitesimal trade tax and redistribute the tax revenue among $A$'s citizens. With this information, we shall be able to say when $A$'s domestic price ratio will fall below, and when it will rise

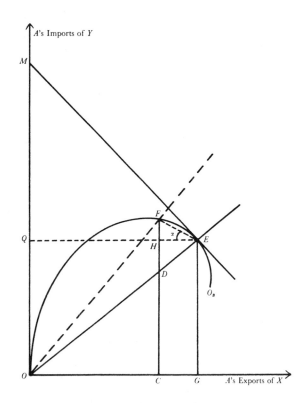

**Figure 18.6** The condition for Metzler's paradox with tax-revenue redistribution.

above, the free-trade barter terms of trade. First consider the case of a finite trade tax; then, through a limiting process, derive the desired condition.

Suppose that $A$ imposes a trade tax $t$ equal to the ratio $DF/CD$. Country $A$'s domestic price ratio will remain at $GE/OG$ if, and only if, at $p = CF/OC$, $A$'s trade point, after the imposition of the trade tax, coincides with $F$. What this means is that a subsidy $DF$ (measured in terms of $Y$ at free-trade prices) given by $A$'s government to $A$'s consumers—which is simply the redistribution of the tax revenue collected by $A$'s government when $A$'s consumers trade at $F$ at the barter terms of trade $CF/OC$—induces $A$'s consumers to increase their consumption and, therefore, imports of $Y$ by $HF$. That is, the ratio $HF/DF$ is simply $A$'s *marginal propensity to import*, $m$—the fraction of each extra unit of income that $A$'s consumers spend on imports of $Y$ (at the free-trade equilibrium prices). We can express $m$ as a function of the slope $\alpha$ of the hypotenuse $FE$ as follows:

$$m \equiv \frac{HF}{DF} = \frac{HF/HE}{DF/HE} = \frac{HF/HE}{(HF/HE) + (DH/HE)} = \frac{\alpha}{\alpha + \bar{p}} \tag{18.18}$$

Keeping the domestic price ratio equal to $\bar{p}$ (that is, the free-trade price ratio), allow the trade tax rate $t$ to approach zero continuously. Point $F$ will then travel along $B$'s offer curve toward the free-trade equilibrium point $E$, and the slope of $FE$ will tend to approach the slope of $B$'s offer curve at $E$, as shown by the tangent $ME$. Accordingly, the critical value of $m$ for which an infinitesimal trade tax in $A$ will leave $A$'s domestic price ratio equal to $\bar{p}$ will be given by eq. (18.18), where $\alpha$ is simply the slope of $B$'s offer curve at $E$, that is, $\alpha = QM/QE$. But since $\bar{p} = OQ/QE$, the critical value of $m$ is actually

$$m = \frac{\alpha}{\alpha + \bar{p}} = \frac{QM/QE}{(QM/QE) + (OQ/QE)} = \frac{QM}{QM + OQ} = \frac{QM}{OM} \tag{18.19}$$

Recall from chap. 6 that the absolute value of $B$'s elasticity of demand for imports $|e_B|$ is given by the ratio $OQ/OM$, that is, $|e_B| = OQ/OM$. Taking the sum $m + e_B$, we get

$$m + |e_B| = \frac{QM}{OM} + \frac{OQ}{OM} = \frac{OM}{OM} = 1 \tag{18.20}$$

In words, *an infinitesimal trade tax in $A$ with tax-revenue redistribution will leave $A$'s domestic price ratio equal to the free-trade price ratio $\bar{p}$ if, and only if, the sum of $A$'s marginal propensity to import plus the absolute value of $B$'s demand elasticity for imports is equal to unity.* Therefore, $A$'s domestic price ratio will rise above, or fall below, the free-trade price ratio $\bar{p}$, depending on whether the sum $m + |e_B|$ is less than or greater than unity.

These results coincide with the case where $A$'s government spends the fraction $\lambda$ of the tax revenue on the imported commodity. The parameter $\lambda$ is now replaced by $m$. However, there is one difference: whereas $\lambda$ ordinarily lies between zero and unity, $m$ can vary over a wider range. Thus, when the imported commodity is inferior, $m$ assumes a negative value; when the exported commodity is inferior, $m$ assumes a value greater than unity. How can our previous conclusion (p. 476) be amended in these two cases? Let us summarize briefly the most important conclusions.

1. When $B$'s demand for imports is elastic at the free-trade equilibrium point and commodity $Y$ is not inferior in $A$, $A$'s domestic price ratio will always fall ($Y$ will become more expensive) after the imposition of the trade tax. However, if $Y$ is inferior in $A$, $A$'s domestic price ratio may rise even though $|e_B| > 1$.
2. When $B$'s demand for imports is inelastic at the free-trade equilibrium point and $Y$ is inferior in $A$, $A$'s domestic price ratio will rise ($Y$ will become cheaper) after the imposition of the trade tax.
3. When commodity $X$ (the commodity imported by $B$) is a strongly Giffen good in $B$ (see curve $HE$ in fig. 18.5), $A$'s domestic price ratio will always rise provided $X$ is not inferior in $A$. On the other hand, if $X$ is inferior in $A$, $A$'s domestic price ratio may fall after the imposition of the trade tax.

# PART B. QUANTITATIVE RESTRICTIONS

Let us consider briefly the second form of trade controls—quantitative restrictions on exports and imports. When the government, for one reason or another, desires to control directly the quantity of imports, it may decree that only a given quantity (import quota) may be imported per unit of time. For this purpose, it may issue import licences that it can either sell to importers at a competitive price or just give away on a first-come, first-served basis. Similarly, the government may desire to control directly the quantity of exports, and it may therefore decree that only a given quantity (export quota) may be exported per unit of time. For this purpose, it may issue export licences that it can either sell or give away.

Consider fig. 18.7. Curves $O_A$ and $O_B$ are $A$'s and $B$'s free-trade offer curves, respectively. Free-trade equilibrium occurs at $E_1$. Country $A$ exports $OX_1$ units of $X$ to $B$ in exchange for $OY_1$ units of $Y$. Suppose that $A$'s government decides to restrict the imports from $B$ to $OY_2$ units of $Y$ per unit of time. Assume that it does this by issuing import licences that it sells to $A$'s importers at a competitive price. Assume, further, that it redistributes among its private citizens all revenue collected from the sale of the import licences. How is equilibrium established under these circumstances?

Country $B$ is forced to trade at $E_2$, and since $B$ remains perfectly competitive, $B$'s domestic price ratio (= barter terms of trade) must be given by the slope of the vector $OE_2$ (not drawn). What is $A$'s domestic price ratio? Draw $A$'s trade indifference curve $I_A^t$ through $E_2$ and then draw the tangent at $E_2$, as shown by $RE_2$. Country $A$'s domestic price ratio is necessarily given by the slope of $RE_2$.

Several observations can be made. First, instead of restricting imports to $OY_2$, $A$'s government could restrict exports to $OX_2$. Therefore, there is a symmetry between export and import quotas, as with trade taxes. Second, $B$ could be forced to trade at $E_2$ with an appropriate trade tax (given by the ratio $OR/RY_2$). Therefore, the effects of export and import quotas are identical to those of trade taxes.

However, there are several fundamental differences between export and import quotas, on the one hand, and trade taxes, on the other. For one thing, the

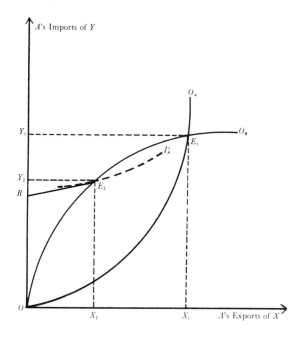

**Figure 18.7** The effects of import and export quotas.

revenue of an import quota, while equal to the tariff revenue of an equivalent tariff, may not accrue to $A$'s government. It may accrue to $A$'s importers (when the government gives the import licences away on a first-come, first-served basis), or it may accrue to $B$'s exporters, when the latter can collude but $A$'s importers cannot. Subsequent shifts in supply and demand in either country cause the equivalent trade tax rate to change while the country continues to export or import, as the case may be, the same quantity as before the change took place. Finally, the conversion of a tariff into a quota that admits exactly the same volume of imports may convert a potential into an actual monopoly by eliminating the threat of competition from increased imports. Conversely, the conversion of a quota into an equivalent tariff may eliminate an actual monopoly by threatening it with potential competition from increased imports.

## SELECTED BIBLIOGRAPHY

Baldwin, R. E. (1960). "The Effect of Tariffs on International and Domestic Prices." *Quarterly Journal of Economics*, vol. 74 (February), pp. 65–78.

Bhagwati, J. N., and H. G. Johnson (1961). "A Generalized Theory of the Effect of Tariffs on the Terms of Trade." *Oxford Economic Papers* (N.S.), vol. 13, no. 3 (October), pp. 225–253. Reprinted in H. G. Johnson, *Aspects of the Theory of Tariffs*, Harvard University Press, Cambridge, Mass., 1972.

Johnson, H. G. (1969). "The Standard Theory of Tariffs." *Canadian Journal of Economics and Political Science*, vol. II, no. 3 (August), pp. 333–352.

——— (1972). *Aspects of the Theory of Tariffs*. Harvard University Press, Cambridge, Mass.

Jones, R. W. (1969). "Tariffs and Trade in General Equilibrium: Comment." *American Economic Review*, vol. LIX, no. 3 (June), pp. 418–424.

———— (1974). "The Metzler Tariff Paradox." In G. Horwich and P. A. Samuelson (Eds.), *Trade, Stability, and Macroeconomics*. Academic Press, New York.

Lerner, A. P. (1936). "The Symmetry Between Import and Export Taxes." *Economica*, vol. III, no. 11 (August), pp. 306–313. Reprinted in R. E. Caves and H. G. Johnson (Eds.), AEA *Readings in International Economics*. Richard D. Irwin, Inc., Homewood, Ill., 1968.

Meade, J. E. (1952). *A Geometry of International Trade*. George Allen and Unwin, Ltd., London, chap. VI.

Metzler, L. (1949). "Tariffs, International Demand, and Domestic Prices." *Journal of Political Economy*, vol. 57, no. 4 (August), pp. 345–351.

Metzler, L. A. (1949). "Tariffs, the Terms of Trade, and the Distribution of National Income." *Journal of Political Economy*, vol. LXII, no. 1 (February), pp. 1–29. Reprinted in R. E. Caves and H. G. Johnson (Eds.), AEA *Readings in International Economics*. Richard D. Irwin, Inc., Homewood, Ill., 1968.

Minabe, N. (1974). "The Stolper–Samuelson Theorem and the Metzler Paradox." *Oxford Economic Papers*, vol. 26, no. 3 (November), pp. 329–333.

Södersten, B., and K. Vind (1968). "Tariffs and Trade in General Equilibrium." *American Economic Review*, vol. LVIII (June), pp. 394–408.

———— and ———— (1969). "Tariffs and Trade in General Equilibrium: Reply." *American Economic Review*, vol. LIX, no. 3 (June), pp. 424–426.

Vanek, J. (1962). *International Trade: Theory and Economic Policy*. Richard D. Irwin, Inc., Homewood, Ill., chap. 16.

(Additional references will be found in "Selected Bibliography" at the end of chap. 19.)

# NINETEEN

## TRADE TAXES AND WELFARE

What are the effects of trade taxes on the welfare of the world, the welfare of the tax-imposing country, and the welfare of such groups as workers and landlords? These are extremely important questions, and we are now in a position to answer them as efficiently as possible.

This chapter is divided into three parts. Part A deals with the effects of trade taxes on the welfare of the world; part B deals with the Stolper–Samuelson theorem; and finally part C deals with the theory of optimum tariffs.

## PART A. TRADE TAXES AND THE WELFARE OF THE WORLD

We saw earlier that free trade enables the world to consume along the world production-possibilities frontier; we also saw how the latter can be derived from the production-possibilities frontiers of the individual countries. Before proceeding any further, however, let us clarify the meaning of the world production-possibilities frontier.

## 19.1 THE WORLD PRODUCTION-POSSIBILITIES FRONTIER IN THE NARROW SENSE

In sec. 16.5 (and see also secs. 2.8, 2.9, and 4.6) we derived the world production-possibilities frontier on the assumption that the world consisted of two countries, $A$ and $B$, whose individual production-possibilities frontiers were given. While the geometrical technique is rather simple, it is important to recall that the frontier we thus derived and shall continue to use shows the maximal quantities of commodities $X$ and $Y$ that the world can produce *under the classical assumption that factors of production do not move internationally.* If this assumption is dropped and factors of production are allowed to move internationally, the world as a whole will be able to consume, in general, beyond the boundaries of what we have called the world production-possibilities frontier, provided that free commodity trade does not bring about complete equalization of factor prices both relatively and absolutely. For instance, if, after commodity trade equalizes commodity prices, the marginal physical product of labor is lower in $B$ than in $A$, a migration of labor from $B$ to $A$ will enable the world to produce more of both commodities. In this case, free trade in commodities alone will not permit the world to produce as much as possible of both commodities. In what follows, we shall be interested in the case where factors of production are immobile between countries; therefore, the term "world production-possibilities frontier" will have the narrower meaning we attached to this term earlier. That is, *the world production-possibilities frontier, in the narrow sense, shows the maximal quantities of $X$ and $Y$ that the world can produce under the assumption that factors, while perfectly mobile within countries, are completely immobile between countries.*

## 19.2 THE INEFFICIENCIES OF TRADE TAXES

The effect of trade taxes on world output is that they interfere with the international resource allocation in such a way as to make it impossible for the world economy to produce and consume along the world production-possibilities frontier (in the narrow sense). This follows from the observation that the world operates on the world production-possibilities frontier when the two countries are allocating their resources in such a way that their respective marginal rates of transformation are equal. In equilibrium, the marginal rate of transformation of a country is equal to its domestic price ratio. Since the existence of trade taxes gives rise to a divergence between the domestic price ratios of the two countries, their marginal rates of transformation must necessarily be different. Hence, the world cannot operate on the world production-possibilities frontier in the presence of trade taxes. *The cum-tax world production-possibilities frontier necessarily lies inside the free-trade world production-possibilities frontier.* But this is by no means the only inefficiency introduced by trade taxes.

Consider two individuals, $\alpha$ a resident of $A$ and $\beta$ a resident of $B$. They both maximize their individual welfares before and after taxes. While, in the absence of trade taxes, the commodity prices paid by consumers are the same everywhere (which implies that the marginal rates of substitution of $\alpha$ and $\beta$ are identical and, thus, they must be consuming somewhere along their contract curve), the same is not true after the imposition of trade taxes. Country $A$'s domestic price ratio will be different from $B$'s and the marginal rate of substitution in consumption in $A$ will be different from that in $B$. Therefore, if the same aggregates of $X$ and $Y$ were made available to $\alpha$ and $\beta$ after the imposition of a trade tax as they were able to consume under free-trade conditions, it would not be possible to make, through lump-sum transfers, both individuals as well off after the trade tax as under free trade. *Because of the divergence between the domestic price ratios of the two countries, the two individuals will not be consuming along the contract curve.* This is a *second inefficiency* introduced by a trade tax (the first being the inability of the world economy to operate along the world production-possibilities frontier).

To summarize, the introduction of a trade tax interferes with the maximization of the potential welfare of the world in two ways: (*a*) the world is forced to produce inside the free-trade world production-possibilities frontier; and (*b*) the allocation of commodities among consumers is inefficient: for the same bundle of commodities before and after the introduction of a trade tax, it is impossible to make all consumers as well off with the trade tax as they were under free-trade conditions. As a result of these inefficiencies, the world as a whole will definitely operate inside the free-trade world utility-possibility frontier. Therefore, from the point of view of potential welfare, the world will be worse off after the introduction of a trade tax. This constitutes, by far, the most important argument against any interference with free international trade.

## PART B. TRADE TAXES AND THE WELFARE OF THE TAX-IMPOSING COUNTRY: THE STOLPER–SAMUELSON THEOREM

The *Stolper Samuelson theorem* purports to determine the effect of trade taxes on the relative and absolute incomes of the tax-imposing country's factors of production.

When a trade tax is imposed, the relative and absolute incomes of the tax-imposing country's factors of production are affected in two ways: (*a*) through the change of the domestic price ratio and the resultant reallocation of resources, and (*b*) through the redistribution of the tax revenue by the government. The Stolper–Samuelson theorem deals primarily with the first.

There are several formulations of the Stolper–Samuelson theorem. After a brief discussion of the most general and correct formulation, we shall consider three other formulations which are not in general correct.

### 19.3 THE CORRECT FORMULATION OF THE STOLPER–SAMUELSON THEOREM

The most general and correct formulation of the *Stolper–Samuelson theorem* is as follows.† The imposition of a trade tax raises, reduces, or leaves unchanged the real wage of factor $F$ used intensively in the production of commodity $C$ (that is, a

---

† See, for instance, Bhagwati (1959) and Kemp (1969). Also, for the generalization of the Stolper–Samuelson theorem to many commodities and many factors, see Chipman (1966, 1969), Kemp (1969), Minabe (1967), and Uekawa (1971).

trade tax raises, reduces, or leaves unchanged the marginal physical product of factor $F$ in every line of production) as the trade tax raises, lowers, or leaves unchanged the domestic relative price of commodity $C$.

The truth of the Stolper–Samuelson theorem follows directly from the discussion of the effect of international trade on the welfare of workers and landlords (chap. 15) and from the discussion of the modern theory (chaps. 8 to 10).

Consider again the two-country ($A$ and $B$), two-factor ($L$ and $T$), two-commodity ($X$ and $Y$) model of chaps. 8 to 10. Actually, in what follows we shall be concerned with one country, say $A$, only—as Stolper and Samuelson (1941, p. 62) point out, the effects of $B$ on $A$ operate via changes in the commodity-price ratio only.

Assume that for $A$'s given factor-endowment ratio ($\rho_A \equiv L_A/T_A$), commodity $X$ is labor intensive relative to commodity $Y$. This assumption does *not* exclude the phenomenon of factor-intensity reversals (see the discussion in part A of chap. 8). In particular, commodity $X$ may be classified as land intensive in country $B$. In the latter case, the Heckscher–Ohlin theorem will not be valid (see chap. 10). Nevertheless, *the Stolper–Samuelson theorem does not depend on the validity of the Heckscher–Ohlin theorem.*

Consider now an increase in the relative price of $A$'s labor-intensive commodity ($X$). How are the marginal physical productivities of labor and land affected in $A$'s industries $X$ and $Y$? Assume that at the higher relative price of $X$, country $A$ continues to produce both commodities. As $p_x/p_y$ increases, country $A$ reallocates its resources from industry $Y$ to industry $X$. Since by assumption commodity $X$ is labor intensive relative to commodity $Y$, the proportion in which labor and land are released by industry $Y$ is not the same as the proportion in which industry $X$ is willing to absorb the two factors. In particular, there emerges an excess demand for labor and/or an excess supply of land; and both of these forces cause the factor-price ratio $w/r$ to rise. As $w/r$ rises, both industries substitute land for labor, i.e., *both* industries become less labor intensive or more land intensive. As a result, the marginal physical product of labor (i.e., the factor used intensively in the commodity which becomes more expensive) increases in both industries, and the marginal physical product of land (i.e., the factor used intensively in the commodity which becomes cheaper) falls in both industries. This completes the proof of the Stolper–Samuelson theorem.

## 19.4 COMPLETE SPECIALIZATION

The assumption of incomplete specialization is important. It was noted in chap. 15 (see also Black, 1969, and Stolper and Samuelson, 1941) that, as $p_x/p_y$ increases continuously, the marginal physical productivity of labor (land) continues to rise (fall) in every line of production *as long as the country continues to produce both commodities.*

When the price ratio $p_x/p_y$ rises to a certain critical value, say $p^*$, the economy specializes completely in the production of $X$. At that point, the marginal physical productivities of labor and land in industry $X$ assume certain values, say $\text{MPP}^*_{Lx}$

and $MPP^*_{Tx}$, which correspond to $p_x = p_A$. Any further increases in the commodity-price ratio $p_x/p_y$ do not affect these factor productivities in industry $X$. However, expressed in terms of commodity $Y$, these productivities become $(p_x/p_y)MPP^*_{Lx}$ and $(p_x/p_y)MPP^*_{Tx}$. Hence, as $p_x/p_y$ continues to increase beyond $p^*$, the marginal productivities of labor and land in terms of commodity $Y$ tend to increase, and both factors tend to become better off relative to their respective positions at $p^*$. Whether land is better off compared to its original position (i.e., before $p_x/p_y$ increased at all) depends on the indifference map of the landlords, and, as we have seen in chap. 15, the outcome can go either way.

## 19.5 DIFFERENT FACTOR INTENSITIES

The assumption of different factor intensities (that is, $\rho_x \neq \rho_y$) is also important for the Stolper–Samuelson theorem. For instance, assume that $\rho_x = \rho_y$ (either because the production functions of $X$ and $Y$ are totally identical, or because of the existence of a factor-intensity reversal at the existing overall labor-land ratio $\rho_A$). The production-possibilities frontier becomes a straight line; and for any commodity-price ratio different from the absolute slope of the production-possibilities frontier, the economy specializes completely in the production of one commodity only.

In the present case ($\rho_x = \rho_y$), the introduction of free trade necessarily makes every factor better off. This is shown in fig. 19.1. The straight line $UV$ is the budget line of a typical worker or landlord in autarky. Its slope shows $A$'s pretrade commodity-price ratio, and its intercepts with the horizontal and vertical axes are given by the marginal physical products of the factor in question (either labor or

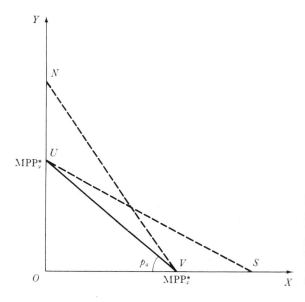

**Figure 19.1** The effect of commodity-price changes on the welfare of a typical worker or landlord when $\rho_x = \rho_y$. The symbols $MPP^*_x$ and $MPP^*_y$ indicate the fixed marginal physical products of labor or land in industries $X$ and $Y$, respectively, for $\rho_x = \rho_y = \rho_A$.

land) in industries $X$ and $Y$, respectively. Allow now country $A$ to trade commodities $X$ and $Y$ in a huge international market at fixed prices. In particular, suppose that $X$ is cheaper in the international market, as shown by the slope of the broken line $US$ which is now the posttrade budget line for the typical worker or landlord. Since $US$ lies uniformly beyond $UV$ (except at the singular point $U$), the introduction of international trade necessarily makes every factor better off.

The same conclusion is true, of course, if $Y$ is cheaper in the international market, as shown by the absolute slope of the broken line $NV$. Then the economy specializes completely in $X$, and the typical worker's or landlord's budget line rotates outward through $V$, as shown by the broken line $NV$. Since $NV$ lies uniformly beyond $UV$ (except at $V$), every factor becomes better off with trade.

In the present case, every factor becomes better off with free international trade (except in the limiting case where the international price ratio is equal to the domestic autarkic price ratio and everybody's welfare remains the same). It follows that a return to autarky makes *every* factor worse off. Further, assuming that the country is already trading internationally, an increase in the relative price of the exported commodity (i.e., an improvement in the country's terms of trade) necessarily makes *every* factor better off. Similarly, a "small" deterioration in the country's terms of trade makes *every* factor worse off. Finally, a *large* reduction in the relative price of the initially exported commodity may reverse $A$'s pattern of trade. In the latter case, the effect on the welfare of workers and landlords is in general indeterminate. In fact, depending on the tastes of each individual, some (workers *and* landlords) may lose and some (workers *and* landlords) may gain, as the reader should be able to show.

## 19.6 OTHER FORMULATIONS OF THE STOLPER-SAMUELSON THEOREM

Bhagwati (1959) observes that there are at least three additional formulations of the Stolper–Samuelson theorem as follows:

**Proposition (a)** "International trade necessarily lowers the real wage of the scarce factor expressed in terms of any good." (See Stolper and Samuelson, 1941, p. 66.)

**Proposition (b)** "Protection (prohibitive or otherwise) necessarily raises the real wage of the scarce factor expressed in terms of any good." Bhagwati (1959, p. 734) attributes this formulation of the Stolper–Samuelson theorem to Lancaster (1957, p. 199).

**Proposition (c)** "Protection (prohibitive or otherwise) raises the real wage of the factor in which the imported good is relatively more intensive." Bhagwati (1959, p. 741) attributes this formulation to Lancaster (1957, p. 199), Metzler (1949, p. 13), and Stolper and Samuelson (1941, p. 72).

The above propositions are not generally true. For instance, proposition (a) depends on the validity of the Heckscher–Ohlin theorem. Does the country export the commodity which uses intensively the country's abundant factor? If not, international trade necessarily causes the country to specialize (and export) the commodity which uses the country's scarce factor; and according to our earlier correct formulation of the Stolper–Samuelson theorem, international trade *raises* the real wage of the scarce factor. We therefore conclude that proposition (a) is valid only when the Heckscher–Ohlin theorem is valid, i.e., when factor-intensity reversals do not occur and (when the physical definition of factor abundance is adopted) tastes are homothetic and similar between countries.

When protection is prohibitive, proposition (b) reduces to proposition (a) and there is nothing to add to the preceding comments. Suppose, then, that protection is *not* prohibitive. In the latter case, proposition (b) is correct when the Heckscher–Ohlin theorem is correct, and in addition the Metzler paradox (see chap. 18) does not occur. On the other hand, if the Metzler paradox does occur, then proposition (b) is correct if, and only if, the Heckscher–Ohlin theorem is incorrect (i.e., if the country in question exports the commodity which uses intensively the country's scarce factor).

Finally, if protection is prohibitive, proposition (c) is correct. In fact, with prohibitive protection, proposition (c) reduces to proposition (a) but with the added assurance that the Heckscher–Ohlin theorem is indeed correct. However, if protection is not prohibitive, then proposition (c) is correct only in the absence of Metzler's paradox. If the Metzler paradox does occur, then proposition (c) is necessarily wrong.

The preceding discussion ignores completely the complications which may arise in the presence of pretrade multiple equilibria.

Although, in their classic paper, Stolper and Samuelson (1941) may have used proposition (a) extensively, there is ample evidence that they had in mind the correct formulation which we considered earlier. Thus, Stolper and Samuelson (1941, p. 72) argue that:

> *It does not follow that our results stand and fall with the Heckscher–Ohlin theorem.* Our analysis neglected the other country completely. If factors of production are not comparable between countries, or if production functions differ, nevertheless, so long as the country has only two factors, international trade would necessarily affect the real wage of a factor in the same direction as its relative renumeration. *The only loss to our analysis would be the possibility of labelling the factor which is harmed as the "scarce" . . . one.* (Italics added.)

## 19.7 REDISTRIBUTION OF THE TAX REVENUE

As mentioned earlier, trade taxes affect the relative and absolute incomes of factors in two ways: (a) through the change of the domestic price ratio and the resultant reallocation of resources and (b) through the redistribution of the tax revenue by the government. Our analysis so far considered the first effect only. For completeness, we now turn briefly to the second effect.

Bhagwati (1959) noted the interesting possibility that under certain conditions the factor whose real wage has been reduced by protection may still become better off if the redistribution of tariff revenue is heavily biased in its favor. There are two obviously *necessary* conditions for this possibility: (*a*) the protection must not be prohibitive and (*b*) the protection must raise the real income of the economy as a whole.

The first condition follows from the fact that when protection is prohibitive, the tariff revenue is zero and no compensation at all can be given to the factor whose real wage has been reduced by protection.

The second necessary condition is also obvious from the Stolper–Samuelson theorem. Thus, when the real wage of one factor is reduced by protection, the real wage of the other factor is necessarily increased. Unless the real income of the economy as a whole is increased, it will never be possible to compensate (by means of tariff-revenue redistribution) the factor whose real wage has been reduced by protection. This means that a small country (i.e., a price taker in the international market) cannot compensate by means of tariff-revenue redistribution the factor whose real wage is reduced by protection. Put differently, a necessary condition for compensating the factor whose real wage is reduced by protection is that the country must have some degree of monopoly-monopsony power in international trade.

Without pursuing any further Bhagwati's interesting insight (for more details, see Bhagwati, 1959), we offer the following example in which compensation is possible. Suppose that protection leaves the domestic price ratio unchanged. (In terms of the analysis of chap. 18, this means that $\lambda + \eta_B = 0$.) In this case, protection does not affect the real wage (expressed in terms of either commodity) of any factor. Hence, tariff-revenue redistribution must make all factors better off.

## PART C. TRADE TAXES AND THE WELFARE OF THE TAX-IMPOSING COUNTRY: THE OPTIMUM TARIFF

From the point of view of the world as a whole, free trade is necessarily the best policy. But is it also true that free trade is the best policy from the point of view of a single country?

Chapter 16 introduces the free-trade consumption-possibilities frontier of a country to show the commodity combinations attainable by the country under free-trade conditions. Is it possible for a country to consume beyond its free-trade consumption-possibilities frontier by imposing trade taxes? When a country is large (in the sense of being able to affect its barter terms of trade), it is always possible (in the absence of retaliation by the other country) to impose an appropriate trade tax and consume beyond the free-trade consumption-possibilities frontier. In other words, despite the fact that the imposition of trade taxes implies that the world definitely operates inside the world utility-possibility frontier, the tax-imposing country can impose an optimum trade tax and improve its potential welfare, with the other country being penalized, so to speak, both by the tax-imposing country's gain and by the inefficiency introduced by the trade tax.

The proposition that a country may, through trade taxes, curtail both imports and exports and thus benefit both as a monopsonist (by forcing the price of imports down) and as a monopolist (by forcing the price of exports up), dates back to John Stuart Mill (1904, pp. 336–342; 1948) and Henry Sidgwick (1887)—if not to Ricardo and Torrens (see Viner, 1965, chap. VI; and Kemp, 1966). It was later formalized by Bickerdike (1906, 1907) and Edgeworth (1925). The argument was later revived by Kaldor (1940), Scitovsky (1942), and others. In particular, Kaldor (1940) referred explicitly to the possibility that a country may gain by a trade tax even though other countries may retaliate. Scitovsky (1942), on the other hand, asserted erroneously that in the presence of retaliation all countries necessarily lose. Johnson (1953) corrected Scitovsky's error and showed that a country may indeed gain by imposing a trade tax even if other countries retaliate.

## 19.8 THE BALDWIN FRONTIER

Consider fig. 19.2. The curve $RVS$ is $A$'s production-possibilities frontier and the curve $MVN$ is $B$'s free-trade offer curve with $V$ as origin. In other words, moving from point $V$ vertically upward, we measure $B$'s exports of $Y$; moving vertically downward, we measure $B$'s imports of $Y$; moving from $V$ to $H$ (that is, leftward), we measure $B$'s imports of $X$; and moving rightward, we measure $B$'s exports of $X$. Point $U$ must necessarily lie on $A$'s free-trade consumption-possibilities frontier: the tangent to $A$'s production-possibilities frontier at $V$ intersects $B$'s offer curve at $U$. Observe that country $A$ can force country $B$ to exchange any commodity

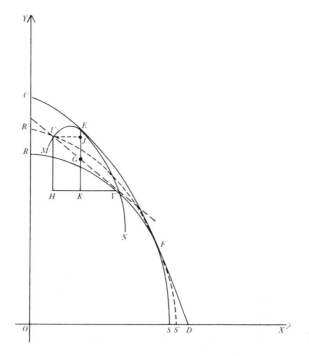

**Figure 19.2** The Baldwin frontier.

combination that lies on the latter's offer curve by simply imposing an appropriate trade tax. Now slide the origin of $B$'s offer curve along $A$'s production-possibilities frontier and trace out the maximal quantity of each commodity available to country $A$ for given quantities consumed (by $A$) of the other commodity. By connecting all points so derived by means of a continuous line, we obtain $A$'s consumption-possibilities frontier that is attainable under an optimum trade tax scheme, as illustrated by the envelope $CEFD$ in fig. 19.2. This envelope ($CEFD$) was first developed by Baldwin (1952) and is known in the literature as the *Baldwin frontier.*

$A$'s free-trade consumption-possibilities frontier ($R'UFS'$) lies inside the Baldwin frontier $CEFD$, except at the singular point $F$. This shows that $A$ can improve its potential welfare by imposing an optimum trade tax and consuming along the envelope $CEFD$ instead of consuming on the free-trade consumption-possibilities frontier $R'UFS'$. Therefore, free trade is *not* the best policy from the point of view of a single country, assuming away any retaliatory action by country $B$.

## 19.9 THE MARGINAL BARTER TERMS OF TRADE AND PARETO OPTIMALITY

Observe in fig. 19.2 that the slope of the envelope $CEFD$ at a point such as $E$ not only is equal to the slope of $B$'s offer curve at $E$ but is also equal to the slope of $A$'s production-possibilities frontier at $V$, the pivot point corresponding to $E$. This follows from the geometrical properties of an envelope, and it has the important economic interpretation that, at an optimal point (i.e., a point on the envelope $CEFD$), $A$'s marginal rate of transformation is necessarily equal to the *marginal barter terms of trade*. This point requires further clarification.

Assume that under free-trade conditions $A$ produces at $V$ and consumes at $U$ by exchanging $HV$ units of $X$ for $HU$ units of $Y$ at the equilibrium terms of trade $HU/HV$ (fig. 19.2). Country $A$'s marginal rate of transformation through domestic production (i.e., the slope of $A$'s production-possibilities frontier at $V$) is equal to $A$'s marginal rate of substitution in consumption; however, they are both higher than $A$'s *marginal rate of transformation through trade* (i.e., the number of units of $Y$ that $A$ is not able to import from $B$ if $A$ reduces its exports of $X$ by 1 unit). Country $A$'s marginal rate of transformation through trade is what we call in the preceding paragraph "marginal barter terms of trade." The average terms of trade at the free-trade equilibrium point are given by the absolute slope of the vector $VU$. How are the marginal terms of trade shown in fig. 19.2?

For the last $UJ$ units of $X$ that $A$ exported to $B$, it received in exchange $EJ$ (negative) units of $Y$. Consider the ratio $EJ/UJ$, which is simply an approximation of the marginal terms of trade at $U$, and then allow point $E$ to approach point $U$. The limit of the ratio $EJ/UJ$ as $E$ approaches $U$ shows the marginal terms of trade at $U$. Graphically, it is given by the slope of the tangent to $B$'s offer curve at $U$.

In the case considered in fig. 19.2, $A$'s marginal terms of trade are negative. That is, not only did country $A$ not receive any positive amount of $Y$ from $B$ for the last unit of $X$ exported to $B$, but, in addition, $A$ had to give up some amount of $Y$ that it was importing when its exports were a little lower. Therefore, it is to the advantage of $A$ to restrict trade and consume more of everything.

In general, $A$ will maximize the amount of $Y$ consumed for any given amount of $X$ if, and only if, $A$'s marginal terms of trade are equal to $A$'s marginal rate of transformation (which, in turn, is equal to $A$'s domestic price ratio). Free trade, however, equalizes $A$'s marginal rate of transformation to the average terms of trade. Finally, note that the average terms of trade are equal to the marginal terms only if $B$'s offer curve is a straight line through the origin.

All optimal points on the envelope $CEFD$ necessarily correspond to points on $B$'s offer curve where the marginal terms of trade (i.e., the slope) are positive, since $A$'s marginal rate of transformation is always positive. This means that all optimal points on $B$'s offer curve imply that $B$'s demand for imports is elastic.

## 19.10 CONSUMPTION EQUILIBRIUM AND THE OPTIMUM TARIFF RATE

Where would $A$ consume along the envelope $CEFD$? That depends on $A$'s demand conditions as determined both by individual consumer tastes and by optimal transfers to achieve an optimum distribution of income and maximize social welfare. Assuming that the final equilibrium point on the envelope $CEFD$ has been determined, can we also determine the optimum tariff (or, in general, the optimum trade tax) that will be required to be imposed by $A$ in order to attain that equilibrium point?

Assume that point $E$ in fig. 19.2 is the final equilibrium point. Country $A$'s domestic price ratio ($= A$'s marginal barter terms of trade) will be given by the slope of $VG$, while $B$'s domestic price ratio ($= A$'s average barter terms of trade) will be given by the slope of $VE$ (not drawn). The implied trade tax rate is given by the ratio $GE/KG$ (compare with eq. (17.6)), which is the optimum rate. But the ratio $GE/KG$ can be quickly recognized as the reciprocal of $B$'s supply elasticity of exports $\eta_B$. That is, the optimum tariff $t$ is equal to the reciprocal of $\eta_B$. Therefore, making use of eqs. (6.6) and (6.7), we obtain

$$ t = \frac{1}{\eta_B} = \varepsilon_B - 1 = \frac{-1}{1 + e_B} > 0 \qquad (19.1) $$

Note that $t > 0$ because $e_B < -1$. This does not imply that the optimum trade tax is uniquely determined. The precise value of $B$'s demand elasticity for imports $e_B$ to be used in eq. (19.1) depends on the precise equilibrium point along the envelope $CEFD$ of fig. 19.2. Since, in general, there is an infinite number of optimal points along the envelope $CEFD$, there will be an infinite number of optimal tariff rates. Accordingly, very little assistance can be offered in the search for the optimum trade tax: the social welfare function needs to be completely specified for this purpose.

## 19.11 SOCIAL INDIFFERENCE CURVES AND THE OPTIMUM TARIFF RATE

Assume now that in each of the two countries there exists a completely specified welfare function and that income is always reallocated among individuals in such a way as to maximize social welfare. Then, as Samuelson has shown, there will be a social indifference map in each country, with all the usual properties of an individual consumer's indifference map, which will summarize social behavior. A movement from a lower to a higher social indifference curve will by necessity imply an improvement in social welfare. Under these conditions, we can be more specific about the optimum trade tax.

Consider fig. 19.3. Free-trade equilibrium occurs at $E$. Country $A$ reaches the broken trade indifference curve $I'_A$ and $B$ the broken curve $I'_B$. Now assume that $B$ continues to trade along its free-trade offer curve irrespective of $A$'s policy. What is the optimum trade tax for country $A$? We must first determine the point on $B$'s offer curve where $A$ would like to trade and maximize its social welfare. (It is assumed that $A$'s government redistributes all tax revenue among its private consumers.) The desired point will be that point on $B$'s offer curve where the latter becomes tangent to the highest possible trade indifference curve of $A$. In fig. 19.3, this occurs at point $Z$. Now the optimum tax rate can be uniquely determined as follows. Draw the tangent to $B$'s offer curve at $Z$, as shown by $UZ$; also draw the horizontal line $RZ$ through point $Z$. The implied tax rate is given by the ratio $OU/UR$, which is simply the reciprocal of $B$'s elasticity of supply of exports at $Z$. Observe that $A$'s domestic price ratio is given by the slope of $UZ$, which is also $A$'s marginal barter terms of trade. Therefore, point $Z$ must correspond to a point on $A$'s consumption envelope.

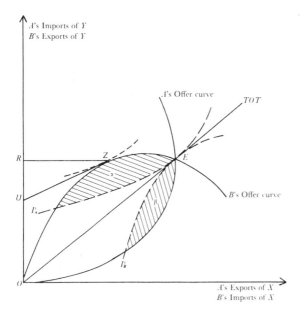

Figure 19.3 The optimum tariff rate and the effects of retaliation.

If $B$'s offer curve were a straight line through the origin, as shown by the free-trade equilibrium terms-of-trade line TOT, the optimum trade tax would be zero. Any other point on TOT besides $E$ would put $A$ on a lower trade indifference curve. This confirms our earlier conclusion regarding a small country that takes international prices as given. There we saw that a trade tax necessarily deteriorates the country's potential welfare, i.e., the optimum trade tax is zero.

## 19.12 RETALIATION

Up to this point, the discussion has been based on the unrealistic assumption that, while $A$ imposes an optimum trade tax, $B$ continues to maintain a free-trade policy. But both countries can play the game. What happens when $B$ pursues an optimum trade tax policy as well?

Beginning from the free-trade position, assume that $A$ imposes an optimum tariff as shown in fig. 19.3. Its trade-tax-distorted offer curve (not drawn) will lie to the left of its free-trade offer curve and pass through $Z$. Country $A$'s welfare improves but $B$'s deteriorates in comparison with the free-trade point $E$. Country $B$ might then retaliate by imposing an optimum trade tax, which will maximize its own social welfare under the assumption that $A$ will maintain the original trade tax rate. However, $B$'s imposition of a trade tax shifts $B$'s offer curve (below $B$'s free-trade offer curve); therefore, the initial trade tax levied by $A$ is no longer optimal. It would thus be profitable for $A$ to change its initial trade tax rate to some new value. But this in turn shifts $A$'s offer curve further, so $B$'s original trade tax rate will no longer be optimal. Country $B$ will be tempted to make a change, and so on in an infinite regression.

Three interesting questions now arise. First, do there exist "equilibrium" trade tax rates which, if they were imposed simultaneously by $A$ and $B$, would call for no further change? Second, will the process described in the preceding paragraph lead to the establishment of the equilibrium trade tax rates? Third, is it possible for at least one country to gain from this tariff war? Clearly, both countries cannot gain because of the inefficiencies introduced by the trade taxes. These questions will not be analyzed in detail.† Nevertheless, the following comments are worth making.

1. Because a trade tax by $A$ shifts $A$'s free-trade offer curve above and to the left, and a trade tax by $B$ shifts $B$'s free-trade offer curve below and to the right, any solution will necessarily occur in the region bounded by the two free-trade offer curves, between $O$ and $E$ (fig. 19.3).
2. If the final equilibrium point lies in the unshaded region $\gamma$ (fig. 19.3), both countries will definitely lose; if it lies in the shaded region $\alpha$, $A$ will gain but $B$ will lose; and if it lies in the shaded area $\beta$, $A$ will lose but $B$ will gain.

---

† On these problems, the reader is referred to Gorman (1958), Johnson (1953), and Kuga (1973).

3. If the barter terms of trade at the final equilibrium position are equal to the free-trade terms of trade, the final equilibrium point will occur somewhere on the straight line $OE$, and both countries will lose.
4. When both countries lose at the final equilibrium point, they can improve their respective levels of social welfare through bilateral trade liberalization.
5. Even when one country gains, the loser will always be able to bribe the gainer through a direct income transfer to abolish all trade restrictions.

## SELECTED BIBLIOGRAPHY

Baldwin, R. E. (1952). "The New Welfare Economics and Gains in International Trade." *Quarterly Journal of Economics*, vol. LXVI, no. 1 (February), pp. 91–101. Reprinted in R. E. Caves and H. G. Johnson (Eds.), AEA *Readings in International Economics*. Richard D. Irwin, Inc., Homewood, Ill., 1968.

———— (1960). "The Effect of Tariffs on International and Domestic Prices." *Quarterly Journal of Economics*, vol. 74 (February), pp. 65–78.

Bhagwati, J. (1959). "Protection, Real Wages and Real Incomes." *Economic Journal*, vol. 69, pp. 733–748.

———— and H. G. Johnson (1961). "A Generalized Theory of the Effects of Tariffs on the Terms of Trade." *Oxford Economic Papers*, vol. 13, pp. 225–253.

Bickerdike, C. F. (1906). "The Theory of Incipient Taxes." *Economic Journal*, vol. XVI, no. 64 (December), pp. 529–535.

———— (1907). "Review of A. C. Pigou, *Preferential and Protective Import Duties*." *Economic Journal*, vol. XVII, no. 65 (March), pp. 98–102.

Black, J. (1959). "Arguments for Tariffs." *Oxford Economic Papers* (N.S.), vol. 11, pp. 191–208.

———— (1969). "Foreign Trade and Real Wages." *Economic Journal*, vol. 79, no. 313 (March), pp. 184–185.

Chipman, J. S. (1966). "A Survey of the Theory of International Trade: Part 3, The Modern Theory." *Econometrica*, vol. 34, pp. 18–76.

———— (1969). "Factor-Price Equalization and the Stolper–Samuelson Theorem." *International Economic Review*, vol. 10, no. 3 (October), pp. 399–406.

Edgeworth, F. Y. (1925). *Papers Relating to Political Economy*, vol. II. Macmillan and Company, Ltd., London. (Reprinted with revisions and omissions from the 1894 *Economic Journal*.)

Gorman, W. M. (1958). "Tariffs, Retaliation, and the Elasticity of Demand for Imports." *Review of Economic Studies*, vol. 25, no. 68 (June), pp. 133–162.

Johnson, H. G. (1953). "Optimum Tariffs and Retaliation." *Review of Economic Studies*, vol. 21, pp. 142–153. Reprinted in H. G. Johnson, *International Trade and Economic Growth: Studies in Pure Theory*. Harvard University Press, Cambridge, Mass., 1958.

———— (1969). "The Standard Theory of Tariffs." *Canadian Journal of Economics and Political Science*, vol. II, no. 3 (August), pp. 333–352.

———— (1972). *Aspects of the Theory of Tariffs*. Harvard University Press, Cambridge, Mass.

Kaldor, N. (1940). "A Note on Tariffs and the Terms of Trade." *Economica* (N.S.), vol. VII, no. 28 (November), pp. 377–380.

Kemp, M. C. (1966). "The Gain from International Trade and Investment: A Neo-Heckscher–Ohlin Approach." *American Economic Review*, vol. LVI, no. 4 (September), pp. 788–809.

———— (1967). "Notes on the Theory of Optimal Tariffs." *Economic Record*, vol. XLIII, no. 103 (September), pp. 395–404.

———— (1969). *The Pure Theory of Internationl Trade and Investment*. Prentice-Hall, Inc., Englewood Cliffs, N.J.

Kindleberger, C. P. (1968). *International Economics*, 4th ed. Richard D. Irwin, Inc., Homewood, Ill., chaps. 7 to 10.

Kuga, K. (1973). "Tariff Retaliation and Policy Equilibrium." *Journal of International Economics*, vol. 3, no. 4 (November), pp. 351–366.

Lancaster, K. (1957). "Protection and Real Wages: A Restatement." *Economic Journal*, vol. 67 (June), pp. 199–210.

Meade, J. E. (1955). *The Theory of International Economic Policy*, vol. II: *Trade and Welfare*. Oxford University Press, New York.

———— (1961). *A Geometry of International Trade*. George Allen and Unwin, Ltd., London, chap. VI.

Metzler, L. A. (1949). "Tariffs, the Terms of Trade, and the Distribution of National Income." *Journal of Political Economy*, vol. 57, pp. 1–29. Reprinted in AEA *Readings in International Economics*. Richard D. Irwin, Inc., Homewood, Ill., 1968.

Mill, J. St. (1904). *Principles of Political Economy*, vol. II. J. A. Hill and Company, New York.

———— (1948). *Essays on Some Unsettled Questions of Political Economy*. London School of Economics and Political Science, London. (Reprinted from the 1844 edition.)

Minabe, N. (1967). "The Stolper-Samuelson Theorem, the Rybczynski Effect, and the Heckscher-Ohlin Theory of Trade Pattern and Factor-Price Equalization: The Case of the Many-Commodity, Many-Factor Country." *Canadian Journal of Economics and Political Science*, vol. 33, no. 3 (August), pp. 401–419.

———— (1974). "The Stolper-Samuelson Theorem and the Metzler Paradox." *Oxford Economic Papers*, vol. 26, no. 3 (November), pp. 329–333.

Samuelson, P. A. (1962). "The Gains from International Trade Once Again." *Economic Journal*, vol. 72, pp. 820–829. Reprinted in J. Stiglitz (Ed.), *The Collected Scientific Papers of Paul A. Samuelson*, vol. 2. The MIT Press, Cambridge, Mass., 1966.

Scitovsky, T. (1942). "A Reconsideration of the Theory of Tariffs." *Review of Economic Studies*, vol. 9, pp. 89–110. Reprinted in H. S. Ellis and L. A. Metzler (Eds.), AEA *Readings in the Theory of International Trade*. Richard D. Irwin, Inc., Homewood, Ill., 1950.

Sidgwick, H. (1887). *The Principles of Political Economy*, 2d ed. Macmillan and Company, Ltd., London.

Stolper, W. F., and P. A. Samuelson (1941). "Protection and Real Wages." *Review of Economic Studies*, vol. 9, pp. 50–73. Reprinted in H. S. Ellis and L. A. Metzler (Eds.), AEA *Readings in the Theory of International Trade*. Richard D. Irwin, Inc., Homewood, Ill., 1950.

Uekawa, Y. (1971). "Generalization of the Stolper-Samuelson Theorem." *Econometrica*, vol. 39, no. 2 (March), pp. 197–217.

Vanek, J. (1962). *International Trade: Theory and Economic Policy*. Richard D. Irwin, Inc., Homewood, Ill., chap. 16.

Viner, J. (1965). *Studies in the Theory of International Trade*. Augustus M. Kelly, Publishers, New York.

# CHAPTER TWENTY

# DOMESTIC DISTORTIONS

The present chapter deals with the theory of endogenous distortions. This theory is applied later in the following chapter to the problem of selecting the least-cost method to achieve a certain noneconomic objective, such as a level of production, consumption, imports, or even employment of a factor of production in an industry.

## 20.1 INTRODUCTION

The desire to accelerate the pace of economic development of the less developed countries and raise their standards of living (through increased capital formation, industrialization, and a larger share of the gains from international trade) gave rise to a renewed interest in the *economic arguments* for protection in the postwar literature. The traditional *infant-industry argument* for protection was restated and expanded to include the whole industrial sector, and many new arguments for protection were advanced by several distinguished economists, most notably Hagen (1958), Lewis (1954), Myrdal (1956), and Prebisch (1959).† These arguments rest, for the most part, on the existence of *external economies* and *factor-price differentials*, which in turn give rise to *domestic distortions* (i.e., divergences between market prices and opportunity costs).

The *theory of domestic distortions* is a direct outgrowth of this activity in the area of economic development and deals primarily with (*a*) the various distortions which prevent the market mechanism from achieving Pareto optimality, and (*b*)

---

† Useful surveys of these arguments have been provided by Meier (1968) and Myint (1963).

the policy recommendations for the neutralization of the domestic distortions and the restoration of Pareto optimality. As it turns out, trade intervention should not be adopted as a means of correcting domestic distortions. The main proposition of the theory of domestic distortions is that *policy intervention must take place at the exact point at which the distortion occurs.*

The development of the theory of domestic distortions owes much to Haberler's (1950) classic paper. Additional important contributions were made by Corden (1957), Fishlow and David (1961), Hagen (1958), Meade (1955), and especially Bhagwati and Ramaswami (1963). The theory was later restated and sharpened considerably by Johnson (1965), and further systematized and generalized by Bhagwati (1971).

The theory of *endogenous* distortions deals with domestic distortions which are primarily due to *market imperfections.*† Nevertheless, as Bhagwati (1971) points out, the main propositions of this theory are easily extended to *policy-induced distortions*, i.e., distortions which are the result of economic policies.

Our discussion proceeds as follows. The next three sections deal with general principles. In particular, sec. 20.2 reviews briefly the Pareto-optimality conditions in an open economy; sec. 20.3 defines and classifies domestic distortions; and sec. 20.4 deals with the general rule for optimal intervention ("first-best" policies). The general principles developed in secs. 20.2 to 20.4 are then applied to monopoly-monopsony power in international trade (sec. 20.5); distortions in domestic production (sec. 20.6); distortions in domestic consumption (sec. 20.7); factor-price differentials (sec. 20.8); and, finally, factor immobility and factor-price rigidity (sec. 20.9).

## 20.2 CONDITIONS FOR PARETO OPTIMALITY

Consider a country (say $A$) endowed with fixed amounts of two factors of production, labor ($L$) and land ($T$), and producing two commodities, $X$ and $Y$, under conditions of *increasing* opportunity costs. Commodities $X$ and $Y$ are traded in world markets. For the most part, the prices of $X$ and $Y$ in world markets will be assumed fixed except when explicitly stated otherwise. In the present section (which gives the Pareto-optimality conditions for the general case) and sec. 20.5 below (which deals with the optimum tariff) world prices are assumed variable.

It is well known that *decreasing* opportunity costs may arise either from increasing returns (see chap. 7) or from the existence of a factor-price differential, as shown by Fishlow and David (1961), Johnson (1966), and Magee (1976). However, in order to simplify the exposition we rule out the phenomenon of decreasing opportunity costs. This simplification enables us to ignore several complications, such as the second-order conditions for welfare maximization, the distinction between local and global maxima, and the possibility of inefficient specialization.

---

† For market imperfections in general, in the context of a closed economy, see Bator (1958).

The tastes of the economy are summarized by a well-behaved social indifference map which either embodies the concept of potential welfare or follows from an optimizing income-redistribution policy (given a Bergson–Samuelson social welfare function), as explained earlier in chap. 5.

Under what conditions is country $A$'s social welfare maximized? Put differently, what are the Pareto-optimality conditions? Drawing on the analysis of earlier chapters (particularly chaps. 4, 5, 16, and 19), and making the simplifying assumption of incomplete specialization in both production and consumption in order to avoid inequalities, we can easily conclude that the necessary (or first-order) conditions for welfare maximization are:

1. The social marginal rate of substitution of $X$ for $Y$ in consumption ($MRS_{xy}$), the social *domestic* marginal rate of transformation ($MRT_{xy}^d$), that is, the opportunity cost of $X$ in terms of $Y$ ($MRT_{xy}^d$), and the *foreign* marginal rate of transformation ($MRT_{xy}^f$), that is, $A$'s marginal terms of trade, must all be equal. In other words,

$$MRS_{xy} = MRT_{xy}^d = MRT_{xy}^f \qquad (20.1)$$

(Recall that the $MRS_{xy}$, $MRT_{xy}^d$, and $MRT_{xy}^f$ are given, respectively, by the relevant absolute slopes of the social indifference curve, the production-possibilities frontier, and the foreign offer curve at the equilibrium point.)

2. The social marginal rate of substitution of labor for land must be the same in both industries. In other words,

$$MRS_{LT}^x = MRS_{LT}^y \qquad (20.2)$$

where $MRS_{LT}^i \equiv$ marginal rate of substitution of labor for land in the $i$th industry ($i = x, y$).

The second condition, i.e., eq. (20.2), implies that the economy allocates its resources at some point on the contract curve. Therefore, when eq. (20.2) is satisfied, production takes place on the economy's production-possibilities frontier. When eq. (20.2) is combined with the equality $MRT_{xy}^d = MRT_{xy}^f$, the economy operates on the Baldwin frontier (see chap. 19). Finally, when eqs. (20.1) and (20.2) are satisfied, the economy operates at a point where the Baldwin frontier is tangent to the highest possible social indifference curve.

## Market Economy and Pareto Optimality

In a socialist state in which, by assumption, all necessary information regarding technology, tastes, factor endowments, and world markets is available to a central planning authority, Pareto optimality can be achieved through centralized decision making based on the solution of an admittedly complex, constrained maximization problem. How is Pareto optimality achieved in a market economy?

In a perfectly competitive economy, the domestic commodity price ratio $p_d$ is equal to the ratio of marginal costs $MC_x/MC_y$ and the foreign price ratio $p_f$. In other words, in a perfectly competitive economy we have

$$p_d = \frac{MC_x}{MC_y} = p_f \qquad (20.3)$$

In addition, in the absence of a factor-price differential (to be discussed below in sec. 20.8), the factor-price ratio in industry $X$, $(w/r)_x$, is equal to the factor-price ratio in industry $Y$, $(w/r)_y$ (law of one price), that is,

$$\left(\frac{w}{r}\right)_x = \left(\frac{w}{r}\right)_y = \frac{w}{r} \tag{20.4}$$

In the absence of any domestic distortions (to be defined in the following section), the domestic commodity price ratio $p_d$ is identified with the marginal rate of substitution in consumption $\text{MRS}_{xy}$; the ratio of marginal costs $\text{MC}_x/\text{MC}_y$ with the domestic marginal rate of transformation $\text{MRT}_{xy}^d$; and the common factor-price ratio $w/r$ with the marginal rate of substitution of labor for land in both industries, $\text{MRS}_{LT}^x$ and $\text{MRS}_{LT}^y$. Finally, in the absence of any foreign distortion (i.e., monopoly-monopsony power in international trade), the foreign price ratio $p_f$ is identified with the foreign marginal rate of transformation $\text{MRT}_{xy}^f$. By making the proper substitutions in eqs. (20.3) and (20.4), we obtain eqs. (20.1) and (20.2). We therefore conclude that *in the absence of any distortion, domestic or foreign, a perfectly competitive economy is Pareto optimal.* This is a central theorem of trade and welfare.

## 20.3 ANATOMY OF MARKET FAILURE

The theory of endogenous distortions deals with certain pathologies (market imperfections) of the economic system. These market imperfections prevent the attainment of one or more Pareto-optimality conditions and render the competitive economy inefficient.

A distortion occurs when a Pareto-optimality condition (see eqs. (20.1) and (20.2)) is violated. First, this section classifies the various types of distortion which may be observed in an economic system. Then it identifies each distortion with the type of market imperfection which may be responsible for it. Finally, it comments briefly on how distortions may actually arise from economic policies.

### Types of Distortion

In general, there are four principal types of distortion which may occur in an open economy. This follows from the fact that there are four different ways in which the Pareto-optimality conditions, as given by eqs. (20.1) and (20.2), may be violated:

$$(a) \qquad \text{MRS}_{xy} = \text{MRT}_{xy}^d \neq \text{MRT}_{xy}^f$$

$$(b) \qquad \text{MRS}_{xy} = \text{MRT}_{xy}^f \neq \text{MRT}_{xy}^d$$

$$(c) \qquad \text{MRS}_{xy} \neq \text{MRT}_{xy}^d = \text{MRT}_{xy}^f$$

$$(d) \qquad \text{MRS}_{LT}^x \neq \text{MRS}_{LT}^y$$

The first distortion ($\text{MRS}_{xy} = \text{MRT}_{xy}^d \neq \text{MRT}_{xy}^f$) is usually called "foreign" since it occurs in the foreign sector. The rest are called "domestic."

Each distortion enumerated above may occur either by itself or in combination with any other(s). For instance, as we shall see later, distortion ($d$) usually implies distortion ($b$) as well.

These are the four principal types of distortion. What market imperfections give rise to them?

## Market Imperfections and Types of Distortion

The first distortion, that is, $MRS_{xy} = MRT^d_{xy} \neq MRT^f_{xy}$, occurs when the open economy has monopoly-monopsony power in international trade. This type of market imperfection and the resultant distortion are discussed further in sec. 20.5 below.

The second distortion, that is, $MRS_{xy} = MRT^f_{xy} \neq MRT^d_{xy}$, occurs when either ($a$) the ratio of marginal costs, even though it is identified with the domestic marginal rate of transformation $MRT^d_{xy}$, is not equal to the domestic price ratio $p_d$, that is, when $MRS_{xy} = p_d \neq MC_x/MC_y = MRT^d_{xy}$; or ($b$) the ratio of marginal costs, though equal to the domestic price ratio, fails to be identified with the domestic marginal rate of transformation, that is, $MRS_{xy} = p_d = MC_x/MC_y \neq MRT^d_{xy}$. The former occurs when either or both commodities are produced under monopolistic or oligopolistic conditions, while the latter occurs when a production externality (economy or diseconomy) exists.

The second distortion ($MRS_{xy} = MRT^f_{xy} \neq MRT^d_{xy}$) may also occur in the presence of a consumption externality combined with monopoly-monopsony power in trade of equal severity so that $MRS_{xy} = MRT^f_{xy} \neq p_d = p_f = MRT^d_{xy}$. This should serve as a warning against the erroneous notion that there may exist a one-to-one correspondence between market imperfections and distortions.

The third distortion ($MRS_{xy} \neq MRT^d_{xy} = MRT^f_{xy}$) arises usually from the existence of consumption externalities, as explained further in sec. 20.7. Bhagwati (1968, p. 23) questions the "empirical significance" of the present case of consumption externalities "from the point of view of official policy," although he admits that "its philosophical importance is quite considerable." Bhagwati (1971, p. 73) prefers to assume that this distortion arises "when sellers of the importable commodity . . . charge a uniform premium on imported as well as home-produced supplies."

Finally, the fourth distortion ($MRS^x_{LT} \neq MRS^y_{LT}$) occurs when either ($a$) a factor-price differential, that is, $(w/r)_x \neq (w/r)_y$, is present, or ($b$) a factor-generated externality exists, as explained earlier in the appendix to chap. 7. In either case, this distortion usually implies distortion ($b$) as well. Factor-price differentials are discussed further in sec. 20.8 below and production externalities in secs. 20.6 and 20.8.

## Policy-Imposed Distortions

Bhagwati (1971) points out that the four principal distortions may also result from autonomous policy measures. For instance, distortion ($a$) occurs when the economy imposes a tariff which is different from the optimum tariff. Thus, a "small" country with no monopoly-monopsony power in trade may impose a positive tariff even though the optimum tariff is zero. Alternatively, a "large" country may impose a tariff which is either smaller or larger than the optimum tariff. Similarly, distortions (*b*), (*c*), and (*d*) occur when, in the absence of any offsetting market imperfections, the economy imposes production taxes (or subsidies), consumption taxes (or subsidies), and factor-use taxes (or subsidies), respectively.

## 20.4 THE GENERAL RULE FOR OPTIMAL INTERVENTION

The theory of domestic distortions is *not* an argument for protection. Domestic distortions violate Pareto optimality, but trade intervention is not the remedy.

In general, there are four points of intervention through taxes and subsidies: international trade (through export and import taxes and subsidies), domestic production (through production taxes and subsidies), domestic consumption (through consumption taxes and subsidies), and employment of factors (through taxes and subsidies on factor use).

Intervention is optimal when it restores Pareto optimality by completely offsetting the existing distortion, without giving rise to a new distortion in the process. This is accomplished when *policy intervention takes place at the exact point at which the underlying market imperfection occurs, and is equal to the degree of distortion* in order to offset the distortion completely. It is the *general rule for optimal intervention*. This important rule is applied to specific market imperfections in the rest of this chapter.

The rule for optimal intervention emphasizes that protection is *not* an optimal policy for correcting domestic distortions. The reason is simple: as shown later in this chapter, *protection remedies a domestic distortion at the expense of a foreign distortion*. Accordingly, in the presence of domestic distortions, protection does not lead to Pareto optimality. What is even worse, protection under these circumstances may even *reduce* welfare—a conclusion which follows easily from the theory of the second best (see sec. 22.2).

In the following sections we deal primarily with "first-best" policies. Nevertheless, where it appears useful, we also consider whether alternative, suboptimal policies may still improve the level of welfare attainable under laissez-faire. This problem becomes important when, for one reason or another, the policy maker is actually denied the use of the policy instrument required for a first-best solution.

Finally, in the case of policy-imposed distortions, the optimal intervention is to eliminate the policy itself. This follows trivially from the general rule for optimal intervention.

## 20.5 MONOPOLY-MONOPSONY POWER IN INTERNATIONAL TRADE

The theory of the optimum tariff studied earlier in chap. 19 rests on the existence of a *foreign* distortion, i.e., a distortion in international markets. This distortion, as we have seen in sec. 20.2 above, occurs when the open economy is "large," i.e., when it has monopoly-monopsony power in international trade. Under these circumstances, free trade equalizes the domestic price ratio (which by assumption is equal to the marginal rate of substitution in consumption $MRS_{xy}$ and the domestic marginal rate of transformation $MRT_{xy}^d$) to the *average* (*not the marginal*) barter terms of trade and results in the following distortion: $MRS_{xy} = MRT_{xy}^d = p_d = ART_{xy}^f \neq MRT_{xy}^f$, where $ART_{xy}^f \equiv$ average barter terms of trade. Accordingly, in the presence of monopoly-monopsony power in international trade, free trade violates Pareto optimality. *The optimum tariff can then be viewed as the first-best policy to offset the foreign distortion.*

It is important to emphasize that the existence of monopoly-monopsony power in international trade results in a distortion *from the national standpoint only.* As we have seen in chap. 19, maximization of world welfare requires the absence of trade taxes or subsidies. In other words, the optimum tariff imposed by our open economy to maximize our national welfare will inflict higher welfare losses to the rest of the world than a direct income transfer (from the rest of the world to our open economy)—a transfer which violates none of the first-order conditions for maximization of world welfare. Consequently, from the cosmopolitan point of view, the tariff is clearly a second-best policy—the first-best policy is a direct income transfer.

Also observe that maximization of national (not world) welfare cannot be achieved through intervention in production, consumption, or factor markets. For instance, an appropriate production tax will restore the equality $MRT_{xy}^d = MRT_{xy}^f$. Nevertheless, it will do so by violating another optimality condition, namely, the equality between the marginal rate of substitution and the domestic marginal rate of transformation. In other words, the production tax converts the initial distortion $(MRS_{xy} = MRT_{xy}^d \neq MRT_{xy}^f)$ into a new distortion: $MRS_{xy} \neq MRT_{xy}^d = MRT_{xy}^f$.

Note that the last distortion $(MRS_{xy} \neq MRT_{xy}^d = MRT_{xy}^f)$ corresponds to distortion ($c$) in our earlier classification in sec. 20.3. It is interesting to note that it is caused not by consumption externalities but by a combination of monopoly-monopsony power in trade plus an economic policy.

The reader should also show that the distortion caused by the existence of monopoly-monopsony power in international trade cannot be offset by means of taxes or subsidies on either consumption or factor use *without creating a new distortion.* This is in agreement with the general rule for optimal intervention. Thus the present distortion occurs in the international markets and must be attacked directly through international trade intervention.

What lessons can be drawn from the preceding analysis? Perhaps the following:

1. Lassez-faire is a first-best policy for a perfectly competitive economy with no monopoly-monopsony power in international trade.
2. In the presence of monopoly-monopsony power in international trade, Pareto optimality (from the national viewpoint) is attained by means of the optimum tariff which attacks the distortion at the source and at the appropriate rate.
3. It is not true that a tariff always increases welfare. The result depends on circumstances.

Having discussed the foreign distortion (monopoly-monopsony power in trade) at some length, we shall assume for the rest of the analysis of this chapter that world prices are fixed (i.e., our open economy possesses no monopoly-monopsony power in trade). Alternatively, we may assume that the optimum tariff is always imposed. This means that in the future we shall ignore the foreign distortion and concentrate on the other three domestic distortions.

## 20.6 DISTORTIONS IN DOMESTIC PRODUCTION

As mentioned in sec. 20.3 above, the second type of distortion ($\text{MRS}_{xy} = \text{MRT}^f_{xy} \neq \text{MRT}^d_{xy}$) occurs when either (*a*) one commodity or both are produced under monopolistic or oligopolistic conditions, or (*b*) when a production externality exists in either industry. When a good is produced under monopolistic or oligopolistic conditions, its price to consumers is raised above its marginal cost of production, and therefore violates eq. (20.3). Similarly, in the presence of production externalities (economies or diseconomies), the ratio of (private) marginal costs $\text{MC}_x/\text{MC}_y$ cannot be identified with the domestic marginal rate of transformation. Both cases result in the following domestic distortion: $\text{MRS}_{xy} = \text{MRT}^f_{xy} \neq \text{MRT}^d_{xy}$. For this reason, these two cases are treated simultaneously in the present discussion.

When the production externality is *output* generated, no other distortion occurs besides $\text{MRS}_{xy} = \text{MRT}^f_{xy} \neq \text{MRT}^d_{xy}$. Nevertheless, if the production externality is *factor* generated, another distortion in factor employment results: $\text{MRS}^x_{LT} \neq \text{MRS}^y_{LT}$. In the present section, the production externality is assumed to be of the output-generated variety so that the additional distortion in factor employment is avoided. Factor-generated production externalities are treated later in sec. 20.8.

The distortion in domestic production is illustrated in fig. 20.1. Under autarky the economy reaches equilibrium at $P_0$; the domestic commodity-price ratio is given by the absolute slope of the straight line $DD'$ through $P_0$; and the domestic marginal rate of transformation is given by the absolute slope of the tangent ($TT'$) to the production-possibilities frontier ($UV$) at $P_0$. By assumption: $p_d > \text{MRT}^d_{xy}$. This means either (*a*) that commodity $X$ is produced under monopolistic or oligopolistic conditions or (*b*) that external economies (diseconomies) exist in the production of commodity $X$ ($Y$).

### Specialization in the Wrong Commodity

Suppose now that our economy is given the opportunity to trade commodities $X$ and $Y$ in the world markets at fixed prices. In particular, assume that the international price ratio is given by the absolute slope of the broken line 1 (through $P_0$) which lies in between the slopes of $DD'$ and $TT'$. In other words, assume that the international price ratio $p_f$ lies in between the autarkic market price ratio $p_d$ and the domestic marginal rate of transformation.

Obviously, our economy's *true* (or real) comparative advantage lies in commodity $X$ since $\text{MRT}^d_{xy} < p_f$. Nevertheless, our economy's *apparent* comparative

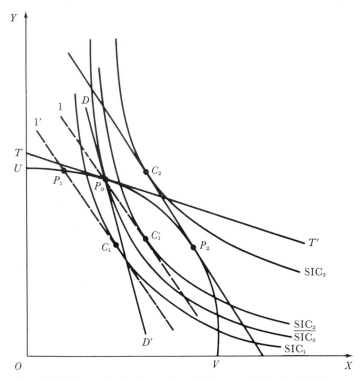

**Figure 20.1** Distortion in domestic production: specialization in the wrong commodity.

advantage lies in commodity $Y$ since $p_d > p_f$. Accordingly, under laissez-faire our economy will specialize in commodity $Y$, that is, the *wrong* commodity. Thus, production moves, say, to point $P_1$ and consumption to point $C_1$. Our economy becomes worse off after the introduction of free trade! Point $C_1$ lies on a lower social indifference curve than $P_0$. Of course, as the reader should show, point $C_1$ *could* lie on a higher social indifference curve than the autarkic point $P_0$.

In terms of the terminology of chap. 5, we can say that the introduction of international trade causes our economy to enjoy a *consumption gain* and suffer a *production loss*. Thus, if production were frozen at the autarkic point $P_0$, the economy's consumption would shift from $P_0$ to, say, $C_1'$, which must lie on a higher social indifference curve. This is the consumption gain. However, production does not remain at $P_0$—it moves to $P_1$. Our economy's income falls (compare the community budget lines 1 and 1'). This adverse shift in production causes the consumption equilibrium to move from $C_1'$ to $C_1$. This is the production loss. In general, the introduction of free trade in the present case may make the economy better off or worse off depending on whether the consumption gain is larger or smaller than the production loss.

If free trade causes our economy to specialize in the wrong commodity, should tariff protection be offered to the industry $(X)$ in which our country has its true comparative advantage? Certainly a tariff on imports raises their domestic price above the world price, encourages their production, and tends to eliminate the divergence between the foreign and the domestic marginal rate of transformation. Unfortunately, trade intervention is not the optimal policy in the present case. In fact, it may even be detrimental to national welfare.

In the first place, as we have seen in earlier chapters, a tax on trade cannot reverse the direction of trade. Accordingly, even a prohibitive tariff cannot restore the equality between the foreign and the domestic marginal rate of transformation, for, by assumption, the foreign price ratio is higher than the domestic marginal rate of transformation under autarky. What is even worse, though, is the fact that protection may even reduce national welfare. For instance, a prohibitive tariff causes the economy to return to the autarkic equilibrium. This reverses the production loss, but it also reverses the consumption gain. If the consumption gain is larger than the production loss (i.e., if the introduction of free international trade makes the country better off), then the prohibitive tariff necessarily reduces national welfare.

What is the optimal policy in the present case? It is to give *a production subsidy to commodity X, or impose a production tax on commodity Y, to make the domestic marginal rate of transformation equal to the given international commodity price ratio without disturbing the equality between the foreign marginal rate of transformation and the marginal rate of substitution.* This optimal policy is illustrated in fig. 20.1. Production equilibrium shifts to $P_2$ and consumption equilibrium to $C_2$.

## Overspecialization in the Right Commodity

If the international price ratio does *not* lie between the autarkic market price ratio and the domestic marginal rate of transformation, then our economy will specialize in the right commodity but the degree of specialization will be either higher or lower than the optimum.

Consider fig. 20.2, which is similar to fig. 20.1, and assume that the international price ratio is smaller than the domestic marginal rate of transformation under autarky, as given by the absolute slope of the broken line 1. In this case, our economy's true comparative advantage lies in commodity $Y$, and the economy actually specializes in the production of $Y$.

In the absence of any domestic distortion, production would be optimized at $P_2$ where $\text{MRT}_{xy}^d = \text{MRT}_{xy}^f$. Since free trade equalizes the domestic market price ratio $p_d$ to the foreign marginal rate of transformation $\text{MRT}_{xy}^f$, and since the domestic price ratio is higher than the domestic marginal rate of transformation because of the distortion in domestic production ($\text{MRT}_{xy}^d < p_d = \text{MRT}_{xy}^f$), production cannot occur at $P_2$ under laissez-faire. In fact, production must occur northwest of $P_2$, as illustrated by points $P_1, P_3$, and $P_4$. Accordingly, the country *over*specializes now in the right commodity.

How does free trade compare with autarky in the present case? The introduction of trade again causes the economy to enjoy a consumption gain. Nevertheless, contrary to the previous case in which the economy necessarily suffered a production loss, in the present case the production effect on welfare may be positive, i.e., a gain (as illustrated by point $P_3$), negative, i.e., a loss (as illustrated by point $P_4$), or zero (as illustrated by point $P_1$). When the country does not suffer a production

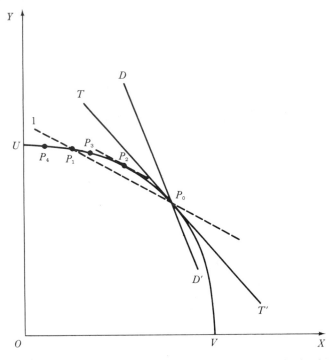

**Figure 20.2** Distortion in domestic production: overspecialization in the right commodity ($Y$).

loss, the introduction of trade necessarily increases national welfare. Otherwise, the overall welfare effect is indeterminate.

The argument for protection in the present case would be that, by means of an appropriate trade tax (an import tax on $X$ or an export tax on $Y$), production could return to its optimum point $P_2$. Unfortunately, this is again a second-best policy and may even reduce national welfare. What the trade tax actually does is to replace one distortion ($\text{MRS}_{xy} = \text{MRT}^f_{xy} > \text{MRT}^d_{xy}$) by another ($\text{MRS}_{xy} > \text{MRT}^d_{xy} = \text{MRT}^f_{xy}$). Thus, while production is optimized at $P_2$, a consumption loss results from the failure to equalize the marginal rate of substitution to the domestic and foreign marginal rates of transformation. As the theory of the second best teaches, the effect on national welfare could be anything.

The optimal policy is to intervene directly at the source of the distortion, namely, production. Thus, the optimal policy in the present case is either a production subsidy to industry $X$ or a production tax on industry $Y$, at an appropriate rate to offset the distortion completely. Such a production tax (or subsidy) offsets the distortion in production completely, without creating another distortion in consumption.

## Underspecialization in the Right Commodity

Consider, finally, fig. 20.3, which is similar to figs. 20.1 and 20.2, and assume that the international price ratio, given by the absolute slope of the broken line 1, is higher than the domestic market price ratio which exists under autarky. In this case, after the introduction of international trade, the economy specializes in the

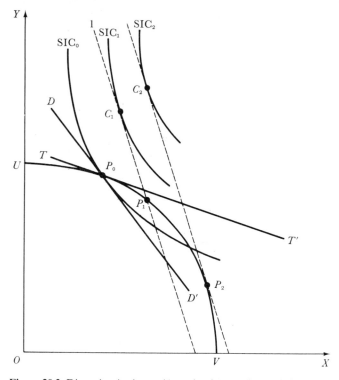

**Figure 20.3** Distortion in domestic production: underspecialization in the right commodity ($X$).

right commodity ($X$), that is, the commodity in which the economy has a true comparative advantage, as shown by point $P_1$. However, the country does not specialize sufficiently in the right commodity ($X$). As a result of the existing distortion in domestic production, $p_f = p_d > \mathrm{MRT}^d_{xy}$, specialization in $X$ cannot proceed up to point $P_2$. Accordingly, laissez-faire leads to production at a point ($P_1$) which lies between the autarkic production-equilibrium point ($P_0$) and the point ($P_2$) where production is optimized, that is, $p_f = \mathrm{MRT}^d_{xy}$. Nevertheless, the introduction of trade makes the country better off (compare points $P_0$ and $C_1$) in the present case—the consumption gain is now supplemented by a meager, but nevertheless positive, production gain.

Again trade intervention is a second-best policy. The optimal policy is a production subsidy to $X$ or a production tax on $Y$, at an appropriate rate to offset the distortion completely (and without creating a new distortion in consumption). This optimal policy is illustrated in fig. 20.3. Production equilibrium shifts to $P_2$ and consumption equilibrium to $C_2$. Note that $C_2$ necessarily lies on a higher social indifference curve than $C_1$.

## 20.7 DISTORTIONS IN DOMESTIC CONSUMPTION

The third type of distortion ($\mathrm{MRS}_{xy} \neq \mathrm{MRT}^d_{xy} = \mathrm{MRT}^f_{xy}$) arises usually (but by no means exclusively) from the existence of consumption externalities (economies or diseconomies).

Consider fig. 20.4. At the given international terms of trade $p_f$ our "small" open economy produces at $P_0$ (where production is truly optimized) and consumes at $C_0$ (because of the consumption externality) instead of $C_1$ (where national welfare is maximized). Thus, by assumption, $MRS_{xy} > MRT^d_{xy} = MRT^f_{xy}$. This situation could arise from the existence of an external economy in the consumption of commodity $X$, an external diseconomy in the consumption of commodity $Y$, or some combination of the two.

Pareto optimality can be fully restored only if the marginal rate of substitution is reduced sufficiently to become equal to the foreign and domestic marginal rates of transformation. In turn, this calls for a reduction in the relative price of $X$ (or, alternatively, an increase in the relative price of $Y$) charged to the domestic consumers. Would a tariff, then, on the imports of commodity $Y$ bring about Pareto optimality? Unfortunately not. A tariff imposed on imports in order to restore the equality between the (social) marginal rate of substitution and the given foreign marginal rate of transformation has at the same time deleterious effects on domestic production. Thus, in terms of fig. 20.4, an appropriate tariff could raise the domestic price of $Y$ sufficiently and encourage the economy to $(a)$

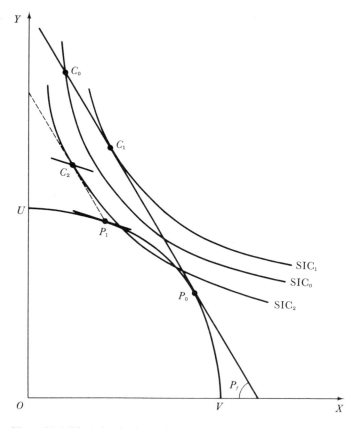

**Figure 20.4** Distortion in domestic consumption.

*increase* the production of $Y$ and *decrease* the production of $X$, and thus produce at a suboptional point such as $P_1$ where the domestic marginal rate of transformation is equal to the new (lower) domestic market price ratio; and (b) consume at a point such as $C_2$ where the social marginal rate of substitution, though still higher than the domestic marginal rate of transformation, is equal to the foreign marginal rate of transformation. The former (i.e., the shift in production from $P_0$ to $P_1$) involves an unnecessary *production loss*. The latter (i.e., the equalization of the marginal rate of substitution and the foreign marginal rate of transformation) involves a *consumption gain* which may be identified with the movement of consumption equilibrium from $C_0$ to $C_1$, assuming for this calculation that production remains frozen at $P_0$.

We therefore conclude that in the present case a tariff gives rise to both a consumption gain (which results from the restoration of the equality $MRS_{xy} = MRT_{xy}^f$) and a production loss (which results from the divergence created by the tariff between the domestic marginal rate of transformation and the given foreign marginal rate of transformation). It is not inconceivable, then, that the production loss may be strong enough to outweigh the consumption gain and actually reduce social welfare as illustrated in fig. 20.4 by point $C_2$.

Similarly, a production tax or subsidy does not restore Pareto optimality either. For instance, a production tax on $Y$ or a production subsidy to $X$, at an appropriate rate which just offsets the divergence between the marginal rate of substitution and the domestic marginal rate of transformation, introduces a new distortion by simply breaking the equality between the domestic and foreign marginal rates of transformation. Accordingly, one distortion ($MRS_{xy} = MRT_{xy}^d > MRT_{xy}^f$) is substituted for another ($MRS_{xy} > MRT_{xy}^d = MRT_{xy}^f$), and national welfare may either increase or decrease.

What is the optimal policy? Either a consumption subsidy (tax) to the commodity whose consumption is subject to the external economy (diseconomy), or a consumption tax (subsidy) on the other commodity. Thus, in the example given in fig. 20.4, the optimal policy is either a consumption subsidy to commodity $X$ or a consumption tax on $Y$, at an appropriate rate to offset the distortion completely. Such direct intervention at the source of the distortion restores Pareto optimality. The optimal solution is indicated in fig. 20.4 by production equilibrium at $P_0$ (where $MRT_{xy}^d = MRT_{xy}^f$) and consumption equilibrium at $C_1$ (where $MRS_{xy} = MRT_{xy}^f$). The consumption tax or subsidy generates a consumption gain without a simultaneous production loss.

## 20.8 FACTOR-PRICE DIFFERENTIALS

This and the following section deal with distortions which originate in factor markets. In particular, the present section deals with the problems created by factor-price differentials and, more specifically, wage differentials. The next section deals with factor immobility and factor-price rigidity.

Concern over wage differentials is not new, as is easily verified by the early works of Cairnes (1874), Manoilesco (1931), Ohlin (1931, 1933), and Viner (1932).

In the postwar literature the subject of factor-price differentials received a great impetus as a result of the increased interest in the economics of the less developed countries. Thus, contributions have been made by Bhagwati and Ramaswami (1963), Eckaus (1955), Fishlow and David (1961), Haberler (1950), Hagen (1958), Johnson (1965, 1966), Johnson and Mieszkowski (1970), Lewis (1954), and others.

Two different types of factor-price differential are usually cited in the literature, especially by writers in economic development. First, there may be a differential between the reward of a factor in different industries. Thus, it is usually alleged that industrial wages are higher than wages in agriculture by a margin which is higher than what can be accounted for by such factors as higher skill, disutility of urban living, investment in human capital (by training), and moving costs from the rural to the urban sector. Second, factor prices may be equal in all industries but factor rewards may not correspond to marginal productivity. Thus, wages may be equal between industry and agriculture but wages in agriculture may be higher than the marginal productivity of labor there. Lewis (1954) assumes that wages in agriculture are equal to the average—not the marginal—product of labor. Both of these types of factor-price differentials give rise to two distortions at the same time:

$$(a) \qquad \text{MRS}_{LT}^{x} \neq \text{MRS}_{LT}^{y}$$

$$(b) \qquad \text{MRS}_{xy} = \text{MRT}_{xy}^{f} \neq \text{MRT}_{xy}^{d}$$

## Reasons for Factor-Price Differentials

What are the reasons for the existence of distortionary factor-price differentials? Factor-price differentials which may indicate genuine distortions (i.e., differential which cannot be accounted for by higher skills, investment in human capital, moving costs, disutility of urban living, etc.) may be due to any number of reasons. Bhagwati (1968, p. 18) lists five such reasons while Magee (1976, pp. 3–4) lists fifteen. Some of these reasons are as follows: lack of information, discrimination (age, sex, or race), prestige and humanitarianism, seniority which does not reflect economic superiority, trade union intervention, differential factor taxation or subsidization, factory legislation, imperfect capital markets, etc. For further details on the causes of distortionary factor-price differentials refer to Bhagwati (1968), Bhagwati and Ramaswami (1963), Fishlow and David (1961), Johnson (1965), and Magee (1976).

## The Welfare Effects of Distortionary Factor-Price Differentials

The discussion of the welfare effects of factor-price differentials dates back to Manoilesco (1931) who observed that the average income in industry exceeds that in agriculture, and concluded that agricultural countries can benefit by providing tariff protection to industry in order to shift workers out of agriculture into industry. More recently, the argument has been revived by Lewis (1954) and Hagen (1958).

Genuine factor-price differentials give rise to two major distortions. First, they prevent the equality between the marginal rate of substitution of labor for land in industries $X$ and $Y$ (that is, $MRS^x_{LT} \neq MRS^y_{LT}$). As a result, they cause a misallocation of resources—the economy does not operate on the contract curve and the production-possibilities frontier is pulled in toward the origin (except at the intercepts). Second, factor-price differentials give rise to a divergence between the commodity market price ratio and the domestic marginal rate of transformation, i.e., they give rise to the distortion: $MRS_{xy} = MRT^f_{xy} \neq MRT^d_{xy}$.

We therefore conclude that, in the presence of factor-price differentials, the economy (whether open or closed) cannot maximize national welfare for two reasons: (a) the economy produces on an inferior, shrunk-in production-possibilities frontier; and (b) in addition, the economy chooses a suboptimal position on this inferior frontier.

## Economic Policies

Can protection improve national welfare in the present case of factor-price differentials? It may and it may not. What is absolutely certain in this case is that protection cannot possibly restore Pareto optimality since it cannot restore the equality between the marginal rate of substitution of labor for land in the two industries. Hence, with protection, the allocation of resources continues to remain inefficient and the economy continues to produce on the shrunk-in production-possibilities frontier. But even if we were to ignore the inferiority of the production-possibilities frontier on which the economy operates, it must be clear from our earlier discussion of distortions in domestic production (see sec. 20.6 above) that protection may even reduce welfare below the level attained under free trade. The same conclusion is reached by Bhagwati and Ramaswami (1963) and Johnson (1965).

A production subsidy to the commodity overpriced by the distortion or a production tax on the underpriced commodity, though still not optimal (or first best), is nevertheless superior to both protection and laissez-faire. The reason is simple. *The production tax (or subsidy) maximizes national welfare subject to the shrunk-in production-possibilities frontier.* This policy does not restore Pareto optimality fully, of course. But it does eliminate the divergence between the market price ratio and the domestic marginal rate of transformation, i.e., it restores eq. (20.1). For this reason, the production tax (or subsidy) enables the economy to increase its national welfare above the level attained under laissez-faire or any scheme of protection.

To summarize: the economic policies of protection and production tax (or subsidy) do nothing to help the economy produce on its optimal production-possibilities frontier. But whereas laissez-faire and protection lead to a second inefficiency (because, in addition to $MRS^x_{LT} \neq MRS^y_{LT}$, laissez-faire also implies $MRS_{xy} = MRT^f_{xy} \neq MRT^d_{xy}$, while protection implies $MRS_{xy} \neq MRT^d_{xy} = MRT^f_{xy}$), the production tax (or subsidy) eliminates the second inefficiency and increases welfare beyond any level attainable under laissez-faire or protection.

Turn now to the optimal (or first-best) policy. How can the economy restore Pareto optimality fully? The answer must be clear from the general rule for optimal intervention. Thus, the economy must attack the distortion at the source which is the *inefficient use of factors of production*. This can be accomplished through appropriate taxes or subsidies on the uses of factors.

We know that the economy operates on the true production-possibilities frontier when $MRS_{LT}^x = MRS_{LT}^y$. This can be accomplished by equalizing the factor-price ratios of the two industries (*inclusive* of taxes or subsidies on factor use), i.e., when $w_x/r_x = w_y/r_y$, assuming that $w_i$ and $r_i$ ($i = x, y$) include taxes and/or subsidies on factor use. Would such policy restore Pareto optimality fully? While the equality $w_x/r_x = w_y/r_y$ leads to production on the true production-possibilities frontier, the economy may still choose a suboptimal position on that frontier unless $w_x = w_y$ and $r_x = r_y$ also. (Of course, these last equalities necessarily imply $w_x/r_x = w_y/r_y$.) Why are the equalities $w_x = w_y$ and $r_x = r_y$ necessary for welfare maximization?

Consider the production functions $Y = Y(L_y, T_y)$ and $X = X(L_x, T_x)$ of industries $Y$ and $X$, respectively. Take their total derivatives as follows:

$$dY = MPP_{Ly} \, dL_y + MPP_{Ty} \, dT_y \tag{20.5}$$

$$dX = MPP_{Lx} \, dL_x + MPP_{Lx} \, dT_x \tag{20.6}$$

It may be convenient (but by no means necessary) to assume that the above changes in $Y$ and $X$ ($dY, dX$) result from a marginal reallocation of resources from industry $Y$ to industry $X$ while the economy operates on its true production-possibilities frontier. In other words, assume that $dL_x = -dL_y = dL > 0$ and $dT_x = -dT_y = dT > 0$. We also know that perfect competition leads to the following equalities (ignoring the possibility that factors may not be remunerated according to their marginal productivity): $w_x = p_x MPP_{Lx}$; $r_x = p_x MPP_{Tx}$; $w_y = p_y MPP_{Ly}$; and $r_y = p_y MPP_{Ty}$. Substitute these assumptions into eqs. (20.5) and (20.6) and then form the ratio:

$$-\frac{dY}{dX} \equiv MRT_{xy}^d$$

$$= \frac{(p_x/p_y)(w_y \, dL + r_y \, dT)}{w_x \, dL + r_x \, dT}$$

$$= \frac{(p_x/p_y)(r_y/r_x)[(w_y/r_y) \, dL + dT]}{(w_x/r_x) \, dL + dT} \tag{20.7}$$

Since by assumption $w_x/r_x = w_y/r_y$, eq. (20.7) reduces to

$$-\frac{dY}{dX} = MRT_{xy}^d = \frac{p_x \, r_y}{p_y \, r_x} \tag{20.8}$$

This last equation shows that the domestic marginal rate of transformation becomes equal to the market price ratio when $r_y/r_x = 1$ or when $r_y = r_x$. Since $w_x/r_x = w_y/r_y$, this implies that $w_x = w_y$ also.

A heuristic explanation of the preceding result can be easily provided. Consider a closed economy which maximizes welfare by producing at a point on its production-possibilities frontier where $MRT_{xy}^d = p_x/p_y$. Freeze production at that point and let both factor prices in industry $X$ increase by, say, 10 percent. Obviously, the equality $w_x/r_x = w_y/r_y$ is preserved. The value of the domestic marginal rate of transformation is also kept fixed by assumption. Does the market price ratio remain fixed also? Certainly not. The relative cost of producing $X$ increases by 10 percent. Hence, the initial equality $\text{MRT}^d_{xy} = p_x/p_y$ is now replaced by the inequality $\text{MRT}^d_{xy} < p_x/p_y$. *The effect of a proportionate increase in $w_x$ and $r_x$ is thus similar to the effect of a production tax (subsidy) on $X(Y)$.*

## An Illustration

We can facilitate the understanding of the preceding discussion by means of a simple illustration. Assume that the wage rate in industry $X$ is higher than the wage rate in industry $Y$, that is, $w_x > w_y$ but $r_x = r_y = r$. Therefore, $(w/r)_x > (w/r)_y$. We can conclude immediately from eq. (20.7) that $\text{MRT}^d_{xy} < p_x/p_y$. This is shown in fig. 20.5. The solid curve $UP_2 V$ is the economy's true production-possibilities frontier, while the broken curve $UP_0 P_1 V$ is the economy's shrunk-in frontier. The fixed international price ratio is given by the absolute slopes of the parallel straight lines through $P_0$, $P_1$, and $P_2$. Under laissez-faire, the economy produces at $P_0$ and consumes at $C_0$. Thus, the economy fails to maximize national welfare

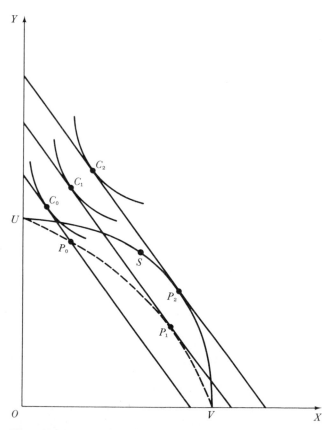

**Figure 20.5** Factor-price differential.

because (a) it operates on the inferior frontier $UP_0 P_1 V$ instead of the true frontier $UP_2 V$, and (b) it chooses on the inferior frontier a suboptimal point $(P_0)$ instead of the optimal $(P_1)$.

Both a trade tax (or subsidy) and a production tax (or subsidy) restrict the economy to operate on the inferior frontier $UP_0 P_1 V$. But whereas the effects of a trade tax (or subsidy) on welfare are uncertain (because of the distortion it creates in consumption), a production tax on $Y$ or a production subsidy to $X$, at an appropriate rate to completely offset the divergence between $\mathrm{MRT}^d_{xy}$ and $p_x/p_y$, can make the country better off. Thus, by an appropriate production tax on $Y$ or a production subsidy to $X$, the economy could be made to produce at $P_1$ and consume at $C_1$.

Full Pareto optimality can only be restored by means of appropriate taxes and/or subsidies on factor use. Here we must be careful. The inequality $(w/r)_x > (w/r)_y$ can be converted into an equality in four different ways: (1) a subsidy to the use of *labor* in $X$; (2) a tax on the use of *labor* in $Y$; (3) a tax on the use of *land* in $X$; and (4) a subsidy to the use of *land* in $Y$. All four ways enable the economy to produce on its true production-possibilities frontier $UP_2 V$. Are they all optimal then? The answer is "No!" Only the first two can restore full Pareto optimality. The reason, of course, is that only the first two methods restore the fundamental equalities: $w_x = w_y$ and $r_x = r_y$.

When a tax is imposed on the use of land in $X$ (third method) or a subsidy to the use of land in $Y$ (fourth method), we have: $w_x > w_y$ and $r_x > r_y$, even though the equality $w_x/r_x = w_y/r_y$ is fully restored. Accordingly, in these two cases, the economy does produce on its true production-possibilities frontier but at a suboptimal point, such as point $S$ in fig. 20.5, as if the factor-price differential did not exist but the economy imposed a production tax on $X$ or a production subsidy to $Y$. (Recall that in the present case $\mathrm{MRT}^d_{xy} < p_x/p_y$.)

We therefore conclude that *full Pareto optimality is restored, in the present case, by means of either a subsidy to the use of labor in X or a tax on the use of labor in Y, at a rate which exactly offsets the distortion.* Such an optimal policy leads to production equilibrium at $P_2$ and consumption equilibrium at $C_2$ (fig. 20.5).

## Factor-Generated Production Externalities†

As mentioned earlier, factor-generated production externalities produce the same distortions and need the same policy remedy as factor-price differentials. We can best illustrate this proposition by pursuing further the example of factor-generated externalities given earlier in the appendix to chap. 7.

Consider again the industry production functions

$$X = X(L_x, T_x, L_0 - L_x) \tag{20.9}$$

$$Y = Y(L_y, T_y) \tag{20.10}$$

---

† This subsection is slightly more advanced than the rest of the chapter. The reader may skip it if he wishes.

and recall that the (social) marginal rates of substitution of labor for land in industries $X$ and $Y$, respectively, are given by

$$\text{MRS}^x_{LT} = \frac{(\partial X/\partial L_x) - (\partial X/\partial L_y)}{\partial X/\partial T_x} \tag{20.11}$$

$$\text{MRS}^y_{LT} = \frac{\partial Y/\partial L_y}{\partial Y/\partial T_y} \tag{20.12}$$

Further, perfect competition leads to the following equalities:

$$w = p_x \frac{\partial X}{\partial L_x} = p_y \frac{\partial Y}{\partial L_y} \tag{20.13}$$

$$r = p_x \frac{\partial X}{\partial T_x} = p_y \frac{\partial Y}{\partial T_y} \tag{20.14}$$

that is, factor prices are equal to their private (*not* the social) marginal productivities. Accordingly, perfect competition leads to

$$\text{MRS}^y_{LT} = \frac{\partial Y/\partial L_y}{\partial Y/\partial T_y} = \frac{w}{r} = \frac{\partial X/\partial L_x}{\partial X/\partial T_x} \neq \text{MRS}^x_{LY} \tag{20.15}$$

and thus the economy produces inside its true production-possibilities frontier. But this is not all.

Consider now the total differentials of eqs. (20.9) and (20.10):

$$dX = \frac{\partial X}{\partial L_x} dL_x + \frac{\partial X}{\partial T_x} dT_x - \frac{\partial X}{\partial L_y} dL_x \tag{20.16}$$

$$dY = \frac{\partial Y}{\partial L_y} dL_y + \frac{\partial Y}{\partial T_y} dT_y \tag{20.17}$$

The assumption of full employment requires that $dL_x = -dL_y$ and $dT_x = -dT_y$. Substituting these assumptions, and also eqs. (20.13) and (20.14), into eqs. (20.16) and (20.17), we obtain

$$dX = \frac{1}{p_x} \left[ \left( w - p_x \frac{\partial X}{\partial L_y} \right) dL + r \, dT \right] \tag{20.18}$$

$$-dY = \frac{1}{p_y} (w \, dL + r \, dT) \tag{20.19}$$

Finally, consider the domestic marginal rate of transformation

$$\text{MRT}^d_{xy} \equiv -\frac{dY}{dX} = \frac{p_x}{p_y} \beta \tag{20.20}$$

where

$$\beta \equiv \frac{w \, dL + r \, dT}{[w - p_x(\partial X/\partial L_y)] \, dL + r \, dT} \tag{20.21}$$

Surely, the market price ratio cannot be equal to the domestic marginal rate of transformation since $\beta \neq 1$. This is a second distortion introduced by the factor-generated externality.

What is the optimal policy in the present case? As with all other types of distortion, the government must intervene at the precise point where the distortion occurs and offset it completely. In the present case, this can be accomplished by an appropriate tax or subsidy on the use of *labor—the factor which generates the externality*. In particular, for an optimal economic policy, the government must establish the following equality:

$$w_y = w_x - p_x \frac{\partial X}{\partial L_y} \tag{20.22a}$$

or

$$w_x = w_y + p_x \frac{\partial X}{\partial L_y} \tag{20.22b}$$

Thus, assuming that $\partial X/\partial L_y > 0$ (that is, that an external *economy* occurs), the optimal policy is either a tax on the use of labor in the production of $X$ or a subsidy to the use of labor in the production of $Y$. In the former case (tax on the use of labor in $X$) the tax must be equal to $p_x(\partial X/\partial L_y)$, that is, the value of the external economy—see eq. (20.22b). In the latter case (a subsidy to the use of labor in the production of $Y$) the subsidy must again be equal to $p_x(\partial X/\partial L_y)$—see eq. (20.22a). On the other hand, if $\partial X/\partial L_y < 0$ (that is, if an external *diseconomy* occurs), the optimal policy is obviously either a subsidy to the use of labor in $X$ or a tax on the use of labor in $Y$.

When the above optimal policy is pursued, the parameter $\beta$ given by eq. (20.21) becomes obviously equal to unity, and, therefore, the divergence between the domestic marginal rate of transformation and the market price ratio disappears. Further, the divergence between the (social) marginal rates of substitution of labor for land in the two industries also disappears. This is verified as follows:

$$\text{MRS}_{LT}^x = \frac{\partial X/\partial L_x}{\partial X/\partial T_x} - \frac{\partial X/\partial L_y}{\partial X/\partial T_x}$$

$$= \frac{w_x}{r} - \frac{\partial X/\partial L_y}{r/p_x}$$

$$= \left( \frac{w_y}{r} + \frac{p_x}{r} \frac{\partial X}{\partial L_y} \right) - \frac{\partial X/\partial L_y}{r/p_x}$$

$$= \frac{w_y}{r} = \text{MRS}_{LT}^y$$

## 20.9 FACTOR IMMOBILITY AND FACTOR-PRICE RIGIDITY

The present section deals with the pathologies known as factor immobility and factor-price rigidity which may exist either singly or in combination. These pathologies have been investigated by Haberler (1950) and Johnson (1965). Both of these authors pose the problem in terms of whether the introduction of trade makes a country worse off in the presence of these pathologies. The problem, of course, arises usually when international trade already exists and the price of imports falls in the international market. We shall presently follow the Haberler–Johnson convention and pose the problem in a similar fashion.

## Factor Immobility and Factor-Price Flexibility

The case of factor immobility dates back to Cairnes (1874) who developed his famous theory of "noncompeting groups" of labor. More recently, both Haberler (1950) and Johnson (1965) discussed the implications of factor immobility within the context of the pure theory of international trade.

Do countries benefit from trade in the presence of factor immobility? Before Haberler (1950) wrote his classic paper, there was some confusion as to whether perfect factor mobility within each country was a necessary condition for countries to benefit from free trade. The root of this confusion, as Haberler notes, was probably the sharp classical dichotomy between perfect factor mobility within each country and perfect factor immobility between countries. Haberler showed that mere factor immobility within a country (which is *not* associated with any factor-price rigidity) does not entail a distortion of the first-order conditions of Pareto optimality. He concluded that free trade is beneficial and that protection necessarily reduces national welfare since, as we have seen, it introduces a distortion.

Consider fig. 20.6. The economy's production-possibilities frontier under perfect factor mobility and factor-price flexibility is given by $UP_0P_1V$. Autarkic equilibrium occurs at $P_0$ where the domestic price ratio is given by the absolute slope ($p_1$) of line 1 (i.e., the tangent to the production-possibilities frontier at $P_0$). Under autarky the economy reaches the social indifference curve $SIC_0$. (Alternatively, we could imagine that initially international prices are equal to the domestic autarkic prices so that the country does not actually engage in international trade even though the opportunity is there.)

Introduce now the opportunity to trade. In particular, assume that the international price ratio is given by the slope ($p_2$) of the parallel lines 2, 3, and 4. (Alternatively, we could assume that the international price ratio increases from $p_1$ to $p_2$.) Under perfect factor mobility (and factor-price flexibility) production equilibrium would shift to $P_1$ and consumption equilibrium to $C_1$. Obviously, the economy gains from trade. More specifically, the economy enjoys both a consumption gain (i.e., the movement from $P_0$ to $C_0$) and a production gain (i.e., the movement from $C_0$ to $C_1$).

In the presence of factor immobility (and factor-price flexibility), the economy's production-possibilities frontier shrinks to the rectangle $OTP_0S$. Does the country still benefit from trade? It most certainly does. Thus, while production remains frozen at $P_0$, consumption shifts to $C_0$. In other words, the country still enjoys the consumption gain even though the production gain is completely wiped out by the immobility of factors.

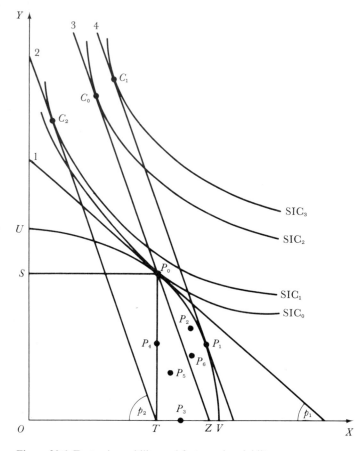

**Figure 20.6** Factor immobility and factor-price rigidity.

Surely, perfect factor immobility is an extreme case. When factors are allowed to be at least partially mobile, some production gain also is enjoyed. Thus, production equilibrium would shift from $P_0$ to some point inside the production-possibilities frontier but beyond line 3, such as point $P_2$, where the value of output produced at world prices is necessarily higher.

We therefore conclude that as long as factor prices are flexible free trade is better than autarky. In addition, in the absence of monopoly-monopsony power in international trade, free trade is an optimal policy. Accordingly, protection necessarily reduces welfare, but not below the level attained under autarky.

### Factor-Price Rigidity and Perfect Factor Mobility

Return again to fig. 20.6 and assume alternatively that there exists perfect factor mobility within the economy and factor-price rigidity. The latter (i.e., factor-price rigidity) may be due to such institutional factors as minimum wage laws, collective bargaining and the like.† Johnson (1965) warns us that in the present context rigidity must be understood in real terms, not in monetary terms as in the money-illusion, Keynesian-type rigidity. In addition, Johnson explains that factor prices may be defined to be rigid downward in terms of one commodity only (either $X$ or $Y$) or in terms of some minimum utility level enjoyed.

When both factor prices are rigid downward, the opening up of the opportunity to trade causes the production of commodity $Y$ (that is, the commodity which becomes cheaper) to cease completely as factors are transferred into the production of $X$ (that is, the commodity which becomes relatively more expensive). However, some of the factor which is used intensively in the production of $Y$ may remain unemployed, so that the actual production point may occur somewhere between points $T$ and $V$, as illustrated by point $Z$ (fig. 20.6), although point $V$ cannot be excluded as a limiting case. As Haberler and Johnson point out, free trade may make the country worse off in the present case, although fig. 20.6 illustrates the opposite case in which the country becomes better off. How is the proposition proved?

If factor prices are rigid in terms of commodity $X$, neither factor's marginal physical product in industry $X$ can be reduced. Accordingly, *factor proportions in industry $X$ must remain constant*. On the other hand, as commodity $X$ becomes relatively more expensive, the marginal products in terms of $X$ of both factors employed in industry $Y$ (that is, $(p_y/p_x)\mathrm{MPP}_{LY}$ and $(p_y/p_x)\mathrm{MPP}_{TY}$) at the autarkic production equilibrium point tend to fall; and, in addition, any variation in factor proportions in industry $Y$ always hurts one factor. Accordingly, the production of commodity $Y$ must cease completely. Nevertheless, since factor proportions in $X$ must remain constant, some of the factor used intensively in producing $Y$ must become unemployed. This case is illustrated in fig. 20.6 by point $P_3$.

Suppose now that factor prices are rigid in terms of commodity $Y$ (that is, the commodity which becomes cheaper after the introduction of trade). In this case there is some flexibility in varying factor proportions in industry $X$ since, at the autarkic production equilibrium point, the marginal products in terms of $Y$ of both factors employed in industry $X$ tend to increase as $Y$ becomes relatively cheaper. The production of commodity $Y$ must again cease completely, however, because any variation in $Y$'s factor proportions necessarily hurts the factor used intensively in producing $Y$. In the present case, however, in which some variation in $X$'s factor proportions is allowed, the production of $X$ will be higher than in the first case in which factor prices were rigid in terms of $X$. In fact, if the relative price of commodity $X$ increases beyond a certain upper limit (which is necessarily higher than the absolute slope of the production-possibilities frontier at its intercept with the $X$ axis, i.e., point $V$), production equilibrium may even occur at point $V$. In this limiting case (which must be obvious from our earlier discussion in chap. 15) no distortion results from the existing factor-price rigidity, since the

---

† As Haberler (1950) and Johnson (1965) carefully explain, factor-price rigidity introduces a distortion only to the extent that it does *not* reflect a perfectly elastic supply of the relevant factor of production, derived, for instance, from an infinite elasticity of substitution between leisure and consumption.

constraint imposed by such rigidity is not binding. The same analysis holds for the case in which factor prices are rigid in terms of a minimum utility level, as the reader should be able to show.

### Factor-Price Rigidity and Factor Immobility

Johnson (1965, pp. 15–18) combines factor-price rigidity and factor immobility, and derives the following additional results.

Consider again the autarkic equilibrium at $P_0$ (fig. 20.6) and assume that the introduction of trade causes the commodity price ratio to increase from $p_1$ (autarkic level) to $p_2$ (international price ratio).

1. If both factors are immobile and both factor prices are rigid in terms of commodity $Y$, production equilibrium remains at $P_0$ as with factor-price flexibility, since no marginal productivity in terms of either commodity is reduced.
2. If both factors are immobile and both factor prices are rigid either in terms of $X$ or in terms of a minimum utility level, the production of $Y$ ceases completely and the factors used to produce $Y$ in the autarkic state remain unemployed. Production occurs at $T$.
3. If both factors are immobile and only one factor price is rigid (in terms of $X$, or of $Y$, or of a minimum utility level), then production of $Y$ does not cease completely. In particular, production equilibrium occurs at some point, such as $P_4$, along the vertical line $TP_0$.
4. If one factor is immobile with a rigid price (in terms of $X$, or of $Y$, or of a constant utility combination of the two) while the other factor is mobile with a flexible price, then production of $X$ increases. Production of $Y$ decreases and actually falls below the level $TP_4$ (that is, the level attained in the preceding case in which both factors were immobile). This case is illustrated by point $P_5$.
5. If one factor is mobile with a rigid price in terms of $Y$ or of a constant utility combination of $X$ and $Y$, and the other factor is immobile but with a flexible price, then some of the mobile factor moves from industry $Y$ to industry $X$ until its marginal productivity in $X$ is reduced to the level set by its price rigidity. This case is illustrated by point $P_6$ which cannot lie above $P_4$.

The proofs of the preceding propositions are left as exercises for the reader.

### Optimal Policy

The optimal policy in the presence of factor-price rigidities is some appropriate scheme of subsidy to factor use. The details for all the cases considered in this section are left to the reader as exercises.

### SELECTED BIBLIOGRAPHY

References will be found in "Selected Bibliography" at the end of chap. 21.

# TWENTY-ONE

## THE INFANT-INDUSTRY ARGUMENT AND NONECONOMIC OBJECTIVES

The theory of domestic distortions surveyed in the preceding chapter is now applied to the infant-industry argument as well as several other noneconomic arguments for protection. As it turns out, protection is not the optimal policy, except in the case where the noneconomic objective calls for the achievement of a certain degree of self-sufficiency (or volume of imports).

The discussion is divided into two parts. In particular, part A deals with the infant-industry argument while part B deals with the theory of noneconomic objectives.

## PART A. THE INFANT-INDUSTRY ARGUMENT

The infant-industry argument is an argument for *temporary* protection to correct a distortion which does not last forever but disappears gradually with the passage of time. This argument, which has always had great appeal to young and developing nations is said to have been formulated in 1791 by Alexander Hamilton, George Washington's Secretary of the Treasury, developed further by Carey and others, and later transplanted into Germany by Friedrich List (see Haberler, 1936, pp. 278–285; 1961, pp. 55–58). Viner (1965, pp. 71–72), however, provides evidence to the effect that this argument is of much earlier origin.

## 21.1 THE FORMULATION OF THE INFANT-INDUSTRY ARGUMENT BY JOHN STUART MILL

Perhaps the clearest formulation of the infant-industry argument is provided by John Stuart Mill (1904). Since Mill's exposition is very concise indeed, we quote it in full:

> The only case in which, on mere principles of political economy, protecting duties can be defensible, is when they are imposed temporarily (especially in a young and rising nation) in hopes of naturalizing a foreign industry, in itself perfectly suitable to the circumstances of the country. The superiority of one country over another in a branch of production often arises only from having begun it sooner. There may be no inherent advantage on one part, or disadvantage on the other, but only a present superiority of acquired skill and experience. A country which has this skill and experience yet to acquire, may in other respects be better adapted to the production than those which were earlier in the field; and besides, it is a just remark of Mr. Rae, that nothing has a greater tendency to promote improvements in any branch of production, than its trial under a new set of conditions. But it cannot be expected that individuals should, at their own risk, or rather to their certain loss, introduce a new manufacture, and bear the burden of carrying it on, until the producers have been educated up to the level of those with whom the processes are traditional. A protecting duty, continued for a reasonable time, will sometimes be the least inconvenient mode in which the nation can tax itself for the support of such an experiment. But the protection should be confined to cases in which there is good ground of assurance that the industry which it fosters will after a time be able to dispense with it; nor should the domestic producers ever be allowed to expect that it will be continued to them beyond the time necessary for a fair trial of what they are capable of accomplishing (pp. 403–404).

Thus, the "Mill test," as Kemp (1960) calls it, for infant-industry protection is whether the infant will eventually overcome its historical handicap and grow up to compete effectively and without protection against early starters.

Bastable (1903, p. 140; 1923, pp. 140–143) objected, however, that the "Mill test," though necessary, is not sufficient, and claimed that, in addition, the infant industry must eventually be able to generate sufficient savings in costs to compensate the economy for the losses (due to higher costs to the consumers) it suffers during the learning period when protection is necessary. Thus, Bastable correctly considered the incurring of costs during the learning period as a type of investment whose returns hopefully accrue to the economy in the form of future cost reductions (relative to the costs which would have to be incurred in the absence of the development of the domestic industry). The "Bastable test," as Kemp (1960) calls it, requires then that the present discounted value of the future benefits are at least as high as the initial costs incurred to help the infant grow.

Johnson (1965, p. 27) notes that even when the "Bastable test" is passed, the infant-industry argument reduces essentially to the assertion that free competition produces a socially inefficient allocation of investment resources. For the validity of the argument, Johnson continues, "it must be demonstrated either that the social rate of return exceeds the private rate of return on the investment, or that the private rate of return necessary to induce the investment exceeds the private and social rates of return available on alternative investment, by a wide enough margin to make a socially profitable investment privately unprofitable." But even if these additional conditions are satisfied, the optimal policy, as Johnson points out, is *not* tariff protection, but rather some sort of *subsidy* to the infant industry, since a domestic, not foreign, distortion is involved.


## 21.2 ECONOMIES OF THE LEARNING PROCESS AND OPTIMAL POLICY

Central to the infant-industry argument is the notion that practice makes perfect. Thus, during the initial stages of development, the "infants" are assumed to learn both from their own experiences and from each other. This learning process, which generally (but not necessarily) involves external economies, is *irreversible*. This is an important feature of the infant-industry argument which distinguishes it from the case of static external economies discussed earlier in chap. 20. Static externalities (economies or diseconomies) form a *permanent* characteristic of the economy's technology and call for a *permanent* government intervention, as we have seen. On the other hand, the infant-industry argument is based on a dynamic learning process which generates external economies over a certain period of time only, and thus calls for only *temporary* government intervention.

When the economies generated during the learning period are *internal* to the firm (e.g., economies of scale), Adam Smith's invisible hand can, in general, be counted on to produce a socially efficient allocation of investment resources, and there is no need for government intervention to protect any "infants." There are, of course, exceptions, as noted by Corden (1965, p. 62) and Johnson (1965, p. 29). Thus, the capital market may be imperfect and as a result the cost of financing investment in new industries may be excessively high, or there may be a difference between social and private time preference, assessment of risk, availability of information, or foresight, and so on. But even in these exceptional cases, tariff protection is not the answer. In fact, tariff protection in these cases is a second-best policy and may even reduce welfare. The first-best policy follows from the general rule for optimal intervention (discussed in sec. 20.4): the government should intervene at the precise point where the distortion occurs. For instance, in the case where an imperfect capital market makes the cost of financing investment in new industries excessively high, the optimal policy is to subsidize the provision of capital to such industries, and so on.

Two major varieties of the externality argument are usually found in the literature. First, it is claimed that, because of the absence of the necessary labor skills, the pioneering entrepreneur into an industry must train his labor force. However, the argument goes, the return from the improvement of labor skills cannot be appropriated by the entrepreneur but is rather imputed to the labor force since his workers, after gaining the necessary skills, could be attracted away by other entrepreneurs who may enter the field later, and who may be willing and able to pay them a higher wage. Accordingly, the private rate of return to the pioneering entrepreneur (who cannot be certain of appropriating all the fruits of his investment) is necessarily lower than the social rate of return. Obviously, the optimal policy in the present case is not tariff protection but rather subsidy to the training of the labor force.

The second externality argument deals with the acquisition of knowledge of production technique. Thus, the acquisition of such knowledge necessarily involves the incurring of costs in the present in the hope of reaping profits in the future. But once created, such knowledge cannot be effectively guarded by the pioneering entrepreneur. Others who enter the field subsequently can certainly make use of it. Once again, the pioneering entrepreneur cannot appropriate all the fruits of his investment, and therefore his private rate of return is necessarily lower than the social rate of return. Tariff protection is again a second-best policy and could hurt the country instead of benefiting it. The optimal policy is merely a direct subsidy to the learning process itself.

Writers in the field of economic development have extended the infant-industry argument to the whole industrial sector. They claim that the external economies which are generated by firms in one industry are not confined to that particular industry alone but instead spread over the whole "infant manufacturing sector." Thus, they think in terms of "infant-economy protection" rather than "infant-industry protection." See, for instance, Corden (1974, chap. 6), Meier (1968, pp. 172–175), and Myrdal (1956, chap. XIII).

## 21.3 GRAPHICAL ILLUSTRATION

The infant-industry argument is illustrated in fig. 21.1. The initial production-possibilities frontier is given by the curve $UV$ and the international price ratio (which remains constant throughout by assumption) by the absolute slope of the lines $L_1 P_1$, $L_2 P_2$, and $L_3 P_3$. Before protection is provided to the infant industry $X$, the economy produces at $P_1$ and consumes at $C_1$. After protection, however, the production-possibilities frontier shifts outward gradually, as a result of the continuous improvement in skills and production techniques, until it attains eventually the position shown by the curve $UZ$. Figure 21.1 illustrates the most favorable case in which the infant industry grows to become a net exporter. Thus, eventually the economy produces at $P_3$ and consumes at $C_4$.

The adjustment process is most interesting but cannot be studied in detail without a lot of additional information. Within our limited scope, however, we can offer some insights. Thus, immediately after a protective tariff is imposed on the imports of $X$ and before any improvement in skills and production techniques takes place, production equilibrium shifts to, say. $P_2$ and consumption equilibrium to $C_2$, where the marginal rate of substitution of $X$ for $Y$ equals the short-run domestic marginal rate of transformation.

If, instead of a protective tariff, a policy of an *equivalent* subsidy to the production of $X$ is pursued, production would still shift to $P_2$ but consumption would shift to $C_3$, where the marginal rate of substitution of $X$ for $Y$ equals the foreign marginal rate of transformation. Thus, the production subsidy to $X$ is superior to the protective tariff, and, as we shall see, this superiority continues through time.

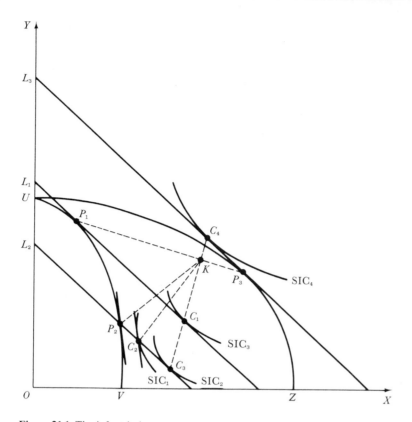

**Figure 21.1** The infant-industry argument.

Imagine now the initial production-possibilities frontier shifting gradually outward, and let the broken line $P_1 P_3$ be the locus of points on the successive frontiers where the domestic marginal rate of transformation equals the foreign marginal rate of transformation (i.e., the line $P_1 P_3$ is the locus of points on the successive frontiers where the slopes are equal to the slope of $UV$ at $P_1$). In addition, let the broken line $C_3 C_1 K C_4$ indicate the income-consumption curve through $C_3$, where the marginal rate of substitution of $X$ for $Y$ equals the given foreign marginal rate of transformation.

The economy will actually follow the consumption equilibrium path $C_3 C_1 K C_4$ when the policy of a production subsidy to $X$ is pursued. When a tariff is actually imposed, the economy will follow a different consumption equilibrium path, illustrated by the broken line $C_2 K C_4$. The precise consumption equilibrium path under a protective tariff is not, however, unique, since it depends on the particular tariff policy pursued through time. Nevertheless, one thing is clear: when point $K$ (that is, the intersection between the broken lines $P_1 P_3$ and $C_3 C_1 K C_4$) is reached, the country becomes self-sufficient in $X$, and, beyond point $K$, it becomes a net exporter of $X$. (Assume that the tariff, or production subsidy, is reduced gradually through time until it is totally removed when point $K$ is reached.) Finally, the production equilibrium path is illustrated by the broken curve $P_2 K P_3$.

Does the economy become better off by assisting the infant industry to grow? We cannot tell from fig. 21.1 alone. All we know is that *eventually* welfare will rise above the initial level at $C_1$. We do not know, however, whether the present discounted value of the future gains in welfare is actually higher than the losses suffered in welfare during the transitional period until the social indifference curve $SIC_3$ is reached.

The problem is actually a little more complex. There is not a single consumption path which moves the economy from the initial equilibrium at $C_1$ to the long-run equilibrium at $C_4$, but many. In fact, there may be an infinite number of such paths, each one depending on a specific economic policy through time. Our analysis clearly shows that a protective tariff can never be the optimal policy since there is always a production subsidy which can do better. But even if attention is confined to policies involving a production subsidy only, a real problem remains: how do we choose the "best" production subsidy scheme? This problem is very similar to the problem of optimal saving posed by Ramsey (1928). Its solution obviously requires knowledge regarding the effect of each alternative production subsidy scheme on labor skills and production techniques through time. This problem, though interesting, is not pursued any further here.

One very interesting feature of the infant-industry argument which must be emphasized is the shift from *static* to *dynamic* comparative advantage.

## PART B. THE THEORY OF NONECONOMIC OBJECTIVES

The theory of endogenous distortions developed in chap. 20 has a direct application to various noneconomic arguments for protection. The purpose of this part is to use the theory of endogenous distortions and throw some light on these non-economic arguments. In particular, this part deals with the desirability of tariffs and alternative policy measures for the achievement of four specific objectives: (*a*) a certain level of *production* (perhaps for military reasons); (*b*) a certain level of *consumption* (usually to restrict the consumption of luxury goods on social grounds); (*c*) a certain level of *self-sufficiency* (i.e., reduce the dependency on imports for political or military reasons); and (*d*) a certain level of *employment of a factor of production*, such as labor (to preserve the national character and the traditional way of life). These objectives are called noneconomic because they essentially originate outside the model. We need not concern ourselves either with the nature or rationality of these noneconomic objectives.

The attainment of a noneconomic objective has an economic cost (in the form of a welfare loss) since it generally involves the violation of one or more Pareto-optimality conditions. The object of our investigation, then, is to determine the optimal policy to achieve a noneconomic objective, i.e., that policy which involves the least welfare loss.

## 21.4 ACHIEVEMENT OF A PRODUCTION GOAL

Suppose that production in an industry which is considered vital to national defense must be encouraged above the level attained under laissez-faire. What is the least-cost method for the achievement of this goal? Corden (1957) showed that the optimal policy in this case is a production subsidy and not tariff protection.

Consider fig. 21.2. Initially (before any intervention), production equilibrium occurs at $P_0$ (where the domestic marginal rate of transformation equals the given foreign marginal rate of transformation) and consumption equilibrium at $C_0$ (where the marginal rate of substitution equals the given foreign marginal rate of transformation). World prices are by assumption fixed and given by the absolute slope of the parallel lines $L_0 P_0$ and $L_1 P_1$. Suppose that the government wishes to shift production from $P_0$ to $P_1$ because for some reason, such as national defense, the production of $Y$ must not be permitted to fall below the level $OJ$.

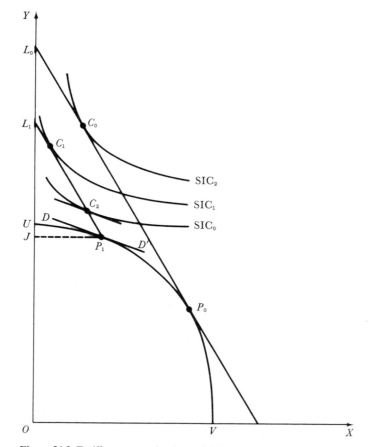

**Figure 21.2** Tariff versus production subsidy to achieve a production goal.

A tariff could achieve the production goal but would lead to an additional, unnecessary, and costly distortion in consumption. Thus, a tariff would cause production to shift to $P_1$ and consumption to $C_2$ (where the marginal rate of substitution equals the *domestic* marginal rate of transformation).

The optimal policy is to subsidize the production of $Y$ so that the marginal rate of substitution of $X$ for $Y$ will remain equal to the foreign marginal rate of transformation. Accordingly, with an appropriate production subsidy to $Y$ (or production tax on $X$), production would shift to $P_1$ and consumption to $C_1$, which lies on a higher social indifference curve than $C_2$.

Corden (1957) has shown that when the economy has monopoly-monopsony power in trade, the optimal policy involves a combination of an optimum tariff plus a production subsidy. The precise optimum tariff rate which must be imposed after the introduction of the additional constraint on production is, in general, different from the tariff rate which is optimum at the initial laissez-faire equilibrium. Corden actually discusses explicitly the case in which the optimum tariff must be reduced below the level which is optimum before the production constraint is introduced—a result which is paradoxical since the import-competing industry must be protected. The paradox, of course, is only apparent because the necessary protection is provided by means of an appropriate production subsidy.

## 21.5 ACHIEVEMENT OF A CONSUMPTION GOAL

Suppose that, alternatively, the government wishes to restrict the consumption of, say, luxuries below the level attained under laissez-faire conditions. What is the optimal policy to achieve this goal? Bhagwati and Srinivasan (1969) have shown that with fixed world prices the optimal policy in the present case is a consumption tax. The tariff is again inferior. (When the economy has also monopoly-monopsony power in international trade, the optimal policy involves a combination of a tariff plus a consumption tax.)

Consider fig. 21.3, which shows the same laissez-faire equilibrium as fig. 21.2. Thus, given the fixed-price ratio in the world markets (shown by the absolute slope of the lines $L_0 Z$ and $C_1 P_1$), the economy produces at $P_0$ and consumes at $C_0$. Suppose, however, that the government wants to restrict the domestic consumption of $Y$ (luxuries) to the level $OJ$. Draw a horizontal line through $J$ and let it intersect the line $L_0 Z$ at $C_2$. Given the production-possibilities frontier, the fixed-price ratio in international markets, and the additional constraint on the domestic consumption of $Y$, it becomes apparent that the best that the economy can do is to maximize social welfare subject to the constraint $JC_2 Z$. Such welfare maximization must occur at $C_2$ since the line segment $C_2 Z$ intersects all (and is never tangent to any) indifference curves.

How can equilibrium at $C_2$ be reached? The economy must continue to produce at $P_0$ and, therefore, tariffs and production taxes and subsidies must be ruled out. An appropriate consumption tax which makes the price ratio to the domestic consumers equal to the absolute slope of the line $L_2 C_2$ (which is tangent to the indifference curve $SIC_1$), and therefore equal to the marginal rate of substitution of $X$ for $Y$ at $C_2$, achieves the desired result.

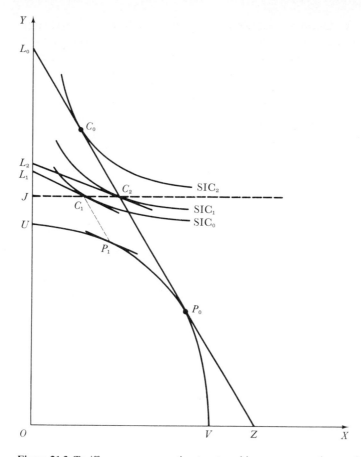

**Figure 21.3** Tariff versus consumption tax to achieve a consumption goal.

A tariff to reduce the consumption of $Y$ is inefficient since it attracts resources into the production of $Y$ and inflicts a needless additional welfare loss to the economy. For instance, as fig. 21.3 illustrates, with an appropriate tariff production shifts to $P_1$ and consumption to $C_1$ (where the marginal rate of substitution equals the domestic marginal rate of transformation and the consumption of commodity $Y$ is $OJ$). But $C_1$ is certainly inferior to $C_2$. The latter ($C_2$), as we have seen, can be reached by imposing an appropriate consumption tax.

## 21.6 REDUCTION OF IMPORTS AS THE NONECONOMIC OBJECTIVE

Turn now to the case where the noneconomic objective is to reduce the volume of imports. Johnson (1965) proved that in the present case a tariff policy is necessarily superior to a production subsidy. Bhagwati and Srinivasan (1969) proved further that the tariff policy is also *optimal*, and extended the proof to the case of variable terms of trade as well.

Consider fig. 21.4. Our economy's offer curve is given by $OO_A$ while the offer curve of the rest of the world is given alternatively by the vector $OT$ (in the case of fixed world prices) or the curve $OO_B$ (in the case of variable world prices). In either case, international equilibrium occurs initially at $E_0$ where our economy reaches the trade indifference curve $I_t^1$.

Suppose now that the government wishes to restrict the imports of $Y$ to the level $OJ$. Assume for the moment that world prices are fixed (i.e., that the offer curve of the rest of the world is given by the vector $OT$). Draw a horizontal line through $J$ and let it intersect the vector $OT$ at $E_1$. Effectively, welfare maximization under the additional restriction on imports means that our economy must try to reach the highest trade indifference curve subject to the constraint $OE_1 Z$. In fact, we may consider the curve $OE_1 Z$ as some sort of offer curve for the rest of the world (as if the constraint on our imports were imposed by the rest of the world), and follow the theory of the optimum tariff to maximize national welfare subject to it. Obviously, maximization of national welfare is achieved when our economy reaches point $E_1$ by imposing a tariff at the rate $OS/SJ$.

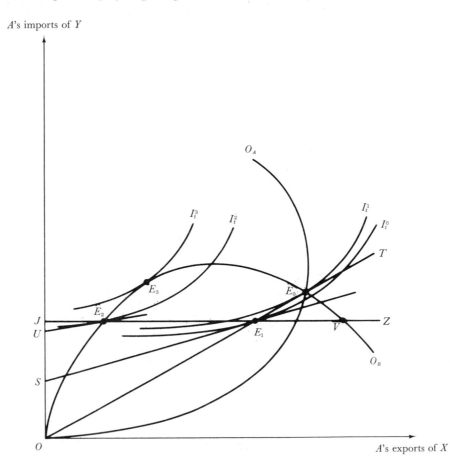

**Figure 21.4** Tariff versus other policy measures to reduce imports.

The analysis remains essentially the same when the barter terms of trade are variable. Thus, suppose that the offer curve of the rest of the world is now given by $OO_B$. The additional constraint on imports means now that our economy must reach the highest trade indifference curve subject to the constraint $OE_2 VO_B$. This is a minor difference from the preceding case of constant terms of trade. Thus, the economy maximizes national welfare subject to the restriction on imports at point $E_2$ by merely imposing a tariff at the rate $OU/UJ$.

In the example of variable terms of trade presented above, the country becomes better off after the imposition of the additional restriction on imports. Thus, point $E_2$ lies on a higher trade-indifference curve than point $E_0$. This paradoxical result is easily explained by the fact that the initial equilibrium at $E_0$ was not optimal from our economy's point of view. Had our economy, before the introduction of the additional constraint on imports, imposed a tariff at a rate which was then optimal, equilibrium would have occurred at $E_3$ initially, and the movement to $E_2$ would have implied a welfare loss.

How do we know that the tariff policy just described is actually optimal for the present case? In other words, is it not possible for our economy to suffer a smaller welfare loss by meeting the additional restriction on imports by means of a production tax or subsidy, or a consumption tax or subsidy, or even a tax or subsidy on factor use? The answer is "No." Any of these alternative policies makes it impossible for the economy to reach a certain consumption indifference curve ($I_c^i$) when trading occurs on a corresponding trade indifference curve ($I_t^i$). Thus, both a consumption tax (or subsidy) and a production tax (or subsidy) introduce a divergence between the marginal rate of substitution ($\mathrm{MRS}_{xy}$) and the domestic marginal rate of transformation ($\mathrm{MRT}_{xy}^d$), and they violate one of the Pareto-optimality conditions on the basis of which the trade indifference curves are derived in the first place. Also a tax or subsidy to factor use causes the production-possibilities frontier to shift inward toward the origin (except at the intercepts) with similar consequences.

We therefore conclude that these alternative policies (production tax or subsidy, consumption tax or subsidy, and factor-use tax or subsidy) imply a higher welfare loss than the appropriate tariff. Thus, with these alternative policies, our economy can still reach point $E_2$, but because of the new distortion introduced by them, consumption will necessarily occur at a lower consumption indifference curve. Accordingly, the tariff is the optimal policy.

## 21.7 ACHIEVEMENT OF A CERTAIN LEVEL OF EMPLOYMENT OF A FACTOR OF PRODUCTION

In some instances it may be desired to raise the employment of a factor in certain activities above the level reached under laissez-faire. This is illustrated in figs. 21.5a and 21.5b. As before, under laissez-faire, production equilibrium occurs at $P_0$ and consumption equilibrium at $C_0$ (fig. 21.5a). Point $E_0$ in the box diagram (fig. 21.5b) corresponds to the production equilibrium point $P_0$ of fig. 21.5a. Thus, $L_x^0$ units of labor are initially employed in industry $X$. Suppose, however, that for some reason the employment of labor in industry $X$ must be raised to $L_x^*$ (see fig. 21.5b). What is the least-cost method of accomplishing this goal? Bhagwati and Srinivasan (1969) showed that the optimal policy is to subsidize directly the use of the factor whose employment must increase (in our case, labor) in the activity where its employment must increase (in our case, industry $X$).

One way to increase the employment of labor in industry $X$ to the desired level $L_x^*$ is to impose an appropriate tariff to increase the production of $X$ as illustrated by point $P_1$ (fig. 21.5a) and the corresponding point $E_1$ (fig. 21.5b). Such a tariff leads to consumption equiliþrium at $C_1$ (fig. 21.5a) where the marginal rate of substitution equals the domestic marginal rate of transformation at $P_1$. It is immediately obvious, however, that the tariff is inferior to an appropriate production subsidy to industry $X$, which also shifts production equilibrium to $P_1$. Thus, unlike the tariff, the production subsidy does not introduce a divergence between the marginal rate of substitution and the foreign marginal rate of transformation. Accordingly, with an appropriate production subsidy to industry $X$, the economy would consume at $C_2$, which is certainly superior to $C_1$.

Nevertheless, a production subsidy is *not* the optimal policy in the present case. Consider fig. 21.5b again. The constraint on the employment of labor in industry $X$ is satisfied when resources are actually allocated along the vertical line $L_x^* R$. First, determine the resultant output combinations of $X$ and $Y$ as the economy moves along the vertical line $L_x^* R$. These output combinations are illustrated in fig. 21.5a by the broken curve $SP_1 T$ which necessarily lies inside the production-possibilities frontier except at point $P_1$ (which corresponds to point $E_1$ in fig. 21.5b). At $P_1$ the broken curve $SP_1 T$ is tangent to the production-possibilities frontier. This property follows easily from the geometrical properties of an envelope, since the production-possibilities frontier can be viewed as an envelope of an infinite family of curves, such as $SP_1 T$, which are obtained in a similar fashion as the curve $SP_1 T$ by varying the parameter $L_x^*$ from zero to the maximum amount of labor available to the economy.

Since the broken curve $SP_1 T$ is necessarily tangential to the production-possibilities frontier at $P_1$, the line $L_1 P_1$ (whose absolute slope indicates the fixed world price ratio) which by assumption intersects the production-possibilities frontier $UV$ at $P_1$ must also intersect the broken curve $SP_1 T$ at $P_1$, as shown in fig. 21.5a. Given all this information, it becomes apparent that the economy can maximize national welfare subject to the employment constraint ($L_x^*$ units of labor employed in industry $X$) by producing on the broken curve $SP_1 T$ at point $P_2$ where the absolute slope of $SP_1 T$ is equal to the fixed world price ratio. What economic policy brings this result about? The answer must be obvious from our earlier discussion of factor-price differentials: in the present case, *the optimal policy is either a direct subsidy to the use of labor in industry $X$ or a direct tax on the use of labor in industry $Y$.*

---

**Figure 21.5** Achievement of a certain level of employment of a factor of production ($L_x^*$). The employment constraint is satisfied when resources are allocated along the vertical line $L_x^* R$ (b) which gives rise to the output combinations illustrated by the broken curve $SP_1 T$ (a). The optimal policy is either a direct subsidy to the use of labor in industry $X$ or a direct tax on the use of labor in industry $Y$, so that the economy produces at $P_2$ and consumes at $C_3$ (a).

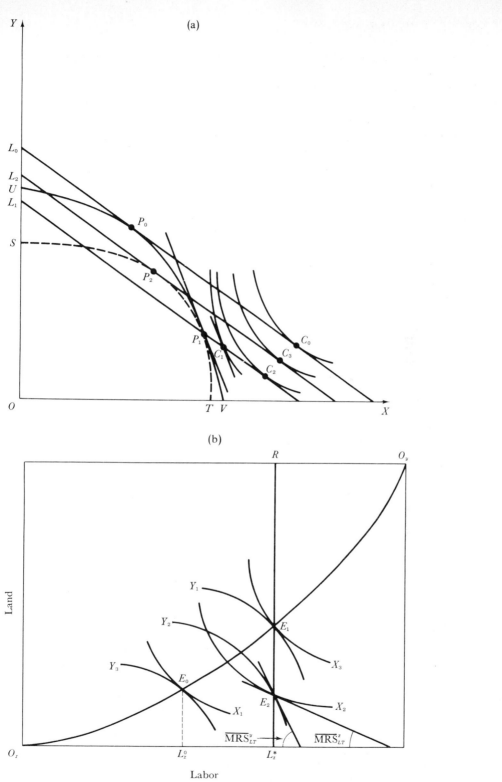

The preceding proposition, first noted by Bhagwati and Srinivasan (1969), is not difficult to prove. In the first place, the factor prices in industries $X$ and $Y$ must be different and, in particular, equal to the respective marginal rates of substitution of labor for land in industries $X$ and $Y$ at point $E_2$, say $\overline{\text{MRS}^x_{LT}}$ and $\overline{\text{MRS}^y_{LT}}$, as shown in fig. 21.5b. In addition, the domestic price ratio $p_d$ must be equal to both the fixed world price ratio $\bar{p}_f$ and the slope of the broken curve $SP_1 T$ at $P_2$.

The absolute slope of the curve $SP_1 T$ at any point is given by the ratio $\text{MPP}_{Ty}/\text{MPP}_{Tx}$. Thus, a marginal transfer of land (the allocation of labor between $X$ and $Y$ remains by assumption fixed) from $Y$ to $X$, say $dT$, causes the outputs of $X$ and $Y$ to change by $dX = \text{MPP}_{Tx}\, dT$ and $dY = -\text{MPP}_{Ty}\, dT$. Hence, the absolute slope of $SP_1 T \equiv -dY/dX = \text{MPP}_{Ty}/\text{MPP}_{Tx}$.

Accordingly, the conditions which the optimal policy must satisfy are

$$\frac{w_x}{r_x} = \overline{\text{MRS}^x_{LT}} \tag{21.1}$$

$$\frac{w_y}{r_y} = \overline{\text{MRS}^y_{LT}} \tag{21.2}$$

$$\bar{p} = p_d = \frac{\text{MPP}_{Ty}}{\text{MPP}_{Tx}} \tag{21.3}$$

Since by assumption $\overline{\text{MRS}^x_{LT}} < \overline{\text{MRS}^y_{LT}}$ (see fig. 21.5b), eqs. (21.1) and (21.2) can be satisfied when (a) $w_x < w_y$, $r_x = r_y$; or (b) $w_x = w_y$, $r_x > r_y$. The first alternative ($w_x < w_y$, $r_x = r_y$) requires either a subsidy to the use of labor in $X$ or a tax on the use of labor in $Y$. The second alternative ($w_x = w_y$, $r_x > r_y$) requires either a tax on the use of land in $X$ or a subsidy to the use of land in $Y$. In all, then, there are four different ways in which eqs. (21.1) and (21.2) can be satisfied. Of these, only the first two (i.e., a subsidy to the use of labor in $X$ or a tax on the use of labor in $Y$, which give rise to $w_x < w_y$, $r_x = r_y$) are also consistent with eq. (21.3), for perfect competition leads to

$$
\begin{aligned}
p_d &\equiv \frac{p_x}{p_y} \\[4pt]
&= \frac{r_x/\text{MPP}_{Tx}}{r_y/\text{MPP}_{Ty}} \\[4pt]
&= \frac{r_x}{r_y}\frac{\text{MPP}_{Ty}}{\text{MPP}_{Tx}}
\end{aligned}
\tag{21.4}
$$

Accordingly, the domestic price ratio $p_d$ becomes equal to the ratio $\text{MPP}_{Ty}/\text{MPP}_{Tx}$ only if $r_x = r_y$.

We therefore conclude that *when the employment of a factor must be increased in a certain industry for a noneconomic reason, the optimal policy is either to subsidize the use of that factor in that industry or to tax the use of that factor in the other industry.* The latter possibility (i.e., taxing the use of the factor in the industry in which its employment must be reduced), though implicit in the analysis provided by Bhagwati and Srinivasan (1969), is not explicitly stated by them.

## 21.8 AN IMPORTANT DUALITY THEOREM

The general rule for optimal intervention, which we studied earlier in chap. 20, states that policy intervention must take place at the exact point at which the underlying market imperfection occurs. By studying the four preceding cases which deal with the achievement of noneconomic objectives (e.g., certain levels of production, consumption, imports, or employment of a factor in an industry), it becomes apparent that the following dual theorem is correct. *When distortions must be introduced into the economy in order to achieve any of the noneconomic objectives just stated, the optimal (i.e., least-cost) policy is to intervene directly at the variable whose value is constrained.* For instance, when the production of a commodity is constrained, the optimal policy involves a production tax or subsidy, and so on. This important theorem was noticed by Bhagwati (1971).

## SELECTED BIBLIOGRAPHY

Bastable, C. F. (1903). *The Theory of International Trade*, 4th ed. Macmillan and Company, Ltd., London.
—— (1923). *The Commerce of Nations*, 9th ed., rev. Methuen and Company, Ltd., London.
Bator, F. M. (1958). "The Anatomy of Market Failure." *Quarterly Journal of Economics*, vol. 72 (August), pp. 351–379.
Batra, R. and P. K. Pattanaik (1970). "Domestic Distortions and the Gains from Trade." *Economic Journal*, vol. 80, no. 319 (September), pp. 638–649.
—— (1971a). "Factor Market Imperfections and Gains from Trade." *Oxford Economic Papers*, vol. 23, no. 2 (July), pp. 182–188.
——(1971b). "Factor Market Imperfections, the Terms of Trade and Welfare." *American Economic Review*, vol. 61, no. 5 (December), pp. 946–955.
Bhagwati, J. (1968). *The Theory and Practice of Commercial Policy*. Special Papers in International Economics no. 8, Princeton University, Princeton, N.J.
—— (1969). "Optimal Policies and Immiserizing Growth." *American Economic Review*, vol. 59, no. 5 (December), pp. 967–970.
—— (1971). "The Generalized Theory of Distortions and Welfare." In J. Bhagwati et al. (Eds.), *Trade, Balance of Payments, and Growth, Papers in International Economics in Honor of Charles P. Kindleberger*. North-Holland Publishing Company, Amsterdam.
—— and V. K. Ramaswami (1963). "Domestic Distortions, Tariffs, and the Theory of Optimum Subsidy." *Journal of Political Economy*, vol. LXXI, no. 1 (February), pp. 44–50. Reprinted in R. E. Caves and H. G. Johnson (Eds.), AEA *Readings in International Economics*. Richard D. Irwin, Inc., Homewood, Ill., 1968.
——, ——, and T. N. Srinivasan (1969). "Domestic Distortions, Tariffs and the Theory of Optimum Subsidy: Some Further Results." *Journal of Political Economy*, vol. 77, no. 6 (September), pp. 1005–1010.

—— and T. N. Srinivasan (1969). "Optimal Intervention to Achieve Non-Economic Objectives." *Review of Economic Studies*, vol. 36 (January), pp. 27–38.

——, —— (1971). "The Theory of Wage Differentials: Production Response and Factor Price Equalization." *Journal of International Economics*, vol. 1 (February), pp. 19–35.

——, —— (1974). "On Reanalyzing the Harris–Todaro Model: Policy Rankings in the Case of Sector-Specific Wages." *American Economic Review*, vol. LXIV, no. 3 (June), pp. 502–508.

Black, J. (1959). "Arguments for Tariffs." *Oxford Economic Papers* (N.S.), vol. 11, pp. 191–220.

Brecher, R. (1974a). "Minimum Wage Rates and the Pure Theory of International Trade." *Quarterly Journal of Economics* vol. 88(1) (February), pp. 98–116.

—— (1974b). "Optimal Commercial Policy for a Minimum-Wage Economy." *Journal of International Economics*, vol. 4, pp. 139–149.

Cairnes, J. E. (1874). *Some Leading Principles of Political Economy*. Macmillan and Company, Ltd., London.

Corden, W. M. (1957). "Tariffs, Subsidies and the Terms of Trade." *Economica* (N.S.), vol. 24 (August), pp. 235–242.

—— (1965). *Recent Developments in the Theory of International Trade*. Princeton University Special Papers in International Economics, no. 7, International Finance Section, Department of Economics, Princeton University, Princeton, N.J.

—— (1974). *Trade Policy and Economic Welfare*. Oxford University Press, London.

Eckaus, R. S. (1955). "The Factor-Proportions Problem in Underdeveloped Areas." *American Economic Review*, vol. 45 (September), pp. 539–565. Reprinted in A. N. Agarwala and S. P. Singh (Eds.), *The Economics of Underdevelopment*. Oxford University Press, London, 1958.

Fishlow, A., and P. A. David (1961). "Optimal Resource Allocation in an Imperfect Market Setting." *Journal of Political Economy*, vol. LXIX, no. 6 (December), pp. 529–546.

Haberler, G. (1936). *The Pure Theory of International Trade*. William Hodge and Company, London.

—— (1950). "Some Problems in the Pure Theory of International Trade." *Economic Journal*. vol. LX, no. 238 (June), pp. 223–240. Reprinted in R. E. Caves and H. G. Johnson (Eds.), AEA *Readings in International Economics*. Richard D. Irwin, Inc., Homewood, Ill., 1968.

—— (1961). *A Survey of International Trade Theory*. Princeton University Special Papers in International Economics, no. 1, International Finance Section, Department of Economics, Princeton University, Princeton, N.J.

Hagen, E. E. (1958). "An Economic Justification of Protectionism." *Quarterly Journal of Economics*, vol. 72 (November), pp. 496–514.

—— (1961). "Reply." *Quarterly Journal of Economics*, vol. 75 (February), pp. 145–151.

Harris, J., and M. Todaro (1970). "Migration, Unemployment and Development: A Two-Sector Analysis." *American Economic Review*, vol. LX, no. 1 (March), pp. 126–142.

Herberg, H., and M. C. Kemp (1971). "Factor Market Distortions, the Shape of the Locus of Competitive Outputs, and the Relation Between Product Prices and Equilibrium Outputs." In J. Bhagwati et al. (Eds.), *Trade, Balance of Payments and Growth, Papers in International Economics in Honor of Charles P. Kindleberger*. North-Holland Publishing Company, Amsterdam.

——, ——, and S. P. Magee (1971). "Factor Market Distortions, the Reversal of Relative Factor Intensities, and the Relation Between Product Prices and Equilibrium Outputs." *Economic Record*, vol. 47 (December), pp. 518–530.

Johnson, H. G. (1965). "Optimal Trade Intervention in the Presence of Domestic Distortions." In R. E. Baldwin et al. (Eds.), *Trade, Growth and the Balance of Payments*. Rand-McNally and Company, Chicago, Ill.

—— (1966). "Factor Market Distortions and the Shape of the Transformation Curve." *Econometrica*, vol. 34, no. 3 (July), pp. 686–698.

—— (1971). *The Two-Sector Model of General Equilibrium*. Aldine-Atherton, Inc., Chicago, Ill.

—— (1972). *Aspects of the Theory of Tariffs*. Harvard University Press, Cambridge, Mass.

—— (1973). *The Theory of Income Distribution*. Gray-Mills Publishing, Ltd., London.

—— and P. Mieszkowski (1970). "The Effects of Unionization on the Distribution of Income: A General Equilibrium Approach." *Quarterly Journal of Economics*, vol. 84 (November), pp. 539–561.

Jones, R. W. (1971). "Distortions in Factor Markets and the General Equilibrium Model of Production." *Journal of Political Economy*, vol. 79 (May–June), pp. 437–459.

Kafka, A. (1962). "An Economic Justification of Protectionism: Further Comments." *Quarterly Journal of Economics*, vol. 76 (February), pp. 163–166.

Kemp, M. C. (1960). "The Mill-Bastable Infant-Industry Dogma." *Journal of Political Economy*, vol. 68 (February), pp. 65–67.

———— and T. Nagishi (1969). "Domestic Distortions, Tariffs, and the Theory of Optimum Subsidy." *Journal of Political Economy*, vol. 77, no. 6 (November), pp. 1011–1013.

Koo, A. Y. C. (1961). "An Economic Justification of Protectionism: Comment." *Quarterly Journal of Economics*, vol. 75 (February), pp. 134–144.

Krauss, M. B., and H. G. Johnson (1974). *General Equilibrium Analysis.* Aldine Publishing Company, Chicago, Ill.

Lapan, H. E. (1976). "International Trade, Factor Market Distortions, and the Optimal Dynamic Subsidy." *American Economic Review*, vol. 66, no. 3 (June), pp. 335–346.

Lefeber, L. (1971). "Trade and Minimum Wage Rates." In J. Bhagwati, et al. (Eds.), *Trade, Balance of Payments and Growth, Papers in International Economics in Honor of Charles P. Kindleberger.* North-Holland Publishing Company, Amsterdam.

Lewis, W. A. (1954). "Economic Development with Unlimited Supplies of Labour." *Manchester School of Economic and Social Studies*, vol. 22 (May), pp. 139–191. Reprinted in A. N. Agarwala and S. P. Singh (Eds.), *The Economics of Underdevelopment.* Oxford University Press, London, 1958.

Magee, S. P. (1971). "Factor Market Distortions, Production, Distribution, and the Pure Theory of International Trade." *Quarterly Journal of Economics*, vol. 75 (November), pp. 623–643.

———— (1973). "Factor Market Distortions, Production, and Trade: A Survey." *Oxford Economic Papers* (N.S.), vol. 25 (March), pp. 1–43.

———— (1976). *International Trade and Distortions in Factor Markets.* Marcel Dekker, Inc., New York.

Manoilesco, M. (1931). *The Theory of Protection and International Trade.* P. S. King and Son, Ltd., London.

Meade, J. E. (1955). *The Theory of International Economic Policy*, vol. II: *Trade and Welfare.* Oxford University Press, London.

Meier, G. M. (1963). *International Trade and Development.* Harper and Row, Publishers, New York.

———— (1968). *The International Economics of Development.* Harper and Row, Publishers, New York.

Melvin, J. (1970). "Commodity Taxation as a Determinant of Trade." *Canadian Journal of Economics*, vol. 3, no. 1 (February), pp. 62–78.

Mill, J. St. (1904). *Principles of Political Economy*, vol. II. J. A. Hill and Company, New York. (The first edition of *Principles* appeared in 1848.)

Myint, H. (1963). "Infant Industry Arguments for Assistance to Industries in the Setting of Dynamic Trade Theory." In R. Harrod (Ed.), *International Trade Theory in a Developing World.* St. Martin's Press, Inc., New York.

Myrdal, G. (1956). *An International Economy.* Harper and Row, Publishers, New York.

Ohlin, B. (1931). "Protection and Non-Competing Groups." *Weltwirtschaftliches Archiv.*, vol. 33 (Heft 1), pp. 30–45.

———— (1933). *Interregional and International Trade.* Harvard University Press, Cambridge, Mass.

Prebish, R. (1959). "Commercial Policy in Underdeveloped Countries." *American Economic Review, Proceedings*, vol. 49 (May), pp. 251–273.

Ramaswami, V. K., and T. N. Srinivasan (1968). "Optimal Subsidies and Taxes When Some Factors Are Traded." *Journal of Political Economy*, vol. 76, no. 4 (July–August), pp. 569–582.

Ramsey, F. (1928). "A Mathematical Theory of Saving." *Economic Journal*, vol. 38, no. 152 (December), pp. 543–559. Reprinted in J. E. Stiglitz and H. Uzawa (Eds.), *Readings in the Modern Theory of Economic Growth.* The MIT Press, Cambridge, Mass.

Viner, J. (1932). "The Theory of Protection and International Trade: A Review." *Journal of Political Economy*, vol. 40 (February), pp. 121–125.

———— (1965). *Studies in the Theory of International Trade.* Augustus M. Kelly, Publishers, New York.

# TWENTY-TWO

## THE THEORY OF CUSTOMS UNIONS: I. THE PARTIAL EQUILIBRIUM APPROACH

This and the following chapter discuss the *theory of customs unions*. In particular, after a brief general introduction to the theory of customs unions and the *theory of the second best*, the present chapter deals with the *partial equilibrium approach* and the following chapter with the *general equilibrium approach* to preferential trading. To be sure, the present chapter touches upon the general equilibrium approach in sec. 22.5 on trade-diverting customs unions and welfare improvement. Nevertheless, a systematic treatment of the general equilibrium approach is postponed until the following chapter.

## 22.1 INTRODUCTION

The standard theory of tariffs surveyed in chaps. 17 to 19 rests on the simplifying assumption that import duties are imposed in a nondiscriminatory fashion, i.e., a uniform ad valorem tariff rate is levied on *all* imports irrespective of the commodity imported or the country of origin. In practice, however, discrimination does occur. Such discrimination takes either one of two forms: (*a*) *commodity discrimination* or (*b*) *country* (or *geographical*) *discrimination*. Commodity discrimination occurs when different ad valorem import duties are levied on different commodities (for example, 20 percent on oil but 50 percent on cameras). On the other hand, country discrimination occurs when different ad valorem import duties are levied on the same commodity imported from different countries (for example, 10 percent on cameras imported from Germany but 60 percent on cameras imported from Japan).

The theory of customs unions is a relatively new branch of the theory of tariffs and deals primarily with the effects of geographical discrimination. In particular, the theory of customs unions deals primarily with the effects of preferential trading. Often a group of countries may decide to form a preferential trading arrangement (e.g., preferential trading club, free-trade association, customs union—all these terms are explained below). This means that all member countries agree to lower their respective tariff rates on imports from each other but not on imports from the rest of the world. Such reciprocal tariff reductions necessarily discriminate against union imports from the rest of the world. How is trade between the union members affected? How is trade between the union members and the rest of the world affected? How is the welfare of the member countries, individually and as a group, as well as the welfare of the rest of the world, affected by this geographical discrimination?

The pioneer in the theory of customs unions is Jacob Viner (1950). He put forth the major proposition that a customs union (or any other form of preferential trading) combines elements of freer trade with elements of greater protection, and argued convincingly that it is not clear that such an arrangement increases (potential) welfare. In particular, Viner argued that a customs union (or any other form of preferential trading) tends, on the one hand, to increase competition and trade among the union member countries (movement toward freer trade) and, on the other hand, tends to provide relatively more protection against trade and competition from the rest of the world (movement toward greater protection).

Viner also explained that the paradox why free traders and protectionists may occasionally agree in the field of customs unions is the result of the strange coexistence of elements of freer trade with elements of greater protection. In their calculations, the free traders tend to exaggerate the elements of freer trade while the protectionists tend to exaggerate the elements of greater protection.

The theory of customs unions is *not* concerned with the Pareto-optimum conditions, i.e., the conditions which lead to maximum welfare. The formation of a customs union necessarily violates the Pareto-optimum conditions because of the existence of tariffs. In fact, the Pareto-optimum conditions are also violated even before the formation of the customs union—tariffs exist before the customs union is formed. Accordingly, the theory of customs unions deals with nonoptimal situations, and therefore is a particular case of the theory of the second best. (The main propositions of the theory of the second best are reviewed briefly in the following section.)

The theory of the second best warns us that no general conditions can be specified under which the formation of a preferential trading arrangement leads always to an increase (or a decrease for that matter) in welfare. This makes the theory of customs unions relatively more difficult than other branches of economic theory. Every case must be analyzed on its own merits—the approach must be taxonomic. Such a taxonomic approach is, of course, very cumbersome, and also cannot be exhaustive. Our object, then, is to provide the necessary analytical framework within which any particular situation may be studied.

Following Viner's (1950) pioneering work, contributions to the theory of customs unions were made by Cooper and Massell (1965), Johnson (1962), Kemp

(1969), Lipsey (1957a, 1960, 1970), Meade (1955a), Vanek (1965), and many others (see the Selected Bibliography at the end of this chapter). A useful survey of recent developments in customs union theory is provided by Krauss (1972), which with Lipsey's (1960) survey offers a comprehensive coverage of the field.


## 22.2 THE THEORY OF THE SECOND BEST

The theory of the second best deals with suboptimal situations, i.e., situations in which not all Pareto-optimum conditions are satisfied. The beginnings of this theory can be traced back to Viner's (1950) path-breaking book. Nevertheless, the theory of the second best was fully developed a few years later by Meade (1955b). Shortly after Meade's (1955b) contribution, Lipsey and Lancaster (1956) restated and generalized the theory.

What is the theory of the second best? Its main theorem is simple. Consider an economy which is prevented from fulfilling one Paretian condition. Then the other Paretian conditions, although still attainable, are in general no longer desirable. That is, when one Paretian condition cannot be fulfilled and thus maximum welfare cannot be reached, maximization of *attainable* welfare requires in general the violation of the other Paretian conditions.

From the above general theorem of second best follows a very important corollary. Consider an economy in a suboptimal situation in which several Paretian conditions are violated (because, say, of the existence of taxes). Suppose now that one or more, but not all, of the previously violated conditions were to be fulfilled (because, say, some of the initial taxes are now removed). Would welfare increase? One might be tempted to answer "Yes," since such a change seems to bring the economy closer to Pareto optimality—more Pareto-optimum conditions are satisfied after than before the removal of some taxes. Yet the theory of the second best teaches us that such a conclusion is simply wrong. The precise effect on welfare depends on circumstances. When two suboptimal situations are compared, there are no general rules in judging which is better than the other.

Meade (1955b, p. 7) offers an illuminating analogy. He imagines a person who wishes to climb to the highest point on a range of hills. Not every step upward helps the person reach the highest summit though. Walking uphill, the person can reach only the summit of the particular hill he happens to be on—not the summit of the highest hill. Thus, while it may be possible to tell that an infinitesimal change in a tariff actually increases welfare (i.e., a small step upward brings the person higher on the particular hill he happens to be on), there is no way of predicting that the elimination of tariffs on trade between the customs union members will actually increase welfare (i.e., there is no way of predicting in a dense fog and without elaborate instruments that when the person switches to another hill that he will actually be higher).

As noted in the preceding section, the theory of the second best is directly applicable to the theory of customs unions since the latter theory by definition deals with suboptimal situations.

## 22.3 PREFERENTIAL TRADING ARRANGEMENTS: DEFINITIONS

Preferential trading arrangements may assume several forms. The purpose of this section is to review briefly the most important forms and acquaint the reader with several terms which have come into fairly standard usage.

**Preferential trading club** Two or more countries form a preferential trading club when they reduce their respective import duties on imports of all goods (except the services of capital) from each other, i.e., when they exchange small tariff preferences. The member countries retain their original tariffs against the outside world. A good example of a preferential trading club is the Commonwealth preference system.

When a group of countries exchange tariff preferences, a policing problem arises. In particular, consider three countries: $A$ (home country), $B$ (partner country), and $C$ (the rest of the world). Suppose that before the formation of the preferential trading club country $A$ imports commodity $X$ from both $B$ and $C$. Assume further that country $A$ levies a duty of, say, 55 percent on all imports of $X$. Countries $B$ and $C$, on the other hand, are net exporters of $X$ and do not levy any import duty on it. After the formation of the preferential trading club, country $A$ lowers its import duty to, say, 50 percent on imports of $X$ from $B$ but not from $C$. For the exchange of preferences to become effective $C$ must be prevented from exporting $X$ to $A$ through $B$. Otherwise, $C$'s exports to $A$ would be treated by $A$ in the same way as $B$'s exports to $A$, since commodity $X$ can enter country $B$ freely. To correct this problem country $A$ must be able to distinguish effectively (perhaps through a detailed examination of the certificates of origin) between goods originating in $B$ and goods originating in $C$.

**Free-trade area (or association)** Two or more countries form a free-trade area, or a free-trade association, when they abolish all import duties (and all quantitative restrictions) on their mutual trade in all goods (except the services of capital) but retain their original tariffs against the rest of the world. An example of a free-trade area is the European Free Trade Area (EFTA) which consists of the "Outer Seven:" Austria, Denmark, Norway, Portugal, Sweden, Switzerland, and the United Kingdom.

The policing problem referred to earlier in relation to the formation of preferential trading clubs exists here too. Actually the problem may be more acute for a free-trade area since by definition the tariff reductions are much greater and the incentive to beat the system stronger.

**Customs union** Two or more countries form a customs union when they abolish all import duties on their mutual trade in all goods (except the services of capital) and, in addition, they adopt a common external tariff schedule on all imports of goods (except the services of capital) from the rest of the world. The adoption of a common external tariff schedule eliminates the policing problem of intra-union trade of commodities originating in the rest of the world.

**Common market** Two or more countries form a common market if they form a customs union and, in addition, allow free movement of all factors of production between the member countries. An example of a common market is the European Economic Community (EEC) which is composed of Belgium, Denmark, France, Germany, Ireland, Italy, Luxembourg, Netherlands, and the United Kingdom. The EEC (also known as the Common Market) already has a customs union and is working toward the implementation of the concept of common market.

**Economic union** Two or more countries form an economic union when they form a common market and, in addition, proceed to unify their fiscal, monetary, and socioeconomic policies. An example of an economic union is the Benelux which was the economic union formed by Belgium, the Netherlands, and Luxembourg (the term *Benelux* is made up of the first letters in each country's name). In fact, Belgium, the Netherlands, and Luxembourg formed a customs union in 1948 which was converted into an economic union in 1960 after the 1958 Benelux Treaty. The European Economic Community plans to go most of the distance to economic union also.

The preceding preferential trading arrangements, i.e. preferential trading club, free-trade area, customs union, common market, and economic union, represent various degrees of economic integration. They start from the lowest degree of economic integration (i.e., preferential trading club) and go through progressively higher degrees until the most complete concept of economic integration (i.e., economic union).

The theory of customs unions does not deal solely with the economic effects of customs unions narrowly defined. It deals also with the economic effects of free-trade areas, common markets, preferential trading clubs, and even economic unions. In short, the theory of customs unions deals with the economic effects of discriminatory systems in general.

## 22.4 TRADE CREATION AND TRADE DIVERSION

Trade creation and trade diversion were Viner's main tools of analysis. Viner himself concentrated on the *production effects* of preferential trading only. It soon became apparent, though, through the works of Lipsey (1957, 1960, 1970), Meade (1955a), and others that the *consumption effects* are also important. Presently, we follow tradition by discussing the production effects first and then extending the analysis to encompass the consumption effects as well.

### (a) Production Effects

Viner (1950) examined the effects of customs unions on the international allocation of resources. Contrary to the general belief which was prevalent in earlier, largely oral discussions (namely, that the formation of a customs union is a step toward free trade and tends to increase welfare), Viner showed that the formation of a customs union could either improve or worsen resource allocation and welfare. Viner proved his proposition by demonstrating that the formation of a customs union could lead either to *trade creation* or *trade diversion*. What did Viner exactly mean by trade creation and trade diversion?

The meaning of the terms " trade creation " and " trade diversion " is relatively simple. The formation of a customs union normally shifts the national locus of production of some commodities. Credit creation refers to the case where the shift in production is from a higher-cost source to a lower-cost source abstracting from duty elements in money costs. Such a shift tends to create trade and is a step toward the free-trade position. This is a shift which the free trader properly approves. On the other hand, trade diversion refers to the case where the shift in production is from a lower-cost source to a higher-cost source, again, abstracting from duty elements in money costs. In this case, the shift diverts trade from the free-trade position. This is a shift of the type which the protectionist approves.

In particular, the formation of a customs union will cause some products which were formerly produced domestically to be imported from other partner countries—the tariffs on such imports are eliminated. Here the shift in production is from a higher-cost domestic producer to a lower-cost producer in a partner country—trade creation. But, in addition, the formation of a customs union will cause some products which were formerly imported from the rest of the world to be imported from a partner country—thanks to the newly formed geographical tariff discrimination. Here the shift in production is from a lower-cost producer in the rest of the world to a higher-cost producer in a partner country—trade diversion.

Broadly speaking, trade creation is good and tends to increase welfare, while trade diversion is bad and tends to decrease welfare. The fundamental notion behind these statements is, of course, that ordinarily trade transfers goods from a low-cost region to a high-cost region. Thus trade increases welfare by reducing costs or, alternatively, by increasing world income. It is in this sense that trade creation is conceived to be beneficial, and trade diversion detrimental, to welfare.

It may be objected that the preceding view of trade creation and trade diversion is an oversimplification of a rather complex phenomenon. In fact, as we shall see later in this chapter, a number of distinguished scholars, most notably Bhagwati (1971), Gehrels (1956), Lipsey (1957a, 1960, 1970), Meade (1955a), and Melvin (1969), questioned seriously the detrimental character of trade diversion. (Their dispute is considered later in sec. 22.5.) It appears that when the simple world of Viner is abandoned for a more comprehensive general equilibrium approach, the concepts of trade creation and trade diversion tend to become obsolete. For instance, Kemp (1969) continues to use the terms trade creation and trade diversion but is careful to warn the reader that the sense in which he is using these terms is very different from Viner's (see Kemp, 1969, p. 36, fn. 4). Nevertheless, Viner's concepts of trade creation and trade diversion still remain the fundamental economic phenomena associated with customs unions, and we must become thoroughly acquainted with them.

**A numerical illustration** The concepts of trade creation and trade diversion are best illustrated by a numerical example. Consider again three countries: $A$ (home country), $B$ (partner country), and $C$ (rest of the world). Suppose that each country produces commodity $X$ at constant average cost as shown in table 22.1.

**Table 22.1  Trade creation**

**Average cost of production of commodity $X$ in countries $A$, $B$, and $C$; and $A$'s cost of importing $X$ from $B$ and $C$**

| Country | Average cost of production, $ (1) | $A$ imposes a uniform 100 percent import duty, $ (2) | $A$ removes the duty on imports from $B$ but not from $C$, $ (3) |
|---|---|---|---|
| $A$ | 50 | 50 | 50 |
| $B$ | 40 | 80 | 40 |
| $C$ | 30 | 60 | 60 |

Under free-trade conditions, country $C$ would export commodity $X$ to both $A$ and $B$ ($30 < $40, $30 < $50). Suppose, however, that country $A$ imposes a 100 percent uniform ad valorem tariff on all imports. While the cost of production of $X$ in $A$ remains at $50, the cost (inclusive of the tariff) of importing $X$ from $B$ and $C$ increases to $80 and $60, respectively, as shown in the second column of table 22.1. Since $50 < $80 and $50 < $60, country $A$ will produce commodity $X$ domestically.

Let now countries $A$ and $B$ form a customs union and eliminate all import duties on imports from each other (but not on imports from $C$). The relevant costs to $A$ are now shown in column (3) of table 22.1. Thus, $A$'s domestic cost of importing $X$ from $B$ falls to $40 (since country $A$ eliminates now the tariff on imports from $B$) and the cost of importing $X$ from $C$ (inclusive of the tariff) remains at $60. Obviously, after the formation of the customs union, country $A$ ceases to produce $X$ and imports it from country $B$ (the other union member). This is an example of trade creation. That is, before the formation of the customs union, $A$ produces domestically $X$ at $50. After the formation of the customs union, $A$ stops production of $X$ and imports it from $B$. Since $B$'s cost of production is lower than $A$'s ($40 < $50), such a shift in the national locus of production represents trade creation and improves the allocation of resources.

Table 22.2 gives an example of trade diversion. The cost of production of $X$ in the three countries is exactly the same as in table 22.1. The only difference now from the preceding illustration is that $A$'s initial import duty is only 50 percent. Accordingly, before the formation of the customs union, country $A$ imports $X$ from $C$ since $45 < $50 < $60 (see column (2)). However, after the formation of the union (see column (3)), $A$ imports $X$ from $B$ since $40 < $45 < $50. The shift in production is now from the low-cost producer, $C$ ($30), to the high-cost producer, $B$($40). This shift in production represents trade diversion and is detrimental to resource allocation and welfare according to Viner.

**Table 22.2 Trade diversion**

**Average cost of production of commodity $X$ in countries $A$, $B$, and $C$; and $A$'s cost of importing $X$ from $B$ and $C$**

| Country | Average cost of production, $ (1) | $A$ imposes a uniform 50 percent import duty, $ (2) | $A$ removes the duty on imports from $B$ but not from $C$, $ (3) |
|---|---|---|---|
| $A$ | 50 | 50 | 50 |
| $B$ | 40 | 60 | 40 |
| $C$ | 30 | 45 | 45 |

In the preceding illustration of trade diversion, higher protection is necessarily offered to $B$'s high-cost producers. This is done not in the customary fashion of a reduction in $B$'s imports of $X$ but rather through price discrimination in $A$ in $B$'s favor. This type of protection offered to $B$'s producers enables them to extend their sales to $A$ by replacing, unfortunately, a more efficient producer $(C)$.

## (b) Consumption Effects

Viner's path-breaking analysis of customs unions, as presented above, dealt with the production effects only. It ignored the consumption effects. This was emphasized especially by Gehrels (1956), Lipsey (1957a, 1960, 1970) and Meade (1955a). In this section, we shall follow Johnson's (1962) paper and bring together both the production and the consumption effects of customs unions.

Consider again the example of trade creation and trade diversion of tables 22.1 and 22.2. In both cases, after country $A$ removes its tariff on imports from $B$ (but not from $C$), the price paid by $A$'s consumers falls, and unless $A$'s demand is perfectly inelastic, $A$'s consumption of $X$ will tend to increase. This increase in consumption (consumption effect) is the element (effect) overlooked by Viner. This new effect must be taken into consideration since it *tends to expand trade—* $A$'s total imports of $X$ tend to expand.

## Trade Creation

The production and consumption effects are illustrated in fig. 22.1. $A$'s demand and domestic supply schedules for commodity $X$ are given, respectively, by $DD'$ and $SS'$. While $A$'s domestic supply curve is upward sloping, for simplicity we assume that $B$'s (that is, the partner's) supply curve is infinitely elastic,† as shown by the horizontal line $PP'$. Adding $A$'s tariff to $B$'s supply schedule, we obtain the horizontal schedule $TT'$. Thus, before the formation of the customs union (and

---

† When the partner and foreign supply schedules are also upward sloping the geometry becomes rather involved. The interested reader is referred to Johnson (1962).

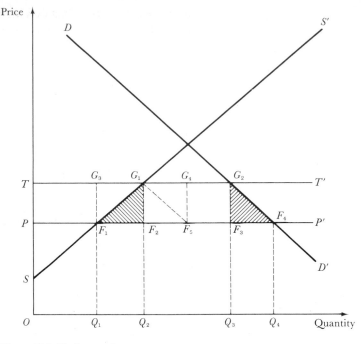

**Figure 22.1** Trade creation.

assuming that $C$'s average cost of production is higher than $OP$), country $A$ consumes $OQ_3$ with $OQ_2$ produced by $A$'s domestic producers and $Q_2 Q_3$ imported from $B$. $A$'s tariff revenue is given by the area of the rectangle $G_1 F_2 F_3 G_2$.

What happens after the formation of the customs union and the elimination of $A$'s tariff? $A$'s consumption increases to $OQ_4$, $A$'s domestic production falls to $OQ_1$, $A$'s imports increase to $Q_1 Q_4$, and $A$'s tariff revenue disappears.

$A$'s consumers benefit from the elimination of $A$'s tariff. By how much? By the area $P F_4 G_2 T$. But not all of this is net gain to country $A$. For one thing, the area $P F_1 G_1 T$ is a producer's surplus enjoyed by $A$'s producers before the elimination of $A$'s tariff and now lost (to $A$'s consumers). For another, the area of the rectangle $F_2 F_3 G_2 G_1$ represents the tariff revenue collected by government before the formation of the customs union. This tariff revenue is now lost, also. Accordingly, the net gain to country $A$ is represented by the areas of the two shaded triangles $F_1 F_2 G_1$ and $F_3 F_4 G_2$.

The shaded triangle $F_1 F_2 G_1$ represents $A$'s saving of real cost on domestic production replaced by imports, and illustrates Viner's production effect of a customs union leading to trade creation. The amount $Q_1 Q_2$ was formerly produced domestically at a total cost given by the area $Q_1 Q_2 G_1 F_1$. This same amount $(Q_1 Q_2)$ is now imported from a lower-cost country at a total cost given by the area $Q_1 Q_2 F_2 F_1$. Obviously there is a net gain of $F_1 F_2 G_1$.

Similarly, the shaded triangle $F_3 F_4 G_2$ represents a net gain in consumers' surplus. It is this consumption effect which Viner ignored. Meade (1955a) classifies this gain as something different from the production gain and in fact states that this gain is due to *trade expansion* (because it represents a net increase in $A$'s consumption that is satisfied from imports and is not just a mere replacement in domestic consumption of goods formerly produced in $A$ as is the production gain). Johnson (1962) adds the two triangles together to obtain the total gain from trade creation.

The total gain from trade creation as represented in fig. 22.1 by the sum of the areas of the two shaded triangles $F_1 F_2 G_1$ and $F_3 F_4 G_2$ depends on three parameters: ($a$) $A$'s initial tariff (i.e., the distance $PT$); ($b$) $A$'s supply elasticity at the pre-union production point $G_1$; and ($c$) $A$'s demand elasticity at the pre-union consumption point $G_2$. In general, the higher the initial level of $A$'s tariff and the more elastic $A$'s domestic supply and demand curves are, the larger the gain from trade creation is.

Draw the broken line $G_1 F_5$ parallel to $G_2 F_4$ (fig. 22.1). Then the sum of the two shaded triangles is equal to the area of the triangle $F_1 F_5 G_1$ which is roughly half the area of the rectangle $F_1 F_5 G_4 G_3$ (that is, the increase in imports times the tariff). This provides a convenient formula for empirical measurement of the trade-creation gains from the customs union. Actually, empirical estimates of this figure run extremely low—one or two percent of the gross national product of the participating countries, sometimes even less.[†] To understand why, assume that a country whose imports ($M$) are 30 percent of her gross national product ($I$) imposes initially a 40 percent tariff ($t$) on imports. Assume, further, that the foreign price of imports is $p_m$ and as the tariff is eliminated imports increase by 50 percent. The total gain given by the earlier formula becomes: $(tp_m \Delta M)/2 = (0.4 \times 0.5 M p_m)/2 = (0.4 \times 0.5 \times 0.3I)/2 = 0.03I$. Thus, even with such an optimistic example, the total gain amounts to only three percent of gross national product.

## Trade Diversion

Turn now to the case of trade diversion. In this case, country $A$ is importing commodity $X$ from the relatively more efficient country $C$ before the formation of the customs union. However, after the formation of the union, $A$ imports $X$ from its partner, country $B$, which, though less efficient than $C$, can sell $X$ to $A$'s consumers cheaper than $C$ since $A$'s tariff schedule discriminates against $C$.

The case of trade diversion is illustrated in fig. 22.2. The lines $DD'$ and $SS'$ are, as before, $A$'s domestic demand and supply schedules. $B$'s and $C$'s infinitely elastic supply curves (before the addition of $A$'s tariff) are given respectively by the horizontal lines $BB'$ and $CC'$. By assumption, $C$'s average cost of production ($OC$) is lower than $B$'s ($OB$). Adding $A$'s tariff to $C$'s supply curve we obtain the schedule $TT'$. ($B$'s schedule including the tariff is not needed. Why?) Before the formation

---

[†] For instance, Johnson (1958) estimates that the welfare gains to Britain expected from freer trade with other European countries are probably in the order of 225 million pounds in 1970—about one percent of the gross national product. See also Balassa (1967, 1974), Sellekaerts (1973), and Verdoorn (1956).

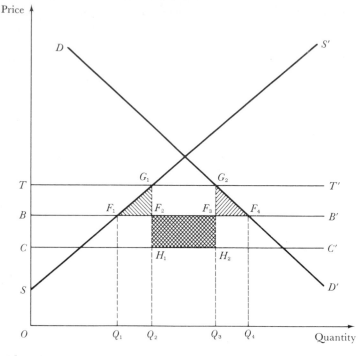

**Figure 22.2** Trade diversion.

of the customs union, $A$ consumes $OQ_3$, of which $OQ_2$ is produced domestically by $A$'s producers and $Q_2 Q_3$ is imported from $C$. $A$'s tariff revenue is given by the area $G_1 H_1 H_2 G_2$.

After the formation of the customs union and the elimination of $A$'s tariff, $A$'s consumption increases to $OQ_4$, $A$'s domestic production decreases to $OQ_1$, $A$'s imports increase to $Q_1 Q_4$ (that is, $A$'s imports increase by the decrease in domestic production $Q_1 Q_2$ plus the increase in domestic consumption $Q_3 Q_4$), and $A$'s tariff revenue vanishes. The consumers' surplus increases again by the area $TBF_4 G_2$. On the other hand, the producers' surplus is reduced by $TBF_1 G_1$ and the tariff revenue by $G_1 H_1 H_2 G_2$. Actually, it is more convenient to divide the tariff revenue loss into two parts: $G_1 F_2 F_3 G_2 + F_2 H_1 H_2 F_3$. Subtracting the areas $TBF_1 G_1$ (loss of producers' surplus) and $G_1 F_2 F_3 G_2$ (first part of tariff revenue loss) from the area $TBF_4 G_2$ (gain of consumers' surplus), we are left with the two shaded triangles $F_1 F_2 G_1$ and $F_3 F_4 G_2$. The sum of these two triangles must now be compared with the second part of the tariff revenue loss, i.e., the shaded area $F_2 H_1 H_2 F_3$. If $F_1 F_2 G_1 + F_3 F_4 G_2 > F_2 H_1 H_2 F_3$, then a net social gain results. On the other hand, if $F_1 F_2 G_1 + F_3 F_4 G_2 < F_2 H_1 H_2 F_3$, a social loss results.

What is the meaning of the triangles $F_1 F_2 G_1$ and $F_3 F_4 G_2$, and the rectangle $F_2 H_1 H_2 F_3$? Well, the rectangle $F_2 H_1 H_2 F_3$ represents the net loss from diverting the *initial* amount of imports $(Q_2 Q_3)$ from a lower-cost source (country $C$) to a higher-cost source (country $B$). This is primarily the detrimental effect of trade diversion referred to by Viner. But as we have just seen, this is not the only effect.

There are another two beneficial effects represented by the triangles $F_1 F_2 G_1$ and $F_3 F_4 G_2$. The former triangle $F_1 F_2 G_1$ represents a production gain, while the latter triangle $F_3 F_4 G_2$ represents a consumption gain.

Implicit in the preceding analysis is the notion that trade diversion need not have a net detrimental effect to welfare as Viner originally thought. This point is pursued further in the following section.

## Some Limitations

The preceding analysis concentrated on the effects of a customs union on a single commodity. But the formation of a customs union will in general affect many commodities. When more than one commodity is admitted various secondary repercussions must also be admitted into the analysis. Thus, various degrees of complementarity and substitutability will exist on the demand side. On the supply side, costs need not be constant.

Further, the preceding analysis assumes implicitly that the increase in imports (following the formation of a customs union) is matched by a corresponding increase in exports at the given terms of trade so that trade remains balanced. This need not be the case, however. In general, the terms of trade will have to change also to reestablish the balance between exports and imports.

These limitations of the partial equilibrium approach to the theory of customs unions point to the need for a general equilibrium analysis. This is actually done in the next chapter.

## 22.5 TRADE-DIVERTING CUSTOMS UNIONS AND WELFARE IMPROVEMENT†

Attempts have been made by several distinguished scholars to show that a trade-diverting customs union may increase welfare. As was natural, these attempts were followed by other attempts to reconcile this apparently paradoxical result with Viner's initial proposition that trade diversion is " bad." The purpose of this section is to review this dispute and offer a reconciliation. The discussion in this section is cast in terms of a simplified general equilibrium model that foreshadows the discussion of the next chapter.

### The Lipsey–Gehrels Argument

Lipsey (1957a, 1960) and Gehrels (1956) advanced the proposition that trade diversion is not necessarily a " bad thing " as Viner had thought. On the contrary, they argued, trade diversion may actually *increase* welfare. This paradox, they explained, is due to Viner's neglect of the consumption effect—a point which was already implicit in Meade's (1955a) analysis.

---

† This section may be skipped on a first reading until the reader becomes familiar with the general equilibrium approach of the next chapter.

*A*'s imports of *Y*

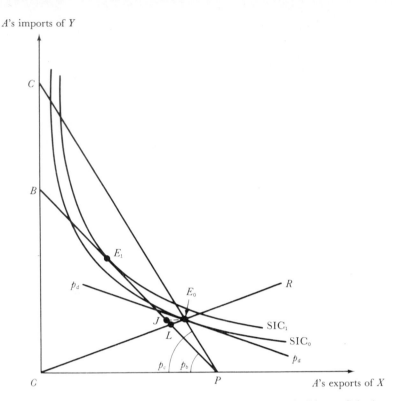

**Figure 22.3** Trade-diverting union and welfare improvement: the Lipsey–Gehrels argument.

The Lipsey–Gehrels argument is illustrated in fig. 22.3. Consider again a model of three countries: *A* (home country), *B* (partner country), and *C* (rest of the world). Countries *B* and *C* are "large" and produce two commodities, *X* and *Y*, at constant marginal rates of transformation given by the absolute slopes of the straight lines *BP* and *CP*, respectively. Country *A* is "small" and specializes completely in the production of *X*. In particular, *A*'s total production of *X* is given by the horizontal distance *OP*. Further, countries *B* and *C* levy prohibitive tariffs on each other's products and do not trade with each other.

Before a customs union is formed between countries *A* and *B*, country *A* levies a nondiscriminatory tariff on all imports of *Y* and redistributes all tariff revenue to *A*'s consumers. As a result *A* reaches equilibrium at $E_0$. Thus, *A* trades with *C* only—imports from *C* are cheaper than imports from *B* by assumption. *A*'s equilibrium must occur on *A*'s consumption-possibilities frontier (*CP*) at a point, such as $E_0$, where the marginal rate of substitution in consumption equals *A*'s (tariff-inclusive) domestic price ratio given by the absolute slope of the line $p_d p_d$. *A*'s pre-union trade with *C* is indicated by the vector $PE_0$ and *A*'s welfare by the social indifference curve $SIC_0$ passing through $E_0$.

After the customs union is formed between *A* and *B*, *A*'s tariff on imports from *B* is eliminated and *A*'s imports shift to *B* at *B*'s price ratio $(p_b)$. Thus, *A*'s equilibrium shifts to $E_1$ which lies on a higher social indifference curve than $E_0$. Hence, $A$'s welfare improves.

The above result is a necessary outcome as long as the line $BP$ intersects the social indifference curve $SIC_0$ as shown in fig. 22.3. If $BP$ lies below $SIC_0$, then obviously $A$ becomes worse off.

Lipsey (1957a, pp. 43–44) explains why $A$'s welfare may actually increase by distinguishing between two effects as follows. First, $A$'s imports become more expensive—the line $BP$ is flatter than the line $CP$, implying that a larger amount of $X$ must be exported after the formation of the union to obtain any given amount of imports of $Y$. Second, the divergence between $A$'s domestic price ratio and barter terms of trade is eliminated after the union is formed. Therefore, $A$'s consumers are able to adjust their purchases to the point where their marginal rate of substitution equals the barter terms of trade—the rate at which $X$ can be transformed into $Y$ through international trade. The former effect is unfavorable (shift of production from a lower- to a higher-cost source) while the latter (consumption effect) is favorable. The final outcome depends on which of these two effects is stronger.

The preceding interpretation is analogous to the earlier comparison between the rectangle $F_2 H_1 H_2 F_3$ and the triangles $F_1 F_2 G_1$ and $F_3 F_4 G_2$ (fig. 22.2), although in the present case the triangle $F_1 F_2 G_1$ is by assumption zero—$A$ does not produce commodity $Y$ at all.

### The Melvin–Bhagwati Argument

The Lipsey–Gehrels argument has been generalized to increasing opportunity costs by Melvin (1969) and Bhagwati (1971). Their graphical illustration is pretty much the same as the Lipsey–Gehrels illustration (fig. 22.3) except that $A$'s production-possibilities frontier is curvilinear and exhibits increasing opportunity costs. For variety, we recast the argument in terms of offer curves and trade indifference curves.

Consider fig. 22.4. $A$'s free-trade offer curve is given by $OO_A$. $C$'s offer curve is given by the vector $OO_C$ and $A$'s (tariff-inclusive) domestic price ratio corresponding to $C$'s prices is given by $OO'_C$. Finally, two alternative offer curves for country $B$ are illustrated by the broken vectors $OO_B^1$ and $OO_B^2$. Before the formation of the customs union between $A$ and $B$, $A$ reaches equilibrium at $E_0$. The broken line $F_0 E_0$ is $A$'s income-consumption curve, as explained earlier in chap. 17.

After the customs union with $B$ is formed, $A$'s tariff on imports from $B$ is eliminated and $A$ reaches equilibrium at the point where $A$'s and $B$'s offer curves intersect. If $B$'s offer curve intersects $A$'s offer curve above and to the left of point $K$ (that is, the intersection between $A$'s offer curve and $A$'s trade indifference curve through the pre-union equilibrium point $E_0$), as illustrated by the broken vector $OO_B^1$, $A$ evidently becomes better off. If $B$'s offer curve intersects $A$'s offer curve somewhere between $F_0$ and $K$, as illustrated by the broken vector $OO_B^2$, $A$ becomes worse off. In general, then, it appears that a trade-diverting customs union may increase welfare.

The Melvin–Bhagwati argument is again analogous to our earlier comparison between the rectangle $F_2 H_1 H_2 F_3$ and the triangles $F_1 F_2 G_1$ and $F_3 F_4 G_2$

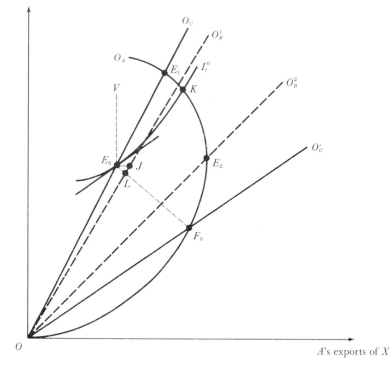

**Figure 22.4** Trade-diverting union and welfare improvement: the Melvin–Bhagwati argument.

(fig. 22.2). In contrast to the Lipsey–Gehrels case, though, Melvin and Bhagwati allow the triangle $F_1 F_2 G_1$ to be positive. Thus, in the Melvin–Bhagwati case, in addition to the gain obtained by consumers who adjust their consumption to the point where their marginal rate of substitution equals the rate at which $X$ can be transformed into $Y$ through international trade, there is a gain by producers who also adjust their production until the marginal rate of transformation equals $A$'s barter terms of trade.

## Conditions for a Trade-Diverting Customs Union to Reduce Welfare

Attempts have been made by both Lipsey (1960) and Bhagwati (1971) to reconcile the apparent difference between the preceding result (i.e., that a trade-diverting customs union may give rise to an increase in welfare) and Viner's initial proposition that trade diversion is always detrimental to welfare. Thus, Lipsey (1960) asserted that Viner had (implicitly) assumed that commodities are consumed in *fixed proportions* irrespective of relative prices—the social indifference curves are L-shaped. Bhagwati (1971) countered that fixed proportions in consumption is not a sufficient condition for a trade-diverting customs union to reduce welfare because variability in production can also be a source of gain. (In terms of fig. 22.2, Bhagwati seems to be saying that even if the triangle $F_3 F_4 G_2$ is eliminated by the fixed-proportions assumption there is still another "favorable" triangle $F_1 F_2 G_1$ which may outweigh the unfavorable rectangle $F_2 H_1 H_2 F_3$.) Bhagwati offered an alternative condition for a trade-diverting customs union to be welfare reducing—that the level of imports, and not the pattern of consumption as Lipsey suggested, be fixed.

The Lipsey and Bhagwati interpretations of Viner are illustrated in figs. 22.3 and 22.4. Consider Lipsey's interpretation first. In fig. 22.3 Lipsey would restrict consumption along the vector $OR$. Accordingly, after the formation of the union, $A$'s equilibrium would shift to point $L$ which is necessarily inferior to point $E_0$ (that is, the pre-union equilibrium point). In fig. 22.4 Lipsey's assumption of fixed proportions in consumption coupled with his assumption of complete specialization implies that $A$'s trade indifference curves become vertical (as illustrated by the broken line $E_0 V$) along the income-consumption curve $F_0 E_0$, which now becomes part of $A$'s free-trade offer curve. Thus, after the formation of the union, $A$'s equilibrium shifts to point $L$, which again is necessarily inferior to point $E_0$ (that is, the pre-union equilibrium point).

Bhagwati (1971, p. 581, fn. 1) notes that under Lipsey's assumptions of complete specialization and fixed proportions in consumption the initial tariff-ridden equilibrium $E_0$ (figs. 22.3 and 22.4) is also the free-trade position. Thus, the original tariff is "ineffective." No wonder, then, the trade-diverting customs union causes $A$'s welfare to fall under these conditions.

Turn now to Bhagwati's interpretation. Keeping imports fixed, the formation of the customs union causes $A$'s equilibrium to shift from $E_0$ to $J$ (figs. 22.3 and 22.4) and obviously $A$'s welfare is reduced.

Kirman (1973) notes the oddity of the Bhagwati assumption regarding consumption behavior and provides some evidence to the effect that Viner had neither Lipsey's nor Bhagwati's assumption in mind.

## The Difficulty Resolved

The dispute over the possibility that, or the conditions under which, a trade-diverting customs union may increase welfare is a sham dispute—a *semantic problem*. As Johnson (1974) correctly points out, the problem arises from a definition of trade diversion which includes, on the one hand, diversion of *initial* trade from a lower-cost source (country $C$) to a higher-cost source (partner country $B$) and, on the other hand, creation of *new* trade between the home country ($A$) and the partner country ($B$), resulting both from the adjustment in $A$'s consumption and the replacement of $A$'s domestic production by $B$'s (partner) production. Analytically, these two elements must be kept apart.

The diversion of *initial* trade from a lower-cost source to a higher-cost source is what we may call *pure trade diversion*. On the other hand, the creation of *new* trade between the home country and the partner country must be considered as trade creation and added to the trade creation proper. Once this is done, then we can always say that trade creation is a "good thing" (i.e., welfare increasing) and trade diversion a "bad thing" (i.e., welfare reducing), with the net effect of the customs union depending on which of these two effects (properly defined) is stronger.

If the above reconciliation is accepted, then we can return to fig. 22.2 and claim that the sum of the areas of the two shaded triangles $F_1 F_2 G_1$ and $F_3 F_4 G_2$ is actually trade creation while the rectangle $F_2 H_1 H_2 F_3$ only represents trade diversion. Similarly, in figs. 22.3 and 22.4 we can decompose the movement from $E_0$ to $E_1$ to (a) a movement from $E_0$ to $J$ corresponding to the increase in cost from *diverting* the initial level of imports from a lower- to a higher-cost source, and (b) a movement from $J$ to $E_1$. The former is trade diversion and reduces welfare while the latter is trade creation and increases welfare.

## 22.6 DYNAMIC EFFECTS OF CUSTOMS UNIONS

Besides the static effects of trade creation and trade diversion whose magnitude, as we have seen, is no more than a negligible percentage of the national income of the participating countries, customs unions have also some interesting *dynamic effects*, such as increased competition, stimulus to technical change, stimulus to investment, and economies of scale. These so-called dynamic effects do not lend themselves easily to systematic analysis. As a result, widespread disagreement and controversy surrounds them. For the benefit of the reader, we discuss these effects briefly. For more information the reader is referred to Balassa (1961), Corden (1972), Leibenstein (1966), and Scitovsky (1958).

### Increased Competition

Competition in this context does not mean many firms selling a homogeneous product. Rather, it refers to the ability and willingness of producers to encroach upon each other's markets. Scitovsky (1958, pp. 19–48) argued that increased competition was very significant in the European Economic Community.

As tariffs are removed and the market expands, the number of potential competitors increases. Monopolistic and oligopolistic market structures become exposed to outside pressures. Inefficient firms must either become efficient or close down. Competition becomes less personal and more effective and leads to research and development of new products.

### Technical Change

As we have just seen, the enlargement of the market leads to increased competition which in turn stimulates research and development. This creates a climate which is conducive to increased technical change and faster economic growth.

### Investment

The increase in competition and technical change leads to increased investment which is necessary in order to take advantage of the newly created opportunities. To be sure, certain import-competing industries are hard hit by the increased competition from more efficient producers located in other union countries. In these industries, of course, a certain amount of disinvestment must be expected. This disinvestment must be subtracted from the positive investment activity in other flourishing industries in order to determine the net effect on investment. The latter is very hard to estimate.

Some union countries may also experience an increase in investment from the rest of the world. Thus, existing foreign firms in the union may expand or regroup in order to take advantage of the newly created opportunities. In addition, foreign firms which in the past used to serve the union countries by exports may now decide to build plants in the union countries—after all, as we have seen earlier in the discussion of trade diversion, these foreign producers are, after the formation of the customs union, discriminated against. This actually may have been the reason for the massive American investment in Europe after 1955, although there are those who believe that this phenomenon was due to a sudden awareness on the part of American corporations of the existence of a growing, vigorous market from which they did not wish to be excluded.

## Economies of Scale

Economies of scale were briefly discussed earlier in chap. 7. Here it is sufficient to note that the creation of a large market leads to a greater degree of specialization which results in a reduction in costs for several reasons: fuller utilization of plant capacity, learning by doing, development of a pool of skilled labor and management, and so forth.

It has been argued that a great advantage of the United States economy is its huge internal market which facilitates the exploitation of economies of scale. Nevertheless, critics observe that, on the one hand, many small companies are efficient while at the same time some large ones are sluggish, and, on the other, countries with relatively small internal markets like Sweden and Switzerland have highly efficient industries and are very affluent.

Economies of scale are particularly important to the less developed countries.

## 22.7 MEADE'S WELFARE INDEX

Before concluding this chapter, we wish to consider briefly a welfare index proposed by Meade over two decades ago.

Meade (1955a, chap. IV and app. II) developed a comparatively simple index of welfare which may be used to assess the effect of a customs union on the welfare of the world. Meade's analysis is based on the "old welfare economics" of Marshall and Pigou. It is a cardinal, not ordinal, index.

Meade argues that the net change in the volume of international trade may be taken as an index of the welfare effects of customs unions. Welfare rises (falls) if the volume of trade increases (decreases).

Meade notes that the imposition of a tax in general creates a wedge (or divergence) between the price which the consumers are willing to pay for an additional unit and the price which the producers are willing to accept in producing the extra unit. The price which a consumer is willing to pay is a measure of the consumer's marginal utility. On the other hand, the price which a producer is willing to accept is a measure of his marginal disutility. Since the price paid by a consumer is higher than the price received by the producer by the amount of the tax, the transfer of an additional unit from the producer to the consumer necessarily raises welfare by the difference between the consumer's marginal utility and the producer's marginal disutility, i.e., the tax.

The above general principle is then applied by Meade to international trade. The price a consumer pays for an imported good is higher (by the tariff) than the price received by the foreign producer. Accordingly, a marginal increase in trade necessarily raises welfare approximately by the amount by which trade increases times the tariff (i.e., the divergence between the two prices). On the other hand, a marginal decrease in trade necessarily lowers welfare by the amount by which trade is reduced times the tariff. To determine the overall effect of a customs union on welfare, Meade (1955a, pp. 58–59) explains that all we have to do is simply (a) add all increases in trade properly weighted by the relevant tariff rates; (b) add all decreases in trade properly weighted by the relevant tariff rates; and (c) subtract the sum of decreases in trade from the sum of increases in trade. The result as determined in step (c) is Meade's welfare index. If this index is positive, then economic welfare has increased; if it is negative, economic welfare has decreased.

When the same uniform tariff rate is applied to all commodities, then Meade's index just reduces to merely the net change in the volume of trade, since the weights are all the same and can be factored out.

## Criticism of Meade's Approach

Unfortunately Meade's elegant analysis rests on several restrictive assumptions which are not necessarily acceptable to the modern economist. Vanek (1965, p. 4) summarizes these assumptions as follows:

(a) The utility of each individual derived from each commodity must be cardinally measurable.
(b) It must be possible to compare, and in particular add, the utilities and disutilities of all individuals.
(c) It must be possible to obtain the aggregate social utility ($U$) as the sum of individual utilities ($U_i$), that is, $U = \sum U_i$.
(d) The marginal utility of income must be the same for all individuals.

(Vanek notes that assumption (c) actually implies both (a) and (b), but nevertheless states them separately for the sake of clarity.)

Finally, Lipsey (1970, pp. 22–23) attacked Meade's analysis on grounds that it rests on partial equilibrium and must be confined to small tariff reductions. For large tariff reductions, Lipsey argued, Meade's index breaks down. Lipsey (1970, pp. 23–27) actually gives a counterexample in which Meade's index does indeed break down. Lipsey's counterexample is illustrated in fig. 22.4. $A$'s pre-union equilibrium occurs at $E_0$. After the customs union with $B$ is formed, $A$'s equilibrium moves to $E_2$ (assuming that $B$'s offer curve is given by the broken vector $OO_B^2$). At $E_2$ the volume of international trade of both commodities is higher than it was at $E_0$. Yet $A$'s welfare (and thus the world's welfare) is necessarily reduced.

## SELECTED BIBLIOGRAPHY

Arndt, S. W. (1968). "On Discriminatory vs. Non-Preferential Tariff Policies." *Economic Journal*, vol. 78 (December), pp. 971–979.

—— (1969). "Customs Union and the Theory of Tariffs." *American Economic Review*, vol. 59 (March), pp. 108–118.

Askari, H. (1974). "A Comment on Empirical Estimates of Trade Creation and Trade Diversion." *Economic Journal*, 84 (June), pp. 392–393.

Balassa, B. (1961). *The Theory of Economic Integration*. Richard D. Irwin, Inc., Homewood, Ill.

—— (1967). "Trade Creation and Trade Diversion in the European Common Market." *Economic Journal*, vol. LXXVII, pp. 1–17.

—— (1974). "Trade Creation and Trade Diversion in the European Common Market: An Appraisal of the Evidence." *Manchester School of Economic and Social Studies*, vol. 42 (2) (June), pp. 93–135.

Baldwin, R. E. (1973). "Customs Unions, Preferential Systems and World Welfare." In M. B. Connally and A. K. Swoboda (Eds.), *International Trade and Money*. University of Toronto Press, Toronto.

Bhagwati, J. (1971). "Trade Diverting Customs Unions and Welfare Improvement: A Clarification." *Economic Journal*, vol. 81 (323) (September), pp. 580–587.

—— (1973), "A Reply to Professor Kirman." *Economic Journal*, vol. 83 (331) (September), pp. 895–897.

Clement, M. O., R. L. Pfister, and K. J. Rothwell (1967). *Theoretical Issues in International Economics*. Houghton Mifflin Company, Boston, Mass., chap. 4.

Cooper, C. A., and B. F. Massell (1965). "A New Look at Customs Union Theory." *Economic Journal*, vol. 75 (December), pp. 742–747.

Corden, W. M. (1965). *Recent Developments in the Theory of International Trade*. International Finance Section, Department of Economics, Princeton University, Princeton, N.J., chap. V.

—— (1972). "Economies of Scale and Customs Union Theory." *Journal of Political Economy*, vol. 80 (3) (March), pp. 465–475.

Floystad, G. (1975a). "Non-Discriminating Tariffs, Customs Unions, and Free Trade." *Kyklos*, vol. 28 (3), pp. 641–644.

—— (1975b). "Trade-Diverting Customs Unions, Welfare and Factor Market Imperfections." *Weltwirtschaftliches Archiv.*, vol. III (2), pp. 243–252.

Gehrels, F. (1956). "Customs Union from a Single-Country Viewpoint." *Review of Economic Studies*, vol. 24 (1), pp. 61–64.

Ghosh, S. K. (1974). "Toward a Theory of Multiple Customs Unions." *American Economic Review*, vol. LXIV, no. 1 (March), pp. 91–101.

Humphrey, D. D., and C. E. Ferguson (1960). "The Domestic and World Benefits of a Customs Union." *Economia Internazionale*, vol. 13 (May), pp. 197–213.

Johnson, H. G. (1958). "The Gains From Freer Trade With Europe: An Estimate." *Manchester School of Economic and Social Studies*, vol. 26 (September), pp. 247–255.

—— (1962). *Money, Trade and Economic Growth*. Harvard University Press, Cambridge, Mass., chap. III and app. (pp. 46–74).

—— (1965). "An Economic Theory of Protectionism, Tariff Bargaining, and the Formation of Customs Unions." *Journal of Political Economy*, vol. 63 (June), pp. 256–282.

—— (1974). "Trade-Diverting Customs Unions: A Comment." *Economic Journal*, vol. 84 (335) (September), pp. 618–621.

—— (1975). "A Note on Welfare-Increasing Trade Diversion." *Canadian Journal of Economics and Political Science*, vol. 8 (1) (February), pp. 117–123.

Kemp, M. C. (1969). *A Contribution to the General Equilibrium Theory of Preferential Trading.* North-Holland Publishing Company, Amsterdam.

Kirman, A. P. (1973). "Trade Diverting Customs Unions and Welfare Improvement: A Comment." *Economic Journal,* vol. 83 (331) (September), pp. 890–893.

Krauss, M. B. (1972). "Recent Developments in Customs Union Theory: An Interpretive Survey." *Journal of Economic Literature,* vol. X (June), pp. 413–436.

Leibenstein, H. (1966). "Allocative Efficiency Versus 'X-Efficiency'." *American Economic Review,* vol. 56 (June), pp. 392–415.

Lipsey, R. G. (1957a). "The Theory of Customs Unions: Trade Diversion and Welfare." *Economica* vol. 24 (February), pp. 40–46.

—— (1957b). "Mr. Gehrels on Customs Unions." *Review of Economic Studies,* vol. XXIV, pp. 211–214.

—— (1960). "The Theory of Customs Unions: A General Survey." *Economic Journal,* vol. LXX, no. 279 (September) pp. 496–513. Reprinted in R. E. Caves and H. G. Johnson (Eds.), AEA *Readings in International Economics.* Richard D. Irwin, Inc., Homewood, Ill., 1968.

—— (1970). *The Theory of Customs Unions: A General Equilibrium Analysis.* Weidenfeld and Nicolson, London.

—— and K. Lancaster (1956). "The General Theory of the Second Best." *Review of Economic Studies,* vol. XXIV (1), no. 63, pp. 11–32.

Loehr, W. (1975). "Notes on Lipsey's Theory of Customs Unions." *Journal of Common Market Studies,* vol. 13, pp. 87–91.

Makower, H., and G. Morton (1953). "A Contribution Towards a Theory of Customs Unions." *Economic Journal,* vol. 63 (249) (March), pp. 33–49.

Massell, B. F. (1968). "A Reply, and Further Thoughts on Customs Unions." *Economic Journal,* vol. 78 (312) (December), pp. 979–982.

Meade, J. E. (1955a). *The Theory of Customs Unions.* North-Holland Publishing Company, Amsterdam.

—— (1955b). *The Theory of International Economic Policy,* vol. 2: *Trade and Welfare.* Oxford University Press, Oxford.

Melvin, J. R. (1969). "Comments on the Theory of Customs Unions." *Manchester School of Economic and Social Studies,* vol. 36 (2) (June), pp. 161–168.

Michaely, M. (1965). "On Customs Unions and the Gains From Trade." *Economic Journal,* vol. 75, pp. 577–583.

Mishan, E. J. (1966). "The Welfare Gains of a Trade-Diverting Customs Union Reinterpreted." *Economic Journal,* vol. 76 (303) (September), pp. 669–672.

Scitovsky, T. (1958). *Economic Theory and Western European Integration.* Stanford University Press, Stanford, Cal.

Sellekaerts, W. (1973). "How Meaningful are Empirical Studies on Trade Creation and Diversion." *Weltwirtschaftliches Archiv.,* vol. 109 (4) (December), pp. 519–553.

Spraos, J. (1964). "The Condition for a Trade-Creating Customs Union." *Economic Journal,* vol. 74 (March), pp. 101–108.

Tinbergen, J. (1965). *International Economic Integration.* Elsevier Publishing Company, Amsterdam.

Vanek, J. (1962). *International Trade: Theory and Economic Policy.* Richard D. Irwin, Inc., Homewood, Ill., chap. 18.

—— (1965). *General Equilibrium of International Discrimination.* Harvard University Press, Cambridge, Mass.

Verdoorn, P. J. (1956). "Two Notes on Tariff Reductions." In International Labour Office, *Social Aspects of European Economic Cooperation,* Geneva, pp. 160–169.

Viner, J. (1950). *The Customs Union Issue.* Carnegie Endowment for International Peace, New York, especially chap. IV.

Williams, J. R. (1972). "Customs Unions: A Criterion for Welfare Gains in the General Case." *Manchester School of Economic and Social Studies,* vol. 40 (4), pp. 385–396.

# TWENTY-THREE

## THE THEORY OF CUSTOMS UNIONS: II. THE GENERAL EQUILIBRIUM APPROACH

This chapter discusses briefly the general equilibrium approach to the theory of customs unions. It considers explicitly a model consisting of three countries: $A$ (home country), $B$ (partner country), and $C$ (rest of the world). Countries $A$ and $B$ will enter into various forms of preferential trading as the discussion proceeds. Each country produces, consumes, and trades two commodities, $X$ and $Y$, and each country's tastes are given by a nonintersecting social indifference map which measures welfare changes also. To simplify the analysis as much as possible, it is assumed that neither commodity is inferior in any country at any relative price or income level. For complications regarding inferiority, the reader is referred to Kemp (1969) and Vanek (1965).

Our discussion is divided into three parts. The first part reviews briefly the free-trade equilibrium position, and then considers the effects of tariffs imposed by either $A$ or $B$ or both. This is done both for the case in which $A$ and $B$ are *similar economies* (i.e., they export the same commodity and also import the same commodity) and the case in which $A$ and $B$ are *dissimilar economies* (i.e., they export different commodities and import different commidities). The second part assumes that $A$ and $B$ are dissimilar economies and considers the effects of various forms of preferential trading into which $A$ and $B$ are allowed to enter. Finally, the third part extends the analysis of the second part to the case in which $A$ and $B$ are similar economies.

The present chapter draws heavily on the works of Kemp (1969) and Vanek (1965)—the two major systematic customs-union studies since Meade (1955).

# PART A. FREE-TRADE EQUILIBRIUM AND THE EFFECTS OF TARIFFS

Before proceeding with the effects of various forms of preferential trading, it seems useful to review our understanding of free-trade equilibrium and the effects of tariffs imposed by either country $A$ or $B$ or both. This brief discussion sets the stage for the analysis of the last two parts of this chapter.

To simplify the discussion as much as possible, it is assumed that country $C$ is a free-trade country throughout, i.e., country $C$ does not impose a tariff. Actually very little is lost when country $C$ does impose a tariff: $C$'s welfare need not be an increasing function of its terms of trade. For further details on this point the reader is referred to Kemp (1969, p. 35).

For the moment it is also assumed that country $C$'s demand for imports and supply of exports are infinitely elastic, that is, $C$'s offer curve is a straight line through the origin. This assumption is dropped later in this chapter to consider the implications of changes in the terms of trade of the union vis-a-vis the rest of the world.

## 23.1 FREE-TRADE EQUILIBRIUM

Consider figs. 23.1 and 23.2 which show the free-trade offer curves $O_A$, $O_B$, and $O_C$ of countries $A$, $B$, and $C$, respectively. Figure 23.1 illustrates the case in which countries $A$ and $B$ are dissimilar, i.e., export different commodities. Figure 23.2

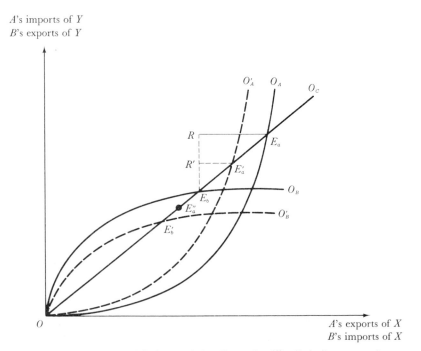

*A*'s imports of *Y*
*B*'s exports of *Y*

*A*'s exports of *X*
*B*'s imports of *X*

**Figure 23.1** Free-trade equilibrium and the effects of tariffs: dissimilar economies.

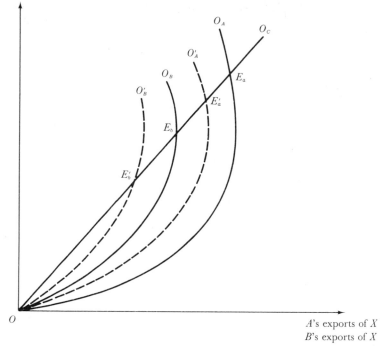

**Figure 23.2** Free-trade equilibrium and the effects of tariffs: similar economies.

illustrates the case in which countries $A$ and $B$ are similar, i.e., export the same commodity. In each figure separately, countries $A$ and $B$ reach equilibrium at points $E_a$ and $E_b$, respectively. Accordingly, in fig. 23.1 the vector $E_b E_a$ shows country $C$'s net trading with $A$ and $B$. In particular, the vector $OE_b$ shows $B$'s trading with $A$ while the vector $E_b E_a$ shows $C$'s trading with $A$. Here, country $C$'s volume of trade is the *difference* between $A$'s and $B$'s volumes of trade, that is, $OE_a - OE_b$. In fig. 23.2 country $C$ imports commodity $X$ from both $A$ and $B$, and exports commodity $Y$ to both $A$ and $B$. Here, country $C$'s volume of trade is the *sum* of $A$'s and $B$'s volumes of trade, i.e., the vector sum $OE_a + OE_b$.

In the case of dissimilar economies (fig. 23.1) trade is disallowed between $B$ and $C$. Otherwise $C$ would have to export and import the same commodity. Similarly, in the case of similar economies (fig. 23.2) trade is disallowed between $A$ and $B$. Otherwise one of these countries would have to export and import the same commodity.

## 23.2 TARIFF-RIDDEN TRADE

We now proceed to show how the free-trade equilibria of figs. 23.1 and 23.2 are disturbed when either $A$ or $B$ or both impose tariffs. In all cases, and in the rest of the discussion in this chapter, it is assumed that each country levying a tariff redistributes all tariff proceeds to its residents in a lump-sum fashion.

## Country $A$ Imposes a Tariff

What happens to the initial equilibria of figs. 23.1 and 23.2 when country $A$ imposes a tariff? Since by assumption country $A$ redistributes all tariff revenue to its citizens, $A$'s offer curve shifts totally to the left, as illustrated by the broken curve $O'_A$. (This has been explained earlier in chap. 18.) Accordingly, $A$'s equilibrium shifts to $E'_a$ and $A$'s volume of trade contracts. Since $B$'s equilibrium is not disturbed, $C$'s volume of trade with $A$ also contracts in both figures.

Actually, in the case of dissimilar economies (fig. 23.1), there is a possibility that $C$'s trade with $A$ and $B$ may be reversed. Thus, if $A$'s tariff is high enough so that $A$'s trade-tax-distorted offer curve intersects $C$'s offer curve at a point between the origin and $E_b$, say $E''_a$, the role of countries $A$ and $B$ as well as the pattern of trade of country $C$ are necessarily reversed. $A$ would now trade with $B$ up to $E''_a$, and $B$ would trade with $C$ from $E''_a$ to $E_b$.

What happens to welfare? Obviously $B$'s and $C$'s welfare remains the same. $A$'s welfare, however, falls—$A$'s trade indifference curve through $E_a$ is necessarily higher than $A$'s trade indifference curve through $E'_a$ (or $E''_a$). In this connection, recall the earlier argument of chap. 19 that the optimum tariff of a small country (i.e., a country facing an infinitely elastic supply of exports and demand for imports by the rest of the world, as is now the case for country $A$) is zero.

## Country $B$ Imposes a Tariff

Return now to the free-trade equilibria of figs. 23.1 and 23.2 and assume alternatively that country $B$ imposes a tariff. In each case, $B$'s offer curve shifts to the position shown by the broken curve $O'_B$, and $B$'s volume of trade is reduced. (Compare points $E_b$ and $E'_b$.) $A$'s and $C$'s welfare remains the same while $B$'s welfare is reduced—$B$'s optimum tariff is zero.

What happens to $C$'s volume of trade? Here we must be careful. In the case of dissimilar economies (fig. 23.1), the reduction in $B$'s volume of trade causes $C$'s volume of trade to *expand*. (Compare the vectors $E_b E_a$ and $E'_b E_a$.) On the other hand, in the case of similar economies (fig. 23.2), the reduction in $B$'s volume of trade causes $C$'s volume of trade to *contract*. (Compare the vector sums $OE_a + OE_b$ and $OE_a + OE'_b$. Why the difference in the two cases?)

The puzzle is resolved when it is recalled that in the case of dissimilar economies (fig. 23.1) country $B$ trades with country $A$ only—not with $C$. Country $C$'s volume of trade is given, in this case, by the *difference*: $A$'s volume of trade *minus* $B$'s volume of trade. Hence, as $B$'s volume of trade contracts, a bigger gap is left in $A$'s foreign trade which is actually filled by trade with country $C$. Hence, country $C$'s volume of trade expands.

On the other hand, in the case of similar economies (fig. 23.2), both country $A$ and country $B$ trade with country $C$ only—not with themselves. Country $C$'s volume of trade is now given by the *sum*: $A$'s volume of trade *plus* $B$'s volume of trade. Hence, as $B$'s volume of trade contracts, $C$'s volume of trade contracts also.

Finally, in the present case where $B$ imposes a tariff, $C$'s pattern of trade cannot be reversed.

## Both *A* and *B* Impose Tariffs

What happens when both country *A* and country *B* impose tariffs at the same time? Here the offer curves of both countries shift as illustrated by the broken curves $O'_A$ and $O'_B$ in figs. 23.1 and 23.2. Their respective equilibria move to $E'_a$ and $E'_b$ as explained above. Hence, the volume of trade of both country *A* and country *B* is necessarily reduced. Similarly, the welfare of both country *A* and country *B* is also reduced—their respective optimum tariffs are zero.

What happens to country *C*'s volume of trade? In the case of similar economies (fig. 23.2), *C*'s volume of trade is necessarily reduced. Recall that in this case *C*'s volume of trade is given by the sum of *A*'s volume of trade plus *B*'s volume of trade, since both *A* and *B* trade with *C* only—not between themselves. However, *C*'s pattern of trade cannot be reversed since neither *A*'s nor *B*'s pattern of trade can be reversed.

On the other hand, in the case of dissimilar economies (fig. 23.1), *C*'s trade may be increased, decreased, totally annihilated, or even reversed. In particular, *C*'s volume of trade increases or decreases according as the decrease in *B*'s volume of trade is larger or smaller than the decrease in *A*'s volume of trade, i.e., according to whether $E'_b E_b > E'_a E_a$ or $E'_b E_b < E'_a E_a$. *C*'s trade is either annihilated or reversed when the reduction in *A*'s volume of trade is either equal to or bigger than the reduction in *B*'s volume of trade by more than $E_b E_a$ (i.e., the initial volume of trade of country *C*). That is, *C*'s volume of trade is totally annihilated when $E'_a E_a = E'_b E_b + E_b E_a$ (that is, when the broken offer curves $O'_A$ and $O'_B$ intersect along the vector $OO_C$). On the other hand, *C*'s pattern of trade is reversed when $E'_a E_a > E'_b E_b + E_b E_a$. All this becomes obvious, of course, when it is recalled that, in the present case, *C*'s volume of trade reflects the difference—not the sum—between *A*'s and *B*'s volumes of trade.

The discussion in the rest of this chapter starts from the tariff-ridden world of figs. 23.1 and 23.2 in which both *A* and *B* impose tariffs and considers the effects of various preferential trading arrangements between *A* and *B*.

## PART B. PREFERENTIAL TRADING: 1. DISSIMILAR ECONOMIES

Turn now to the effects of preferential trading. For pedagogical reasons our discussion is divided into two parts. In this part of the chapter, we discuss the problem of preferential trading arrangements under the assumption that *A* and *B* are dissimilar economies (i.e., they export different commodities and actually trade between themselves, and only one of them trades with the rest of the world). In the following part of the chapter, we discuss the problem under the assumption that *A* and *B* are similar economies (i.e., they export the same commodity, and each trades with the rest of the world only).

## 23.3 FREE-TRADE ASSOCIATIONS

Return to fig. 23.1 and consider the tariff-ridden equilibrium in which both $A$ and $B$ impose tariffs on their respective imports. Assume that this equilibrium is disturbed by the formation of a customs union between $A$ and $B$. What are the effects on the volume of trade, terms of trade, and welfare of each country? Is the formation of a customs union potentially beneficial to $A$ and $B$? To the world as a whole?

For the moment assume that world prices remain constant. This assumption is dropped later in this section when the analysis is extended briefly to variable world prices.

### Customs Union Versus Free-Trade Association

Essentially the formation of a customs union between $A$ and $B$ means that $A$ and $B$ abolish tariffs on imports from each other and at the same time establish a *common* tariff on imports from country $C$ (that is, the rest of the world). In our present simplified model this arrangement differs little from the formation of a free-trade association between $A$ and $B$. In the latter case, $A$ and $B$ agree to abolish tariffs on imports from each other but retain their own tariffs on imports from the rest of the world (that is, $C$). In the present case in which only one member country ($A$) is actually trading with $C$, it makes no difference to our discussion whether a free-trade association or a customs union is formed between $A$ and $B$, provided only that the union adopts as the common tariff on imports from $C$ the tariff of that partner country which actually trades with $C$ in the post-union equilibrium.

In what follows, we find it convenient to discuss the formation of free-trade associations, noting where necessary any important differences from customs unions.

### Pre-Association Equilibrium

Consider fig. 23.3, which is largely similar to fig. 23.1 except for some minor differences to be noted presently. The free-trade offer curves of countries $A$, $B$, and $C$ are again given by the solid curves $O_A$, $O_B$, and $O_C$, respectively, as before. Country $C$'s offer curve is again drawn as a straight line through the origin—an assumption to be dropped later in order to consider the effect on the union's terms of trade. However, instead of the tariff-distorted offer curves of countries $A$ and $B$ which were given in figs. 23.1 and 23.2, only the respective domestic price ratios (corresponding to the fixed-price ratio of country $C$) are given. Thus, $A$'s domestic price ratio is given by the slope of the vector $OP_a$ and $B$'s by the slope of $OP_b$. These price ratios exist in $A$ and $B$ before the formation of the free-trade association. The pre-association equilibria of $A$ and $B$ occur at $E_a$ and $E_b$, respectively, along $C$'s offer curve. (Points $E_a$ and $E_b$ of fig. 23.3 correspond to points $E'_a$ and $E'_b$ of fig. 23.1.)

A's imports of Y
B's exports of Y

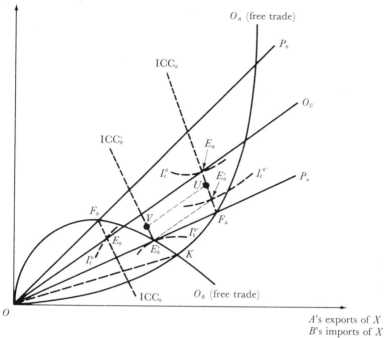

**Figure 23.3** Customs union between dissimilar economies.

How are points $E_a$ and $E_b$ determined? Draw the respective income-consumption curves of countries $A$ and $B$ through points $F_a$ and $F_b$ (the latter being the intersections between the vectors $OP_a$ and $OP_b$, on the one hand, and the corresponding offer curves, $O_A$ and $O_B$, on the other). The intersection between $A$'s income-consumption curve through $F_a$ (ICC$_a$) and $C$'s offer curve gives $A$'s equilibrium offer $(E_a)$. Similarly, the intersection between $B$'s income-consumption curve through $F_b$ (ICC$_b$) and $C$'s offer curve gives $B$'s equilibrium offer $(E_b)$. All this is known to us from chaps. 17 and 18.

To summarize: before the formation of the free-trade association between $A$ and $B$, $A$ trades with $B$ up to $E_b$ and then with $C$ from $E_b$ to $E_a$. $B$ does not trade with $C$.

## Post-Association Prices in $A$ and $B$

Assume now that countries $A$ and $B$ abolish tariffs on imports from each other while they retain their respective tariffs on imports from country $C$. That is, assume that $A$ and $B$ form a free-trade association. What can be said about the post-association equilibrium prices in $A$ and $B$?

Necessarily, $A$'s and $B$'s prices must be equalized after the formation of the free-trade association (except for transport costs, of course, which are presently assumed to be zero). Thus, $A$'s and $B$'s pre-association price ratios must necessarily be replaced by a single common price ratio. Is there anything we can say about this common price ratio before we determine the post-association equilibrium? We can definitely specify some limits for it.

As it turns out (see also chaps. 17 and 18), the common post-association price ratio may coincide with either $A$'s or $B$'s pre-union price ratios, or lie in between the two. In other words, we must have $p_a^0 \leq p \leq p_b^0$, where $p_a^0$ and $p_b^0$ are $A$'s and $B$'s pre-association price ratios, and $p$ is the association's common price ratio after $A$ and $B$ remove the tariffs on imports from each other. The outcome depends on which one of the two partner countries trades with country $C$ after the formation of the free-trade association. If in the post-association equilibrium country $A$ trades with $C$, then $A$'s pre-association price ratio will prevail. If $B$ trades with $C$, then $B$'s pre-association price ratio will prevail. Finally, if all trade with $C$ is totally annihilated, then the common post-association price ratio will lie between $p_a^0$ and $p_b^0$ (although the values $p_a^0$ and $p_b^0$ themselves must be retained as limiting feasible values, even in the present case).

Implicit in the above proposition is another proposition: the formation of a free-trade association between $A$ and $B$ may result in expansion, contraction, total annihilation, or even reversal of $C$'s trade. These cases are considered separately below.

### Expansion or Contraction in $C$'s Trade

The case in which $C$'s trade contracts after $A$ and $B$ form a free-trade association is illustrated in fig. 23.3. Here the association continues to export commodity $X$ to, and import commodity $Y$ from, country $C$. In particular, country $B$ trades with $A$ along the vector $OP_a$. Since $B$ does not collect any tariff revenue, $B$'s equilibrium necessarily occurs at $E_b'$, that is, the intersection between $B$'s free-trade offer curve and the vector $OP_a$. From this point $(E_b')$ country $A$ continues to trade with $C$ at $C$'s prices until point $E_a'$ (on $A$'s income-consumption curve through $F_a$). Hence, $B$'s equilibrium shifts from $E_b$ to $E_b'$ and $A$'s from $E_a$ to $E_a'$.

In the example given in fig. 23.3, country $C$'s volume of trade changes from $E_b E_a$ to $E_b' E_a'$. In general, $E_b' E_a' \gtrless E_b E_a$. Figure 23.3 illustrates the case in which $C$'s volume of trade contracts $(E_b' E_a' < E_b E_a)$. The reader should draw another similar diagram illustrating the other possibility: $E_b' E_a' > E_b E_a$. This can be accomplished when the line $E_b E_b'$ (not drawn) is steeper than the line $E_a' E_a$ (not drawn).

### The Association's Effect on Welfare

Before moving to the cases of trade annihilation and trade reversal we must pause for a moment to consider the effect of the association on welfarre. In particular, what is the effect on $A$'s and $B$'s welfare? Is the association potentially beneficial?

It must be clear from fig. 23.3 that the partner country which does not trade with the rest of the world in the post-association equilibrium (in this case, $B$) necessarily becomes better off. On the other hand, the country which trades with $C$ (that is, $A$) becomes worse off. To verify this, merely compare $A$'s trade indifference curves which pass through points $E_a$ and $E_a'$ and also $B$'s indifference curves which pass through points $E_b$ and $E_b'$.

Is it possible for the country which gains ($B$) to compensate the country which loses ($A$) and still remain better off after the formation of the free-trade association? In other words, is the association potentially beneficial? Unfortunately, anything is possible. The association may or may not be potentially beneficial.

Return to fig. 23.3 and let country $B$ make a series of lump-sum transfers to country $A$ in very small installments. As these transfers proceed, $A$'s and $B$'s equilibrium points ($E_a'$, $E_b'$) will be traveling northwest along their respective income-consumption curves ($\mathrm{ICC}_a$, $\mathrm{ICC}_b'$). (During this process, the association's domestic price ratio remains constant and equal to the slope of the vector $OP_a$. Assume, for the moment, as in fig. 23.3, that the income-consumption curves $\mathrm{ICC}_a$ and $\mathrm{ICC}_b'$ do not cross in this region, and the association continues to export commodity $X$ to the rest of the world.) Country $A$ will attain the pre-association level of welfare when point $E_a$ is reached. If at that time country $B$ is still on a higher trade indifference curve than that passing through $E_b$, then the association is potentially beneficial. A quick test is to draw the tangent to $A$'s trade indifference curve at $E_a$ and observe if it intersects $B$'s trade indifference curve through $E_b$. If it does, the association is potentially beneficial; but not otherwise.

Suppose that the income-consumption curves $\mathrm{ICC}_a$ and $\mathrm{ICC}_b'$ intersect each other somewhere in the cone $O_C OP_a$. Then as country $B$ makes the lump-sum transfers to country $A$, all trade with $C$ will cease once that intersection is reached. In this case, the association is potentially beneficial if and only if $A$'s and $B$'s trade indifference curves through $E_a$ and $E_b$, respectively, intersect each other. When the income-consumption curves $\mathrm{ICC}_a$ and $\mathrm{ICC}_b$ do not intersect in the cone $O_C OP_a$, this condition, though sufficient, is not necessary for a potentially beneficial association, as the reader should verify.

### Trade Annihilation

So far we have considered the case in which countries $A$ and $B$ as a group continue to export commodity $X$ to the rest of the world ($C$), even though such trade may either expand or contract. This is not a necessary outcome, however. As noted earlier, $C$'s volume of trade may be totally annihilated or even reversed. We wish now to consider briefly the case of trade annihilation. The case of trade reversal is considered in the following subsection.

As noted earlier, the post-association domestic price ratio $p$ in $A$ and $B$ must satisfy the following inequalities: $p_a^0 \leq p \leq p_b^0$ where $p_a^0$ and $p_b^0$ are $A$'s and $B$'s pre-association domestic price ratios. To determine quickly whether trade between the association ($A$ plus $B$) and the rest of the world ($C$) is completely annihilated, merely consider the free-trade point between $A$ and $B$ only, i.e., the intersection between $A$'s and $B$'s free-trade offer curves, as illustrated by point $K$ in fig. 23.3. If point $K$ lies somewhere in the cone $P_b OP_a$ (including the limiting vectors $OP_b$ and $OP_a$), then the association's trade with $C$ is totally annihilated. On the other hand, if point $K$ lies outside the cone $P_b OP_a$, as illustrated in fig. 23.3, then the association's trade with $C$ continues.

There is an important difference here between a free-trade association and a customs union. Suppose that instead a customs union is formed between countries $A$ and $B$, and the union adopts $A$'s tariff as the common tariff on imports from $C$.

Country $A$ imports commodity $Y$ only, and therefore imposes a tariff on commodity $Y$ only. In this case, the union's domestic price ratio $p$ must vary within the limits $p_a^0$ and $p_c$ ($C$'s fixed-price ratio)—not $p_a^0$ and $p_b^0$. (When the union actually imports commodity $X$, free-trade is completely restored.) In other words, the union's price ratio must be included somewhere in the cone $O_C O P_a$ (fig. 23.3), which is certainly smaller than the free-trade association's corresponding cone $P_b O P_a$. If the free-trade point ($K$) between $A$ and $B$ lies in the cone $O_C O P_a$, then both a customs union and a free-trade association will lead to a complete annihilation of trade with $C$. On the other hand, if the free-trade point ($K$) between $A$ and $B$ lies in the cone $P_b O O_C$, then a customs union will lead to a complete trade liberalization, whereas a free-trade association will lead to a complete trade annihilation.

What happens to the welfare of the two partner countries, $A$ and $B$, when all trade with $C$ is completely annihilated? Again, anything is possible. Thus, when trade with $C$ is completely annihilated, equilibrium occurs at the free-trade point between $A$ and $B$. This point necessarily lies in the cone $P_b O P_a$. If the pre-association trade indifference curves $I_t^a$ and $I_t^b$ (fig. 23.3), which necessarily lie in the cone $P_b O P_a$, intersect each other, then obviously either (a) both partner countries benefit (when the equilibrium point lies in the hull determined by the two trade indifference curves) or (b) at least one country benefits. On the other hand, if the trade indifference curves $I_t^a$ and $I_t^b$ do not intersect each other, then either (c) both partner countries lose (when the equilibrium point lies between the two trade indifference curves $I_t^a$, $I_t^b$) or (d) one country benefits while the other suffers.

Is the free-trade association potentially beneficial when all trade with the rest of the world ($C$) is completely annihilated? Given the above analysis we must conclude that in this case the free-trade association is potentially beneficial if and only if the trade indifference curves ($I_t^a$, $I_t^b$) through the pre-association equilibrium points ($E_a$, $E_b$) actually intersect each other. In general, there is no reason why this condition should be satisfied.

## Trade Reversal

Consider finally the case of *trade reversal*. This is an extreme case of trade contraction in which, at the final equilibrium point, the association's trade with the rest of the world ($C$) continues but with a different structure: a different commodity is exported to $C$ by the association ($A$ and $B$) after the formation of the association than before it.

The case of trade reversal is illustrated in fig. 23.4, which is similar to fig. 23.3 except for some minor differences to be noted presently. Before the association is formed, countries $A$ and $B$ trade at points $E_a$ and $E_b$, respectively. Thus, jointly, countries $A$ and $B$ export commodity $Y$ to country $C$, and import from $C$ commodity $X$ ($OE_b > OE_a$). (This is a minor difference from fig. 23.3 in which initially $A$ and $B$ export commodity $X$ and import commodity $Y$.) After the free-trade association between $A$ and $B$ is formed, trade with $C$ must obviously continue since the free-trade point between $A$ and $B$ (that is, $K$) lies below the cone $P_b O P_a$. Where

A's imports of Y
B's exports of Y

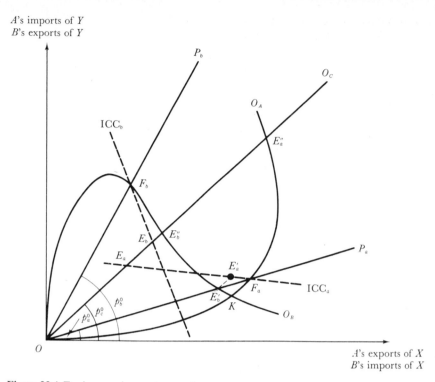

**Figure 23.4** Trade-reversing customs union.

do countries $A$ and $B$ trade in the post-association equilibrium? At points $E'_a$ and $E'_b$, respectively. Obviously, after the free-trade association is formed, $A$ and $B$ jointly export to $C$ commodity $X$, and import from $C$ commodity $Y$. Country $C$'s pattern of trade is reversed.

A necessary condition for the occurrence of trade reversal (fig. 23.4) is that $B$'s offer curve must be inelastic. This is easily verified by observing that $B$'s offer curve must be to the right of $E_b$ (which in turn must lie to the right of $E_a$) and then pass through $K$. Thus, $B$'s offer curve must necessarily be negatively sloped. In particular, $B$'s offer curve must be downward sloping and steeper than $A$'s income-consumption curve through $F_a$.

It is interesting to note the difference between the formation of a free-trade association and a customs union in the present case in which a free-trade association leads to trade reversal. Consider fig. 23.4 again and suppose that a customs union, instead of a free-trade association, is formed. Suppose further that, because initially $A$ and $B$ export jointly to $C$ commodity $Y$ in exchange for $X$ ($B$'s imported commodity), $B$'s tariff is adopted as the union's common tariff on imports from $C$. In this case, the union's domestic price ratio can vary within the cone $P_b OO_c$ only. Certainly $A$'s pre-union price ratio ($p^0_a$) cannot be an equilibrium price ratio. Actually, the post-union equilibrium price ratio coincides now with $C$'s fixed-price ratio. Hence country $A$ trades at $E''_a$, $B$ trades at $E''_b$, and jointly $A$ and $B$ export commodity $X$ and import the duty-free commodity $Y$. We therefore conclude that in the present case the formation of a customs union (instead of a free-trade association) leads to complete liberalization of trade, and both $A$ and $B$ become better off.

## Variable World Prices

The preceding analysis was carried out under the assumption that world prices are constant, i.e., that $C$'s offer curve is a straight line through the origin. We wish now to discuss briefly the case of variable world prices.

We can infer what happens to $C$'s prices by concentrating on what happens to the association's volume of trade with $C$ at $C$'s pre-association prices. Thus, in the case of trade expansion, the union's barter terms of trade with $C$ will tend to deteriorate—at the initial terms of trade there emerges an excess supply of the commodity exported by the union and an excess demand for the commodity exported by $C$. This works in favor of the partner country which does not trade with $C$ and is detrimental to the welfare of the partner country which does trade with $C$. Accordingly, the earlier conclusions reached under fixed world prices are now reinforced.

When at fixed world prices the association's volume of trade with $C$ tends to contract, the association's terms of trade with $C$ tend to improve. This works in favor of the partner country which continues to trade with $C$ and is detrimental to the welfare of the partner country which does not trade with $C$. Thus, in this case, the terms-of-trade effect works against the effect on $A$'s and $B$'s welfare at constant world prices which we discussed earlier. In the final equilibrium position at least one partner country becomes better off.

Consider again fig. 23.3 which illustrates the case of trade contraction. With constant world prices, $A$ moves from $E_a$ to $E'_a$ and $B$ from $E_b$ to $E'_b$. $B$ becomes better off and $A$ worse off. Now let $C$'s price ratio rise. As $C$'s price ratio rises, both the vector $OO_C$ and the vector $OP_a$ become steeper. Suppose that $C$'s price ratio increases sufficiently so that the vector $OP_a$ assumes the initial position of the vector $OO_C$. By inspecting fig. 23.3 it becomes apparent that in this case both $A$ and $B$ become better off. Now if $C$'s price ratio were to increase further from this position, $A$'s welfare would continue to increase and $B$'s would continue to fall. Thus, when $C$'s price ratio increases beyond a critical value, country $B$ actually becomes worse off while country $A$ is necessarily better off. On the other hand, if $C$'s price ratio does not increase sufficiently to make the vector $OP_a$ assume the initial position of the vector $OO_C$, then $B$ definitely becomes better off while $A$ may become better off or worse off with the formation of the free-trade association.

Trade reversal and trade annihilation can be viewed as extreme cases of trade contraction. The welfare effects in these two cases are similar to those of trade contraction which we studied above. For further details see Kemp (1969, pp. 81–82).

What happens to $C$'s welfare? If $C$ is a free-trading country (and we are presently assuming that it is) its welfare always increases (decreases) as its terms of trade improve (deteriorate), except when its pattern of trade is reversed. Thus, in the case of trade expansion, $C$'s terms of trade improve and, therefore, $C$ becomes better off. In the cases of trade contraction and trade extinction, $C$'s terms of trade deteriorate and $C$ becomes worse off. However, in the case of trade reversal, we must be careful. $C$'s welfare tends to fall as $C$'s terms of trade deteriorate only up to the point of complete trade annihilation. At that point, country $C$ reaches the autarkic level of welfare which is an absolute minimum. As the price ratio continues to change in the same direction and $C$'s pattern of trade is reversed, $C$'s welfare starts to improve—the same price-ratio change is now converted into a terms-of-trade improvement since $C$'s pattern of trade is reversed. Thus, in the case of trade reversal, $C$'s welfare may deteriorate, remain the same, or even improve.

## 23.4 EXCHANGE OF PREFERENCES BETWEEN $A$ AND $B$

Turn now to the third possibility of partnership between countries $A$ and $B$: exchange of preferences, i.e., a mutual small reduction of tariffs on imports from each other.

The tariff changes involved with the formation of free-trade associations and customs unions are "large." The formation of a preferential trading club, on the other hand, involves "small" (infinitesimal) tariff reductions. As a result of the *infinitesimal* tariff changes involved, the analysis of preferential trading clubs is relatively simpler.

This section analyzes briefly the effects of a preferential trading club between $A$ and $B$.

### The Setting

Return to fig. 23.3 and recall that initially country $A$ exports commodity $X$ to country $B$ and the rest of the world ($C$) in exchange for commodity $Y$. There is no trading between countries $B$ and $C$, and $C$'s terms of trade are constant—$C$'s offer curve $O_C$ is a straight line through the origin. (The implications of variable world prices are considered below.) The solid curves $O_A$ and $O_B$ are $A$'s and $B$'s free-trade offer curves, while the vectors $OP_a$ and $OP_b$ represent their respective domestic price ratios corresponding to the given world prices. Both $A$ and $B$ impose tariffs on their imports. In the initial tariff-ridden equilibrium configuration, $A$ and $B$ reach equilibrium at points $E_a$ and $E_b$, respectively. How is this initial equilibrium affected when $A$ and $B$ reciprocally reduce their tariffs on their mutual trade? For convenience, the essential elements of fig. 23.3 are reproduced in fig. 23.5.

### The Effects of the Preferential Trading Club on Domestic Prices

For small tariff reductions, the *pattern* of trade between the club ($A$ plus $B$) and the rest of the world ($C$) will definitely remain the same even though the *volume* of trade will probably change. What this means is that $A$ and $B$ jointly will continue

A's imports of Y
B's exports of Y

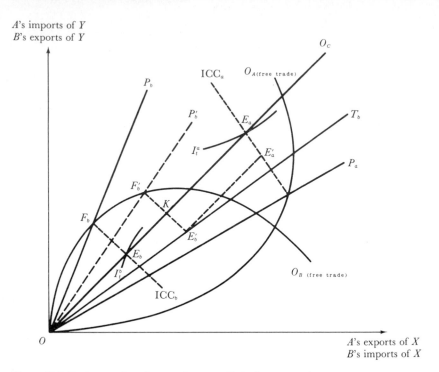

A's exports of X
B's imports of X

**Figure 23.5** Exchange of preferences between dissimilar economies.

to export commodity $X$ to country $C$ in exchange for commodity $Y$. If this is so, $A$'s domestic price ratio (which is rigidly determined by $C$'s fixed-price ratio and $A$'s import duty on imports from $C$) must remain constant. Nevertheless, $B$'s domestic price ratio is pegged to $A$'s price ratio. In particular, $p_b = (1 + t_b)p_a$, where $p_a$ and $p_b$ are $A$'s and $B$'s domestic price ratios and $t_b$ is $B$'s tariff rate on imports from $A$. Thus, as $t_b$ falls, $p_b$ falls also, since as we have just seen $p_a$ remains constant. This is shown in fig. 23.5 by the vector $OP_b'$. As $t_b$ falls, $B$'s domestic price ratio falls from $OP_b$ to $OP_b'$.

We are not out of the woods yet. We know that $A$'s domestic price ratio $(p_a)$ and barter terms of trade with country $C$ $(p_c)$ remain constant, while $B$'s domestic price ratio $(p_b)$ tends to fall. What we do not know yet is what happens to $B$'s barter terms of trade $(T_b)$. Before the exchange of preferences, $A$'s and $B$'s barter terms of trade necessarily coincided with $C$'s fixed price ratio $(p_c)$. What happens after the exchange of preferences? This is an important question. We can answer it after we look closer at $B$'s equilibrium.

## Some Fundamental Relationships

Since country $B$ trades with country $A$ only, $B$'s balance-of-trade equilibrium may be written as

$$p_x^a X_{ab} = p_y^b Y_b \tag{23.1}$$

where $p_x^a$ = price of $X$ in $A$, $p_y^b$ = price of $Y$ in $B$, $X_{ab}$ = $A$'s exports of $X$ to $B$, and $Y_b$ = $B$'s exports of $Y$ (to $A$, of course). From eq. (23.1) we obtain

$$T_b = \frac{Y_b}{X_{ab}} = \frac{p_x^a}{p_y^b} \tag{23.2}$$

We also have

$$p_y^a = (1 + t_{ab})p_y^b = (1 + t_{ac})p_y^c \tag{23.3}$$

$$p_x^a = p_x^c \tag{23.4}$$

$$(1 + t_b)p_x^a = p_x^b \tag{23.5}$$

where $t_{ab}$ = $A$'s tariff rate on imports of $Y$ from $B$, $t_{ac}$ = $A$'s tariff rate on imports of $Y$ from $C$, $p_x^c$ = $C$'s fixed price of $X$, and $p_y^c$ = $C$'s fixed price of $Y$.

From eqs. (23.3) to (23.5) we easily obtain the following fundamental relationships:

$$\begin{aligned}
p_a &= \frac{p_x^a}{p_y^a} \\[2mm]
&= \frac{p_x^b/(1 + t_b)}{(1 + t_{ab})p_y^b} \\[2mm]
&= \frac{1}{(1 + t_b)(1 + t_{ab})}p_b \\[2mm]
&= \frac{1}{1 + t_{ac}}p_c \tag{23.6}
\end{aligned}$$

Accordingly, in general $p_a < p_b$ and $p_a < p_c$. Also when $t_{ab} = t_{ac}$, as is the case before the formation of the preferential trading club, we have $p_b = (1 + t_b)p_c$, that is, $p_b > p_c$. That is, when $t_{ab} = t_{ac}$ we have $p_b > p_c > p_a$. However, when $t_{ab} < t_{ac}$, as is the case after the formation of the preferential trading club, $p_b$ may actually fall below $p_c$. Thus, we may have $p_b > p_c > p_a$ or $p_c > p_b > p_a$.

When $p_c$ and $t_{ac}$ remain constant a reduction in $t_b$ and/or $t_{ab}$ causes $p_b$ to fall while $p_a$ remains constant.

Turn now to $B$'s barter terms of trade ($T_b$). Substituting eq. (23.3) into eq. (23.2), we obtain

$$T_b = \frac{p_x^a}{p_y^b} = (1 + t_{ab})p_a > p_a \tag{23.7}$$

Further, substituting from eq. (23.6) into eq. (23.7), we obtain

$$T_b = (1 + t_{ab})p_a = \frac{1 + t_{ab}}{1 + t_{ac}}p_c \tag{23.8}$$

Thus, before the exchange of preferences (i.e., when $t_{ab} = t_{ac}$), $B$'s barter terms of trade are equal to $C$'s fixed-price ratio, that is, $T_b = p_c$. After the exchange of preferences though, we have $T_b < p_c$ since $t_{ab} < t_{ac}$.

Finally, note that

$$T_b = (1 + t_{ab})p_a$$

$$= (1 + t_{ab}) \frac{1}{(1 + t_b)(1 + t_{ab})} p_b$$

$$= \frac{1}{1 + t_b} p_b < p_b \tag{23.9}$$

Therefore, $B$'s barter terms of trade $(T_b)$ are always smaller than $B$'s domestic price ratio $(p_b)$ as long as $B$'s tariff on imports $(t_b)$ is not totally eliminated.

We can summarize the above results as follows. Before the exchange of preferences we have $p_b > T_b = p_c > p_a$. After the exchange of preferences, i.e., after $t_{ab}$ and $t_b$ fall, we have $p_b > T_b > p_a$ and $p_c > T_b > p_a$, although nothing can be said about the relationship between $p_b$ and $p_c$.

Equipped with these fundamental relationships we return now to the determination of the international equilibrium which will prevail after the exchange of preferences.

## Equilibrium After the Exchange of Preferences

Return to fig. 23.5. Assume that after the small exchange of preferences between $A$ and $B$, $B$'s barter terms of trade and domestic price ratio fall to $OT_b$ and $OP'_b$, respectively. The international equilibrium is now easily established. At the new (lower) domestic price ratio, country $B$'s offer would be given by $F'_b$, if $B$'s tariff revenue were ignored. (In the earlier cases of free-trade association and customs union $B$ had no tariff revenue—its tariff was completely wiped out. In the present case, of course, $B$'s tariff is only slightly reduced.) As $B$ spends the tariff revenue, its equilibrium point moves along $B$'s income-consumption curve $(F'_b E'_b)$ to the vector $OT_b$, as illustrated by point $E'_b$. In short, country $B$ trades with country $A$ at point $E'_b$. As before, country $A$ then continues to trade from point $E'_b$ with country $C$ at $C$'s prices. Hence, country $A$ reaches equilibrium at $E'_a$. (The vector $E'_b E'_a$ is necessarily parallel to the vector $OO_C$.)

The club's volume of trade with the rest of the world $(C)$ may expand, contract, or remain the same. The crucial comparison is between the slopes of the lines $E_a E'_a$ and $E_b E'_b$ (not drawn). As is easily verified, any relationship $(\gtreqless)$ is possible between these two slopes.

## Welfare Changes

Figure 23.5 makes it abundantly clear that, after the exchange of preferences, country $B$ (that is, the country which does not trade with the rest of the world) becomes better off but country $A$ (that is, the country which does trade with the rest of the world) becomes worse off. Thus, $B$'s trade indifference curve through $E'_b$ necessarily implies a higher level of welfare for $B$ than $B$'s trade indifference curve through $E_b$. Similarly, $A$'s trade indifference curve through $E'_a$ necessarily implies a lower level of welfare for $A$ than $A$'s trade indifference curve through $E_a$.

Is the exchange of preferences *potentially* beneficial to $A$ and $B$? In other words, is it possible that after the exchange of preferences country $B$ might be able to compensate country $A$ for its losses and still remain better off than before? The answer is "Yes." Return to the equilibrium reached after the exchange of preferences in fig. 23.5, and let country $B$ make a continuous lump-sum transfer to country $A$. As the transfer increases from zero to larger and larger amounts, $B$'s equilibrium travels from $E_b'$ toward $F_b'$, and $A$'s equilibrium from $E_a'$ toward $E_a$. When $B$'s equilibrium point coincides with $K$ on the vector $OO_C$, $A$'s equilibrium point coincides with $E_a$ (that is, $A$'s initial equilibrium point). Accordingly, when $B$'s transfer to $A$ is such that $B$'s equilibrium returns to point $K$, country $A$ recovers all welfare losses. However, $B$ is still better off: point $K$ necessarily lies on a higher trade indifference curve for $B$ than point $E_b$, as the reader should verify by inspecting fig. 23.5.

We therefore conclude that *sufficiently small mutual tariff concessions are always beneficial*. At this point it should be recalled that, in the case of free-trade associations and customs unions where import duties are completely eliminated between the partner countries (and therefore "large" tariff changes occur), potential welfare need not increase. This confirms an earlier conjecture of Meade (1955, pp. 50–51), and Lipsey and Lancaster (1956, p. 21).

## Variable World Prices

So far we have been assuming constant world prices. We wish to extend our discussion to the case of variable prices.

As with free-trade associations and customs unions, we can infer what happens to $C$'s prices by concentrating on what happens to the club's volume of trade with $C$ at $C$'s initial prices. If this volume of trade tends to expand, the club's barter terms of trade with $C$ will tend to deteriorate, i.e., the vector $OO_C$ (fig. 23.5) will tend to become flatter. On the other hand, if the club's volume of trade tends to contract, the club's barter terms of trade with $C$ will tend to improve—the vector $OO_C$ will tend to become steeper. It goes without saying that if the club's volume of trade remains constant, the club's barter terms of trade will also remain constant; then our earlier analysis would hold word for word.

Consider the case of trade expansion first. It must be obvious from eq. (23.6) that as $C$'s price ratio $(p_c)$ falls, $A$'s and $B$'s domestic price ratios $(p_a$ and $p_b)$ also fall. Similarly, it follows from eq. (23.8) that as $p_c$ falls, $B$'s barter terms of trade $(T_b)$ tend to fall also. Now return to the equilibrium of fig. 23.5 $(E_a'$ and $E_b')$ and let the vectors $OP_b'$, $OO_C$, $OT_b$, and $OP_a$ rotate clockwise. Then observe the movement of the equilibrium points $E_a'$ and $E_b'$ and conclude easily that country $A$ would tend to become worse off and country $B$ better off. Accordingly, the earlier conclusions reached with constant world prices are now reinforced.

Turn now to the case of trade contraction. Here $C$'s price ratio $(p_c)$ tends to rise and, therefore, $p_a$, $p_b$, and $T_b$ tend to rise also. Accordingly, the vectors $OP_b'$, $OO_C$, $OT_b$, and $OP_a$ rotate counterclockwise now. The reader should be able to show that the welfare changes which we studied earlier in connection with fixed world prices tend to be reversed. As a result, in the present case the final outcome can be anything except that it is not possible for both *A* and *B* to become worse off after the formation of the preferential trading club. In other words, either one partner country (*A* or *B*), or both, will become better off. (Why?)

## 23.5 OPTIMAL POLICY

We have now concluded our discussion of the effects of various preferential trading arrangements between dissimilar economies. Before we proceed with the discussion of preferential trading arrangements between similar economies there is one final question which must be settled: what is the *optimal* policy for the dissimilar economies *A* and *B*? In other words, what policy should they pursue to maximize their potential welfare? The answer must be clear from our earlier discussion (chap. 19) of the optimum tariff. Countries *A* and *B* ought to eliminate all tariffs on their mutual trade and impose a common optimum tariff on imports from the rest of the world. The distribution of income between *A* and *B* can be adjusted, of course, by means of lump-sum transfers.

## PART C. PREFERENTIAL TRADING: 2. SIMILAR ECONOMIES

We turn now to the case of similar economies as illustrated in fig. 23.2. In this case, both *A* and *B* export to the rest of the world (*C*) commodity *X* in exchange for commodity *Y*. Countries *A* and *B* trade with *C* only—not between themselves.

The formation of a free-trade association between the similar economies *A* and *B* (that is, the reciprocal abolition of tariffs on their mutual trade), as well as the exchange of preferences between them, changes absolutely nothing. The reason is simple: countries *A* and *B* just do not trade between them by assumption. For this reason we only have to consider the formation of a customs union between *A* and *B*.

## 23.6 FORMATION OF A CUSTOMS UNION

A customs union between two similar economies (*A* and *B*) becomes effective only if the common tariff adopted by the union is different from the pre-union tariff rate of at least one of the two union members. When *A*'s and *B*'s tariff rates are equal in the pre-union situation and the union's common tariff rate is equal to them, then the formation of the customs union changes nothing. Thus, when the pre-union tariff rates of *A* and *B* are equal, the customs union will become effective only when the common tariff rate on imports from the rest of the world adopted by the union is different from *A*'s and *B*'s pre-union tariff rates.

In general $A$'s and $B$'s pre-union tariff rates are not equal, and the common tariff rate adopted by the union need not be equal to either one of them. This general case can be decomposed into the following two steps. First, change the tariff rate of one of the union members and make it equal to the tariff rate of the other union member; second, adjust the new common tariff rate to the level adopted by the union. The second step involves merely an adjustment of a tariff rate and should present no problems to the reader who mastered the analysis of chaps. 17 to 19. (See also sec. 23.8 below.) For this reason, we concentrate on the first step only.

To fix ideas, assume that in the pre-union situation country $A$'s tariff rate is higher than $B$'s. We wish to discuss the following two possibilities: ($a$) the customs union adopts $B$'s (lower) tariff rate on imports from $C$; and ($b$) the customs union adopts $A$'s (higher) tariff rate on imports from $C$. We discuss briefly these possibilities in the next two sections.

## 23.7 THE UNION ADOPTS THE LOWER ($B$'s) TARIFF RATE

Consider fig. 23.6, which is similar to fig. 23.2. Only the free-trade offer curves of $A$ and $B$, $O_A$ and $O_B$, are shown—not their respective tariff-distorted offer curves. In addition, the vectors $OP_a$ and $OP_b$ indicate the pre-union domestic price ratios of

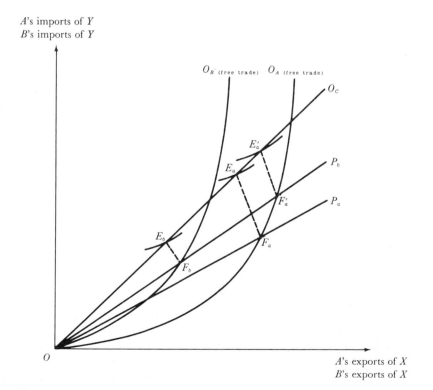

**Figure 23.6** Customs union between similar economies. The union adopts the lower ($B$'s) tariff rate.

countries $A$ and $B$, respectively. The vector $OP_b$ is steeper than the vector $OP_a$ since, by assumption, $A$'s pre-union tariff rate is higher than $B$'s. Both vectors $OP_a$ and $OP_b$ must, of course, be flatter than the vector $OO_C$ which stands, for the moment, for the offer curve of country $C$ (that is, the rest of the world). The assumption that $C$'s prices are constant is dropped below in order to consider the consequences of variable world prices. The initial pre-union equilibrium of countries $A$ and $B$ is given by points $E_a$ and $E_b$, respectively. The broken lines $F_a E_a$ and $F_b E_b$ are, as before, $A$'s and $B$'s income-consumption curves, respectively.

After the customs union is formed, and assuming that $B$'s lower tariff rate is adopted on imports from $C$, $B$'s equilibrium must and does remain at $E_b$. On the other hand, $A$'s equilibrium shifts to $E_a'$. Thus, as country $A$ allows its tariff rate to fall to $B$'s tariff rate, $A$'s domestic price ratio rises and becomes equal to $B$'s and thus $A$'s equilibrium moves to $E_a'$. (The broken line $F_a' E_a'$ is $A$'s income-consumption curve corresponding to $B$'s pre-union domestic price ratio.)

The effects of the customs union are simple in the present case and can be summarized as follows:

1. $B$'s equilibrium (volume of trade, domestic prices, barter terms of trade, welfare, etc.) remains the same.
2. $A$'s, and therefore the union's, volume of trade with the rest of the world ($C$) necessarily expands.
3. Country $A$ necessarily becomes better off; $A$ moves from a lower to a higher trade indifference curve.
4. The union's welfare improves; country $A$ becomes better off without country $B$ becoming worse off.
5. The welfare of the rest of the world remains the same; $C$'s offer curve is infinitely elastic by assumption.
6. As a result of conclusions 3 to 5, the welfare of the world as a whole improves.
7. The union's optimal policy is to eliminate all tariffs altogether.

## Variable World Prices

How should the preceding conclusions be amended when world prices are variable? We have seen that at constant world prices the union's volume of trade with the rest of the world ($C$) tends to expand. Accordingly, $C$'s terms of trade improve, and the union's deteriorate. The rest of the world becomes better off. On the other hand, $A$'s and $B$'s welfare tends to fall from the respective levels attained with fixed world prices. As a result, country $B$ becomes worse off while the final outcome on $A$'s welfare is indeterminate.

The preceding conclusion that country $B$ becomes worse off is true only if $B$'s pattern of trade is *not* reversed. Actually, a large improvement in $C$'s terms of trade may actually reverse $B$'s pattern of trade. Then, country $B$ may actually become better off as the reader can verify easily.

We, therefore, conclude that when world prices are variable both $A$ and $B$ may become better or worse off, or one may become better off, the other worse off. For further details, see Kemp (1969), pp. 110–112. The union's optimal policy is to impose an optimum tariff on imports from $C$.

## 23.8 THE UNION ADOPTS THE HIGHER ($A$'s) TARIFF RATE

Turn now to the second possibility: the union adopts the higher ($A$'s) tariff rate. This case is slightly more complicated than the previous one.

Consider fig. 23.7. It is similar to fig. 23.6 with some additional information added to it. In particular, the branch of $B$'s free-trade offer curve which ordinarily lies in the third quadrant has been rotated by 180° and placed in the first quadrant as shown by the curve $OO'_B$. By necessity this curve ($OO'_B$) must be tangent to $OO_B$ (the branch of $B$'s free-trade offer curve which does belong to the first quadrant) at the origin, and must lie totally below the vector $OP_a^2$ which is tangent to both $OO_B$ and $OO'_B$ at the origin. The reason for drawing the curve $OO'_B$ in the first quadrant is simply this: $B$'s pattern of trade may be reversed now, and it is convenient to show what happens in the first quadrant.

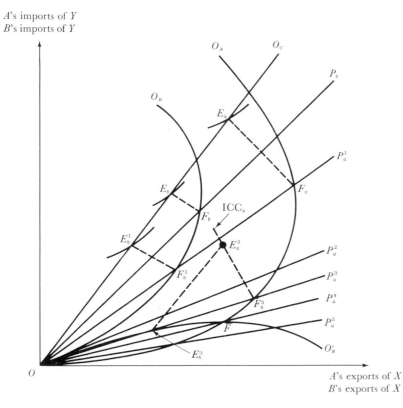

**Figure 23.7** Customs union between similar economies. The union adopts the higher ($A$'s) tariff rate.

We must distinguish among several possibilities according to whether $A$'s pre-union domestic price vector intersects $OO_B$, is tangent to $OO_B$ and $OO'_B$ at the origin, or intersects $OO'_B$ above, at, or below point $F$, the latter being the free-trade equilibrium point between $A$ and $B$. These possibilities are illustrated in fig. 23.7 by the price vectors $OP_a^1$, $OP_a^2$, $OP_a^3$, $OP_a^4$, and $OP_a^5$. We consider each of these cases separately.

Before proceeding any further, it is important to recall the following rule which we established earlier: the union's equilibrium domestic price ratio must lie in the cone (including the boundaries) which is formed by $C$'s infinitely elastic supply curve $(OO_C)$ and $A$'s pre-union price vector.

**Case (1)**  If $A$'s pre-union price vector intersects $B$'s offer curve $OO_B$, as illustrated by the vector $OP_a^1$, then $A$ will continue to trade at $E_a$ but $B$ will move to $E_b^1$. In this case, $A$ is not affected at all, but $B$'s volume of trade with $C$, and therefore the union's volume of trade with $C$, contracts. Similarly, $B$'s welfare also falls. Hence, in this case, the union is detrimental to the potential welfare of $A$ and $B$.

**Case (2)**  If $A$'s pre-union price vector is tangent to $B$'s offer curve at the origin, as illustrated by the vector $OP_a^2$, then again $A$'s equilibrium (not shown) and welfare will remain the same but $B$ will move to its autarkic point. Thus, $B$'s volume of trade is completely annihilated, and therefore the union's volume of trade with $C$ contracts. $B$'s welfare is again reduced, and the customs union proves to be detrimental to the potential welfare of the union members.

**Case (3)**  $A$'s pre-union price vector intersects $B$'s offer curve $OO'_B$ above and to the left of point $F$, as illustrated by the vector $OP_a^3$. Here $B$'s pattern of trade is *reversed*. Thus, $B$'s trade with $C$ is completely annihilated, and $B$ starts trading with $A$ at point $E_b^3$. Then, as explained earlier, country $A$ continues to trade with $C$ along the vector $E_b^3 E_a^3$ which is parallel to $OO_C$. Country $A$ actually reaches equilibrium at $E_a^3$—the point of intersection between the vector $E_b^3 E_a^3$ and $A$'s income-consumption curve through $F_a^3$.

To summarize: $B$'s pattern of trade is reversed, the union's volume of trade with $C$ falls (why?), and $A$'s welfare also falls (why?). Country $B$ may become worse off or better off (why?).

**Case (4)**  $A$'s pre-union price vector passes through point $F$, as illustrated by the vector $OP_a^4$. In this case, the union's trade with $C$ is totally annihilated. The union members ($A$ and $B$) trade now by themselves only. Country $A$ necessarily becomes worse off, but country $B$ may become better off or worse off as in case (3) above.

**Case (5)**  $A$'s pre-union price vector passes below and to the right of point $F$, as illustrated by the vector $OP_a^5$. As explained earlier in this chapter, all union trade with $C$ is now totally annihilated, and the union members trade between themselves only at point $F$ as in case (4) above.

It is interesting to note that the present case in which the union adopts the higher ($A$'s) tariff rate is actually composed of the following steps: (a) the union adopts the lower tariff rate as done in sec. 23.7 above; and (b) the union increases to the appropriate level the common tariff rate on imports from C. When viewed in this light, and the present effects are combined with those determined earlier in sec. 23.7, the effects of an increase in the union's common tariff rate on imports from C can also be discovered.

## Variable World Prices

In all cases studied above, the union's volume of trade with C tends to fall at constant world prices. Accordingly, C's terms of trade and welfare deteriorate. However, the effect on $A$'s and $B$'s welfare remains indeterminate as the reader can easily verify. Thus, both $A$ and $B$ may benefit, both may suffer, or one may benefit while the other suffers.

## SELECTED BIBLIOGRAPHY

Kemp, M. C. (1969). *A Contribution to the General Equilibrium Theory of Preferential Trading.* North-Holland Publishing Company, Amsterdam.

Lipsey, R. G. (1970). *The Theory of Customs Unions: A General Equilibrium Analysis.* Weidenfeld and Nicolson, London.

——— and K. Lancaster (1956). "The General Theory of Second Best." *Review of Economic Studies,* vol. XX (1), no. 63, pp. 11–32.

Meade, J. E. (1955). *The Theory of Customs Unions.* North-Holland Publishing Company, Amsterdam.

Vanek, J. (1962). *International Trade: Theory and Economic Policy.* Richard D. Irwin, Inc., Homewood, Ill., chap. 18.

——— (1965). *General Equilibrium of International Discrimination.* Harvard University Press, Cambridge, Mass.

(Please find additional references in "Selected Bibliography" at the end of chap. 22.)

# NAME INDEX

# NAME INDEX

# SUBJECT INDEX

# SUBJECT INDEX

Market imperfection:
  and Pareto optimality, 503
  and types of distortion, 504
Marshall-Lerner condition, 177–179
Marshallian stability analysis, 191
Meade's geometric technique, 7, 145,
    155–171
  and tariffs, 444–445
Metzler case, 474
  commonsense explanation of, 478–480
  graphical illustration of, 476–478
  mathematical analysis of, 475–476
Microeconomics, 3, 4, 6, 8, 9
Mill test, 526
Minimum wage laws, 522
Modern theory, 8, 16, 56, 68, 203–309, 319,
    362, 363
  standard model of, 206–222, 235, 256–257
Monetary controls, 442n.
Money illusion, 523
Monopolistic market, 70, 504, 507, 558
Monopoly, 185
  potential, 483
Monopoly-monopsony power in trade,
    492–493, 501, 503–507, 522
  and achievement of consumption goal, 532
  and achievement of production goal, 532
Monotonic function, 119, 259
Moving costs, 514
Multiple exchange rates, 442n.
Multiple pretrade equilibria, 149–151, 171,
    197, 205, 254, 264–265, 283


National income, 3, 4, 314
  net, at factor cost, 449, 451
  per capita, 368–371
National income accounting, 449
National locus of production, shift in, 547, 548
Natural resources, 303–305
Negative definite, 123
Neoclassical theory, 7, 16, 31, 56, 83–201,
    205, 282, 319
Neo-neoclassical growth theorem, 382
Nonappropriable factor, 281
Noncompeting groups, 22, 521
Noncompetitive imports, 299n., 304
Noneconomic objectives, 500
  consumption goal, 530, 532–533
  employment of factor, 530, 535–539

Noneconomic objectives:
  optimal policy for, 530
  and Pareto optimality, 530
  production goal, 530–532
  reduction of imports, 530, 533–535
  theory of, 8, 525, 530–539
Nontraded goods, 285, 343n.


Offer, 189, 193, 195
Offer curve:
  derivation of, 56–61, 282
  elasticity of, 172–175
  and Graham, 54
  and increasing opportunity costs, 145, 155
  under increasing returns 189–197
  and international equilibrium, 61, 155,
    168–170
  and law of comparative advantage, 62–63
  and Meade's geometric technique,
    155–157, 163–171
  and multiple equilibria, 180
  properties of, 166
  and stability of international equilibrium,
    63–64, 179
  subsidy-distorted, 461
  and terms of trade, 61–62, 170–171
  trade-tax-distorted, 463–469, 568
    intersection with free-trade offer curve,
      467
    with tariff-revenue redistribution,
      468–469
    when tariff revenue is spent: on exported
      goods, 464–467
    on imported goods, 466–468
Oligopolistic market, 70, 283, 504, 507, 558
Open economy, 5, 37–40, 116–118
  simple, 47–51, 129, 140–147, 156,
    193–195, 251
Open region, 28n.
Opportunity cost, 7, 85, 129
  and comparative advantage, 23–24, 33–34
  constant, 155, 400–403
  decreasing, 501
  and factor abundance (lemma), 260
  and Graham, 54
  increasing, 110, 115, 117, 140, 141, 145,
    150, 160, 163, 244
  and many countries, 80
  and marginal cost, 110–115, 117